during the Early Modern Period

⫷ W9-AMX-507

FREDERICK WILLIAM III
(son)   1797-1840

AUSTRIA
(and Holy Roman Empire,
except as noted)

Hapsburg

MAXIMILIAN I, Archduke of Austria, Holy Roman Emperor	1493-1519
CHARLES V (grandson)	1519-1556
FERDINAND I (brother)	1556-1564
MAXIMILIAN II (son)	1564-1576
RUDOLPH II (son)	1576-1612
MATTHIAS I (brother)	1612-1619
FERDINAND II (cousin; grandson of Ferdinand I)	1619-1637
FERDINAND III (son)	1637-1657
LEOPOLD I (son)	1657-1705
JOSEPH I (son)	1705-1711
CHARLES VI (brother)	1711-1740
MARIA THERESA, Archduchess of Austria, Queen of Bohemia and Hungary	1740-1780
[CHARLES VII of Bavaria, Holy Roman Emperor	1740-1745]
[FRANCIS I, Holy Roman Emperor; husband of Maria Theresa	1745-1765]
JOSEPH II, Archduke of Austria (son of Maria Theresa)	1780-1790
[HOLY ROMAN EMPEROR	1765-1790]
LEOPOLD II (brother)	1790-1792
FRANCIS II (son)	1792-1806
[EMPEROR OF AUSTRIA	1804-1835]

SPAIN

ISABELLA, Queen of Castile	1474-1504
FERDINAND, King of Aragon	1479-1516
JOANNA, Queen of Castile (daughter of Isabella and Ferdinand)	1504-1516

Hapsburg

CHARLES I (Emperor Charles V) (son)	1516-1556
PHILIP II (son)	1556-1598
PHILIP III (son)	1598-1621
PHILIP IV (son)	1621-1665
CHARLES II (son)	1665-1700

Bourbon

PHILIP V (grandnephew)	1700-1724
LOUIS (son)	1724
PHILIP V (father)	1724-1746
FERDINAND VI (son)	1746-1759
CHARLES III (brother)	1759-1788
CHARLES IV (son)	1788-1808
[FERDINAND VII (son)	1808]

Bonaparte

JOSEPH	1808-1813

Bourbon

FERDINAND VII (son of Charles IV)	1813-1833

MUSCOVY
(Russia after 1547)

Rurik

IVAN III, Grand Prince of Muscovy	1462-1505
VASSILI III (son)	1505-1533
IVAN IV, the Dread, Tsar of Russia from 1547 (son)	1533-1584
THEODORE I (son)	1584-1598
BORIS GODUNOV (brother-in-law)	1598-1605

Shuiski

VASSILI IV	1606-1610

Romanov

MICHAEL I (grandson of Ivan IV)	1613-1645
ALEXEI I (son)	1645-1676
THEODORE III (son)	1676-1682
IVAN V (brother)	1682-1696
PETER I, co-tsar with Ivan V (half-brother)	1682-1725
CATHERINE I (widow of Peter I)	1725-1727
PETER II (grandson of Peter I)	1727-1730
ANNA (niece of Peter I)	1730-1740
IVAN VI (grandnephew)	1740-1741
ELIZABETH (daughter of Peter I)	1741-1762
PETER III (nephew)	1762
CATHERINE II (wife)	1762-1796
PAUL I (son)	1796-1801
ALEXANDER I (son)	1801-1825

A History of
Early Modern Europe
1500-1815

D'YOUVILLE COLLEGE
LIBRARY

A History of
Early Modern Europe
1500-1815

by

HERBERT H. ROWEN

Elmira College

Holt, Rinehart and Winston, Inc.
New York

Copyright © 1960 by

Holt, Rinehart and Winston, Inc.

Library of Congress Catalog Card No. 60-6032

27600-0110

Printed in the United States of America

D 209
. R 9
1960

MAY 1 7 1993

Preface

THE WAYS OF TEACHING HISTORY are many, more than can be served by any one textbook. Yet this introduction to the history of Europe in the early modern period is designed to meet the needs of most methods. It does not clamp upon the teacher a rigid pattern which determines for him how he must shape his course. Instead, by providing the student with a clear expository and narrative account of the principal institutions and events, it gives the instructor greater freedom. It enables him to build upon this foundation his own structure of analysis and interpretation, and to introduce more effectively into the classroom and into collateral reading the major debates among historians.

To be sure, the historical picture here presented rests upon the author's own reading of the meaning of the past, but he has sought to embody therein the discoveries and judgments of recent scholarship. He has endeavored to keep his focus fixed upon specific people, not faceless groups: to tell what kind of persons these men and women were, what problems they met, how they sought to solve them, and what were the consequences of their acts. He has sought to tell this tale with clarity, vigor, and color, not just in order to keep the student from dozing over it, but simply because he does not believe that history is dull and sees no reason why it should be made dull.

The manner of presentation has been adapted to the character of the material. The first chapter describes the geographic, demographic, social, and political structure of Europe in the early modern period; the discussion of these factors within the chapters devoted to the histories of the states is therefore confined to noting how the particular country fits within the large pattern. Chapters 2-6 and 25-27 treat the economic, religious, artistic and intellectual life of Europe, as well as its overseas expansion, as general European phenomena. Political history is told for each country in narrative sequence. For the convenience of those who wish to use the book over two semesters, it is divided into two approximately equal parts, with the mid-seventeenth century as the place of division; but it may be easily used for a one-semester course.

It is even more pleasure than duty to thank those who have helped me to bring this work to completion. Among those who have read sections lying within their fields of interest, and have given me the priceless benefit of their corrections and suggestions, are Professors Charles Gibson and

John C. McGalliard of the State University of Iowa; Nicholas V. Riasanovsky, William J. Bouwsma, and Thomas Kuhn of the University of California, Berkeley; Eugen Weber of the University of California, Los Angeles; Donald Weinstein of Roosevelt University; Martin Wolfe of the University of Pennsylvania; and George W. Forell of the Lutheran Theological Seminary of Chicago. Yet, the responsibility for the book being mine alone, I had to decide which of their criticisms to accept and which, at my peril, to decline. At greater distance the book owes much to my own masters at Columbia University; among them I should like to include the late John Bartlet Brebner, a scholar and a man of vision, no less than Garrett Mattingly, Shepard B. Clough, and John H. Wuorinen, with whom I worked more closely. I wish to give special thanks to Dr. E. Gunter Troche, Director, and Mr. Dennis Beall, Curator, of the Achenbach Foundation for Graphic Arts of the California Palace of the Legion of Honor, San Francisco, from whose collection of prints came many of the illustrations in this book; Dr. Troche, in particular, suggested many of the prints, and he and Mr. Beall were unfailingly courteous and helpful even when confronted with the vagaries of a historian's judgment and taste. President J. Ralph Murray of Elmira College graciously provided the services of his secretarial staff for typing the manuscript. The greatest burdens have fallen upon my wife, Mildred Ringel Rowen, and the greatest services have been hers too; I cannot express my gratitude to her better than to say that this book is hers, and our children's, no less than mine.

H. H. R.

Berkeley, California
March 21, 1960

Contents

8. France: The Cruel Century   1483-1589   163

9. France under the Early Bourbons   1589-1661   186

Part Two. The Old Regime and the Revolution

17. France under the Grand Monarch   1661-1715   389

27. Arts, Thought, and Science in an Age of Reason 1650-1815

28. France in Revolution: I 1787-1795

IV. The Settlement at Vienna, 681
   *The Congress of Vienna · The Peace of Vienna · The Holy
   Alliance · Europe in 1815*

1

Patterns of People and Power

I. The Land

EUROPE, a large peninsula jutting westward from the immense land mass of Asia, scarcely deserves the grandiose name of "continent" given to it by early geographers. But their exaggeration contained much truth. For the men who lived in its relatively small space as the sixteenth century began, Europe did possess the scope and attributes of a continent: the wide variety of geographic potentialities wherein human labor and ingenuity had already erected a distinctive and vigorous civilization.

Shape and Space. The shape of the continent had guided the movement of peoples in the past and it continued to influence their later activities and mutual relationships. Europe is in broad outline a right-angled triangle. The southern side runs along the Mediterranean and Black Seas. The eastern boundary extends perpendicularly along the low mountains of the Urals to the Arctic Ocean; though the Urals are in many respects a boundary of mere convenience from the strict geographic point of view, they did demarcate different patterns of civilization to the east and west. The hypotenuse runs from the tip of Portugal northeast along the Atlantic Ocean and the North and Baltic Seas.

But Europe is much more than a triangle. Three great peninsulas thrust out from its mainland: on the north, the Scandinavian peninsula, with the Baltic Sea and the gulf of Bothnia separating it from the continent; on the south, the long narrow boot of Italy; and directly across the Adriatic Sea to the east, the broader peninsula of the Balkans. To these might be added the Iberian peninsula of Spain and Portugal, though it may rather be viewed as the expanded tip of the European mainland. Off the west shores of the continent lie the British Isles. Everywhere lesser promontories break up the evenness of the coastline: capes and bays, straits and river mouths, all protect the sailor from the fierceness of the sea and contribute to the maritime destiny of Europe. Generally, therefore, Europe affords more space in the east and less as one moves westward toward the Atlantic.

But men need more than just space to live in. Whether they live in bounty or penury depends in large part upon the climate, the landscape, and the soil. These geographical characteristics tend to be more favorable, however, toward the west and south of Europe than toward its east and north.

Europe lies almost wholly within the temperate climatic zone; the portion north of the Arctic Circle has few inhabitants and its historical importance has been very limited. But moderate temperatures in Europe are due as much to warm winds and ocean currents as to distance from the equator. The huge air masses baked by the Saharan sands blow across the Mediterranean most of the year to bathe southern Europe in their warmth; but the mountains just to the north slow the passage of the hot winds and cause much of their moisture to fall as rain before they penetrate far inland. The countries on the Atlantic have mild winters and even rainfall; while eastern Europe, beginning with the Polish plain and extending across Russia, suffers from the extremes of temperature and the low precipitation characteristic of continental areas.

Mountains and Plains. Three mountain groups form the stone skeleton of Europe. Largest and most important is the southernmost, made up of the Pyrenees on the west, separating Spain from France. The Alps, in the center, arch around the northern end of the Italian peninsula. The Balkan range, on the east, forms the backbone of the peninsula of the same name. The coastal plain of southern France, between the Pyrenees and the Alps, forms the only wide gap in this hard underbelly of Europe. Skirting these high ranges to the north are a series of lower, rolling mountains covered with forests: the Jura in eastern France, the Black Forest country of southern Germany, the Erzgebirge (Ore Mountains) and Sudeten ranges on the border of Bohemia, and the Carpathians at the easternmost end of the system. Furthest north are the more rugged mountains of the Scottish highlands and the Scandinavian peninsula. On the extreme southeast, the lofty Caucasus separates Europe from the southwestern regions of Asia.

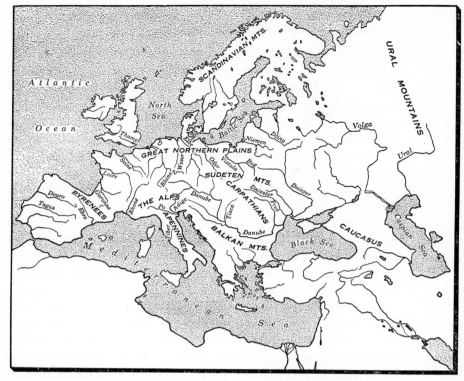

EUROPE: Mountains, Plains, and Waterways

The mountain ranges have economic values in their forests and minerals (not yet in water power during the early modern period), and strategic value in that control of these barriers gives control of the passageways between the plains.

The areas of densest human habitation are the plains. In these low and flat regions, fertility of the soil is higher, communications are easier, and less land is lost from use than in mountain areas. The principal plain of Europe occupies the land between the Alpine ranges and the western and northern seas; it begins at the Pyrenees, extends across France, the Low Countries, northern Germany, and Poland, until it passes into the vastnesses of Russia. The other plains, enclosed more narrowly within islands, peninsulas, or mountain ranges, are much smaller; these include the lowlands of the British Isles, the valley regions of northern Italy, the Hungarian and Bohemian plains between the Alps and the lower ranges to the north, and the coastal plains of Rumania and Bulgaria along the Black Sea, of southern Spain on the Mediterranean, and of southern Sweden along the Baltic.

The soils of Europe are extremely diverse and differ widely in fertility. The Mediterranean seaboard is not too well favored. Most of its soils are sandy, with only a thin cover of topsoil to nourish the crops, although the Po

3

valley of northern Italy and the volcanic soils of Sicily and the Neapolitan region are extremely productive. The great European plain is largely composed of rich loamy soils in the west, in France and the nearby Low Countries, but the rim of the plain along the shores of the North and Baltic Seas coalesces with sandy dunes, pine barrens, and marshlands. In Russia the black earth (chernozem) of the Ukraine is highly fertile; the degraded chernozem of the wooded steppe to the north is less productive, but still easily cultivated. The mixed-forest lands further north are not fertile in their natural state, except briefly when burned over or under artificial fertilization. Throughout this area the continental climate limits crops.

Routes. Trade and travel in Europe have been favored by the extent of her plains and by the intervals between the mountains, but most of all by the many waterways which run from the mountains across the plains to the seas. The larger rivers in Europe are navigable quite far inland. The greatest, the Volga, runs through the easternmost region of European Russia, but leads only into the landlocked Caspian sea. The Danube, next in length, drains the whole inner plain southeast of the Alps; the Rhine, on the other hand, is only one, though the most important, of a whole series of rivers running roughly parallel from the Alps across the northern plain to the North and Baltic Seas. The Vistula and Niemen rivers drain the Polish plain. Most other rivers are short and of local importance only.

Historical Effects. The broad pattern of European historical development, up to and during the three centuries which concern us in this book, was greatly influenced by this geographic environment.

The resiliency that has characterized European society in great measure derives from its ecological strength. The land springs back to vigor when cultivation ceases; rain clouds, not rivers and irrigation works, furnish the water on which agriculture depends, and both drought and excessive rain are far rarer than in most other sections of the world. Thus the penalty for political error and defeat was not, in the ages of which we write, the downfall of human society itself, at least in its complex and developed forms. Europe did not suffer the experience of such regions as central Asia, where conquest sometimes meant the destruction of the irrigation system which permitted large numbers of men to live; nor did any part of Europe live as did the tropical kingdoms of central America and southeast Asia, which only persistent labor safeguarded from the encroachments of the jungle.

The traditional primacy of the Mediterranean region, which still held in 1500, had rested more on the convenience of its great waterway than on the inherent productivity and wealth of its seaboard. Atlantic coastal trade was pushing hard on the older trade from the Mediterranean by way of northern Italy and the Alps into central Europe. The recent successes of Portuguese and Spanish navigators in the more distant reaches of the ocean seas presaged the end of the Mediterranean states' domination of waterborne commerce. The rise of France to pre-eminence in the centuries immediately before 1500 was a harbinger of future developments, for France drew her principal strength from her northern provinces, which were part of the north European plain and looked out upon the Atlantic Ocean.

The multiplicity and variety of European geography—the islands, peninsulas, and valleys as well as the broad plains—furnished a basis for the existence of many societies in separate zones. The highlands west of the Rhine terminate in the Ardennes forest and pinch the plains into a narrow corridor south of the Rhine river delta; this is the site of the Low Countries, which are not set off by natural features from either France or Germany, and yet as a region keep apart the peoples of these two distinctive portions of the great plain. Further east, the absence of any major natural barrier makes the location of ethnic and political frontiers more a matter of historical accident than of any geographical necessity, even though the huge, almost impassable region of the Pripet marshes at the eastern edge of Polish settlement dissects the plain—and beyond begins the zone of the Russian-speaking eastern Slavs.

The geography of Europe did not, however, isolate these separate societies and states from each other. The physical barriers between them are important, but not impossible to surmount or bypass. The variety of the cultures and institutions which we shall study existed within an all-encompassing single general European civilization. The differences between the peoples consisted chiefly in their individual ways of combining the same social elements. He who studies European history both in its general and its particular aspects finds constant recurrence of the familiar, though in unfamiliar ways. The very structure of the land on which the Europeans lived helped them to form many peoples, and still in many ways to be one people.

Until the period at which our survey begins, European society had been enabled to maintain itself aloof from other civilizations, though not wholly isolated from them. On the east, the European plain ran on into the steppelands and forests of central Asia; but these regions were thinly populated, hard put to support the conquests of their nomadic peoples, as was visible in the decline of the Mongol hordes. On the southeast, the Crusades had ended in a stalemate between Moslem and Christian. The Moslem continued to hold the whole long extent of the shores of North Africa, but the Sahara at his back denied him landward resources far more inexorably than the Alpine barrier denied them to the Christian on the northern shores of the Mediterranean. The surge of the Ottoman Turk, who had just taken Constantinople (1453), was a new threat, but it pressed hardest on Europe in the mountainous regions of the Balkans and the eastern Alps. Europe faced difficulties rather than disaster in its relations with other, hostile civilizations.

II. The Population

Man's physical environment forbids him from doing some things and virtually compels him to do others, but in rather more numerous situations it gives him opportunities and obstacles. What he achieves with his possibilities is up to himself and his fellowmen. Most of man's conquest of nature depends upon the combined activities of large numbers of men; reciprocally, the ability of society to sustain itself in such numbers depends upon making the earth fruitful. Thus, states are powerful according to the size of their population as well as their situations, their physical and economic resources, and their social structure. "The strength and wealth of kings and sovereign princes consist in the opulence and numbers of their subjects," declared the French King Henry IV.

Nothing like exact figures, or even close guesses, is available for the population of the European states before the latter part of the eighteenth century. It is evident, nevertheless, that by 1500 Europe's population was overcoming the drastic slump brought on by the Black Plague during the middle of the fourteenth century. Yet there were probably not as many people in 1500 as there had been in 1350. France, which had perhaps as many as 20,000,000 at the earlier date, had only about three-quarters of that number in 1500. Spain at the latter date had a little more than 7,000,000, England (including Wales) about 5,000,000. The next two centuries displayed differing trends for different countries. England continued to have a stable population until the beginning of the eighteenth century, while Spain suffered a decline to about 5,000,000 during the same period. France increased her numbers during the seventeenth century, reaching 18,000,000 by 1650 and 20,000,000 by 1700.

During the eighteenth century, the curve of population begins a sharp upsweep throughout Europe. The table on the next page indicates this change for some European states.

The reasons for this upsurge remain very unclear. It has not been possible to demonstrate significant increases in the percentage of marriages or in the birth rate, or similar declines in the death rate, especially among infants. Explanations based on hygienic improvements or economic expansion have been found inadequate; on close examination the changes prove not to coincide even approximately with the areas where these supposed causes were operative. At best, these factors were contributory. But the economic consequences—the growth of the available manpower and the increased pressure upon the means of sustenance and livelihood in Europe—are both obvious and significant.

POPULATION CHANGES DURING THE EIGHTEENTH CENTURY

	Approximate Population, millions	
	1700	*1800*
France	20	28
Spain	5	10.4 (1787)
Italy	11	18
England (including Wales)	5	9
Ireland	1.1 (1672)	4 (1788)
Russia*	14	30
Hungary (including Transylvania)	2	8.2
Austria (all Hapsburg lands) *	20	27
Bohemia	1.5	3 (1804)
Europe as a whole	118	188
World	330	575

* The possessions of the Romanovs and the Hapsburgs varied widely in this period. These figures therefore indicate the number of their subjects rather than the inhabitants of a fixed area.

III. Society

Such commonplace social arrangements as class and family are among the most powerful forces shaping human affairs. Their effect is easily overlooked because they seem natural to those brought up under them. Yet a full comprehension of historical events requires attention to these patterns of social organization. One factor in the general unity of European history from the medieval period onwards has been the considerable similarity of these institutions in most parts of the continent.

Class. The sense of class has always been strong in Europe. Except in a few recesses of slow development, like mountain valleys or poor fishing villages, the majority of men in 1500 were an inferior group set apart from their "betters."

Economically, the lower classes comprised the poor, those who labored for a livelihood. The upper classes were the prosperous and the rich; some were active, like military leaders and government officials, while others were idlers.

Psychologically, a clearly apparent emotional distance separated these upper and lower classes. The two were different, and they knew it. They did not dress alike, they obeyed different standards of conduct, they spoke different languages or spoke the same tongue differently. The little men stood in awe of their superiors, but often felt for them a gnawing hatred that occasionally became slashing violence. The upper class looked down on the lower with contempt, antipathy, and lurking fear. Living in the same society, the two groups had only a limited feeling of shared purpose. Reminiscence of common tribal origins, a growing provincial or national allegiance, a common Christian creed, some sense of mutual need and responsibility—all existed to some extent and muted the hostility between the classes; but they did not extinguish it.

Like high and low, rural and urban also were separated by an important cleft within European society. Countryfolk and townspeople eyed each other with distrust and dislike. Similarity of social status did not dispel this hostility; peasant and artisan cheated and duped each other with delight. Nor were landlord and burgher in general any closer; they were too much rivals for political influence and social prestige. The crossing of these lines of cleavage defined four major groups: the nobility and the peasantry in the countryside, the patricians and the commoners in the towns.

The Nobility. The preponderant social class in almost every country was the landed nobility. It was usually the wealthiest group, for landed estates represented the largest single source of wealth everywhere but in a few commercial centers. It virtually monopolized political and military offices. Throughout Europe it formed a self-perpetuating intermarriage group: a nobleman who married beneath his rank lost face, unless the bride was very rich (in which case he was "manuring his land"). Legally, a nobleman was one who held, directly or by inheritance, a title bestowed by a ruling prince.

In western and central Europe, titles of nobility were arranged in an elaborate pyramid of dignity and importance. At the bottom came the most numerous group, simple gentlemen or knights, known in England as "Sir" followed by the complete name (Sir Francis Walsingham, for instance), in France as *chevalier* and in Germany as *Ritter*, followed by *de* or *von* (= of) and the name either of an estate or of the family. Next higher, in England and Germany, came barons; above them, or directly above knights in other regions, followed, in progressively decreasing numbers, viscounts, marquesses (the French form *marquis* being also common in English), counts (earls in England), and dukes; these took the names of estates or territories after their titles. The title *prince* was accorded to sovereign rulers who were not kings, like the Prince of Orange, and to the eldest son of the British sovereign; it was also used as a descriptive general name, though not as a title, for the almost-sovereign great vassals in the Holy Roman Empire.

Nobility also consisted in a claim to be of stock superior to the common herd of men. Nobles were "gentlefolk" and "well-born." In continental countries, the children of a nobleman shared his position, sometimes with a title of lesser rank. In England, however, the rule of primogeniture extended to the right to a title; the heir was considered to be noble and carried a courtesy title (like Lord William Cecil); his sisters and brothers were usually commoners, though of "gentle" birth and with special forms of honorable address. They shared this in-between status with the "gentry," who numbered all well-born people who did not possess a title, like many prosperous landlords who on the continent would have held a noble rank. Thus the English gentry and nobility together comprised about the same groups as the continental nobility; the difference lay in their legal status.

The nobility in Europe east of Germany were not distributed into such an elaborate array of ranks; within their class formal equality prevailed. In Poland, for instance, all were known as *pan*, which meant no more than "Sir" though it was often translated as "count." The difference between such a great magnate as a Radziwill, with estates covering hundreds of square miles, and a simple *pan* owning a smidgen of land, was very real, to be sure, but it arose only from wealth and influence, not from prerogative.

The Peasantry. The peasantry, the most widespread of all groups, were nonetheless a local class. Normally the village bounded their lives; they felt few ties of familiarity and sympathy beyond the province in which their dialect was spoken. Economic changes had established significant gradations within the class; in the center were the mass of self-employed peasants, above them a small group of well-to-do peasants whose conditions of life often did not differ greatly from those of the poorest nobles, beneath them landless peasants with little hope and less status. Especially in western Europe, the isolation of the peasantry was being slowly eroded by emigration of the more ambitious and more desperate to the towns, and by other contacts with urban life.

The Townsmen. The urban population was split between rich and poor. Wealthy townsmen, chiefly merchants and bankers, felt themselves to be a patriciate, a well-born group though usually not noble. They felt toward the town poor the same distaste and fear that the landed nobility felt for the peasants. In general, people of this class had a common pattern of life. They were also attached to more narrow associations, the guilds which functioned as corporate bodies with both legal and social status. Each such group had its own distinct loyalty. The poor in the towns, jumbled together in crowded quarters, had less of such sense of special identification with narrow groups, except where occupational differences remained strong, as in the Low Countries.

The class structure of European society in 1500 had not crystallized into impassable caste lines. Movement up and down the social ladder, especially in western countries, occurred though it was hardly frequent. Some paths of ascent were respectable, like careers in the church or the university. Others emphasized more dubious talents: adventurers made gambles of their own lives; ladies achieved social eminence by becoming mistresses of kings or great nobles. In general, however, the accumulation of wealth was the means of rising out of one's class to a higher one; its loss, the cause of falling from exalted position.

The Family. The historical role of the family continued strong in European society during the early modern period. Its consequences were especially significant in such areas as economics and politics. Powerful as was the institution of the family in Europe, it frequently operated in confusing and contradictory fashion because of its own peculiar structure.

European families, unlike those in societies with a strong system of clans, were not distinctly set off from each other like squares on a checkerboard. The broad family or clan, which gave individuals a sense of single and specific family membership, had disappeared from Europe except in a few regions like the highlands of Scotland. Instead the European family system was a web of overlapping "narrow" families of husband, wife and children. It was both patriarchal (ruled by the father) and patrilineal (traced by his line and name). The interests of husbands, fathers and sons outweighed those of wives, mothers and daughters; often the eldest son was favored above all other children. Each such family nonetheless represented the meeting point of two opposing pyramids, one of ancestors and the other of descendants, in which both the female and the male line were equally present. Only the direct patrilineal line—father through grandfather, great-grandfather and so on—was clearly felt; but its influence was muddled by the seldom wholly lost interests brought in by the mother, the grandmother, and so on. For the wife and mother, the interests of her own family-by-birth often conflicted with those of her family-by-marriage, particularly with respect to her children and their welfare.

The broad family, as well as the narrow family of complete consanguinity, was an institution of mutual support and encouragement. But the individual was not lost in the family; rivalries between cousins, between brothers, and even between father and son were frequent and all the more bitter because of their closeness. When these crosscurrents of purpose and hope flowed into the world of politics by the channel of the dynastic state, in which rule belonged to families, the consequences affected not merely a small number of individuals but millions.

IV. The State

The political organization of Europe drew more attention from contemporaries and later observers than did its social institutions. The structure of governments was more varied and more variable, and their actions affected the lives of people in more obvious ways. Men do not fail to notice the workings of an institution which can take away their lives, their money, or their freedom of movement and choice, but which defends them against crime and invasion.

The Sovereign State.   Since the collapse of the Roman empire in the West a thousand years before, political order had slowly evolved by the fusing of Germanic and Roman political institutions.

The characteristic medieval form of government which resulted by the year 1000 was feudalism.   In form it consisted essentially in the grant of fiefs, principally land, to vassals in exchange for services, principally military; the heart of the system consisted in the inclusion of almost all powers of government as well as extensive economic rights in the grant of the fief. The decentralization of political authority under feudalism was intensified by the practice of great vassals granting fiefs to subvassals in their turn; this process was frequently repeated several times, creating a pyramid of government from the mere knight, usually the lord of a manor, to the king himself as the capstone of the feudal state.

By the time another five centuries had passed, the revival of more centralized authority in the state had hollowed out the feudal element while frequently retaining the feudal forms and names.   Vassals lost many of their rights of government and became only the more powerful and influential among subjects.

In contrast to the overlapping and conflicting jurisdictions of the feudal authorities, the new state claimed a total and exclusive right to rule within its frontiers.   It recognized no rival for control among its subjects and rejected the right of any foreign power to intervene in its affairs.   It took as an axiom the principle of Roman law that "the will of the prince has the force of law."   These principles formed the basis of the definition of sovereignty given by the French thinker Jean Bodin (1530-1596); for him, sovereignty was unique and indivisible within a given state.   All sovereign states were formally equal; their decisions might be criticized by moralists or limited by practical considerations, but could not be appealed to any higher legal authority.   Even Roman Catholic rulers turned aside, when they did not deny outright, the assertion of the papacy that it could dethrone sovereign princes.   Because the new kind of state put forward its claims only within the boundaries of a specific territory, in contrast with the universal aspirations of the Holy Roman emperor and the more personal allegiances of feudalism, historians have also given it the name of "territorial state."

Government by Administrators.   Although the territorial state displaced the previous feudal state, it resulted from the triumph of the more powerful over the weaker forces within feudalism.   It was not, however, the ordinary victory of greater pluck, luck, or ability among contenders commanding similar sources of power; it was the achievement of a more efficient means of rule.   This was government by professional administrators instead of by an unspecialized governing class performing all tasks of rule, whether military, judicial, fiscal, or political. Such specialized administrators are often called "bureaucrats," indicating that they ruled from an office (*bureau* in French); their instrument of government was the pen rather than the sword.

Unlike the older type of feudal governors, who held semi-independent power, the new administrators were wholly dependent for appointment and advancement on the ruler, who could dismiss them at will; thus their obedience, the most essential attribute of a government servant, was assured. Furthermore, being normally at some distance, they were less subject to the wiles and pressures of those they governed. From his worktable or desk, the bureaucrat could pay attention to and direct a far greater region than one who governed in the field; and a number of such administrators, obeying the same orders, could apply an identical policy over the whole of a great state. Policy could be maintained without break over time, instead of following the vagaries of knowledge and judgment of an individual; bureaucrats kept records and thus passed on their experience to their successors.

Full-time administrators required support, since they could not earn their livelihood in other occupations during their spare hours. At first the feudal technique of granting estates as fiefs was frequently employed, but this in the long run resulted in the government servant slipping into the class of vassals. By the end of the fifteenth century, almost all state officials were receiving regular salaries.

Professional Armies. The emergence of the territorial state was also furthered by the superiority of professional soldiers over feudal levies. Armies consisting of knights furnishing their military service usually melted away after little more than a month. The *ban* and the *arrière-ban*, or levies of feudal knights, fell into disuse; the obligation of knight's service was often commuted into a money payment. The payment of troops to remain for the whole period of campaigning from spring through autumn led to the development of a mercenary military system.

Armies were recruited from volunteers who signed up with any commander able to pay them. Captains organized military companies as a business venture; they sold their services to rulers on a contractual basis, at specified rates for a fixed time. In Italy, they were called *condottieri* (conductors, captains, leaders). Their troops were sworn to obey them, rather than the prince for whom they fought. In countries with strong central governments, like Spain, France, and England, captains were not allowed to organize companies on their own initiative; the state issued "patents," or licenses to recruit troops for its service, as they were needed. Otherwise, the system was much the same everywhere: the captain received a blanket payment for the service of his company, out of which he paid his men; they usually armed and outfitted themselves at their own expense, and bought their own food. Supplying troops was not ordinarily a direct function of the military organization, but was entrusted to businessmen who maintained the supply train.

Most armies moved with the accompaniment of wives, laundrywomen, hangers-on; they formed ambulatory little worlds separate from the life around them. A peasant lad who accepted an enlistment bonus, either because he could not eke out a livelihood at home or because he hoped to rise by his talents and perhaps amass some wealth by judicious looting, was cutting himself off from his familiar world of values and opportunities and building himself a new and different career.

New Weapons. There was much more to the success of these new professional armies than the use of firearms. To be sure, by the end of the fifteenth century guns had replaced crossbows (and longbows in England). Despite the prowess of the English longbowmen at Crécy and Agincourt during the Hundred Years' War, little emphasis was placed upon projectile weapons for halting the charge of heavy armored cavalry, the most formidable military force then known in Europe. This task was not given to the primitive matchlock, with its slow and uncertain fire, but to an infantry lance weapon, the pike. At the battles of Granjon (1476) and Nancy (1477), the serried ranks of Swiss pikemen had held and destroyed the crashing cavalry of Charles the Bold, duke of Burgundy. Soldiers like these Switzers could not be improvised, however; they required the strenuous training and discipline possible only with long-service professional troops. The Spaniards were the first major power to adopt the new technique; their infantry dominated Europe militarily for the next century and a half.

Artillery were chiefly useful for siege warfare; large-scale fortification of cities became more important, while the construction of relatively small fortresses of the old medieval type came to a halt. The improvement in firearms was slow; it was not until the seventeenth century that a serviceable flintlock was introduced and field artillery began to play a battle role as significant as it was dramatic. Cavalry continued to be useful for the shock action of thundering squadrons. For mounted soldiers, slashing swords were to remain for a long time far more important weapons than puny pistols.

As armies grew larger, their weapons more varied, and their organization more complex, success in battle came less and less from impetuosity, for which the French were particularly famed, and increasingly from the combination of arduous preparation of the troops, the dull but necessary organization of supplies, and wise strategy, with bold tactics and battle leadership. During the sixteenth century, campaigning continued to be intermittent, mainly because no state proved able to sustain uninterrupted large-scale operations for very long.

The Navies. Seapower developed with equal vigor during the sixteenth century. Better ships and weapons, as well as improved ship-handling and combat methods, all made the power of states effective at sea as well as on land. In the Mediterranean, the galley, a long and narrow vessel driven by oarsmen in several banks as well as by sails, was the most dependable warship; it could sail in calm weather or windy, and was useful for the boarding operations which remained the principal form of naval battle until late in the sixteenth century.

Improvements in sailing ships made by Atlantic shipbuilders, first the Portuguese and then their various neighbors to the north, were adapted to combat purposes; ships became more responsive to control; they could sail close-hauled to the wind and could hold the sea in storms; high castles fore and aft facilitated boarding operations, while cannon, used in increasing numbers for broadside fire, prepared for a revolutionary shift in naval combat operations. Fleet actions became the key to victory in both the inland and the open seas, although the individual operations of cruising privateers were more effective against merchant shipping.

Despite these developments, naval power contributed much less than land forces to building up the new territorial states. It was seldom useful against feudal magnates, the principal foes of the sovereigns within the state. Only Venice and Genoa, the Italian trading republics, maintained large professional navies in the late fifteenth and early sixteenth centuries; elsewhere merchantmen were usually armed and often sailed together for self-defense. The Atlantic powers developed their own sea power, especially for protection of their overseas activities in America and Asia.

Taxes. These instruments of the territorial state—the professional administrators and the mercenary armies—were not only powerful and efficacious in its growth and consolidation; they were also immensely costly. In a society which produced relatively little beyond its bare needs, a very high proportion of surplus goods and services had to be devoted to maintaining the armies. The narrow revenue sources of feudal kings, largely dues and rents from their own domains, were grossly inadequate; taxes directly upon the sovereign's subjects became the principal source of income of the territorial state.

Since the land remained the largest body of wealth in most countries, taxes upon agriculture provided the most considerable revenues. As feudal dues and manorial rents decreased in real value during the sixteenth century owing to the steady inflation of the currency (see ch. 2, pp. 41-42), the governments expanded their own claim to a portion of the farmers' income. But the amount which finally fell clinking into the coffers of the state was substantially reduced by the costs of collection; there were too many taxpayers, too widely dispersed, who were difficult to assess and to make pay. Cadasters, or detailed and permanent public records of land ownership, were infrequent and usually incomplete; taxation was normally fixed by the central government not upon the individual farmer, therefore, but upon the village, which was compelled to collect and pay over to the tax collectors the sum due.

Commerce, too, was a rich vein for the tax collector to mine. Articles of trade were necessarily visible and were sold at a public price in a public place; if imported or exported, they had to pass through specified customs houses at or near the frontiers; it was simple, therefore, to assess and collect taxes upon goods in transit or for sale. If the tax was equal for all and moderate in amount, it could be passed on to the consumer and did not harm the seller.

Industry counted for relatively little as a source of taxes, not only because the total value of its product was small compared to agriculture, but also because producers could easily conceal their actual wealth from all but fellows in the craft. They usually paid taxes not in terms of their economic activity, but as urban residents; the town government, not the central government, normally assessed them upon the value of their residences and collected the sums due.

Personal income was almost invariably refractory to taxation. It was easy to conceal, and inquiry by the government as to its size and source was resented as unwarranted intrusion into private affairs. Only landowners could be fairly taxed on income, at least insofar as it was directly proportional to their holdings; but such an impost could scarcely be distinguished from agricultural taxation in general.

Tax Collectors. The tax collectors typified the new administrators of the territorial state. They did not share in making policy. They were agents only, of authority which they did not possess in their own name. They were not usually permitted to pass judgments upon delinquents, and even less to punish them; these were prerogatives vigorously defended by the courts. The tasks of the tax collector were assigned to distinct individuals according to function: there were receivers, treasurers, recordkeepers, and supervisors of accounts at local, provincial, and national levels.

All too frequently, the increasing efficiency of these officials in the extraction of funds from the population could not keep pace with the demands which the rulers placed upon their revenues. Wars, in particular, consumed money with a voracity which those who embarked upon them seldom anticipated. Money to pay armies was needed before it was collected.

Governments resorted to loans from individuals and banking families, but the recurring bankruptcies and repudiations of even the wealthiest states tended to dry up this source of assistance. To obtain credit, rulers sometimes were forced to give control over tax revenues to the lenders, who drew off the sums owed them before passing on the remainder to the treasury. This practice was called "tax farming" (the French word *ferme* originally indicated a firm payment, hence a rental). Whenever, as in France, monarchs began to "farm" out the taxes years in advance of the collection date, the specter of state bankruptcy began to loom up.

Forms of the State. Although contemporaries knew clearly the individual characteristics of the territorial state, they continued to distinguish between existing states according to the way in which power was held in them. In monarchy, authority belonged to a single person, usually called the "king." Where power belonged to many, as in Venice and Genoa, the government was called a "popular state" or a "republic." (The term "republic" [Latin *res publica*, public thing] was used in political theory for any organized state, including monarchy, under the rule of law; Bodin called his study of the French monarchy *The Six Books of the Republic* [1576].)

Monarchy. Monarchy was the more prevalent form of government in early modern Europe. The ruler, often called the "prince" in works of political theory, directed foreign policy, made the laws, was the supreme judge and final court of appeals, and commanded the armed forces. His decisions overrode all others: he was executive, legislature, and judiciary wrapped up in one man. Most of these tasks he normally performed by delegation; the government of even a small state was more than one person could direct personally.

The advice and assistance of a council were necessary. The typical "council of state" had developed out of the *curia regis*, the feudal king's council; its judicial functions, though not abolished outright, usually remained only residual prerogatives. The council members brought to the ruler their knowledge, their judgment, their proposals and—when he was fortunate—their force of character; they also aided him in the execution of policy. In most countries, members of the council seldom had specific responsibilities as heads of administrative departments before the end of the sixteenth century. Though one or a small group normally took leadership in the council, in the typical case all its members were formally equal. Political struggle within the ruling class customarily took the form of efforts to win a preponderant position within the council—the visible and effective sign of royal favor.

The royal (or princely) court also played an important political role. As the broad group of companions among whom the king resided, the court formed his immediate world of face-to-face experience. Most of the courtiers were no more than noble hangers-on, idling away their empty hours in gossip, gambling, flippant affairs of the heart, paying attendance upon the king in endless ceremonies, and having little to do with politics.

A smaller number, however, were deeply involved in problems and business of state: they sought to persuade the king to follow their own views, partly by means of personal appeals and arguments, often by more devious influences like winning over a royal favorite, male or female. To gain a king's ear by giving him a mistress from one's own circle was a political triumph not to be despised. For the first business of politics was to hold the king's favor.

The court was usually divided between informal groups of like-minded men, linked by ties of family and friendship, whom the English came to call by the descriptive name of "connections." Political forces in the wider circles of the nation usually endeavored to attain their objectives by means of adherents at court; only if such a method failed did they resort to others, more dangerous. Thus "connections" at court and in the country were political parties in an incipient form.

The "Estates." Although the king or prince was the ultimate source of all political authority in monarchies, government was shared in practice with portions of the population at the beginning of the sixteenth century. Vassalage, the most important form of such participation during the period of the feudal kingdoms, gave way during the late middle ages to assemblies representing important and influential segments of the population. These segments were the two, three, or four "orders" or "estates" * of the realm. The representative bodies were frequently known as "assemblies of estates" or as "States" or as "parliaments." The nobility was always, and the clergy almost always, represented in these assemblies; towns frequently sent members, as did occasionally the peasantry.

These assemblies usually had evolved out of the king's practice of calling local and provincial leaders to his council to give advice and accept responsibility for raising emergency taxation. Such assemblages frequently held the right of consenting to extraordinary taxation; in some case, as in the Low Countries, the Holy Roman Empire, and some French provinces, they also saw to the collection of these grants by their own tax officials. In England, legislation had come to consist in "acts" of the Parliament put into effect by the king's signature, but elsewhere an explicit legislative function of these "assemblies of estates" was rare.

Kings usually considered these representative assemblies to be impediments to their authority, and sought to reduce their powers or to eliminate them entirely. The kings who held their thrones by election, as in Poland and Hungary, found they could do so only by winning military victory over the assemblies of estates which elected them. The kings by hereditary right, or dynasts, were more successful in their struggle against the influence of the estates. The kingdom was their property, just as the kingship was their office; the feudal practice of combining rights of government and property in land

---

* "Estates" and "States" in this sense are identical terms. The French word *état* stands for such "estates," but capitalized (*État*) it stands for "state" in the sense of "government." "Estates" is found commonly used for the assemblies of France and Germany, "States" for those of the Low Countries.

in the same person was continued in the institution of dynastic monarchy, although the decline of vassalage meant the elimination of the same practice at lower levels; doctrines of royal absolutism were also encouraged by the rise of Roman-law theories of the unlimited sovereignty of princes.

Republics. In republics, all powers of government normally resided in assemblies of estates of the kind just outlined. Some kind of executive agency, with authority delegated from the estates, was formally established, as in Venice, or improvised, as in the Dutch republic during the periods when there was no stadholder (see ch. 7, p. 147; ch. 24, pp. 542-545). A separate judiciary was common, however. Ultimate authority did not reside in the representative assemblies, but in their electors. Suffrage was almost always limited to more or less narrow groups; democratic notions were rare. Such republics resembled contemporary monarchies more than modern parliamentary democracies. The ruling classes in the republics increasingly became patrician oligarchies ruled by burgher dynasties. Those who held power in the early modern republics sought to perpetuate their positions in their families. Those entrusted with executive authority and military command likewise frequently endeavored to make their offices hereditary, and sometimes to transform them into regal form.

Incipient Nationalism. The early modern territorial state, whether monarchical or republic, possessed many elements of the nation-state which became characteristic of the history of Europe after 1815. Many of the territorial states, though by no means all, were inhabited mainly by one nation—that is, a group speaking the same language, of the same ethnic origin, and with the same cultural habits and attitudes. Questions of specifically national character did not arise frequently in this period, however. Dynastic families placed their members on thrones without concern for the language or stock of those they would rule. National attachments weighed least heavily with the nobility, the most powerful political class; burghers felt their strongest loyalty for their own towns; the peasant world was the parish. Nonetheless, as the potency of state action grew and affected more and more profoundly the lives of subjects, and as the support of subjects for their governments became important in political struggles, there began to develop those coinciding interests of the people and the state out of which grew the typical nationalism of a later period.

Order and Law. To those who were ruled, the supreme benefit of government was to be safeguarded in person and possessions. Professional criminals who deliberately flouted law and order were few, although hardship and despair constantly recruited new bandits and thieves. The treatment of culprits, suspected or condemned, was universally cruel and stern. Torture to extract confessions was employed without doubt as to its validity or morality; mutilation and branding were common; capital punishment, as the

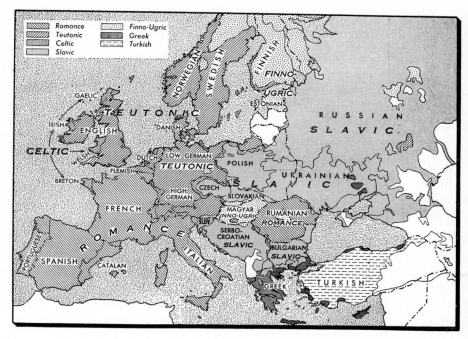

The Languages of Europe

supreme penalty, seemed the surest and was applied for a wide range of crimes. Executions, conducted in public, were spectacles that contributed more, it would seem, to the general taste for gore than to the reduction of the rate of crime. Whatever the limitations and faults of the law, a rough justice and peace were maintained; to contemporary men, these were the very purpose of the state.

By 1500, trial of offenders in both civil and criminal cases was almost everywhere the business of special courts of justice. Lawyers and judges had evolved elaborate systems of jurisprudence. In some countries, courts followed statutory enactments as well as traditional native practices called "customary law"; English jurists placed particular emphasis upon prior judicial findings (precedents), which they incorporated into a "common law." Elsewhere, as in Scotland and southern France, the legal codes of the late Roman empire, fixed in the *Corpus juris civilis* (Body of civil law) and commented upon by hosts of late-medieval legists, formed the basis of court decisions; Roman-Byzantine law thus interpreted became known as "written law," in contrast to "customary law."

In actual practice, most countries depended neither on the "written" nor on the "customary" law exclusively. Medieval political thinkers usually denied that new law could be established. Arising out of divine will and natural reason, all law was immutable and already in existence, they asserted; it needed only to be discovered and proclaimed. Nonetheless, governments issued edicts and ordinances which only legal artifice could interpret as being merely old law made newly known. By the end of the fifteenth century, enactment of statutes was accepted everywhere as a fact. Both "customary" and "written" systems of law were thus modified by statute, which became the usual way of making major changes in the laws. Furthermore, judges and lawyers in countries under "customary" law habitually referred to "written" law when they ran across gaps in their own systems; and "Roman" lawyers did much the same with "customary" law, though more surreptitiously. "Customary" law was written down precisely like Roman law; it usually arose from the merging of already established Roman doctrines with Germanic codes established during the period of the invasions of the Roman empire.

Legists supporting the rulers of the new territorial states found the Roman law congenial, for it proclaimed the prince as the sole all-powerful source (or interpreter) and enforcer of law. Roman law was also more easily adaptable to the definition of nonfeudal freehold property than the customary law had been, though lawyers in England and northern France found no difficulty in making their customary systems do service for the new needs.

The Uses of the State. To those who ruled, whether in a monarchy or a republic, there were many uses of the state. It gave them a matchless source of wealth and prestige in a world where these ranked high in most men's desires. The power of the state was no less desirable: it extended the individual ruler's will over millions of men. At the strictly personal level, it provided a means of doing good to one's friends and harm to one's enemies; at the political level, it enabled one to seek the achievement of good for mankind, or for whatever segment of mankind held one's affection, and to prevent evil being done to them.

The use of power was not as simple a thing as enjoying it. Power was dangerous to hold: rivals within the country, fellow-rulers outside, were eager and ready to take advantage of any weaknesses; the overthrow of princes and republican governments was too frequent for comfort. Power was difficult to handle. The situations confronting rulers were complex, uncertain, and constantly changing. Though the consequences of action were fraught with danger, it was impossible to forecast them with any accuracy. Yet the penalty for inaction, loss of initiative, was even greater.

Power was the tiger of the Chinese fable: those who rode it dared not dismount. Political struggle was a constant drama, often wretched, sometimes dull, but now and again reaching heights of immense tragedy.

PART ONE

The Emergence of the
Territorial State

Europe in the Sixteenth Century

Map labels:

HOLY ROMAN
EMPIRE

R U S S I A
(MUSCOVY)

FINLAND
(to Sweden)

TEUTONIC ORDER

LITHUANIA

TEUTONIC ORDER

P O L A N D

BLACK SEA

O T T O M A N   E M P I R E

CYPRUS

AEGEAN
SEA

CRETE

HUNGARY

AUSTRIA

GERMANY

SWEDEN

NORWAY
(to Denmark)

SKAGERRAK

DENMARK

BALTIC SEA

NORTH
SEA

SCOTLAND

IRELAND
(to England)

ENGLAND

ENGLISH CHANNEL

NETHERLANDS

F R A N C E

ATLANTIC
OCEAN

GULF
OF BISCAY

PORTUGAL

SPAIN

Castile

Aragon

Granada

CORSICA

SARDINIA

SICILY

Naples

Papal
State

Venice

SWITZ.

Savoy

ADRIATIC   SEA

IONIAN
SEA

MEDITERRANEAN   SEA

2

The Development of Commercial Capitalism

1500 - 1650

ALTHOUGH MAN does not live by bread alone, neither does he live without it. The production of goods and the provision of services are only part of man's activity, but a necessary part. The history of the three centuries after 1500 cannot be understood apart from the great economic transformation that began to take shape in those years. At the beginning of our period, Europe was a continent mainly agricultural; at its close, the transformation of the world by industrialism was already clearly foreshadowed—the age between was that of triumphant commerce.

I. Agriculture

In 1500 Europe was moving from a simple to a complex economy. Though at least four out of every five of her people still had to devote themselves to the task of raising food, they supported a nonagricultural population large by comparison with other lands and earlier times. The time was slowly approaching when a relatively small number of people would remain on the land while the rest, eating food grown by others, would serve commerce, industry, government, arts, and letters. Such a transformation required the integration of the peasantry into an all-encompassing market system.

It was not easy to make over the European peasant into a producer of commodities. He was not eager to sell what he produced in order to buy what he consumed. Nowhere do peasant communities easily or quickly abandon their safe and familiar self-sufficiency; those in Europe did not do so in this age of transition. They continued to grow their own food, weave their own cloth, sew their own garments; a few blacksmiths and harness makers, as well as traveling tinkers, did tasks of special difficulty or requiring special skill. But European peasants could very seldom meet this goal of sufficing to themselves. They had to import some products: salt for the livestock came from distant mines or from the salt pans along the beaches of France and Portugal; iron for plows and other farm tools was mined and smelted in few places; millstones were seldom locally available. But even more important in drawing commodities from the rural communities were the taxes exacted by the state and the rents and dues paid to landlords, contributions that could not be evaded or put off. Only a small part was consumed directly by those who collected them; the rest entered the channels of trade and furnished the provisions for the growing urban population.

The transformation of the agricultural communities became much more rapid as they were meshed into the broad system of European commerce. Each of the major patterns of agricultural organization was differently affected. The communal pattern prevailed throughout the great European plain; west of the Elbe river, the manorial form was usual, while to the east the peasant community itself was the unit of agricultural enterprise. Where agricultural activity was based upon the peasant community, the changes were most striking; where the system of individual ownership and tillage prevailed, it was consolidated.

Manors. The manor had been the typical form of agrarian organization on the northwest European plain for at least five centuries. The manorial unit did not always coincide with the village community. In many cases there were two or more manors associated with a single village; the village provided the residential and social framework of peasant life, the manor the economic framework, combining the systems of property holding and tillage. Some governmental functions belonged to the manor, others often to the village. Though the manor has often been linked by historians with the feudal system, it was actually quite distinct from it. Feudalism was a form of power distribution among the political rulers (see ch. 1, p. 11), manorialism a way of assuring cultivation of the land by peasant communities which neither owned nor controlled it. Manors existed before feudalism and continued, though greatly modified, after it was gone; where they existed together, the manors provided the feudal lords with their most important revenues.

During the sixteenth century, the distribution of land within the manors

FARM LIFE IN THE SIXTEENTH CENTURY. Engraving by Jan Baptiste Collaert, after a drawing by Tobias Verhaecht, about 1600.

"The Age of Silver" *(Aetas Argentea)* is one of a series of engravings illustrating the "four ages of Man." It shows the techniques of agriculture in Flanders at the end of the sixteenth century. The varieties of farm tools and the number and kinds of livestock are notable. *(Achenbach Foundation)*

continued relatively unchanged. Some of the land belonged to the peasants; some, the "demesne," to the manorial lord; and the rest was "common" land, the property of the manor as a community. Large "open" fields were the major divisions of manorial land. Each such field was divided into sections of perhaps ten or more acres given over to the cultivation of a single crop at any one time. These sections were further subdivided into strips separated by balks, or unplowed sod. Peasant holdings consisted only of these strips; a family usually held one or more in each of the crop sections.

A peasant could not till his own strips as he thought best; the whole section was cultivated as a unit, according to a customary pattern which the manorial community alone might change. Plows, wagons, hoes, livestock used for traction, were individually owned. Especially on the northern plain, the work of cultivation was frequently co-operative. The demesne sometimes included strips interspersed among the peasant holdings in the open fields, but usually consisted chiefly of one or more large tracts tilled as units. The customary source of labor for cultivating the demesne was the labor service of the peasants, part of their regular obligations to the lord of the manor; increasingly, however, the landlords relied upon hired labor, which was easier to control and hence more efficient.

The common land was an essential element in the manorial economy. Both peasants and lord held rights to utilize the pasture and the woodland which made up this common. The lords usually retained the sole right to hunt in the woods, while the peasants could take a limited amount of wood for burning. The number of livestock each family could graze on the pasture and in the woodland was calculated according to the size of its holdings in the arable land. This arrangement was characteristic of the manorial method of combining individual and group interests; collaboration was necessary and frequent, but almost never was there an egalitarianism of rights.

Manorial Decline. Outwardly, the manorial system continued to prevail in the pattern of western European agriculture after 1500. It was a sick system, however. Its efficient functioning depended on tight control of its labor supply by means of serfdom, which in much of western Europe the peasantry had thrown off.

The development of trade and the wider use of money transformed the duties and the rights of the peasantry in western Europe. In many places, they purchased release from the legal status of serfs; impecunious lords of the manor were eager to receive a tidy sum in exchange for the services and the irregular payments due from serfs. The lords of the manor gladly joined, too, in changing the character of the rents and dues which continued in effect. Once given in goods and services, these came more and more frequently to be paid in cash; they often ceased to be obligations upon persons and fell instead upon the land.

Peasant tenures, once the inalienable birthright of long-established families, gradually became objects of sale and purchase. The sense of property changed. Increasingly it referred not to the place of the peasant and his family within the manorial community, but to the land itself, with its customary rights as part of its worth and its obligations as an encumbrance upon it. Frequently, the person who held a tenure came to feel himself to be the true owner of the land.

One could now hold a tenure without being a peasant who toiled upon it for his living. Townsmen bought peasant tenures for the sake of their income; enterprising manorial lords rounded out their demesne lands in the same way. But burghers had no claim upon peasant labor, and manorial lords had frequently bartered away their rights for cash commutations. The land therefore could either be operated as a capitalist enterprise with hired labor or rented to peasants for fixed sums and limited periods on leasehold. In either case, manorial collaboration gave way to individual operation. (The rise of leasehold renting of land is reflected in the changed meaning of the word "farmer." Originally "farm" referred to the fixed, or "firm," payment for the hire of land, and a "farmer" was what is now called a "tenant" or renter: a farmer owning his land would have been a contradiction in terms.)

Thus transformed, the manor ceased to be the self-sufficient peasant community of earlier centuries. It became instead little more than the legal form of agricultural enterprise. The peasant still produced for his own use as much as he could, but a very large amount of his crop entered the channels of trade to feed and clothe towns both nearby and distant.

East Europe: The New Serfdom. A parallel but far from identical transformation of rural life took place in eastern Europe. The rise of towns and the growth of trade and industry in the West created an almost insatiable demand for grain; the open plains of eastern Europe were better able than any other area to be the granary of the continent. This combination was opportunity itself for the ruling classes, who wanted the luxuries produced in the West. Their problem was to obtain the grain in order to supply the demand; they could not solve it without reversing the conditions of the peasantry.

During the high middle ages, the peasantry east of the Elbe river had come to live much better than their western brothers. Especially in eastern Germany and western Poland, many peasant settlements had originally been colonies of immigrants attracted from the overpopulous West (mainly Flanders and the Rhineland) by favorable conditions offered by landowners and ruling princes. The mass of the Polish peasantry had benefited in the same way by "settlement with German law," that is, by the grant of conditions like those of the newcomers. Peasant holdings had been considerably larger than in the West, while the landlords kept relatively little land to be tilled by hired hands. The landlords' revenues in fixed rents decreased steadily in value during the fifteenth century. The peasants largely governed themselves in their villages, which provided the economic and governmental as well as the residential and social structure of their activity. As long as these conditions remained, the landlords were in no position to ship to the West the quantities of grain it demanded.

The nobility held in their political powers the resource for breaking, to their own advantage, the self-sufficiency of the peasant communities. The rights of village government which they had granted to the peasants during the earlier stage of colonization they now drew back to themselves; the kings and princes deprived the peasants of the protection of the national courts and left them defenseless before the arbitrary decisions of the landlords, who were their only judges. To the fixed fees which the peasants had paid as tenants, the landlords added more and more compulsory labor service. Where the peasants had been obligated to do no more than two or three days of work for the landlord a year, they were now compelled to do as much in a single week; they also had to transport the grain to the market, or to the barges on which it would move down the rivers to the great ports on the Baltic.

To prevent them from fleeing to milder masters or freer lands, the governments curtailed or even destroyed the personal freedom of the peasants. Laws were established requiring peasants to meet all obligations to their landlords before they could quit the land; increased tax burdens were placed upon their villages as well as upon them individually. Serfdom, or compulsion upon the peasant to remain on the soil, came to millions of free peasants in eastern Europe at the very time when it was disappearing in most of western Europe. Nor were the peasants allowed to retain the land they had received on direct leasehold in earlier centuries; the landlords used any pretext to recapture every possible acre so that the peasants' labor could be put to the fullest use. Thus it was in the East that large-scale farming was first introduced into modern Europe, though upon the basis of bondage, not of free hired labor.

By the end of the sixteenth century the success of the landlords in transforming agriculture as they had desired was clear. The exports of grain from Poland are vivid evidence. Some 600,000 bushels of grain were shipped annually through Danzig (which handled about nine-tenths of the total) around 1500; a century later this amount had increased to no less than 4,500,000 bushels.

Individual Agriculture. Individual agriculture, as distinct from the manorial or village patterns, was also widespread in Europe, especially away from the great northern plain. In the uplands, which remained economically retarded, private ownership of arable land was usual, though combined with village rights over pasturage. In the lands along the Mediterranean, manorialism had always been weak, and outright ownership of land was common. Rental tenancy, usually on a sharecropping basis (*mezzadria*), was the prevalent system in northern Italy; direct cultivation of landed estates by hired labor was also introduced. In England, where manorialism had once been strong, its demise in the fifteenth and sixteenth centuries was all the more evident. Copyhold tenures deriving from manorial custom were weakened and frequently gave way to leaseholds for limited periods of time.

The enclosing of common lands as private property, to be used for sheepwalks or for capitalist farming with hired hands, was the most remarked aspect of the change. Demesne land, as the landlords' own, was the easiest and the first to be enclosed; then ordinarily came the commons, to be followed by the open-field strips, which had to be redistributed at the same time. Individual agriculture achieved its greatest successes across the North Sea in the Low Countries. There the manorial system had never been strong, and was virtually absent from the coastal strip, where the "polders," lands below sea level reclaimed by diking and drainage, were always privately owned, frequently by rich townsmen who had borne the heavy expense of their establishment.

Improved Methods. Except in the Low Countries and (later) in England, little advance in agricultural technique accompanied the great transformation in rural property relationships.

Crops. The most important crops continued to be cereal grains; bread was the basic item in the European diet, and flour could be stored safely for long periods of time. The principal cereal grains (collectively called "corn" in English usage) were wheat and rye; winter wheat for milling into a pure white flour provided the bread of the more prosperous classes, while rye, sturdier and cheaper, was the common bread "corn." Barley, to be fermented into beer, and grapes for wine, were also common crops; grapes could be grown on sandy or hilly terrain unfavorable to cereals. Oats and legumes were used to feed both human beings and livestock. Flax provided the principal vegetable fiber for cloth; sheep were raised, especially in England and Spain, primarily for their wool, while animal hides were of essential importance in supplying leather.

The Problem of Soil Fertility. The principal problem continued to be maintaining and reviving the fertility of the soil under sustained cultivation. The amount of arable land available influenced the methods employed by farmers to achieve continuous crops. In the forest regions of central Russia, the primitive technique of slash-and-burn persisted even into the sixteenth century, but the fertility of the burned clearings was soon exhausted and constant movement from clearing to clearing was necessary. The much more common method in regions where more land than labor was available was to sow a field to a single crop for years on end until the harvest yield declined too greatly; then it would be allowed to lie fallow while another field was put under the plow.

Where the land had a thin cover of humus and limited fertility, especially in the Mediterranean area, a two-field system was common; in this arrangement, a field was tilled and left fallow on alternate years. A three-field system, adaptable to more fertile land, was most widely employed. In this rotation, one field was sown to the bread grains (rye or wheat), another to barley, oats, or peas, and a third remained fallow. In the subsequent year, the fallow field was sown to rye or wheat, the other fields were likewise shifted forward in the rotation pattern. Thus only one-third of the land was withdrawn from cultivation at any one time. At best, however, the harvest remained small; the yield was seldom more than four or five times the quantity of seed put into the soil, sometimes as little as three. Little attention was given to selection of better-quality seeds; the ordinary practice was merely to take a portion of the previous crop at random. The yield may be compared with modern seed-to-harvest ratios of 10, 20, or more.

None of these various systems of field utilization adequately replaced the organic materials (principally nitrogenous compounds) taken from the soil by the growing crops. Leguminous plants, as used in three-field rotation, helped nitrogenous regeneration; near the coasts seaweed provided a rich fertilizer but in limited amounts. Animal manures continued to be the only adequate fertilizer in most places. Because of the value of the droppings left by the livestock, the provision for allowing farm animals to graze on the stubble in the fields after harvest was usually considered to be a right of the landholder, not a burden upon him. Nevertheless it was difficult to maintain herds large enough to produce as much manure as the fields needed. From spring to autumn, cattle, pigs and goats browsed in the pasture and woodlands, where their droppings were lost from use. There was seldom enough hay to keep much livestock over the winter. Only what hay could be gathered from the pastureland, especially the marshes good for little else, was available for winter storage.

A vicious circle dominated agriculture: the need for cereal grains was too crying to permit much planting of hay crops like alfalfa and clover in the regular fields, but without the livestock which hay kept alive, there was not enough fertilizer to maintain high fertility in the arable land. Thus the herds remained quite small, limiting the production not only of crops but also of meats and dairy products. Accessory sources of foods, like fishing and beekeeping (reminiscent of the primitive times when men were food gatherers as much as food growers), continued to be important in the economy of the peasant household.

Innovations. The Low Countries showed how the problem of sustained intensive cultivation could be solved. Here neither custom nor manorialism were strong enough to hamper experiments in improved agricultural techniques. Not only were the usual crops cultivated, but garden crops and livestock raising were also emphasized. By the early part of the seventeenth century, clover was introduced; it improved the soil for subsequent crops and provided fodder for large numbers of cattle. Turnips, too, proved useful as food for people and animals, and did not deplete the soil. The herds could be maintained at full strength, and contributed their droppings to reinvigorating the soil. Netherlandish farmers made use of every opportunity to obtain fertilizer from other sources as well. They bought the night soil (human excreta) accumulated in the many nearby towns; they also imported burned peat from the eastern provinces of the country, thus adding needed potash to their land. The innovations in the Low Countries were studied and imitated, especially in England, during the seventeenth and eighteenth centuries.

II. Trade

The ability of the European countryside to supply food well beyond the needs of the producers themselves made possible the development of a numerous commercial and industrial population. The visible sign of the transformation was the growth of cities; capitalists are usually city dwellers, as appears from the modern use of the word *bourgeoisie* (French for "townsmen") for this class.

The Towns. Even at the high point of rural self-sufficiency, from about the eighth to the tenth centuries, traders continued to travel across Europe, but in small numbers and with tiny stocks; commerce concerned little beside a few luxuries and did not require established urban market places. Beginning with the eleventh century in western and central Europe, the relative stabilization of political life by means of feudalism, the improvement in agriculture, and the growing general prosperity combined to facilitate the rise of towns. The modern city* began as a fortified place of safety, a *burg;* or as a market place that grew up where customers came to the tradesmen and not vice versa; or as a residential center built specially for possessors of accumulated wealth. Whichever of these factors had given its first impulse to any particular town, the other characteristics tended to develop as well. All three elements continued to shape the physical appearance and social life of the European town in 1500 much as they had for the five previous centuries; its economic function likewise remained, as the slowly but steadily beating heart of local trade. Hundreds of such towns dotting the countryside formed the prevalent urban pattern almost everywhere in Europe through the whole early modern period. A few grew into specialized industrial or governmental centers; the rest remained local market towns with a few thousand inhabitants or less.

Market Towns. The market towns were not purely places of trade, however; in general, what the market town sold, it first made. Industrial tasks once the virtual monopoly of the villages, manors, and great estates passed increasingly into the hands of town artisans during the latter middle ages.

By 1500, makers of cloth and clothing, tanners, leatherworkers, ropemakers, carpenters, and blacksmiths were usually townsmen, though wandering tinkers and shoemakers continued to bring their skills to rural folk for many centuries. Urban craftsmen supplied not only their fellow townsmen but all the countryside roundabout. Able therefore to devote themselves to a single craft, they became more skillful than their rural competitors and could produce more cheaply.

* The distinction made in American English between the "town" as a *small* and the "city" as a *large* urban center is absent in British and continental usage; in this book, the words are used interchangeably, except where specifically noted.

The artisan was usually his own shopkeeper. He might sell in his own shop, like the tailors; or he might have a stall in the market place where he put out his goods for sale, especially on the weekly market day. It was to the market place, too, that the peasants from the neighboring area brought their surplus food to sell; with the money thus obtained, they bought the fabricated articles they needed. But the market town was more than the self-sufficient rural community writ larger. Articles from more distant places, usually semiluxuries, also were sold in the market place, though they formed only a small proportion of the turnover. The money the peasants acquired was also used to pay taxes and rents owed to governments and landlords who spent them elsewhere. The broader regional and interregional commerce of Europe thus ultimately rested on the underpinnings of local trade.

Large Towns. Cities larger than these market towns were few in number. Some were political capitals, like Paris and London, which tended to grow more rapidly than other towns. Large numbers of persons came together to pay attendance upon the king in his court and to serve him in agencies of state; these in turn gave employment to many others who fed, housed, and clothed them, and otherwise cared for their needs. Thus capitals became ready-made markets of considerable size, permitting even greater specialization than was possible in local market towns; some trades and crafts could be plied only where such great wealth was concentrated.

Other large cities arose because of favorable locations on major trade routes. Such were Venice and Genoa. Their strategic positions at the heads of inland seas placed them astride of the best routes between the Mediterranean and the interior of Europe. Antwerp, on the Scheldt river in the Low Countries, served trade between southern and northern Europe.

Towns specializing in some phase of industrial operations might grow to considerable size, as in the Low Countries, but seldom became as big as capital cities or trading centers; huge factory towns were still part of a far-off future.

Trade at a Distance. These larger cities formed the nodes of a vast network of regional and interregional trade. It is impossible to estimate with any exactness the size of this commercial activity at the turn of the fifteenth to sixteenth centuries. Although the total amount of local trade was certainly much larger, the commerce at the higher level, between big cities over long distances, bore the seeds of historic changes of great consequences.

Wares. Local and long-distance commerce had different origins. Market-town trade reflected the uniformities of Europe: the exchanges involved were much the same everywhere, the produce of the farm for the handiwork of the nearby town. Trade between the larger cities, on the other hand, rose out of the variety and disparities characteristic of Europe as a whole: it depended on the fact that goods found or made only here and there were wanted everywhere. Mineral ores were found spottily, usually in the mountains; timber for ships came mainly from the evergreen forests of the North and the oak woods of the warmer climates; salt, from a few springs or from the seaside in the hot South; fish, from the sea and then not off every shore; grain, from the low plains; sheep and their wool, from their high plateaus. Often the skill to transform raw materials into particular products was limited to the inhabitants of a few areas or localities; at least until such skill spread, it was an element favoring trade between its possessors and all others.

Transport. Local and long-distance trade also differed in the demands they placed upon the organization of transportation, and hence in their consequences for economic arrangements. Local trade required only simple methods of transport; almost any peasant's cart could convey even bulky goods from farm to market town without much difficulty. Interregional and international trade, on the other hand, involved distances not of a few leagues but of hundreds and even thousands of miles. Transportation then could not be only one among a number of activities of the man who grew or made the goods himself; it became instead the task of a relatively small number of specialists.

For efficiency, water transport was preferable to the movement of goods by land. Ships carried large and heavy cargoes in their holds at low cost, especially if propelled by sails, unaided by oarsmen. At the start of the early modern period, the improvements in ship construction had progressed to the point where ships were no longer passive to the wind; deep-keeled bottoms, variable-angle rigging of the sails, and large hinged rudders made it possible to sail them into the wind as well as before it. Yet there were hazards. Though the ships were fairly sturdy, great storms still took a steady toll of foundered vessels. Piracy and its legalized companion, privateering, also created a frequent and very real danger. Navigation remained difficult; seamen preferred to hug the coast, guided by landmarks rather than by instruments.

Rivers furnished the means of waterborne transportation inland. Barges carried bulky loads downstream, driven by the current; but movement of vessels upstream remained difficult and expensive. Shifting sandbars and channels were usual where the rivers ran slowly; swift streams, on the other hand, presented dangers in rapids and hidden rocks. River traffic was subject, too, to the exactions of lords through whose lands the streams passed; on many rivers, the numerous tolls increased costs well beyond purely technical needs.

Overland commerce, on the other hand, was limited by the means of transport. Wagons could move only short distances, all the more since roads usually lacked any kind of paving or drainage and slowed the traveler by mire in the wet months and by deep ruts in the dry. Pack-borne transport on horse- or donkeyback was necessarily limited to valuable articles of small size and weight.

The Southern System. Distant commerce was confined to a comparatively few routes distributed into three major groups. Of these the southern trading network was the oldest, and until the end of the fifteenth century, the most important as well. It derived its strength from the advantages of the Mediterranean, a protected inland sea linking more than two thousand miles of European, Asian, and North African shores. The southern region of general European commerce included directly only about one-third of the vast Mediterranean seaboard, the northwestern segment comprising Italy and the southern shores of France and Spain; the rest, under Islamic control, traded with Europe chiefly through these lands. Some Moslems preyed on the Christians instead of trading with then; the principal danger to Christian merchantmen on the Mediterranean came not so much from storms and rocks as from pirates cruising out of Algiers and other North African ports.

A considerable amount of exchange took place within the region, especially between Spain and Italy; major elements of this trade consisted of Spanish merino wool sent to the clothmaking cities of northern Italy, and Sicilian wheat shipped to the grain-hungry Iberian peninsula. It was not the movement of such bulky, low-value products as these which nourished the prosperity of Mediterranean commerce, however, but the export of manufactured articles and the trade with the Levant. The north Italian cities were famed for many skilled crafts; goods such as the fine woolens of Florence and the sturdy cordovan leathers of Spain were desired throughout Europe. The products manufactured in the Mediterranean region of Europe were chiefly luxuries or semiluxuries for the prosperous and the wealthy.

Commerce with the Levant, which loomed even greater in the trade of this region, was likewise a matter of luxuries. For centuries the spices of southeast Asia and the silks of China had come by ship and caravan to Syria and Egypt, where Europeans bought them partly with their own manufactures, but mostly with precious metals. The wars of the Ottoman Turks had briefly ruffled the even flow of this exchange, but the conquerors of the Byzantine empire soon re-established the transit trade of the Levant, which paid them rich tribute. The fall of Byzantium (Constantinople) to the Turks in 1453 was significant chiefly for finally cutting off Italian trade, principally Genoese, with the grain-producing regions of Crimea and southern Russia and with the overland silk route terminating at the Black Sea. Difficulties for Genoa meant advantage to Venice, its archrival, whose trade ran predominantly to the spice-selling cities near the isthmus of Suez, particularly Alexandria. Venice rose to its greatest wealth and power at the end of the fifteenth century, when it held in its hands virtually the entire supply of spice for Europe.

The Northern System. The trade of the North, like that of the South, was chiefly water-borne. The many rivers flowing across the great northern plain carried the products of a vast inland region to the North and Baltic Seas and the Atlantic Ocean, which formed the main pathway of northern commerce. The fundamental difference between the southern and northern trading regions consisted in the goods involved. The North shipped and sold principally products taken from its soil and the surrounding seas, not manufactured goods or imports from faraway lands. In western Europe, where industrial populations were most numerous, agriculture was seldom able to produce any great surplus of food; indeed, though agrarian conditions were generally good, local crop failures were not infrequent.

The shortages had to be made good by imports, primarily from the Baltic. Down to Danzig, and other Baltic ports, came the grain of the east European plain, where agrarian changes made an unusually large surplus available for export (see above, pp. 27-28). Ships from further south, particularly the Low Countries, carried the grain to their home ports, where some was distributed to local markets, some was reshipped to the Iberian peninsula or even to the Mediterranean, and the rest was warehoused until demand came from a region needing a supplement to its own supplies of the basic carbohydrate in the European diet.

The shipbuilding industry not only provided the vessels to carry the trade of the North, but contributed to its volume by a voracious demand for naval stores and supplies. The straight, slender fir trees of the thick northern forests produced the best ship masts; timber for hull construction was also shipped out in large quantities; resinous evergreens supplied pitch, tar, and other essential products for ship construction and maintenance. Thus the materials of northern commerce were fundamentally bulky and low in per-unit value. The total volume of this trade was immense by the standards of the period, however, and by the turn of the fifteenth century it was probably greater than that of southern trade.

The North-South System. The third network of trade routes ran between southern and northern Europe. The South sold to the luxury-craving North its own manufactures and the wares it imported from the East; the North sent down the raw materials which the South lacked. This trade went partly overland between Italy and Germany through the Alps, but about 1500 the maritime route by way of Gibraltar and terminating at the Low Countries was becoming more important. The Low Countries, at the intersection of the major north-south and east-west routes, continued their powerful economic growth as the main agents of European interregional trade.

The development of this commercial system embracing all Europe had immense social and political as well as economic consequences; at the very time when the religious unity of Latin Christendom was breaking apart, when the rise of territorial states was dissipating the sense of European political unity, the interdependence of European economic life was being intensified and magnified.

The Shift to the Atlantic. The general pattern of European trade changed surprisingly little during the early modern period. The southern and northern systems of trade remained distinct and yet interrelated, as they had been ever since the high middle ages. The principal cause of change was the expansion of the European commercial system as a whole to include vast overseas empires in the Orient and America (see ch. 6, pp. 122-140). Economic predominance shifted away from the Mediterranean to the Atlantic seaboard. The southern region thus subsided into relative backwardness, beginning shortly after 1500 and becoming sharply marked a century later. The northern region grew rapidly, both in comparison with the South and in absolute volume of trade. The interregional trade route was modified mainly in that Lisbon and Seville displaced Venice and became the principal southern termini of the system, while in the Low Countries first Antwerp and then Amsterdam became the principal intermediate port of transfer and warehousing.

III. Industry

Manufacturing industry, as a specific branch of economic activity distinct from both agriculture and commerce, was not the characteristic economic type of medieval life and did not become so during the early modern period. Agriculture continued to occupy the vast majority of hands; commerce began to equal ownership of wide landed estates as a producer of great wealth; but the manufacture of goods for sale was the work of fewer men and produced less wealth. Even so, the expansion of commerce and the rise of large towns encouraged the formation of substantial industry in Europe by 1500, and increasingly thereafter.

The process of production in most industries changed little between the late medieval and the early modern periods. This continuity was particularly evident in the local market towns, where butchers, bakers and candlemakers plied their crafts in much the same old way. The artisan in the small town usually did the whole work of fabrication, beginning with the raw material and ending with an article ready for use which he sold directly to the consumer. Indeed, tailors and shoemakers could not work to general sizes, but only to the measurements of a customer. Although the artisans in the local market towns together accounted for the great bulk of production, the output of a single artisan was necessarily limited.

Regional and interregional commerce created a wide market for such industries as textile manufacture, mining and metalworking, and shipbuilding. The spur of demand and the whip of competition encouraged significant advances in the technique of production.

Textiles. The biggest of these industries was the manufacture of textiles, concentrated in northern Italy and in the Low Countries. Cloth was produced in many grades, from shoddy mixtures to the finest woolens and damasks; wool was the principal fiber, although linen was also popular and silk was in demand among the prosperous. Some peasants continued to weave coarse homespun for their own use, but more prosperous farmers joined with the nonagricultural population in buying the cloth they wore.

Cloth production was one of the most complex of industrial processes, comprising such varied stages as the combing of the raw wool, the spinning and the looming, and the elaborate finishing of the woven cloth. The work in these various stages tended to become differentiated skills, performed by special crafts; in the Low Countries, where division of labor was most advanced, various towns performed different phases of the total process of clothmaking or specialized in manufacturing special fabrics.

Many of the operations were subject to performance by machine; mechanical fullers quite early replaced human workmen in the difficult and dirty process of cleansing, matting, and toughening the cloth. The tendency of guilds to impede or even prevent the introduction of improved techniques in some instances impelled merchants to move the manufacture of cloth out of town limits to the freer countryside.

Metals. Such hindrances played a smaller role in the metal industry. There was an almost insatiable demand for its products. On the whole, requisite capital investment was large and in the nature of the extractive and productive process the mines and plants tended to be located deep in the countryside, often in mountainous or forested regions, where town guilds were powerless.

Mining and smelting of the ores constituted one of the most massive industrial operations known to the period. Shallow surface mining had long since given way to pit workings; numerous technical difficulties, such as raising the ore to the surface and draining underground water, tested the ingenuity of the miners and encouraged a quest for improved methods. To convert ores to usable metals was not easy. Iron ore could be reduced by crushing and heating in a furnace, but silver ores gave up their whole treasure only after the amalgam method of extraction with mercury was invented in the mid-sixteenth century in Spain.

Iron and the alloys of copper (bronze and brass) were the most used of base metals. Iron was used mainly in the form of wrought iron. The manufacture of ironmongery, metal products in common use, was highly developed, especially in England. Pure copper was little used, but the technique of casting bronze was fairly well developed. Gold and silver working were handicrafts, more matters of skill than of complex or large machinery. The manufacture of arms was basically part of the metalworking field, like other parts except for the intensity of the demand for improvement of the product. Cannon were the biggest metal articles manufactured at the time in any numbers; the processes of casting and boring artillery pieces required establishments far larger than the small shops which made articles of hardware.

Shipbuilding. Shipbuilding, even more than the metal industries, was necessarily a large-scale operation. The Arsenal at Venice was the model of advanced methods of ship construction in the late middle ages; but in the next centuries the shipwrights of Holland and Zeeland took over leadership in their art. In the Dutch yards wind and water power were used to drive mechanical saws; interchangeable parts were employed to an unprecedented extent; rapidity and cheapness of construction were emphasized rather than careful and narrow traditionalism.

IV. Forms of Organization

The process of production as well as the conditions of trade were reflected in the character of industrial organization. Where the market remained fairly stable and the amount of capital investment needed was neither insignificant nor immense, the guild system usually prevailed; otherwise, "free" (nonguild) methods of various kinds were found.

The Guilds. Early European guilds had been so-called "merchant guilds," which included in their membership virtually all the resident merchants and skilled artisans in a town with distinction of craft or commodity. Such guilds protected the interests of the general business community primarily against outside competition; only members of the guild were permitted to conduct business within the town, with such specific exceptions as annual fairs. As European cities grew larger and more complex, the simple structure of the merchant guild proved inadequate. By the end of the fifteenth century, it had been replaced almost everywhere by the "craft guild," which lasted in some countries well into the nineteenth century.

The principle of occupational specialization controlled the organization of the craft guild. Although in theory each line of trade might have been supposed to possess its own guild, the practice was quite different. The number of guilds varied from a dozen or so in a small town to as many as 140 in a city like Paris.

The security of its membership in the pursuit of their trade and livelihood was the central economic function of the craft guild. By strictly forbidding any hoarding of raw materials or stockpiling of finished goods, especially if produced by others, it prevented any single person from establishing a monopoly over the market. The guild ideal was equality of its members; it set identical prices for all guildsmen and enforced identical standards of quality upon them. In so doing, it often safeguarded the interests of the consumer. Often, however, the town councils had to keep watch over the individual guilds lest they seek their own advantage too brazenly at the expense of the general community.

Masters, Journeymen, and Apprentices. The central figure in the guild was the master, the owner of a shop in which he himself was the principal workman. He was a full-fledged member of his guild, with the right to vote for its officers and to enjoy all its benefits. These were many, for the guild was a social and religious as well as economic organization; it provided help for its members in the event of need, succored the master's widow when he died, had its own feasts and festivals, and, not least, was a lay fraternity within the church with its own patron saint (in Roman Catholic lands).

Apprentices and journeymen worked beside the master in his shop. The apprentice was a boy entrusted by his parents to live in the master's home and be trained in his craft. The apprentice learned by imitation and by the performance of simple and then successively more difficult tasks until after a number of years—the average number in England was finally set at seven— he was a competent workman, able to do a master's work. He was not ready to set up his own shop, however, for usually he lacked the money to purchase his tools and materials and had no wife to run his household, to which the shop was closely attached. A stage as a journeyman therefore intervened between apprenticeship and mastership. During this period the craftsman worked in the shop of a master for daily wages (hence his name, "journeyman," from the French *journée*, day); unlike the apprentice, he did not have to live in the master's household or obey him in his personal life. After he had accumulated savings and taken a bride, he was ready for mastership in his trade.

The Oligarchic Trend. During the high middle ages, the reality of guild life often corresponded to this idyllic picture, especially in small-scale trades providing for local needs. It did not survive where the costs of setting up shop were inordinately high, as with gold and silversmiths, or where the guild form actually covered the development of a complex, large-scale industry, as in Netherlands textiles. It became impossible for virtually every apprentice to rise through a relatively brief period as a journeyman to mastership and independence. The guilds came under the control of the masters in possession, who treated their positions as property to be handed down to their heirs. Obstacles of expense and labor were usually put in the way of acceptance of candidates for mastery: a costly and difficult specimen of his handiwork, the "masterpiece," might be required; he had to prove his competence by examinations of excessive harshness, and to pay for banquets and

other festivities for the assembled masters. But for the son or other designated heir of a master, these almost impossible requirements were very often
put aside or eased. Thus, in the centuries immediately before and after 1500,
the large majority of journeymen in oligarchic guilds had no hope of becoming masters and formed a class of lifelong wage workers.

A master was ordinarily no longer limited to a few apprentices and
journeymen, but could put to work as many as he could pay. Sharp conflicts
of interest between masters and journeymen ensued; the strike and the lock-
out were invented, and frequently employed despite strict governmental bans.
Journeymen formed their own protective associations or *compagnonnages*
(from the French *compagnon*, companion or journeyman); they also often
traveled from town to town to ply their trade, sharpen their skills, and seek
better conditions.

Capitalist Business. The guilds did not form the basis for the development of the capitalist forms of commerce and industry most characteristic of
the following stage of economic life. For one thing, the guilds were too much
monopolistic associations of masters protecting their narrow interests and
barring the introduction of new and usually improved methods of production
and organization. Even more important, the guild system was fundamentally
suitable to self-employed craftsmen with a few helpers, rather than to large-
scale operations requiring great sums of capital and using many workmen.

Specifically capitalist forms of industrial organization developed slowly.
By the early sixteenth century, most mines had passed from the ownership of
co-operatives of the miners themselves into the hands of joint-stock companies, with princes, noblemen, and rich merchants holding the shares; the
workmen became mere hired hands. Heavy metalworking plants likewise
used many hands, though they usually belonged to individual owners. A more
widespread form of capitalist production was the so-called "putting-out"
system, or cottage industry; the organizer of production was a merchant who
purchased raw material and distributed it to home workers for each phase
of production. The workers were paid a piece rate, and although they worked
at home and supplemented their incomes with the produce of garden plots,
they were often wage-workers as truly as factory hands.

Organization upon a capitalist basis came more quickly to commercial
enterprises. The earliest, and until the nineteenth century the prevailing,
form of organization was the family business. It was familiar, because the
guild shop was such an enterprise; it required no novel legal arrangements or
moral justifications, for there was no distinction between the obligations of
an individual and the obligations of his firm. Such an organization was most
easily expanded by the inclusion of the owner's sons; companies with names
like "John Doe & Sons" remain common to the present day. Companies
including brothers, cousins, and nephews were next to come; they arose first

in Italian and later in German trade and banking. More significant as a harbinger of the future was the partnership. This arrangement might include both active and "sleeping" (investing, not managing) partners, but the rule of unlimited legal liability usually extended to all partners, as to all members in a family firm.

Other forms developed which made greater expansion possible. The regulated company was an association of individual traders under government sponsorship and control; the Hanse of the northern German cities and the Company of Merchant Adventurers in England were fundamentally of this type. The joint-stock company, which was the direct forerunner of the modern limited-liability company, developed first in shipping enterprises, especially in Italy, whence it spread to other maritime countries. The earlier companies were organized for one or at most for a few voyages; capital and profit had to be redistributed after a short period.

Around the turn of the sixteenth century, however, the Dutch and British companies for colonial trade were organized on a long-term basis; profits were paid out periodically, but the capital invested as shares remained in the enterprise to finance continued operations. Such an organization combined the permanency of the family firm with the power of bringing together masses of capital which even the wealthiest families could not furnish. The age had relatively little need for such joint-stock enterprises, but the device was known and available from the mid-sixteenth century.

The "Price Revolution." The lifeblood of this expanding capitalism was money, the means of exchange and payment. During the middle ages, especially after 1300, a shortage of currency had resulted from the decline in silver production and the constant drainage of precious metals to Asia as payment for imports of spices, silks, and the like. A renewal of silver mining on a large scale in Europe during the late fifteenth century, especially in Germany and Austria, brought some relief. The discovery of America transformed the scarcity of coin into surplus. The silver and gold mines opened up in Spanish America poured precious metal, especially silver, into Europe at an increasing volume during most of the sixteenth century, and continued, though more slowly, thereafter. Economic historians estimate that the gold and silver in Europe, mostly in the form of coin, increased about four times from 1500 to 1650.

A steady and rapid rise of prices resulted, first in Spain and then gradually through the rest of Europe. The cost of goods in Spain rose on the average about 300 per cent between 1500 and 1600, while wages, typically lagging behind, increased only about 275 per cent (according to the researches of E. J. Hamilton). In France during the same period, prices rose 220 per cent, wages only 140 per cent; in England, the spread was even wider, reaching some 250 per cent for goods and 130 for wages about 1600, and 350 per cent for goods and 190 per cent for wages about 1650. It has been estimated that prices increased between two and three per cent a year on the average in Europe during this period. This immense inflation has been named the "price revolution" of the sixteenth century by economic historians.

Contemporaries sought for an explanation of the skyrocketing prices. One was that the money was being debased by reduction of its precious-metal contents. The French thinker Jean Bodin demonstrated the shallowness of this theory; even where debasement occurred, he showed, it was not adequate to explain the price increases. He indicated the true nature of what had happened: a vast increase in the amount of money available to pay for the quantity of goods available.

The consequences of the price revolution upon the European economy were varied. Fixed rents dropped rapidly in value, sometimes pulling land-owners down into poverty; people with fixed incomes also suffered. Wages were more flexible, but seldom caught up with the cost of living. Manufac-turers employing any of the capitalist systems of organizing production usually benefited, because costs usually lagged behind selling prices; com-merce found its advantages, too, especially in the loosening of credit.

Banking. Banking, the one form of economic enterprise which does business with money and not with the goods or services which money buys, expanded rapidly during the early modern period. The dual functions of banking consist in facilitating payments, especially in a Europe marked by the presence of numerous currencies of differing worth, and in credit. Both aspects of banking were present from the beginning, but they were performed by other institutions before banks were developed; banking preceded banks by decades and even centuries.

Fairs, which had arisen as market places during the middle ages, con-tinued to provide the occasion for settlement of accounts long after their original function was abandoned; at these gatherings of merchants and moneychangers, an elaborate technique of "clearing" accounts was used to minimize the need for actually transferring money at a time when its trans-port was expensive and dangerous. At the end of the fifteenth century, Geneva and Lyons, along the western overland route between Italy and northern Europe, were competing for this role; Lyons won out not long after, with important consequences for both political and economic developments. The bank of the Rialto at Venice and the bank of Saint George at Genoa met a similar need; the bank of Amsterdam, formed when that city became the commercial metropolis of Europe early in the seventeenth century, further developed the system of making payments for and against depositors' accounts.

The function of lending grew more haphazardly and with greater diffi-culty. Its basic impediment was the ban in canon law against usury, or the taking of interest on loans. This rule fitted the usual need in an agrarian society beset by crop failures; a loan of money or grain came out of surplus and was repaid in full, leaving the lender as rich as before; it tided a victim over his bad times. The ban on interest fell more uncertainly upon the economically different case of business loans, which really were forms of providing business capital. The canonical rule was too clear to permit open charging of interest in such cases, but medieval and early modern businessmen and casuists (theologians concerned with application of moral rules to particular cases) circumvented the limitation by inventing various ways to permit business loans which brought profit to the lender as well as to the borrower. Such loans, however disguised, were made mainly by private businessmen, especially goldsmiths. Banks as such entered the business of making loans slowly and unevenly until late in the seventeenth century. Governments borrowed even more frequently than private persons, but were bad risks because against their default there was no recourse but refusal to grant further credit.

V. The Business Spirit

Long-distance trade and large-scale industry encouraged and necessitated a more deliberate and informed conduct of affairs than was characteristic of medieval economic life. The simple record keeping of a small craftsman was grossly inadequate; a cash box for income and expenditure, a spike on which to stick bills—these could not handle any large volume of business. Special ways of keeping records became necessary. Journal bookkeeping (daily entry of all transactions in a single book) came into use first; it sufficed for keeping track of purchases and sales, but not for defining the profit status of a firm. For this purpose, double-entry bookkeeping was invented and gradually improved in Italy, where commerce was most advanced; in this system of keeping accounts, the position of a firm with regard to all sums owing by it and to it was made clear. With such records, it became possible to develop a science of accounting, or analysis of the financial status of a firm and the profitability of its operations. Without ceasing to be an art, running a business was slowly becoming more of a science.

Such new and gradually evolving economic institutions as banking, accounting, and capitalist forms of the firm all pointed to profit making as their primary goal, yet the men who built and operated them seldom had so distinct or exclusive a purpose in mind till after the new system had been functioning for a considerable period of time. Then the institutions slowly and uncertainly, but in many respects relentlessly, imposed their own character on their creators and operators. Profit came to the surface as a frank motive in human conduct, and after a period of sharp criticism, it achieved almost universal moral acceptability. The give-and-take between men and institutions still continued: men in business were driven to make fuller use of the new capitalist business forms.

It is difficult to sum up the spirit and character of large groups of people, but it is possible to speak of the kind of people whom these new economic institutions tended to form in increasing numbers in this period. These were men more deliberate, purposeful and rational in the conduct of business and the search for profit than the medieval age usually knew. Earning a livelihood by the sweat of one's brow had always occupied most of the energies of the great majority of mankind, who dreamed of wealth as an escape from drudgery. But among those who won success by the new economic methods were some who took pride in their exertions and called work a joy as well as a duty.

Thus economic life at the beginning of the early modern period was varied and even contradictory. In some ways it was little changed from what it had been centuries before; in others, it was quite new. The separation of management and ownership from labor; large-scale operations culminating in the big integrated factory; a new spirit of rational enterprise and frank profit taking—all these could already be observed in 1500, if only in incipient form. During the next three centuries these essential characteristics of capitalism continued to grow in vigor and significance until they came to dominate the entire economy of Europe in the nineteenth century.

3

Letters and Arts in the Age of the Renaissance

1450 - 1650

THINKERS AND ARTISTS at the beginning of the sixteenth century rejoiced in the triumphant newness of their own age. They boasted of their new learning and their new style. Original and creative minds of the time turned against their predecessors of the centuries just past. The bright young men of around 1500—earlier in Italy, later elsewhere in Europe—characterized medieval philosophy, literature, and art as ugly barbarism. Men now should think, write, paint in the new ways these new leaders had discovered.

But these bold innovators were also imitators. Their novelty consisted in recapturing the lost arts of classical Greece and Rome, which had come to an end a thousand years before. So proud were they of this achievement that they celebrated the "rebirth" of good literature, of fine arts, and of true philosophy. This name, "Renaissance," has come to be applied to the whole time roughly from 1400 to 1650.

But in the realm of spiritual creativity, as in human life in general, things changed more slowly than it may seem. Renaissance men did not totally transform their attitudes toward life, their intellectual assumptions, their standards of beauty and truth. They retained the medieval manner even when they thought they were abandoning it. They usually rejected only those aspects of their tradition which directly conflicted with revived classical forms. Beneath the classical surface of many a poem or edifice created during these years, we now see without difficulty the same basic structures that medieval poets and builders had used. Medieval and neoclassical themes were juxtaposed and harmonized, in defiance of the theorists, because the new way of looking at antiquity was not so wholly different from the old as they thought.

The debate among historians as to the essential characteristics of "the Renaissance" as an entity is in large measure a war of words. The variety of experiences found during these fifteen or twenty decades precludes any simple and inclusive definition beyond the commonplace observation that it was the time of the New Learning of the humanists and the New Style of the artists. The period of the Renaissance is not clearly distinguishable from the ages that came before and after. The Renaissance is medieval insofar as it continued and developed the institutions, attitudes, methods, and manners of the previous period; but it is not just medieval, because it developed characteristics of its own. Similarly, the Renaissance underlies many modern developments, but it is significantly unlike them in many ways. The relationship between the Renaissance and the preceding and following periods is thus compounded of both continuity and change.

I. Humanism

Philosophy and literature in the Renaissance form the twin elements of a broad movement called humanism. In a general or philosophic sense, the word "humanism" means the study of man rather than of nature or God. Renaissance scholars, however, used it in a more special way; they revived the classical Latin use of the term *humanitas* for literary activity, and applied the word "humanities" to the study of the classical languages (Greek and Latin) and the rhetorical form and intellectual content of the great classical authors.

Neo-Latin Classicism. Renaissance humanism, then, required a new educational system designed to take the place of the method of instruction which had prevailed in European universities since their first formation in the eleventh and succeeding centuries. Except for a minority who took degrees in civil law or medicine, most students in medieval universities prepared for careers in the church. They all used a common language of the learned, which we call medieval Latin. Its grammar and basic vocabulary were much the same as those of classical Latin, but its diction and rhetoric had been adapted to new needs linked with the professions of most educated men—theologians, lawyers, and medical doctors—who had come to use technical jargons that were the despair of laymen.

Medieval students began their study of Latin from introductory grammars of fairly recent date, but soon passed on to selected readings from ancient authors. Thus, though the graces of good literature held no independent place in education, these students read books written in styles subtler, more varied, more deeply moving than those of most contemporaries.

At various times during the medieval period, sensitive authors had tried to recapture this "pure" classical style, as well as to write in a grammar more nearly like the classic; their sporadic endeavors in part constituted what have been called the early renaissances of the ninth and subsequent centuries. From the time of Petrarch (ca. 1304-1374), increasing numbers of learned men undertook to master the classical style. The essential characteristic of an educated man, by their standards, came to be the ability to write like the authors of antiquity. A humanist education consisted in such linguistic and literary studies as were needed for acquiring this new art of good writing.

The rhetoric of Cicero, the orator of the late Roman republic, was adopted by the humanists as their model for an obviously exalted style, far above the drabness of everyday speech and the technical precision of most medieval philosophers. It became a matter of prestige in governmental and especially in ecclesiastical offices to have documents composed in such Ciceronian Latin; diplomats were expected to be able to speak and write like ancient Romans.

Neo-Greek Classicism. For the most enterprising humanists, there was another linguistic ability whose mastery marked a man as possessing rare and valued equipment for the new learning. This was Greek, the language which the Romans themselves had learned in order to rise to a higher cultural level. Wide ranges of ancient learning, including much of the important early Christian theology, were available only in Greek. In a modern vernacular form, the language was still spoken in parts of the Levant, but western students wished rather to learn the tongue of ancient Greece. This classical Greek had survived among Byzantine scholars, some engaged in government service or education, others in monasteries. Professors of Greek were recruited from among them and came first to Italy, carrying with them precious manuscripts in the language they were to teach. After the fall of Constantinople to the Turks (1453), refugee scholars increased the number of teachers of Greek in Italy; a small number also took posts in France, Spain, England, and other western lands. But even by 1500 a command of Greek remained exceptional. It was not a necessary, though an increasingly desirable, part of a humanist education.

The Search for Manuscripts. Eager scholars hunted through the libraries, especially in old monasteries, for neglected manuscripts. Hundreds and thousands of handwritten books were brought to light. Sometimes they found the same book, frequently some tract of medieval piety, copied over innumerable times. But now and then an ancient work was discovered in what proved to be the sole example or one of the few surviving copies. All of these were transcripts made from the brittle papyrus books of antiquity to the sturdy parchments of medieval bookmaking. The copyists had been monks working in the early medieval centuries (ca. 600-1200), the very period which Renaissance scholars loathed as the "dark ages."

Especially when there was more than one copy of an ancient work, it was possible to make careful comparison and analysis of the text. Such precise philological scrutiny was one of the striking novelties of the period, for medieval scholars had almost always assumed the accuracy of their books and concerned themselves with understanding what they read. Some scholars learned to distinguish the literary and linguistic patterns of different centuries. The development of textual criticism served primarily to make possible a more correct and profound understanding of the classical writers.

Erasmus.   No one was more influential in the development of literary scholarship than the famed Desiderius Erasmus. Completely at ease in classical Latin and familiar with Greek, Erasmus worked with great diligence and intelligence to prepare critical editions of numerous Latin and Greek authors, especially early Christian theologians. His supreme achievement was his own annotated translation of the New Testament from Greek into Latin.

Erasmus earned his living, once he achieved success, as a writer: an increasing number of humanists were enabled to do so after 1500 by the vast expansion of book printing. Printers eagerly sought out the works of writers who could keep their presses at work. Writers thus began to achieve greater literary freedom, depending rather on the favor of a broad and impersonal market of book buyers than on the support of patrons. Scholars also frequently served as editors and proofreaders.

II. Philosophy

Erasmus illustrated the way in which study of the classical authors modified but did not revolutionize the pattern of European thought. The basic problems with which it grappled had already been propounded by the great medieval thinkers.

Christian Humanism.   The central question was the place of man in the universe, his relation to God and the world. Virtually no one doubted the scriptural answer that the natural world of things mineral, vegetable, and animal existed for man's sake; nearly everyone also believed that man had been created in his turn to serve God.

Late medieval philosophers had made no important new contribution to answering such questions. They gave their principal attention instead to the formal implications of philosophical and theological propositions. Their debates, although at their best extraordinarily subtle, tended to neglect the human implications of Christian doctrine. They were logicians, not shepherds of men.

When the humanists began to read the Latin and Greek authors more closely and accurately, they found it increasingly difficult to reconcile classical and Christian doctrines. Nonetheless the humanists remained strongly Christian in their beliefs and motives. Repelled by the logic-chopping of the scholastics, they turned instead to classical thinkers for answers to the ever-recurring problems of man and the universe.

Cardinal Nicholas of Cusa, the most original and encompassing of fifteenth-century thinkers, was both medieval scholastic and Christian humanist. He stressed the neo-Platonic principle that the world as created by God is ultimately describable in geometrical and arithmetical terms. This view was a restatement in neo-Platonic phraseology of the fundamental view of the natural world accepted by the major scholastic thinkers; it differed mainly in its emphasis upon the mathematical character of essential things. Such theories, fostered by neo-Platonists active later in the century, particularly the group of the Platonic academy of Florence around Marsilio Ficino and Pico della Mirandola, kept before thinkers the principle that the world possessed a "numerical" structure. Erasmus, the "Prince of the Humanists," had a powerful influence in the religious life of the early sixteenth century. (See ch. 4, pp. 76, 84.)

Secularism. Christian humanism, though far stronger than other Renaissance humanism in influence and number of followers, did not command the beliefs of all thinkers. Pietro Pomponazzi, for one, in his *Tractatus de immortalite animae* (*Treatise on the immortality of the soul*, 1516), rejected as fictions fit only for lowly minds many of the crucial Christian dogmas like the doctrine of rewards and punishments in the after life; for himself, he preferred the aristocratic doctrines of the stoics to Christian ethics.

Secular attitudes grew stronger among the thinkers of the sixteenth century, yet the general mood of the time was not antireligious. Men continued to accept ultimate religious norms, although some neglected or minimized them. In general, the purpose of intellectual activity remained judgment and evaluation rather than mere description and analysis. Institutions and individuals were judged on the basis of what they should be, rather than studied directly to discover what they actually were. Standards of judgment were believed, as before, to have their origin in divine ordinance and prescription, directly through revelation and indirectly through the natural order of the universe.

The increasing secularism of the sixteenth century may be seen in three quite different thinkers from three countries. Erasmus' friend Sir Thomas

More, a scholarly English lawyer and statesman, was beheaded for his refusal to betray his Roman Catholic faith and principles. In his famous book *Utopia,* More satirized the greed, cruelty, passions and irrationality of the world in which he lived. Yet this Catholic martyr, in describing the imaginary perfect world of Utopia, left it without any Christian church.

The Italian Niccolò Machiavelli won a reputation for utter immoralism in consequence of his great work of political analysis, *The Prince;* his name, in the form "Old Nick," was made synonymous with the devil. Yet Machiavelli, though as nonreligious in his interests and standards as any man of his time, did not actually reject the Christian code of right and wrong; instead he put alongside this religious rule of conduct a potentially competitive set of standards, the interests of the state and the people.

The great French essayist Michel Eyquem de Montaigne took little active part in the world; unlike More and Machiavelli, he was a man of contemplative thought. Gently yet profoundly skeptical, doubting the validity of human knowledge and scornful of the certitudes for which men died and killed, he seems to have remained a sincere Catholic believer nonetheless.

Philosophy in Literature. In the study of man, Renaissance thinkers were less systematic than their medieval predecessors. They based their works more on personal experience and literary reminiscence and less upon formal analysis of revelation and philosophy. They cited authority as frequently as medieval writers, but called more upon the great thinkers and writers of antiquity and less upon the usual Catholic commentators.

Perhaps the biggest change of all was that even the best of formal thinkers in the Renaissance proved on the whole less successful in describing and understanding men in their real situations, confronted with their specific human problems, than did the poets and dramatists. The supreme psychologist of the age was the Englishman William Shakespeare, by profession an actor, playwright, and poet. In his novel *Don Quixote,* the Spaniard Miguel Cervantes depicted the fate of man, suspended between unattainable ideals and scorned reality, more profoundly than any philosopher of the time.

III. Natural Science

During the Renaissance, as during the medieval period, only a small number of thinkers gave much attention to natural science. The larger number carried over into the effort to understand the physical world the same fetishism for antiquity which literary men displayed. Many thought it unnecessary, even improper, to check the assertions of an ancient author. Even when conflicting evidence based on direct observation was put before them, they endeavored to retain respectably antique notions. Map makers clung to Ptolemaic descriptions of the world long after geographical explorations made them untenable.

Yet there was also another continuing strong tradition of scientific inquiry, equally concerned with the science of classical antiquity but different from and even hostile to the rhetorical spirit of the new humanists. This more specifically scientific tradition rested upon the recovery of many ancient works of science, especially during the twelfth century, as transmitted usually by Arabic translators and commentators and translated in turn into forthright medieval Latin; during the thirteenth and fourteenth centuries, European scientific thinkers, in analyzing these works, already formulated many of the problems that occupied the scientists of the period after 1500.

Observation and Authority. Progress in scientific endeavor in the sixteenth and early seventeenth centuries was rapid particularly in the fields of obviously practical importance, like medicine, mining and metallurgy, and military engineering. The domination of the classical authors was strongest in medicine, where the writings of the ancient Greek, Galen, were still the fundamental textbook. The conflict between personal observation and the ancient authorities, evident at least as early as the fourteenth century, became inescapable in anatomical studies, especially when artists like Leonardo da Vinci and inquisitive professors like the Netherlander Vesalius did their own dissections instead of taking their data from Galen. Leonardo confided his observations to secret notebooks, but Vesalius was concerned with training medical practitioners.

Educated at Paris and Montpellier, Vesalius became professor of surgery at Padua. It was a fortunate appointment for him, for no other university in Italy or all Europe was so favorable to rationalist thought and scientific activity. Vesalius emphasized the importance of dissection; when his own observations conflicted with Galen's statements, he called the Greek wrong, albeit sometimes timidly. His own discoveries, embodied in the book *De corporis humani fabrica* (*The structure of the human body*), published in 1543, were individually of little significance though substantial in their totality. But nobody before Vesalius's time applied dissection to make detailed anatomical description in such detail, varying from tradition, in such scope. This represented a major shift of direction.

Other scientists trained in humanist learning made important discoveries. The German Georg Bauer, better known by his Latin name Agricola, based his study on observations of the work of existing crafts in mineralogy and mining, *De re metallica* (*Of metals*), published in 1556, the year after his death, upon his own observations. On the other hand, the Frenchman Ambroise Paré, a military surgeon, and Bernard Palissy, a worker in ceramics, were successful inventors without humanist training. Palissy boasted that he was "neither Greek nor Hebrew, neither poet nor theoretician, but only a plain workman with little education." Throughout the sixteenth century science continued to be mostly bookish. Only after 1600 did modern science begin to develop in a clear and vigorous way.

Astronomy. The one field of science which seems to contradict this statement—astronomy—actually confirms it.

The Ptolemaic Tradition. It was not accidental that astronomy was the area of knowledge where the fundamental methodology of modern science was developed. The primary facts of observation were easily accessible in the sky overhead. There was a long tradition of geometrical description of the movement of the heavenly bodies; it began in the ancient world and was reinforced by the rise of neo-Platonic ideas in the fifteenth and sixteenth centuries. The necessary mathematical tools for analyzing all the immediately accessible data were already invented.

The prevalent cosmological system, during the medieval period and through the sixteenth century, was that of Ptolemy, the famous second-century Alexandrian astronomer and geographer, who placed the earth at the center of the universe. Aristotelian philosophers accepted this theory, as did the scholastic Christian thinkers, who attempted to make it accord with the biblical account of creation.

Copernicus. But with the publication in 1543 of Nicholas Copernicus' *De revolutionibus orbium coelestium* (*On the revolution of the heavenly orbs*), a new astronomical theory began to win men's minds, even though it violated common sense by putting the sun at the center of the universe. Born of German parents in the Polish town of Toruń (Thorn), Copernicus was typical of the scholars and scientists of his age in that he belonged not to a local but to a general European tradition. He studied mathematics and medicine at Cracow and then at Italian universities. After taking degrees in these fields, he added a doctorate in canon (church) law from Ferrara, and thenceforth earned his living as an ecclesiastical official in the duchy of Prussia. From his student days at Bologna, Copernicus rejected the Ptolemaic geocentric cosmology in favor of a heliocentric system. Copernicus found support in his own astronomical observations for the principle that the sun was the hub around which the universe turned. He assigned circular orbits to the planets, including the earth as one of these, and emphasized the revolution of the earth on its own axis, causing the alternation of day and night. Copernicus emphasized that lighter bodies moved towards the heavier, and the heaviest of all he believed to be the sun.

Copernicus knew only too well that his cosmology, by disputing the astronomy accepted by the scholastics, seemed to call into question Christian theology as well. He was reluctant therefore to publish his great work during his lifetime. When it went to press shortly before his death, the Lutheran scholar Andreas Osiander wrote a preface designed to ward off hostile criticism. He presented Copernicus' study as a mere hypothesis. It was, he wrote, no more than a mathematical curiosity not intended to describe the real world of nature. But he was distorting Copernicus' own opinion. For all his caution, the staid old churchman believed that his description of the universe corresponded with reality. Osiander's precaution was hardly necessary, for the work attracted little attention except among astronomers.

The Conflict of the Systems. Nonetheless it was astronomy, and with it the fields of mechanics and optics, which experienced the most rapid and successful growth of any natural science in the early modern period. Only these fields had—and had had from antiquity—the equipment and the concepts enabling them to make a mathematical description and analysis of the natural world. In all other fields, description had to remain primarily or exclusively qualitative, and hence closer to the old Aristotelian science. The Aristotelian system, as developed by the scholastics, consisted in the refinement of common-sense observations; its insights came through the logical implications of the obvious rather than from the discovery in objects of characteristics which did not accord with ordinary observation and meaning. Copernican heliocentrism was symbolic of the movement of physical science toward explanations of nature in drastic conflict with what men could see for themselves—is anything plainer than that the sun moves around the earth once a day? Yet it was these "fantastic" explanations which proved more successful than any other in the long run.

For the moment, however, the only advantage of the Copernican system over the Ptolemaic was its greater mathematical simplicity; it brought no practical advantage otherwise in the description of the skies. The astronomers' critical problem was to account for the movements of the planets, the sun, and the moon. The fixed stars stay in the same constant relationship to each other, but all together they are seen to revolve about the earth. The planets, on the other hand, wander (their name being derived from the Greek word for "wanderer") through the fixed stars; it is not possible to describe their behaviors in terms of single uniform circular motions. Since it was assumed in the Ptolemaic system that the earth was the center of their rotations as well as that of the fixed stars, it was necessary to explain the planets' aberrations from circularity. This explanation was accomplished by describing them as moving in orbits around centers which themselves in turn moved in other orbits around other centers, and so on until the ultimate resulting motion corresponded fairly closely with the observed paths of the planets. Copernicus slightly reduced the number of these secondary orbital motions or "epicycles," and simplified the geometrical pattern by placing the center of the first circle at the sun, not the earth.

Brahe and Kepler. The Copernican system, though it gained increasing acceptance during the later sixteenth century, did not win all astronomers to its principles. The greatest astronomical observer of the entire period, the Dane Tycho Brahe, for instance, continued to prefer Ptolemy's system. Tycho, however, accumulated vast amounts of data on the movements of the heavenly bodies based on much more precise techniques of observation than any devised before him.

His pupil and successor as imperial astronomer, Johannes Kepler, devoted himself far more to the problem of finding mathematical formulas applicable to the amassed data. He was a much more proficient mathematician than his master, and held to Copernicus's theory. He further reduced the complexity of mathematical description of the course of the planets (including the earth) by regarding their paths not as circles and epicycles but as ellipses. This left only the movement of the moon with an epicycle, and greatly reduced the number of assumptions required for geometrical analysis of the planetary orbits.

Galileo.   Until the seventeenth century, astronomical observations had been confined to what the unaided eye could see. One path of development lay in improvement of the mathematical analysis of what was known on this basis. Another consisted in the invention of new devices to extend observation to the still unknown. The most important of these new instruments was the telescope.

An Italian physicist, Galileo Galilei (usually known by his first name), learning of the device in 1608, grasped its significance for astronomy. In the following year, he constructed a primitive telescope with a magnification of three diameters, which he presented to the Senate of Venice. Shortly after, he built one with a magnification of thirty diameters, which proved useful in scanning the heavens. With it Galileo perceived the Milky Way as a collection of stars, observed the similarity between the phases of Venus and those of the moon, and discovered the rings of Saturn and the satellites of Jupiter. Jupiter and its moons provided him with a parallel to Copernicus' heliocentric system. In 1610 Galileo described his discoveries in the *Nuntius sidereus* (*Messenger of the stars*). Other men began to build telescopes, and new discoveries were frequent. Not least was Galileo's own observation of sunspots in 1611.

Galileo was interested in terrestrial mechanics as well as in astronomy. He undertook to define more exactly how far and how fast objects moved. He developed the theory that free-falling objects have a constant acceleration, and prepared many further developments in mechanics.

Galileo and the Church.   It was as an astronomer that Galileo won fame and found himself in difficulties. Roman Catholic authorities, sensitive after the Council of Trent, did not disregard Galileo's presentation of the heliocentric theory as they had done with Copernicus' almost a century before. The conflict between the new cosmology and the letter of the Bible was now too dangerous to be overlooked. Within a few years of publication of the

Nuntius sidereus, the Congregation of the Index criticized Galileo for teaching a "false Pythagorician doctrine" leading to "destruction of Catholic truth." The Inquisition (Holy Office) forbade Galileo to teach Copernican doctrine, and the astronomer, a pious Catholic and not a foolhardy man, accepted the decree.

But he could not remain silent about his discoveries and his theories; he believed too strongly that they were true. In 1632 he presented his subtle defense of Copernicanism in the *Dialogues on the Great World Systems;* on the surface, this book was a defense of the Ptolemaic system and it received church permission to be published. But the defender of scholastic cosmology, Simplicius, obviously had the worst of the argument. When the pope, till then friendly to Galileo, was persuaded that the astronomer was mocking at him in the person of Simplicius, he permitted the Inquisition to bring Galileo to trial for breaking his promise not to publish anything concerning the Copernican theory. In 1633 the Inquisition sentenced Galileo to life imprisonment and compelled him to abjure his "errors and heresies." A venerable tradition tells us that the aged astronomer, after speaking his recantation, murmured *"Eppur si muove"* ("And still it [the earth] moves") ; the story lacks any verification, and yet it reflects what we know Galileo felt. Before long, the sentence was commuted to internment at his country estate, where Galileo died.

Physics, Chemistry, and Biology. Not the earth only, but the scientific endeavor also moved. After 1600 the initiative in the study and explanation of nature passed into the hands of experimental scientists. Even Galileo's unfortunate experience with the Inquisition represented a mishap rather than a total commitment of the Roman Catholic church against the new science; in any case, scientists who confined themselves to their specific work, leaving unremarked any possible discrepancy between their discoveries and theories, on the one side, and religious doctrine on the other, were left unmolested in both Catholic and Protestant countries.

The attack on Aristotle and the Aristotelians was vigorous and unremitting. One French professor defended new theories on the nature of comets in 1618 with the comment, "How can the authority of a single man, who bases his doctrine neither on observation nor on mathematical proofs, serve as an article of faith in celestial and subliminal things!"

Physical inquiry developed at an accelerating rate after 1600 in many parts of Europe. In that year the Englishman William Gilbert described the fundamental characteristics of magnetism. He explained the operation of the compass for the first time by describing the earth itself as a great magnet. The Italian Torricelli continued Galileo's study of the laws of falling bodies. In chemistry descriptive studies continued, though more slowly than in physics.

In biological science the most important discovery during the entire period was made by an English physician trained at Padua as well as at Cambridge. In 1615 William Harvey, court physician of James I and professor at the College of Physicians in London, announced discovery of the circulation of the blood, though he did not describe his discovery in detail until 1628, in a book printed at Frankfurt, Germany. His method was based on rigorous and systematic observation and analysis. He dissected living animals, made direct and comparative studies of the movement of the heart, examined the hearts of embryonic chickens, and experimented with the effects of ligatures on various arteries and veins.

The Scientific Academies. Scientific researchers were a proud and sensitive band. They haggled and fought with each other for the honor of having been the first to invent a new scientific instrument, to formulate a new theory, or to propose or solve a mathematical problem. But they preferred to have their tempests within associations of their own.

Science was a collective as well as an individual enterprise. Finding little interest in their work at the universities, the scientists formed their own societies. The first such groups arose in Italy. One of the best known was the *Accademia dei Lincei* (Academy of the Lynxes), formed in 1601. It took its name in 1609 because the lynx was supposed to have eyes that penetrated secrets. Galileo's difficulties in the 1630's hurt the influence of these scientific lynxes, but their organization lingered until 1657. Similar societies were established in Germany. One stated its purpose forthrightly in its name, the *Collegium naturae curiosorum* (College of natural curiosities), formed in 1652.

A group destined for much longer life and greater influence began less pretentiously in 1631 in Paris. Its guiding spirit was a Roman Catholic friar, Father Marin Mersenne; he was both an experimenter and a philosophical thinker of considerable power, but excelled as an organizer. The scientific minds of the French capital assembled under his leadership from 1631 to 1637, and the resulting group continued in various forms until 1666, when the French minister Colbert reorganized it into the *Académie des Sciences* (Academy of Sciences) under government sponsorship. In London a similar association was formed in 1645 at Gresham College; reorganized as the Royal Society in 1662, it became the most important scientific society in Europe.

The Philosophy of Science. After 1600 science rose rapidly in the scale of recognized intellectual values. Philosophical inquiry became increasingly concerned with the analysis of the assumptions and requirements of science.

Descartes. The most fundamental contribution to the philosophical basis of modern science was made by the Frenchman René Descartes. He began as a mathematician, his most important work being the application of algebraic methods to geometry. Although this analytic geometry ultimately provided the fundamental mathematical method for modern physics, Descartes' philosophical ideas had even more immediate impact upon scientific thinking. He set up an almost complete cleavage between mind and matter, thus freeing the study of physical nature for description in terms of time, space, and motion only. Matter itself he defined as that which took up space, or pure extension. Such ideas made possible the study of the physical universe on the analogy of a self-operating machine.

Francis Bacon. The prophet of the new science was the English statesman and thinker, Francis Bacon (Lord Verulam). Bacon presented theories both of science and of its place in human affairs. From his early *Advancement of Learning* (1605) to his posthumous *New Atlantis* (1627), he attacked Aristotelian conceptions, emphasized the importance of discovery by observation, and urged the formation of special institutions to maintain well-supported and well-organized scientific study. He visualized scientific knowledge as power over nature, by which man could put the physical world at his service as he had never done before. He glimpsed in the future the industrial revolution which made science man's servant in the factories and the fields. But he underestimated the difficulty of formulating scientific theories. His command of science as a practitioner was small and his grasp of current developments limited; he continued to reject Galileo's theories like the most adamant Aristotelian.

A Soulless Science? Some of those caught up by the new scientific studies became deeply troubled by the implications they discovered in them. The world as the Aristotelians and scholastics had understood it was meaningful in all its reaches. Divine purpose and control extended everywhere; the order of nature was created by God for man's use. Directly or indirectly the whole universe was moral in nature. The Ptolemaic cosmology fitted this conception: the earth, man's residence, was at the center of all things. Copernican theory revised this comfortable cosmology. If the ideas of physical order must be so radically changed over by new learning, what foundation was there for the ideas of moral and social order? Permanence was no more. The English poet John Donne wrote despairingly of a world with "all coherence gone." The Cartesian concept of space proved especially disturbing. Descartes described mind and matter as wholly different things. If mind remained the possessor of knowledge and faith, then space, as the field of matter, was left utterly without connection with the mind or soul, and hence was also unconnected with ultimate meanings.

None protested more vigorously against such a soulless universe than one who understood the new science as well as anyone of the time. This was the French mathematician and physicist Blaise Pascal, for whom science could not take the place of moral purpose. The universe of Cartesian extension, with its spiritual emptiness—"the eternal silence of these infinite spaces," he called it—terrified Pascal. But the immediate future lay not with the Donnes and the Pascals. As men grew more accustomed to the new mechanist conception of the physical universe, they felt fewer terrors in its silent vastnesses and more confidence in their ability to be its masters.

IV. Literature

The pre-eminence of literature over formal thought was characteristic of the Renaissance period as a whole. The choice of the language—vernacular or Latin—therefore became a central problem.

Vernacular or Latin? In the later middle ages, writers began to use the vernacular languages with increasing frequency for works of literature, although they continued to use Latin for works of formal thought. France was the heartland of medieval literature, while England, Spain, Germany, and the Low Countries all developed native writers of great power and talent. Italy was the last major country to develop a literature based on the use of the native tongue; but Dante and Petrarch both drew inspiration from the Provençal poetry of southern France, which had been the accepted medium of expression of their predecessors in northern Italy. Poetry, the most compressed and memorable of the verbal arts, was dominant. There was no dearth of literary inventiveness; new poetic forms of great virtuosity flourished. Thus the great shift in literature caused by the rise of humanism consisted not in creating an interest in esthetic forms, but in transferring it to Latin to a much greater degree than before.

Petrarch, who followed Dante as a master of Italian poetry, turned against his own superlative achievements in his native language, as lacking true dignity and permanence. He did more than any other single man to persuade writers to use Latin rather than their mother tongues for works of literary art.

Italy. By the beginning of the sixteenth century, although humanist education had spread to other countries, Italy retained the leadership in the new literary mode. In Rome, Naples, Ferrara, and elsewhere, academies (as almost all assemblages of men for a literary or intellectual purpose were called) were formed to encourage the art of writing well. If mere diligence and the strict imitation of revered models were sufficient to create great literature, this should have been an age of unequaled accomplishment. But rhetoric was soon pushed to excess. At the academies, the wits who gathered to admire each other and themselves put elegance all too frequently in the place of ideas and sincere feelings. Most of the neo-Latin works were little more than highly polished pieces displaying much virtuosity but communicating little feeling of direct experience or creative originality. Ancient models were taken to be perfection itself; they were admired and adored rather than analyzed and evaluated.

Nonetheless, where a writer had something to say as well as the skill to say it, a work of high value could be created. Such, for instance, was the *Syphilis sive de morbo gallico* (*Syphilis or the French disease*). In this work the Veronese doctor Girolamo Fracastoro, described in excellent verse and skillful composition the spread of a new malady (for which he invented the medical name—the people usually called it after a recent invader or hated neighbor). Some of these neo-Latin works had Christian subject matter, like the poetry of the monk Battista Spagnuoli, which was particularly admired as equaling Vergil's, or the *Christiade*, an epic on Christ's life by Marco Girolamo Vida. Even more prevalent were works on elegiac and pastoral themes. However artificial and empty, these rustic pieces delighted contemporaries and were assiduously imitated wherever the new esthetic penetrated in Europe. It seems clear that it was actually the form of the ancient writers which was being sought after: their art of easy, smooth-flowing expression, their lofty, exalted manner.

Although the stricter humanists restricted the new style to works in Latin, literature in the vernacular reasserted itself strongly in Italy after 1500. It was not bound to imitate antiquity as closely, and medieval and classical themes were joined together with astonishing frequency. This mingling is nowhere clearer than in the *Orlando furioso* (*Roland the Furious*, 1516) of Lodovico Ariosto. His hero is the favorite of medieval epics, Roland, his subject the battles of Charlemagne and his hosts against the Saracens. But Ariosto told the story without the elaborate overlay of symbol and allegory customary with the medieval authors, in a language and manner shaped by imitation of Vergil, Ovid, and Homer, and with an uproarious irony at the expense of his heroes. After Ariosto the vein of originality and creativity ran thin for many decades. Only the ill-starred Torquato Tasso, whose genius was struck down by madness, achieved greatness with his *Gerusalemme Liberata* (*Jerusalem Delivered*, 1580). As befitted an epic of the Crusades written after the Catholic Reformation had already put its mark on Italian life, Tasso added an intensely religious element to the chivalric and epic elements Ariosto had used.

The Italian theater developed an engaging and resourceful form during this period, though it was only slightly affected by the general humanist movement. While some authors endeavored to write classical plays after the models of Terence and Plautus, their work was less vital and appealing than the *commedia dell' arte* (loosely, "the professional theater") begun at Mantua in 1567. Strolling players performed, using fixed characters like the soldier, the flirt, the rustic, in fixed situations, but with only approximate plot definitions and improvised dialogue. At their best, the players achieved immediacy of communication and were able to adapt quickly to current interests and events.

Humanism gave to Italy an independence and leadership in the field of literature she did not possess before. Like France in the medieval period, she became the master of other lands in the arts of the word. But where the medieval Italian literary tradition had been largely derivative, such countries as France, Spain, and England had vigorous medieval literatures to which the peoples were still devoted. Despite talk among extreme humanists about abandoning all medieval literature as barbarism, the Renaissance brought increased variety of form, style, and content to literature without wholly eliminating its medieval origins.

France and the Netherlands. In France and the Low Countries the traditions of the "rhetoricians" remained strong in the early sixteenth century. They had treated poetry as a kind of literary challenge where victory was the greater in proportion to the difficulty overcome; they had developed complex systems of meter and rhyme, and their forms, especially the rondel, ballade, and some others, remained popular. In the Low Countries, Jean Lemaire des Belges was one of the first to respond to Italian neoclassicism; but he used a medieval theme in his *Illustrations de Gaule et singularités de Troie* (*Notabilities of Gaul and Individuals from Troy*, 1515) on which to embroider his Italianate effects.

A purer neoclassicism developed in France, particularly thanks to the activity of a wealthy Parisian merchant, Guillaume Budé. After becoming the foremost Greek scholar in Europe, Budé persuaded the king, Francis I, to found and support a college to teach the humanistic disciplines of linguistics and philology which the scholastics at the University of Paris still rejected. The *Collège de France* (College of France) grew very slowly for many years after its foundation (ca. 1522), but eventually its instructors and students provided the basis for the broad expansion of classical training in France.

Paduan rationalism was taken up at Lyons, the city of wealth and trade in eastern France where no university existed to dominate intellectual life. Some of the Lyons intellectuals turned against Christianity and became deists who believed only in an impersonal God; even those who remained sincere Christians took part in freer discussion of religious doctrine than was usual. Out of the Lyons circle came a humanist who retained all the earthy vitality of the medieval folk literature. François Rabelais, a monk released from his vows, earned his living as a medical practitioner who followed Galen and Hippocrates only too faithfully. His great achievement was the vast mock-heroic tale of two giants, father and son, *Gargantua and Pantagruel* (1532-1564). Rabelais mixed medieval folktales with humanist aspirations and learning in a deliciously personal and unique way that nonetheless illustrates the prevalent duality of Renaissance literature.

After mid-century, Latin ceased to be the vehicle for most literary activity in France, although it remained the almost universal tongue for formal studies. Classical imitation and reminiscence were continued in works in the vernacular. The theorist of this new development was Joachim du Bellay. His *Défense et illustration de la langue française (Defense and glorification of the French language,* 1549) was a plea to French writers to use their native tongue in order to achieve the grace and power of the ancients. In poetry the work of Pierre Ronsard and his friends in the group called the *Pléiade* (the Pleiades, the name of a star group) were an illustration of the success that could be achieved on du Bellay's lines. In prose the *Essays* of Montaigne developed a powerful form for the exploration of ideas in a flexible, variable way quite unlike that of the rigid, syllogistic structure of the medieval thinkers. Even so, Montaigne's prose style was as much linked to the past as to the future, because of its loose and meandering pattern.

The early seventeenth century brought a major change to both prose and poetry in France. The critic Guez de Balzac laid down rules for writing a prose style as orderly as that of the ancient authors. This new attitude took hold of the promising writers of the period. The lengthy novels which emanated from the salon of the marquise de Rambouillet, where the literary and intellectual élite of Paris gathered, were among the first to show the results of this new conception. Endlessly subtle in the analysis of the emotion of love, they were nonetheless written in a lucid, disciplined prose which quickly outmoded Montaigne's meanderings. The mathematician-philosopher Descartes proved in his *Discours de la méthode (Discourse on method,* 1637) that the same style could be adapted to works of philosophical power and precision. Similar rules for the writing of poetry of like qualities were enunciated by the critic François de Malherbe. The tragedies of Pierre Corneille demonstrated that this ideal of clarity and control could be achieved in plays with a psychological insight and dramatic intensity unmatched in France.

Spain. Spain responded unevenly to the influence of humanism and the new vernacular literature of Italy. The universities did not impede the spread of humanist education as they did in France; spurred on by leaders in church and state like Cardinal Jiménez de Cisneros, they undertook the teaching of the classical languages and rhetoric at the same time that they revived Thomism. Many of the humanists acknowledged Erasmus as their master. Juan Luis Vives, the most gifted among them, was a thoughtful educator. When Erasmus came under attack by Spanish theologians as the progenitor of the Lutheran heresy, humanists who retained their identification with him were discountenanced, and at last in 1538 the government ruthlessly destroyed them.

Medieval literary traditions continued little affected at first by the new esthetic and intellectual forces which came into the land. The native vigor and pithy realism of Spanish writers were not easily bent towards the neo-classical ideal of lucidity and smoothness of expression. The romance of chivalry, *Amadis de Gaula* (*Amadis of Gaul*), became even more popular after printing had reduced book prices; numerous editions appeared both before and after 1500. It was mainly the poets who looked to Italy for inspiration and refinement of forms, but they paid a penalty in the loss of originality. After mid-century, Italian influence on the poets became so strong that advocates of the traditional national forms were moved to protest the importations from Italy.

But outside poetry the medieval tradition continued unimpeded. *Amadis de Gaula* remained popular and was imitated widely. The *Vida de Lazarillo de Tormes* (*Life of Lazarillo de Tormes*, 1554) introduced a new literary form of much different character, the picaresque novel. In it the adventures of lovable rascals from the depths of society were depicted with brutal cynicism and scorn for the proclaimed moral values of the time.

Spain's "age of gold" came after 1560, when the Counter Reformation was triumphant throughout the Iberian Peninsula. The prose pastoral, introduced in 1559 with the *Diana* of the Portuguese Jorge de Montemor (in Spanish, Montemayor), was taken up by Miguel Cervantes de Saavedra in his *Galatea* (1585) and others, but the picaresque novel grew even more rapidly. Even though the *Lazarillo* was put on the Index in 1560, the picaresque form became dominant. Its cynicism culminated in the bitter *Guzman de Alfarache* (1599, 1605) of Mateo Aleman. The independence of Spanish literature received further emphasis when Cervantes turned away from the Italian tale to write brief adventure novels. Social and moral criticism became more difficult as the Inquisition sharpened its vigilance, but it did not cease. It merely slipped beneath the surface, resulting in the addition of the dimension of subtlety to the realistic honesty of Spanish literature. Again it was Cervantes who initiated the new form.

Cervantes was no bookish commentator upon the world; he knew the hectic uncertainties of life from his own experience. An impoverished student, then a soldier wounded at the great naval battle of Lepanto, he was captured by Algerian pirates and spent some years in slavery before he was bought back into freedom. A career as a minor government servant only brought new hardships; he was in prison in 1601-1602 for delinquency in his duties when he began his *Don Quixote*. First published in 1605, this greatest novel of the century resembled Rabelais's work in its use of medieval forms which the author both mocked and liked; he blended the pastoral and the picaresque novels, in an enchanting world of imagination and incisive satire, of realism and idealism. It achieved enormous popularity and was soon translated into

French and English. Hilarious adventure delighted the ordinary reader, while the more sensitive were moved by its subtle and compassionate irony.

Popular realism, which in his *Novelas ejemplares* (*Exemplary tales*, 1613) Cervantes showed need not be decked out in picaresque garb, proved distasteful to some who thought it more important to imitate the ancients. After 1600 Luis de Góngora y Argote led in the elaboration of a specialized language and forms, such as the classical odes, to lift literature above the mundane and everyday. This movement, called Gongorism after him, had parallels in the Italian movement called Marinism.

The theater was even more popular. Its unquestioned master was the amazing Lope de Vega, who after 1609 wrote no less than 1800 plays as well as other shorter works, only some of which have survived. These are comedies of "cape and sword," based on a kind of continual improvisation by the author upon fundamental themes of complicated intrigue; but his verve in expression and his knowledge of the human passions keep him from the insipidity which might be expected to result from such enormous productivity. His successor to the stage, Pedro Calderón de la Barca, paid more attention to the new conventions and used a more cultivated style, as befitted the nobility and court who were his audience.

England. England began the sixteenth century, as did Germany, with relatively small literary activity. It was not until the fourth and fifth decades of the century that the influence of the Italian poets, not least Petrarch and his followers, made itself felt. Several more decades passed before the efflorescence of literature now associated with the name of Queen Elizabeth I could be seen. In the two years 1578 and 1579 appeared the *Euphues* of John Lyly and the *Shepheardes Calender* of Edmund Spenser. Lyly's main concern was to prove that English need not remain a rough, workaday tongue, but could equal the graces of the Italians and French at their best; his style was too self-conscious, too elaborately wrought, to maintain itself as a common pattern, but his interest in elegance and nicety of diction was passed on to other, more gifted writers. In the *Shepheardes Calender*, Spenser successfully combined English subject matter with humanist learning and the deliberate artistry of the Italians and French. His *Faerie Queene* (1590, 1596) greatly resembled Ariosto in its mingling of medieval chivalry and contemporary humanist elements. With Sydney, Spenser gave the tone to many subsequent English poets.

The theater, even more than poetry, became the characteristic art form of English literature toward the end of the sixteenth century. Though medieval dramatic forms had died away, the study of the ancient plays revived theatrical interest, particularly in boys' schools. With the establishment of the theater at Shoreditch in 1576, plays began to be performed for a wide public, ranging from the common folk to the great noblemen who patronized the playwrights and players and protected them against repressive measures. The furious crudity of the early plays caused the more sensitive, attuned to Italian delicacy, to demand lilt and lightness, rather than the thunderous violence of Thomas Kyd and Christopher Marlowe.

The youthful player-playwright William Shakespeare met this demand with his *Love's Labor Lost*, but as he achieved success for himself and his company he encompassed all the types of drama then in use—comedy, tragedy, and history. He made poetry part of the very essence of the play, conveying the innermost feelings of the characters as no prose could ever do. His extraordinary insight into the character of human beings and the drollery and tragedy of their lives gave a reality and vitality to his plays matched only by a single contemporary work, Cervantes' *Don Quixote*.

After Shakespeare, both poetry and theater had to labor on with supreme achievement behind them. But continue they did. John Webster, Thomas Middleton, John Fletcher, and Francis Beaumont all wrote plays notable for their construction, their realism, and their vigor. Ben Jonson patterned his plays upon the Latin dramatists, but his sense for the varieties of human types saved his work from bookish slavishness.

The concern for the play of ideas and concepts which Shakespeare had sometimes shown became almost an obsession with the poet John Donne. His dense, hard-wrought verses reflect a tortured demand for faith and certainty which the previous age had not known. Neoclassicism continued in the hands of a young poet of extraordinary learning and poetic sensitivity, John Milton. He interwove Latinity and true English diction in works of intense Christianity and moral sensitivity.

V. The Arts

The Renaissance interplay of medieval and neoclassical elements held true in art as it did in literature, but in different ways and with different results. Historians and critics have given the palm to painting as the characteristic art form of the Renaissance; the imitation of antiquity played a lesser role in painting than in sculpture and architecture. In music, Renaissance antiquarianism was purely an affair of the theorists; the actual writing and playing of music were hardly affected.

Painting. By the end of the fifteenth century, two regions led in the field of painting, the Low Countries and Italy.

Realism. In the Netherlands, the indigenous artistic tradition grew directly out of the medieval pattern without interruption. Favored forms were miniatures and book illustrations, and devotional and altarpiece decora-

PRIMAVERA (SPRING). Painting by Sandro Botticelli, about 1478. The Uffizi Gallery, Florence.

Medieval and neoclassical themes and techniques are subtly blended in this painting by the famed Florentine artist. The figures—Venus in the center, the Graces on her left, the Spring goddesses Primavera and Flora on her right—are drawn from classical mythology, and their garb and actions obey the symbolism of this literary tradition. The design is largely Gothic in origin: the triptych pattern evokes the pointed arch; the modeling of the figures follows medieval patterns. *(Bettman Archive)*

tions. Remarkable achievements were the naturalistic detail and psychological veracity in the portraiture of individual persons.

Italian painters sought a different kind of truth: the exactness of the scene depicted as if the event had been stopped by magic, with the frame a window opening upon it. The primary means for achieving this realism were the representation of perspective (upon the basis of precise mathematical construction of the composition according to the rule of vanishing perspective) and the use of lighting and shadow to round out the elements of the scene. Before 1500 mastery of these techniques had been achieved; the principal question remained the use to which they would be put.

Neoclassicism. The principal purposes of painting during the fifteenth century in Italy had remained religious, as before. The rise of humanism brought some desire to follow literature in recreating the art forms of antiquity. In painting this recreation was particularly difficult because virtually no Greek or Roman pictures survived to be studied and imitated. One solution was to depict classical subject matter, especially Greco-Roman mythology. This was the way taken by Sandro Botticelli, a member of the neo-

Platonic academy in Florence, in such paintings as "The Birth of Venus" and "Primavera" ("Spring"). Technically these paintings have virtually no element of neoclassical imitation; Botticelli continued to use many patterns of arrangement and manner from traditional religious painting, such as the triple distribution of figures, two groups around a central subject.

The new style of painting spread soon after 1500 from its home in Florence to the rest of Italy, notably to Venice and Rome. The work of experimentation had held the major attention of painters in the previous century; their human figures had been pallid as portraiture and placid psychologically. More attention was now paid to making good the neglected qualities. Especially at Venice, Giorgione innovated the use of vivid color, which in the hands of his pupil Titian and the Venetian school generally came to equal or dominate other elements of painting. Under the influence of Netherlandish masters, Italian portraits came to life: again it was Titian who achieved supreme mastery in creating a sense of psychological and visual immediacy, as did Raphael, who worked at Rome.

Michelangelo, by the rounded dimensions of his figures in the Sistine Chapel ceiling paintings in Rome, revealed his primary training as a sculptor. Even more important and influential was his strength of expression. He held the viewer not by creating an illusion of physical reality but by appealing to his emotional responses. He was not satisfied to portray figures exactly like real persons or according to the precepts of ideal proportions; he exaggerated to intensify, and thus began the break-up of Renaissance naturalism.

Mannerism. After these masters, Italian painters worked in many directions, combining and recombining the basic elements of their art. As the Catholic Reformation grew in strength, it influenced developments in two closely allied ways. By greater emphasis on the inner self of the devout soul, and by frank emotionalism in the expression of the new piety, it encouraged an intensity more like the passionate Gothic works than the fifteenth-century art from which it more immediately derived. This "mannerist" method and attitude culminated outside Italy in the work of a Cretan, Domenico Theotocopuli, who went to Spain where he was known as El Greco (The Greek). El Greco often combined distorted, tortured shapes and violent, almost ugly colors with dramatic composition and subjects to create a mystical world where the soul of man sought escape from this world's hell.

Pictorialism. Pictorialism was the prevalent Italian manner which spread over Europe during the sixteenth century. In France, the Low Countries, and Germany it contributed to strengthening the penchant for portraiture. Such artists as Albrecht Dürer, Lukas Cranach, and Hans Holbein retained the quality of psychological penetration, but embodied the elements of color and composition which the Italians had developed. But the Germanic countries also possessed a tradition of fantastic imagination, repre-

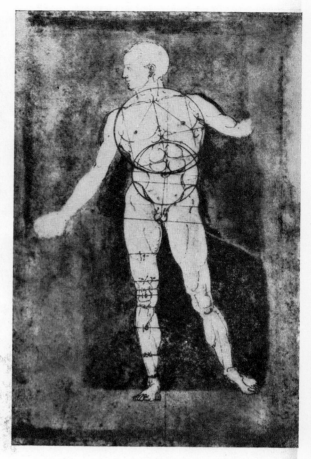

PROPORTIONS OF THE BODY. Drawing by Albrecht Dürer, a study for his Adam and Eve, early sixteenth century. Albertina Museum, Vienna.

Dürer is the representative figure of the German Renaissance, in whom merge the enduring interests of the German Gothic—in particular its intense religiosity and its obsession with death —and the new themes and techniques he learned during his visits to Italy. This drawing illustrates the Renaissance artists' concern for accuracy of anatomical depiction, as well as the geometrical means of achieving desired bodily proportions. (Bettman Archive)

sented by the diabolic scenes of Hieronymus Bosch and the visualization of Death in the works of Dürer. The same fantasy, in the hands of a tragicomic satirist like Pieter Breughel, depicted the vanity of all life in the follies and foibles of peasant life.

When the great Brabant port of Antwerp was closed off from its life-giving trade by Dutch control of the Scheldt river early in the seventeenth century, the artists in the moribund Belgian town expanded their activity to rival the Italian cities as producers of paintings for sale in many lands. The foremost of these was Peter Paul Rubens, who combined the overt religiosity of the Catholic Reformation with voluptuous scenes from classical mythology.

In Spain in the same period, Renaissance naturalism reached the summit of achievement in the work of Velásquez. The same stringent realism that marks the best of Spanish literature characterized the work of this painter of royalty and court. His individual and group portraits at first glance seem no more than impeccably accurate observation; but they continue to hold the onlooker by a sense of subtle and pitiless psychological insight, on the one

FALL OF THE DAMNED. Painting by Peter Paul Rubens (with an addition in the lower part by another hand), about 1620. Altere Pinakothek, Munich.

This painting by the great Flemish artist exemplies both the characteristics of the baroque style and the qualities of Rubens himself. The subject is the fall of the damned in the Last Judgment. The ordeal of the damned souls is depicted in the fearful contortions of the bodies, just as the vigorous movement of the design conveys the drama of History's end. Yet the individual figures are drawn with anatomical precision, without exaggeration, and with the same fleshly accuracy as Rubens' secular nudes. (*Bettmann Archive*)

hand, and by uncanny beauty of color and composition, on the other. A blunter and more sentimental Spanish realism than that of Velásquez was represented in the work of his contemporary, Murillo.

Rembrandt. Across the Rhine from the Spanish Netherlands, the Dutch republic gave rise to a vigorously independent movement. Two of its characteristic types were the pure landscape and the homely interior; the intense

TOMB OF GIULIANO DE' MEDICI. Sculpture by Michelangelo Buonarotti, 1520–1534. The New Sacristy, Church of San Lorenzo, Florence.

The neoclassical subjects and techniques of the Renaissance are exemplified in this monumental sculpture, which is part of Michelangelo's tomb of the Medici. The seated central figure wears the dress of a Roman ruler, while the half-reclining nudes are in the vigorous dramatic tradition of Hellenistic sculpture. The background duplicates the architectural forms and compositions of the Roman epoch. Nonetheless the total impact of the tomb, with its huge proportions verging on exaggeration, is Michelangelo's own. *(Bettman Archive)*

civil life of the land was reflected in group portraits of town regents. But it was a successful painter in the civic style who broke loose to open up a new and powerful style of painting. This was Rembrandt, who built out of somber colors and shadowy depths a sense of penetrating into the innermost secrets of the human soul. Where Velásquez may be looked upon as the acme of Renaissance naturalism, Rembrandt transcended the forms of which he was equally the master to make technique the merest servant of his veracity and pity.

Architecture and Sculpture. Architecture and sculpture were able to achieve the neoclassical ideal more easily than painting, thanks to the presence on Italian soil of ancient Roman buildings and statuary. Little was known of Greek work, especially from the "golden age" before the rise of Rome; "Greek" to the early Renaissance meant Hellenistic, the variety of styles that developed upon the original Hellenic base especially after the Roman empire took over the entire Mediterranean world.

Neoclassicism. During the fifteenth century the designers of buildings and the carvers of statues eagerly studied the available monuments of antiquity. Leon Battista Alberti, an artist of many-sided talents, embodied his observations in rules for architecture. But the works which came from the drawings of Alberti and other architects of the period revealed that "classical" for them meant the elements of external decoration more than the basic structure of the edifice itself. Many neoclassical buildings were constructed according to familiar medieval ways, but with an overlay of classical columns, Roman arches, entablatures, and devices; yet the inherent taste and judgment of the designers assured a visual balance and rightness in most of these buildings that kept them esthetically appealing, however incongruous historically. The vigor and naturalism of the statues excavated at an increasing rate during the century encouraged sculptors to undertake portraits of successful military commanders and like works of civil character as well as the niche statues, altars, and tombs that were traditional church pieces. Elsewhere on the continent builders and sculptors at the beginning of the sixteenth century still worked within the pattern of the late Gothic, proving the vitality of the medieval style.

The development of architecture in the sixteenth and early seventeenth centuries affected almost solely two types of public buildings, churches and palaces (including palatial homes). The fundamental techniques of construction changed little. Only the abandonment of the Gothic style, with its flying buttresses and ogival (pointed) arches, made a difference in structure as well as appearance; the classical column and the rounded dome took their place. Renaissance architecture, beginning in Italy in the fifteenth century as an overlay over medieval edifices, produced works in the next period which moved away from the older pattern. The masterpiece was the basilica of St. Peter's in the Vatican at Rome; several of the greatest artists, not the least of them Michelangelo, proposed successive designs for the vastest building in Christendom. The pattern of the great domed church continued to be used in much of Europe.

Baroque. Toward the end of the sixteenth century a new style developed, more closely associated with Spain. This was the so-called "baroque" church, characterized by intricacy of design and a striving for an immediate impact upon the onlooker. The changes in sculpture paralleled to some extent those in architecture and painting. The naturalism of the fifteenth century continued throughout the period thereafter, but Michelangelo opened a new pattern as well. This was sculpture and painting of intense emotionality. This development culminated in the baroque works of Luigi Bernini, highly dramatic and verging on exaggeration.

4

Religious Reformation:
The Emergence of Protestantism

1500 - 1560

DURING THE SIXTEENTH CENTURY a religious revolution split Christendom in Western Europe into Catholic and Protestant forms, and Protestantism in turn ultimately into half a hundred sects. Yet this was not the first division in Christianity; the faith, like universal religions of any age, had been torn by schism and heresy through its course of fifteen centuries. Long before Martin Luther appeared in Saxony to launch the Reformation, Christian Europe was divided between Roman Catholic and Greek Orthodox churches. Because Christianity was a religion proclaiming its unique validity, Latin and Greek denounced each other's views as false and schismatic. Thus the two great groups of Christendom entered the modern era in independence and apartness.

I. The Church of The West

Within its own domain, the region west of a line running across the continent from the Adriatic sea to the gulf of Finland, the Roman church was the one institution shared by all peoples and states.

Rites and Structure. This unity rested on the sacraments. According to accepted doctrine, these rites transmitted divine grace to men by the miracle of their performance. The first five sacraments—baptism, confirmation, penance, the Eucharist or Lord's Supper, extreme unction—were considered to be necessary for the salvation of all men; the sixth, marriage, legitimized and sanctified the family; and the seventh, ordination, transmitted to priests, and to no others, the power to administer the other sacraments. Only bishops, as successors to the original apostles, could perform the rite of ordination.

The structure of the church derived from these sacramental functions. The ordinary Christians formed the flock confided by God to the care of the shepherds, the priests, who were in turn established and controlled by bishops. Latin Christendom was distinguished from its Greek brother by the special powers attributed to the bishop of Rome, the Pope. Since early centuries he had claimed and ultimately had been accorded throughout the West the position of Christ's vicar over all Christians, the supreme ecclesiastical lord over all men.

An Agency of Men. The religious unity of the West did not mean uniformity. In its many different functions, the church made use of the hermit and the organizer, the gravedigger and the intellectual, the spellbinder and the bureaucrat. In an extraordinary variety of institutions, the church had endeavored to meet the spiritual needs of all groups in society rather than thwart or deny any of them. But the reconciliation of clashing interests had not been easy, and a general spirit of dissatisfaction and uncertainty hung over Latin Christendom. For the church had in many respects ceased to function primarily for the central task laid down for it by its own doctrines.

The opportunity to serve had long since ceased to be the only reason for entering holy orders, or even the most important. Greed gnawed at the moral integrity of churchmen great and small. Church posts were sought for the revenues attached to them—rentals on church lands, the tithe, fees for administration of the sacraments, the fees charged by ecclesiastical courts. This infection was the price paid by the church for the way it had managed to maintain its personnel and support its work during the medieval period, when it could depend neither on voluntary contributions nor on government salaries. The status and influence of various classes in society were precisely reflected in the kind of church positions they were able to claim for their sons and daughters: the local parishes, commanding small revenues, found mainly sons of peasants or poor townsmen for their priests, while more remunerative benefices became the preserve of the wealthy and the influential. Plums like rich abbeys and bishoprics aroused fierce competition, the contending candidates using both bribes and threats upon the chapters or monastic foundations which had the right of nomination.

The papacy itself had become the most valued prize of all. Immense revenues poured into its coffers. Bishops and abbots paid for confirmation of their appointments, for the emblems of their office, and sent to Rome a portion of their first year's revenues (annates). All Christians (except where political authorities forbade it) paid the papacy a tax called Peter's pence. The papal curia, which handled appeals from local ecclesiastical courts to the supreme jurisdiction of Rome, exacted numerous and heavy fees for the performance of its services. Finally, the faithful everywhere made special payments for a multitude of exemptions and authorizations. Of these the indulgence, which provided the issue on which the Reformation began, was the best known.

No one ventured a theoretical defense of simony, the purchase of ecclesiastical office, but there were many critics to call attention to other abuses. The monastic orders were freely criticized. They had been founded on the principle of poverty, lest worldly possessions distract or tempt the man given over to the life of meditation, prayer, and service. But the orders had grown wealthy, and in the popular mind, monks had become fat, idle, and ravenous.

The rule of celibacy was frequently flouted; in local parishes, tongues wagged about the priest's housekeeper who was also his concubine, and great churchmen often flaunted their mistresses and publicly acknowledged their bastard children.

The rule of residence was broken with equal ease and carelessness. Often a churchman held several benefices at once. He himself might be in residence at none of them; in his place he would send a vicar entrusted with performance of the duties of the office, for which the vicar received a pittance called a "congruent portion."

Ignorance, illiteracy, and inadequate training for their tasks, were common failings among churchmen. Though outright disbelief was rare among them, as among Europeans generally, many churchmen were indifferent to the content of their faith. Theological questions had become chiefly the concern of professional theologians in the universities, who tended to be more interested in the technical niceties of their craft than in its meaning for mankind. In many states, the rulers called upon the most intelligent and competent churchmen to undertake responsible duties in the government, and rewarded able civil servants by the grant of benefices in their control. Thus the church had become more and more a subordinate agency in the world of laymen.

Competition for Control. The power for improvement rested with the great prelates and the pope, on the one hand, and with the mighty princes in the new territorial states, on the other. But, being the beneficiaries of these malpractices, they were reluctant to act in accordance with their responsibilities and powers. The pious and the thoughtful joined with the disappointed and the jealous in clamoring for reform of the church "in the head and in the members," that is, from supreme pontiff down to simple parish priest.

Most advocates of such reformation continued to look toward general councils of the church to accomplish their aims. These councils, in which cardinals, prelates, and heads of the monastic orders were the principal members, were, according to the adherents of this doctrine, the ultimate authority within the church, and could even depose popes. Such claims seemed stronger than reality in 1500, however, for during the fifteenth century the general councils of Constance (1414-1418) and Basel (1431-1449) had met without wresting control of the church from the pope, or imposing measures of reform upon him. Nonetheless, the possibility that several powerful kings might combine to enforce upon the Holy See a council with more effective powers remained a threat to which the pontiffs were most sensitive.

The demand for reform was also taken up whenever a pope died and the Sacred College of cardinals met in conclave to elect his successor. They imposed upon their nominee a "capitulation," or promise to undertake specified reforms (which included increased power and revenue to the cardinals). But once the Sacred College had given its votes to a new pontiff, it retained no means of control over him. Popes thus disregarded these capitulations with impunity.

General councils and cardinals were not the only competitors of the papacy for control within the church. The bishops, as local administrators, also sought to magnify their own role and to develop their independence of the central authority at Rome. Episcopal autonomy was greatest where it was combined with the exercise of political power, as in the ecclesiastical principalities of Germany. In most cases, however, secular princes came between the papacy and the bishops; they protected the prelates against papal domination only in order to impose their own. This process had been carried farthest in Spain, France, and England, while the fragmentation of political authority in the Holy Roman Empire meant that a national church there was more a dream than a fact.

Conflicts arose easily out of the complexity of church organization. For centuries the great religious orders, especially the mendicant friars (Dominicans and Franciscans), had clashed with the secular clergy. Parish priests disliked the presence among their flock of begging friars and the competition of preaching monks. Bishops resented the exemption of monastic houses from their jurisdiction.

Disputes over Doctrine. Intellectual life within the church was likewise marked by the struggle of contradictory elements. Wide liberty of thought had been permitted, even encouraged, in the medieval church. Mystics and rationalists, Platonists and Aristotelians, disciples of Thomas Aquinas the great systematizer, of Duns Scotus the subtle skeptic, of William of Ockham the master of logicians, all confronted each other within the same edifice of learning and speculation. Boldness of mind by itself brought little danger. There was no conformity, and no requirement of conformity, about the exact meaning of the truths to which all assented.

Not that all men had accepted Catholic dogma in its entirety. Movements like the Brethren of the Common Life in the Low Countries and adjacent lands arose to intensify personal piety and to expand the role of the laity in the church. But when such movements began to deny either the sacraments or the monopoly of the priesthood in their performance, the dread charge of heresy fell upon them and they were suppressed as the Albigensians and the Lollards had once been. Important in their time, these were little more than memories at the beginning of the sixteenth century. They had failed to win the support of the secular governments, and persecution had wiped out all but tiny remnants. The Waldensians lurking in the fastnesses of the Savoyard Alps, the few Lollards among the artisans of the English towns, were no danger to the existing religious order.

Christian Humanism. Despite the obvious difficulties facing them, the advocates of reform did not despair of success. They were confident that the new learning, by restoring Christian teaching to its first purity, would generate new piety. Erasmus of Rotterdam, the greatest living classical scholar, was certain that the restoration of "good letters" would bring with it a clearer understanding of man's religious duties and a greater readiness to overcome abuses. In his *Handbook of the Christian Knight* (1503), he put forward a simple picture of Christian ethics; in the *Novum instrumentum* (1516), he reprinted the Greek text of the New Testament with his own Latin translation and notes; and in *The Praise of Folly* (1511), he satirized the weakness of all men, churchmen most of all.

Other Christian humanists were eminently successful in many parts of Europe. In Spain, Cardinal Francisco Jiménez de Cisneros was their sponsor. Acting for and by means of the state, Jiménez extracted from the papacy virtually absolute control of the Spanish church. On the one hand, he vigorously suppressed many abuses and consolidated Spanish orthodoxy; on the other, he founded the university of Alcalá de Henares to teach theology in combination with the new learning. In France, the kings, especially Francis I, supported the teaching and reforming activities of the humanists. Their leader was the gentle but zealous Jacques Lefèvre d'Étaples, who turned his learning to Biblical studies. In England, the new scholarship, especially in the persons of John Colet, dean of St. Paul's in London, and Sir Thomas More, lawyer and statesman, was winning both influence upon the mighty and prestige for the new piety based on the humanists' methods. In Germany, where Italian and Netherlandish influences merged, humanism was predominantly Christian and pious from the beginning.

The support which secular and ecclesiastical princes gave to the humanist cause led the reformers to feel that success was near and certain. How could it be otherwise, when the powers of the world, both temporal and spiritual, were behind them? Such serene self-confidence was as much a matter of faith, however, as of careful and honest weighing of the real situation.

Savonarola. The tragedy which overwhelmed Girolamo Savonarola (1452-1498) in Florence might have served as a warning of the difficulties faced by earnest reformers. To be sure, he was an ascetic Dominican monk, not a humanist; but he won the adherence of humanists and common folk alike in his campaign to make over both Florentines and the social and political order of their city closer to his image of Christian piety and righteousness. His stern puritanism, which wrenched Florence from its beauty-seeking arts and its moral laxity, won him enemies, but none so dangerous as Pope Alexander VI.

Unable to tame Savonarola's vehemence by the rebuffed offer of a cardinal's red hat, Alexander sought at least to quiet him by an order to cease his preaching. The wrathful monk responded by proclaiming that when the pope erred, good Christians must refuse to obey him, and by calling for a general council to act against the sinful pontiff. In 1497 Alexander excommunicated Savonarola, whose enemies among the Franciscans and the wealthy patricians of Florence then accomplished his downfall. In 1498 he was tortured, forced to recant, and burned as a heretic. Yet his memory was preserved by many as the image of selfless devotion to the cause of a purer church and a better humanity.

The humanists, who in general did not look upon Savonarola, triumphant or defeated, as one of their own, knew no such uncertainty when Johannes Reuchlin, a German scholar, came into conflict with the Dominican theologians who dominated the university of Cologne. Prompted by a converted Jew, Jacob Pfefferkorn, who made a career of denouncing the people into which he had been born, the Dominicans had demanded that all Jewish books be burned on the emperor's orders as blasphemous. Reuchlin, who was Germany's leading Hebraist, opposed such blanket condemnation; most Hebrew works were useful in philosophy, science, linguistic studies, and theology, he averred. Accused of heresy before the court of the Inquisition at Cologne, Reuchlin appealed to Pope Leo X. A commission appointed by the pontiff cleared Reuchlin in 1514. The humanists followed up this victory (which was reversed after 1517) with a satire upon their opponents. In the *Epistolae obscurorum virorum* (*Letters of obscure men,* 1515, 1517) they mocked savagely at the scholastics for their awkward Latin, their creaking philosophy, and their loose morality.

II. The Lutheran Revolt

The conflict between the defenders and attackers of the status quo in the church suddenly took on a more somber aspect in 1517. Three years before, the papacy had agreed to permit Albert of Hohenzollern, youngest brother of Elector Joachim of Brandenburg, to add the archbishopric of Mainz to the sees of Magdeburg and Halberstadt which he already held. Albert had to pay 10,000 ducats above the usual fees for this exemption from the canonical law forbidding the holding of more than one see. In order to repay the 34,000 ducats he had been compelled to borrow from the banking house of Fugger, Albert agreed to permit the issuance of the Jubilee Indulgence (designed to pay the costs of rebuilding the Roman basilica of St. Peter's) in his territories, and persuaded his brother Joachim to do likewise in the lands of the house of Hohenzollern.

The Indulgence Controversy. Albert named John Tetzel, prior of the Dominican monastery in Leipzig, to conduct the distribution of the indulgence in Halberstadt and Magdeburg. Tetzel was a dramatic salesman. By vivid descriptions of hell and purgatory, he stirred the crowds into frenzied fear. Then he assured them that the paper he brought would rescue them and their departed loved ones from these torments; for the pope had power to draw upon the merits earned by saints beyond their own needs of redemption, in order to remit the penance due by sinners who bought the indulgence. He skipped lightly over the requirement that indulgences were effective only for the remorseful who had received absolution in confession.

Protests against this traffic in the salvation of souls mounted rapidly, not least among the members of Tetzel's own order of Dominicans. When he began to promote the indulgences in Jüterbog and Zerbst, not far from Wittenberg, capital of electoral Saxony, Tetzel met a new and formidable obstacle to his work. Because the indulgence was not on sale in Saxony, a number of Wittenberg citizens obtained it from Tetzel. Dr. Martin Luther, preacher in the Wittenberg city church and professor of Biblical literature at the university, heard in confessional of these sales and was stirred to indignation.

The Entry of Luther. The issue of the indulgences was of intense personal concern to Luther. He felt the whole course of his religious development during the previous decade to be involved. Ever since he had joined the Augustinian order of Eremites in 1506, he had grappled with the question, "How shall I know I am saved?" Baffled by his inability to find certainty of divine grace and eternal salvation in the mere reception of the sacraments or in his vows as a monk, Luther had feared the condemnation of God, in whom, as was usual at the time, he saw an implacable judge. Finally, in the works of St. Paul and St. Augustine, the first and last of the great founders of Christian theology, he discovered an answer which relieved his awful sense of sin. Sinful man was made just by faith, not by works. Justification was the inward transformation of the sinner, who accepted the fact of his sinfulness and trusted in God's mercy to enable him to combat it.

Luther therefore decided to initiate public debate on the indulgences. He did so in the customary way of scholars, by posting theses, ninety-five in number, on the door of the castle church. These were Latin propositions in which he stated his objections to the indulgence system. Such remission of penalties applied only to the living and then only for what the church itself inflicted, Luther maintained. He denied that there existed a treasury of merits upon which the church could draw for rescuing souls in purgatory. In any event, the pope should be willing to grant indulgences, assuming their efficacy, in simple charity without requiring money, he concluded. Yet he affirmed that he wished only to strengthen the pope's true authority against false doctrines which endangered it.

The Charge of Heresy. Luther anticipated an academic debate upon the principles he had set forth. He hoped to win the leadership of the church to his views, and even sent a copy to Archbishop Albert for his approval. That prelate responded instead with an appeal to Rome to cut off the activities of the Saxon troublemaker. Pope Leo X, thinking too much was being made of a quarrel between Dominican and Augustinian monks, declined to act. Luther continued confident that his enemies acted without Leo's approval; he misread the pope's complacency for something like readiness to agree with him. Yet he endangered such leniency as he found in the pontiff by hinting that popes and church councils could err in propounding doctrine. Furthermore, he had sent copies of his propositions to friends in Erfurt and other towns, and they had at once reprinted them. In this form the Ninety-Five Theses were distributed far and wide.

Within a short time the sale of indulgences fell off almost to nothing. Leo X finally accepted the Dominicans' proposal that Luther be called to Rome to answer accusations of heresy. In August, 1518, Luther received an order to appear in the Holy City within sixty days; an accompanying document accused him of heresy, but refused to rebut his opinions on the grounds that the pope was infallible and his power absolute.

Luther now had to choose between what he believed to be gospel truth and the obedience he had wished to maintain to the church and to the pope. If he went to Rome, he realized that death at the stake or life in a dungeon cell awaited him. He turned at once to his prince, Elector Frederick of Saxony, known as "the Wise." On the advice of his counselors, Frederick arranged for Luther's case to be heard at Augsburg before the papal legate, Cajetan. This confrontation (October, 1518) made the contrary attitudes clear: Cajetan, general of the Dominican order, endeavored to win over the

Wittenberg professor by kind words, but would not abandon either the tenets of scholasticism or the rights of Rome; Luther seems to have been surprised that he did not persuade the legate, who was the leading Roman theologian of the day, of the rightness of his views.

Rejection of the Papacy. Luther appealed "from the pope badly informed to the pope to be better informed" for proofs clearly drawn from the Bible that he was wrong. But Leo had already declared him to be a notorious heretic (August 23, 1518). On seeing the papal brief, Luther sought refuge in the defeated conciliar doctrines of the fifteenth century, but it was the strength of Elector Frederick which proved his shield. The elector, though himself annoyed by the unbending stubbornness of his now famous subject and not fully sympathizing with his theological innovations, would not permit a German to be condemned out of hand in a foreign country.

Early in the summer of the following year, Luther at last faced the fact that a chasm had opened between himself and the rulers of the church. He defended his views at Leipzig during a famous debate (June 27-July 16, 1519); at Luther's side was his colleague at Wittenberg, Andreas Carlstadt, who had sponsored Luther for the doctorate. Johannes von Eck, the outstanding Catholic theologian in Germany, intervened in the debate. A wily debater, Eck drove Luther into positions he had not yet been ready to announce; the reformer now denied that either pope or general council was infallible, that the church of Rome held any supremacy over other churches, and that there was any authority in the church, in the last analysis, other than Holy Scripture.

Definition of Doctrine. As a consequence of the debate, Luther gave increased emphasis to the Bible: not only did he claim for it absolute primacy in all theological questions, but he also came to deny more and more firmly that it needed interpretation. Luther felt with passionate sincerity that such a certainty as to the meaning of scriptural text as he himself possessed could be explained only by the ineffable and unerring guidance of the Holy Spirit; therefore, whatever their apparent logic, his opponents were necessarily wrong.

Luther next turned his attention to the question of the sacraments. He abandoned the traditional Catholic view that they miraculously transmitted divine grace by the very fact of their administration (*ex opere operato*, by the doing of the thing done). Instead he accepted the sacrament as a sign of the promise of salvation by Christ. He also reduced the true sacraments to two, baptism and the Lord's Supper (the Eucharist).

The definition of the Eucharist became a central theme in sixteenth-century theological debate between Catholics and Protestants, as those who quit Rome came to be called (see ch. 13, p. 306), and among Protestants themselves; the relationship between priests or ministers, on the one side, and the laity, on the other, was ultimately shaped by the answer given to this question. Luther, who sought to make only those changes in theological doctrine which he felt flowed inevitably from his basic views, modified the Catholic position regarding the Eucharist rather than rejecting it outright. He continued to believe in the real presence of Jesus Christ in the bread and wine of the sacramental sacrifice, but not that they actually became his body and blood (the Roman Catholic doctrine known as "transubstantiation"). Though preferring to have both bread and wine administered to the communicants ("in both kinds"), he did not consider it necessary.

Luther accepted the administration to infants of the sacrament of baptism, whereby all persons may be brought into the church immediately after birth. He defined penance as the forgiveness of sin consequent upon faith in the divine promise of redemption. Such faith, he said, led to good works which in themselves were powerless to achieve salvation.

Leadership of Reform. As his views became more and more widely known, Luther appeared to advocates of reform not alone in Germany, but in most parts of Europe, as the boldest and best leader their cause had produced. Those who had already developed a strong antipathy for the papacy, such as the scholarly German knight Ulrich von Hutten, urged him to take the lead in a revolutionary movement of independence from Rome. But the older school of Christian humanists, however sympathetic with his criticism of abuses, did not wish to see the very edifice of Latin Christendom destroyed. They urged Luther to seek reforms in a calm, persuasive manner. He could not accept such counsel when wrath raged within him against what he now felt to be utterly intolerable evils. During 1520 he published three pamphlets which set forth his position clearly, and thereby he virtually accepted leadership of the revolution against Rome.

In his *Address to the Christian Nobility of the German Nation*, he turned to the state as the major instrumentality for reform of the church. He called upon the political leaders of Germany to undertake this task, in accordance with their God-given duty of keeping good order among men. They should halt the flow of money to Rome, and forbid obedience to her orders. The mendicant orders should be suppressed. In the universities the educational methods of the Christian humanists should replace scholastic teaching.

In *The Babylonian Captivity of the Church*, he argued that all Christians were truly priests, and that the right to administer the sacraments and to preach belonged to those they selected, not to a special group of ordained priests. He reaffirmed his new doctrines on the sacraments, which underlay his conception of the proper relationship of churchmen and laity.

In *The Freedom of the Christian Man*, Luther again argued for justification by faith alone. The Christian was in bondage only to God, but such was true freedom, which no other human being could touch. Christians were held, however, to obey the secular rulers, who could command only the flesh, not the spirits, of their subjects. Christians gladly accepted, too, the duty of service to fellow men.

Excommunication and Outlawry. During the same year, 1520, Leo X struck the rebellious Wittenberger from the community of Roman Catholics by publishing the bull *Exsurge domine* (*Arise O Lord*), condemning Luther as a heretic. He confirmed the bull a year later. Luther's supporters rallied only the more strongly behind him, and began to denounce the pope as Antichrist.

In 1521, he received at last the opportunity he had long sought for a hearing before the highest authority in Germany, the Holy Roman emperor. Given a safe-conduct to appear at the diet of Worms, he came to defend his views before Charles V and the papal legate Aleander. He acknowledged authorship of the books on which the charge of heresy against him was based.

Commanded to retract what the church, whose true doctrines were clear and unarguable, had declared false, Luther replied by reaffirming his principles: "Unless I shall be overcome by the testimony of Scripture or by clear reason (for I trust neither in pope nor in councils alone, it having been established that they often err and have contradicted themselves), and because I am bound by the writings set forth by me and because my conscience is held bound by the word of God, I am not able and do not wish to retract anything, since it is neither safe nor righteous to go against conscience."

Again the plea went out to the accused heretic: Come back to the true church. He turned to the emperor, and spoke, in German, the simple words: "I cannot do otherwise. Here I stand, may God help me. Amen."

It is scarcely possible that any more sincere or dramatic plea for the rights of conscience has ever been uttered, and yet Luther could not comprehend how the conscience of other men could differ from his, unless the devil misled them. Luther was asked, Was not Emperor Charles bound by his conscience to suppress the heretics? "We know that he neither is nor can be certain, for we know that he errs and does battle with the Gospel," he replied. "The emperor is duty-bound to acknowledge God's word and to do its service, as do we, with all his strength."

Charles's conscience was as clear and certain as his subject's, though where Luther sought absolute certitude about the content of his faith, Charles accepted his Catholic religion as part of his inheritance. He believed it implicitly to be true, but was ready, when political interest dictated, to let the theologians effect a compromise on its meaning if they could. In any event, after Luther's responses, Charles knew him to be a heretic. In an edict dated May 8 but signed May 26, 1521, at Worms, the emperor put Luther under the ban of the empire. As an outlaw, the reformer could be seized, robbed, and killed with impunity.

Yet the emperor respected the safe-conduct he had given Luther and permitted him to leave Worms. On the journey back to Wittenberg, Luther was "kidnaped" at the orders of Elector Frederick and taken to a safe hiding place at Wartburg castle, near Eisenach. There, except for one brief visit to Wittenberg, he stayed for almost a year, engaged in the translation of the Bible into German.

Building a New Church. The supreme rulers of both church and empire had condemned Luther. He could now direct his appeals only to the councils —now a vain hope—or to the lesser princes and to the people at large in Germany. Henceforth his principal concern was to build up a church based on what he was convinced was a true reading of Scripture, to re-establish its doctrines on that basis, and to organize it as an enduring and effective institution. One by one he decided to abandon numerous practices of Catholicism. He vehemently condemned the monastic system as false to the principle of poverty on which it had been founded, and contrary to nature in its vow of chastity. He himself married, proving a more contented husband and father than he had been a monk.

To encourage and direct religious studies in his new way, he remained ceaselessly engaged in the ensuing decades in writing tracts and studies, not only in his rough-hewn though serviceable Latin but also in the German of ordinary men. Luther used his mother tongue with a power and skill hardly rivaled before the eighteenth century. The forthrightness and vigor of his language made his German version of the Bible one of the greatest triumphs in the whole history of scriptural translations.

Luther never acted for the sake of change itself. He had intended no more than to set church and theology right again, to undo what he saw as the work of Antichrist in the centuries between the apostles and himself. He modified only such doctrines and institutions of the Catholic church as he could not fit into his fundamental pattern of beliefs. His reform of the liturgy consisted mainly in pruning it of elements he considered as medieval overgrowth and presenting it in German, enhanced by German hymns of great power and beauty. Luther was in heart and mind, though not in language, a complete conservative. He wished to bring about necessary changes by the action of the established political authorities, not by the rebellion of subjects.

But a religious revolution is a revolution, which, like any other, is easier to unleash than to contain. The unbudging conservatism of the masses was subject to almost instantaneous transformation into violent outbursts of savage hatred and desperate attempts to attain a justice which they had hardly dreamed was possible in this life. Moderation was no part of their makeup, and once aroused by the bold and passionate words of Dr. Martin Luther, they would not stay within the cautious limits he put upon his purposes.

Church, State, and People. The issue of whether the reforms should be conducted by the state or by the people was posed almost at once in Wittenberg itself. Carlstadt, Luther's fellow-professor at the university, took the lead of the popular forces during his friend's absence at the Wartburg. He directed them in destroying images in the churches and in enforcing a ritual according to the new ideas. Luther left the safety of Wartburg for a brief visit to Wittenberg in order to bring an end to the turbulence. After his definitive return to Wittenberg, he tried to restrain Carlstadt's fervor, but was compelled finally to have him expelled from the city. Reform should be effected by preaching and persuasion, not by violence, Luther told the too-hasty and overardent.

The reformer found no easy or ultimately adequate answer to the knotty question of the proper relationship between church and state. His preference ran to a democracy in church administration; congregations should pay their own expenses and select their own officials. But the secular princes of sixteenth-century Germany, least of all those who adopted Lutheranism, would not gladly be deprived of the rights of supervision and direction over the church which in large measure they already possessed and wished to enlarge. Nor did independent congregations prove capable of co-operating among themselves without coercion.

Thus Luther was compelled to assent to direction of the territorial churches by the great princes. Visitors, acting on the authority of the elector of Saxony, took over the functions and after a while even the name of bishops; they supervised the local churches, enforcing correct doctrine, selecting personnel, and controlling finances. This became the general pattern of Lutheran state churches, so that what to Luther had been at first only a device became the central institution of the church he founded. In the towns, the Wittenberg pattern, in which the municipal authorities designated a superintendent of churches from among the clergy, was widely imitated.

Melanchthon. Luther's principal assistant in the work of theological and institutional renovation was Philip Melanchthon, Reuchlin's grand-nephew, who came to Wittenberg to teach Greek and Hebrew at the university. The brilliant young humanist continued his classical and linguistic studies, and became Luther's most effective apostle among the growing humanistic circles in Germany. Despite their close affection and steady collaboration, tension developed between the two men. Luther was a daring and creative innovator, whose torrential ideas Melanchthon took and systematized, though it was not always easy to fit them together. More serious was Melanchthon's fundamental bent as a compromiser; he was willing to compromise with other sects of Protestants and even with the Roman Catholics on what Luther considered to be essential points. Luther summed up his own views in two didactic tracts, usually known as the Small and the Large (or German) Catechisms, of 1529.

The leaders of the Lutheran movement came from many different ranks of life. Most numerous and influential were those who had already assumed the religious life as their profession, priests and monks who quit their Catholic robes but not their functions as spiritual leaders. Some humanists took on responsible tasks because of the opportunity to achieve reforms they had discussed only in theory before. From among the common people arose a relatively smaller number of new leaders, who though neither trained nor experienced in such work felt the call to preach the evangels. Among the general population, virtually every group felt the appeal of the new movement; but there were some also in every class who would not be swayed from the old faith.

The Break with Erasmus. Nor did many years pass before Luther began to lose followers among those who had been the first to join him. He was friendly to the humanists, and might even be considered one of them insofar as he favored their linguistic and rhetorical system of education. But when they tended, as did Erasmus, to see literary excellence as a method for the achievement of piety, and to disregard the importance of a clear and definite body of beliefs, he was their enemy. To be sure, he had enunciated the doctrine of private judgment, but he had been confident that his own interpretation of Scripture would win the voluntary and total adherence of all fair-minded and well-instructed Christians. However, the method of free interpretation could not easily be halted at the point he himself had reached. Many of the humanists who had hailed him for his revolt against papal authoritarianism and dogmatism were indignant at the strictness of interpretation which he in his turn considered necessary. He was not tolerant toward dissent and disagreement.

The divergence was widest and most significant between Luther and Erasmus. Erasmus respected the traditions of the church and the church as a tradition; his religious feeling, though fully as real as Luther's, was different in character: Luther's was intense, passionate, and centered in a quest for certitude; Erasmus's rested on a gentle skepticism, less concerned with the nature of an unknowable God than with that of imperfect man. Luther had rebelled against the old church in order to establish doctrine on a clear, more definite basis; Erasmus placed character above dogma, loving-kindness before truth.

The clash between them came into the open in 1523, when Luther attacked Erasmus for cowardice. The great humanist made his defense in a *Diatribe on Free Will* in which he disputed Luther's doctrine that man was powerless, his will enslaved to God: man, he replied, had the liberty to choose meaningfully between good and evil. Erasmus failed to understand that Luther reintroduced something like free will into his doctrine, but it was possessed only by the true Christian on whom divine grace had fallen. By

1527 the break between the two men was complete. Erasmus remained loyal to the Roman church which he had so trenchantly criticized, and did not wish to be known as the prophet of a schismatic faith he had not meant to help create.

The Peasant War. Others broke with Luther because he was too little the revolutionary, not too much. Those who passionately desired to improve the social and economic conditions of man's life interpreted Luther's ideas—especially the freedom and equality of the Christian man—to apply here. They felt justified in employing violence to attain their purposes, for were not their enemies servants of the devil? Luther, on the other hand, declared that God had entrusted the sword to the state, and to no others, to maintain order and law, not to destroy them. The just man, he said, was honest, industrious, and moved by love for his fellows, and would be such in his worldly endeavors as well as in religious life. To use the Gospel as justification for rebellious violence was blasphemy. He urged the nobles to give up their avaricious and oppressive conduct toward the peasantry, and called upon the princes to seek their subjects' welfare, not their harm.

But the peasants rose in desperate revolt (see ch. 13, p. 301), proclaiming that they were only seeking the rights assured them by Scripture. Luther would not countenance what he felt to be perversion and misuse of his doctrines. He denounced "the murderous hordes of the peasants" and demanded their merciless suppression. Yet, when the rebellion had once been put down, his wrath softened and he demanded again that the nobles treat the peasants with human decency and fairness. But he did not waiver in his belief that government is divinely instituted and that political and social revolution is the devil's work. A major result of the episode was to turn much of the peasantry against Luther while strengthening the princes' confidence in him as well as their insistence on controlling the church within their lands.

The Lutheran Reformation was adopted by most of the states in the northeastern part of Germany, though it won adherents almost everywhere else in the country. A fully legalized status for Lutheranism was finally achieved by the Peace of Augsburg, under the terms of the "Recess" of September, 1555 (see ch. 13, p. 313). One consequence of this settlement for the Lutherans was to make both the princes and the churchmen adhering to the new faith highly conservative, satisfied with their present position rather than seeking further gains, more interested in the consolidation and specification of doctrines than in fervid winning of new converts.

The Winning of Scandinavia. Only in neighboring Scandinavia did Lutheranism also emerge triumphantly as the state religion. The new ideas from Wittenberg spread easily into these northern lands, for they moved along established channels of cultural and economic influence. Hanseatic merchants, in particular, became sources of Lutheran ferment.

DESIDERIVS ERASMVS ROTTERODAMVS.
Qui Patrie lumen qui nostri gloria seca.
THOMÆ HOWARDO, COMITI ARVNDELIÆ, & SVRREIÆ, PRIMO ANGLIÆ COMITI, DOMINO HOWARDO
MALTRAVERS, MOWBRAY, SEGRAVE, BREVS, CLVN, & OSESTRIÆ, COMITI MARESCALLO ANGLIÆ,
NOBILISSIMI PERISCELIDIS SIVE GARTERY ORDINIS EQVITI & SERENISSIMO REGI
CAROLO MAGNÆ BRITANNIÆ, FRANCIÆ & HIBERNIÆ, REGI AB INTIMIS CONCILYS, *artium&*
omnium liberalium Mecoenati maximo, hanc Erasmi effigie amoris ergo humiliter Lucas
Vorsterman Sculptor D. D: Hansus Holbenius *pinxit*   *Cum Priuilegio Reg*

"DESIDERIUS ERASMUS OF ROTTERDAM." Engraving by Lucas Vorsterman, seventeenth-century Dutch artist, after the painting by Hans Holbein, about 1630–1640.

"The Prince of Humanists" in a characteristic pose—thoughtful, mild, but not without concern for his bodily comfort. The original painting is by one of the greatest portraitists of the sixteenth century; the engraving is dedicated to Thomas Howard, earl of Arundell and Surrey. *(Achenbach Foundation)*

Fundamentally, the royal government in Sweden took the initiative in reorganizing the religious life of these realms on the Lutheran pattern.

The movement was royal from the start. The king was the unquestioned supreme governor of the church, selecting its officials and deciding upon its doctrines as the final authority. The Roman Catholic bishops were replaced by a Lutheran episcopate, for there was never any question of self-government by the local churches. In Denmark the people came to Lutheranism first, and its acceptance by the king was a central issue of political struggle during the 1530's.

As in Germany, the vernacular became the language of liturgy and scripture in the Scandinavian countries. The Bible was translated into both Danish and Swedish before mid-century. The principal difference between the Lutheran state churches in Denmark and Sweden consisted in the theological basis for the episcopate. In Denmark the new bishops were instituted by Johannes Bugenhagen, one of Luther's collaborators who had never been consecrated as a Catholic bishop; the direct line of apostolic succession was therefore broken. In Sweden, on the other hand, the government took particular precautions to assure that John Magnusson should be consecrated by Rome. Then in turn he consecrated national bishops whose powers could be presented as deriving without interruption from St. Peter's.

Triumphs and Defeats. The influence of Luther's doctrines was not confined to these Teutonic lands. To the east of Germany, they were taken up widely, but, because the leaders of the Lutheran movement were usually local nobility, the new movement tended to weaken rather than strengthen central governments. The Baltic seaboard, from East Prussia to Estonia and Finland, became a Lutheran stronghold. In Poland, though Lutheranism won numerous adherents, it was only one of several creeds adopted by the dominant nobility for their own territories. In Bohemia, efforts to establish a friendly collaboration between the Lutherans and the Bohemian Brethren failed despite much effort. Both German townsmen and Magyar noblemen flocked to Lutheranism; for them it was linked both to humanism and to their education in German universities. The easternmost part of Hungary, Transylvania, went over to the new church most strongly. The hereditary lands of the Hapsburgs, notably Carinthia, witnessed a similar shift of the landed aristocracy, followed by the peasantry, to Lutheranism.

In the western and southern lands, Lutheranism failed to win and hold broad sections of the population. In the Low Countries, it found followers among the middle and lower classes, but the repressive measures of Charles V prevented any consolidation of this heresy. In the Latin countries Lutheranism was an affair only of some intellectuals, reaching few others. Its reception in Spain was mixed. Many humanists were attracted to it, and the new ideas even reached close to the throne of the king, Charles I (Charles V, as emperor), in the person of his secretary Alfonso Valdes and the latter's brother Juan. But the monarchy, having already achieved control of ecclesiastical affairs within its boundaries and having made great progress in eliminating the most notorious of the abuses, gave no quarter to those infected

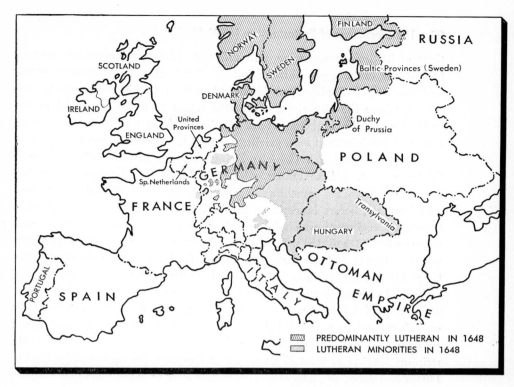

The Lutherans in Europe, 1648

with Lutheranism. By 1521 the reading of Luther's works, which had been translated into Spanish and imported from Germany, was officially forbidden. Outright Protestants remained few in number, strictly hunted; some were burned at the stake, others fled abroad.

In Italy, Lutheran penetration was impeded by the strong sense felt in most places that the country derived important economic benefits from the papacy. Nonetheless a number of independent individuals did break with Catholic doctrine, but almost all embraced some form of Protestantism other than Lutheranism. In France, Lutheran ideas held the attention of many who were discontented with the old church, but the Sorbonne, the theological faculty of the University of Paris, watched with hawklike closeness and persistence for the appearance of heretical doctrine. Though the reformers were soon labeled "the Lutheran sect" by their opponents, few of them became specifically disciples of the Wittenberger.

III. Calvinism

Across the Holy Roman Empire from Saxony, another form of Protestantism arose. Its doctrines were those of Luther at the start, but the conditions of its development were quite different. Christian humanism had long been strong in the upper Rhineland and Switzerland, as in the Low Countries, and the laity had played an important part in religious affairs. In this region, where the city states dominated rather than the territorial principalities as in the Lutheran areas, religious reform tended to merge with measures for defense of local privilege against foreign domination.

Zwingli. Huldreich (Ulrich) Zwingli was the first important leader of this movement. Unlike Luther, who came to classical learning rather late and always remained something of a stranger within it, Zwingli was trained as a humanist before becoming a theologian. Appalled by the fate of Swiss mercenary regiments which he served as chaplain during the Italian campaigns of 1513 and 1515, he won public attention by his attack upon the whole system of hiring out as mercenaries. He became a parish priest in the Great Minster of Zürich in 1519, where his attacks on abuses, more political and social than religious, made him a leader of the reformers.

Study of Luther's writings carried him away from his early Catholic orthodoxy, and he persuaded the Zürich town council to order abandonment of numerous Catholic practices in the churches of the city (1524). He stripped religion of most of its ceremonial aspects, far more ruthlessly than Luther had done; all pictures and ornaments were removed from the churches, the organs were dismantled and music abandoned. The preacher's sermon became the heart of the Zwinglian church service.

Accepting the principle of literal biblical truth, Zwingli interpreted its meaning as common sense and plain reason seemed to dictate; unlike Luther, he would retain only what the Gospels specifically required. He amplified and modified the notion of predestination, to which Luther had given little attention. According to this doctrine, which St. Augustine had put at the center of his theology, God selected those who would be saved and those who would be damned from the beginning of creation; the former would receive his grace, the latter would be left to sin and pay the penalty. Zwingli differed sharply with Luther concerning the Eucharist. He interpreted the communion in a symbolic sense; to him the bread signified Christ's body but did not actually become present in it, as Luther held. The sacraments were only signs of divine grace, not means for its transmission.

The controversy threatened to divide the two main branches of Protestantism at a time of severe struggle with Charles V, and a debate was organized at Marburg in 1529, in an effort to overcome the differences. Zwingli came more willingly than Luther, but proved less willing to make a settlement. He rejected a compromise statement by Luther because it did not clearly emphasize the purely spiritual character of the communion. Luther wished mainly to consolidate the changes he had already wrought, while Zwingli feared that he was allowing Catholic errors to remain in his doctrines. The Colloquy of Marburg, as the debate was known, marked the final break between the two camps of Protestants.

In social and political matters, Zwingli remained a strong conservative, to whom the use of the sword came easily. His readiness to employ force in the service of religious doctrine finally accomplished his undoing, however. The "Kappel War" of 1531 resulted from the efforts of Zürich, under Zwingli's leadership, to crush the Catholic cantons of central Switzerland. After the defeat of the Zürichers at Kappel (October 11, 1531), Zwingli was found wounded on the battlefield and immediately slain by the victors.

Bucer. A unique role in shaping the general character of Protestantism outside the Lutheran area fell to the city of Strassburg, on the Rhine, and to its chief theologian, Martin Bucer. Much of the impetus for reform in the cities of upper Germany came originally from Zwingli, but as the movement spread north into the Rhineland it changed character under Bucer's leadership.

Called to Strassburg as its leading pastor in 1523, Bucer continued the policy of toleration already favored there. He endeavored by patient persuasion to bring the various Protestant groups to agreement, so that they could achieve their common aims. But he could not brook Anabaptists, who wished to separate the "elect," or chosen of God, from the body of all Christians. Though he accepted the doctrine of predestination, he believed it was the duty of the "elect" to direct the one true church by means of firm ecclesiastical discipline. The sinner and the false believer should be punished by excommunication.

Bucer argued that the church should hold a position equal to the state's, but the magistrates of Strassburg, who gave him their backing on most issues, refused to admit that the church did not lie within their proper jurisdiction. He wavered in his opinions concerning the sacraments, but ultimately joined Luther in the belief that Christ was really (substantially) present in the eucharist. In 1548, Bucer refused to condone Strassburg's temporary bowing before the might of Charles V. He went off to England, then just entering its period of strenuous Protestantizing under Edward VI, but died two years before the advent of Mary Tudor and Catholic reaction.

The Rise of Calvin. A young Frenchman whom Bucer befriended and assisted was able to create a broad and powerful new movement upon the basis of a city-state much like Strassburg. John Calvin founded a new form of Protestantism in the city-republic of Geneva upon which were patterned most major Protestant groups formed after the middle of the sixteenth century.

Calvin, like Zwingli, received his first education in strictly humanist fashion, till, at the age of fourteen, he was sent to Paris to study at the university. Enrolled at the orthodox College of Montaigu, he acquired a firm command of scholastic theology in its Ockhamite and Scotist forms. In 1528, he transferred to the study of law at Orléans, where the new learning was emphasized, and continued these humanist interests on returning to Paris in the early 1530's. But he did not turn from the traditional Erasmian humanism and piety dominant there until 1533, when he became associated with evangelical reformers. One of these was Nicholas Cop, newly elected rector of the University of Paris. Neither Cop nor his young friend had much time to enjoy the benefits of this office, for they were forced to flee when Cop's inaugural sermon, much of it drawn from a sermon by Luther, drew the accusation of heresy. Calvin remained in hiding within France.

In 1534 he began writing his *Institutes of the Christian Religion.* Later that same year he was compelled to take refuge outside of France. He went first to Strassburg and then to Basel, working all the while to complete his *Institutes.* Technically an expanded catechism, this work developed into a systematic exposition of Calvin's version of Protestant doctrine. Its logical coherence contrasted sharply with the erratic and thematic character of Luther's writings, though most of the doctrines differed little from Luther's. The book was originally written in Latin, but in 1541 Calvin published his own translation into French; in this form it won many adherents to his ideas, and its lucid, vigorous style helped also to shape the form of modern French prose.

Geneva as "God's City." After brief visits to Italy and France, Calvin set out in 1536 for Strassburg. The presence of Charles V's troops on his route compelled him to take a detour through Geneva. There the reformer Guillaume Farel prevailed upon him to remain in order to take over from him the task of completing reform of the church in that city. Thus did chance lead Calvin, who wished to remain a scholar, into his other great life work, the creation of a church centered in Geneva but extending to many parts of Europe.

The previous year Farel had persuaded the city council that only religious reform would safeguard the town's autonomy against the dominance of the bishop of Geneva and the duke of Savoy, who shared its overlordship. In 1536, before Calvin's arrival, a meeting of the citizenry agreed to reorganize life and government upon the basis of the Gospels. The town government was unprepared to direct such changes, however, because it had hitherto been excluded from the business of the church by the bishop. Farel was unable to cope with the crisis which followed, and thus had been moved to take advantage of Calvin's passing through Geneva. Calvin soon proved to have the vigor of personality and the assurance in decision and action which Farel lacked, but he continued to work in intimate collaboration with his sponsor and friend. Their purpose was to create on earth, first of all within the confines of the city on Lake Leman, a City of God as nearly as man could build it.

Their system has often been called theocratic because it made church-men so strong, but its ecclesiastical organization was not the monopoly of churchmen; the laity played an essential role in the system. The highest clergy were pastors, who preached, administered the sacraments, and con-trolled the moral activities of their flock. They were subject to mutual self-criticism; if they disagreed, the elders, and ultimately the city government, acted as arbiters. Beneath the pastors Calvin set the teachers of the youth, whom he also considered as clergy; then the elders, or presbyters, laymen who kept watch over the discipline of the people; and lastly deacons, who saw to the social duties of the church, such as supervision of aid to the sick and the poor.

Above all these he put a consistory as the supreme government of the church. Its members included all the pastors and twelve of the elders; laymen outnumbered professional churchmen.

Calvin drew his line of demarcation not between laity and priesthood, as in the Roman system, but between church and state. He did not define the state's function as simply to keep law and order, as did Luther, but rather he wished it to employ its force directly for the achievement of morality. The ultimate purpose of the state, for Calvin as it had been for theologians and political thinkers for almost two thousand years, was the good of the people; since that good was defined by God in revelation, who could set it forth for statesmen to follow but godly men, notably those trained in the Gospels and called to the leadership of God's church? Thus Calvin, in the last analysis, left the state organizationally separate from the church but subordinated to its policies. Active citizenship depended upon church membership, but only those who kept to the straightest path of moral rectitude and church fervor were safe from excommunication. This dreadful weapon Calvin placed in the hands of the ministers, or pastors, who could call upon the city government to enforce their decisions. On the other hand, Calvin assigned to the state judgment of matrimonial matters, involving the always thorny questions of property ownership; such cases had been in Catholic lands the close preserve of ecclesiastical courts.

Aristocratic Resistance Quelled. Such a system, in order to function, required mutual respect and good will on both sides, or control by one only. The strict and strenuous moral life which Calvin sought to impose upon the Genevans aroused the opposition of many. Yet for years Calvin lacked the power to eliminate them and their influence.

Leaders of the old aristocratic families of Geneva took up the struggle against him. They did not wish to lose into the hands of Calvin and his associates the political authority which they had wrested from the bishop of Geneva and the duke of Savoy. In 1538 they were able to regain control, and Calvin and Farel were expelled. At Bucer's insistence, Calvin returned to

Strassburg, where he took over a pastorate and continued his theological studies. He was deeply influenced by Bucer's liturgical and governmental innovations.

When his supporters regained power in Geneva three years later, Calvin, after initial hesitation and on the basis of far-reaching promises, heeded their call to return. He wished to apply what he had learned about effective church administration and church-state relationships at Strassburg. In 1541 Calvin, aged only thirty-two, returned to Geneva, where he remained till his death. The Ecclesiastical Ordinances which were drawn up and adopted under his guidance provided greater independence for the church than it possessed in Lutheran or other Protestant territories.

Calvin's attempt to govern the moral conduct of Genevans aroused wide antipathy. The consistory pried into the slightest details of personal life; it was, if anything, stricter than the Spanish Inquisition. It was not enough to refrain from evil doing, such as singing ribald folk songs, playing cards, or quarreling with one's family. It was necessary to conform in a positive way, and diligent and attentive presence at sermons was the most important of these duties. Calvin was a man utterly without a sense of good humor such as lends appeal to Luther's otherwise so serious personality. He did not distinguish between criticism of himself and a direct attack upon "the honor of Christ." By 1553, Calvin's opponents were again able to muster a large majority in the councils, but Calvin was able to rescue his position in the crisis which developed over the trials of Michael Servetus.

Servetus. Servetus was a Spanish-born physician long resident in France who had escaped into obscurity under a false name after publishing tracts against trinitarian doctrines while in Strassburg more than a decade earlier. His decision to reprint his books led to his exposure, and he fled from France. En route to Naples, Servetus, who was as bold in religion and in personal conduct as he was in scientific investigation, passed through Geneva. He was recognized, arrested, and finally convicted of heresy.

Calvin assented to his execution, though he sought a less horrible death for him than burning at the stake. Most Protestant leaders hailed the condemnation and destruction of the troubled and troubling genius; only a few found fault, one being Sebastian Castellio, who argued against burning men for holding different opinions on matters which the Bible does not set out clearly, and in violation of the spirit of a God of mercy and a Christ of pity. But Castellio had already been defeated by Calvin, who had prevented his appointment as a regular pastor in Geneva.

From this period until his death in 1564, Calvin's grip on the government of Geneva remained firm. He consolidated his system. In 1559 the Genevan Academy was established; it contained both a secondary school and what amounted to a university, except that it did not grant a formal degree.

The Calvinists in Europe, 1648

Under the guidance of Theodore Beza, its rector, the academy trained youths in Calvinist doctrine and from its benches went forth ministers to carry the new militant Protestant creed to many lands.

Elaboration of Doctrine. In his social and economic views, Calvin was, like Luther, a staunch conservative. He approached matters always from the point of view of religion. Though he required an ascetic pattern of life from his followers, he rejected both the monasticism of Roman Catholicism, which made self-denial primarily the virtue of a few monks, and the cursory religion of the ordinary man who would not let its prescriptions change his everyday conduct. Christians, he held, should apply the moral law in their economic and political activity. Thus, in the question of whether or not interest on loans constituted forbidden usury, Calvin followed St. Thomas Aquinas, who emphasized fairness and equity as the essence of proper economic relationships, rather than the usual medieval method of condemning interest as a question of law while devising means to permit it in practice.

Theology remained Calvin's central concern during the final decade of his life. He continued to revise his *Institutes*, which was published in final form only in 1559. Translations appeared in many languages during and after his lifetime. Calvin contrasted the worthlessness of sinful man with the pure righteousness and absolute sovereignty of God. He avoided, by placing upon the sinners alone the blame for their misdeeds, the perennial problem of explaining the presence of sin in a world created and ruled by an almighty and benevolent God. Calvin placed greater stress upon the doctrine of pre-destination than either Luther or Bucer had, though whether or not it is the central doctrine of his system remains in dispute among historians of reli-gion. Only those elected by God's primal decision, with His eternal fore-knowledge, received His grace and thereby the life of a good Christian in this world and eternal salvation in the next.

But Calvin's principal attention was not directed to this "terrible decree," as he called it, against those whom God, almost inexplicably, damned or at least refrained from saving even before they had been created. He was inter-ested in the way in which man's struggle against evil is a sign of his election though not a means of obtaining it. Thus Calvin managed not to limit God's omnipotence and still provided psychological motivation for a vigorously responsible life, dominated by personal initiative rather than fatalism and moral unconcern.

Calvin desired the unification of all Protestant churches, but could envisage it only through acceptance of his doctrines substantially as they were. Like Luther, he was utterly persuaded that his basic ideas did not come from his own mind, but were the work of the Holy Spirit; to abandon them was therefore to turn against God. He saw without much regret the failure of efforts to achieve a compromise with the Lutherans, and the great hatred which developed later in the century between his followers and Luther's was already foreshadowed.

The Zwinglians, on the other hand, under the leadship of Zwingli's suc-cessor Heinrich Bullinger, in 1549, worked out a compromise with Calvin and Farel. This was consolidated by a subsequent agreement in 1566, and the two trends merged both inside and beyond Switzerland. After 1580 they came to be called by the single name of "Reformed." The spread of Cal-vinism to other lands, though begun during Calvin's lifetime and under his leadership, did not make great progress till after the completion of his work of reorganization in Geneva.

IV. Anabaptism

Despite their mutual hatreds and struggles, Roman Catholic, Calvinist, and Lutheran all joined to repress various smaller groups of Christian reformers who are known by the general name of Anabaptists. Some of them offended the general body of Christendom by combining religious revolution

CALVINISTS PREACHING OUTSIDE ANTWERP, 1566. Etching by an unknown seventeenth-century Dutch artist. The dark line in the center results from a fold for binding the original print in a book of Dutch historical prints put together late in the seventeenth century.

Three Calvinist ministers may be seen preaching to an assemblage of faithful of varied ages and classes. The armed protection given to the meeting by retainers of the nobility is indicated by the presence of the soldiers. *(Achenbach Foundation)*

with political, social, and economic demands which endangered the existing order of the world. Others preferred to turn their back on the world of sinners, seeking refuge in isolated communities of the "elect" or refraining from the work of the state. Most of these groups rejected the baptism of children, and thus they came to be called Anabaptists (Greek for "rebaptizers").

The Swiss Brethren. Their movement had begun in Switzerland, where it was known as the "Swiss Brethren." Conrad Grebel, its first leader, had been a member of the Zwinglian circle in Zürich. His demand for absolute literalness in reading the Bible was only a strict application of Zwingli's own principles, but Grebel, by his demand that the church should be free of the state and include none but those who freely confessed its faith, denied the common practice of requiring all members of a community to belong to an inclusive church standing in a fixed relationship to the state. The Anabaptists thus overthrew the Augustinian distinction between the "invisible" church of the righteous and the saved, and the "visible" church to which all men belong.

The Anabaptists adopted extremely rigorous standards of judgment and conduct. They simplified ritual to the extreme, rejecting whatever they could not find in the Bible. They reduced the Eucharist to a memorial service to be celebrated not in churches but in private homes. Their congregations selected their own lay ministers, and were otherwise self-administering. Only mature persons, aware of the meaning of their deeds and beliefs, could truly belong to the church, into which they were initiated by baptism as adults.

The movement spread to many parts of Europe. The fate of its adherents was everywhere tragic, for they were the bane of all established religious creeds. In Germany Catholics and Lutherans joined in condemning them and agreed to suppress them (1529-1530). In Switzerland, Zwingli, always ready with the sword, began to persecute the Anabaptists in 1525; first they were driven out, then they were burned at the stake, and ultimately drowning, in ghastly mockery of their beliefs, was introduced. But the movement spread nonetheless. Though it had been initiated by members of the educated upper classes, it grew especially among the sorely oppressed of the lower orders of society. Congregations were established throughout Germany and in other parts of central Europe, especially Moravia and Hungary. In Austria, Jakob Huter organized Anabaptist communities upon the basis of communal economic and social forms. In Strassburg, Anabaptists took advantage of the atmosphere of tolerance to form their own communities, though they tried and finally broke Bucer's patience.

Münster and Menno. In the Low Countries, led especially by the mystic poet-painter David Joris (1501-1556), the movement emphasized millenarian beliefs, that is, the expectation that the end of the world was imminent. Forced to flee by the persecution of Charles V's government, Joris took refuge in Basel and lived a double life there: known to the world as a plain man who practiced the same religion as his neighbors, he continued to lead his followers in secret, urging them to prepare for imminent Judgment Day. Most of the Dutch Anabaptists remained peaceful citizens who withdrew from the sinful world rather than oppose it; they preferred to suffer martyrdom rather than take up arms in resistance.

Others, made of different stuff, wished to crush sinners. They followed a baker, Jan Matthys, and a tailor, Jan Beuckelsz, in seizing the town of Münster, in Westphalia across the frontier (1534). Supported by the craft guilds and the common folk, Beuckelsz' adherents held the town for more than a year. Beuckelsz set himself up as a ruler under the name King Jan of Leiden. His introduction of polygamy and economic communism intensified the revulsion and hatred of the outside world, and Catholics and Lutherans combined to crush the movement in a bloody siege (1535).

Menno Simons took over leadership of the peaceful Anabaptists who had not been drawn into the Münster adventure. A Catholic priest who had become a Lutheran, Menno reacted to the events of Münster, in which a brother had been slain, by undertaking to form more Anabaptist communities on a peaceful basis. He forbade service to the state, yet approved obedience to its orders; he expounded trinitarian doctrine without using its terminology. Under his guidance the movement of Mennonites, as his followers were called, spread from their first seat in the westernmost German province of East Friesland through the Low Countries and northern Germany. Though their oppression continued, the Mennonites had thus begun the process which eventually led to their acceptance as a legitimate group within the fabric of society.

5

Religious Reformation:
Anglicanism and Catholic Reform

1517-1660

AT MIDPOINT in the sixteenth century, little more than three decades after Dr. Luther posted his theses at Wittenberg, the greatest kingdoms in Europe remained steadfastly Roman Catholic. Had they not persisted in warring among themselves, they might have overwhelmed their Protestant rivals for the allegiance of Christian believers. The new forms of Christian organization had gained control only of some lesser realms and city-states, and of the English monarchy, the one Protestant state of substantial strength.

I. The Anglican Reformation

Still, the course of religious changes in England till that moment gave limited comfort to thoughtful Protestant leaders on the continent who looked to London for aid and succor. Everything in England seemed to depend upon the personality of the reigning monarch, and nothing seemed less certain than the dynastic succession in that turbulent land.

Defender of the Faith. When Henry VIII began to reign in 1509, the English nation was overwhelmingly Catholic. Remnants of Lollardry, the heresy of an earlier age, escaped extirpation only by dozing away in obscurity. But loyal as Englishmen remained theologically to Rome, there was widespread antipathy to the pope and to the clergy generally. Papal power, relatively distant since the days of King John, was brought too close to home when Thomas Cardinal Wolsey, the king's principal minister, was named papal legate in 1518; Wolsey wielded to the advantage of his own wealth and domination the virtually complete jurisdictional rights which the pope granted him in England.

Nonetheless the first stirrings of the new heresy born in Germany were few and mild. At the universities, bolder spirits among the young scholars began to study the works of Luther and his followers which were smuggled into the country; from the ranks of these "Germans," as they were called at Cambridge, came many future leaders of the English Reformation. More daring even than these was William Tyndale, who made it his life work to translate the Bible into English. His version, based on Erasmus' edition of the Greek New Testament and the Hebrew text of the Old Testament, was first printed clandestinely at Worms, Germany, in 1526. It was followed by seven editions.

Nonetheless, public supporters of the new religious ideas were rare. To advocate them was dangerous. The monarchy burned convicted heretics; even the gentle Sir Thomas More, as the royal chancellor, grimly sent Protestant martyrs to the stake. King Henry boasted of his loyalty to the old faith. In reply to Luther's doctrines, he wrote (or helped to write) a tract, *The Defense of the Seven Sacraments;* the pope in recognition bestowed upon the royal theologian the honorific title "Defender of the Faith."

"The King's Business." Yet it was this very king who cut England out from the Roman allegiance. The occasion for this great transformation was a little thing, as historical causes go: the desire of Henry VIII to divorce his wife, Catherine of Aragon, and marry Anne Boleyn. To the king, his request to Pope Clement VII to annul his marriage seemed most reasonable. The earlier papal dispensation permitting him to marry the widow of his elder brother Arthur (despite the prohibition in Leviticus 18:16 and in the canon law) had not been truly efficacious—was not Catherine's failure to bear him a male heir who lived past infancy proof of God's wrath with him? In any case, popes had been notoriously ready to juggle with marriage laws for kings and great nobles; if one pope could permit a violation of canon law, why could not another permit the violation to be corrected? The issue was clear to Henry: he deserved well of the papacy by his suppression of the new heresy in his realm; it was Clement's duty to declare the marriage with Catherine null and void if so powerful and faithful a son of the church requested it.

The issue was by no means so clear at Rome. In the first place, Catherine denied that her marriage to Arthur had ever been consummated, and thus the original dispensation had not been really necessary. In the second place, it was one thing for the pope to grant a dispensation from canon law, and another to announce to the world that in a specific case his predecessor had not possessed power to do so; Roman theologians had already cited this very dispensation as proof that popes had full powers to interpret and apply the law of the church.

Such difficulties as these might have been circumvented, but not the insistence of Emperor Charles V, nephew of the forlorn queen, that the pope maintain the sanctity and intactness of her wedlock. For the emperor was a mighty man, and though a pious and loyal Catholic, he had already displayed his readiness to impose upon the pope his own interpretation of papal duties. The course of the "king's business," as the divorce proceedings were called, falls within the bounds of chapter 10 (p. 220) but the consequences to religion in England need description here.

Unable to move the papacy to do as he wished, Henry in desperation accepted the proposal of Thomas Cromwell, an up-and-coming government official, that the case be tried in the king's own courts. To make the outcome more certain, Cromwell also suggested that the king declare himself head of the church in England. Just what being the head would mean remained unclear. When, in 1531, the leading churchmen of the land, assembled in Convocation, assented to a declaration that the king was supreme head of the church in England, they appended to it the words "as far as the law of Christ allows." Under this definition, Henry might be claiming for himself no more power over the church in England than the kings of France and Spain possessed over ecclesiastical affairs within their own territories, and no one doubted that they were Roman Catholics.

The next step, taken the following year, made the split from Rome definite. Convocation voted, at the king's behest, in favor of revision of the ecclesiastical laws of the country; the task was entrusted to a committee of clergy and laymen selected by Henry. Sir Thomas More, the king's chancellor, had painfully accepted the royal actions to this point as still tenable within the Roman communion; but now he resigned his post in protest against this casting off from Roman jurisdiction. Henry went ahead, however; Parliament voted to prohibit payment of annates to the pope and forbade taking appeals from an English court to any foreign tribunal, including the papal curia. Nevertheless, when Henry named Thomas Cranmer, a teacher of theology at Cambridge, as archbishop of Canterbury in March, 1533, the pope issued the bulls confirming the appointment. Whatever hopes for reconciliation were held in Rome were vain; Cranmer at once arranged for his own archiepiscopal court to proclaim the divorce of Henry from Catherine (formally, the annulment of their marriage as invalid). Henry thereupon married Anne Boleyn.

Catholic but Not Roman.   Religious Reformation had begun in England, but in a most anomalous way. On the continent, religious innovation had come into being by the efforts of religious thinkers and leaders, and then had won the adherence of peoples and rulers; in England, on the contrary, the king rejected all these new doctrines, except one—antipapalism—and that one only under the press of his personal business. What had been begun could not be stopped, however; the question remained: how far would the Protestant Reformation proceed in England?

In 1534 Parliament confirmed the royal power over the church, including a supreme headship; but the king assumed no priestly powers as such. In 1536 and 1539 the government dissolved the monasteries and took their immense wealth into its own hands; a few new bishoprics were created, but most of the church's property passed out of its hands. Church officers continued to draw their revenues as before from the earnings of the manors, tithes, and other holdings of the benefices; but the value of such livings diminished drastically.

Submission of the church to the royal will seemed complete. Henry wished no more; he desired to keep the church as close as possible to the doctrines and organization which had prevailed before the separation from Rome. The prelates, most of them legally trained administrators much more than professional theologians, shared this attitude with the king. Their primary concern was to assure the solidity and unity of human society; they could not conceive of maintaining it otherwise than by the leadership of the crown, to which all owed obedience. Like the king they remained at heart Catholic, although they were willing to be with him no longer *Roman* Catholic.

The Pull of Protestantism.   But it was not easy to sit between two stools, or on both. To reject the supremacy of the Roman pontiff was to accept the one tenet shared by every Protestant creed; in Rome's eyes it was as totally and reprehensibly heretical as all the many aberrations of the Anabaptists.

The state had initiated the schism from Rome; it wished to keep all further changes under its own control. It strove to confine discussion of religious theories to educated folk, especially to the theologically trained. King Henry, of course, counted himself among these latter. An English translation of the Bible, modified from Tyndale's version, was published for use in churches in place of the Latin Vulgate. But simple laymen began to use it too, to the dismay of officialdom, both ecclesiastical and governmental. In 1543 Parliament solemnly forbade women and persons without learning to peruse the sacred pages, and two years later Henry complained that the "most precious jewel, the Word of God," was being "unreverently . . . disputed, rhymed, sung and jangled in every alehouse and tavern contrary to the true meaning and doctrine of the same."

Cranmer was the principal artisan of the new definitions in theology.

He inclined further towards specifically Protestant views than did his master, but Henry kept his affection for the churchman who had helped to arrange his divorce. Questions of doctrine arose over the liturgy to be used as well as the credos to be established for the nation. In 1536 Convocation summed up official dogma in ten articles of faith indicative of a growth of semi-Protestant sentiment; there was no mention of "transubstantiation" in the article on the Eucharist.

Though royal authority enforced these articles with the penalties of law, views more strongly Protestant were debated and more and more widely adopted. The king, angry at this growth of religion beyond his own opinions, set Parliament to work in 1539 upon a new credo; virtually every element of Roman Catholic theology compatible with the abandonment of papal supremacy was specifically reaffirmed. The punishments provided for denying any of the six articles of faith were so harsh—even death—that the people called the new law the "Whip with the Six Strings."

Edward the Protestant. This experiment with a religion neither Catholic nor Protestant ended when Henry VIII died in 1547. The new king, Henry's son Edward VI, was a mere boy; the regents who governed in his name were strongly Protestant. Parliament speedily repealed the Act of Six Articles and established a single form of church service for the whole country in the first Act of Uniformity (1549). The litany provided in the Book of Common Prayer was made compulsory for all churchmen. To continental Europe went a call to Protestant leaders to aid the English reformers, still relatively few in number; the most eminent of those who crossed the Channel was Martin Bucer, the embodiment of the cause of Protestant union.

The archbishop consolidated his own theological ideas in the forty-two articles of faith approved by the royal council. Much like Bucer, he found good in both Lutheran and Calvinist schools of thought, and added ideas of his own; no longer hampered by the reluctance of Henry VIII to move any further from Catholicism, Cranmer now emphasized above all the general theme of opposition to Rome shared by the major Protestant groups. The government began to take sterner measures to enforce religious uniformity; it forbade laymen to absent themselves from Sunday church services according to the new liturgy, or to attend religious ceremonies according to any other rite.

What the state had done, it could try to undo; and the state did what the reigning monarch wished. Edward VI died in 1553, and his six years' reign was too brief for Cranmer's new, frank Protestantism to root itself widely among the people.

Mary the Catholic. The crown passed to the head of Mary Tudor, who shared the staunch Catholic beliefs of her mother, Catherine of Aragon. The supreme headship of the church of England, which by law she inherited from her father and brother, she abhorred as schismatic and heretical; but she gladly used that power to bring the nation back to the olden faith and the Roman obedience. Within two years of her accession Parliament repealed the ecclesiastical innovations of the previous two decades. Catholic prelates took over the sees of Protestant bishops. It remained only to return to the church its purloined possessions.

The attempt to divest the new owners of the secularized church and monastery lands stirred up a hornet's nest among the politically most influential groups in the country; the great nobles and wealthy gentry and commoners who had received these lands, whether by purchase or royal gift, looked upon them as their own rightful property.

Rome gave Mary no help, but rather only hindrance, in her enterprise, designed though it was to restore its ecclesiastical supremacy in England. Pope Paul IV did not comprehend the difficulties of her position and felt both suspicion and antipathy for her cousin, Reginald Cardinal Pole, who had been named papal legate to England. The pope deprived Pole of his post of legate after the queen named him archbishop of Canterbury in 1556, and then ordered the aged clergyman to return to Rome for possible trial on suspicion of heresy. But Pole died before he could leave England.

Under Mary's rule, the government was ready to burn out heresy, as governments in England and everywhere else were and had always been. Almost three hundred Protestants died at the fiery stake during her reign. Even this persecution was too brief, sporadic, and unsystematic to destroy all the convinced Protestants, and those who survived bore a bitter and undying hatred for the queen they called "Bloody Mary." Many, leaders and simple believers alike, fled to the continent for safety. Exile confirmed them in their beliefs, and they absorbed at first hand the experience of successful Protestant communities in the Rhineland and Switzerland.

The mass of Englishmen were frightened rather than converted. They tended, like ordinary men at most times in history, to accept the religious pattern of their state and society—but that pattern was changed three times within a quarter century. The government ruthlessly enforced each form of faith in turn, but achieved principally a widening cynicism and passive conformity rather than deep and true religious belief. One observer bewailed the growth of a "third religion" of mere outward observance disguising inner indifference.

Elizabeth the Ambiguous. With the accession of Elizabeth I as queen in 1558, the character of Anglican religion was transformed again. Till then the rulers had endeavored to make wholly clear what was commanded of the people in the way of faith. Elizabeth took a new turning. As concerned as any of her predecessors had been with establishing the religious unity of her state, she desired to hold as many of her subjects as possible within its accepted bounds. The key to such a policy was doctrinal ambiguity. Thereby divergent views might exist simultaneously within the one general religion as long as none attempted to exclude the others by too precise a definition of the true faith.

Like her father Henry VIII, Elizabeth tried to keep her church Catholic though not Roman. The church in England, according to official doctrine, was part of the universal church, as it had always been; nothing had been changed in this regard when the supremacy of the bishop of Rome had been cast off. Because Elizabeth relied upon the episcopate as the natural instrument of her own domination of the church, it was important to preserve and enhance the power of the bishops. Three bishops, who had fled abroad during Mary's reign and returned to their sees under the Protestant queen, consecrated Matthew Parker as the new archbishop of Canterbury; Anglicans accepted this ceremony as maintaining the uninterrupted apostolic succession on which the episcopal order rested, and the "Catholicity" of the Anglican church was thereby further strengthened.

The Anglican Settlement. Archbishop Parker took the lead in shaping the conservative religious settlement. Two acts of Parliament in the year after Elizabeth's coming to the throne provided the basis for the new arrangement; the Act of Supremacy and the Act of Uniformity consolidated the principle that crown and Parliament legislated for the church and all religious business, though with the advice and consent of the leading churchmen meeting in Convocation. The statutes of Mary's reign restoring Roman Catholicism were repealed; Elizabeth was proclaimed the sole "supreme governor" in matters of religion as well as of politics. The term "governor" made it clear that she laid no claim to specifically priestly or ministerial functions, such as preaching or administering the sacraments, but would abate not an inch of control over religion in her realm.

Where religious uniformity was required, heresy had to be defined. Doctrines contrary to the Bible or decrees of early councils of the church fell under the ban, as before, but to dispute dogma as laid down by Parliament with the assent of Convocation also became heresy. Whoever held office, whether religious or civil, was required to take an oath acknowledging the queen's supremacy over the church; refusal meant at least the loss of office, but heavy fines and even the death penalty also awaited offenders. A body of commissioners was set up to act as supreme ecclesiastical court and to supervise church affairs generally; this Court of High Commission acted in the queen's name.

Catholic Recusancy. Repression of Roman Catholics was constant and vigorous. Most of the Catholic prelates remaining from Mary's reign refused to accept the new order; they were removed from their functions, imprisoned in the Tower, and brought to trial. But during the first half-decade after

1558 there was action against only about two hundred "recusants," as the Protestants called those who stubbornly adhered to their Roman Catholic faith. Elizabeth and her ministers insisted upon outward conformity, but no more. Those who continued the old practices privately, while attending Anglican services publicly, were not yet molested; the queen said she wished to open no window into any man's soul. The hope behind this leniency was that Catholicism would shortly become extinct, and this expectation proved correct for most ordinary Englishmen, who could not stand against the dictates of the ruling powers. A small number of wealthy and noble families kept to the old faith, though under the penalty of losing all political influence.

The major problem facing the English Roman Catholics was to maintain their integrity while avoiding extermination. The first need, therefore, was for missionary priests to administer the sacraments and guide the consciences of pious Catholics. William Cardinal Allen, an exile from England, took over the leadership in this difficult task. At Douai, he organized a seminary for training priests, later transferred to Reims. Though not himself a member of the order, Allen worked particularly closely with the Jesuits.

When Pope Pius V issued a bull in 1570 excommunicating Elizabeth and declaring her deposed, Parliament replied in 1571 by making it treasonable to call the queen a heretic who might be deposed, to bring the pope's bull into the country, or to distribute it. Allen's purposes were both aided and hindered: aided by his having the authority of the Roman pontiff in warning English Catholics that they could not attend Anglican services with mental reservations; hindered because the papal decree seemed to require rebellion against the "wicked Jezebel" who ruled in England.

Allen and the large majority of English Catholics endeavored to evade the strait choice embodied in the decree from Rome; they reiterated their political fidelity, but the words of their admitted spiritual overlord, the pope, weighed more heavily than their own assertions. The very success of the mission into England undertaken by two Jesuit priests, Edmund Campion and Robert Parsons, indeed intensified the repression of Catholics by the royal government, for Englishmen had welcomed and safeguarded the two missionaries on their journey through peril. Campion met a martyr's death and Parsons went abroad to endless exile, but others came after them into England.

Rise of the Puritans. The royal authorities continued to follow their goal of an ambiguous moderation in setting forth the creed and services of the established Anglican church. Something of a Catholic atmosphere was retained in the service, based on Cranmer's second Book of Common Prayer: the clergy wore vestments and crucifixes, music was played. A more marked Protestant feeling dominated the new creed drawn up in Thirty-Nine Articles and enacted by royal decree in 1563 after approval by Convocation: its definition of the Eucharist was conciliatory toward both Lutherans and Calvinists.

This settlement appealed to those who looked upon the church primarily as the bulwark of society and the state, none more so than the queen herself; it was also acceptable to those relatively indifferent to the theological issues. But it aroused persistent opposition from the religiously earnest who wanted to rid the national church of every vestige of Catholicism in liturgy and doctrine. This desire to cleanse official religion prompted their opponents to label them derisively as "Puritans."

The name "Puritan" soon was used for all groups demanding exact obedience to the system of church doctrine and government they believed the Bible prescribed. On many things these groups disagreed among themselves, but they all rejected the "Catholicism" of the Anglican church and stressed individual conversion of the believer as the inflowing of divine grace and redemption. They set apart the "saints" and the "sinners," whereas the Anglican officialdom favored what might be called "community religion," that is, the acceptance of the individual into the Christian community as a birthright from which he would become excluded only after specific and persistent adherence to doctrines clearly irreconcilable with the broadly permissive official creed.

The reformers took the initiative in 1563. They proposed in Convocation that the forms and ceremonials utilized by Roman Catholics be dropped from the Anglican liturgy; though defeated, they came within two votes of victory in one house of the assembly. The Puritans did not seek religious freedom as such; they wanted freedom for themselves to establish their own creed as the national religion, to save their church from perilous concessions to Roman Catholicism, the enemy equally of the English nation and true religion. They were ready to punish dissenters as sternly as Calvin had done at Geneva.

A theologian of little personal influence, Richard Hooker, gave classical expression to the Anglican position in his *Laws of Ecclesiastical Polity* (1594-1597; additional books 1648-1662). God did not make salvation depend upon any specific kind of church organization, Hooker argued; ecclesiastical government was something for human experience and judgment to decide. Yet he denied, as a defender of the Anglican order had to, that any man could take himself out of the national church if he found fault with it; it was not for the individual to set his limited knowledge and wisdom against the ordained authority of the state.

Separatists. Puritan and Anglican were not yet contrary terms, however. Many Puritans, probably most, wished only to make over the Anglican church, not to leave it. No more than Hooker did most Puritans, especially in the earlier decades, believe in individual choice of faith; they denied that toleration was proper in matters of religion or that a number of Christian churches could properly co-exist. But when they began to hold conventicles, or private services according to their own principles rather than the Book of Common Prayer, Archbishop Parker pounced upon those who took part in these "prophesyings."

The more obdurate Puritans were not deterred; they even began to favor actual separation from the "sinful" national church. These separatists drew sharp warnings from the Swiss theologians to whom the reformers turned for counsel and consolation. Stay within the Anglican fold and seek establishment of a governing synod free of state domination, was the advice from Zürich. Such strategy was not wholly unrealistic. The government acted only sporadically and indecisively against the Puritans, who had important supporters at Court and in Parliament; the state, faced by threats of war and invasion from Catholic states, could not afford to destroy utterly those whose support it might at some time need. But the official creed continued to maintain the semi-Catholicism the Puritans so much abhorred, the Anglican bishops were not loath to punish opponents when they could, and the reformers were therefore driven to advocate ecclesiastical reorganization on presbyterian lines. In the place of the episcopalian system they called for councils of laymen and clergy to function as an aristocratic self-government in the church.

Though many Puritans looked upon the queen as the inevitable defender of Protestantism in a world where it was under an immense threat and were reluctant to attack her personally, others, less ready to compromise with the needs of the world, attacked her as vigorously as did any Roman Catholic. These radical Puritans repeatedly formed into splinter groups within the body of the movement of reform. They differed with the majority of Puritans in that they desired to abandon almost all ritual in the service and to do without theologically trained ministers. They thought laymen reading the Bible for themselves and moved by divine grace were sufficient leaders of their meetings.

One of the first of such leaders was Robert Browne, who formed a conventicle of nonconformists at Norwich in 1580. Forced to flee the country, he organized a similar group at Middelburg in the Dutch province of Zeeland. The government, Browne said, should administer the property of the church, but leave to the congregations the choice of their ministers and their beliefs. He did not favor complete independence for each congregation, and rejoined the Anglican communion before a decade was past. His followers, still called Brownists after him, moved strongly in the direction of separatism. Many of the sects which rose up in England in the early seventeenth century were offshoots of the Brownist movement.

"No Bishop, No King." When James VI, king of Scotland, followed Elizabeth upon the throne of England in 1603 as James I, the Puritans looked forward eagerly to having the state on their side, not against them. James had been educated as a strict Protestant and was known for his strong theological interest.

This expectation proved false. James accepted Calvinist doctrine but not presbyterianism, such as had cramped his authority in Scotland. He believed as strongly as had Elizabeth that royal power depended upon the maintenance of episcopalianism; in his own phrase, "no bishop, no king." But he proved no more successful than she in extirpating the Puritans. During the reign of James and his son Charles I, Anglican theologians began to minimize or even reject the Calvinist tenet of predestination, which seemed to them to make the church unnecessary for salvation.

William Laud, who became archbishop of Canterbury under Charles, pointed up the Catholic and episcopalian element in Anglican doctrine. Laud's Catholic predilections were so strong that only the Roman doctrine of papal supremacy deterred him from joining the old church. He became the object of the Puritans' most bitter hatred. They called him, and those who accepted similar doctrines, by the detested name of "Arminians," after the party in the contemporary Dutch religious controversy which rejected strict predestination beliefs.

As the conflict between Anglican and Puritan grew into a struggle between two separate and antithetical parties, several characteristic developments occurred among the Puritans, particularly their most extreme elements. Some fled abroad to be able to worship according to their own lights; the Dutch Republic, where religious tolerance, especially toward divergent Protestant creeds, was already broad, provided the most important haven for these exiles. From 1620 onward, those attracted by the opportunity to build a "city of God" in the wilderness emigrated across the Atlantic to New England.

Among all Puritans the inner fire of righteousness was displayed to the world as moral fervor, an insistence upon the precise observance of the Sabbath and repression of all "worldliness," such as the traditional joys of Englishmen—dancing, sports, festivals, and the like. The theology of Puritanism became more and more closely linked to the doctrines of the Parliamentary party in its struggle with the monarchy, especially under the reign of Charles I; the story of the Puritan part in overthrowing the king and setting up a republic must be told as part of the history of England in that period (ch. 11, pp. 256-258).

II. The Catholic Reformation

Thus far we have given our attention to the rise of Protestantism in its various forms. Nevertheless the persistence of the old church has been a distinct and ever-present element in the background of our story.

The Start of Change. Roman Catholicism, when embodied in such stalwarts as Cardinal Allen, the Englishman, and Cardinal Borromeo, the Italian, obviously had ceased to be the tired and lackadaisical institution it had so frequently been when Luther and Calvin put it under attack. Vigor, clarity, self-assurance and self-assertion—these were the characteristics that began to appear ever more prominently in the Roman church after the middle of the sixteenth century.

In the struggle against Protestantism, the Catholic position in the issues at debate had to be clearly defined. There was, however, an ingrained reluctance among the Roman theological leaders to rush into statements of irrevocable dogma. Furthermore, influential Catholic rulers, especially in Germany, were opposed to closing off the avenues of possible reconciliation. The acrimonious dispute between scholastics and Christian humanists over the general character of Catholic theology also impeded coming to a decision.

Nonetheless the two groups, faced by the same enemy, at last discovered that they could draw increased strength from each other. Neoclassical rhetoric was universally accepted, but the precise and powerful weapon of analysis created by the scholastics came back into its own within the Roman church as a weapon for theological attack upon the religious innovators.

In any case, until the church began the difficult task of institutional reform, Catholics were hard put to rebut the Protestant charge that abuses arose from erroneous Roman doctrine. Their first reaction was to deny that the shortcomings really existed. But many Catholic leaders realized that the weaknesses were too notorious to be denied; the more deep-seeing among them knew, too, that the abuses were gravely harming the church and had to be removed. The abuses resulted not from the doctrines that Rome preached, they proclaimed, but from violation of their true meaning and intent.

But mere affirmation of correct doctrine was not enough to undo the evil. The church was a vast, complex institution. Its effective functioning depended upon the good will of a multitude of officials who benefited by the very abuses they were called upon to remedy. Only when a sufficient number of men should enter the ecclesiastical career primarily for the opportunity of service, instead of seeking to enjoy the great accumulated revenues of the church, could reform in the Roman church begin to take shape and make progress. Reform of souls had to precede renovation of the institution. The manner in which the Catholic clergy, or at least crucial elements among them, was regenerated, differed greatly from the way in which Protestant ministers were formed. Lonely meditations in a monastery, punishment of the body to break its hold over the soul, all the self-denials of asceticism—these were the primary instruments in the spiritual regeneration of the Catholic clergy. Thus the thousand-year-old pattern of Catholic revival—a rebirth of monasticism leading to broad results throughout the church—was once more repeated.

The New Orders. A millenium before, the hermit's life had been the ideal of the regular orders (the orders, that is, under a monastic rule or *regula*) ; they founded their new centers of civilization and religion in wilderness and isolation. Only a few hundred years before, the Franciscans and Dominicans, regulars still, took over the task particularly of supplementing the secular clergy in the towns. The characteristic religious orders of the Catholic Reformation had as their object service "in the world," like seculars.

In 1517, before the onset of Protestantism, several score of priests and pious laymen in Rome joined together in the Oratory of Divine Love. Their purpose was to emphasize individual piety and deeds of charity. After the sack of Rome a decade later, the members of the Oratory dispersed to many other towns of Italy and became leaders in the internal reform of the church. Those who became bishops, notably Jacopo Sadoleto and Gian Pietro Caraffa devoted themselves to their diocesan duties with rare diligence.

When Caraffa became general of the Theatine order, he changed his position but not his aim. The Theatines recruited their members from among the Italian aristocracy, the same class which furnished almost all members of the episcopate. The primary purpose of the Theatines was reform of the secular clergy, but their method was to set a model of severe poverty and devoted service by their members. The order remained small in size, though not in scope; it was a seedbed for future leaders of the church, and a source of inspiration even for those outside its ranks.

In an hour when millions of Europeans were quitting the Roman church, the performance of charitable works by religious orders helped to hold the affection and loyalty of untold members of others for the old church. Perhaps most successful of all these new orders was the Oratorians, founded by Philip Neri, the son of a lawyer and a noblewoman, who became a missionary to the people in Italy. Characteristically, the Oratorians were not monks, but secular priests. A similar group, the Capuchins, were not a wholly new creation, but a reformed off-shoot of the Franciscans. Their program of absolute obedience to the strict rule of St. Francis was symbolized by their founder's insistence that they wear a hood, or *cappuccio* (whence the popular name for the order), of the exact design he believed the saint had ordered.

The Capuchin and Theatine patterns of monastic reform came from the minds of men trained as priests and monks. They were concerned with making the institutional system they knew work better, rather than with changing it. Thus they retained much of the character of the medieval church—provincialism, dispersal of responsibility and authority, a considerable amount of self-government. Their orders were built on a scale mostly local, not one of nations and continents. They were better adapted to works of charity than to vast campaigns for the reconquest of lost lands for the Catholic faith. This was the task assumed by the most novel and successful of all the new orders formed in the sixteenth century, the Society of Jesus (Jesuits).

The Society of Jesus. A Spanish army officer, Ignatius Loyola, created the Jesuit order on the pattern of the most efficient instrument then known by which men imposed their will and leadership upon their fellow-men—the professional army. The very name he first gave to his order, the "Company of Jesus," was indicative of its military inspiration.

A wound had ended Loyola's military career. During an extended convalescence, he turned to reading works of piety and meditation. By a series of inexorable self-examinations and ceaseless prayers, he overcame his sense of spiritual uncertainty. Henceforth all truth and right for him were what the church desired and decided; her orders were beyond the full comprehension of men, but men could obey them. Loyola took his own experiences as a program for training other souls. His *Spiritual Exercises*, as he called the book in which he laid down these rules, were designed to produce for the church spiritual soldiers, such as he had resolved to become himself.

To do the work he had chosen, Loyola needed a command of theology, the church's own weapon. He studied first at Spanish universities, but went to Paris to complete his training. Fellow-students at the Sorbonne were drawn to the Spanish ex-soldier, already in his thirties, with his stern determination and lofty ideals. A small group followed his spiritual exercises and took vows of service to the church. In 1537 they went to Venice en route to Jerusalem to become missionaries to Islam; unable to find passage because of war conditions, they decided to continue their work in Europe under the name "Society of Jesus." Local prelates, impressed by their enthusiasm and resolution, persuaded the pope to grant formal authority for their order in 1540. Though originally they engaged in work of practical charity like the older order, Loyola's soldierly bent soon turned them to the tasks of reconquest and reconsolidation of the church.

At the top, the general of the order ruled absolutely; within the order no council or chapter could stand against his will. Other orders wore distinctive garb and frequently assumed responsibility for an associated order of nuns; Loyola kept the Jesuits a purely male order, dressed in the usual habit of the secular priest, or indeed like laymen when their duties required. Even more distasteful to the older orders was the exemption allowed the Jesuits from the daily performance of the liturgical offices which comprised the essence of most monks' duties. The order grew to great strength, even after Loyola's death in 1556; in 1624 there were more than 16,000 members.

The Jesuit order, large as it was, did not disperse its efforts. Its strategy was clear and effective; to win influence over the political rulers, to educate the youth, to gain converts in Europe and overseas. The Jesuits provided fathers confessor for kings and great nobles, stiffening their fidelity to Rome but often trimming the commands of Christian morality to the human frailties of those for whom they were spiritual guides. As educators they were active in organizing preparatory schools and in providing professors for Catholic universities; at both levels they were leaders in combining humanist and scholastic disciplines. Within Europe they made vigorous efforts to win back Protestants, by subtle argument, by appeals to worldly considerations like wealth, safety, or status, and when possible by the action of the states whose rulers they guided. As missionaries, they served not only in the American colonies of Spain, Portugal, and France, but they also penetrated to the farthest East; Francis Xavier, one of Loyola's first companions at Paris, engaged in mass conversions in India, and lost his life while attempting to spread Catholicism to Japan and China.

Reform in Rome. The approach of the religious orders to the key problem of reform in the church—improvement in the spiritual leadership of the secular clergy—was indirect, even if essential. The direct remedy lay with the great prelates and ultimately with the pope. The attack of the Protestants upon the papacy had consolidated its position as the central institution of the Roman church. From the time of the election of Pope Paul III in 1534, the Roman pontiffs remained committed to the program of reform. Nonetheless they could not simply use their enhanced prestige to proceed as they pleased in the work of renovation. They had to accomplish their purposes in collaboration with the papal administration, especially within Rome, and with the episcopate throughout Catholic Europe.

The principal means by which the papacy could exert its authority and initiative was its own officials. But the papal administration, with its offices filled by purchase instead of by appointment for merit, with its bureaucratic self-sufficiency and complacency, was the seat of some of the worst abuses in the church; antipathy to the Roman officeholders was widespread even where loyalty to the Catholic faith was strongest. Officials who had bought livelihoods, not sought opportunity to serve God and mankind, could not be expected to carry through reforms at their own expense. It was financially impossible in most cases to replace corrupt or hostile administrators except by expropriating them.

The popes had to go cautiously, for the administration was the agency by which they exerted their own direct control over the church. But time, and the new piety working among the higher leaders and personnel of the church, could do what blunt efforts at immediate reform could not. Even Leo X, with his small comprehension of the religious revolution that took place during his reign, knew the need for better men in the church; his appointment of the devoted and capable Cajetan to the college of cardinals showed the way for later popes. Paul III, two decades later, continued to nominate strongly reformist cardinals during a long fifteen-year reign. Lesser appointments, too, were made with greater care for the quality of the men who would represent the church.

How the times had changed was proved in 1537 when a commission named by Paul III to propose reforms submitted its report. It was confident enough of his support to blame earlier pontiffs as well as prelates for their venality; it called the widespread utilization of appointments to offices in the church for secular purposes the root of the shortcomings in the ecclesiastical organization. To admit so many of the Protestants' charges was a bold action, but a wise one, for it made effective remedies possible.

The Council of Trent. The traditional way to rally the whole church for a difficult task like reform was to call together its leaders in a general council. Leading Catholic rulers and influential churchmen pressed persistently for convocation of another council.

Preliminary Controversy. The proposal was a ticklish one for the popes. A century before, two councils had almost wrested leadership of the church from the pontiffs. On the other hand, the Fifth Lateran Council (1512-1517), which the popes effectively dominated, had proved so lethargic, so uncertain of its role, that it had been of little use in achieving improvement.

Even more important was the question of the goal of a council. Some princes and churchmen, especially in Germany, desired to win back the less refractory of the heretics by accepting a few of their innovations, particularly the cup for the laity in the mass and permission for clergymen to marry. Others, notably the Spaniards and Italians, insisted that no heresy be introduced into the doctrines of the church, which needed nothing more than stricter defining and stronger defending. Finally, the problem remained of utilizing the councils as instruments for strengthening the authority of the papacy, and therefore of reaffirming the subordination of the episcopate to the supreme pontiff.

In 1542, Paul III decided to call a general council. He chose Trent, a town in the Austrian Alps, as the meeting place; though legally within the boundaries of the Holy Roman Empire, it was geographically on the southern slopes of the mountains. Meetings were distributed over three periods (1545-1547, 1551-1552, 1562-1563). The objectives of the pope and the emperor were in conflict almost at the outset; the papal representative proposed that doctrinal questions be debated first, in order to make clear the heresy of the Protestants, while the spokesmen for Charles V urged primacy for organizational reform, in the hope that the Protestants, not offended by too blunt a statement of dogma, might be tempted back into the old church. Each side feared that if the other approach were taken, its own demands would be disregarded.

The final compromise was significant of the changes within the church: formally both groups of questions were to be discussed simultaneously, but actually the papal legates, having the direction of the sessions in their hands, gave emphasis to doctrine. Only the highest officeholders within the church—bishops and archbishops, generals of orders and influential abbots—were given the vote, individually instead of by nation. This arrangement made the more numerous Italians even more influential. Clergy of lesser rank were excluded, except for theologians called in to take part in the debate without a casting vote.

The First Assembly. The first period (1545-1547) of the council's meetings were marked by the consolidation of doctrine. Replying to the exclusive stress of most Protestants upon the Bible, the council declared that Scripture and tradition were equally authoritative, but that the power to define the meaning of both was given to the "teaching church." Neither the literalism of fundamentalists nor the sophistication of the historical-philological school of commentators was permitted to override the interpretation of doctrine by the pope and general council. The Vulgate, the Latin translation of the Bible by St. Jerome, was declared to be authentic.

On the central question of the sinfulness of man, the council reaffirmed the Thomistic position, which avoided the extremes; on the doctrine of justification, it asserted the freedom of will of man, who could work for or against divine grace by rejecting it sinfully or by accepting it with God's aid. The seven sacraments were declared to be necessary to salvation. Only the clergy could administer them, the council held, thus reaffirming the central role of the sacramental priesthood in the Roman church. The compulsion upon bishops to reside in their dioceses was reaffirmed; in general, the administrative system of the church was improved and long-existing abuses abolished.

The Second Assembly. The second assembly of the council (1551-1552) accomplished little. When Protestant armies swept down from Germany to a point not far from Trent, the council was suspended. Thereafter Pope Paul IV, the former Cardinal Caraffa, conducted reforms on his own initiative and authority, but would not permit the council to meet again. He acted with great sternness against simony, and reduced the expenditures of the cardinals and his own as well. Pope Pius IV, who succeeded him in 1559, represented a change in the church; he came not from the aristocracy, but from a lower-class Milanese family.

The Third Assembly. Sharp conflicts marked this final period of meet-

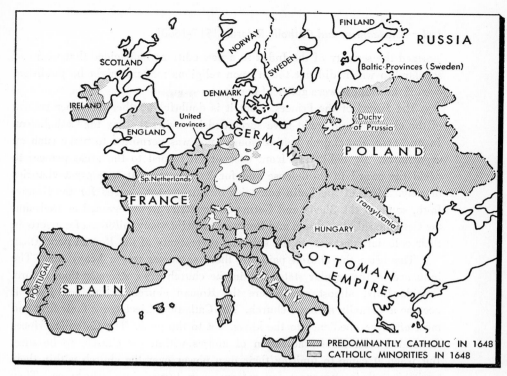

The Catholics in Europe, 1648

ings after the council reassembled at Pius' order in 1561. On one side was the papal party, comprising most of the Italians; on the other, the prelates from Spain, France, and Germany. The representatives of all three nations wished to restrict the power of the popes, but disagreed violently on doctrine. The French and Germans pleaded that reforms, such as the use of the national languages in the liturgy, particularly the mass, would bring at least some of the milder Protestants back to the church, but the Spaniards stood firm, as did the papal representatives, against any such concessions. The legates used the dispute among the national prelates to reinforce papal domination of the council, but were unable to achieve any important limitation upon the power of the Catholic rulers over the church within their own lands. The council finally closed in January, 1564. Significantly, the decrees and canons of the council were promulgated by a papal bull, and interpretation of their meaning was reserved to the pope. The pontifical character of Roman Catholicism was reaffirmed.

The precise definition of dogma by the Council of Trent was not enough, however; faithful Catholics had to be warned against the perils of heretical books. In 1559 Pope Paul IV had published an Index of Prohibited Books; with his characteristic severity, he banned any work faintly heretical in tone or implication, or by an author of less than perfect orthodoxy. Pius IV lessened the severity of the Index in a new edition; he decided that works of scholarship which did not touch upon religious matters might be published even if the authors were guilty of heresy.

The Sword of the Princes. But it is doubtful whether the inner reform of the church alone could have succeeded in saving the day for Catholicism. In any case, the church neither sought nor was permitted to make such an experiment. By habit and from necessity it turned to the great princes to wield the sword in its defense and for its progress. It won great victories thereby. Most of the Latin countries of Europe were saved for the Roman faith, some of the Slavic and Germanic countries were regained as well, and the Catholic rulers of Spain and Portugal brought many millions of converts in their colonial conquests to the spiritual sovereignty of the Roman pontiff.

The price the church paid for these successes was a heavy one. The influence of the secular states within the church grew stronger than before. Outside Italy, almost everywhere the Roman church maintained itself it became a virtually national church. The Catholic subjects gave their first and most effective obedience to the kings, not to the pope. The Catholic princes demanded immediate eradication of abuses within the church, to be sure. But when it came to limiting their own power over the church within their territories, their eagerness for reform soon turned into reluctance. They continued, more strongly than before, to exploit the ecclesiastical establishment for meeting the economic needs of royalty and nobility.

III. A New Phase

Thus far, in these two chapters, we have surveyed the Reformations in Europe—Protestant and Catholic—from within, from their own vantage-point of description and analysis. We have seen a single religion dominant over almost an entire continent give way to several major creeds and many minor ones, all deriving from the same tradition, all built in some way upon the teachings and experience of Christ. For most of them, Christ remained the son of God and God himself, a divine Savior, a Redeemer who had sacrificed Himself for the salvation of mankind. As almost all of them saw it, Christ had laid down a single religious truth, the only path to righteousness and eternal bliss—and to deny that truth was heresy, damnable in the eyes of God and punishable by the courts of men. Such beliefs followed easily and naturally from the monotheistic character of Christianity, particularly as interpreted in an age of growing legalism and rationalism. Latin Christendom in the medieval period had not been able to prevent the rise of heresy, even less the schism of the Eastern church, but it had been able to drive down the heretics and minimize the influence of the schismatics.

The Reformation exploded the religious unity of western and central Europe, but it did not destroy the belief in the ideal of a single religion, of one Christendom. Contending groups of Christians did battle with each other for the cause of the same Lord and Savior, because to do less was to deny one's own version of the common faith. Only the most downtrodden, the poorest in wealth and power, such as the Anabaptists, abandoned the ideal of a single religion in the state; but they also gave up effective claim to universality, and were content to form communities of saints who turned their back upon the sinful world instead of redeeming it. Some, like Castellio, could not reconcile Christian love with burning heretics at the stake, but in their own age their voices often seemed to echo emptily in a wilderness of clashing religions.

The Reformation represented an extraordinary intensification of religious feeling and passion, but it gave to the states vastly extended control over religion within their boundaries. The necessities of state, being primarily political, had already led to the subordination of religious interests during the sixteenth century. It was only a foretaste of what was to come. Many abuses were abolished, but not those which gave the secular powers a dominant voice in the affairs of the church. Kings and nobles continued to use, more flagrantly than ever, ecclesiastical appointments for secular purposes. Religion was ceasing to have any history significantly its own, and was becoming an integral and inseparable part of the general political and social history of the lands of Europe.

6

Europe beyond the Seas

1492 - 1650

EARLY IN THE sixteenth century Europeans took the first steps in a world-encompassing enterprise: first of exploration and discovery, and then of exploitation, commerce, and colonization. A hundred years later, they were moving outward from their continent in ever increasing numbers.

Peoples at every level of political development received new European masters in place of, or above, their old rulers. The interests of the European "homelands" took primacy over those of the "colonies." Much of the wealth of the newly discovered lands was drained off to Europe. In return the Europeans, unasked, brought to the peoples they met and conquered their religions and their accumulated experience of social and intellectual life. Few of the societies they confronted were totally static, and some were already in the throes of considerable changes; but all were transformed, for ill or good, under the impact of this alien European culture. In a few areas where the climate and soil were favorable and the native population was small, settlers from Europe built duplicates of their homelands as they thought they were or should be. The Europeanization of the world was under way.

I. Search for the Indies

By the year 1400 Europe already possessed the requisite energies and purposes for expansion overseas. Though the large majority of her people seldom traveled far from their homes, some were willing to go adventuring abroad. The process of "internal colonization" within Europe itself was substantially over; there was little useful land open for occupation at home. Yet the population, reduced by plague and economic retrogression, was again beginning to grow. The numbers required for overseas ventures were at first fairly small: a few thousand men in the maritime nations at the Atlantic edge of Europe sufficed.

Motives. A variety of motives prompted them to sail, explore, and conquer. One was religious: Europeans, taught that their faith was the only true one and that they had a duty to bring its gospel to the heathen, were confident of their right to overthrow the infidel, especially the Moslem. During the twelfth and thirteenth centuries, the Crusades had carried unprecedented numbers of Europeans to Palestine and adjacent countries and had resulted in the formation, although only briefly, of Latin kingdoms on the shores of the eastern Mediterranean (the Levant); the memory of the Crusades encouraged European Christians to attempt the defeat of the Moslem in some other way.

Another motive was economic: trade, especially over great distances, had long produced large and dramatic profits as compared with the slow though steady return from workaday activities at home. Products from the distant East—China and the Indies—were in strong demand in Europe. Spices in particular were desired to preserve meat and to make foods more palatable; pepper from India and the East Indies and cloves from a few islands in the East Indies were the most important, but cinnamon, mace, and nutmeg were imported as well. Other goods conveyed from the East were silk from China, cloth of cotton from India, rhubarb used as a pharmaceutical, and precious stones.

War and political changes in the Middle East had cut down the overland trade in these goods, but the sea-land route terminating at Alexandria and the ports of Syria remained open. There the Venetians continued to buy these wares for transport and resale in central and western Europe. Envy of the Venetian monopoly was strong, especially in Genoa; but the only effective way of breaking it was to circumvent it. Whoever found a new route to the sources of supply would garner great wealth for himself.

Parallel with this desire for profitable trade was a hunt for precious metals; gold and silver were the very essence of wealth in the conceptions of the period. The explorers looked for hoards that they could seize or obtain by trade, and for signs of placer deposits and subsoil veins of gold and silver that they could mine. Closely connected with this economic drive was a political interest in expansion: increased territory usually meant additional revenues, the basis of the strength of states. Conquests overseas might prove easier to make and more productive of income than small and difficult seizures of land within Europe itself.

Nor can the quest for adventure and glory be neglected as a motive: it was a deeply rooted tradition in European life, reflected and encouraged in the popular literature of chivalric romance. The records of the journeys made by a few bold Europeans beyond the Levant into central and further Asia fed this venturesome spirit. Marco Polo's account of his overland trip (1272-1295) to distant Cathay (China) was read with particular eagerness and enlivened men's imaginations with notions of a fabulous and wealthy East.

Techniques and Theories. For converting these drives into successful discoveries and conquests, a broad basis of scientific and technological competence was necessary. The first requirements were ships capable of sailing into the open ocean and men capable of handling them. By the beginning of the fifteenth century, shipwrights in the Atlantic countries had developed sturdy vessels which easily made the coasting voyages that were usual in these waters. Large, square-rigged ships were used instead of the oared galleys characteristic of the Mediterranean. Excellent for sailing before the wind, these ships were too clumsy for journeys into unknown waters along strange shores. For such purposes the Portuguese adapted to their own hulls the "lateen" rig, based on a triangular sail suspended from a long slanted yard. Late in the century, Portuguese and Spanish designers developed the square-rigged caravel; by putting square sails on the forward mast and lateen rig on the two other masts, they retained the size and speed of the square-rigged ship and the maneuverability of the lateen-rigged vessel.

Explorers obviously could not expect to sail with detailed and precise maps, such as the portolano charts which European mariners used in their home waters, but they did require some general geographical knowledge and principles to guide their journeys. The fund of these had been enriched in the fifteenth century. No educated person doubted that the earth was round; classical geography, culminating in the work of Ptolemy (around A.D. 130), accepted the doctrine of the sphericity of the world, and it was continued by the scholastics in the West and the Arabs in the Near East throughout the middle ages. Their theories, especially in the late medieval period, drew very little from contemporary voyages, however. The *Imago Mundi* (*Image of the World*, written 1410, printed 1483), of Pierre Cardinal d'Ailly, was an enormous compilation of the classical and Arab authorities on geography; through Christopher Columbus, who studied it closely, it contributed to the enterprise of exploration. Even more influential was Ptolemy's *Geography*, recovered in the same year 1410. It both encouraged and misinformed oceanic explorers; Ptolemy rejected Eratosthenes' accurate estimate of the circumference of the globe in favor of his own, which was about one-quarter

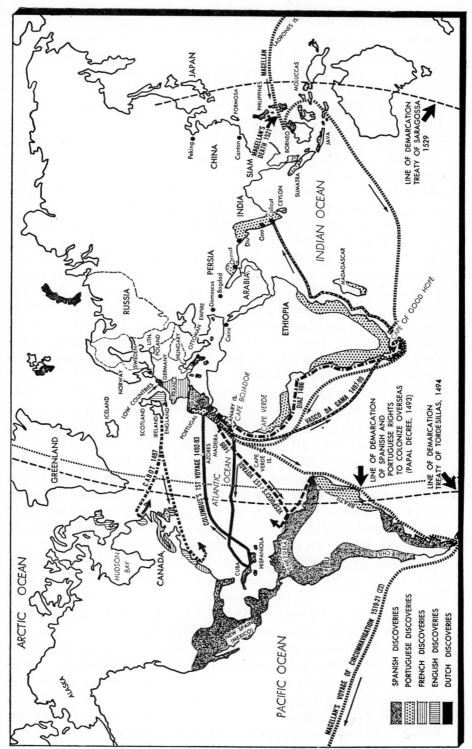

Overseas Discoveries of European Explorers, 1492-1650

too small; and he depicted the Indian Ocean as an enclosed sea, bounded by a land connection between Africa, China, and an antarctic continent. His theory that the torrid zone suffered from unbearable heat worried those who began a southerly voyage.

Navigators during the fifteenth century relied almost completely on dead reckoning, which combined compass direction and a rough estimate of distance sailed. Those who could do so added celestial navigation for estimating latitude, but this was a rare skill during the period of the first discoveries; the astrolabe and quadrant were effective for finding latitude on land, but difficult to use at sea even if one knew how. There was no accurate way of establishing longitude before the eighteenth century.

When the explorers reached inhabited land, they had to be able to maintain themselves in the face of hostile native populations. The superiority of European military and naval power was crucial, therefore. The Portuguese, unlike the Venetians, depended upon artillery rather than upon boarding troops for naval fighting; they used their cannon to attack the hostile vessels, and proved the efficacy of this tactic against the best native fleets in the Indian Ocean during the early sixteenth century. On land, European military technique—based on light armor, the pike, sword, and firearms, the use of horses, and especially on operation in organized units—also proved superior to that of most native armies.

Henry the Navigator. The pioneer country in European overseas exploration was Portugal, a nation which seemed scarcely equipped, at first glance, for such momentous accomplishments. Portugal was a poor land, thinly populated; her farmers were hard put to feed themselves, her fisherfolk did not venture very far from the safety of her shores, and her rulers, with their limited resources, were poor relations in European royalty. But Portugal, poised at the southwestern tip of the continent, possessed a position of great advantage for the enterprise of exploration; and her long crusade to expel the Moors from her territory and her subsequent wars against the Christian states of Spain had stiffened her people's resoluteness and warlike qualities.

It was one man with a dream who launched them on the far seas. The dreamer, Prince Henry, a younger son of King John I, was also a doer. Henry became convinced that a strait or open sea connecting the Atlantic and Indian Oceans lay south of Africa, and set himself the task of finding such a seaway to the Indies. Drawing upon his revenues as head of Portugal's military-religious orders and as governor of Algarve, the southernmost province of Portugal, Henry assembled experts of every kind useful to nautical exploration—mapmakers, astronomers, sailors, and shipbuilders—in the little village of Sagres, at the tip of Cape St. Vincent looking off into the Atlantic. With their work, Portuguese ships and maps became the best in Europe during the fifteenth century, especially for oceanic ventures.

The captains whom Henry, year after year, sent exploring down the coast of Africa never reached the realm of Prester John, the legendary Christian priest-monarch somewhere on the other side of the Moslem world, with whose help Henry hoped it might be possible to defeat the "infidel" in an immense pincer attack. Their exploits were not negligible, however. In 1418-1419, they discovered the island of Madeira; between 1427 and 1432, the archipelago of the Azores, off the Portuguese coast; in 1434, the difficult barrier of Cape Bojador was doubled; and by the time of Henry's death in 1460 Portuguese ships had begun to sail round the great western bulge of Africa.

The Eastern Successes. All the subsequent successes of the Portuguese explorers were built upon Henry's initiative, persistence, and patience; though he seldom went to sea himself, Henry nevertheless deserves the name of "the Navigator" given him by admiring English historians in the nineteenth century.

The opening up of the Guinea coast, where the Portuguese began to take slaves, ivory, gold, and pepper during the 1470's and 1480's, did not long delay the search for the southern tip of Africa. It was reached and passed during 1487-1488 by Bartolomeu Dias, who called the great promontory the Cape of Storms; but King John II, on Dias's return, gave it the happier name of Cape of Good Hope. The good hope was realized when Vasco da Gama, sailing from Portugal in 1497, reached Calicut, a spice port on the west coast of India, on May 16, 1498. After picking up a cargo of pepper and cinnamon, despite the opposition of Moslem merchants, Da Gama made the return journey to Lisbon. Prince Henry's dream was achieved at last—a Portuguese navigator had gone around Africa, bypassing the centuries-old spice route through the Levant and the Mediterranean. An empire in the fabled faraway Indies was in the making for the little kingdom at the edge of Europe.

Da Gama's exploit thus regained for Portugal the lead in the work of exploration she seemed to have lost six years before to her more powerful neighbor, Spain. In 1492 an expedition sailing for Queen Isabella of Castile had reached land due west across the Atlantic.

The Western Project. Christopher Columbus, who made his historic voyage under Castilian banners, was born (ca. 1446) an Italian, like so many other master mariners of his age (though a host of other nations have claimed him as a native, with more pride of place than solidity of scholarship). His family were weavers of Genoa, but he soon chose the sea as his calling. Shipwrecked on the coast of Portugal in 1476, he sailed thereafter on Portuguese ships, to the British Isles, possibly to Iceland, and down the coast of west Africa; from 1479 to 1485, he lived on the islands of Madeira and Porto Santo close by.

Even before he had left Italy, Columbus had conceived the "enterprise of the Indies," that is, to reach Japan, China, and India by sailing directly across the Atlantic to the west. He submitted his proposals first to his "own" king, John II of Portugal, who named a committee to consider them. These experts rejected as scientifically unwarranted Columbus' calculation of the distance from Europe to the coast of Japan as less than 3,000 nautical miles. They were right and Columbus wrong, because he made much too small an estimate of the size of the earth (the actual distance between Europe and Japan is 10,600 nautical miles along the great circle route). Columbus, who hunted for every shred of evidence in his favor and read it in the most favorable way possible, impressed the king as a "big talker," on whom there was no reason to gamble the sums he demanded for his expedition. In any case, plans already afoot to send Dias to find a southerly route around Africa promised more success than Columbus' wild ideas.

Columbus now turned to whatever monarch he thought might support him; his brother Bartholomew, a chart maker, journeyed in vain to France and England, while Christopher himself went to Spain in 1485. Only in 1491, when the war against Granada was about to end victoriously, did Queen Isabella at last accept the proposals of the then despairing and hapless Columbus.

The Voyages to America. Columbus' journey in three small but sturdy ships (anything but the cockleshells of the popular imagination) lasted from August 3 to October 12. The first land reached was the cays of the Bahamas, followed by other islands to the south in the Caribbean sea. The stone-age peoples he found did not fit the image of Indians loaded with gold and precious stones he had expected to meet; but he still imagined himself at the rim of the Asiatic mainland or Japan itself. On his return, a storm forced him to run into Lisbon port for shelter; Bartolomeu Dias, his own great voyage apparently overshadowed by this boastful rival's exploit, came aboard to order him to court to give account of his journey to the king. Skeptical of Columbus' boast to have found a new route to Asia, John II laid claim to the islands he had discovered as outlying parts of the Azores. When Columbus reached the Spanish court, he was given a hero's welcome, proclaimed Admiral of the Ocean Sea, and made hereditary governor of the new lands over which the queen of Castile took sovereignty.

The bulls issued on her behalf by Alexander VI, a notoriously pro-Spanish pope, were no more than chips in an elaborate game of diplomatic poker that followed between the Spaniards and the Portuguese. In the treaty of Tordesillas (1494) a line of demarcation was set down 370 leagues west of the Cape Verde Islands, all new lands found to the east thereof being Portuguese, all to the west Spanish.

Columbus himself returned three more times (1493, 1496, 1502) to the scene of his triumph, but each journey brought him increasing disappointment: no sign of China or India was visible. By the turn of the century almost everyone lacking the admiral's invincible self-confidence—which had buoyed him during the first epoch-making journey—realized what he would not admit, that these were unsuspected lands in the midst of the ocean.

Vespucci and the "New World." By an irony of fate due in no small part to the discoverer's own stubbornness, not his name but that of a fellow-Italian, Amerigo Vespucci, was given to the New World. Vespucci, an alert and intelligent observer though a latecomer and dilettante in the field of exploration, described his four voyages to the western lands between 1497 and 1503 in letters to friends; when these appeared in a best-selling book printed in Germany in 1507, the *Cosmographiae introductio* (*Introduction to cosmography*), the geographer Martin Waldseemüller decided to call the new regions America, in his honor. Usage soon fixed this name, though later historians, concerned at such "cheating" of the honor from the discoverer, too long discounted Vespucci's own qualities.

The quick acceptance of Vespucci's description of the New World as a continent, not an archipelago, did not instantly dash hopes that the true Indies—as distinct from the misnamed "West Indies"—could still be found by sailing west. Portugal held the route around Africa firmly in her control, and none dared attempt to wrest it from her. The discovery of a sea across the isthmus of Panama by Vasco Nuñez de Balboa in 1513 encouraged such hopes. Up and down the shoreline of Central, South, and North America probed the mariners of Spain, France, and England; the sight of great river mouths and bays briefly raised their expectations, until the explorers realized they were not channels to the Pacific.

The Passage to the Indies. Not until October 1520 was the desired passageway found by the Portuguese-born navigator sailing in the service of Spain, Fernão de Magalhães (usually Anglicized as Ferdinand Magellan, after the Spanish form of his name). Magellan fought his ships through the stormy straits henceforth named after him, till thirty-eight days later he reached calm ocean beyond, which he gratefully called the Pacific. The subsequent journey across the Pacific bore Magellan to a violent death in the Philippines, but a faithful captain took one ship home by way of the Indian Ocean and the Cape of Good Hope. The first circumnavigation of the globe did not disturb Portuguese domination of the East; only the Philippines fell into Spanish hands. Meanwhile the persistent explorations of the eastern shores of the American continent brought a clear knowledge of their outlines and character from the Tierra del Fuego (Land of Fire) at the south to Labrador and even further north.

For the next century, maritime explorers continued to seek still other water routes to the Indies. They hoped to duplicate in the northern hemisphere, by sailing to the north of either the European or the American continents, what the Portuguese and Spaniards had achieved in the southern. Dutch and English mariners penetrated into Hudson Bay, a huge arm of the sea on the rim of North America, and to the White Sea and Archangel on the northern coast of Russia. But the close-packed ice of the Arctic Ocean proved impenetrable to even the sturdiest of ships and the most valiant of crews; the luckless left their lives in the white wilderness, while the more fortunate returned home with their discouraging tales, which by the early seventeenth century brought these northern voyages of exploration to a halt.

Land Exploration. The work of exploring the American continent continued on land. Most of the journeys of discovery were simultaneously expeditions of conquest; those to Mexico and Peru are only the best-known of many. Some, however, were productive of little or nothing besides knowledge; such were Hernando de Soto's (1538-1541) and Francisco Vasquez de Coronado's (1540-1542) expeditions through what is now the southern and southwestern United States. As the sixteenth century wore on, the initial work of exploration was accomplished and the first stage of discoveries brought to an end.

II. The Patterns of Empire

Wherever discovery led to conquest or settlement, the new phase of European empire began, even while explorers continued to probe the unknown further on. Distinctive patterns of European domination resulted from the intermingling of several factors: the geographical character of the region, including its distance from Europe; the structure of the native society; and that of the European nation which conquered it. Varied as were these systems of imperial rule, they resembled each other in their fundamental elements. Thus did Europe transplanted overseas duplicate its characteristic multiplicity-within-unity at home.

Initiative Private and Public. The initiative in imperial activity frequently came from private individuals or groups, spurred by hopes of profits or seeking refuge from hardship and tyranny. They worked in relative freedom from the vagaries and uncertainties of politics, but they seldom possessed resources sufficient to maintain themselves for long when difficulties proved greater than anticipated—and colonizers, like most dreamers and speculators, usually underestimated the magnitude of the problems they were to face. State sponsorship, on the other hand, had mixed merits.

Governments were richer than private men, and their armed forces gave comforting assurance against manifold perils. But the demands upon states were more numerous, complex, and distracting; hence colonial enterprise directed by governments frequently faltered for want of home support. Government-chartered joint-stock companies kept some advantages of both systems. But the companies, organized to trade for profit, looked upon their governmental functions as hindrances in their rightful activity: they built empires despite themselves.

The Spread of Religion and Culture. Though in doctrine all Christian groups accepted the duty of converting the unbeliever, practices differed widely. In the first centuries of European colonization, only the Roman Catholics gave themselves eagerly and energetically to the missionary task outside the European continent. Where the conquerors took over whole societies, as in Hispanic America, all inhabitants under their effective rule were Christianized, however superficially in many cases; but the aboriginal religions were suppressed and much of the native cultures sacrificed in the process. Where the Europeans could do no more than seize footholds within densely populated lands, as in Portuguese India, they seldom converted further than the reach of European guns. In the forests of Canada, however, where French regiments had not yet penetrated, adaptable French Jesuits persisted in converting those who had martyred the first missionaries; but to win these souls, they accepted the tribal societies much as they found them. Protestant creeds remained stiffly European and even national. The English in America drove out or destroyed the native "Indians" without much thought for the possibility of winning them to their own religion. The Dutch in the East Indies, with an eye for profit, carefully avoided the Portuguese "error" of mixing faith with trade; Calvinism was their own affair, and heathens no doubt deserved the damnation to which (by Dutch lights) they were certainly doomed.

European languages and culture had similarly differing fates in the process of colonization. Where wholly European societies arose, as in British America, the tongue and habits of the homeland were transplanted but underwent transformation under the new conditions. In Hispanic America, Spanish and Portuguese became the general language of the people, and Iberian culture the heritage of both Creoles (those of European stock born in America) and natives. In the region of the Indian Ocean, the Portuguese language lasted longer than the Portuguese empire; in a simplified form it has continued as a *lingua franca* (a generally utilized second language). The Negro population brought into America as slaves from the early sixteenth century lost the use of the native African languages and adopted their masters' speech; they retained other aspects of their African culture, especially their musical heritage, mingling them with their masters' culture.

III. The East Indies

The opportunity to make good the dream of the fifteenth-century explorers—to reach the Indies by sea and bring home a share of their vast riches—came first to the Portuguese.

The Portuguese and the "Arabs." It was an opportunity bristling with difficulties, as Vasco da Gama learned when he landed at Calicut in 1498. "Arab" merchants (actually Indian Moslems) showed little desire to buy the Portuguese wares. There was little demand in the tropical subcontinent for woolen cloth, such as the Venetians had carried to the Levant, or for the hardware and gewgaws such as the Portuguese themselves sold along the West African coast.

Although the Portuguese represented little direct threat to their trading monopoly, the Arabs still feared the intruders. In 1500, a second fleet from Portugal met resistance from them and the local Hindu rulers. Da Gama's next fleet, in 1502, was larger and more heavily armed; he bombarded Calicut into submission and almost completely destroyed a much more numerous Arab fleet, thanks to the superior artillery and maneuvering skill of his squadron. But even if the Arabs had welcomed them, the Portuguese would not have been satisfied; their plan was to replace the Arabs in control of the spice trade, not to share it with them. Nor could the Portuguese depend upon the precarious permission to trade accorded them by Hindu rulers.

Creating Portugal's Empire. To drive the Arab traders off the Indian Ocean, to establish their own naval and trading bases along its shores—this was the task the Portuguese assigned to the great viceroy, Alfonso d'Albuquerque, in 1509. The very next year Albuquerque accomplished the central part of his plan by the capture of Goa, a well-protected harbor on an island immediately off the west coast of India. To pinch off the ancient spice route to the Levant, he seized Ormuz (Hormuz) and Socotra, islands commanding the entrances from the Indian Ocean to the Red Sea and to the Persian Gulf respectively. At the other extremity of the trading system of the Indian Ocean, he found a place of similar decisiveness, Malacca, which controls the strait connecting the Indian Ocean with the China Sea. The seizure of Malacca in 1511 completed the essential parts of Albuquerque's strategy. Within two years a Portuguese ship sailed into Canton, on the southwestern coast of China; after a while the Portuguese received the island of Macao, down river from Canton, as a trading post. The Portuguese also reached the islands of the Moluccas, where most of the spices they wanted were originally produced.

Albuquerque thereafter consolidated Portuguese control of the spice trade in all parts of the Indian Ocean. He restricted the carrying of spice for Europe to Portuguese ships sailing around the Cape of Good Hope, and permitted native shippers to carry spices and other goods within the confines of the Indian Ocean only with the permission, given for a price, of the Portuguese authorities. The tribute and taxes they exacted provided the Portuguese, directly and indirectly, with the spices they coveted; they did not have the needed wares nor the desire to conduct a trade of simple exchange. The Portuguese empire in the Indies thus rested upon the use of armed force for economic exploitation—this was no innovation in the East, but had been the pattern of repeated conquests in Asia over the centuries.

By chancing to launch his grandiose plan at an unusually favorable moment, Albuquerque succeeded beyond normal possibilities. The powerful Moslem states on the Indian mainland had been prevented from concentrating their efforts to expel the Portuguese interlopers by constant wars with the great Hindu kingdom of Vijayanagar, in the south. Only after the Portuguese position at Goa had been consolidated did Vijayanagar begin to suffer a decline, and not until 1565 was it destroyed by the Moslems. The Moslem siege of Goa began within four years, but by then the Portuguese were ready. They held out against immense odds for two years until the sultans withdrew; the Moslems were unable to capture a naval fortress with uninterrupted access at sea controlled by its own ships. Although Moslem strength was reestablished in the Mogul empire, the Portuguese were able, partly by deliberate policy and partly by accident, to avoid conflict with it, at least until the death of the Mogul Akbar in 1605. But the Portuguese position upon the Indian mainland remained no more than a toehold a century after the conquest began.

The Downfall of the Portuguese. Building an empire in the distant Indies severely strained the limited resources of Portugal. Her population was steadily depleted; though few of the thousands who went out to the East every year desired to remain permanently, many died there. Portuguese missionary zeal, though limited in its achievement, nonetheless offended the native peoples and rulers. The expenses of empire devoured the direct revenues of the Portuguese authorities in the Indies; the net profits came chiefly out of the spices imported through Lisbon, but most of them were used to pay for the extravagances of the Portuguese rulers in policy and courtly display. The Portuguese nation grew weaker even while her monarchs rivaled the greatest in Europe.

Even more dangerous to the preservation of Portuguese rule in the Indies was the decline in Portuguese sea power. The excellence of the first Portuguese fleets could not be maintained; the number of ships lost en route increased from less than one in ten before 1580 to almost one in three in the next three decades.

Some hope of support was found in the personal union of Portugal with Spain, her old rival for empire, under Philip II in 1580. The Hapsburg kingdom was the strongest naval power in Europe and controlled the Philippine Islands, not very far from the East Indies where the Portuguese position was most shaky. Instead of assistance, the Spanish connection brought only increased peril to the Portuguese empire in the East. The most implacable enemies of the Portuguese after the turn of the sixteenth century became not local kings and sultans, but two European sea powers gripped in war with Spain. The question thereafter was not whether the Portuguese dominions in the Indies would survive, but who the heirs would be—the English or the Dutch?

The English and Dutch East India Companies. The fear of trespassing upon Portuguese overseas possessions, so marked earlier in the century, evaporated during its closing decades. English mariners had sailed into the forbidden waters beginning with Francis Drake's circumnavigation of the globe (1577-1580) and had seen the flimsiness of Portuguese power; Dutch sailors made the Indies voyage as crew members aboard Portuguese ships. Even more essential to the success of interloping attempts was the book of sailing directions, the *Itinerario*, published in 1595-1596 by the Dutchman Jan Huyghen van Linschoten after his return from Goa, where he had lived during the 1580's.

The first English and Dutch voyages for commercial purposes were discouraging in result, though not total failures; the necessity of large-scale organization of fleets and trading posts was soon evident. Companies for East Indian trade were soon formed in both England and the Netherlands. The English company, chartered in 1600, was soon outdistanced by its Dutch counterpart, established in 1602 by the States-General, which compelled a number of small and competing local companies to merge for the sake of the general interest of the nation. The English organization depended upon court favor and had much smaller invested capital than its Dutch rival; the English company continued to function upon the basis of distribution of invested capital and profits every three years, after which it was reorganized; the Dutch company was soon put on a continuing basis. As traders, the Dutch demonstrated their ability in this novel market; unlike the Portuguese, they brought wares desired in the East, particularly the excellent weapons manufactured in Europe. Militarily, too, they were as superior to the Portuguese as the latter had been to the Arabs a century before; they won a naval battle against the Portuguese at Bantam in 1601 by means of better artillery and fleet handling.

Creating the Dutch Empire. The Dutch at first directed their principal efforts toward the spice islands of the East Indies, where they drove out the Portuguese with the aid of the local rulers. Gradually they subordinated these princes to the authority of their East India company, by treaties of trade, alliance, and protection. Before these first advantages could be lost, the ruthlessly efficient governor-general, Jan Pieterszoon Coen, took over in

1618. He established the company's naval power securely upon the base constructed at the new city of Batavia, on the northern coast of Java; Batavia became the company's headquarters and capital in the Indies, from which Coen directed the crushing of resistance to its authority. The Portuguese were driven from their last important positions in Malacca and Ceylon during the 1640's and 1650's.

The English—whom the Dutch government at home did not wish to offend needlessly—represented more of a problem. Collaboration between the Dutch and English companies, enforced by the home governments, broke up as a result of the superior strength and drive of the Dutch. A tragic episode at the island of Amboina in 1623 marked the end of this interlude of uneasy alliance. A small group of dissatisfied English merchants plotted to overthrow the local Dutch authorities with the aid of Javanese mercenary soldiers; the Dutch officials seized the conspirators, tortured confessions from them (in accordance with the usual practice), judged them guilty in a trial in which important legal procedures were neglected, and executed them without waiting for the confirmation of the governor-general. In England, the affair aroused roaring anger: the "massacre of Amboina" became the standard theme of anti-Dutch propaganda for half a century.

The Dutch East India company built its policy during the seventeenth century upon the program devised by Governor-General Coen. Supplying spices to Europe across the immensities of two oceans could bring in continuously high profits only if the produce of Asia were obtained and transported virtually without cost; the problem was to make trade within the Indies bear the expenses of maintaining the company and its power.

Although the Dutch were more efficient traders than the Portuguese, Coen recognized that only by the use of force could his countrymen overcome the greater skill of native merchants. The Dutch knew from their experience in Europe the importance of the profits to be garnered from shipping. The company therefore reserved for itself the major traffic of the eastern seas, barring other European ships and confining native ships to short-haul routes. It also built Batavia into another Amsterdam, a central warehouse for the goods of Asia.

The constant necessity of enforcing this policy against European and Asiatic interlopers and recalcitrant princes compelled the company to expand its possessions despite its desire to trade rather than govern. But even where it ruled directly, the company concerned itself almost solely with commercial matters. It did destroy unwanted spice production to safeguard its monopoly of the supply, without pity or recompense for the natives whose livelihood was thus torn from them; but it did not needlessly interfere with the lives of the natives in other respects.

English India. Driven from the East Indian islands by Coen and his successors, the English East India company continued its activities on a limited scale on the Indian mainland. It was particularly successful in the northern part of the peninsula, where it traded in cottons, indigo, and saltpeter at Surat. Thanks to the protection of the local Mogul rulers, it maintained itself against Dutch competition. In the southeast, along the Coromandel coast, the Dutch were more troublesome, until the establishment of a fortified English trading post at Madras in 1639. This gave the English company control of its own territory, however small, and provided a base for protecting its interests more effectively. The English position on the Indian mainland was modest in scope, but great growth was possible.

IV. The New World

The American islands and continents discovered by Columbus and his successors seemed "fool's gold" at first alongside the true metal of the Portuguese empire in the Indies. The Spaniards sought a more direct route to the Indies, and a huge land mass barred their way; they wanted spices, and discovered a new world whose resources had scarcely been tapped. But the Portuguese empire in the East survived only in weak and small fragments after a century, while the Spanish dominions in America proved before long to be both vigorous and profitable to Spain.

England, France, and the Dutch Republic, all latecomers in colonization, failed to established any permanent footholds in America during the sixteenth century. Their first, usually desultory efforts were easily crushed by the Spaniards, whose prowess was still formidable. Two stretches of unoccupied territory alone seemed fairly safe: the steaming tropical lands of Guiana and the densely forested coastland of continental America north of Florida.

The three powers were able to set down colonies in various parts of Guiana and to maintain them; but they were costly in money and manpower, and returned little for the expenditures. North American colonization came later, when the decline of Spanish power was already evident; the sparsely inhabited regions held little attraction for the Spaniards, intent upon exploitation of native labor.

The Economy of Spanish America. The precious metals seized as treasure in Mexico and Peru, or dug from the earth in the mines of Upper Peru (Bolivia) and Mexico, adequately justified the colonial enterprise to the government of Spain. Most of the mines were operated as private businesses, on a capitalist basis, under government license; the state exacted a fifth of the metal as its share. This provided about one-sixth of the ordinary royal

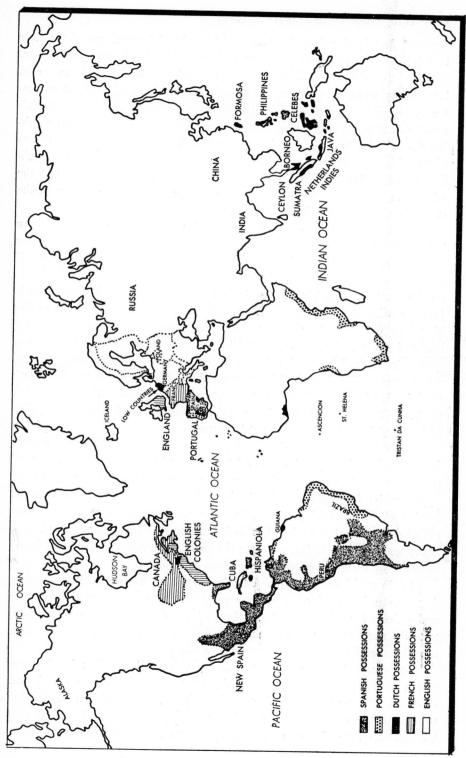

Colonial Expansion of European Powers, 1492-1650

ARCTIC OCEAN

ALASKA

HUDSON BAY

CANADA

ENGLISH COLONIES

CUBA

HISPANIOLA

NEW SPAIN

PACIFIC OCEAN

GUIANA

PERU

BRAZIL

ATLANTIC OCEAN

ICELAND

LOW COUNTRIES

ENGLAND

FRANCE

GERMANY

POLAND

SPAIN

PORTUGAL

RUSSIA

• ASCENCION

ST. HELENA

TRISTAN DA CUNHA

INDIA

CHINA

CEYLON

SUMATRA

FORMOSA

PHILIPPINES

CELEBES

BORNEO

JAVA

NETHERLANDS INDIES

INDIAN OCEAN

SPANISH POSSESSIONS

PORTUGUESE POSSESSIONS

DUTCH POSSESSIONS

FRENCH POSSESSIONS

ENGLISH POSSESSIONS

revenues, less by far than the taxes paid by the rich provinces of the Low Countries; but it was a steady income, collected without difficulty or resistance.

Had Spanish colonial activity been restricted to the exploitation of lucrative mines, the empire would have had too narrow a base for permanence. English, French, and Dutch rivals all wished to capture Spain's sources of treasure in America, but they could not do so without first crushing the colonies in which her mines were located. The would-be destroyers of Spanish colonial power found the broad-based agrarian societies established in Spanish America invulnerable to their jabs and thrusts. Not the mines but rather the ranches and plantations proved the true source of the strength and stability of Spanish America.

The ultimate character of the Spanish empire was foreshadowed even before 1520 in the Caribbean islands where the Spaniards first set foot. Placer mining for gold yielded little; the raising of cattle soon became the principal industry on Hispaniola and Cuba. After the conquest of more extensive lands on the continent, ranching was quickly introduced. Spaniards were already familiar with livestock-raising from their experience at home, where the Mesta, or guild of sheepherders, dominated the Castilian economy. Great herds of sheep and cattle were established wherever the terrain and climate were suitable, and horses for the herdsmen, as well as for military and private use, were likewise raised in great numbers. The principal products were wool for local use and leather for export to Europe. Tilling the soil was left to the Indian natives, but under a system which assured adequate supplies of food and labor to the new Spanish masters.

Spain needed the colonies more than they needed her. Her advantages from the American provinces consisted chiefly in the annual shipment of treasure and other supplies, the taxes upon exports to the colonies, and the opportunities for mainland Spaniards to find lucrative employment in the service of the colonial governments. The compensating cost of protection afforded the colonists against hostile incursions was not negligible, but their safety was also due in large part to the difficulty prospective invaders found in mounting sustained offensive operations deep inland.

Spain could not supply the colonists' needs by its own efforts. To some degree, merchants of other nations participated in the colonial commerce under the cover of Spanish firms; but smugglers and interlopers who came to trade, not loot, were almost always welcomed by the colonists in America, though not so frequently by government officials.

Spain and the Indians. The problem of the Indian in Spanish America was a disturbing one for the Spanish state. The *conquistadores* and later colonists, with very few exceptions, had no qualms about reducing the Indians to a condition of virtual slavery. They argued that the natives were barbarians incapable of reason (usually equated to understanding European law and religion), who were properly placed under the lordship of their betters. The royal authorities in Spain, and many Spanish theologians, could not accept these theories easily. The practitioners of centralized monarchy in Spain looked askance at the tendency of colonial magnates to set themselves up as almost independent powers; when the nobles of Spain had been subjected to royal authority, their colonial counterparts could hardly be allowed to go their own way. Furthermore, the sense of law was vigorous and effective in Spain; the kings and their lawyer-administrators were concerned with the rights of the native peoples in America. Their cause was taken up by an influential ecclesiastic, the Dominican Bartolomé de Las Casas, who emphasized the conversion of the Indians to Christianity and their full rights as subjects of the crown.

Official policy followed Las Casas' principles. The Indians were proclaimed to be subjects only of the crown of Castile, with a right to their property and personal freedom; they were to be governed only by the Council of the Indies, a separate agency of government for the overseas dominions of the king.

But the principles were bent to the advantage of the colonists. Influential and wealthy Spaniards in America were assigned the labor tribute imposed on particular villages; this grant of *encomienda* was specifically nonfeudal, as the *encomendero* received no rights of government. The parallel system of the *repartimiento* provided for forced labor by the villagers; though the authority came from the state, the Spanish colonists received the work of the Indians as needed. Yet the supervision of royal officials served as a brake upon the worst extremes of exploitation, such as prevailed in the mines; harsh as the *encomienda* and *repartimiento* undoubtedly were, the Indians probably suffered more severely from the European diseases to which they were exposed. Indian population declined severely during the sixteenth century, the growth in population which began in the next century was due to an increase in the numbers not of the purebred natives but rather of an Indian-Spanish (mestizo) class.

Spanish Colonial Government. In general, Spanish colonial society was marked by a high degree of self-sufficiency. Spanish America developed a vigorous urban culture, with splendid buildings, great universities, and other evidences of wealth and creative power. The basic instrument of government was a central bureaucracy directed from Seville by the council of the Indies. The chief administrators were provincial governors (called viceroys in the two most important "kingdoms," Mexico and Peru); they did not rule by themselves, but with the advice and consent of *audiencias*, appellate courts functioning as governors' councils. This distribution of authority had a twofold purpose: it checked the danger that any single branch of government in the colonies might arrogate undue power to itself, and it assured the strict legalism dear to the Spanish governmental mind.

Brazil. Brazil, under Portuguese domination, developed a pattern of colonial society and government distinct from that of Spanish America. During most of the sixteenth century, Brazil was little more than an appendage of the great Portuguese empire in the East Indies; her harbors served as ports of call for ships sailing the south Atlantic route to the eastern empire. The rise of sugar plantations late in the century in the northeastern region provided the basis of economic development. Vast strips of territory were granted upon a semifeudal basis to captains-donatory; efforts to imitate the Spanish system of colonial government after the union of the Spanish and Portuguese crowns in 1580 limited the autonomy of the great planters to a small extent.

After the renewal of the Dutch war of independence in 1621, control of the main Brazilian ports and nominal rule over the rest of the colony was seized by the Dutch West India company. When the mainland Portuguese rose against Spain in 1640, their Brazilian brothers turned against the Dutch and soon drove them first from the entire inland region and then even from the port of Recife (Pernambuco). The rebels then voluntarily returned the country to the sovereignty of the now independent Portuguese crown.

The Caribbean Colonies. The character of the Caribbean colonies changed after the first century of European rule. The English and French put down settlements in the islands of the Outer, or southern Antilles, where the strong prevailing southerly winds made it extremely difficult for the Spaniards to attack them from their bases to the north, especially those in Cuba. Cattle-raising declined in relative importance; the half-wild producers of smoked and jerked beef, called *boucan* in French, eventually turned to piracy in large numbers, whence the name "buccaneers." Tobacco was introduced as a large-scale crop, and then sugar, for which the rich soil and hot climate were particularly well adapted.

The bitter commercial rivalries and the habit of semilegalized smuggling and interloping resulted in a sharp increase in piracy in the whole region; the distinction between privateering under letters of marque, which gave legal status to ship capture under contemporary ideas of international law, and outright piracy, was often difficult to draw; in any case, it was a line often crossed.

Newfoundland. Far less spectacular than Caribbean plantations, Peruvian mines, or Mexican ranches as a source of wealth, but of no less importance for the people of Europe, were the American fisheries in the North Atlantic. They supplied a mass need for food in Europe and provided work for multitudes of fishermen. The rich cod banks of Newfoundland, discovered by John Cabot in 1497, at once attracted Portuguese, French, and English fishermen. The original practice of returning to the home ports as soon as the hold was filled with fresh fish, as was customary in European waters, involved the loss of considerable time in traveling, as well as a large danger of spoilage. Smoking and salting the catch in temporary beachside settlements in Newfoundland made it possible to return with cargoes of "dry" fish equivalent to several holdfuls of "green" fish. Such working camps were not maintained over the winter. The fishermen opposed proposals to establish permanent settlements on these bleak coasts; the eventual rise of fishing fleets based on nearby New England proved that their concern about local competition was not unfounded.

French and Dutch Settlements. The French and Dutch settlements were directed primarily toward trade. The first French colony, founded in 1605 by Huguenots in Acadia, was strictly agricultural, to be sure; but it was followed within three years by Quebec, established by Samuel de Champlain as a trading post. Colonization by peasants played a secondary role in the work of the Company of New France established by the French minister Cardinal Richelieu; the manorial system, already decadent in the homeland, was transplanted to French America. Some of the settlers came from Normandy, on the west coast of France; many were soldiers who took their discharge in the colony. A stable, largely self-sufficient agricultural society arose, valuable chiefly as a basis for military defense of New France; but the prosperity of Quebec rested upon the activities of the fur traders, the *coureurs du bois* (woods runners) who roamed through the northland forests on friendly and intimate terms with the Indians.

The Dutch colony of New Netherlands, in the valley of the Hudson River further south, was very similar in character. Commanding the best route to inland America, it prospered commercially; but the Dutch West India Company, to which it belonged, never succeeded in inducing many settlers to take up farming on the manorial estates granted to the *patroons:* Dutch farmers, free of seigneurial overlordship in their homeland, were understandably reluctant to accept its burden in the colony.

English Settlements. To the north and south of New Netherlands were two areas of English settlement. The English colonists were like the Spanish in their emphasis upon establishing replicas of their native societies; they founded not trading posts but "new Englands." Unlike the Spaniards, however, they were unable to put subjugated native peoples to performing the hard menial labor of the society. The forest Indians of North America were a thinly dispersed population, living by hunting and primitive agriculture. The English soon discovered that they might exterminate or expel the Indians but they could not enslave them; in any event, even if the Indians had been docile enough there were too few of them to have furnished the labor force for the English colonies. The settlers therefore had to bring their working force, as well as a ruling class—for which candidates were easier to recruit. The great majority of English colonists were voluntary settlers, some paying their own way, others indentured servants bound to service for a period of years. Criminals sentenced to transportation to the colonies soon merged with the class of indentured servants.

The first settlements were private ventures organized by two chartered companies, the Virginia Company in the southern region and the Massachusetts Bay Company in the north. The companies differed in two essential points. As to government: the officers of the Virginia Company remained in England, while those of the Massachusetts Bay Company joined the settlers in New England. The northern colony was virtually independent in its internal affairs from the very beginning, while the development of local control was slower in Virginia, where the governor was appointed, at first by the company and later, when the crown took over the colony, by the king. As to religion: the settlers in Virginia were predominantly Anglicans, and therefore adherents of the state religion in the homeland, as was required by all other colonizing countries; the Massachusetts Bay settlers were religious dissenters whose emigration to overseas territories under its domination was uniquely favored by the British authority.

Other English colonies formed subsequently in the intervals between southern and northern settlement were granted to individual proprietors; like the chartered companies, these proprietors were semifeudal in character though wholly dependent upon the favor of the crown, unlike their medieval counterparts.

The relationship between the English colonies and crown rapidly developed towards a self-government unique in the period. This rise of effective self-government in the English colonies did not at once cause sharp conflicts of economic interest between them and the homelands. After initial periods of peril and hardship, the colonies soon prospered, but only the southern colonies, where tobacco production became the principal activity, fitted in with the mercantilist notions of the colonies as an economic dependency of the homeland; the northern colonies not only were self-sufficient but even produced a salable food surplus from their farms and fisheries.

7

The States of Italy

1494 - 1650

AT THE END of the fifteenth century, as for a thousand years preceding, the Italian people formed a single nation but not a single state. They spoke and wrote one language, the most common characteristic of national unity. To be sure, popular dialects differed greatly in Italy, as elsewhere, so that the ordinary Sicilian and Venetian could scarcely speak to each other; but the genius of Dante and Petrarch and the cultural predominance of Florence had won considerable, though hardly universal, acceptance for the Tuscan form as the literary language. Social life was basically similar; the differences between customs of localities within Italy were considerably less than those between Italian and foreign folkways. Likewise, Italians shared a common history. They all took pride in Italy's having ruled "all the world," long ago, during the resplendent centuries of ancient Rome.

I. A "Geographical Expression"

The intervening centuries were more painful to recall, for they emphasized Italy's decline from glory and her persistent political disunity.

Italy and the "Barbarians." After the fifth century A.D., though a rump empire continued in the East under the rule of Byzantine Greeks, the Italians had lost leadership in the West to the very peoples they had raised to civilization. Frenchmen, Germans, and Spaniards at various times established their domination in parts of Italy. In 1500 more than a dozen Italian states still maintained their independence; four—Venice, Milan, Florence and the Papal State—were "big" states, at least by peninsular standards, but even they were smaller by far than the countries beyond the Alps. The bickering and wrangling among Italian states sharpened the skill of their leaders at the game of politics.

Thus, though the Italians recognized their weakness in numbers and territory compared to the foreigners, they were confident late in the fifteenth century that they could outwit these "barbarians," as they called them. Undismayed by greater force, they trusted the fate of their states to their own superior guile. Few possessed any sense of a possible common goal for the Italian nation in politics, and none saw any way to achieve it except by the triumph of his own state. Politically, Italy continued to be no more than a "geographical expression," in the witty and supercilious words of a foreign statesman three centuries later when they still remained true.

The invasion of Italy in 1494 by Charles VIII, king of France, put to the test not only the subtle plans of the Italian princes but also the reliability and durability of the states they ruled. Within a decade or two, the rulers proved inadequate. Italy lay almost helpless before the new "barbarians." How each state met the crisis depended in very large part upon its own internal history and organization.

Social Changes. The Italian economic system shuddered but did not shatter under the first impact of the opening of the sea routes to the two Indies by Portugal and Spain. Trade with the Levant and with the rest of Europe continued though on a reduced scale. Handicrafts and larger industrial enterprise in turn were diminished in scope as their market fell off. Agricultural activity, making possible greater local and regional self-sufficiency, assumed increased importance.

The position of the various groups in society was similarly transformed. The urban groups, notably the businessmen who had given the tone to the Italian city in the middle ages, became mute and passive as the sources of their strength were sapped. Infrequent rebellions of the city poor were little more than hopeless rioting, while banditry, especially widespread in central and southern Italy, constituted a kind of perpetual low-flame insurgency of the impoverished peasantry.

The landed aristocracy established itself as the paramount political and social class, less and less in rivalry with the ruling princes and more and more their well-rewarded and privileged servants. Noble rank and title

Italy, about 1600

became the proper garb for all wealthy, not only in the countryside but also in the towns, where the right of citizenship increasingly became the prerogative of those who did *not* besmirch themselves by earning their livelihood as tradesmen or worse.

II. The Papal State

One Italian state stood out from all the others because of the unique basis of its authority. This was the State of the Church or Papal State.

Papal Monarchy. The Papal State was neither republic nor hereditary monarchy nor tyranny based on mere force. The pontiff, not the people, possessed all sovereign rights in the name of the church; he was, at least in theory, as absolute a prince as any in Christendom. Rome and its environs had belonged to the pope in one fashion or another for some ten centuries. Though the famed "Donation of Constantine," a pious forgery dating probably from the eighth century, had been repeatedly exposed by the year 1500, papal sovereignty did not depend upon it, and few questioned the right of the papacy to rule its own lands. Holding his office purely by election, the pope could not pass it on to heirs of his own family. Those who tried to endow either a son or a nephew permanently with some portion of the papal domains were despoiling the church of its property.

Two strongly felt needs impelled the papacy to build and maintain its own territorial state. First, without a state of his own, the pope ran the danger of becoming the pawn of any potentate able and willing to impose his rule upon Rome, so that the very performance of the pontiff's sacred duty seemed to require a buffer of lands to protect him in his seat of government. Second, popes insisted upon matching the full scope and prestige of secular princes, of which possession and control of a state were the supreme sign: less would detract from the dignity of Christ's vicar on earth.

Rome and the Provinces. The city of Rome and the outer regions of the State of the Church differed fundamentally in economic and political characteristics. Rome existed by and for the church. Without independent importance as a center of trade or industry, it served the ecclesiastical office-holders who worked and dwelt within its walls. Even those Romans who resented government by ecclesiastics knew that the papacy was the ultimate source of all their livelihoods. The decision of the Council of Trent to enforce residence in their dioceses upon bishops therefore aroused deep anxiety among Romans lest, "if Rome ceases to be the haunt of the priesthood," as one foreign observer put it, they should all be ruined.

Outside the Eternal City, however, no such exchange of service and advantage prevailed. The papacy ruled there as suzerain over self-sufficient localities to whose life it contributed little; at best, its failure to collect taxes with efficient rigor was a compensating gain. Its inability to establish tight control over the feudal lords who parceled out domination of the State of the Church outside Rome did positive harm: neither trade nor industry developed beyond the limits characteristic of somnolent market towns.

The Papacy in Active Politics. Despite the absoluteness of their authority, the popes were unable to establish strong government in the State of the Church. It was not for lack of trying, especially after Rodrigo Cardinal Borgia was elected pope as Alexander VI in 1494. He took it as his paramount goal to provide his illegitimate children with states and titles. His favorite son, Cesare, named gonfalonier (captain) of the Church, used both his military prowess and his utterly ruthless treachery to crush the feudal lords in the districts of the Romagna and the Marches; when this task was completed in 1501, the pope gave his son the title of duke of Romagna. Other potential rivals and opponents Cesare exterminated with fabulous duplicity and cruelty. Alexander's death in August, 1503, proved the fragility of his dream of establishing Cesare as an independent and sovereign prince. Cesare being ill at the moment of his father's demise, the surviving lords whom he had despoiled recaptured their lands. To escape their vengeance, Cesare fled to the Spaniards, who took him prisoner. The new pope, Giuliano Cardinal della Rovere, who adopted the name of Julius II, at once re-established papal sovereignty over the lands bestowed upon the fallen Cesare.

Pope Julius took as his central purpose the establishment of the State of the Church upon a sounder political footing. First he limited the feudal jurisdictions of great noble families; then he took the field to wage war against foreign enemies, first Venice and then France. He built up the temporal greatness of the Papal State to an unprecedented degree. Unlike his predecessors, he did not mar his achievement by nepotism. Yet, though he achieved unwonted success as a temporal prince among temporal princes, he forgot that the primary duty of the bishop of Rome was religious: the leadership and guidance of a universal church.

The personal interest of the pope came to the fore again with the election of Giovanni de' Medici as Leo X. His first intention was to "enjoy the papacy," and insofar as his pleasures lay in great works of art, mankind thereafter benefited by the munificence and splendor of his patronage. The perils implicit in a vigorous territorial policy for the Papal State came to fruition during the reign of Clement VII (Giulio de' Medici). His participation in war against the Emperor Charles V led to the sack of Rome in May, 1527, and the collapse of the State of the Church as an effective political force. The efforts of Paul IV (Giovanni Pietro Caraffa) to organize a league against domination of Italy by the Spanish Hapsburgs failed dismally in 1557. This was the last venture of a pope into the dangerous game of big politics.

The Papacy and the Catholic Reformation. To save the independence of the Papal State, the popes had not only to abandon any major initiative in international affairs apart from purely theoretical pronouncements of their rights; they also had to play off the great Catholic kings against each other —thereby weakening the Catholic front against the Protestant Reformation. In contrary effect, the pontiffs turned their attention thereafter almost exclusively to their religious duties: self-reform of the Roman Catholic church on its own fundamental principal of papal supremacy became possible.

Even nepotism, one of the worst excesses of papal administration in the fifteenth and early sixteenth centuries, changed in character and lost much of its general perniciousness. Although it persisted as an important element of Roman government for more than a century, it was no longer directed toward the vain enterprise of carving out hereditary principalities from the State of the Church for members of the pontiff's family. Its primary purpose became to provide him with reliable advisors. The popes began to name a "cardinal nephew" to act as principal minister of government. The pontiff, who possessed the title-granting prerogative of secular princes, usually elevated his family into the high aristocracy of Rome, while he enriched them with lucrative offices in church and state.

Decline. Internally, the government of the Papal State fell into decrepitude. Its laxity and inefficiency became notorious. The finances of the state were incredibly bad. Most of the tax revenues went to pay interest on an immense state debt: by 1640 the incredible proportion of 85 per cent was reached! The practice of selling governmental offices, which only worsened conditions, was extended for the sake of temporary income.

Despite employment of a numerous police force, the government could not maintain law and order for its subjects. Highwaymen infested the countryside, preying on travelers, often with the connivance of local barons. Within the city of Rome, the great nobles lorded it like independent princes.

Excessive pride cost the aristocracy dearly. They refused to reduce expenditures even when their fortunes declined, as happened widely throughout Europe during the inflationary sixteenth century. Nobles they were, and nobly they would live. To do so, they borrowed beyond their ability to repay. In 1596 Clement VIII recognized the weakness of the haughty aristocrats by ordering that the estates of insolvent creditors, whether freehold or feudal, be sold. For lesser folk life continued on its usual course, but lazier than ever. A visiting French diplomat during the 1640's admired the Roman antiquities all about, but felt only contempt for the do-nothing Roman populace of his own day. Like government, like people. Drowsy quiet ruled: the age of bustle and endeavor was past.

III. Venice

Venice, the "bride of the sea" at the northeastern corner of Italy, joined together splendor and power around the end of the fifteenth century. Like the other states of Italy, she fell from the dizzy heights of great-power status during the sixteenth century, but more slowly and safely. Her government remained robustly efficient and resourceful through years of trial and defeat. Her economic system, stabbed in the vitals by the Portuguese discovery of the Cape route to the Indies, survived thanks to the persistence, ingenuity, and adaptability of her merchants. Venice suffered decline but not disaster.

Merchants and Merchantmen. The greatness of Venice was the work of time, not the creation of a moment. For long centuries her merchants had gone out in her ships to the far corners of the Mediterranean world, and beyond. By the fifteenth century all trade roads led to Venice; rivals like Genoa and Pisa who had challenged her supremacy in the inland waters had failed. Venice treated the Adriatic as her own sea: others sailed on it only if she permitted. Even after the Ottoman Turks completed their conquest of the Levant, whence came the most important of Venetian goods of commerce, this route was not closed; but it was the new masters of Constantinople,

Damascus, and Alexandria who laid down its conditions, not the Venetian visitors. Spices, silks, and other wares for the well-to-do continued to reach Venice. There they were stored in warehouses or sent out to be converted into articles of use.

To purchase these goods from the East, merchants from many lands in Europe came to the city on the lagoon, where they found themselves as dependent on Venetian good-will as the Venetians themselves were on Turkish sufferance. The grandiose establishments for foreign traders, like the famed *Fondaco dei Tedeschi* (German House of Trade), were actually enclosures outside of which they were not allowed to do business.

The Edifice of Government. The profits of commerce provided the foundation for an edifice of state of remarkable solidity and stability. Venice was the customary example of republican organization in Europe, for it did not belong to a single prince, like hereditary monarchies and principalities. But the Venetians themselves did not consider their state as abstract and impersonal. During the fifteenth century, its simple, age-old designation as the Venetian Republic was abandoned in favor of the more pretentious *Serenissima Signoria Veneta* (Most Serene Lordship of Venice). This designated specifically the doge, six ducal councilors, and three chief judges of the tribunal of the *Quarantia* (Forty). The visible head of the state was the doge (literally, "leader"); his powers, however, were as limited as his dignity was great. The Grand Council, the source of all authority in the state, comprised all members of the nobility. An astute foreign observer emphasized their hereditary status and their absolute power. "The monarch in Venice, whose name is the Grand Council, has a thousand heads, but his character and methods are identical."

Until the fifteenth century, the aristocracy had been a fairly numerous and open class. It included most wealthy tradesmen, for enrichment was almost always followed by ennoblement, at least until the sixteenth century. The slowing of the process and then its virtual halt was recorded in the Golden Book, a register of all births and deaths in the families of the Venetian aristocracy, instituted in 1506. It numbered 1,671 names at its inception, less than three hundred more half a century later, and only about 1,200 when the republic fell three centuries afterward. During this same period, office-holders came to be recruited more and more from a small circle of extremely wealthy noble families; the rest of the aristocracy, except for the honors of their titles and their membership in the Grand Council, had little more chance of high office than the common folk.

Regular responsibility for the conduct of government was given to a Senate of 160 members; its tasks of legislation and direction of foreign affairs were entrusted in turn to an executive, the *Collegio* (committee). But even this group proved too large and cumbersome. More and more during

the sixteenth century, the Council of Ten, elected annually by the Grand
Council, came to be the lord of its masters. This permanent body of state
was given power to act swiftly and energetically on all business requiring
immediate decision or secrecy, or involving conspiracy or treason against the
state. In practice, these were the most important affairs of government and
the mighty ten were able to control the fundamental policy of Venice.

The Practice of Government.   For its work of internal guardianship, the
Council of Ten relied upon three Inquisitors of State, first named in 1539.
Their formal title, given to them later in the century, became a watchword
for the most effective and dreaded political police in Europe. Its operations
were silent, its sentences swift and harsh; it seemed like an irresponsible monster. Yet dispassionate historical studies, without ascribing to the inquisitors
an incongruous gentleness, have shown, more significantly, the precautions
taken by the Venetian authorities to keep them servants, not masters of the
state, or reckless tyrants over its people. The inquisitors had to confine themselves to established law; they could not follow whims nor satisfy personal
grudges.

The unparalleled stability of the Venetian state did not rest only on the
stern discipline imposed by the inquisitors. More important and ultimately
safer was the political education of the nobility. Aristocratic Venetian youth
early learned, by precept and by example, the sense of responsibility to the
welfare of the state. Its service was a duty to be neither evaded nor assumed
at will: tasks were assigned, not sought. Training for careers, which included
both domestic and foreign service, was lengthy, careful, and elaborate. Venetian ambassadors proved its worth to the world; they won well-deserved fame
for their extensive and detailed knowledge, their easy competence in negotiations, and their ability as accurate observers and fluent reporters. Yet a
change in the character of Venetian society became visible during the sixteenth and seventeenth centuries. Seriousness of purpose gave way to festivities, carnivals, and infamous debaucheries, which attracted visitors from
other lands and early made this incipient tourist trade into an important
source of Venetian earnings.

The "Terrafirma."   The unusually high political maturity of the Venetian governing class was reflected in its treatment of the Terrafirma, the
mainland adjacent to Venice's lagoons which had been annexed during the
past few centuries. The conquered peoples gave a surprising degree of loyalty
and support to their masters. The towns and villages were not stripped of
their rights of internal self-government. Venice used their territories not
primarily for exploitative profit but as a buffer against hostile invasion. In
return, they were assured protection and stability. The nobility of the Terra-

firma, on the other hand, were watched with hawklike vigilance for signs of disaffection or rebellion; they were granted no participation in the government of Venice itself.

IV. Florence

Florence, southwest of Venice across the peninsula, rivaled it in power and prestige. Yet the Tuscan city had the smallest territory and the fewest inhabitants (about 750,000) of any of the Italian "big five."

Industry, Trade, and Banking. Industrially, however, it led them all. The manufacture of woolen cloth, especially in the fine varieties, remained its principal industry, although its exports to the south were beginning to lag behind those of Lombardy. On the other hand, the new and profitable silk-weaving industry was beginning to develop strongly. Overseas, Florentine merchants competed effectively with the Venetians and Genoese in the Turkish empire, where they sold cloth and ironware, and bought dyestuffs, wax, spices, and alum; in Egypt and Tunisia, they inherited the trading privileges of Pisa, which they had conquered. Florence competed with Genoa in international banking; the famed banking family of the Medici had long handled the lucrative exchange business of transferring papal revenues to Rome.

Rule of the Medici. Florence resembled Venice politically too. It also possessed a republican city-state form of government and held in subjection towns and territories for many miles roundabout. For centuries civil strife had scarred its history, till in 1434 the city found its masters in the Medici bankers. They did not change the form of government, nor did they need to. By persuasion and manipulation, by repression of opponents if necessary, they established effective leadership of the Florentine state. Such an indeterminate situation was tainted with illegitimacy, however: Medici power derived neither from the hereditary right of a dynasty nor from the elective grant of a popular state. The death of Lorenzo de' Medici in 1492 brought to an end the long period of relative calm and order that the Medici had given to Florence. With the advent to power of Lorenzo's son Piero began the city's time of troubles.

The French invasion of Italy proved too much for Piero. The French king, Charles VIII, easily frightened him into accepting his alliance on humiliating conditions: passage south, French control of Tuscan ports and border fortresses, and large gifts of money by Florence to him. The Florentines, in indignation, threw off the Medici rule: the republic was again its own master. When Charles, demanding that the Florentines stand by Piero's treaty, threatened to have the trumpets blow his army's call to attack, one of their leaders replied with the fierce resolve of an armed and aroused city:

"Then we shall ring our bells!" It was Charles of France who backed down. The alliance stood, however, on terms acceptable to Florence. While the French marched southward to the conquest of Naples, the Florentines undertook the reconquest of Pisa, which had revolted from their dominion.

Savonarola. Florence was free now to go her own way. Which way would it be—the rule of the leading families which had chafed under Medici ascendancy and wished to replace it with their own, or that of the broad populace, hating all oligarchical control but incapable of self-government and seeking little but violent vengeance and destruction? The answer remained unclear for the next four years. During the turmoil of the rebellion, a Dominican preacher of wide popularity, Fra Girolamo Savonarola, won leadership of the city. His sermons were hotly democratic in mood, but the constitution adopted at his suggestion provided for a temperate government by patrician families, much like Venice's. His own dream, however, was to bring about Christ's reign on earth; his followers intoned his hymn to "Jesus, king of Florence."

Before long, Savonarola's efforts to remold a joyous and active people on the ideal of the monk proved vain. Hostile parties formed against him. he fell from power, and was burned at the stake (1498), when he ran foul of the papacy (see ch. 4, p. 77). The *Piagnoni* (weepers), as their foes called Savonarola's supporters, lost control of the government to the anti-Medici patricians, dubbed by their opponents the *Arrabbiati* (mad dogs).

The new rulers were little more effectual at the head of the state than Piero de' Medici had been. The Pisans held out against their armies until 1509. An experiment with a militia army, instigated by the secretary of the government, Niccolò Machiavelli, was a debacle. The new regime fell ignominiously when the army of the "Holy League" invaded Tuscany to punish its failure to join it in war against France.

Return of the Medici. In 1512 the Medici came back into Florence and resumed control of the city. They held it for fifteen years, thanks especially to the support of Cardinal Giovanni de' Medici, who in 1513 became pope under the name of Leo X. But the debacle of Leo's whole policy of using the papacy as an instrument of family advantage, culminating in the sack of Rome in May 1527 during the reign of Clement VII, brought the overthrow of Medici government in Florence in the very same month.

To regain the city of their ancient power for his family, Clement went over to the camp of Emperor Charles V. Imperial troops easily reconquered Tuscany in 1530; the Medici took over again in Florence. The following year Charles V instituted Alessandro de' Medici as head of the republic of Florence and its hereditary duke. The *signoria,* or sovereign lordship, of Florence was abolished in 1532. Though the power of Alessandro and his successor Cosimo (1537) equaled that of any other Italian prince, they were no more than hereditary dukes of Florence and Siena, ruling over a republic. Cosimo set himself to achieve a loftier title, so important in an age where precedence counted for so much. In 1569 Pope Pius V proclaimed him "Grand Duke of Tuscany," a title confirmed seven years later by the emperor. The republic of Florence existed no longer, in either fact or name.

The Grand Duchy of Tuscany. The days of tumult and vitality were past; the days of calm came. Tuscany became the model state in Italy. Cosimo's government was efficient and just, though he suppressed threats to his rule with utmost harshness. Under Cosimo and his successors the commercial life of the country was expanded. Pisa's tradition of hostility to Florence made it unsafe to develop its port facilities, though it lay conveniently at the mouth of Florence's river Arno. Instead, nearby Livorno (Leghorn) was built up into the principal seaport of Tuscany. Proclaimed a city in 1577 and later declared a free port (exempt from customs duties), Livorno soon attracted Greek, Jewish, and Levantine merchants from the east and Englishmen and Hollanders from the Atlantic. The peasants of Tuscany, on the other hand, continued to be out of favor with the government that sat in Florence; their conditions worsened under the Medici grand dukes. When the Thirty Years' War broke out in Germany, small merchants and manufacturers suffered direly from its repercussions on trade.

V. Savoy-Piedmont

On the threshold of the sixteenth century, the duchy of Savoy-Piedmont did not seem distinctly Italian. Its lands lay astraddle the mountains and valleys of the southwestern Alps between France and Italy.

Half French, Half Italian. Savoy itself, on the western slopes, was strongly French in tongue and traditions; Piedmont, on the eastern inclines, with the ducal capital of Turin, was more Italian in character, but still with a large admixture of French influence. The political interests of the duchy were directed more toward France than Italy. In its origins and character, the Piedmontese state resembled France, where feudal monarchy had grown over into incipient absolutism, rather than the principalities of Italy, where power ultimately derived in most cases from popular grant or violent seizure of the state. Like France, Piedmont had an ancient and vigorous dynastic tradition with deep roots among the people.

By unintended historic irony, the shift of Piedmont toward more complete and intimate participation in the life and pattern of her Italian neighbors was initiated by the act of a French king. For the dukes of Savoy as for so many others, Charles VIII's invasion of Italy marked the beginning of a new age. Both Charles VIII and Louis XII were able to cross the Alps through Piedmontese territory whenever they pleased, meeting their first resistance further inland. In the subsequent wars between the French kings and their Hapsburg foes, both sides used the Piedmontese passes without question. They occupied and administered the territories of the duke of Savoy as their own interests dictated.

Emanuel Philibert. The first glimmer of improvement came when Duke Emanuel Philibert took service with Charles V, commanding a Spanish army at the victory of St. Quentin, in northern France (1557). By the treaty of Cateau-Cambrésis (1559), Emanuel Philibert regained possession of his dynastic lands, although it was not until 1574 that the last of the French forces withdrew; the marquisate of Saluzzo, which thrust uncomfortably between the duke's states, remained under French sovereignty.

Emanuel Philibert, strong with his prestige as a general under Charles V and relatively free of dependence upon local factions, re-established a firm and efficient government in his states. French administrative reforms remained in effect; the *parlements*, or supreme appellate courts, instituted by the French in Turin and Chambéry, were retained under the name of senates. Emanuel Philibert did not call the old assemblies of estates into session, but collected taxes on his own authority and by agreement with local groups. Though he exacted large revenues from his people, he used them with care and wisdom; the state debt was reduced by more than half, and economic development in agriculture, industry, and mining was encouraged. Since the highlands of Savoy and Piedmont produced a meager, hard-won living for their people, the combined effort of government and subjects was needed to make their work more productive and the state's tax income more ample. The duke also built new roads, tying his states more closely together.

He drew upon his military experience to organize an effective army; its basic force was composed of professional soldiers, recruited principally from among his own subjects; the obligation of feudal service remained for the nobility, but the duke encouraged them to receive exemption by payment of a special tax. In foreign policy, he took a neutral stand between France and Spain, despite his long service with Charles V; he also reached a settlement with the Swiss cantons by which, acknowledging the independence of Geneva, he regained the lands along the southern edge of Lake Geneva. Thus, the duke assured a long period of peace to his exhausted states. His subjects responded to his policy of stability and prosperity by giving to him, and to his dynasty, an allegiance based on gratitude as well as historic tradition.

Uneasy Independence. Emanuel Philibert's son, Charles Emanuel I, succeeding him in 1580, turned to a more adventurous policy. He alternated alliances with France and Spain instead of remaining neutral between them; he regained Saluzzo for some decades, only to lose it a week before his death in 1630. Nonetheless the vigor of his conduct won new prestige for his state and crown. "The Lord Duke of Savoy," wrote an Italian commentator, "is the defender of the liberty and reputation of the Italian princes, because he was the first to show the face of a free prince, who when pressed hard put his hand to the sword, protesting that he would live free by it or die."

His successors followed his policy of swinging between France and Spain according to the advantage of the moment. Their highest goal was conquest of Milan, and perhaps a royal crown. But the outbreak of civil strife between rivals for the regency during the reign of Charles Emanuel II, which began in 1638, distracted Piedmontese attention from grand policy for many decades.

VI. Milan

The duchy of Milan, like Venice, its neighbor to the east, had a reputation for both political stability and economic wealth. Lombardy, the historic name for the region, was favored with a fertile soil, mild climate, and adequate rainfall. Milan itself lay at the crossroads of a net of trade leading from upper Italy to northern Europe through the Alpine passes. The people of the duchy, in Milan as well as in its dependent towns and territories, were numerous, industrious, and prosperous.

The Sforzas. By the second half of the fifteenth century, Milan's political future was already shadowed over by uncertainty. The reigning dynasty, the Sforzas, had a disputed title to the ducal throne: their claim rested on marriage to a daughter of the Visconti, the hereditary dukes, shortly before the extinction of the direct line, and on the success of a rebellion against the short-lived Ambrosian republic (1447-1450). After 1480 power came into the hands of Ludovico, nicknamed *il Moro* (the Moor), uncle of the reigning duke, Gian Galeazzo, as his guardian. His nephew's marriage endangered Ludovico's control over the state; the youth's death about two years later was blamed by many on his uncle. Ludovico nonetheless at once had himself proclaimed duke and received the seal of legitimacy by the emperor's investiture.

Imperial backing did not save him the duchy when Louis XII of France coveted it, however. Captured by the French in 1500, Ludovico lost his freedom and the state for which he had risked his life and perhaps his soul. During the next thirty-five years, possession of the duchy alternated between the king of France and a Sforza duke according to the fortunes of war. Then the death of the last duke returned the duchy, as an imperial fief, to the control of Emperor Charles V. Five years later the emperor regranted the duchy as a fief to his own son, Philip of Spain.

Spanish Rule. A new era began for Milan. Though technically still part of the Holy Roman Empire, it became in practice a Spanish crown land. In some respects this change was of great moment, in others of little. In all matters of relations to other states, Milan gave of its substance and people to serve the high policy of the king of Spain, like any other of his dominions. The Milanese played no part in the formulation of that policy; their particular interests received no special consideration except within the over-all pattern of Madrid's concerns.

Internally, Milan's government was hardly touched: the duke happened to be king of Spain, to be sure, but he made no effort to remake Lombardy in the image of his homeland. No effort was made to unify the government of the duchy beyond what the previous rulers had accomplished. The various counties and provinces retained their traditional administrative and financial autonomy, with distinct privileges and customs. Hence, though the sovereignty of the king of Spain was absolute (except for the theoretical subordination to the Empire) and unquestioned, in practice it was exercised with limitations. Philip II allowed no tampering with his prerogative, especially as regarded the church; he did not scruple to enter a bitter controversy with Cardinal Borromeo, the doughty archbishop of Milan, over control of the church of Lombardy.

In general, however, he did not seek to undermine local government in the duchy; he confirmed the senate, the high court and council, in its privilege of rejecting three times any decree of the governor which it deemed contrary to the interests of the country. No more than three of the fifteen senators were Spaniards; the rest were Lombards or subjects of the king in his other lands. All other offices of state were also open to the Lombards, though on the same shared basis. But no longer were they confined to careers in their own duchy, as before; they now could serve wherever the flag of Spain flew. Many entered military service under their new master, and rose to high posts in the Spanish army.

These opportunities were confined almost exclusively to the Lombard nobility, however, who broke their historic connections with commercial enterprise; in 1593, noble rank and commerce were declared incompatible. The career of jurisprudence became a noble preserve, leading to careers in the administrative service. This tight dependence upon the nobility by the Spanish authorities represented the one important change from the earlier policies of the Visconti and the Sforzas; they had begun to undercut and abolish the privileges of the feudal aristocracy, but the Spaniards now reaffirmed and consolidated the privileges of the large landed proprietors within their own estates.

VII. The Two Sicilies

South Italy belonged to two closely related states. One, the kingdom of Sicily proper, occupied the island of that name; the other, occupying the peninsular mainland south of the State of the Church, was the kingdom of Naples.

Union with Aragon. At the end of the fifteenth century, both states were connected with the royal house of Aragon, in Spain. Sicily proper had been joined to Aragon by union under a single dynasty since the late thirteenth century; during the recent period, the kings of Aragon took the Sicilian crown for themselves, but they resided in Aragon and left the government of the island to a viceroy. Naples, on the other hand, had come into Aragonese hands from its previous holders, the house of Anjou, as recently as 1443. The two Sicilies had then been joined under Alfonso V of Aragon till 1458; thereafter Naples went to his illegitimate son Ferdinand (Ferrante) I, his other lands to John II and then Ferdinand II, known as "the Catholic," of Aragon. After 1494, when Ferrante died, the kingdom of Naples passed back and forth through the hands of the kings of France and Ferrante's son and grandson.

In 1503, Ferdinand of Aragon took over the Neapolitan realm, but continued to govern Sicily and Naples, although reunited under his crown, as separate kingdoms each under its own viceroy. Otherwise they were administered on the same lines as Milan: local traditions were generally observed; the local nobility was utilized at home and elsewhere in the Spanish dominions; and the resources of the lands were employed for the common policy imposed by Madrid in foreign affairs. The parliaments of both kingdoms remained in existence, but represented only the tax-exempt classes although their main function was to vote taxes. Most of the powers of the Sicilian parliament passed in 1567 to a standing committee, the Deputation of the Kingdom.

Decline and Hardship. Though Naples and Sicily had been productive and populous during earlier centuries, both countries were already in the grip of severe hardship when Aragonese rule began. Conditions became more difficult during the sixteenth and seventeenth centuries. Ordinarily the only visible symptoms of distress were the prevalent banditry which no measures of repression could prevent, and the open display of grinding poverty in the cities.

Popular revolts broke out in 1647 in Naples and Palermo. The deep hatreds and sufferings of the common folk found outlet in these uprisings. They followed common patterns of development: resistance to a new tax spread with unexpected vigor and rapidity; a popular leader—in Naples a fisherman from Amalfi named Tommaso Aniello, but better known as Masaniello; in Palermo first Nino La Pelosa and, after his execution, the boatman Giuseppe de' Alesi, took command of the movement, which caught the Spanish authorities unawares and unprepared; the disputing noble leaders made a quick reconciliation with the viceroy; the popular leaders were unable to set up a program or escape the intoxication of their sudden elevation; their downfall and death, and the easy crushing of the insurgent forces, soon followed.

VIII. Genoa

Spanish domination of the Italian peninsula during the sixteenth and seventeenth centuries depended in very large degree upon the collaboration of a small independent state, the republic of Genoa. Genoa was the main port by which Spanish troops passed on their way to Germany and the Low Countries; its bankers financed the operations of the Spanish armies. This city-state upon the Ligurian Sea south of Piedmont and Lombardy both resembled and differed from Venice, its onetime hated competitor.

Like Venice, Genoa drew its original sustenance from seaborne commerce; the decline of its trade began well before the opening of the sea routes to the Indies. But it developed banking as an independent economic activity to a far greater extent. Its basic system of government was similar to Venice's, even to calling the head of the state a "doge." Party conflict, a pallid business in Venice, recurred frequently and sometimes riotously in Genoa.

Foreign conquest, too, was a never-absent danger to the Ligurian port; its landward defenses, the mountain ranges immediately to the north of the coastal plain, were more easily crossed than Venice's lagoons. The French repeatedly occupied the republic during their wars with Spain, but were finally expelled in 1528 when the Genoese admiral Andrea Doria broke with them and joined the Spanish-Imperial camp. Doria gave the republic a new constitution frankly oligarchical in character; political power was henceforth confined to the great aristocratic families. Opposition to Doria within his city continued; in 1547 an uprising against his authority led by Gian Luigi Fieschi, a nobleman with a considerable popular following, came close to success. Its failure was also a defeat for France, which had supported Fieschi in the hope of regaining influence in Genoa. The capture of the island of Chios by the Ottoman Turks in 1566 completed the loss of the once-great Genoese empire in the Levant; the continued retention of the nearby island of Corsica, immediately south of Genoa, brought no advantage but that of a little prestige.

IX. The Lesser States

Besides these half-dozen Italian powers of some weight and moment, there continued in existence an assortment of small to tiny states. Some were totally independent; others, theoretically dependent on the Holy Roman Empire, were virtually so. Some were republics, others principalities. Some maintained reputation by the endeavors of their rulers, not least the Este princes of Ferrara and Modena; others, especially in the mountainous regions, slumbered safely away from the world's concerns. But one by one the number of such independent states was reduced over the decades; some passed to a foreign dynasty on the extinction of a local line of rulers, others were conquered outright. Nonetheless these little states continued to be a feature of the Italian scene, especially immediately to the north of the Papal State, for the next three centuries.

X. Wars in and for Italy

Penned within Italy's boundaries of rock and water, all these states formed a little, almost self-contained world. It was a world in political turmoil: war and preparations for war never ceased; each state was the foe of all the others, friendships mere temporary expediencies; alliances formed, dissolved, and reformed perpetually as states sought every possible sliver of advantage in their mutual competition for power.

The System of Powers. Yet there existed a tradition of order and ultimate stability beneath the turbulence. With all the warring, no state had been able to bring all the rest to heel. Whoever strove to establish his own predominance and reduce his rivals to dependence and obedience thereby brought into existence a coalition of individually weaker but more numerous states able to thwart his ambitions. Political analysts began to explain this situation in theoretical terms as a "balance of power"; some even claimed that statesmen actually pursued the goal of such an equilibrium, but self-interest rather than common welfare motivated almost all those in power. Thus the states system of Italy before the final decade of the fifteenth century already foreshadowed the developing continental pattern of international relations.

The isolation of the Italian system from the larger world was incomplete, however. On the one hand, the states of Europe beyond the Alps had important interests within Italy which they never neglected for long; on the other hand, the issue of peaceful intercourse or open hostilities with the states of Islam to the east and south remained a constant problem, especially pressing and difficult with regard to the Ottoman empire.

As the fifteenth century moved toward its close, the part played by foreign states in Italy's affairs seemed to be diminishing. Even in the south, where members of the house of Aragon ruled the two kingdoms of Sicily, the illegitimate origin of Ferrante I of Naples made him more foe than friend to his legitimate cousins of Aragon, who by law should have sat on his throne. Italian rulers had grown accustomed to treating their affairs apart from general European connections, although they did not scruple to seek the assistance of foreign states for some immediate advantage within Italy. They were confident they could make the "barbarian" do their work. How could he best them when—or so they presumed—he lacked their wiles and tricks?

The Foreign Invasions. Thus it came about in 1493 that Ludovico il Moro of Milan and Cardinal Giuliano della Rovere, an opponent of Pope Alexander VI, encouraged the young king of France, Charles VIII, to invade the kingdom of Naples. In August of the following year, Charles VIII sent his army into Italy to make good his claims upon Naples as inheritor of the Angevin line. The numbers and ruthlessness of the French forces, who still lived in the traditions of the Hundred Years' War, astonished and frightened the Italians, for whom warfare had come to mean the relatively mild operations of the *condottieri*. By February of 1495, Charles had conquered Naples. A month later he faced a coalition of states to thwart his aim; this "Holy League" consisted of three Italian states—Milan, Venice, and the Papacy—and two foreign potentates—the Emperor Maximilian and Ferdinand of Aragon. To expel the "barbarian," other "barbarians" were called into Italy: a curious reminiscence of the declining days of ancient Rome! The French quit Italy, but only for three years.

In 1499 the new French king, Louis XII, returned to attempt the conquest not only of Naples, like his predecessor, but also of Sicily and Milan. His diplomacy was more adroit and his military forces were strengthened by Swiss infantry, famed for their pike formations. The progress of Louis's troops was marked by more resistance than Charles's had seen, but they too came to Naples and conquered. They were not alone, however: Louis XII had agreed to divide the realm with Ferdinand of Aragon, his rival claimant. Ferdinand, as devious and astute a politician as any in Europe, had let the French clear the way: now it was they who had to go. Their sending was neatly and expeditiously accomplished by Ferdinand's "Great Captain," Hernández Gonzalo de Córdoba, who used the new Swiss pike tactics for his infantry regiments in defeating the French on the Garigliano River in the fading days of 1503. On New Year's Day the French commander accepted a truce; the next year, Louis XII accepted Ferdinand's sovereignty over the whole kingdom of Naples in a treaty of peace.

War soon broke out again, with Venice, the last large and independent state in Italy, as the target of a grand coalition. The republic had continued to expand its territory of the Terrafirma, but its fearful neighbors did not begin war upon the Most Serene Lordship until the Emperor Maximilian had opened hostilities and been defeated; then he joined the league formed under the auspices of Pope Julius II at Cambrai, December 10, 1508, including France, Spain, and a half dozen lesser states. The French defeated the Venetian army at Agnadello five months later, but the astute leaders of the endangered republic divided their opponents, conceding to the pope and the king of Spain territories the Venetians could no longer hold in any case. France then became the principal danger in Julius's eyes, and he formed an alliance with Venice and Spain (1510), consolidated the next year in a "Holy League." When the French lost to the Swiss forces of Maximilian Sforza at Novara in 1513, they had to quit Italy entirely.

The Triumph of Spain. The tables were turned two years later by the new king of France, Francis I. The duke of Milan, though supported by the emperor, the pope, and Spain, and though he had excellent Swiss troops under his command, was defeated in a two-day battle at Marignano (now Melegnano). When Francis renewed hostilities in 1521, his opponent was the king of Spain, Charles I, now Emperor Charles V as well; the Swiss, who had entered Francis's service, again faced opponents who had mastered their tactics, and were again defeated, this time by Charles's German and Spanish infantry at Bicocca (1522). They put the capstone on this victory by defeating Francis in person at Pavia (February 24, 1525).

Even though the French king, who was taken captive at Pavia, signed a peace treaty at Madrid early the next year, war was soon resumed in the peninsula of Italy. Before long the emperor re-established his superiority over all foes below the Alps; Spain ruled much of Italy, and what she did not rule, she tried to dominate by force, threat of force, and more gentle persuasion. Spanish predominance in Italy was recognized when Henry II, Francis's son, made a peace treaty with Philip II, Charles's son, at Cateau-Cambrésis in 1559.

The classic age of Italian high politics was at an end. Italian soldiers still fought with valor and skill, but for foreign lands; Italian diplomats still plied their craft with their customary adroitness, but their range of action was smaller and the stakes involved fewer and of less importance. Besides Venice, only Piedmont-Savoy retained any independence of policy; it could not, however, stand aside from the struggle of the great powers, but only choose freely which of them to support. Even the war of the Mantuan succession (1627-1631), resulting from the death without direct heirs of the duke of Mantua, Vincenzo Gonzaga, was an Italian war only in the sense that it was fought in Italy for possession of an Italian land—but the principal contestants were, as for the past century, the Hapsburgs of Spain and Germany and the kings of France. The outcome of the war, a compromise

settlement at Cherasco (1631), indicated the declining fortunes of the Hapsburgs but gave no promise of lessening foreign domination as such.

The Turks and Lepanto. The looming power of the Ottoman empire
presented a different kind of problem for the states of Italy. Having conquered Constantinople in 1453, the Turks were free to employ their exuberant
energy wherever opportunity suggested. If, as seemed possible, the Ottoman
drive were directed due west, Italy would soon face the full weight of Turkish arms. Yet the princes of the peninsula devoted little attention to this
peril, a little too far beyond the tips of their noses. Only Venice and Genoa,
owing to their historic trade with the Levant, and the pope as the head of
Latin Christendom, were concerned in more than words. But Genoa, driven
from her eastern colonies, was already giving her main attention to the
western Mediterranean, while Venice, similarly despoiled, found compensation in the acquisition by gift of the island kingdom of Cyprus in 1489.

The popes' vehemence on behalf of a united crusade against the Turk
was matched only by the passivity of states in Italy and beyond for the
project. The burden of effective resistance fell chiefly upon the Venetians,
whose naval power was superior to that of the Ottomans. The lagoon city
could not employ that strength without compunction, however. Its indispensable grain imports came from the Balkans, where the Turks now ruled,
and from southern Russia, by the route through the Dardanelles; and, after
Sultan Selim I's annexation of Syria and Eygpt in 1517-1518, Venice's imports of the goods of the East likewise passed through territories under
Ottoman rule. For the Venetians, therefore, war with the Turk was a last
resort, when the sultan would not give them peace or allow them to trade
even under difficult and onerous conditions.

Until well past the middle of the sixteenth century, Turkish naval power
grew ever stronger, particularly when the corsair chieftains of North Africa
put themselves under the nominal suzerainty of the sultan. Italy, like most
other European states on the Mediterranean, suffered severely from their
piratical ravages. Warning towers along the coastline did not prevent the
incursions of the Moslem rovers, for the Italian states were unable to unite
their efforts in self-defense.

The initiative in combating the Turks and their North African vassals
came from the kings of Spain, Charles V and Philip II. Only a Turkish
invasion of Cyprus spurred a league of Italian states and Spain to aid the
Venetian defenders; the succor was too late to save them. The assembled
armada, under the command of Philip's half-brother, Don John of Austria,
defeated the Turkish fleet at Lepanto, on the west coast of Greece, on October 7, 1571.

For Spain, her monarch, and his brother, the glory was immense: the
age-old legend of Ottoman invincibility was shattered. For Italy as a whole,

Lepanto ended conclusively the threat of Turkish attack. But for Venice, its fruits were bitter. Cyprus was gone and Philip was unwilling to aid in its reconquest. Within two years Venice made a separate peace with the sultan; she abandoned Cyprus and paid a large war indemnity, but received back her coveted trading privileges. Except for the island of Candia (Crete), the Venetian colonial empire was lost; to safeguard her trade, the Venetians henceforth maintained a policy of prudent defense, avoiding offense to the Turks in the effort to meet the competition of rivals for Levantine trade, notably the Dutch and French.

XI. Political Thought

As political life in Italy subsided from its scurry and strain at the start of the sixteenth century to the placidity which marked it during the century that followed, the character of Italian political thought also changed in roughly parallel fashion. During the decades before and after 1500, political theorists of every stripe—republicans and monarchists, advocates of liberty and of authority—laid down their rules for statesmen and judged their conduct thereby. Characteristics they all shared were their humanist training and familiarity with classical antiquity. They were not confined within a single mold thereby: the wide variety of Greek and Roman experience and ideas provided them with examples and judgments of every kind.

Machiavelli. The most influential among them was Niccolò Machiavelli, the Florentine secretary of government. His most important single work, *The Prince,* was superficially another of the long series of "mirrors for princes," wherein were painted the character and conduct of a model ruler; Machiavelli adapted this form to a description of the way statesmen actually took and kept power. His predecessors as formal theorists all accepted the scholastic definition of the goal of the state as service to the people; Machiavelli observed the practice of narrow egoism by all successful princes. The rules for success chiseled into the stony sentences of *The Prince* constituted a new political morality in direct violation of the old: murder and assassination, deceit and duplicity, hatred and distrust of fellow-men, instead of the Christian virtues of truth, charity, and love.

Machiavelli's apparently forthright defense of evil-doing frightened and fascinated his readers. If, as may well have been his intention, he was actually satirizing the recently re-established Medici to whom it was dedicated, his intention remained the secret of his friends; others took the book at face value. In his other works, notably the *Discourses on the Ten Books of Titus Livius,* Machiavelli upheld a belief that the best ruler served the interests of the majority of his subjects, which ultimately did not conflict with his own.

Even in *The Prince*, he portrayed as foes of the state only the ruler's rivals among his own class, not the generality of his subjects.

"Reason of State." Though Machiavelli's works were soon translated and read in other countries, his fellow Italians soon invented a term for his central idea. The doctrine of the supremacy of the interests of the state and ruler over all other interests they called *ragione di stato*, or "reason of state." * The character of political analysis thereafter emphasized the problem of the conflict between political success and common notions of morality. Some thinkers, satisfied with a facile utilitarianism, derived from Machiavelli merely the notion of a political craftsmanship which disregarded ethical considerations.

Others, including Giovanni Botero, whose *Della ragion di stato (Concerning reason of state*, 1589) became the best known of the school, sought to reconcile reason of state with traditional morality. Their "sweet harmony" consisted in the doctrine that success in politics depended upon the morality of action; they set honest "prudence" against immoral "astuteness." But by the end of the sixteenth and early seventeenth century, their debate was little more than idle prattle, for Italian political leaders, as we have noted, lacked the independence of action by which they could have tested these theories.

In 1650, the Italian states' decline from power and importance in the ranks of European countries was virtually complete. Yet Italy's quietude was not wholly passivity. In the arts, she continued to give even more than to receive; her powerful traditions of intellectual activity were not wholly dissipated; patterns of proper conduct for the nobility emanated from the peninsula as before. The economic life of the people, modified by the changes in Italy's position in the world of trade, remained steady in many areas. Recovery depended upon circumstances, but events no longer depended upon Italians. Her great culture was Italy's hope and her feeble power her tragedy in mid-seventeenth century.

* *Reason* here means "consideration" or "interest."

8

France: The Cruel Century

1483 - 1589

NATURE MADE FRANCE a fair and flourishing land. A poet called it *"la douce France"* (sweet France), and the country merited the loving phrase. The climate was mild, the rainfall even, the soil productive. A varied economic life easily sustained some fifteen million people at the beginning of our period, and it could support many more. The realm of France was not only sweet but strong. More people lived in it, and paid more taxes, than in any other European state. In the nobility, France possessed a numerous, skilled, and valorous military class. Agriculture and industry met all the essential needs of the country. Yet men, by blundering and savagery, have often brought desolation and despair to France. Never was this irony of its history more cruelly exhibited than during the century that began auspiciously with the advent of Charles VIII in 1483 and ended blackly with the dagger death of Henry III in 1589.

I. "Sweet France"

The Land. By 1483 France had come close to whatever natural barriers lay between her and her neighbors. On the seaward side, she had everywhere reached the water's edge, except for the English-held port of Calais on the strait of Dover; the duchy of Brittany, on France's westernmost peninsula, although in practice virtually independent, was legally a fief under the French crown. Within its outer boundaries, the monarchy ruled everywhere, except for the independent principality of Orange and the papal territories of Avignon and Comtat-Venaissin.

The situation of the land frontiers remained less definite and settled. The Pyrenees and the Alps formed the rough boundary of the kingdom, but with major interruptions. In the southwest, the independent kingdom of Navarre straddled the western range of the Pyrenees, while the adjacent region of Béarn was also a free principality; the tiny shepherd's republic of Andorra, further east in the high ranges of the Pyrenees, was a fief conjointly under France and a Spanish bishop. On the east, the duke of Savoy held the western slopes of the lower Alps, while further north the dukes of Burgundy held Franche-Comté (the "free county" of Burgundy), an imperial fief on the western slopes of the Jura range. On the northeast, ducal Burgundy and Champagne formed the boundary of France along the edges of the Holy Roman Empire in Lorraine; in their geography both French and imperial areas were almost alike and had no significant natural barrier between them.

Similarly the plain of northern France continued unchanged past the boundaries of the French state on the extreme north; there the situation was politically intricate, though legally clear. The counties of Flanders, Artois, and Hainaut, admittedly fiefs of the French crown, were held by the duke of Burgundy and formed part of the Low Countries; the jurisdiction of the French courts in these counties was highly problematical, for during the fifteenth century the dukes of Burgundy had established their virtual independence of France.

The People. Within those boundaries prevailed a single dominant people and culture, the French. Ethnically the French were as much a conglomerate as any European people. The ancient Gauls furnished the basic element of the population, to which had been added numerous Latin elements during the period of Roman rule and a sparser Germanic component (from the Franks, who gave their name to the country) at the beginning of the medieval period.

Their varied cultures had merged to form a single civilization before the year 1000 and the untutored speech of the Roman citizenry and soldiery in Gaul had produced the common tongue, French. It was still spoken, like most European languages, in a score or more dialects; the widest divergence in these *patois* lay between the patterns of the South and North. There was only one literary language, based mainly on the usages of Tours and Paris, which was beginning to undergo the direct influence of classical Latin by way of the Renaissance grammarians.

The long continuity of rule by kings of France had produced a considerable degree of identification with a "general fatherland"; but the sense of belonging to a local parish or town, and beyond it to a province, was still usually stronger.

Along the edges of the kingdom, distinctive ethnic groups continued to maintain themselves. A Germanic group, the Flemings, peopled the county of Flanders; a Celtic people, the Bretons, the peninsula of Brittany. In the extreme southwest, the Basques, speaking a language unrelated to any other European tongue, inhabited the westernmost Pyrenees, including Navarre; at the other end of the range, Catalan was the tongue of the people of Cerdagne and Roussillon. Only the Bretons were confined to the territory of France; all the other groups were parts of peoples inhabiting the adjacent countries as well.

Economic Life. Economically and socially France's uniqueness may be said to have consisted in her striking typicality. Her economic institutions were generally characteristic of those of western Europe, neither so far advanced as those of Italy and the Low Countries toward a preponderant commercial capitalism nor so laggard as those of Spain or Scotland. Agriculture remained primary. Most areas were self-sufficient in their basic needs, as was the country as a whole. The growing of cereal grains for the production of bread flour prevailed in the northern plain, while excellent wines, produced especially in the sandy southwest near Bordeaux and in the hill country of Burgundy, provided the most important French export commodity.

Most commerce continued within a local and regional framework, but a sizable export and import trade was carried on, principally in foreign ships. Banking, with an emphasis on currency exchange, was concentrated in the city of Lyons, on the Rhône river, where easy connections could be maintained with Italy, Germany, and the Low Countries; Italian banking houses did most of the business. Industrial production remained mainly in the hands of artisans; the makers of French luxury wares were already well known for their skill and taste.

Classes. The character and relative numbers of the social groups in France were likewise much like those of western Europe as a whole. The peasantry was the most numerous segment of the population. Living in modified manorial communities, most peasants were free persons, though in a few regions in Brittany, Hainaut, and Burgundy serfdom continued in a mild form.

The landed nobility comprised several levels of rank and importance. The poorest nobility, generally having the title only of *seigneur* (lord), managed to live only little better than the more prosperous peasants; their privileges of tax exemption frequently made the difference in their living standards and marked them off socially from their inferiors. The middle ranks of the nobility lived safely away from the brink of poverty, in more adequately aristocratic fashion. The high nobility lived and felt almost like independent princes, and were often closely linked by friendship and marriage with the royal family. All noble groups shared a sense of distant superiority over all commoners, though the practice of marrying wealthy though untitled heiresses was frequent.

The town population comprised the patricians and prosperous men of business and professions, customarily known as the *bourgeoisie*, with, beneath them, the common workpeople. The *bourgeoisie*, particularly as they acquired wealth and consolidated their control of the town governments, modeled themselves on the nobility and intermarried with them.

The State: Powers. The similarity of the French monarchy to other European states was less marked. It was the most nearly perfected princely government in western Europe. The subjects of the king, whether organized into broad estates (see ch. 1, pp. 17-18) or particular groups, did not share authority with him; the monarch retained control of government almost completely in his own hands.

The kings of France, even at their weakest, were more than mere feudal suzerains; they were the general sovereigns whose rights extended everywhere in the "common fatherland," especially in matters of justice. Legists drew upon the arsenal of the revived Roman law for precepts of royal absolutism: "the will of the prince has the force of law," they repeated; state courts, or *parlements* (not to be confused with the English "parliament"), increasingly replaced baronial courts or at least encouraged appeals to their own jurisdictions.

More and more, feudal and manorial obligations once met by personal service were replaced by financial payments. Especially during the Hundred Years' War, direct taxation upon the subjects of the king came to supply an increasing proportion of his revenues; the taille, a personal tax upon all nonexempt subjects, provided at least half of the amount in the treasury by the time of Charles VIII. The gabelle, or compulsory purchase of salt at exorbitant prices, was another lucrative source of revenue, and one especially obnoxious to the population. Much of this money was used to maintain royal armies apart from feudal levies, on the basis of regular pay and voluntary service.

Important as were the various agencies of his authority, the king also drew strength from a quite immaterial but always powerful tradition; he was a half-magical person, entrusted by God with the government of his realm, able to cure scrofula by the touch of his hands, embodying the majesty of a supremely exalted office which he, and only he, held within his lands. As such, the king was given a personal loyalty, reinforcing, though distinct from, the more specific obedience due him as suzerain and ruling prince.

French lawyers and foreign observers agreed in the dictum that the "king of France is more of an emperor in his own realm than any other prince in Christendom."

The State: Brakes. To employ these large powers effectively was not easy or simple, however. Numerous brakes upon the initiative of the monarchy were still built into the structure of the state and society. Above all, the courts, one of the most essential instruments of royal authority, maintained a vigorous tradition of established law. They resisted the notion of arbitrary government and substantially protected the personal and property rights of the king's subjects against the whims or greed of his officials.

Furthermore, the king did not rule over a uniform body of subjects, all equally obedient to his will. Frenchmen were distributed into a hierarchy of hereditary rank and influence, with the nobility at the top. The nobles of France looked upon participation in political affairs as a birthright and they retained a lively tradition of resort to arms in defense of their rights and honor. Even when they did not go beyond the limits of legality into active rebellion, they had often been able to frustrate the king's will by passive disobedience or merely by doing nothing to support him. No king of France was strong enough to overcome their united opposition.

Yet, great as were their powers of resistance, the nobles had not been able to build them into positive control of the state. They possessed no permanent agency to represent them as a group; they rallied round individual leaders, usually malcontents in the royal family. It was these most elevated of noblemen—the king's brothers, cousins, nephews, even his sons—who had come to represent the most immediate peril to this authority.

Cities posed a less difficult problem for the king and his ministers. The wealthy patricians who already virtually monopolized urban governments continued to exercise more extensive rights than most noblemen. They were usually responsible for the maintenance of order; municipal police were seldom in the king's own service. Thus the urban aristocracies kept the habit of rule and acquired extensive experience in local government through organized representation.

The more lowly classes in society—the peasantry in the countryside, the workingmen in the towns—seldom presented as grave difficulties to the state as their social betters. They lacked all tradition of participation in its affairs, or observed the scant traditions indifferently except when they were immediately affected; at most they followed one or another dominant party without playing any independent role. Yet they were a force of immense potentialities that could not be safely forgotten; peasant rebellions and urban riots lay not far below the habitual surface passivity of the poor. Such movements usually affected ordinary political controversies only as troubling and complicating factors; while the *bourgeoisie* and aristocrats might use them as sticks for beating opponents, there was always a danger of their striking at the whole established order.

II. The Time of Adventures

The year 1483, when Charles VIII came to the throne of France, brought both need and opportunity. The need was the country's, for peace and internal consolidation; the opportunity the government's, to meet these needs under favorable circumstances and with the ample means of the French monarchy. The country had passed through the long calamity of the Hundred Years' War (1337-1453) and emerged victorious; now, thirty years after the English withdrawal, the damage wrought by marauding soldiery, repeated sieges, and exorbitant taxation and requisitions had not yet been fully undone.

Charles VIII. What the French monarchy did with its chance depended largely on itself. The events of the first decade of the reign of Charles VIII typified in many respects the way it would go at its problems, as well as what they would often be. The very first problem involved the king's age; French kings attained their legal majority at thirteen. Though Charles was exactly two months beyond that point at his accession, he was too young to govern. His strong-minded sister, Anne of France, and her husband, Pierre de Beaujeu, an experienced administrator, took over guidance of the government. Regents at best lacked the prestige and the certain authority of kings ruling in their own person: kings' minorities were the endemic weakness of dynastic monarchies. Princess Anne's opponents concentrated their fire on several of her counselors. Her attempt to disarm her foes by dropping several of their most hated targets—a common method of calming movements arising more from personal jealousies than from widespread discontent—did not work.

Resistance to her rule by those who demanded a share in government continued so strong that Anne finally convoked the Estates of the kingdom. The clergy, the nobility, and the commoners—the three orders of the community—sent deputies to Tours in January, 1484. This was the first such meeting to which the name of Estates-General was given. A spokesman for the crown deftly identified the power of the crown with the interests of the people at a time when peace and order were necessary to both. A reduced grant of taille was voted. However, once the Estates-General disbanded, the government easily re-established its prerogative of setting the amount of taxation, the taille included.

The Incorporation of Brittany. The next crisis involved no danger to the country but only to the regency of Anne of France. In 1487 the duke of Orléans, the king's restless, jealous cousin, led a rebellion against the regent's authority; the duke of Brittany and the counts of Foix and Albret were his allies, while behind the scenes the king of England and the Holy Roman emperor supported him in this *guerre folle* (crazy war), as it was called. Its ending, however insane according to later political notions, was quite normal for the times. When superior royal forces crushed the revolt, the rebels submitted and were pardoned: the full penalty of death was not customarily employed against princes of the blood or great nobles once they laid down their arms and abandoned their objectives.

Brittany, to be sure, soon felt the weight of vengeance. The duchy, nominally under the suzerainty of France, had been virtually independent on its far western peninsula away from the centers of royal strength. When it came into the hands of a thirteen-year-old heiress, Anne of Brittany, the French claimed the duchy had reverted to its overlord. The young duchess was compelled to save her duchy by marrying Charles VIII. Brittany was linked to France only by this personal union; but Anne had to promise to marry Charles's successor if their own marriage produced no children. The wedding heralded Charles's own proclamation of political manhood. Aged twenty-two, he pushed his sister from control of the government and began to rule in his own name and person.

The Descent into Italy. The vanity of Charles VIII soon became a force of great historical consequences. When Ludovico il Moro, the duke of Milan, called him down into Italy in 1492, Charles responded with gay enthusiasm. The heritage of Naples was his by way of the Angevin dynasty, a branch of the French royal family, and he would make his claim good. He felt himself to have the makings of a hero, though his poor, malformed body, subject to epileptic fits, hardly resembled the doughty champions in the romances of chivalry on which he fed his dreams. He had no training in coping with the complex and brutal reality of politics to give him pause as he faced decision. And his counselors urged him on—there were rich lands to be conquered in fabled Italy!

The campaign began in 1494 with storybook ease, thanks to a policy of buying peace on all other frontiers by facile concessions to England, Spain, and the emperor. The swiftness of French success was matched only by French ignorance and ineptness in the swirling currents of Italian politics. A coalition was formed which drove the French out of the peninsula within a year. The disconsolate Charles, once back in France, did not quit his dream of heroism. Preparations were under way for a new descent into Italy when he died in 1498, short of his goal and not yet twenty-nine years of age.

The new king, Louis XII, had been the leader of the aristocratic opposition as duke of Orleans. As monarch, he continued in the path of the predecessor he had once envied. To keep Brittany within the kingdom, he divorced his wife, the ugly and saintly Jeanne of France, and took Anne of

Brittany for his bride—but with the provision that their second son would inherit the duchy, which would thus be loosened from the French tie.

Then Louis turned to the Italian enterprise left hanging by Charles VIII. To the Angevin claim on the kingdom of Naples he added a pretension to the duchy of Milan; he was the grandson of Valentine Visconti, and thus held a sounder title to it than Duke Ludovico. Fortune did not smile on him as quickly as it had on Charles VIII; conquest of Milan in 1499 came only after considerable difficulties. On the other hand, disaster to his enterprise did not come as swiftly either: it was not until 1512 that all his successive campaigns came to final and total failure, and then it was France itself which faced invasion on several frontiers.

Francis I. When Louis XII died on the first day of 1515, the situation on his own accession was repeated. It was an envious cousin who succeeded him, as Francis I, and like him continued to pursue his predecessor's ambitions. Externally, a hero's role fitted Francis better, for he was a stalwart figure, an excellent soldier and huntsman. The failure of the Italian campaigns of the previous reigns might have made him wary of the enterprise beyond the Alps, but the king's youthful companions eagerly urged him to renew it, for "war is the most noble exercise there is for a prince." Again the adventure began well, with the victory at Marignano (see ch. 7, p. 159).

Emperor Maximilian's death at this time took him out of the picture as a problem for France, but his grandson Charles I of Spain more than took his place. Charles pretended to the status of duke of Burgundy, though Burgundy had reverted to the French crown when Charles the Bold died leaving only a woman for heir; nonetheless he continued to use the title and he put to the fore of his ambitions the conquest of the duchy. Since Charles already held Spain, the Low Countries, and Franche-Comté, he thus connected the century-old vendetta between the French royal house and its severed branch of Burgundy with the recent clashes of the French kings with the emperor and Spain over domination of Italy.

The threat became all the greater when Maximilian died in 1519, leaving Charles as the Hapsburg candidate for the imperial throne. Francis thereupon flung a mortal challenge to Charles of Hapsburg by declaring his own candidacy. His motives were double: to weaken the chain of Hapsburg positions circling France by striking at its key link; to take down the presumption of this upstart Austrian who dared vie with the king of France for the highest station in Europe. Despite the threats, promises, and bribes of the French ambassadors, Charles was elected (see ch. 14, p. 300), but his feud with Francis now seemed beyond reconciling.

War with Hapsburg. Their rivalry soon flared into open war. After skirmishes on other frontiers, Italy became the main battleground. The Swiss now were in the French camp. In 1516 the cantons had reached an agreement by which their mercenaries entered the French service. Charles's troops drove the French from Milan, however, and then destroyed the army, Swiss and all, which Francis took back across the Alps in 1525 to recapture lost Lombardy. Francis himself, fighting for his life, was saved by a Spanish officer; from his prison tent, the king wrote his mother, Louise of Savoy, who governed the realm in his absence, that "all is lost save honor." The most illustrious prisoner taken in Europe in the sixteenth century, he was brought to Madrid to meet his captor.

Charles V could not follow up his victory on the battlefield: though triumphant, he was almost as drained of strength as his vanquished foe. Instead, the emperor relied upon his prisoner's need to extract from him a truly royal ransom—the full cession of the duchy of Burgundy and the counties of Flanders and Artois; abandonment of all French rights and claims in Italy; Francis's sons to take his place as hostages for performance of these clauses. Yet the French monarch had no need to fear for the safety of his kingdom. His captivity had not disconcerted his mother, much though she adored him: she continued to rule France in his name with courage and skill, meanwhile seeking an alliance of European rulers to effect her son's release.

In dreary close confinement, Francis lost his courage and swallowed his pride; he accepted his captor's terms (the treaty of Madrid, 1526), intending deliberately to reject them once free. Charles, to his sorrow, relied upon Francis's vaunted honor and sent him home. The French monarch refused to ratify the treaty and arranged for the provincial Estates of Burgundy to proclaim their desire to remain French.

The play of the alliance system now ran in Francis's favor, for there were many who feared the emperor's overgrown power. Francis spoiled his chance, however, by offending the Genoese admiral, Andrea Doria, whose defection to the imperial side in 1528 opened the Mediterranean seaways for the safe passage of Spanish troops and supplies to Italy and Germany. Lack of means continued to beset both Francis and Charles, till mutual exhaustion led them to make peace in 1529 at Cambrai. Francis, a widower, married Eleanor of Portugal, Charles V's sister. The Italian adventure had again miscarried.

Neither Victory nor Defeat. But it had not ended. Francis I did not abandon the dream of toothsome Lombardy, nor Charles V that of his ancestral Burgundy. Their war spread far beyond its original limit. First Francis renewed his thrust at the emperor's position in Germany, more deftly than in 1519. When a group of imperial princes and cities banded together in 1531 in the Schmalkaldic league to restrain the growth of imperial supremacy, Francis quickly gave them his support, despite their predominantly Protestant faith. Finicky Catholics condemned this dual standard of policy, but Francis did not doubt that he was the sole true champion of the church, which therefore benefited by whatever made him strong.

This kinky argument was further twisted when Francis, self-proclaimed crusader for the Christian faith, took the Ottoman sultan as an ally against the emperor. He needed the Turk to distract Charles's attention on the frontiers of Austria and Hungary in central Europe, and in the Mediterranean Sea. A year after a French ambassador set up a permanent legation at Constantinople in 1535, a commercial agreement was reached with the Turks returning to France its former trading privileges and its protectorate over Catholics in the Levant. An informal, but no less effective, collaboration between French and Turkish forces ensued; the most dramatic instance was the clearing of all Frenchmen from Toulon, a Mediterranean naval base, to permit the Turkish fleet to winter there in 1543-1544.

The fighting between the French and imperial forces continued indecisively. Each side proved able to thrust across the other's frontiers, but not to sustain the offensive. The statesmen did no better than the soldiers. Truces solved nothing. Forlorn campaigning followed intervals of tentative, half-hopeful, half-mistrustful friendship. In 1547 Francis I died, neither beaten nor victorious.

"A King of Beasts." Within the boundaries of his own state, Francis knew no such cramping of his will and power. The Emperor Maximilian envied him because he was a king of beasts: "in whatever he commands, he is obeyed instantly, as man is by beasts." He collected taxes virtually at will, without obtaining the consent or even advice of those who paid them. The Italians expressed their admiration by calling Francis "His Majesty," a title hitherto reserved for the emperor.

The government of France remained very much the personal affair of the king and his immediate entourage. The work of making policy and supervising the conduct of the business of state fell increasingly into the hand of a small group to whom the king gave large trust, the "council of affairs." In the provinces, where he could not be in person all the time, the king delegated authority to governors; when some of them began to act independently of his control, Francis reduced their functions to military command after 1542. The chief civil function, especially the maintenance of law and order and the administration of justice, was placed under the supervision of special officials, the bailiffs and seneschals. All feudal jurisdictions, even the most complete, were brought fully under the royal courts by the ordinance of Villers-Cotterêts (1539): the arm of the king's judges now extended everywhere in the kingdom. The unification of the judicial system received a further buttress by the provision of this ordinance that French—in the form of the language used by the Parlement of Paris—was to be obligatory for all other courts.

However, like so many other kings, Francis I experienced the bitterness of rebellion within his own family. His cousin Charles, the duke of Bourbon, held a group of apanages, fiefs, and other domains in the center of France, which his officials administered virtually as a separate state within the state. The duke's power was all the greater because his office of constable of France gave him command, at least in name, over the royal armies. Francis compelled the Parlement of Paris to dispossess the duke from his lands in favor of the queen-mother, who had a rival claim to them. In the hope of winning back his lands, Duke Charles joined the service of the Emperor Charles V. His plans for rebellion were detected and he was declared a traitor; no one stirred in his behalf inside France. Writers in the royal pay made much ado about his treason, but it was indicative of the strong grip of feudal ideas that most noblemen and lawyers defended the legality of his action, on the principle that his liege lord had played him false, though they called it politically unwise to rebel without powerful companions on his side.

The Concordat of Bologna. The most effective measure taken by Francis to consolidate the power of his throne came very early in the reign. In 1516, with his prestige won at Marignano still intact, Francis persuaded Pope Leo X to agree to a concordat for the future government of the church in France. The king accepted the doctrinal and sacramental sovereignty of the papacy over the Gallican (French) church; in return, he received very extensive rights of appointment to all its major benefices. This Concordat of Bologna made the Gallican church a virtual national church within the Roman communion: its fate was linked almost inextricably for the next three centuries with that of the Capetian monarchy.

Pope Leo's concession proved most timely. When the storm of the Reformation began to be felt in France in the next decades, the monarchy, though slow and hesitant in beginning repression, never wavered in its commitment to the Catholic side; like the Catholic kings of Spain, the Most Christian kings of France already held control over their national churches equal to or greater than that attained by princes who went over to Protestantism.

Rebels against Orthodoxy. Followers of Erasmus and Lefèvre d'Étaples found a center for their work at Meaux when the earnest reformer Guillaume Briçonnet became its bishop in 1518. The king protected them against the University and Parlement of Paris, the strongholds of orthodoxy; Francis still looked upon the reformers primarily as humanists, who brought his reign fame and glory. His sister Marguerite, who went to Navarre as queen in 1527 and made it a haven of reform, encouraged his policy of clemency, but Louise of Savoy urged him to root out the heretics.

The spread of new ideas to the common folk, among whom it merged with moods of social protest (a popular uprising in Lyons in 1529 combined hatred of the rich and the clergy), began to turn Francis away from his mild attitude. He lost all patience when the reformers, in a daring and dramatic action, put up placards in the great cities of the kingdom, and even on the king's own bedroom door in the castle of Amboise, denouncing the Roman Catholic sacrament of the mass. This "affair of the placards" (October 17-18, 1543) resulted in vigorous repression of the heretics. All printing was placed under the censorship of the *parlements*. Many of the reformers fled the country.

III. The Wars of Religion

Henry II, the sole surviving son of Francis I, therefore inherited in 1547 a state of great powers and few pressing problems. But difficulties did not have to come to Henry II: he managed to find and create them. He was a morose and reticent man, all the more sensitive in his pride because he lacked self-confidence; he had spent three years as a hostage in Madrid and resented the father who had bought his own freedom at the expense of his sons'. Henry's pride gave him ambitions, not the qualities needed for achieving them.

He contented himself with government by counselors. His royal independence went no further usually than to choose between two sets of advisors with alternative policies. On the one side were the Guises, a branch of the ducal family of Lorraine, who had entered the service of France and numbered among their members a great military leader and the outstanding churchman of France. Their great rivals were the constable of France, Duke Anne (then a man's name also!) de Montmorency and his nephews the Châtillons, who also included military and church leaders. The contest for influence was further complicated by the activities of a group of Italian exiles, connected with the Lyons banking circles, who were close to the queen, Catherine de' Medici (in French, de Médicis).

Henry II decided to complete what his father had begun late and ineffectually—the destruction of the Calvinists. In this policy he received the united support of the otherwise hostile Guise and Montmorency factions; although the former supported the papacy and Jesuits, and the latter the autonomy of the Gallican church, they were equally hostile to the new heresy. A special chamber of the Parlement of Paris was organized to try heresy cases from the whole country. It received the popular name of *Chambre ardente* (fiery chamber) in recognition of its readiness to burn those it found guilty. Henry himself often went to watch the heretics die: for him, as for the kings of Spain and Portugal, the ceremonial executions at the stake were an "act of faith."

The Expansion of Calvinism. The new creed nonetheless spread more rapidly than ever. The conduct of its martyrs—meekly submissive to death, but proudly expecting salvation in eternal life—won it new adherents. The ever worsening hardship of life among the common people, in a period of steady inflation and recurrent wars, made them ready for a message of hope. But not only the small people went over to Calvinism; some Catholic clergy-men were also converted, and often their flocks followed them; so did the peasantry on the estates of the many noblemen who quit the old faith.

These converted nobles brought more than followers, however. Theirs was a new spirit; they were not meek in the face of the established power, but proud and defiant: they were ready to take up the sword for their beliefs. They were also prepared to protect their positions in society when attacked by the onmoving progress of centralized monarchy and economic change. The new character of Calvinism began to be clear in 1558 when such notable personages as Antoine de Bourbon, the king of Navarre, and Francis d'Ande-lot, Montmorency's nephew, became Huguenots (as the Calvinists began to be called). King Henry was not deterred, but only stirred to great wrath. He issued the stern Edict of Écouen in 1559 against the heretics and prepared to wage war upon them.

Again War with the Hapsburgs. Against foreign enemies, Henry's armies had been less successful than they promised to be against his own subjects. When he began to reign, the contrary tugs toward war and peace were embodied in the persons of his great counselors. Montmorency, although the ranking military leader, had become a man of peace; he distrusted adven-tures abroad and urged friendship with the emperor. The Guises wanted war, especially in Italy, where they coveted the kingdom of Naples. The Italian exiles also advocated an active French policy in Italy, hoping to regain their lost positions in their native states.

The Guises gained the first victory, though the direction of French activity was Germany, not Italy. Henry II continued his father's policy of opposing Charles V in Germany with the aid of the Protestant princes. They gave him permission to occupy three imperial fortified cities—Metz, Toul, and Ver-dun—on the western bank of the Rhine; a French army seized them in 1552 and Duke Francis of Guise held off an imperial army which Charles V brought to Metz under his own command. This eastward move of the French might was almost haphazard in its origins, but the strategic value of the three cities (or "Three Bishoprics," as they were frequently called) soon became evident. French armies then crossed over into Italy, but did good only for the exiles.

Influence over Henry then swung toward Montmorency, who negotiated an armistice with the emperor (1556). The exiles won the king's ear long enough to bring renewal of war; it was fought in the North, however, under Montmorency's command, and led to his ignominious defeat and capture at

Saint-Quentin (1557) and then to the victories of the Guise duke, Francis, who stopped the weakened imperial army and recaptured Calais from the English (1558).

The Peace of Cateau-Cambrésis. The king, yearning for Montmorency, plagued by financial need—in 1558 the government had been compelled to suspend payment of its obligations—and eager to use his armies to enforce the Edict of Écouen, accepted peace in 1559 at Cateau-Cambrésis. France abandoned its positions in Italy, but retained its hold over the Three Bishoprics; the peace was sealed by the marriage of the king's daughter Elisabeth to Charles V's son Philip II, now king of Spain.

The hasty ineptness of Henry II in the negotiation of the peace shadowed his reputation, but in fact he had done little more than recognize the situation as it actually was. France was strong within its shell of defenses, but unable to strike effectively to destroy the encircling girdle of Hapsburg power. French armies had reached across high mountains and long distances to win triumphs at the beginnings of their campaigns; they had not been able to maintain themselves far from home, and were ill-equipped to occupy the countries they conquered. During the years of the Italian wars, the French forces had seen their adversaries, notably the Spaniards, improve steadily in quality. France had also lost control of the sea in the western Mediterranean; thus French communications with the peninsula remained fragile while Spain's were strong and safe. During the seventy-five years since the advent of Charles VIII, the immense potentialities of French power had again and again tempted those who wielded it to bold deeds beyond the frontiers; again and again that same might had then been needed to hold off in defensive battle the foe whom headstrong policy had helped call into action.

But Henry II was little troubled by such considerations. He played, like a noble knight of yore, at chivalry. During a joust in full armor with a Scottish officer in his service, he was felled by a fragment of a broken lance that came through the eyepiece of his helmet. A few days later, in mid-July 1559, Henry II died raving.

Crisis in the Kingdom. The three sons of Henry II who followed each other upon the throne during the thirty years after his death might have ruled adequately in calm years, but theirs was a time that tested the mettle of men, not least of their kings and governors. The fatal joust came at a critical moment for France. Age-old problems persisted and new ones rose up; all combined with each other in perplexing complication. Monetary inflation and rapid economic development unsettled the pattern of livelihood for all classes and worsened it for many; since any change seemed to promise only improvement, men became readier to overturn the existing situation.

The system of government and political relationships was not finally fixed and accepted by all. Royal officials and legists claimed absolute power for the king, but many of them continued to teach medieval theories that a king who did not serve the welfare of his subjects was a tyrant; thus the readiness of the monarch's subjects to obey him without debate or dispute on all occasions was still limited. The politically and socially influential classes had not forgotten that they once had participated in the government of the country as a right, not by the king's pleasure. So long as the hand at the helm of the state was strong, they obeyed; but once it faltered, they were ready to take advantage of the opportunity to regain what they had lost. Catherine de Médicis, the queen-mother during these three reigns, put the obstacles in the way of arbitrary royal rule in a few words: "France cannot be governed like a small state in Italy. This kingdom is composed of a great nobility and lives under laws which it is not easy to change."

The political situation was further complicated because the conflicts between Frenchmen were not confined within the boundaries of the state. The feeling that Frenchmen owed political loyalty and service only to the French state and its ruler, though it had grown far stronger over the preceding centuries, was still incomplete; it was not yet clearly treasonable to treat with foreign powers concerning the affairs of one's own country. Religious difference accentuated the readiness to go abroad for support; French Catholics and Huguenots felt closer to those of the same faith in other countries than to their compatriots of different religion. Religious controversy, by bringing into play some of men's most dearly held beliefs and convictions, made other conflicts more sharp and bitter; in this sense, these three decades between 1559 and 1589 were truly a period of "wars of religion."

Francis II. The first of Henry II's sons to reign was Francis II. Fifteen years of age when he came to the throne, he was neither boy nor man. Although past the age for a formal regency, he was nonetheless too young to govern in person; as with Charles VIII in 1484, others had to rule for him. His mother, Catherine de Médicis, shared guidance of the state with the Guises, whose niece, Mary Stuart, the queen of Scotland (see ch. 10, pp. 224, 232), was Francis's wife.

Catherine, a neglected, almost despised spouse during the lifetime of Henry II, now seized the opportunity to play a truly regal role through her son. Among European royalty the Medici of Tuscany were upstarts, still to attain grand-ducal rank; Catherine had been given to Henry as a wife for political advantage when he was a younger son of Francis I. But Catherine reduced kingship, like all political life, to the dimensions of the purely personal. She had no grasp of the historic controversies of her time, which incited multitudes to venomous hatreds, violent hostilities, and noble sacrifices. She remained committed to no party except herself and her sons; she had no cause except their power and their royal inheritance. Thus she gained in freedom of maneuver—no mean advantage in an age of extraordinarily complicated political alignments—but lost that solidity and fidelity of support that can be won by those who hold to principles shared by vast numbers of fellow men.

The Guises, on the other hand, intimately associated their private family interests with the cause of militant Catholicism. In their struggle with more supple personalities, like Catherine or, later, Henry of Navarre, this commitment was to be both their strength and their weakness. The other great clans seeking control over power were the Montmorency-Châtillon group, still Catholic in sentiment, and the Bourbons, with the Huguenot King Antoine of Navarre at their head.

The "Tumult of Amboise." The initial victory in this many-sided contest went to the Guises: Francis II reigned and the cardinal of Lorraine ruled. Their personal influence over the king gave the Guises their trumps in the struggle for leadership of the state. The prince of Condé and many of the Huguenot gentry who followed him planned a bold strike against the Guises: to seize the king while he stayed at the castle of Amboise during the winter of early 1560. Betrayal and loose organization undid the conspirators; the lesser culprits were ruthlessly hunted down and punished, while Condé kept his life but went to prison.

The decision to take up arms was a fateful one, for it loosed the demon of civil war in France. Calvin, from Geneva, had opposed resort to force; he moved slowly and reluctantly toward acceptance of insurrection as a weapon in the cause of religion. But he had not held back from their desperate step the violent nobles who now led the Huguenots, and in the next decades their political conceptions and practice came to be shaped even more by the forge of events than by the theories of their theological teacher.

The fruits of the royal triumph in the "tumult of Amboise," as the nipped rebellion was called, went not to the Guises but to the queen-mother. She sought to end the incipient clash of religious parties by winning the Calvinists back to their proper obedience to the king (and herself). The first of a long series of edicts granting the Huguenots limited toleration came from the royal pen at Amboise (March, 1560).

The Politiques. In this novel policy of permitting freedom of conscience, however restricted, to loyal subjects, Catherine received invaluable support from a skilled jurist, Michel de l'Hôpital, whom she named chancellor of the kingdom. L'Hôpital gradually formed around himself a party of moderate Catholics who came to be known as *Politiques* (political men) ; emphasizing the primacy of the interests of the French state, they favored gentler methods than the stake and the gallows for bringing the Huguenots back to the Catholic fold if possible, and were ready to accept, if they had to, some form of lasting compromise which would enable the Huguenots to maintain themselves within the state, although in a subordinate position.

Meanwhile the growing violence and disorder in the country, by interfering with the collection of taxes and imposing additional expenses upon the government, further worsened the financial difficulties inherited from the reign of Henry II. In the hope of gaining additional funds without too blunt an exercise of the royal authority, Catherine ordered the meeting of the Estates-General. The death of her tubercular son shortly after the Estates convened again threw open the problem of the control of the state and the direction of its policy.

Charles IX. The throne passed to the next younger son of Henry II, the ten-year-old Charles IX. Catherine cajoled the council of state into making her sole regent for her son, with a council of regency having a purely advisory capacity. The power of the French state, despite its many difficulties, still appeared immense to foreign observers. "This vast and powerful kingdom," wrote the Venetian ambassador, "with its great population and abundance of goods and wealth, is wholly dependent upon the supreme power of the king, who is the natural leader beloved and obeyed by the people and controlling absolute authority."

To maintain that power was not so easy as the diplomat implied. Neither the Estates-General which was in session at Orléans when the new reign began, nor another which followed it soon after at Pontoise, would grant the government the increased taxes for which the queen-regent and her spokesmen pleaded. Instead she was compelled to turn to the clergy for some immediate additional revenue, although they possessed theoretical exemption from taxation. To make them more amenable to this unpleasant burden, the government played up the threat of outright confiscation of church property; reference to the Protestant secularizations made plain the penalty for excessive parsimony.

In 1561, an assembly of the Gallican church at Poissy agreed to pay off specific debts of the state. This "ecclesiastical tenth," as the grant was called, was to run for sixteen years, by which time the government presumably would have emerged from its fiscal difficulties. Thus the church became, at first only temporarily, one of the most important taxpayers in the country. It escaped, however, the danger of coming under the heavy hand of the government tax collectors by itself undertaking to collect the agreed sum from its own members. In this way the church was enabled, with the encouragement of the government, to establish its own fiscal administration. It also established its right to meet every five years in national assemblies for the purpose of fixing the amount of taxes it would pay. After 1561 the Roman Catholic church was the only order in the French state to have and maintain a permanent formal organization.

Meeting with Words. At the very time that her government was thus returning to the Catholic church in France part of the autonomy it had lost by the Concordat of Bologna and earlier pacts, Catherine continued her efforts toward reducing the hostility between the Catholics and Calvinists and thus stiffening the fidelity of the whole population to the crown. Like many other princes who were committed not to the exclusive truth of a particular body of religious dogma but rather to the desirability of having a single religion in their states, Catherine fostered attempts to find a meeting ground on which both creeds would meet and eventually reunite. This was a hard task. At the opening session of the Estates-General at Orléans (December 13, 1560), L'Hôpital had seen the difficulty. "It is madness," he cried out, "to expect peace, quiet, and friendship between persons of different religion." But such "madness" was in fact his aspiration and the queen-regent's.

The supreme effort was made by Catherine when she compelled the Catholics to accept a conference to explore the possible area of doctrinal agreement with Calvinist theologians. The Colloquy of Poissy (1561), as it was called, proved worse than nothing. The rigidity of the theologians on both sides destroyed Catherine's hopes; when Theodore Beza entered the hall with his colleagues, the cardinal of Tournon exclaimed, "Here are the Genevan dogs!" The hostility of the two camps became more clear-cut than before. The Catholics rallied more closely to their own cause; Montmorency and the Guises sank their differences for the sake of collaboration in this impending trial of arms. The Huguenots, too, were ready for defense and attack.

Meeting with Weapons. In March 1562 began a long civil war which it has become customary to divide into eight "wars of religion." Actually it was a single conflict, but neither of the contending parties was able to rouse up sufficient strength permanently to defeat and destroy the other. Each so-called "peace" proved—all but the last—to be a temporary truce, a period of recuperation for new military exertions. In that decisive month of March, a year after Charles IX began his reign, a force of Catholic troops under the command of the duke of Guise surprised and slaughtered a group of Huguenots at services in a barn outside the small town of Vassy. The scattered fighting thereupon increased in tempo and intensity, till this first "war of religion" ended a year later with the assassination of the duke and the declaration of a peace.

Catherine endeavored to dissuade all parties from returning to arms by giving them places in the council of state; meanwhile, to strengthen loyalty to the boy king, she took Charles IX for a two-year journey around the provinces. In 1567, the fighting resumed for a year, subsided, was renewed, and then came to a longer halt in 1570 with the peace of St. Germain. This treaty granted the Huguenots the right to garrison and govern certain fortified towns, one being the port of La Rochelle on the western coast of France, the other Montauban, inland. The right of the Huguenots to bear arms in their own cause was thus implicitly recognized.

The need for peace was great. The people were already beginning to suffer from the widespread though intermittent fighting, while the efforts of the government to strengthen its finances were being imperiled by the constant drain of military expenditures. In order to bring the two religious parties closer together, Catherine de Médicis arranged the marriage of her daughter Margaret, the king's sister, to Henry of Bourbon and Navarre, a staunch Calvinist by upbringing.

St. Bartholomew's Day. The ray of hope for civil peace proved only a false dawn. Catherine's success depended on her royal son's acceptance of her leadership. But Charles IX, having reached man's age, wished to throw off his mother's domination. Unable to take charge of affairs himself, he gave himself the sense of independence by becoming dependent on another person, a man who could play the part of the father and guide he had lost when a small boy. This was the admiral of France, Gaspard de Coligny, a Châtillon who had become a devout Huguenot and the leader of his party. Coligny encouraged the young king in his self-assertion and boldly guided him toward a policy of war with Spain. At a meeting of the council, he accused the Guises to their face of having "a Spanish cross in their bellies" because they resisted such a war between Catholic kings.

Meanwhile Catherine's whole edifice of influence and command was crumbling. In August, 1572, she plotted an attempt upon Coligny's life, but an harquebus shot only wounded him. The king ordered an inquiry. Fearing detection and disgrace, Catherine revealed her guilt to the king and frightened him with the prospect of an insurrection by the Huguenot nobility assembled in Paris for the marriage of Henry of Bourbon, since June the king of Navarre.

In dismay and panic, the king permitted his mother to unleash the fervently Catholic mob in Paris, under the leadership of the duke of Guise, to slay and slaughter the Huguenots. Few of them escaped; Henry of Navarre hastily feigned conversion to the Catholic faith to save his life, but Coligny died bravely. This massacre in Paris on St. Bartholomew's Day (August 24, 1572) was followed for two months by similar blows against the Calvinists throughout the country; sometimes the local authorities undertook the task of extermination themselves, sometimes they permitted bloodthirsty mobs to do the work, but sometimes they protected the intended victims. Nonetheless the number of those killed ran to many thousands, at least three thousand in Paris alone. Catholics in other lands greeted the news with exultation. The pope viewed the massacre as divinely ordained punishment for the mass-haters, and Philip II gloated with expectation of new successes for his policy.

The "Little Genevas." But the deed of violence misfired. The Huguenots, though badly hurt, were not destroyed. Instead they turned against the monarchy itself, and the civil war resumed with greater fury than ever. The Huguenots became a well-organized revolutionary political party with its own armed forces. Once the king of Navarre was able to escape back to his own camp, the Huguenots also possessed a commander of great energy on the battlefields and even greater subtlety and competence in the more difficult craft of political leadership. Huguenot arms were successful especially in the south and southwest. There government by Huguenots displaced a very large proportion of royal authority; Calvinist noblemen ran their estates like little kingdoms, and towns under Huguenot control became little Genevas.

Meanwhile in the royal camp the massacre had brought neither confidence nor agreement. The duke of Guise took firm leadership of the Catholic cause, to the dismay of Catherine, who had not wished him in Coligny's place. The king himself, wracked by remorse over his assent to the foul act, gave way to the tuberculosis that had already killed Francis II; he died in 1574, a sorry king not yet the man he had hoped to be.

Henry III. The new reign brought the downfall of her ambitions to Catherine, because Henry III, her third son on the throne of France, at once threw off her domination. For France it was a period of far greater grief and pain, because the civil wars raged on, worsened by the slackening of supreme authority in the state. France was slipping into a state of dispersed and uncertain political power reminiscent of the earliest years of the Capetian monarchy. The deep centuries-old love and respect for the monarch and the monarchy faded as Catholic and Calvinist found themselves forced to work variously without the king or against him; the magic aura around the crown of France dissipated, and men began to examine its nature and its right to existence.

In works such as the *Vindiciae contra tyrannos* (*Defense against Tyrants*, 1579), the Huguenots emphasized that kings ought to rule for the sake of their peoples; if they failed in this duty, especially by oppressing the true church, they became tyrants. To this traditional doctrine of political thought, they added an important idea: that tyrants could be legitimately killed by their subjects, or even an individual. This belief was not wholly novel, though it had been minimized by earlier political writers; and a similar doctrine was enunciated at about the same time by Jesuit theorists, especially in Spain. In France, however, Catholic writers for the moment continued to be royalist, in contrast to the tendency of the Huguenots to stress ultimate popular sovereignty in the persons of the lesser magistrates or intermediate agencies of government.

Henry III was not a man to save a threatened crown either by the splendor of his personality or by the vigor of his policies. Despite his quarrel with his mother, he was much like her in character and policy. His personal life was marked by effeminate vices that shocked even an age used to loose living; yet he was fond of ceremonial religion. He wanted to be free of masters, but managed to be always dependent on one or another camp. His reign began with a war against the Huguenots; the fighting ended ignominiously two years later with further concessions to them. The policy of St. Bartholomew's Day was reversed.

The Catholic "League." The Catholics reacted against royal authority with a new weapon. These were conspiratorial confraternities, known as "Leagues," first established in 1568 and then re-formed in 1578 to defend the Catholic cause by arms against the Protestant threat; they operated without government supervision or participation, duplicating on the Catholic side the formation of a revolutionary party by the Huguenots. Provincial leagues of these armed confraternities merged into a single League under the direction of the duke of Guise, who began to support theories of provincial autonomy while maintaining a face of dynastic loyalty. More significantly, however, he also required the adherents of the League to give an oath of loyalty to himself. The disintegration of the French state was gathering speed, while Philip II of Spain looked on happily, ready to use the League for his own ulterior purpose of destroying or subordinating the monarchy of France.

At wit's end, Henry III took increasingly desperate and contradictory measures to reassert his vanishing leadership. First he declared himself the head of the Catholic League. It ceased to be revolutionary in law but not in fact; its obedience to the king was dependent upon his acceptance of *its* program and the domination of *its* real leader, the duke of Guise. Furthermore, such use of a conspiratorial organization only further weakened the already imperiled supremacy of the regular government and its administrative machinery.

The king, to further his new policy, called the Estates-General into session for aid in suppressing the Huguenots. This instrument too proved useless, though the government nominally had a majority of supporters in each of its three orders. The Politiques, once the most royalist of parties, refused to follow the king in his alliance with the League. The Estates voted in favor of religious unity, but refused to approve either war for that purpose or the new taxes necessary to wage it; the best the government could do was to prevent any movement for limitation of the royal absolutism. But its monopoly of power was becoming more and more of a fiction; the king talked but the duke of Guise and the king of Navarre acted.

The fiscal crisis grew steadily worse; current revenues declined; loans at high interest rates and currency manipulation for the sake of immediate profits were temporary solutions that created grave dangers for the future.

The constant recurrence of the wars of religion made reform of the finances of the state a hopeless dream. The economic life of the country began to suffer severely from the disorder created by the depredations of the armies and their insatiable demands for money and supplies.

The Crisis of Succession. The age-old problem of dynastic monarchy— the succession to the crown in the event of failure of the clear line of royal descent—began to loom up during the mid-1580's. It muddled and magnified the existing crisis. Disquiet had begun when no son was born to the king, and increased in 1584 after the death of the duke of Anjou (formerly duke of Alençon), the youngest son of Catherine de Médicis, who might have replaced his brother on the throne. According to the so-called Salic law, which prescribed inheritance of the crown in the most direct line of male descent, the natural heir was Henry of Navarre, as head of the Bourbon branch of the royal family.

Salic law or not, the Catholic majority of France did not want this Calvinist as their king; to bar him, they invented a new "fundamental law" of the kingdom, to the effect that the king of France had to be a Roman Catholic. The throne could be given, on Henry III's demise, to the elderly Cardinal Charles of Bourbon, the uncle of Henry of Navarre; but he was so aged that the problem of succession would recur within a short time. Thus other candidacies began to appear for that tempting occasion. The Guises claimed descent from Charlemagne to demonstrate a claim antedating all Capetian lines. Philip II of Spain put forward the candidacy of his daughter Isabella; but she seemed barred because her claim came through her mother, Elisabeth of Valois; furthermore, fear of her subservience to her father troubled many Catholics.

The debate which ensued soon involved the whole question of the nature of the monarchical state, though the positions of the parties were reversed: the Huguenots now emphasized dynastic right in the hope of putting their leader on the French throne, while the extreme Catholics began to play their opponents' recent tune of popular sovereignty.

"War of the Three Henrys." The king commanded little but his immediate bodyguard. The southern part of France was under Huguenot sway, and much of the north and east obeyed the duke of Guise and his League. Lacking any independent support, Henry III swung to and fro between his great rivals in the last phase of the "wars of religion," called "the war of the three Henrys" because the kings of France and of Navarre and the duke of Guise all shared the same first name. The king first remained with Guise, but lost the last shreds of his own personal authority and prestige to his nominal servant, particularly after Paris rose against the king in defense of the duke (May, 1588). It was the first revolutionary riot in Paris in almost two centuries; under the sponsorship of preaching monks, extreme democratic doctrines were put forward; but the leadership of the movement soon passed to the Guises.

Henry III fled his capital. When he called the Estates-General to meet at Blois later in the year, he discovered that the League commanded a majority of its members; the assembly made ready to assert its control over the royal authority. To defend himself in these straits, Henry III turned to murder. At his command, the duke of Guise and his brother the cardinal of Guise were assassinated, while the cardinal of Bourbon was imprisoned. The king turned to Henry of Navarre; together they undertook a siege of Paris which put itself under the leadership of the surviving Guise brothers, the dukes of Aumale and Mayenne.

Henry of Navarre tried to soften the Calvinist fervor of his own followers and urged a policy of toleration and conciliation as a basis of continued collaboration with Henry III. On the other hand, the king's dependence upon the Bourbon claimant to the succession intensified the hatred of the League for him. The clamor against the tyrant besieging Paris inspired a monk, Jacques Clément, to remove him; he made his way to the king's camp and stabbed him (August 2, 1589). Henry III was the first king of France to meet death at a subject's hand.

9

France under the Early Bourbons

1589 - 1661

BY LAW AND CUSTOM, at the instant a French king died, his successor began to reign. *"Le roi est mort! Vive le roi!"* ("The king is dead! Long live the king!") ran the traditional cry of mingled mourning and rejoicing as one reign ended and another began. Thus an interregnum, always a breeding time of troubles, could not exist.

I. King Henry IV

But *who* was the king? The duke of Mayenne, as lieutenant-general of the realm for the Catholic League, proclaimed the cardinal of Bourbon as "Charles X." But this phantom king was his enemies' prisoner, and Mayenne continued to rule in his name most of the northern half of the country, as well as most of the important cities, except Bordeaux and Tours.

The Declaration of Saint-Cloud. Some Catholic royalists were in a more difficult position. They would not abandon the Salic law, but neither would they accept Henry of Bourbon and Navarre, whom it designated as the new monarch, because he remained a heretic. Not even Henry III's death-bed designation of the king of Navarre as his successor shattered their determination. "Better a thousand deaths!" they muttered ominously in the royal camp at Saint-Cloud.

The Huguenot chieftain bent before the rising wind. He negotiated with the royalist Catholic leaders a formal declaration promising not only to maintain the full rights and privileges of the Catholic religion, but also to take instruction himself in its doctrines, the prelude to conversion. Only then, two days after his reign had begun, did they shout *"Vive le roi!"* and proclaim him as Henry IV.

With the royal armies accepting his command, Henry IV began the conquest of his kingdom. Only the southwest, the traditional Huguenot stronghold, was firmly his; in the southeast, his fellow-Calvinist Lesdiguières, held the outpost province of Dauphiné, while a Catholic Politique, Montmorency-Damville, gave him the support of Provence, the key to the south. In the western and central provinces, royalist and League forces struggled for domination. Henry's first objectives, however, were to regain Normandy and Picardy and then to recapture Paris. Several times he defeated Mayenne, but Spanish troops rushed from the Low Countries to the Guise leader's rescue and thwarted Henry's sieges of Rouen and Paris. By 1592, it was clear that neither side could crush the other by military means.

Abjuration: the "Perilous Leap." In both camps, the attempt was then made to achieve a political solution of the stalemate. Mayenne called a meeting of the Estates-General in Paris (January, 1593). A majority favored election of a king in place of "Charles X," who had died, but could not settle upon a candidate agreeable to themselves and to Philip II of Spain, whose troops provided them with their best military forces.

One group in the League, troubled particularly by outbursts of mob violence in Paris, began to seek a settlement with the royalists upon the basis of the conversion of Henry IV. Although, by the declaration of Saint-Cloud, he had indicated his willingness to consider becoming a Catholic, Henry had not wished to bemean himself by unseemly haste; he wished, too, to strengthen his hand by triumphs on the battlefield. Now he concluded that he could not safely delay any longer. He had to make the "perilous leap," as he called it. In the basilica of Saint-Denis outside Paris, the archbishop of Bourges accepted his abjuration and received him back into the Roman communion. Early in 1594, Henry IV was formally consecrated at Chartres; he was anointed with sacred oil and even swore the traditional oath to extirpate heresy in his kingdom.

The "leap" succeeded. In Paris, the public abjuration of the king— throngs from the capital had defied a ban by the duke of Mayenne to attend the ceremony—and the continuing hardships resulting from the siege combined to produce an uprising against the League. Henry IV was welcomed into his capital, while Spanish troops garrisoned there were permitted to withdraw to the Low Countries. The cause-and-effect relationship between his conversion and the action of Paris was so patent that wits soon ascribed to Henry the cynical remark, *"Paris vaut bien une messe"* (Paris is well worth a mass). In the provinces, other cities, notably Lyons, also threw off the authority of the League and accepted Henry for king.

The End of the League. Mayenne continued to hold out in Burgundy, and other League leaders in Brittany, Picardy, and the south. They maintained that only the pope, not an archbishop, could absolve Henry from his sin and receive him back into the church. This event they did not expect to happen, for Pope Clement VIII seemed as adamant against Henry as his predecessors had been. However, the same pressure to serve Spanish interests which Mayenne knew and resented was also felt and feared by Clement, who began to look to the king of France as a possible counterweight. In 1595, therefore, the pope accepted terms negotiated with Henry's ambassadors at Rome. The latter admitted the inefficacy of the archiepiscopal absolution, though not of the royal authority since 1589; in turn, Clement absolved the errant king.

The Leaguers soon acknowledged Henry IV, but haggled with him over terms for accepting his authority. His minister in charge of finances protested indignantly against their demands—huge outright grants of money, lucrative appointments for themselves, their relatives, and their henchmen, hereditary governorships in the provinces. Henry observed coolly that the cost of subjecting them by arms would be ten times larger. He refused them only outright possession of the governorships, though granting the posts for their own lifetimes. "They did not return my kingdom to me," he commented sardonically, "they sold it back." After more than three decades, the civil wars in France had come to an end.

The Edict of Nantes. All the while, the Huguenots watched, indignant and troubled. As early as 1591, Henry issued an edict at Mantes to confirm their rights as laid down in enactments by his predecessors: they could not be prosecuted for their beliefs and could practice their own rites wherever they did so at the time, including at least one town in every district (*bailliage*) and the houses of all noblemen of a certain rank; provisions were also made for their equal treatment in the courts and in appointment to offices. After his consecration in 1594, Henry assured the Huguenots that when he swore to destroy heretics, he was not thinking of his former comrades-in-faith. They wanted more solid guarantees: the right to practice their religion everywhere, equality with Catholics in the courts, and payment by the king of their garrisons in their "places of safety." To grant such terms would provoke the just-reconciled Leaguers into new rebellion; to refuse would mean driving the Huguenots to the same act of desperation.

Instead, Henry IV entered into an elaborate discussion with the Protestants, resulting in the famous Edict of Nantes (April 13, 1598). It improved the Edict of Mantes by increasing the number of Huguenot places of safety from ten to one hundred, opening all government offices to them, and establishing chambers of mixed membership to try cases involving them. The new law ran without time limit; yet a clear, though faint, hint of possible eventual abandonment might be heard in the explanation that it had been adopted because "it has not *as yet* pleased God to allow France to have single form of religion."

The manner of the edict's making demonstrated how far Henry had moved: it was not the gift of an inwardly Huguenot king to reward his friends, but a negotiated treaty of peace between a Catholic monarch and a group of his subjects, designed to end a new civil war before it began. Moreover, it was a compromise peace, satisfying neither Catholics nor Huguenots. For the former, the concessions to the heretics implied Henry's insincerity in his conversion. For the latter, their legal inferiority was galling; and dependence upon the good-will of future monarchs, who would be born and educated as Roman Catholics, was filled with easily envisioned perils. Left to themselves, the opposing parties were almost certain to come to blows in an effort to change the terms of the settlement, or destroy it altogether. If it endured, it would take the constant efforts and will of the reigning kings.

Triumph at Vervins. France needed foreign as well as domestic peace before she could effectively begin her work of recovery. Henry IV's chief foe was the implacable Philip II, who hated him as a heretic and a rival for the throne of France. Until 1595-1596, Henry had to concentrate his efforts on conquering the rebels within France; during that period, however, he did not face the main forces of Spain, but only "auxiliary" troops sent by Philip to serve in the armies of the League. In 1595, Henry decided that he was strong enough to take the initiative of declaring war himself. The forces brought together for defeating the rebels must be used against the foreign threat.

At the same time, Henry increased diplomatic pressure upon England and the Dutch Republic for a formal alliance against Spain. Queen Elizabeth in England met with bland cunning his attempt to guide her into renewal of strong measures of war against Spain. She did enter into the proffered alliance but displayed more interest in getting Spanish-held Calais into her own hands than into Henry's. The Dutch, too, though they joined the alliance, distracted relatively few troops from the French front; their captain-general, Prince Maurice, preferred to besiege enemy cities rather than risk his forces in the open against the Spanish infantry.

The triple alliance nonetheless served the French purposes, for Philip II, faced with the exhaustion of Spain's resources for waging war, finally abandoned his refusal to acknowledge Henry IV or make peace with him. In

1598, at Vervins, his negotiators concluded a treaty with France. Its formal terms provided little change from the treaty of Cateau-Cambrésis, made four decades earlier. For Henry IV, a stand-off peace was victory: he had preserved his own country from conquest and dismemberment, and had maintained his own rule over it.

The Tasks of Peace. Now that peace had come, its tasks fell partly to the government and partly to the people. The success of each depended upon that of the other. The nation could rebuild from the damage of war only if protected against its recurrence; the state needed the resources to be drawn from a prosperous people to sustain itself and to defend them.

At the moment, the administrative disorganization in government resulting from the long period of civil war confronted the king and his ministers with their most pressing problems. In the border provinces, where troops were normally stationed, governors possessed general military powers of command; but, as one commentator remarked, "in times of civil strife, every province is on the frontier." Henry dared not strip them of their privileges all at once, lest he goad them into rebellion; they had too much real power to be treated roughly. Instead, in his characteristic manner, he conciliated them as he disciplined them. He fed their avarice with grants of funds he could ill afford, as he had done with the leaders of the League. He avoided, whenever possible, giving orders they were likely to disobey; but when he commanded, they had to comply. "I want to be obeyed" was a phrase that recurred constantly in his letters. Within the area he considered proper for the king's authority, he would brook no power of decision other than his own; but he did not seek to extend the range of his authority.

Sully. The work of reconstruction and the maintenance of adequate military forces depended upon the expenditure of large funds and the presence of a reserve in the coffers of state. But the royal treasury was empty. To replenish it, Henry IV depended upon his old comrade-in-arms, Maximilien de Béthune, baron de Rosny, whom he made superintendent of finances. Rosny (from 1606 duke of Sully) had proved his mettle as an administrator by the efficient handling of his regiment during the civil wars. Now the whole kingdom became his field of operations. Sully did not attempt to modify the system of taxation and expenditure, but concentrated his attention on reducing waste, preventing fraud, and assuring to the central treasury the full sum due it after local expenses had been met. He reduced the tax burden on the peasantry by lowering the taille more than a quarter between 1597 and 1609; but the gabelle, or salt tax, remained in full force.

In order to tap the wealth of townsmen, who escaped most direct taxes, Sully accepted the practice of creating new government offices for sale and also their conversion into the virtually absolute property of their holders. The method involved a tax known as the *paulette,* which enabled an office-

HENRY IV.   Engraving by Pierre Firens, 1610.

A print made shortly after the assassination of Henry IV on May 14, 1610. He is characterized in the lower caption as:

> A great king and captain, great too in his mercy.
> He ruled his people in peace, enlarged France
> More than any other king, subjected rebels
> To his valor, and kept his oath faithfully.

(Achenbach Foundation)

holder to transmit his post to his heirs upon payment of an annual tax of one-sixteenth of its value. The salary received seldom adequately compensated for these costs of acquiring and keeping office, but indirect benefits were very great. These included exemption from the taille and often from other taxes, and in most of the higher offices the grant of noble title. Under Henry IV's

191

firm hand, government servants continued to do the king's bidding, but thoughtful observers foresaw much danger when a less forceful monarch sat upon the throne or when government policy came into conflict with the interests of servants whom it could not dismiss except with great difficulty.

Sully also worked to improve the economic conditions of the country, notably agriculture (and its accompaniment, pasturage) which he considered to be the basic source of national wealth. Royal decrees forbade the seizure of farm equipment and livestock for payment of debts, aided the repurchase of common lands and the re-establishment of customary rights of usage, and permitted the transport and export of grain during good crop years. Additional land was brought into cultivation by means of marsh-drainage operations, although frequently the local population, more interested in the fishing than the tillage, resisted the creation of these "little Flanders."

Sully also worked to improve internal communications. As *grand voyer* (grand master of the roads), he directed the rebuilding of bridges and the filling in, and sometimes the paving, of roads neglected during the civil wars. The long-term advantages of these improvements meant little to the local peasantry, who were compelled to labor on repairing the highways (the royal *corvée*). Waterways too received Sully's attention; river channels were cleared and canals dug.

Laffemas. Industrial activity also received the attention of the government. Henry IV's adviser on questions of manufactures and trade was his personal tailor, Barthélemy de Laffemas, who stood firmly on the principle that the country should export as much as possible and import as little as it could, thereby increasing its monetary wealth. The most important project designed to attain this goal was the introduction of silk-growing to meet the large French demand for this cloth. Though the government supported the cultivation of mulberry trees and the care of silkworms, the experiment failed after a decade, apparently because the climate was too cold; the silk manufacturers of Lyons and Tours alone remained active.

Economic prosperity came back widely and steadily, though not equally to all or everywhere in the country. It arose primarily from the pent-up initiative of the people, released by the return of peace, rather than from the activity of the government. The re-establishment of agriculture underlay all other gains. Deserted villages and unplowed fields—the by-products of the movement and quartering of troops—saw people returning and the crops coming up again. The beneficial effects soon made themselves felt in the towns, where trade quickly improved. Next commerce between France and other nations increased, with the Dutch—allies of the French—carrying the cargoes. The fundamental vitality of the French people had reasserted itself. Nonetheless, rebellions and riots of peasantry against increased taxation and other burdens like the *corvée* for Sully's roads continued to sputter throughout the reign. Yet, if peace continued, the general pattern of increased productivity and welfare could be expected to continue too. The dependence of the people upon the policies of their government remained unchanged.

End of the Reign. The absence of an heir to the throne created one peril to the state that Henry IV could not solve by general policy. He had been separated from Queen Marguerite of Valois for more than a decade; the pope was willing to grant an annulment, and she would not resist it provided her hated rival, the king's mistress Gabrielle d'Estrées, did not take her place on the throne. In 1599 Gabrielle died, the annulment was duly granted, and the next year Henry married Marie de Médicis, of the Florentine grand-ducal family, who at once began to bring sons into the world. Queen Marie intensified Henry's turn toward Catholicism, to which he became strongly devoted. Even though the Jesuits had been expelled from France after an attack upon Henry's life by one of their students, Jean Chastel, in 1594, he welcomed the order back within a decade. He took a Jesuit, Father Coton, for court preacher and then as his private confessor, a post of powerful and scarcely hidden influence. The king's Huguenot friends found him less attentive to their appeals: "He has Cotton (*du Coton*) in his ears," they jested sadly.

Meanwhile Henry gradually turned from a tentative to a bolder foreign policy. The Hapsburg power, in both its German and Spanish branches, continued to be his principal target. In the Low Countries, he aided the Dutch to continue their resistance to Spanish reconquest, though their truce in 1609 was not to his liking. In Italy, he reconciled the papacy and Venice when they entered into a quarrel, thus disputing Spain's leadership in affairs of the peninsula after a half-century of French weakness. Events in Germany pushed to the forefront late in the decade with the controversy over the succession in Cleves-Jülich. To prevent the emperor from seizing these valuable lands, he prepared to send troops to support the Protestant claimants. Catholic opinion in France was much perturbed by Henry's renewed policy of alliance with Protestant powers against Catholic princes. Their protests did not avail, however. The troops were ready to march when, on May 14, 1610, a former Leaguer, Ravaillac, stabbed the king to death on a Paris street.

II. Louis XIII

The new king, Louis XIII, was not yet nine years of age. In accordance with custom, as well as the intention of Henry IV, Marie de Médicis, his mother, assumed the regency.

The Regency of Marie de Médicis. Mistrustful of rivals for authority among the great princes of the blood, she sought and received confirmation of her office from the Parlement of Paris. In so doing, however, she broke with the policy of Henry IV, who had shorn the Parlement of its prerogative of rejecting as well as registering royal edicts; thus she revived the political role which it had lost. Although a devout Catholic who disliked aiding Protestants in Germany, Marie hesitated to change Henry's plans there. The French army marched, captured Jülich, and permitted the Protestant claimants to establish themselves.

The victory gave her confidence, and she veered around to the very opposite policy—friendship with Spain. She made an alliance with Philip III and opened negotiations with him for a double marriage between their children; these culminated in 1615 with the wedding of Louis XIII and the Spanish *infanta*, Anne of Austria, as well as that of Louis's sister Elisabeth and the *infante* Philip, the later Philip IV. The Spanish ambassador, along with the papal nuncio, entered the circle of the queen mother's most trusted advisers. That her strongly Catholic bent was ultramontane, not Gallican, became clear when her officials drove Edmond Richer, *syndic* (provost) of the Sorbonne, from his post for publishing a book denying complete papal authority over the Catholic church in France.

Though regent, the queen-mother did not undertake the detailed conduct of the day-by-day affairs of state, but chose, as was to be expected, a chief minister to act on her behalf. She did not name one of the several French officials experienced in the conduct of high government business, or any of the great nobles who claimed by birthright a place of leadership in the state. Instead she turned to a Florentine of uncertain talents and great ambitions, Concino Concini by name. Concini's principal qualification was his marriage to Leonora Galigaï, whose mother had been Marie's wet nurse. The queen-regent named him marshal of France in 1613, assisted him to purchase the French marquisate of Ancre, and permitted him to lord it over the haughty French aristocrats. Concini, his wife, and their benefactor became the object of bitter hatred. The great nobles reasserted their own claims and rose in rebellion. The pattern of the reign had been set.

The civil war ended quickly when the queen-mother promised them substantial pensions (annual grants from the treasury). There was no money to pay them, however: the cupboard was bare, for Concini had already been in it. The Estates-General, convoked in 1614 at the demand of the rebellious princes, did not help; the various orders were more concerned to tussle with each other than to provide new revenues to the crown. But Marie used the opportunity to strike at the great nobles; they rebelled again, and again she had to make concessions to buy their peace.

"King at Last!" The queen-mother had reckoned without her son, from whom all her power derived. At thirteen, Louis XIII had been declared of age, but though her regency was legally over, Marie continued to rule as before. She gave little attention or affection to the youthful monarch. Concini ran the government and snubbed his royal master for three more years, until the envious and resentful king summoned up the courage, in 1617, to command his murder. When the captain of his bodyguard had done the deed, the sixteen-year-old exulted, "I am king at last!"

He missed the underlying paradox of his action. The French monarchy rested upon a long tradition of law, embodied in the rule that subjects acted against each other, and the king against a subject, only by means of the royal courts, not according to the law of the jungle. The assassination of the overmighty Concini was not ultimately different in kind from the murder of King Henry when a subject had taken upon himself the right of judgment. The example of a *coup d'État* (stroke of state), as a violent and irregular deed of this kind was called, was only too contagious.

In any case, Louis XIII was truly king only to the extent that his mother ceased to function as regent; the lad, lacking all training for business of state, uncertain of himself and given to outbursts of temper and impulsive action, could not personally conduct the government. Another "first minister" was needed to take Concini's place. The king's choice fell upon a young nobleman, Albert de Luynes, who as his falconer had befriended him in his loneliness.

The Administration of Luynes. The task of governing France proved, however, to be far beyond Luynes's abilities. A period of confused struggles developed, marked notably by rebellions of the queen-mother, bitter hateful "wars of mother and son," as one of them was called. Once a peace had been patched up between them, Luynes, with the support of the young king, who was also a fervent Catholic, drove the Huguenots to rebellion; at the same time he abandoned France's Protestant allies in Germany. Promoted to constable of France, Luynes failed to put down the Huguenots and died while besieging Montauban, even while the king, disappointed, was planning his dismissal. Louis could do no better than recall his mother to power, and then the surviving ministers of his father, the *"Barbons"* (greybeards), with the exception of Sully, the Protestant. But they had lost the secret of success; French foreign policy remained passive and ineffectual.

Internal Developments. Fortunately, these civil wars had been brief and had caused little damage. As long as they did not expand into the kind of savage, widespread hostilities which had filled the final decades of the previous century, the slow silent processes of national development could go on uninterrupted.

The two great religious movements entered new phases. The Catholic Reformation deepened and widened, and for the first time took strong hold in France. Increasing numbers of the churchmen and lay persons turned to the work of recapturing souls lost to the Protestant heresy, of educating born

Catholics in their own faith, and of giving charity to the needy and the helpless. So began another age of French saints, among them the gentle man of the people, Vincent de Paul, as well as the nobleman, Francis de Sales.

Protestant fervor turned from the work of conversion to the organization of the Huguenot community within French society. The French Calvinists were ready and able, if permitted, to live as a tight-knit minority and also to serve the French state.

The country remained prosperous. The very absence of a strong foreign policy saved it from involvement in major war and hence from heavy taxation. Still, there might remain only a short time for France to go about her domestic business, neglectful of events in other lands. For half a decade, Germany had been gripped by the ever-widening struggle between Protestant and Catholic. The first successes in the Thirty Years' War had gone to the Hapsburg emperor, supported by his Spanish cousin. Total Catholic victory would tighten again the Hapsburg ring encircling France and bring closer the danger of renewed assault. France might not seek war, but war could find her.

III. Richelieu

By 1624 almost all the triumphs of Henry IV had been dissipated. The succession of governments given to France by Marie de Médicis and then by Louis XIII had lost control of events, domestic and foreign. At their worst they had been weak of nerve and mind, capitulating to the first difficulties and contriving policies of self-defeating inconsistency; at their best, they had possessed energy, but without the necessary boldness and grandness of general policy or subtlety and suppleness in the manipulation of men. The king sensed the need, but the man he named seemed a surprising choice.

A Man of Energy. Cardinal Armand Jean du Plessis de Richelieu, named to the council in April, 1624, had been the queen-mother's follower. However, when she had slipped into the morass of rebellion against her king and son, it was Richelieu who returned from exile in Avignon to persuade her to make peace with him. The cardinal did not at once receive complete authority to direct the government nor was his leadership over the other members of the council clear; but he set to the work of recovery with extraordinary vigor, ready not only to act but also to learn from events.

The first two years of his administration were filled with renewed activity, especially in foreign affairs. To halt the progress of Spain was already his central goal; pamphleteers in his service advertised this as the cause of "good Frenchmen," and impugned the loyalty of those who resisted it for the sake of religion. His first steps were to renew the alliance with

CARDINAL RICHELIEU. Line engraving by Michel Lasne and Isaac Briot, 1633.

This portrait of the great Cardinal-Minister reveals his intensity of spirit and purpose. The caption identifies him as "Cardinal, Duke and Peer of France, Grand Master, Chief and Superintendent of Shipping, Governor and Lieutenant General for the King in the land of Brittany." *(Achenbach Foundation)*

the Dutch Republic and to arrange the betrothal of Henriette Marie, the French king's sister, to the heir to the English throne, the prince of Wales, Charles Stuart. These initial successes of Richelieu's policy were almost destroyed at their inception. The Huguenots revolted and Richelieu was compelled to strain the sympathies of his English and Dutch allies by calling on them for naval assistance to put down their fellow-Protestants. Even worse,

197

the Catholic party in France aroused great anger in England by persuading Henriette Marie, who had married the newly enthroned Charles I in 1625, to demand the grant of free worship to English Catholics.

Richelieu had learned one lesson, painfully but surely. Before he could act with assurance and effectiveness abroad, he would have to be in control of the situation at home. His first task was to consolidate the authority and strengthen the functioning of the French state. The sovereignty of the monarchy, however complete in the theory of many legists, was crippled in fact by the readiness and ability of many Frenchmen to take up arms against the state, as well as against each other, in defense of their principles, their rights, and their privileges. Richelieu faced three different kinds of rebellion: the religious risings of the Huguenots; the political and personal insurgencies of the great nobility; and the social-economic outbursts of peasants desperately resisting the enforcement of tax collection beyond their capacities.

Rebellion of the Huguenots. Richelieu's policy toward the Huguenots was the most difficult to evolve and conduct. Inconsistency plagued any useful plan of conduct with regard to this large and restive minority. Outright concession to their demands was impossible: it meant not only permitting them to maintain a state within a state, pursuing its own goals often in opposition to those of the monarchy; it also meant inciting the vehement resistance of the Catholic majority of the nation, which had never been wholly reconciled to the policy of the Edict of Nantes.

Total suppression of the Huguenots was no better. In the first place, it would deeply, perhaps irreconcilably, offend the Protestant powers who were the principal allies of France in the inevitable coming struggle with the Hapsburgs. Furthermore, Richelieu did not believe in the use of the sword to win back souls. He did not doubt that Calvinism was a heresy destructive of the individual soul and dangerous to the state, but he was confident in the efficacy of a persistent and intelligent campaign of conversion by argument, especially when backed by substantial rewards of money and office to converts. Toleration, to be sure, was not a God-given right of the Huguenots, but a grant of the state. When they took up arms to make good their claims, they must be crushed, not as heretics but as rebels; and when they were defeated, their political not their religious privileges must be shorn from them.

The peace with the Huguenots in the spring of 1626 had been no more than a mistrustful armistice. In the autumn of the following year, the Huguenots rose again in rebellion in southern and western France under the leadership of Duke Henry of Rohan and the militant Protestants of La Rochelle. Catholic and Protestant Frenchmen once more warred upon each other and called upon foreign powers of their own faith for assistance. Spain served the French government as a naval ally, while the English sent an expeditionary force under the duke of Buckingham to aid La Rochelle.

The Huguenots Subdued. Richelieu took personal command of military operations designed to reduce the Huguenot stronghold by siege. Twenty-five thousand troops easily hemmed it in by land; but the small royal naval force, with a token reinforcement of Spanish ships, proved inadequate for breaking the port's communications with the sea. Not until a dike and breakwater were constructed between the port and the open sea, and Buckingham had been driven off, could Richelieu break the defenders' will to resist; even then, a full year of siege passed before they capitulated.

Even in this moment of victory Richelieu continued his fundamental policy toward the Huguenots. He deprived the town of its self-government and fortresses and re-established Catholic worship within its walls, but did not subject the Protestant inhabitants to further persecution. Meanwhile, troops under the personal command of Louis XIII brought the remaining rebels to heel. Similarly moderate terms were accorded them; the Edict of Nantes remained intact except for abolition of the "places of safety," the autonomous Huguenot fortresses on which their status as a "state within the state" depended. It was significant that the settlement finally ending this rebellion was not called a treaty, as before, but "the grace of Alais" (June 1629), the free gift of the king. Even the duke of Rohan, the archrebel, was permitted to emigrate abroad.

Aristocratic Insubordination. The nobility, apart from the small segment involved in the Huguenot struggles, presented a different kind of problem to Richelieu. He did not contest their position as the dominant political, economic, and social class in the country; he felt himself to be wholly one of them. But he demanded that they accept subordination to the king's authority—which he wielded.

The aristocracy's readiness to rebel was closely associated with its habits of easy violence. For most French noblemen, a ready challenge and an undaunted defiance were points of honor, so that dueling had become a kind of perpetual warfare among them. To curb this fury of self-destruction, Richelieu persuaded the king to renew in 1626 the earlier edicts against duels, and then to enforce them sternly, as had never been done. He even insisted on the execution of several duelists guilty of repeated offenses. Another edict required demolition of fortified castles at a distance from the frontier; since most of these were badly dilapidated, it was a gesture of symbolic rather than practical importance, but one which struck at a beloved prerogative of the nobility. Such measures were means to chasten and discipline the aristocracy of France, and harness them to the king's service.

Battle for the King. Far more important for Richelieu in maintaining his ascendancy was the battle of influence with his fellow-noblemen over the mind and feelings of the king. The cardinal knew that he was utterly and absolutely dependent upon Louis XIII; one word of command from the monarch and he would be cast out of office; another word, and he would be slaughtered by the nobility as the harshest taskmaster they had ever known. For his own class hated and feared him, both for his relentless chastisement of its members and for his depriving them of their accustomed and valued rights of influencing royal policy. Richelieu had to battle for the king's ear against a horde of courtiers, including many leading churchmen offended by the cardinal's courting of foreign Protestant states.

The lead in the struggle against Richelieu was taken by the king's own brother and, in the absence of a son, his heir, Duke Gaston of Orléans. Twice in the eventful year 1626 he fomented rebellion with the cardinal-minister as a principal target, and twice, when exposed, he came cringing back to gain pardon by betraying his fellow-plotters, who bent their necks to the executioner's great sword. Richelieu had to prove to the king that his royal authority, the defense and aggrandizement of his state, and the satisfaction of his self-esteem, all depended upon the political skills and steely determination which the cardinal, alone in France, possessed.

As soon as war against the Huguenots had been brought to a victorious end, the opposition to Richelieu broke into the open. For three years his foes stormed at his position in the king's confidence. The first initiative was taken by the party of the "devout" Catholics, as they were called: the queen-mother, gripped by hatred for the "traitor" Richelieu, was their leader, and their policymaker was the chancellor, Michel de Marillac, Richelieu's chief rival. In line with the general interests of his party, Marillac urged the king to end the covert struggle against Spain which Richelieu had renewed, to continue the Catholic counterattack upon the Huguenots, and to begin measures of internal reform. The cardinal did not deny the gravity of the domestic situation, but warned that the king had to choose between remedying these weaknesses and defeating the Hapsburg encirclement while there was still time and opportunity: the resources of the monarchy were inadequate for both enterprises.

The King Won. The choice fell, finally, upon Richelieu's program of sacrificing the needs of domestic policy to victory abroad, but not until his adversaries had almost overthrown the cardinal. The king fell gravely ill in September of 1630; his mother wrenched from him a promise to dismiss Richelieu. On his return to Paris, in a meeting of passionate tears and pleas at the Luxembourg palace, she won (or thought she had) his assent to fulfilling his word. Richelieu, seeking out the distraught and harried monarch the next morning at the royal hunting lodge in Versailles, recovered his master's confidence. Not daring to push his luck too hard, he agreed to a compromise with the queen-mother, but her hatred for him and her desire to re-establish her sole dominance over her son led her to reject it. The king put her under guard, but she escaped, and fled the next year to Brussels, under the protection of the king of Spain, never to return again to France or see her first-born son.

Gaston of Orléans led another insurrection in 1631, but soon he too was fleeing before the armies of the king and his imperious minister. When the duke of Montmorency, governor of Languedoc, took up arms in Gaston's cause, he was defeated and at Richelieu's rigid insistence, beheaded, despite numerous pleas that so great a nobleman be spared. The lesson was taught: it was death to take up arms against the king.

Peasant Rebellions. Marillac, in pleading for the primacy of internal reform, had posed the problem of peasant uprisings, the third kind of resistance faced by Richelieu. Such rebellions had erupted sporadically during the reigns of Henry III and Henry IV and began to recur frequently during the 1620's, with the renewal of an active—and costly—policy by the government. Though reminiscent of the Jacqueries or peasant wars of the medieval period, the rebellions of the French countryfolk in the sixteenth and seventeenth centuries differed crucially in having as their main target the tax gatherer rather than the lord of the manor. It was the state whose exactions now drove them to the desperate act of taking up arms. Their power lay in their numbers and in their geographical location far from the border provinces where the main military forces were stationed. Their weaknesses were many, and fatal to any prospect of success: they could not stand against the attacks of trained and organized troops; they had to return to their fields at frequent intervals to perform the necessary tasks of tillage and harvest; and they had no general program.

In consequence, these rebellions, rooted in desperation and the bitterest hatred, were soon crushed without imperiling the state; but they distracted the attention of the government from other matters for a time, and cost scarce money to put down. They were pinpricks, not swordstrokes. This was their principal importance to the cardinal: they impeded him in the pursuit of his goals of high policy. He had only contempt for the common people, "asses who worked best when heavily loaded," he said; he had neither pity nor understanding for those who paid the price for glory and did not reap its benefits.

The Intendants. Although Richelieu turned his back on reform, he wrought many important changes in French political life. It was rather the way that institutions worked than their structure which he transformed. In conformity with his central concern for power, he directed reorganization of the department of war under a busy and subservient aide, Sublet de Noyers. Existing military organizations were not abolished but compelled to accept central control and direction. The instruments of the new policy were the "army intendants"; these were officials who did not own their posts, as did most government servants in France, but served "by commission," subject to dismissal at the will of the government. They began to take increasing charge of all aspects of military administration, leaving only command functions to the commanders, who owned their regiments.

Similar officials, frequently called "intendants of justice," were used to control civil administration; they were usually judicial counselors sent into provincial towns to oversee the general business of government, particularly the operation of the courts and the collection of taxes. Though similar officials had been appointed in the French monarchy as far back as Charlemagne's reign, with the *missi dominici*, their sustained and widespread use by Richelieu fundamentally created a new system of government parallel to the old, controlling but not replacing it. Yet they did not achieve fixed and permanent status and function, but derived their power only from the personal confidence and specific authorization of the principal minister; the *parlements*, the core of France's traditional government, subjected them to relentless attack as irregular and irresponsible rivals.

Trade and Finances. Richelieu was acutely sensitive to the state's need for revenues and accepted the mercantilist argument that a "favorable" balance of trade, that is, an excess of exports over imports, increased the amount of money in the country and therefore the taxes it could pay. He devoted considerable attention particularly to expanding France's commerce and establishing her as a colonial power. His instruments for achieving these closely related goals were joint-stock companies for the various enterprises he supported; he designed them to be like the Dutch trading companies, notably the East India company, but the French companies were the result of government initiative, not of private enterprises co-ordinated and unified by the state, as with the Dutch. Richelieu expanded the French navy and improved its functioning under his own direction as "grand master of navigation"; its role in protection of commerce was particularly important in his mind.

Despite his strong economic interest, the cardinal never attempted to achieve control over the fiscal apparatus of the state, its most sensitive economic aspect. He permitted the tax farmers to maintain their effective domination of the revenues of the state, because they alone could meet his imperious demands for immediate funds to maintain French armies and pay French subsidies. The cost to the French state was immense; even though taxes were raised to unprecedented levels, a huge proportion of the collections stuck to the fingers of the tax farmers, much of it illegally. Furthermore, the necessity for funds drove the government to create more and more offices, for which there was no need, merely for the sake of the purchase price it received.

Public Opinion. Richelieu also devoted constant attention to winning support for his policy. He supported a pack of pamphlet writers and encouraged a Protestant doctor, Théophraste Renaudot, to establish a weekly news summary, *La Gazette*, as agencies of what nowadays is called "public relations." The pamphleteers in his pay defended the cardinal's actions and policies with the doctrine of "reason of state" and the necessary secrecy of its business. But the arguments inevitably included explanations of his triumphs and excuses for his setbacks, so that public opinion began, however slowly and invisibly, to assume the role of critic and judge of affairs of state.

Thus, a striking paradox marked Richelieu's administration. On the one hand, he struck down the traditional rivals of the monarchy, or at least forced them into surly obedience; and therefore he is correctly known as the creator of absolute monarchy in France. On the other hand, he helped to bring up new competitors for authority, the venal officialdom and the tax farmers, whose peril to the monarchy seemed less real and immediate because it was relatively novel. The change, fraught with significance for future development of French life, was the result not of Richelieu's deliberate policy, however, but of his incessant and ever growing demand for funds with which to make France safe from the Hapsburgs and predominant in Europe.

War at Second Hand. Even before the final defeat of Gaston's last rebellion in 1632, Richelieu was able to turn his major energies to his central purpose of defeating the Hapsburg power. During the years when he had been consolidating the royal hold over France and his own hold over the king, the imperial forces in Germany had swept to new successes under the leadership of Wallenstein (see ch. 14, p. 326), while Spain displayed unexpected energy under the leadership of the count-duke of Olivares (see ch. 12, p. 287). The cardinal undertook a delicate and complicated policy designed to undermine the Hapsburg position with least harm and expense to France.

Richelieu's first moves in Germany were preparatory. Gustavus Adolphus, the king of Sweden, was persuaded, in part by French arguments and in part by his own interests, to transfer his army from Poland to Germany. Though he halted and even reversed Wallenstein's gains, the resources he commanded in Sweden were insufficient to maintain his forces in this new theater of war. Richelieu willingly doled out subsidies from the French treasury to pay the Swede, but at the same time endeavored to subordinate him to French policy. The self-reliant Gustavus Adolphus, on the other hand, did not truckle to his ally. The French began to play upon the possibility of persuading the elector of Bavaria, a Catholic, to turn against the emperor.

Meanwhile, the French-Swedish alliance approached the breaking point. It was saved when Gustavus Adolphus fell during his victory at Lützen; the tension between the allies lessened, but did not disappear. Richelieu did not scruple to negotiate with Wallenstein when the imperial commander began to break away from his sovereign, but the emperor struck this weapon from the cardinal's hand before he could use it—Wallenstein was slain as a rebel in 1634.

Open War. The policy of fighting the Hapsburgs with the hands of third parties becoming ineffective, France could no longer remain on the sidelines. In 1635 Richelieu brought France into direct and open war against Spain, though not yet against the emperor; to buttress his policy he tightened the alliance with the Swedes, renewed that with the Dutch, and sent the duke of Rohan, the exiled Huguenot, into the Valtelline passes, between Italy and Austria, with a French army to break the Spanish line of communications with the Empire. The Spaniards slashed back with unexpected vigor. Employing troops and commanders already hardened in the war, they drove south from the Low Countries to Corbie, and Paris was gripped with fright lest they cross the seventy miles to the capital. Richelieu inspired the Parisians with fresh courage and organized new military forces, which recaptured Corbie in less than four months. By 1638 Richelieu had regained the lost initiative, and French and French-aided armies began to capture key positions in Germany and Italy.

Two years later, a double opportunity to strike at the Spaniard in his own peninsula was given to the French. Catalonia, in the northeast corner of the kingdom, revolted against Philip IV and offered the title of count of Barcelona to Louis XIII. Portugal, united with Spain by personal union since 1580, also threw off Spanish authority with French assistance. Richelieu began to smell victory.

Factions at Home. He needed respite from foreign war, for domestic difficulties were again pressing in upon him. Factions at court had recovered from their dazed fear of the cardinal and begun to oppose him and his policies. Another queen, the reigning Anne of Austria, took the lead among Richelieu's adversaries. She was all the more dangerous to him because she gave birth to a son and heir in 1638 and to another son two years later. Her antipathy to the ruling cardinal arose in part from opposition to his anti-Spanish policies, and in part from pique at his enjoyment of her husband's confidence and friendship during the long chill years when she had been an unvisited, almost abandoned spouse.

The Parlement of Paris resumed its practice of remonstrating against government edicts, but in 1641 Richelieu sent the king to the palace of justice to limit these rights of criticism and withholding assent by means of a *lit de justice* (bed of justice: a formal meeting of the Parlement in the king's presence). Provinces protected by their Estates against the full impact of the royal tax collectors were forced to pay more heavily; in Provence the Estates were abolished.

The impoverishment of the population as a consequence of wartime taxation brought a fresh outbreak of popular riots and rebellions. The salt tax was particularly hated, and led to the uprisings of the *Croquants* (Clodhoppers) in 1635 and of the peasants of Normandy under "Jean Va-nu pieds" (John Barefoot) and "Bras-nu" (Bare Arms) from 1639 to 1641. The year 1642 was marked by the half-pathetic, half-contemptible conspiracy of the king's young friend, the marquis de Cinq-Mars. To oust Richelieu and install himself at the head of the government, he arranged to take Spanish aid, but was caught and beheaded. The cardinal, worn out by illness and exhaustion, died not long afterwards (December, 1642).

The king's own death, as he knew himself, would not be long delayed, for he too was the victim of a mortal malady. Distrusting his wife's pro-Spanish proclivities, Louis XIII issued a declaration in April, 1643, establishing a regency to take over the government for his son and heir, Louis. The queen and two princes of the blood were made members, in deference to their well-established prerogatives, but they would be outvoted by four other regents, all friends of the late cardinal. On May 14, assured that his and the cardinal's handiwork would not be flightily destroyed by his widow, the king gave up his soul.

IV. Mazarin

Within four days, the will of the late king had been undone, and yet his deeper intention was achieved.

Queen-Regent and Cardinal Minister. On May 18, the queen-mother went before the Parlement of Paris, like Marie de Médicis thirty-three years before, to obtain its declaration that she should govern as sole regent. When she named one of the proposed regents of the opposing camp, Cardinal Jules Mazarin, as her principal minister, the courtiers gloated; he was a foreigner, an Italian introduced into the French diplomatic service by Richelieu and only recently naturalized; he was pleasant, conciliatory, a weakling in the common opinion, and obviously an easy mark for manipulation.

The great nobles, aided by ambitious duchesses and abetted by the power-hungry Parlement, attempted to seize effective control of the government from the queen-mother. To their indignant surprise, she held fiercely to power. Anne of Austria built her policy not on her past attitudes and actions, but on her son's future: to keep his kingdom intact and his power strong, she did not hesitate to continue Richelieu's policy of waging war against her own brother, Philip IV of Spain. Furthermore, she promptly gave to Mazarin a confidence and steady backing such as Richelieu had had to win by the most difficult struggles of his career. Mazarin had already won her ardent affection, and their intimacy became so close that many claimed they were secretly married (although a cardinal, Mazarin had never taken priestly orders) or, worse, mistress and lover. In any case, Mazarin possessed the total measure of Anne's authority as queen-regent.

Westphalia: Incomplete Triumph. Mazarin turned to achieving victory over the Hapsburgs with a single-minded intentness greater if possible than Richelieu's. He found funds by every expedient to pay the troops, and was able to mount increasingly effective campaigns against the Hapsburg armies. At the same time, trustful in his art of diplomacy, he sent French negotiators to the peace conferences which opened in 1644 at Münster and Osnabrück in Westphalia.

Mazarin's fundamental objectives were to split the Hapsburg states, compelling each to make a separate peace; to break up the centralizing efforts of the emperor and rally the lesser princes of Germany around France as their protector; and to extend the boundaries of France, particularly along the northern frontier with the Spanish Low Countries and on the eastern border in Alsace. He succeeded only in part. The emperor did make peace with France, transferring his rights in Alsace to the French king; "German liberty," as the privileges of the imperial princes were called, received French (and Swedish) guarantees. But the Spaniards persuaded the Dutch, who were dismayed at the prospect of French conquest of the southern Netherlands, to make a separate peace with them. Thus the imperial defection from Spain was counterbalanced by that of the Dutch from France, and the king of Spain took courage to continue the war with France. He was encouraged in this unexpected firmness of resolve by the upsurge of resistance within France to the government of Mazarin.

The Fronde. The French nation was to Mazarin primarily a source of revenue for the conduct of France's foreign policy. He was totally devoted to her interests, though he conceived them in narrowly royal terms of the defeat of her foreign enemies and the conquest of new territories. The rebellions against high taxes which raged in the south during the first years of his administration did not deter Mazarin from increasing existing impositions and introducing new ones. Unwary of the sensitivity of the urban rich on the matter of their prerogatives as holders of state loans and owners of government offices, he fixed new taxes upon them. When forced by resistance to withdraw or reduce one tax, he turned quickly to another. But it was not until he struck at the Parlement of Paris by creating new offices in their own sacrosanct ranks that he met a resistance that he could not turn by his wiles. When he attempted to split the various *parlements* by exempting only the Parisian from an edict depriving the high courts of four years of pay as the price of continuing the *paulette* for nine years, he met with point-blank refusal to register the edict.

The Parlement, encouraged by external similarity of name to the English Parliament, then at the height of its triumphs in the Civil War, pro-

France in 1648, with Provinces

claimed its own political powers and rights of criticism. The four chambers of the Paris courts united their ranks, in violation of existing law; when Mazarin retaliated by removing from them the protection of the *paulette*, they proclaimed (Declaration of the Chamber of Saint-Louis, June 15, 1648) a theory of quasi-constitutional monarchy, with themselves as its guardians. That the monarchy as Richelieu had built it was their target for destruction became clear when they demanded the abolition of provincial intendants; Mazarin, without troops to spare from the embattled frontiers, did not dare reduce their resistance by force until the victory of Condé over the Spaniards at Lens (August 20).

The Rebellion of Paris. At once Mazarin ordered the arrest of the leaders of the Parlement; in reply the magistrates, encouraged by the coadjutor (assistant bishop) of Paris, Paul de Gondi, called upon the populace to raise barricades in the streets. The government gave in and released the prisoners, but after the signature of peace in October ordered Condé to march

207

his army toward Paris, relying on the customary slump in wintertime military operations for protection against the Spaniards. With his approach, Anne removed the king and court to the nearby palace of Saint-Germain, in safety from the rebellious Parisians. Then she issued commands to the Parlement and other courts to quit Paris for exile in other cities and began a siege of Paris.

The city, under the leadership of defiant members of the courts, defended itself; it found allies in several provincial *parlements* and governors as well as in Spain. But the royal forces proved too strong, and a compromise peace was negotiated, based on an amnesty and the obedience of the Paris Parlement. Further violence within Paris was short-lived; the population, having engaged in the grandiose game of insurrection (which they had called a *"fronde,"* after a game played with balls and slings in the streets), had tired and desired quiet and peace. The "parliamentary" Fronde was at an end.

The Princes in Revolt. The troubles of the queen-regent and her principal minister with rebellious subjects continued. Now the leadership of opposition fell to Condé, the army commander, Turenne, France's other outstanding general, and bishop Gondi. The principal object of each was to oust Mazarin, and each desired for himself the post of first minister. Mazarin fought this new Fronde by diplomatic as well as military techniques. Playing upon a conflict of interests between Gondi and Condé, he arrested the prince, then subdued the rebellious provinces by force. Victorious, he did not keep his promises to the Parlement, nobility, and clergy; the Frondeurs reunited their forces and successfully compelled the queen-mother to release Condé and dismiss Mazarin (February, 1651). The cardinal withdrew across the frontier into the territory of the elector of Cologne, but continued actually to direct the government of France by correspondence and couriers: in ostensibly dismissing Mazarin, Anne of Austria had acted at his instructions and retained her confidence in and dependence upon him.

Civil war, till then sporadic and local, spread widely; all of Mazarin's ruses and dogged persistence on the part of the queen-mother were required to overcome forces which were more powerful than those which operated in the name of the king. Three of Mazarin's adversaries came around to the royal cause: Gondi, rewarded by French support which gained him appointment as cardinal de Retz; Turenne, whose venture into the Fronde had been largely prompted by infatuation with one of the intriguing duchesses; and the Parlement of Paris, troubled by the persistence of disorder. The queen-mother, in order to make further resistance the crime of *lèse-majesté*, had Louis XIV proclaimed of legal age on September 7, 1651, two days after his thirteenth birthday.

Condé continued his struggle, with Paris and Bordeaux on his side; he was beaten by Turenne just outside Paris, but was given control of the city by his sister, the famous *Grande Mademoiselle*, the duchess of Longue-ville, and by the poor of the capital, who rose in insurrection. The richer elements of trade and government service, with the prompting of Retz, finally regained power in the city and called back the king (October 21). Condé fled across the border into the Low Countries and was made the commander-in-chief of the Spanish armies still waging stubborn war against France. The royal cause was triumphant at last: Retz, though archbishop of Paris, was imprisoned; Mazarin was called back (February 1653); and Bordeaux, where a popular insurrection broke out in favor of continued resistance, was subdued (August). The second Fronde, or "Fronde of the Princes," had ended.

The Work of Peace. From 1653 all was quiet within France. Mazarin governed without difficulty over a nation in which all voice of opposition had been muted and those who sang the monarchy's praises became more numer-ous and vociferous. The victory of absolute monarchy, according to the prevailing political theory, brought peace, the most urgent of needs; its opponents, with their selfish aspirations toward re-establishment of lost pre-rogatives and their lofty dreams of limited and constitutional monarchy, brought only war and devastation. Personal devotion to Louis XIV, then already a youth of striking personal qualities, handsome and winning in his ways, became almost a cult.

General economic life began to prosper with the years of peace, although the struggle with Spain continued on a lessened scale. For the poor, as usual, the improvement of conditions came more slowly and less certainly. The government and the church engaged in a wide work of charity to relieve conditions, and Vincent de Paul dedicated the last decade of his life to this task.

Mazarin needed money for the state, especially since the war with Spain continued, but how it was obtained did not interest him, despite the experience of the Fronde. He entrusted the direction of the fiscal affairs of the state to Nicholas Fouquet, the superintendant of finances, who met all Mazarin's demands but continued to use all the old outworn devices: the sale of offices; loans against the security of the revenues of future years; concession of tax collections to tax farmers at exorbitant rates (he partici-pated covertly in their operations, to his own immense enrichment). No one of influence in the government thought to urge that the opportunity be used to reform known malpractices and costly improvisations.

Defeating Spain. In completing his lifework of making France great and bringing down the Hapsburg power, Mazarin continued as persistent and resourceful as he had always been. He brought the lesser princes of Ger-many together into a "League of the Rhine," with France as a member, in order to prevent the emperor from weakening their cherished "German liberty." Then, when the imperial diet was convened to choose a "king of the Romans" as emperor-elect, Mazarin energetically though unofficially put forward the candidacy of Louis XIV. The French king was not elected, but his interests were served when the electors used his candidacy to extract further concessions from the new designate, Leopold I.

The main business of Mazarin's foreign policy, however, was to drive Spain to accept France's final triumph and make peace. To achieve this goal, the cardinal went so far as to take the alliance of Cromwell, the lord protector of the English Commonwealth and the bane, supposedly, of all monarchies. French and English forces combined to win the battle of the Dunes (1658), which wrested from Spain the port of Dunkirk, at the southwestern tip of the Low Countries. Although Dunkirk had to be turned over to Cromwell as an English foothold on the continent, the price was small compared to the immediate gain.

Spain began serious peace negotiations, which were concluded in 1659, one hundred and one years after the treaty of Cateau-Cambrésis; this Peace of the Pyrenees was an overwhelming French triumph. The formalities of signature of the treaty on the Isle of Pheasants, in the middle of the Bidassoa river between France and Spain, provided for the most exact equality imaginable; but the terms of the treaty embodied Mazarin's conception of France's advantage. All Spanish territory to the north of the Pyrenees, primarily the county of Roussillon, was ceded to France; a strip along the southern edge of the Spanish Netherlands was the other French territorial gain.

But Mazarin had not finished; he eyed not merely segments of Spanish territory, but the Iberian monarchy itself as a future conquest for his king and master. To establish a claim on the Spanish crown, Marazin's negotiators exacted a marriage between Louis XIV and Maria Theresa, daughter of Philip IV, as the central provision of the peace. To strengthen that claim the chief French negotiator, Hugues de Lionne, slipped into the treaty a proviso that the *infanta* renounced her claims to the Spanish royal succession "*moyennant*" (on the basis of and subject to) payment of an immense dowry —which the impecunious Spanish treasury could not be expected to pay. The marriage was celebrated without delay, and the French king returned to Paris with a royal bride as his most important trophy of war.

The Young King.   In the sixteen years since his father's death, Louis XIV had grown to manhood. Yet no crisis in his relations with his mother or the cardinal-minister had arisen. Mazarin had given kindness and attention to the fatherless boy-king, thus firmly establishing their relationship upon affection and trust. Though he had neglected Louis's formal education in the over-busy years of the Fronde, when the king became a youth he began to prepare him for the coming tasks of ruling France. He introduced him into the councils where the highest state business was discussed, gave him the background of events, and explained the reasons for decisions; thus the young man received a "political," as distinct from a humanist, education. Mazarin thereby solved one of the most difficult of all problems in dynastic monarchy, where the reigning kings tended to look with distrust upon their heirs, around whom centered unsatisfied ambitions, disaffected hopes, and worse. The cardinal survived, tired but victorious, till 1661, when he died, in a quiet country where memories of the Fronde already grew dim.

For more than half a century after the death of Henry III, the same broad pattern dominated the history of France as during the previous three decades of the wars of religion. Civil turmoil balked her skilled and industrious people in the performance of their labors, turning the land into a jungle of violence and misery. Yet they were the makers of their own bedevilment. Their passions, aspirations, and ambitions led them again and again to take up arms against each other until the middle of the seventeenth century the crown emerged as the solitary victor.

10

Britain: The Tudor Period

1485 - 1603

FACING WESTWARD toward the vast Atlantic and eastward toward narrow waters and the mainland of Europe, the British Isles seem wedded to the all-encircling sea. Yet the three kingdoms comprising the islands in the sixteenth century—England, Scotland, and Ireland—were societies firmly rooted upon the land. Fishing and shipping—the seagoers' livelihoods—occupied only an outer rim of population.

Nonetheless insularity had already given to the history of these islands a distinctive character. The sea provided safety; not since the descent of William the Conqueror upon the south English shore in 1066 had the wide moats of the English Channel and the North Sea been crossed by successful invaders. Behind these water barriers, the peoples of Britain were able to work out their problems with an unusually large margin for experiment and error.

I. Henry VII

On August 22, 1485, the armies of two noble factions contending for the throne of England met and fought at Bosworth Field, in the central county of Leicestershire. Before the day was out, the reigning king, Richard III, was dead. With Richard fell for the moment the hopes of the line of York. The royal crown, found beneath a hawthorn, was placed upon the head of the pretender, Henry Tudor, earl of Richmond and leader of the Lancastrians.

A New Dynasty. The red rose, badge of the line of Lancaster, had vanquished the white rose of York. For how long? During thirty years the vicissitudes of the Wars of the Roses had shuffled possession of the crown between the rival dynasties, but seldom had a victor held a flimsier claim to it than the new king, Henry VII. Leadership of Lancaster had passed to him by way of the Beauforts, who were descended from a bastard son of John of Gaunt and had been excluded from the succession by act of Parliament.

Henry Tudor moved at once to seal the victory of his arms by the processes and ceremonies associated with a rightful reign. First came coronation, the supreme symbol of kingship with its mystical and religious rites. Then, in a more mundane approval, Parliament proclaimed Henry VII legitimate king of England, but left in careful silence the dubious aspects of his inheritance. Finally, in January 1486, the Lancastrian king took for his queen Elizabeth of York, daughter of Edward IV; henceforth his dynasty was neither Lancastrian nor Yorkist, but, after his own name, Tudor. It was a generous and politic action, such an extinction of a political feud as Shakespeare may have had in mind when writing *Romeo and Juliet*.

False Pretenders. Elizabeth proved a loving and loyal wife, but could not stay Yorkist sympathizers from attempting to overthrow her husband. The conspirators drew heavily on support from outside the kingdom but were hampered by the absence of any free member of the house of York to lead them or provide a rival claimant to the throne. In desperation, they twice put forward false pretenders. One, an Oxford lad of ten named Lambert Simnel, was crowned in Ireland as Edward VI; the other, a Fleming in his early twenties named Perkin Warbeck, claimed to be Richard, duke of York, second of the two sons of Edward IV whom Richard III had slain in the Tower. Simnel was captured in 1487, but the king, in a gesture of mercy and mockery, sent him into the royal kitchens to scrub pots and pans. Warbeck was more ambitious, more dangerous, and less fortunate. Captured in Cornwall in 1497, he was sent to the Tower, where he was executed two years later after an unsuccessful plot to escape. Henry VII foiled and frustrated rivals for his throne with ease largely because of his success in winning the loyalty, or at least the acquiescence, of the English nation. For the mass of Englishmen, the verdict of Bosworth Field was God's own verdict, at least until someone upset it or royal misrule made them ready to follow a pretender's banners. The re-establishment of good government, shattered by three decades of civil turmoil, was their first interest.

Fortunately for Henry, the task of good governance was within his capabilities. The realm did not require extraordinary exertions by the state to aid recovery from the civil wars. A marveling continental observer had called it England's "particular mercy" that the Wars of the Roses had not "wasted, destroyed, or demolished" either the country, its peoples, or its houses: "the calamities and misfortunes of the war fell only upon the soldiers, and especially upon the nobility." Thus English society remained productive and resilient.

The Land's Wealth. The land, its first resource, was fertile and well-watered; only the hill country of the north and west was less rich, and there abundant grass fed great numbers of sheep. Around 1500, as for centuries thereafter, England fed herself without difficulty, growing all the cereal grains she needed. There was land to spare for the more lucrative enterprise of growing wool, which was the best in Europe. Nevertheless in some areas many landowners transferred so much land from arable to pasturage, "enclosing" former open-field or common lands, as to raise fears that sheep were taking the food out of the mouths of men. The difficulties resulted more from the displacement of labor than any actual shortage of food production. The export of wool was the country's "prodigy of trade," its most important contribution to the international economy. Previously the English shear had been sent as raw fiber to the looms of Flanders, but by the closing decades of the fifteenth century a domestic textile industry, located mainly outside the guild-dominated towns, had taken over production of rough woolen cloth, mostly sent to the Low Countries to be further finished into fine cloths. Other industries, metal manufactures being the most important, remained small. Agriculture and trade continued to be the economic sinews of England.

The Fabric of Society. English society was not in crisis. Its structure was based on the same elements—laboring peasantry, wealthy countrymen, townsmen—that prevailed in continental Europe, but differed in several significant respects. The manorial system had virtually disappeared. Serfdom had given way almost everywhere to personal freedom for the tillers of the ground; thus the venom of servitude was absent from tenancy relationships.

The rural rich dominated the countryside without difficulty. They included not only a titled nobility, but also a more numerous gentry of prosperous though untitled landowners. The strict rule of primogeniture made the younger sons and the daughters of the nobility legally almost indistinguishable from all others of "gentle birth." Intermarriage between gentry and nobility was becoming frequent. No patent (legal grant) of title was necessary to become a "gentleman"—only sufficient wealth and good manners to act like one for a long enough period. Prosperous townsmen bought estates and became country squires; marriage further increased the movement back and forth between the two groups. No sharp cleavage had formed between urban and rural wealth such as held true in most of conti-

nental Europe. Therefore English society did not require direction and control by the crown, but the bare minimum of protection and maintenance of
public order.

Rule Both Firm and Cheap. Henry VII was ready to give the realm the
government of strength and moderation it required. He was himself a fitting
leader for such a state. Before his return to England he had drunk the sour
wine of exile, and it had made him wise in the ways of men. The means for
re-establishing stable government were at hand. The Wars of the Roses had
shredded the edges of royal authority but not its center. York and Lancaster
alike had always endeavored ultimately not to destroy or limit the royal power
but to seize it for themselves. Thus the centuries-old process of royal centralization needed only the spur of definitive victory by one party to be
renewed. The tradition of the king's supremacy was ancient and powerful;
the Norman conquest in 1066 had brought together all political power and
authority in the monarch's hand, and throughout the medieval period the
feudal dispersion of government had been limited by the overriding claim of
the king to the ultimate loyalty of all Englishmen.

Henry discerned clearly the two elements necessary to safe and good
government in his reign. The first was to rule firmly, the second to rule
cheaply. Firm rule required that the turbulent nobility be tamed, not ruined;
they were a born and trained ruling class whose strength was the monarchy's
strength so long as they were not permitted rugged independence. Henry
made no effort to destroy them but punished any hint of plotting or rebellion.

He kept the direction of policy in his own hands, depending upon an
active yet obedient royal council to give him advice, execute his commands,
and act on his behalf in the multiple business of state which did not require
his own decision. Henry limited the number of high-ranking noblemen in
the council and entrusted the most important tasks to "small men" whose
promotions were solely his gift.

The "Star Chamber." Strong government also required the ending of
the "bastard feudalism" of the great nobles, who kept private armed bands
at the very time when the monarch himself did not possess a permanent
bodyguard. This task could not be entrusted to the regular courts, bound
as they were to the narrow rulings and elaborate procedures of the common
law, with juries subject to the hints and threats of local magnates. Instead
Henry returned to his royal council as the fountainhead of justice given in
his name. Under former reigns, a section of the council had begun to spe-
cialize in the function of intervening in judicial proceedings. Between 1487
and 1504, statutes laid down the duties and rights of this administrative court
for the first time. It held its sessions in secret, was permitted to use torture,
but could not inflict the supreme punishments of death and confiscation of
goods because these required conviction by a jury. The court, which met in

a room with a blue ceiling studded with stars, became known as the "Star Chamber." Backed by the king's stern authority, the Star Chamber stiffened the whole process of justice in the country. It ended the maintenance of private armies and reaffirmed the supremacy of the royal government.

It was a commonplace among experienced statesmen that "the gatheringe of money"—in the words of Sir Thomas More—"withdraweth the hearts of Englishmenne fro the Prince." To keep his expenditures within bounds, Henry avoided as much as he could the usual extravagances of royalty— ostentation and war. After spending freely on an imposing coronation, he lived modestly, content with the fact of power, not needing its outward show.

Limited War. To avoid war took greater effort and ingenuity. The Hundred Years' War (ca. 1337-1453) had ended three decades earlier, but England and France continued to glare at each other across the Channel like tomcats edging toward a fight. Henry knew how limited were the resources of his kingdom for another major war, yet he dared not imperil his hard-won prestige by backing away. He went to war in 1492 against Charles VIII on behalf of the rulers of Brittany, but made peace after nine days' fighting which won him the credit of military triumph and the cash of a French war indemnity. The support given to Perkin Warbeck in the Low Countries, where the widow of Duke Charles the Bold, Margaret of York, still wielded influence, resulted in a break with England's great wool market and traditional friend in 1493. Henry transferred the "staple" of English wool, as the continental outlet for this valuable export was called, from Antwerp to Calais, but gladly came to terms with the ruler of the Low Countries, Duke Philip the Fair of Burgundy, when he abandoned Warbeck's cause. The peace was capped by a commercial treaty favorable to England, the *Magnus Intercursus* (1496); the "staple" moved back to Antwerp.

The English commitment to arms in both conflicts was limited; Henry fought his wars, as he ruled his state, as cheaply as possible. Henry VII preferred to stay at peace while others fought; his safety lay in their quarrels.

Filling the Treasury. Nonetheless his wars cost too much. Even small wars undid the greatest frugality. A strong tradition, to which Henry VII adhered as long as he could, held that the king should "live of his own," that is, on the revenues from the royal domain and various feudal dues. Henry's income from these sources increased considerably during the reign, particularly when confiscated estates of rebels and plotters were added to the royal domain. To wage his campaigns against Scotland and France, the king needed additional revenues, for which parliamentary approval was legally necessary. Parliaments convoked in 1491 and 1496 granted the necessary funds, but rebellions against the collection of these levies flared up, briefly but hotly, in impoverished districts in the North and in Cornwall. Henry did not limit himself to revenues approved by Parliament. He extracted considerable sums from the clergy, while his officials strictly enforced his varied feudal rights for the sake of their associated revenues. Forced loans from wealthy citizens came closer to violating parliamentary prerogatives, and aroused hatred for the responsible officials. By the time the reign ended in 1509, the royal treasury was heaped high with coin.

When Henry married his children to foreign royalty, he knew that Europe no longer doubted the finality of Bosworth Field. In 1502 his eldest daughter, Margaret, became the wife of King James IV of Scotland, tying that restless realm in the North closer to English interests. More important was the marriage concluded a year before between Henry's eldest son Arthur and Catherine of Aragon, daughter of the reigning king and queen of Spain. When Arthur died in 1502, Ferdinand of Aragon hastened to obtain a papal dispensation for Catherine's marriage to the prince's surviving twelve-year-old brother, Henry. The wedding was delayed till he reached the years of manhood.

II. Henry VIII

When the first Tudor king died in 1509, none stirred to prevent his son from following him upon the throne as Henry VIII. The youth of eighteen was his father's unquestioned heir, and those who doubted or denied his father's title had been stilled by exile or the executioner's axe. Most of the country had grown accustomed to comfortable peace and obedience; the rest were prudent and quiet. Caution, moderation, and tranquillity did not mark the new king himself. Henry VIII, unlike his father, had been a king's son, well-schooled in sports and books but also petted and flattered, and for the last six years sure of his inheritance, so that his pride swelled at his royal state.

Wolsey: Man of All Work. He was not ready, however, to accept the burdens of governing in person. Instead he placed all the major responsibilities of government one by one upon the shoulders of a single man, Thomas Wolsey. Through him Henry governed the Roman Catholic church in England as well as the civil administration of the country. At his behest the pope in 1514 named Wolsey, who had been no more than court chaplain in 1509, to be archbishop of York, and bestowed the scarlet hat of a cardinal upon him a year later. Rich abbeys and other lucrative benefices flowed into the cardinal's possession until he possessed probably the largest revenues in the kingdom after the king himself. In 1518 the pope rounded out Wolsey's ecclesiastical powers by naming him legate *a latere*, with disciplinary powers over the English church hitherto reserved to the papacy. At the same time Wolsey rose to command of the civil government. His appointment in 1515 as chancellor, the supreme legal officer in the realm, capped his control of the king's confidence and policy.

Wolsey exercised all his varied functions with enormous diligence and considerable intelligence, yet his long administration spun itself into a record of grandiose plans ending in small successes and large failures. Seeking no reconstruction of society or politics, he nonetheless undercut existing institutions by his disregard for traditions and established interests. Although of middle-class family, he bore himself with the imperious majesty of a born king. His policy, like his manner, was absolutist: he gladly governed with a hard hand. He disliked persuading Parliaments, which could not be pushed easily or far, to meet the growing financial demands of the state. He preferred to extort "benevolences" (forced loans) from the wealthy. When these did not suffice, he imposed an "Amicable Grant" (1525) upon the poor. The peasants in a number of counties drove off the collectors of the tax by armed force. The emergency revealed what Wolsey had forgotten—that the government, without a standing army, had few means for imposing its will upon large numbers of recalcitrant subjects. Wolsey abandoned the tax and called upon the dukes of Norfolk and Suffolk to pacify the embattled peasantry. But most domestic affairs went smoothly during all but the final years of Wolsey's administration.

Wily Diplomacy. Wolsey could feed the king's vanity and his own ambition only by triumphs visible to the wide world, in the arena of war and diplomacy. There the great minister played his game with all his skill until England began to stand forth among the European powers with an importance beyond that justified by her economic resources or her military prowess. Wolsey's system depended upon the existence of a relative balance of strength among the contending forces, primarily the Hapsburgs (ruling in Spain, the Empire, and the Low Countries) on the one side and the Valois kings of France on the other. England's weight, in itself small, could then throw the scale either way.

This wily diplomacy conflicted, however, with two powerful forces: a deep and persistent English antipathy toward France and an equally strong inclination towards the cause of King Charles of Spain, based on the historic connection of trade with the Low Countries and the more recent family connection, established when Henry VIII married Catherine of Aragon, Charles's aunt, shortly after his reign began. A war against France in 1512-1513 brought advantage only in Scotland, which came strongly under English influence after the death of King James IV during an attempted expedition into England.

War against France having proved unproductive, Wolsey tried to play the part of peacemaker. He arranged a short-lived peace between the hostile parties in 1518, but then fell victim to his royal master's boundless ambition.

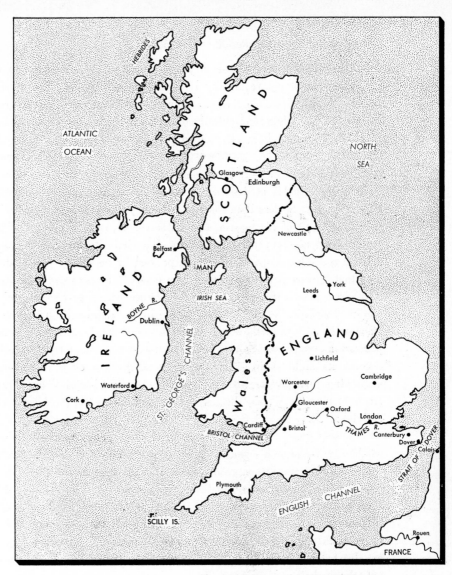

The British Isles in the Sixteenth Century

Henry VIII put in his candidacy for election as Holy Roman Emperor, thus antagonizing both the main rivals, Charles of Spain and Francis I of France. Wolsey's own ambition led him to seek election to the papacy in 1521 and 1522. Both king and minister failed of their goals, to their public discomfiture. Further attempts to reap advantage, first by supporting the Hapsburg ruler, now Emperor Charles V, and then Francis I, brought as little result as before. The failure of Wolsey's foreign and domestic policy began to shatter the king's hitherto granite confidence in his minister. It was exploded by the cardinal's mishandling of "The King's Business" of divorce from Queen Catherine.

"**The King's Business.**" Henry VIII could not endure the thought that his family might not remain upon the throne of England. But in the mid-1520's, his only descendant (apart from an illegitimate son) was the Princess Mary. All the other four children born to the queen had died in infancy. In 1525 Mary had been proclaimed princess of Wales, heir to the throne. But would some male rival, descended from earlier royal stock, contest her right and overthrow her, as the earl of Richmond, her grandfather, had done to Richard III at Bosworth Field? The monarch's fear for the future of his dynasty, no less than his lust for saucy Anne Boleyn, decided him to seek annulment of his marriage to Catherine (see ch. 5, pp. 101-102).

Wolsey, accepting this assignment, fell victim to the evasions of papal diplomacy. When Pope Clement VII, pressed by the emperor, ceased to pretend that he was preparing to grant the divorce, the king struck in his wrath at Wolsey. The cardinal gave up the chancellorship to Sir Thomas More, admitted violation of the ancient statute of praemunire by having accepted office as papal legate (though at the king's command!), lost his innumerable possessions, and went up to York to reside, for the first time since he had become its archbishop. There he brought the axe close to his neck by attempting to negotiate with the ambassadors of Charles V and Francis I. Arrested in 1530, Wolsey died, weary and despairing, on the road to London and the block.

Wolsey gone, Henry VIII floundered for a policy for three years. He would not abandon his goal of winning papal approval for his divorce but could contrive no better means for achieving it than intimidation of the pope. A Parliament convened in 1529 increased the king's power over the church in England, recognizing him in 1531 as "Supreme Head of the Church" in the realm though not explicitly throwing off the ultimate authority of Rome. Early the next year another parliamentary act suppressed the papal annates but left it open for the king to suspend its operation; the pope did not take the bait.

Divorce Personal and Religious. Suddenly, in the space of a few months, hesitancy vanished from royal policy. Henry VIII had found another instrument for his business. Thomas Cromwell, a former agent of Wolsey's who had entered the king's service in 1529 and won his confidence by his energy and devotion, persuaded the king in 1532 to act with new directness. He pointed out that Henry, by confining all judicial processes, including the ecclesiastical, within England, could have his case for divorce tried within his own realm, where his might prevailed, not the emperor's. No change was necessary in the doctrine or practice of the church, apart from this affront to the pope—hardly distinguishable from those perpetrated by the kings of France and Spain, good Catholics both. So Henry VIII blinked at schism because he intended no revolution in religion.

"The King's Business" moved to fulfillment. Henry VIII married Anne Boleyn, some months pregnant, in January 1533, a month before the new archbishop of Canterbury, Thomas Cranmer, pronounced the king's earlier marriage invalid. The next year brought completion of the separation of the Anglican Church from Rome. The Act of Supremacy proclaimed as treason any refusal to recognize the king as "Supreme Head, on earth, of the Church of England." Two years later the suppression of the monasteries, begun under Wolsey, was resumed; under Cromwell's direction as vicar-general for ecclesiastical affairs, the lands of the abbeys were confiscated by the crown and then sold, usually at a small fraction of their true value, or given away as outright gifts. Thus within a few years one-sixth of the land in England was redistributed to the advantage of those who commanded funds or influence. The beneficiaries of this immense transfer of wealth were henceforth welded by common interest to the king's cause.

The religious transformation shattered the country's traditional friendship with the Empire and the Low Countries. The ambassador of Charles V in London risked his life to organize insurrection against Henry VIII on behalf of Catherine of Aragon; he reported wide success in his preparations until the deposed queen and wife refused to countenance his efforts to incite civil war in her adopted homeland. Without her assent, nothing could be done. Cromwell and his master received time to do their work of change and to consolidate the crown's power without having to crush a rebellion of the still numerous English Catholics. Instead, those who chose the old faith rather than obedience to the king faced the fate of Sir Thomas More, who died on the block in 1535.

Thomas Cromwell. Cromwell, who as a young man had brought back with him from Italy Machiavelli's *Prince* as a manual of practical statesmanship, had triumphed over More, who in 1529, when Cromwell was entering the king's service, had urged him always to tell Henry VIII "what he ought to do, and never what he is able to do." For, More had warned, "if a lion knew his own strength, hard were it for any man to rule him." If Cromwell remembered that caution he doubtless smiled: by 1535 he was already chancellor of the exchequer, the king's secretary (and was remaking this office into the most important administrative post in the state), and the most trusted and powerful councilor and agent of the crown. A year later he was made a baron, and in 1540 an earl. The summit had been reached.

Then came the cliff. The king's matrimonial affairs, which had been the occasion of Cromwell's ascent, brought about his fall. He had successfully passed through the crises of Anne Boleyn's disgrace and execution (1536) and the death of Jane Seymour, Anne's successor, a few days after giving birth to a boy Edward. To strengthen English ties with the German Lutheran princes, against the common foe Charles V, Cromwell negotiated a marriage between Henry and Anne, daughter of the duke of Cleves; but the German Protestants patched up their dispute with the emperor, and Henry, laying eyes upon his new queen, found her ugly beyond hope. The lion of England speedily divorced Anne of Cleves and sent her to peaceable retirement at a country estate; his paw fell instead on Cromwell, who had made two mistakes too many. The minister was dismissed from his offices and convicted of treason. He pleaded for "mercy, mercy, mercy"; the king, moved, permitted him to die beneath the executioner's axe instead of in the hangman's noose.

Changing England. The first decade of Reformation had come to an end. England was changing. The ease and quiet of the first years of the reign of Henry VIII were vanished; a new turbulence could be felt in English life, deeper and more powerful than that of the previous century. The patterns of life were losing their fixity, and the state, to which men traditionally had looked for preservation of the established order, was the agent of the change. Those who sought change therefore were encouraged to look to the state to effect the results they wished. The tie between monarchy and people was growing tighter and more vital; the ruler was becoming more immediately concerned in the welfare of those he ruled and his subjects more involved than ever in the affairs of the dynasty and the decisions of state.

For the moment, however, most of these changes were concealed within deep, almost invisible historical processes. The state still did not command large regular armies with which to impose its will upon its own people. The creation of a modern navy, designed for combat upon the high seas, was begun; a navy board was formed with central responsibility for its administration. But the effect of a fleet upon a people's life is indirect. Despite the turmoil in high policy, the people's activity in gaining their livelihood was affected only intermittently. The realm continued to prosper despite occasional wars and consequent interruptions of trade. The inflationary surge of sixteenth-century prices was only beginning; England was still apart from the mainstream of economic change.

The King His Own Minister. Henry himself had been profoundly affected by the events of those years. He had tasted personal power and his arrogance fed upon it. He relished the godlike right of life and death he held over the subjects, but lost the ancient sense of the king's duty to serve his people as a selfless, dispassionate judge. For personal and dynastic reasons, he had ripped and rearranged the complex web of social and political relationships in England; now he wished calm again, for he disliked change for its own sake. But he would not turn back, and he could not without catastrophic loss of prestige and power.

After Cromwell's fall, Henry faced out the remaining seven years of his reign without the advantage and convenience of a great principal minister.

He supervised in person the administration of his government and the elaboration of its policy. Although he lacked Cromwell's ingenuity in meeting the perplexing problems of a confused situation, he displayed both energy, as might have been expected, and a surprising prudence.

In foreign affairs the king proved more successful, though on a more limited scale of activity, than either of his great ministers. His chief triumph consisted in subordinating Scotland to his own interests and control. The Anglican schism from Rome caused conflict with Henry's nephew, James V, who reigned at Edinburgh; the Scottish king was intensely loyal to the old religion. To strengthen his hand against the ancient enemy to the south, who was now a heretic to boot, James renewed the "Auld Alliance" with France; he married a daughter of Francis I and, after her death, Mary of Guise, a member of the ducal family that reigned in Lorraine and exerted strong influence at the French court. In 1542 war broke out between England and Scotland; by November, the English were victorious at Solway Moss; a month later, James V was dead, succeeded by a week-old daughter, Mary. The queen mother, Mary of Guise, continued to resist the English, but the invaders were aided by Scottish Protestant rebels, who slew the bishop of Saint Andrews, the Catholic leader. By 1546 the queen-mother was compelled to make peace. English power had not been effectively distracted from Scotland by a small-scale parallel war with France, which ended with peace in the same year. Henry retained the port of Boulogne, on the French coast.

Heirs Male and Female.   Domestic problems, apart from Henry's besetting trouble with confirming his succession, proved relatively easy to handle as well. The Catholics in the northern counties had risen in rebellion in 1537 in a desperate but ineffectual movement called the Pilgrimage of Grace. To establish a tighter rule over this outer portion of his kingdom, Henry established a kind of viceregency at York, the council of the North, which largely duplicated the privy council in its broad powers of government in the king's name and interest, but exercised them with even greater autonomy (like the similar council of Wales).

Assuring a safe passing of the royal crown to an heir of his own descent was more difficult. Catherine of Aragon had been put aside because she had provided only a girl, Mary, as heir; Anne Boleyn, who displanted her, did no better in giving birth to Elizabeth. Jane Seymour, who came next as queen, bore a boy, Edward, but none of the subsequent wives—Anne of Cleves, Catherine Howard, and Catherine Parr—produced children. Edward was heir to the crown, but was a sickly child who might not outlive his father or himself sire an heir. Hoping to prevent dispute over the succession, Henry had Parliament fix the line of royal succession. Mary and Elizabeth were established as successors in order to Edward if he died without heir.

If their lines failed, the throne would go not to the descendants of Henry's elder sister, who formed the hostile royal family of Scotland, but to those of his younger sister, who formed the ducal line of Suffolk within England. Then, in 1547, his own energies exhausted and vanished, Henry VIII died. His political and dynastic handiwork would be put at once to the test.

III. Edward VI

The late king's fateful insistence upon obtaining a male heir, though his realm be turned topsy-turvy to do it, seemed justified when his son succeeded him, easily and uneventfully. Nothing Henry VIII had done, however, could prevent the common difficulties of a royal minority, for Edward VI was a boy of nine in January 1547.

Protector Somerset. The council named as co-regents the king's uncle, Edward Seymour, earl of Hertford, and John Dudley, viscount Lisle. They immediately used their power to climb up the rungs of noble rank: Seymour became duke of Somerset and Dudley earl of Warwick; but Somerset assumed sole effective charge of the government with the title of "protector." A staunch Protestant, he encouraged Archbishop Cranmer to continue the construction of the new religious order in England.

In the hope of preventing Catholicism from becoming strong again in Scotland, the protector sought for Edward VI the hand of Mary, the queen of the Scots. When Mary of Guise refused her daughter to the English, the protector sent an army of invasion to persuade her. The Scots resisted fiercely and the French came to their aid with an expeditionary force and an attack upon Boulogne. Marriage between Queen Mary and the French dauphin, Francis, sealed this renewal of the "Auld Alliance" and doomed Somerset's dynastic design for Anglo-Scottish union. The English were compelled to leave Scotland and give up Boulogne.

Somerset's prestige reeled under the defeat. The inconsistency of his domestic policy brought him down. He disliked social change and sympathized with the little folk who took the brunt of the movement for enclosing of lands. This view placed him in opposition to the majority in the council and Parliament, representing the sections of the nobility which, like Somerset's own clan of the Seymours, had multiplied their wealth and magnified their influence by the acquisition of expropriated church lands under Henry VIII. Already offended by the protector's haughty disdain for them, they took the initiative against him when he acted softly in putting down a peasant rebellion against enclosures in Norfolk. In 1549, under the leadership of Somerset's long overshadowed coregent, Warwick, the royal council dismissed the protector from his offices.

The Government of Warwick. Warwick assumed his duties, though without his high title of protector. Under his sponsorship, the shift away from Rome continued, while bishops began to lose their "temporal" possessions to the state, as the abbots had done before them. Nor did Warwick fear economic change: with his encouragement, the state no longer resisted but encouraged enclosures. As a result, Somerset's popularity revived. Warwick, playing upon the young king's fears, won his assent to the execution of Somerset in 1552, and was himself rewarded with the title of duke of Northumberland. Edward VI, a tubercular adolescent, admired the virile duke with the hard fist. When the duke expressed his concern lest princess Mary, a Catholic, come to the throne, the king, on his own authority without parliamentary enactment, abolished his father's rule of succession and named Lady Jane Grey, the daughter of Henry Grey, duke of Suffolk, to follow him. Northumberland married his own son to the reluctant Lady Jane, who loved her books rather than power or glory; but her father wanted the regent's support for establishment of a Suffolk dynasty. In 1553, Edward VI died, not yet a man, having reigned but never ruled.

IV. Mary I

Which rule of succession would hold—Henry VIII's, which confirmed the ordinary rule of primogeniture, or his son's, which established a reigning monarch's arbitrary choice of his successors? The memory of the Wars of the Roses proved more powerful than the troops with which Northumberland supported his proclamation of Lady Jane Grey as queen. Northumberland found himself isolated and helpless, and Mary, daughter of Henry VIII and Catherine of Aragon, took the crown. Northumberland lost his head for rebellion; Lady Jane, innocent of any crime but the ambitions others held for her, went to the Tower.

Back to Rome. Mary I began her reign with the support of the nation against a usurper; her ability to retain their favor depended upon her policy. As a fervent Catholic, Mary constantly held it her highest purpose to bring England back to the Roman allegiance in religion. In 1553 it was not a purpose impossible of achievement, for the majority of Englishmen (as far as modern historical scholarship can determine), disturbed or shaken by the events of the past two decades, had not firmly decided for either the old or the new faith (see ch. 5, pp. 104-105). Her essential problem consisted in making return to Catholicity palatable to this middle majority.

She bungled this task. Her efforts to give the confiscated lands back to the church brought her into direct conflict with Parliament, which refused to enact the necessary legislation even though it was subservient to her wishes in most other matters affecting religion. In 1554 she married Philip, heir of Charles V. To placate parliamentary hostility to this foreign connection, the marriage contract provided that Philip would not reign as king in England nor interfere in English policy. It soon became clear nonetheless that Mary's policy was almost identical with her husband's.

Protestant Revolt. Rebellions against her rule broke out. The duke of Suffolk led one rising in the Midlands on behalf of his daughter the imprisoned Lady Jane; Sir Thomas Wyatt led another in Devonshire. Suffolk was easily defeated, but Wyatt held out for a longer time before capture. The duke, his ill-fated daughter, and Wyatt all met death on the block.

Protestant hopes inevitably fell upon the queen's half-sister, Elizabeth; to save her head, Anne Boleyn's child attended mass and denied, with every appearance of sincerity, all treasonous thoughts against her sister. Mary permitted her to live, first as a prisoner in the Tower and then in seclusion at the country house of Hatfield; but, at Philip's suggestion, she reaffirmed Elizabeth's right of succession. Open and unrepentant Protestants met harsher "justice"; the burning of heretics became frequent in 1555, and a number of Anglican bishops, including Cranmer, went to the stake in 1558. Later that year Mary declared war upon France in alliance with Spain, where Philip reigned since 1556. The war went badly; Calais, the last English-held port across the Channel, was lost to the French. On this final note of failure, Mary died November 17, 1558.

V. Elizabeth I

Elizabeth I followed her half-sister upon the throne. Though at the moment none opposed her advent by force of arms, the shadow of illegitimacy hung over the new queen. Her own father had once proclaimed her a bastard after her mother's execution, and his later withdrawal of this denunciation of his own blood did not wholly whiten its dark implications as to her rights. Catholics, of course, affirmed her illegitimacy on the ground that the divorce of Catherine of Aragon had been invalid. On the other hand, Elizabeth's succession was eased because England (unlike France) had no Salic Law limiting succession to males.

The question whether Elizabeth I reigned and ruled by right of true inheritance mattered to the English nation as much as it did to her; the possibility of a renewal of the Wars of Roses, with the more terrible impulse of a crusade for faith added to dynastic rivalries, rose up before every eye. The answer to this searing question depended not only on subtle syllogisms, but far more on the grim conflicts of beliefs and passions—and on the ability of the young queen to master a maze of difficulties.

Master of Self and State. What kind of woman had come out of the semiexile of Hatfield House to assume the power, the majesty, and the perils of royal state? The years of change, turmoil, and danger through which she had passed had forged her personality into a distinctive pattern. She had learned how to submit humbly when she was weak, and now she was avid of command; yet she sensed that power was most safely used when it did not impose burdens men would rebel to throw off. Reticence and dissimulation had saved her life, and now she knew how to make her own decisions. without proclaiming her innermost purposes or reasons to the world; sometimes even her most trusted intimates did not know her full mind.

Elizabeth soon showed herself to be a master of the difficult art of government. Like her grandfather, she retained close personal control over the administration without hamstringing it. Because she had confidence in her own judgment. she listened to her ministers' counsel; because she knew she controlled them, she trusted them to act on her behalf and in her name. She did not choose any "principal minister"; instead she relied upon a small group of officials, chief among them Sir William Cecil, who served her from her advent until his death forty years later.

Burghley and Walsingham. As her principal secretary of state, Cecil performed a multitude of duties with untiring diligence and uncommon skill; but even more important to Elizabeth was his wisdom in policy. Like herself, Cecil was sober, cautious, but. when he acted, forthright and energetic; like herself, he had bent to the Catholic wind during Mary's reign, but supported the Protestantism of the new period in the queen's "middle way." As the Catholic peril rose during the later decades of her reign, Elizabeth gave an increasing part in her inner councils to Sir Francis Walsingham, who was equally devoted to her interests but saw them with the eye of a Puritan sympathizer. She named Walsingham her second secretary of state in 1571, but reaffirmed the predominance of Cecil by elevating him in the same year to the peerage as Baron Burghley and in the next year naming him lord high treasurer. Walsingham, as secretary of state, continued to increase the importance of that office; its control of the royal correspondence enabled him to play an ever larger role in the conduct of foreign affairs; his organization of an efficient secret service within the country protected the regime against plotters, while his influence among the more vehement Protestants tended to keep them safely, although restively, in her camp. Burghley and Walsingham might have fought each other to a standstill under a less firm mistress, but she made them serve together loyally and effectively.

Councils and Parliament. The fundamental instrumentality of government remained the privy council, with its parallel councils in the North and in Wales. Elizabeth kept the privy council a working body of about twenty; some of its members sat in the House of Commons to guide its proceedings, while others headed the principal agencies of state. The council met regularly to debate all important matters of state; the queen did not attend its meetings, but received reports of its discussions and decided upon major proposals of policy. Subject to her disapproval, it had the power of decision. Its members held their offices for extremely long periods of time, amassing great knowledge and skill in the performance of their duties and developing a strong sense of professional obligation as servants of the state as well as of the queen personally.

Parliament played a less central role in Elizabethan government. The queen tended to view it as a disturbing element but did not wish to forgo its valuable contribution to the stability of her regime. She knew that only Parliament's laws carried the fullest weight of authority among the people and in the courts of law, and were therefore the safest way of embodying her will. She knew, too, that the views of influential sections of the nation were most accurately and responsibly mirrored in its proceedings, and that it could rally the English people around her person.

But during her reign the dominant role in Parliament shifted increasingly toward the House of Commons, which began to show unprecedented self-assertion and even independence. She granted wider rights of debate to this lower house, but refused to permit it to debate "matters of state," which included such topics as the question of her marriage, demands that she name a successor and heir, her governance of the church, and foreign relations. Those who spoke too freely in Commons on such matters met sharp punishment, including the Tower; but she preferred to guide debates in the house by means of the privy councilors who sat on its benches. She persuaded rather than compelled whenever possible, and when the time came, she could sweep Commons to her way with eloquence and affection.

Proposals of Marriage. During her entire reign, no important issue arose which did not involve many interests and passions, often entangled in exasperating confusion. Every question of domestic policy had important consequences in foreign affairs, and vice versa. Elizabeth herself gave first attention to two domestic interests: to preserve herself upon her throne, and to advance the interests of the people she ruled and loved. Three problems thrust themselves before her government as soon as she began to rule: proposals for her marriage; the character of Anglican religion and its place in the state; and the economic recovery of the nation.

When Elizabeth Tudor came to the throne, a young woman of twenty-five, it was taken for granted that she would marry; a husband would govern for her and father heirs of her body to follow her upon the throne. The only question was her choice of a mate and master. The first candidate to present himself was Philip II of Spain, her erstwhile brother-in-law; a fervent Catholic, he assumed that Elizabeth, if she became his wife, would follow him in faith and policy as docilely as had Mary. Elizabeth did not reject his offer out of hand; a French alliance with Scotland made Spanish amity, or at least neutrality, desirable. The consolidation of Protestantism in England soon made this proposed marriage a practical impossibility. Her heart chose a man of her own years and nation, Robert Dudley, son of the duke of Northumberland. The obstacle to their marriage fell away when his wife, Lady Amy (Robsart), was found dead at the foot of a staircase. The widespread horror at the murder—for so it was taken to be, despite official explanations of accident—gave Elizabeth pause in her passion. She abandoned whatever plans she had for marrying Dudley: the safety of her rule came before the demands of her heart. She kept Dudley as her favorite till his death in 1588, naming him earl of Leicester once the Robsart affair had quieted.

The "Virgin Queen." But her growing political astuteness warned her that to raise a subject to regal rank as her consort would rankle with the host of noblemen not so honored; and her personal reluctance to share her authority with any one she could not easily command only reinforced her refusal to treat any Englishman thereafter as a serious matrimonial prospect. Only foreign royalty, notably the youngest son of Henry II of France, the duke of Alençon (Anjou), were given consideration. Even in considering him, although titillated by the make-believe of official romance, Elizabeth always kept before her the icier goal of diplomacy, to attach France to her policy as an ally. She had no intention whatever of accepting a foreign consort as master of English policy.

Such playing with marriage proposals left her subjects unamused; voices were constantly raised in the House of Commons to demand that she marry. These irked supporters, usually vigorous Puritans in policy, declared that her first duty consisted in providing an heir to the throne, thereby preventing war over her succession and safeguarding Protestantism in England. The queen, angered at their intrusion into matters affecting her person and crown, prohibited any further discussion of the topic in Parliament; and she began to parade her unmarried state as a boon, not a bane, to England. Poets began to flatter the "Virgin Queen," and a courtier, Sir Walter Raleigh, called his projected colony in America "Virginia." At last advancing age "solved" the question of the queen's marriage by rendering it meaningless.

The Protestant Queen. The status of religion in the state permitted neither evasion nor delay. The ancient principle of a single religion within the country, upholding and upheld by the crown, was not questioned. The queen, herself without deep-felt dogmatic convictions in matters of faith, attempted to establish a broad-based national church taking in all loyal subjects. Numerous and influential Englishmen would not fit themselves docilely into the queen's pattern of a *via media*, a middle way half-Catholic, half-

Protestant. At the beginning of the reign, Catholics presented the more obvious threat to the crown's policy. Probably half of Elizabeth's subjects (even the best estimates are no better than informed guesses) would have gone back to the Roman Catholic fold if they had an unhampered choice. Elizabeth and her advisers, particularly the cautious and sober Sir William Cecil, avoided presenting them with clear-cut alternatives of conscience.

Nothing could conceal the fundamental Protestant character of the new regime, however. No Catholic could accept in good conscience Elizabeth's control of the Anglican church as its supreme "governor," or the Book of Common Prayer, reissued in 1559, which defined its doctrine. It was these same issues—the queen's governorship and the Book—which aroused against Elizabeth a more baffling, if less dangerous, opposition. This came from Puritan elements within the Anglican church, who endeavored to throw off its Catholic vestiges in ritual and doctrine. Their further purpose was to persuade and coerce the queen into taking the lead among Protesant states. Elizabeth held off their demands as long as she could, but the pressure of the Catholic danger prevented her from turning the power of the state against these recalcitrant subjects, whose support she would need in the event of crisis.

Economic Growth. For almost two decades, she managed to live mainly "of her own," by the revenues which fundamentally came to the crown as the greatest landowner in the country and as suzerain over all who held land by feudal tenures. Expanding economic activity also enabled the queen to live without constantly seeking grants from Parliament. She tapped the growing foreign trade of the country by means of the customs duties of tonnage and poundage, voted to her by Parliament at the beginning of the reign.

Elizabeth, with Cecil at her right hand, gave systematic encouragement to English economic life. The most efficacious measures were those which concerned her own government. Probably the most important was the reestablishment of a stable and honest coinage. With the guidance of Sir Thomas Gresham, an English merchant who had gained an insight into the operations of a money system at Antwerp, all silver coins, of varying values, were called in and reissued at a single fair rate. With a steady restraint unmatched by most of her fellow-monarchs, Elizabeth thereafter maintained the English coinage unchanged, providing unparalleled stability for commercial transactions.

The strengthening of the debt structure of the government was almost equally significant. State expenditures were kept within the revenues taken in; debts incurred by the queen's predecessors at extortionate rates of interest were paid off quickly, especially if owed to foreign lenders. It was not long before the English crown found sufficient credit for its needs within the country at reasonable cost. English taxpayers reaped the benefits as well as the queen's government.

Reasons of Faith and State. A strange paradox prevailed in England during the reign of Elizabeth I. Powerful groups of her subjects—the Puritans and their friends—disagreed sharply with her purposes and methods in the conduct of foreign affairs, yet they remained bound to her cause because it was ultimately their own. The queen for her part could not part with their support in a world of always lurking perils. Thus mutual fondness and admiration between nation and monarch found frequent expression in sharp demands, harsh recriminations, and stern warnings.

The conflict of states was a conflict of faiths, pitting adversaries against each other according to the simple principle of their acceptance or rejection of the Roman allegiance. But only in the minds and hopes of religious stalwarts on both sides did the battle of nations retain such awful simplicity. The particular interests of states—their preservation, their aggandizement, their glory and greatness, in brief, "reason of state"—shaped their policy as much as the issue of supreme principle. In practice, religion became an instrument for the achievement of state policy against brothers in the faith as well as against enemies across the line. Elizabeth saw this brute fact of international life with utter clarity and without complaint; she was ready to seek her own advantage and the preservation of her realm and people without enslaving her policy to automatic support of Protestants against Catholics everywhere and in every case. The chill deliberateness of her conduct of foreign affairs appalled the growing multitude of persuaded Protestants in England. They did not understand her unwillingness to risk the security of her throne or country; for them power had been given to the prince by God for no other purpose than to advance His cause.

The Scottish Problem. At the outset, she faced the implacable necessity of keeping Scotland friendly or at least neutral; a hostile regime in the northern kingdom would afford any continental foe of England a beachhead on her own side of the narrow seas. The goal of a Scotland safe for England was more easily defined than attained.

In the middle of the sixteenth century Scotland was a turbulent land which seemed beyond control of all men, native or foreign. It was a poor country where the Highlanders, driven by the inadequacy of tillage and pasturage, raided the Lowlands for a pittance of booty, and the Lowlanders in their turn often raided the border counties—the poorest part of England— for similarly meager gains. Scottish society retained a largely tribal form; the power of its nobility rested less on the ownership of land than on their positions as clan chieftains. The monarchy had possessed limited means of rule. The support of the Catholic church, however, had provided the kings with an invaluable base among the people.

Thus, when Calvinist ideas penetrated the country and won the allegiance of numerous noblemen who swore fidelity to the new faith and to each other in the first Covenant (1557), the struggle for political power took on the form of repeated bloody civil wars between the rival faiths. The accession of Francis II, husband of the Scottish queen, Mary Stuart, to the French throne in 1559, drew very tight the traditional alliance between the starveling kingdom of the Scots and the wealthy, powerful realm of France. The continued presence of French troops in Scotland, aiding Mary against the Calvinist rebels, endangered English security even though peace had been made between France and England earlier in the year at Cateau-Cambrésis. Elizabeth dared not withhold English assistance to the insurgents, lest French domination be consolidated at Edinburgh; her troops helped the rebels to defeat the French and compel them to withdraw from Scotland in 1560.

Mary, Queen of Scots. Queen Mary sailed off to her husband's land, but soon returned a widow (1561). In her absence, the Calvinist reformers had strengthened their grip on Scotland. In John Knox, who had learned at Geneva how to be the Scottish Calvin, they possessed their own religious leader of genius and unbounded vigor; in James Stewart, earl of Moray, the queen's half-brother barred from the throne by illegitimacy, they had a political chieftain of cunning and obduracy. Mary briefly accepted the accomplished revolution in politics, but her taste for power, made keener by her experience of the more absolute authority of the French monarchs, and her unchanged Catholic faith, prompted her to break loose from the control of Knox and Moray. She could not concentrate her energies on this single ambition, however; an unrestrained sensuality crossed her purposes and trapped her in repeated tragedy. In 1566 she married a cousin, Henry Stuart of Darnley; as a strong Catholic with an excellent claim to the English throne, Darnley presented a threat to the dominant Calvinists in Scotland and to Elizabeth in England. Moray rose in rebellion with Elizabeth's encouragement, but was defeated and fled below the border. Mary's triumph over rebellion was reversed by her break with her husband, who slew her secretary, David Riccio, shortly before she gave birth to a son James. Darnley died in turn at the hands of James Hepburn, earl of Bothwell (1567); the queen's marriage to Bothwell shocked the world and left her helpless before the rebels. Mary, briefly captured, escaped south to seek the protection and assistance of Elizabeth, who had been aiding the rebels.

Moray took over rule in Scotland as regent for Mary's infant son, who was proclaimed as king James VI. The country fell back into political turmoil. Moray ruled only until 1570, when he was assassinated; fierce civil war followed for three years, then the Calvinists regained supremacy. In 1579 a Catholic cousin of the king, Esme Stuart, count of Aubigny, won the boy's confidence, but the Calvinist clergy and nobility rose again in arms to drive out the intruder.

The Unwelcome Prisoner. Meanwhile, Mary's presence in England confronted Elizabeth with a host of problems that defied satisfactory solution. Elizabeth's principal advisers urged her to send Mary back to Scotland, but England's reigning monarch, keen to the implications of abetting regicide, refused to doom her unwanted guest to certain death at the hands of a Scottish court. If Mary were permitted to go on to the continent, she could rally Catholic potentates to support of herself as leader of an endeavor to restore Catholicism in England. If she were permitted to go free in England, the numerous English Catholics would find in her a leader who possessed the best claim to the throne if Elizabeth were unseated. So Mary remained under guard, a pampered prisoner.

Events proved this perhaps the worst of solutions: every one of the consequences Elizabeth had sought to avert came upon her, sooner or later. In 1569 a rebellion broke out among Catholics in northern England on behalf of the queen of Scots; it was put down with pitiless repression, more than 800 rebels losing their lives on the gallows; but Elizabeth continued to protect her cousin from the vengeance of English Protestants. The next year Pius V excommunicated Elizabeth by the bull *Regnans in excelsis*. The bull also declared the queen's tenure of the throne invalid. The implication that Catholics had a duty to rebel against Anne Boleyn's daughter was only too clear; Parliament retaliated by making support of papal authority and claims an act of treason. From that time Catholics who died in England for their faith were punished not as advocates of false religion but as traitors, a distinction they undoubtedly found it difficult to make. Many Catholics did die, as traitors or as martyrs; for plotting and preparations for rebellion, in collusion with foreign Catholic princes and in anticipation of their invasion, became almost constant. The beginning of the Jesuit missions to England by Campion and Parsons (see ch. 5, p. 107) sharpened Protestant fears.

Nonetheless the likelihood of aid to English Catholics by foreign armies remained small during the decade of the 1570's. Philip II, the sword of Counter Reformation, still avoided direct action against England; his attention was held by the rebellion of the Low Countries and the wars of religion in France. Elizabeth, too, refused to take open command of European Protestantism against the Spaniard and his allies. She permitted English sailors to undertake semipiratical excursions against Spain in the Caribbean, and even shared surreptitiously in their financing and their profits; she cautiously aided French action against Spain in the Low Countries. Not even Spanish efforts to support enemies of Elizabeth in Scotland and Ireland stirred her from this limited program.

Conspiracies and the Block. When a plot of English Catholics was discovered in 1583 with the aim of killing Elizabeth and putting Mary of Scots on her throne, the implicated Spanish ambassador was expelled from the country. The privy council took the lead in forming a private association of Protestants pledged to slay any person on whose behalf an attempt might be made against Elizabeth's life; two years later Parliament enacted a law embodying the same principle. The imprisoned Scottish queen, regardless of this menace and encouraged by messages from Spanish officials, continued her support for conspiracies against her patient host.

Walsingham brought her to doom in 1586, however, when he trapped her into sending patently seditious letters by supposedly safe devices actually under his agents' control. Mary was tried by a special commission; Parliament confirmed the sentence of death. Elizabeth held back her approval as long as she could; even when she signed the order of execution, the privy council had to dispatch it on its own authority. Mary Queen of Scots died on the block at Fotheringay (February 1587), mourned by her cousin; but she ceased to be the hope and banner of English and European Catholicism for restoration of the Roman faith in England.

The Armada Repulsed. The tragedy at Fotheringay marked the end of the process by which Elizabeth gradually and reluctantly abandoned her policy of avoiding direct war with Spain. English seamen began to take a more aggressive and independent share in oceanic enterprise at Spain's expense as early as the decade of the 1560's. John Hawkins, who had undertaken slaving expeditions from Africa to Spanish possessions in the Caribbean, had been a smuggler without any bellicose intentions. His cousin Francis Drake, when he seized a Spanish treasure train (Panama, 1572) and raided Spanish cities on the western coast of America during his circumnavigation of the globe (1577-1580), was more than a smuggler; but his piracy did not involve Elizabeth's responsibility, not at least as long as the queen's participation (as "Miss Elizabeth Tudor") in financing the bold sailor was concealed.

In 1585 Elizabeth, in order to forestall the danger of reconquest of the northern Netherlands by Alexander Farnese, duke of Parma, sent an expeditionary force under the command of her favorite, the earl of Leicester, to aid the Dutch. Philip, still technically at peace with England, began to build and equip an "Invincible Armada" (*armada*, Spanish for "armed fleet") for invasion of the island kingdom. Drake became Elizabeth's instrument for interfering with the Spanish preparations; in 1586 he was permitted to strike again at Philip's possessions in the Caribbean as a diversion of Spanish energies, and the next year he hit directly at the coasts of Spain and Portugal, raiding their shipping so effectively that the expedition against England had to be put off till 1588. Only then did open, large-scale war develop, when Philip sent forth his immense fleet to conquer England. Before it could reach the southern Netherlands, where Parma had an army waiting to embark, the Armada had to run the gantlet of English naval power along the southern

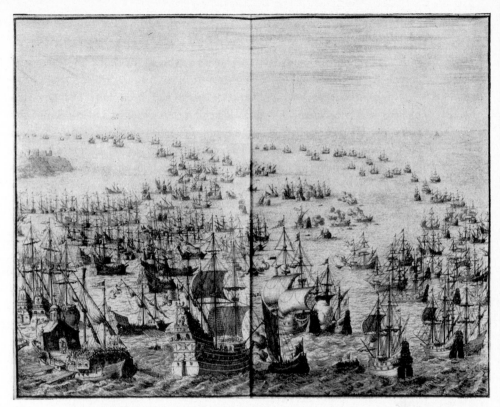

THE SPANISH ARMADA OF 1588. Etching by Jan Luyken. The dark line in the center results from a fold for binding the original print in a book of Dutch historical prints put together late in the seventeenth century.

The shape of sixteenth-century warships—the pure sailing ships characteristic of the Atlantic fleets, as well as the oared galleys brought up from the Mediterranean—is visible in this print, which suggests the immense numbers of the Spanish fleet sent against England in 1588. *(Achenbach Foundation)*

shore of England. The defending fleet, depending on its greater speed and superior gunnery, raked the larger but slower foe till the Spaniards lost their tactical array; a storm ("an English wind") rose which flung the tattered Armada northward through the North Sea. Thence it worked around the west coast of Ireland to its home ports, after losing scores of ships sunk or wrecked.

Greatness and Swagger. England's year of greatness was 1588. Exultation and pride reigned supreme. No other people. had ever inflicted so total and shameful a defeat upon Europe's greatest power. The surging energies of the English people seemed to double and redouble under the inspiration. The note of confidence became louder in the works of poets and playwrights, culminating in the genius of Shakespeare and an imposing array of lesser talents. England came of age in the creativity and quality of her civilization, although its achievements still made little impact outside her boundaries in continental countries and few foreigners bothered to learn the islanders' language.

English swagger was premature. Spain had been hurt but not vanquished, and subsequent expeditions against her coast and her colonies by Drake and Hawkins ended in failure and ultimately in the deaths of the two sea dogs. Spanish naval power learned the lesson of the defeated "Invincible": the new Spanish ships embodied the principles of speed and gunnery taught by the English. Although direct operations against Spain brought few results, Elizabeth achieved greater success in her preferred method of indirect action. After 1589, Philip gave his principal attention to unseating Henry IV in France; by aiding the Bourbon king, Elizabeth effectively pinned Spanish power until in 1598 Philip made peace with France. To be sure, war between Spain and England continued, but in desultory fashion marking the difficulties in the way of negotiating peace rather than any strong will to continue war.

Ireland under the Tudors. Meanwhile rebellion in Ireland flared again in 1597, revealing a dangerous weakness of England's defenses on her western flank. The outer island of Britain had been theoretically under the dominion of the kings of England since the twelfth century, but their power had seldom extended far beyond an area on the central eastern coast known as the Pale. Within this district Anglo-Norman landlords dominated a society roughly like England's in economic form, but increasingly Irish in culture; outside the Pale, the Irish native population of Celts, most of them speaking their own Gaelic language rather than the imported English tongue, continued to live under a thin overlay of English political forms. At the end of the fifteenth century, Henry VII had placed all agencies of local Irish government under the specific control of the English crown and parliament (Poyning's Law, subjecting Irish legislation to English approval). The English interest in Ireland consisted rather in excluding penetration of any influence or domination by a great continental state than in extracting wealth from the country; its tax revenues were so meager that they never covered the expenses even of the small military force usually maintained in the Pale.

The Irish economy for the most part combined subsistence agriculture with livestock raising; before Elizabeth's reign few Englishmen held much land in Ireland from which sizable rents could be taken. Irish society retained its tribal forms, but the traditional clan pattern was breaking up. The clan leaders had been partly Anglicized when the English crown granted them as the proprietors the lands occupied by their clans. The result had been to weaken the fidelity of the tribal followers to their leaders, who began to treat as their own lands and rights hitherto controlled by the law of the sept (clan). The power of the chieftains was not strengthened by counterbalancing English support; the overlords from across the Irish Sea continued to distrust them.

Catholic Erin.   To the English, the entire pattern of Irish life—cultural, social, economic, political—remained strangely backward and barbaric. Their resulting scorn and fear were accentuated when the Irish failed to accept the Anglican revolution in religion. The conflict of cultures was doubled by the clash in faiths, for only within the Pale did even a small number of Irishmen support the church of Ireland, as the local counterpart of the Anglican church was called.

English authority in Ireland had been theoretically tightened when Henry VIII had taken the title of "King of Ireland" instead of the previous "Lord of Ireland," but neither he, Edward VI, nor Mary I had been able to extend or strengthen English power in the island to any important extent. Elizabeth was at first ready to permit the Irish to rule themselves under her nominal overlordship, but she would not brook their continued allegiance to Rome nor their readiness to take Spanish aid. She began to employ military force against them despite her general antipathy to war; the reduction of hostile and intractable subjects to obedience was for her a necessity, not a question of choice. She also initiated a program of establishing English "plantations" in and near the Pale; Sir Walter Raleigh and other royal favorites sent Englishmen to settle in Ireland under English forms of land ownership with English culture and loyalties. It was easier to bring over English landlords than English peasants, and a characteristic new pattern of Irish life began to develop: the land continued to be cultivated by Irish peasants, henceforth tenants who paid rents to English landlords. A clash of economic interests between English and Irish was superimposed upon the already existing cultural and religious hostilities.

O'Neill's Rebellion.   Rebellion, especially in the North in Ulster under the leadership of the O'Neills, became endemic; a combined Irish insurrection and Spanish invasion in the Southwest was defeated with difficulty in 1579, and the danger to the English flank became all the greater after England entered open war with Spain in 1588. Yet Hugh O'Neill, flattered by English honors, remained outwardly loyal for a decade; not until 1598, when the Anglo-Spanish war was subsiding, did he lead a new island-wide insurrection. Although English military prowess had been multiplied many times during the war, the first expedition against O'Neill failed badly. It was commanded by the queen's favorite, the dashing earl of Essex, son of her beloved Leicester. Essex, whose bungling matched his vanity, frittered away the English strength, was recalled to London, attempted a mad, hopeless, rebellion, and died on the block as a traitor (1601).

A modest and skilled captain, Charles Blount, baron Mountjoy, took over command. He adopted a strategy designed to win against a dispersed enemy, poorly trained and equipped but with the support of virtually the entire population; he employed the greater resources of England to seize and hold vital points and tighten a net around O'Neill's field forces, until they were trapped and crushed. Lord Mountjoy's strategy succeeded, but the English royal treasury, zealously replenished and protected by all of Elizabeth's wiles and precautions, was emptied. The sore on the western flank had drained England's strength even more dangerously than the more easily limited campaigns against Spain.

Wales. Wales, the Celtic land from which the Tudors first came, took a path of development utterly unlike Ireland's in the sixteenth century. Henry VII was still largely a Welshman ruling in England. Henry VIII, wholly English in spirit, replaced the traditional tribal system of Welsh government with the more efficient and direct English system; a council for Wales supervised the whole administration in the outlying country, which began to send members to sit in Parliament. English became a second tongue for an increasing number of Welshmen; but English culture did not displace the indigenous pattern of life. The Welsh adopted English intellectual and religious values; the Anglican church took root, further uniting the two peoples.

The Scottish Heir. Scotland continued its own independent life in the north. James VI began his personal rule, gaining experience in the art of government by manipulating the rudimentary Scottish regime, which had a Parliament possessing fewer powers than its English counterpart. He shared the Calvinist faith of his subjects, but disliked the presbyterian form of its organization; the Anglican method of episcopal government provided a more effective way for a king to control the church. In foreign policy he docilely followed the lead of Elizabeth of England; more and more the succession to her throne seemed to be his for the waiting. But the aging queen would not declare her wishes on the succession. "Can I love my winding sheet?" she asked peevishly. James waited, quietly impatient; the English people waited, restlessly patient.

The only action came from Sir Robert Cecil, the queen's chief minister since the death of his father, Lord Burghley. Reluctantly, fearing the penalty of disgrace or worse if discovered, Cecil opened secret negotiations with James to assure him the English royal title, while the Scot, less guardedly, sought by his personal diplomacy to win the approval of his fellow-monarchs for his accession in England. Cecil was concerned not only for his own future as a royal servant, but even more to avert civil war such as contested successions had so often brought to the country; James was more interested in attaining his rights by inheritance and extending his power. At last the queen, growing feeble of body though not of mind, named James as her successor. Cecil's secretive negotiations were capped with the safeguard of legality.

Then, in the year 1603, more than forty-four years after ascending the throne, Elizabeth I died. Her handiwork passed into new hands. What would they do with it? Was it a reign only that ended, or a whole age?

II

The Crisis of the British Monarchy

1603 - 1660

I. The Reign of James I

THE ACCESSION OF James VI of Scotland as King James I in England and Ireland, by unifying governance of all the realms of Britain in a single person, marked an eventful change in the public life of the island peoples. The pivot of their common history remained England, where the ultimately effective decisions were made; but what occurred in England depended in large part upon events in the brother kingdoms to the north and across the Irish sea.

Britain in 1603. As the new reign began, the peoples of Britain were cleft into bitterly hostile groups. Although religious unity was the almost universal ideal, religious dissension was the fact. The official religion in England and Ireland was Anglican, but it had not won the allegiance of any but a minority in Ireland. Its principal competitor was Calvinism, in the shape of the Presbyterian church of Scotland and the rising Puritan forces in England. The old faith, Roman Catholicism, retained the loyalty of a great majority of the Irish as well as of a substantial minority of Englishmen, especially in rural areas. Separatist groups maintained themselves fitfully in England. Although the monarchy had not been able to enforce unity, its efforts to achieve this ideal had sharpened the hostility between the various faiths; they were all unwilling to live in peace with each other, except for hopelessly small and weak groups like the Separatists.

Wealth was increasing, but so was economic instability; some men could hope for fortune, others faced difficulties or even impoverishment. Below the level of the propertied classes, the poor and the poverty-stricken felt sharply the pangs of distress and hoped vaguely, though deeply, for some kind of improved life.

Different patterns of life were adopted by different groups, but each maintained that only its own was worthwhile and proper. Traditional habits in England were boisterous, joyous, and often violent, with strong vestiges of the ancient pagan past; court life, superficially more refined, possessed many of the same characteristics, with amorous gallantry, ostentatious display, and bitter backbiting rivalries added. In England, the Puritans attacked the usual ways of life among both the common people and the courtly nobility as wicked and blasphemous; they sought to impose upon all men their own half-ascetic habits, with their emphasis upon the abolition of sports, dances, and all Sunday pleasures except the sermon. The Puritan goal was substantially achieved in Scotland, but there the Presbyterians found it attacked by the power of the state. The Irishry still lived much as they had for centuries, in a way the English thought barbarous and attempted to eradicate, with slow success at best.

All these conflicts were reflected in a variegated intellectual life. Men probed more deeply for the ultimate reasons and purposes of their activity. England was becoming again a leader in philosophy, as she had been in the high middle ages. But as the controversialists came to know their opponents' beliefs better, they fought them with increased rancor and raucousness. Debate made political life more violent, not less.

A "God upon Earth." James I did not doubt his ability to govern his peoples, for all their irascible squabbles, with strength and wisdom. He considered himself such a philosopher-king as Plato had dreamed of. He was a learned man, able to hold his own in controversy with all but the greatest thinkers of his age. He had a clear theory of the nature of the state and the character of kingship which guided his purposes. He saw all the realms he ruled—England, Scotland, and Ireland—as his grand estates, inherited from ancestors who had conquered them by arms. As supreme lord, he claimed the unquestioning and unlimited obedience of those he governed; as a Christian prince, he acknowledged his duty to rule in their interests, but according to his own judgment and wisdom. Monarchy, he asserted, derived its powers from God, and God alone; kingship was *de jure divino*, by divine right; and kings themselves, in their potency and sagacity, were "gods upon earth." No institution in the state existed except by the king's command or permission;

The British Isles in the Seventeenth Century

all power of making and enforcing laws ultimately and essentially belonged to him.

James I was learned, however, in more than theories. As king in Scotland, he had wrung the royal power from the hands of arrogant nobles and haranguing divines; he knew his Scots, and how to govern them, molding his policy to the possibilities for action. But such rule required constant labors. In England, on the contrary, he expected to govern easily and pleasantly. This anticipation was not unwarranted. The English people were accustomed to depending upon royal government for decisions of general policy, and no revolutionary party dedicated to the overthrow of the existing state found place among them. The tradition of centralized royal government was more vigorous than ever after the reign of Elizabeth I. The growth of bureaucratic government, requiring the guidance of a supreme controller, continued to strengthen the position of the king as the final authority and maker of decisions.

The Shoals of Policy. Nonetheless James I could not hope to attain either greater glory for his dynasty or the religious unity of his peoples—the grand aims of his policy—without pains and exertions. Riot and rebellion were no longer a constant plague in England and Scotland, but restive-ness and readiness to resist unliked policy lurked beneath the surface; the danger in England was hidden from the king, who knew the country from books and reports but not from personal experience.

Englishmen had a long and strong tradition of obedience to royal gov-ernment, but they retained a lively sense of their right to be consulted about decisions affecting their lives and purses; the institution of Parliament rested not only upon the impulse of the monarch but also upon the memories and affections of the people.

The English legal system, the very foundation of everyday royal power in the enforcement of the laws, had achieved substantial autonomy; the common law could not be twisted or thwarted by the king without rousing the lawyers, a dangerous political pack when angered. Though local govern-ment continued to exist by royal authority and under supervision of the royal council, it was not a docile instrument of central government; it drew its strength not only from the king, far above, but at least equally from the local nobility and squirearchy from which it was selected. The declining value of money in an age of constant inflation made it more difficult than before for the monarch to live, according to the tradition, "of his own," for the permanent crown revenues were fixed in amount; but new taxation, which could be adjusted to changed conditions, normally required the assent of Parliament.

In Scotland the Parliament was feebler, but the king's subjects were readier to take up arms; in Ireland, resistance to the English conquest con-tinued to flare and flame after centuries. Although personal union of the three crowns afforded the king a measure of tactical freedom in his relations with the realms individually, it also increased the danger that insubordina-tion in one country would be encouraged and reinforced by similar move-ments in the others.

Wrangles with Parliament. Soon after his arrival in England, James received his first lesson in the facts of English political life. When he sum-moned Parliament in 1604, he ordered that election returns should be submitted to the court of chancery for verification; the House of Commons stubbornly refused to abandon its traditional privilege of judging the validity of its members' election. James, unready for such resistance, conceded the right, which limited his control over its membership. He also met defeat when he put before Parliament a plan to introduce free trade with Scotland and to grant all Scots the rights of free-born Englishmen. James for his part rejected a parliamentary plan for "perfect union," which by embodying Scotland within the English legal and governmental system, would reduce his hard-won powers in his native country. When Parliament refused to grant him a new regal title, he proclaimed himself nonetheless "King of Great Britain."

These issues were small compared to that of taxation. The king needed additional revenues to cover the expenses of his costly court, the rounds of his hunting, and his gifts to favorites. He was willing to ask Parliament for the funds, but considered it bound to grant what he requested. His first Parliament demanded that he make reforms and economies first, and would not accept his promise to consider their grievances after it voted funds. After he dissolved the Houses in 1611, he attempted to obtain extra revenues by imposing additional customs duties on merchants without parliamentary approval, and by rigorously enforcing payment of antiquated feudal dues; the result was more resentment than money. In 1614, he summoned another Parliament, but the same wrangle over the priority of grants or grievances developed and spilled over into denunciation of royal bounty to favorites. Two months and two days after it assembled, this "Addled" Parliament (so-called because it enacted no legislation) was dissolved.

Rule by Prerogative. When the king began to employ the old device of asking subjects for "benevolences," he discovered that his mere word did not move local officials any more effectively than it did Parliament. Sheriffs and justices of the peace in the counties balked openly, or simply sat on their hands, when the privy council instructed them to "persuade" wealthy residents to give to the king. They disapproved unparliamentary taxation like the "benevolences," and when they resisted together, they were too numerous to be replaced. James's attempts to tax by his own prerogative also brought him into conflict with the common-law courts. The judges, led by Sir Edward Coke, chief justice of the court of common pleas, resisted such taxation as depriving Englishmen of their property without proper process of law (that is, without either trial in court or enactment of a general tax by Parliament and king). In 1616 the king dismissed the unduly independent Coke.

James managed to govern without Parliament until 1621, when the plight of his son-in-law, Frederick V of the Palatinate and expelled king of Bohemia (see below, p. 246), created a need for more funds than the expedients of the previous decade could provide. Parliament, though favorable to Frederick's cause, demanded that the king explain his policy; he refused to explain, and they to give more than a small and inadequate amount.

Instead they took the offensive against the instruments of the king. Their first target was the corruption in the circle around his favorite, George Villiers, duke of Buckingham. Two of the duke's friends, Sir Francis Mitchell and Sir Giles Mompesson, were convicted by the House of Lords on charges brought by the Commons that they had extorted bribes from innkeepers in exchange for licenses, of which they held the monopoly. James had permitted their trial to divert criticism from himself and Buckingham. Parliament, thus encouraged, turned next upon a mightier offender, the lord high chancellor, Sir Francis Bacon, just named Viscount St. Albans. Bacon confessed to taking presents from persons involved in cases before him. The unstated offense for which he was really convicted was having supported the king's claim of absolute prerogative.

"Subjects' Birthright and Inheritance." Commons, further emboldened, returned to the question of foreign policy. In reply to the king's charge that they were meddling in his business, they issued a protestation (December 18, 1621) affirming their right to discuss and vote upon anything which affected the kingdom. Commons' prerogatives were "the ancient and undoubted birthright and inheritance of the subjects of England." James retaliated by dissolving Parliament (1622) and imprisoning the most outspoken leaders of Commons, including Coke, who had been elected a member after his dismissal as lord chief justice.

A change came over the king when he summoned his fourth and last Parliament in 1624. Physically, he was tormented by arthritic disorders; politically, he had learned the difficulties of enforcing an unwanted policy upon England; most of all, however, his Spanish policy (see below, p. 247) had failed. Now he asked the representative assembly for its advice, and later accepted their demand for war against Spain. He realized that a new power was rising in the state. "Chairs for the ambassadors!" he exclaimed when receiving a parliamentary delegation. Parliament was no longer satisfied merely to petition for redress of grievances, to legislate on matters put before it by the crown, and to grant taxes when requested. Commons in particular was more self-assertive than ever, although its specific claims did not go beyond its prerogatives of judging its members' election and its freedom of debate.

Puritans and Catholics. James's contest with his indocile English subjects over their legal and political rights was connected with and exacerbated by another struggle with the numerous Englishmen who would not accept the Anglican establishment in religion.

He first attempted to subdue this Puritan aberration by force of argument. Anglican bishops and Puritan theologians met at his command and under his supervision in a conference at Hampton Court in January, 1604. There the Puritans discovered that the king had acquired in Scotland a strong hatred for self-rule by the church; far from becoming their willing leader in the presbyterian transformation of the Church of England, as they had expected, he would be their bitterest foe in the enterprise. He warned the Puritans to conform or be harried from the land, and carried his threat into deeds. The Elizabethan Act of Uniformity was reinvigorated; the Anglican doctrine was stiffened by canons so rigidly anti-Puritan that some three hundred dissenting clergymen gave up their positions rather than force their consciences.

The re-establishment of episcopacy in Scotland in 1606 signalized the new situation: the king was able to rely on his strength in England to engage in his own kind of ecclesiastical reform in his native country. It was the Scottish kirk which was to be remodeled on the Church of England, and not vice versa.

The Puritans, though hurt, were not destroyed. Their cause became involved with that of the Parliamentarians, so that the king's inability to reduce opposition in the national assembly weakened his efforts to destroy the Puritans.

Relations between James and his Catholic subjects were more complex, never quite friendly and often openly hostile. On the one hand, the king, though loyal to Anglicanism, did not share the bitter hatred of most of his Scottish and English subjects for the old faith. On the other hand, as long as Rome permitted influential Catholic theologians to teach tyrannicidal doctrines, he feared that his Catholic subjects were potential traitors. He continued therefore to enforce Elizabethan anti-Catholic laws. The unsuccessful Gunpowder Plot (1604) of a small group of desperate Catholics to blow up the king and Parliament resulted in greater restrictions. The custom developed of burning the principal conspirator in effigy every November 5, on Guy Fawkes' Day; it helped to rivet in the memories of English Protestants a belief that English Catholics had a penchant for treason. Nonetheless, not many years after the conspiracy itself, repression of Catholics was relaxed. Queen Anne became a convert to Catholicism, and the king sought friendship and marriage alliances with Catholic kings, first of Spain and then of France.

Foreign Affairs: The King's Business. The personalism so characteristic of James I's policy was nowhere more evident than in his conduct of foreign affairs. The determination of policy toward other states and potentates belonged only to himself; his subjects had no right whatever to inquire into what was the king's private business, even less to demand any particular program of action. To buttress these claims, James referred back to the centuries-old royal prerogative of conducting foreign relations without the intervention of Parliament; but he failed to realize that English monarchs had usually sought the views of influential subjects, particularly merchants whose very livelihood depended upon the state of peace and war with their customers or competitors.

The first act of James's foreign policy was to end the long-sputtering war with Spain by a compromise peace in 1604. Relations between the governments improved rapidly, but the English nation remained hostile to the Spaniards. Its Protestantism was moved to anxiety by Spanish leadership of the embattled Catholic Reformation. Its sense of justice and quest for profit were offended by the Spanish practice of seizing English ships and crews despite the advent of peace.

The king and people differed less in their attitude toward the Dutch. James disliked them as successful rebels; the people were more concerned with the Dutch as mighty rivals in trade, fishing, and shipping, whose success was all the more distasteful because they exploited in high-handed fashion the Channel and the North Sea, which the British considered their own. The conflict of interests extended to the new markets of the East Indies; Dutch expulsion of English merchants from the Spice Islands aroused English wrath, especially after the execution of English factors at Amboina (see ch. 6, p. 133). Whenever the threat to the Protestant cause rose high, however, Englishmen tended to forget other matters and seek closer alliance with the United Provinces for the sake of their common Protestant faith.

Protestant Leadership and a Catholic Courtship. This duality of English policy towards the Dutch was simplicity itself compared to the complications of James's policy toward Germany and Spain in the latter part of his reign. On the one hand, he played the part of a leader of Protestantism against the counterassaults of the Catholic Reformation; on the other, he sought the favor of Catholic Spain, which led the attack upon Protestantism. In 1608, James joined the Protestant Union in Germany, and five years later married his daughter Elizabeth to its leader, Frederick V of the Palatinate.

The arrival in England that same year of a guileful Spanish ambassador, Diego Sarmiento de Acuña, later named count of Gondomar, brought the doom of James's frankly Protestant policy. The British monarch made the worldly-wise Gondomar a confidant into whose cynically receptive ears he poured out his complaints against his own subjects and their institutions. "It is one of my greatest services," Gondomar informed his royal master in Madrid, "that I have been able to rouse such bitterness and mistrust between the king and the lower house." Gondomar deftly plied the English monarch with the value of Spanish friendship. Negotiations for marriage between a Spanish *infanta* and the prince of Wales, Charles, proved a lure which held James with almost magic attraction. James panted for the £600,000 the princess would bring as a dowry, but the Spaniards raised demands—the suspension of penal laws against Roman Catholics in England; the baptizing and education of children resulting from the proposed marriage as Catholics, and their right to retain their faith if they inherited the throne—which James could not grant.

A French Bride and Spanish War. Frederick V's fling at kingship in Bohemia in 1619-1620 (see ch. 14, p. 323) had briefly both appalled and delighted James, who disliked rebellion for any cause but gladly saw a queen's crown on his daughter's head. English opinion took up their cause, and James asked Parliament for money with which to support them; but he would not abandon his quest of a Spanish bride for his son, and fondly deceived himself, with Gondomar's help, into believing that Madrid would abandon the Hapsburg emperor for the sake of an English marriage. The conflict between Parliament and king played into Gondomar's hands, at least until the prince of Wales, accompanied by the duke of Buckingham, went uninvited to Spain to seek the *infanta's* hand in person. There they were put off with vague words, until they realized that the whole business had been a farce from the beginning. Thus personal indignity at last caused James to accept the anti-Spanish policy his subjects had been demanding.

War with Spain, the reversal of a whole reign's efforts, resulted. Alliances were arranged with the Dutch and the Danes, and the French proved willing to give Henrietta Maria, the French king's sister, as bride to the prince of Wales. The marriage treaty was already concluded, but the wedding had not taken place when James I died in 1625.

II. The Reign of Charles I

The new king, Charles I, though born a Scot, had been reared in England and was in language and manner an Englishman. Yet he had little sympathy for or understanding of the minds and motives of his English subjects and felt toward them no such obligation of honorable conduct as he observed toward his family and friends.

The Choice before the King.   His position when he began to rule was on the whole favorable. Although political and religious opposition was as vigorous as it had been under his father, it was dispersed; unless the king summoned Parliament and kept it in session, opponents lacked any effective channel for their activity. Charles could do without Parliament, however; the fixed revenues of the crown, supplemented by income from expedients, provided a bare adequacy for maintenance of the government and the court. Avoidance of expensive foreign entanglements and war was consequently necessary, but insular Britain could easily remain out of the broils of the powers across the Channel and the North Sea. Time, by creating and reinforcing new habits, could strengthen the basis for the king's endeavor to rule by prerogative and to put down Puritanism. Such a policy, however, meant forgoing the public prestige on which the king doted and the free-handed expenditures on which the queen, Henrietta Maria, insisted as her regal right.

In 1625, however, Charles I did not think it necessary to accept frugality and inaction as the basis of his policy. The war with Spain was as much the result of Parliament's clamor as of his own policy while prince of Wales; the assembly would certainly grant him funds to fight the Spaniard. When it assembled in June, he was quickly undeceived. Commons voted only a seventh of what he asked, and compounded the affront by granting the customs dues ("tonnage and poundage") for a single year, instead of for the whole reign as had been customary.

Parliament's Grievances. Members reiterated that redress of grievances must precede further grant of funds. When it was hinted that the duke of Buckingham, Charles's favorite like his father's, was the greatest grievance of all, the king dissolved Parliament: he would not allow it to touch his friend. The war with Spain continued, but it was so badly directed by Buckingham, and so loosely fought, that it brought the English only shame; an English alliance with Louis XIII proved useless, since he insisted on using English ships against the Huguenots at La Rochelle and was indignant when the crews balked at fighting fellow Protestants.

The need for funds became so urgent that Charles summoned another Parliament in 1626. It gave him not support but bitter criticism. In Commons Sir John Eliot hinted at treason. Buckingham was named as the author of the country's woes and an impeachment against him begun. To save him from almost certain conviction, Charles dissolved his second Parliament. The first had met for less than two months, the second for little more than four.

The Petition of Right. The slovenly conduct of foreign policy led to war with France, yesterday's ally. An effort to aid the defenders of La Rochelle won the support of the British nation, but Buckingham's ignominious failure in the expedition sent to its relief (see ch. 9, pp. 198-199) raised hatred against him to a new pitch. To raise money, the government asked for "benevolences," but those who refused to contribute were imprisoned as if they had been guilty of nonpayment of taxes.

The issue of the forced loan dominated the elections for the Parliament which Charles summoned in March, 1628. Again the opponents of the king's policy won a majority in Commons. Sir Edward Coke took the lead in proposing a petition for the redress of grievances not of individuals but of the whole nation. The Petition of Right, as it was called, called on the king to end taxation without parliamentary legislation, to reaffirm the right of prisoners to seek writs of habeas corpus (requiring that the cases against them be stated and brought to trial), and to cease compulsory quartering of troops upon the civil population or any action by martial law.

Charles attempted to equivocate, but Parliament would not be put off. Desperate for funds, the king at last gave his assent. The Petition was not a statute but a mere promise, however, and Charles felt free to act according to his own judgment. Parliament voted additional taxes, and forced loans ceased; but the conflict with the monarch was soon resumed when he continued to collect tonnage and poundage by his own prerogative, the parliamentary grant having expired in 1626. When Commons drew up a remonstrance against unparliamentary taxation, Charles adjourned Parliament until the following January.

In August 1628, the duke of Buckingham was slain by an assassin; the public rejoicing was a sign that the king was losing popular affection. Blind to this peril, Charles continued with his basic program of prerogative government and Anglicanism. Nonparliamentary taxes were maintained. The appointment of William Laud, the leading "Arminian," or anti-Puritan, as bishop of London marked the resumption of the king's drive to enforce religious uniformity.

Taxation and Religion. These two issues—taxation and religion—became the principal business of the new session of Parliament called in January, 1629. Eliot introduced three resolutions opposing papist and Arminian innovation in the church and denouncing as treason to the king and kingdom either levying or paying tonnage and poundage without authorization by Parliament. When the speaker of the House of Commons attempted to rise, thereby ending the sitting and preventing a vote, he was held down in his chair by violent hands and the resolutions were passed.

Commons was claiming more than it ever had before: the king's policy, it asserted, required its approval; resistance to its decisions therefore was treason. If he granted these demands, Charles accepted Parliament as an equal partner in his sovereignty. He had no intention of accepting any such equality.

Instead he dissolved this third Parliament (March) and determined upon a new course—to rule permanently without Parliament. It was a bold gamble for high stakes. If Charles succeeded, the politically powerful classes in the country would be bridled. But if he failed, they would confront him again, more resolute and embittered than they had ever been before.

Ship Money. Charles recognized that his whole policy hung upon the question of finances. Eking out the fixed revenues of the crown by all possible devices; frugality in domestic expenditures; and avoidance of war, the great devourer of money—these were the necessary conditions for his success. The land forces in England were allowed to decline, but the navy could not be slighted without danger. Other expenses were ruthlessly cut. The immense royal debt of more than £1,000,000 went unpaid; the more fortunate creditors were given monopolies or other means of recouping their losses at the expense of the populace. Old feudal dues were resurrected and enforced with implacable vigor.

Still the king could not "live of his own." Other revenues had to be found. Royal officials continued to collect tonnage and poundage without parliamentary authorization; the increasing prosperity of trade made these customs duties more remunerative than ever. Ship money, a tax levied during medieval times on coastal towns to pay the expense of maintaining a fleet for their defense, was resurrected in 1634. The next year it was extended to inland counties, where it had never been paid; by 1636 it was evident that the government intended to make it a permanent and general tax.

To test its legality, John Hampden, a Buckinghamshire country gentleman of Puritan sympathies, refused to pay ship money; he was tried and found guilty. The legal basis of his conviction was the absolutist doctrine of Roman law that the king's will was law. In the traditional view, however, a prince who took money from his subjects without their consent, that is, without parliamentary grant, was a tyrant.

Decisions like that against Hampden did not gain respect because of this tradition and also because there was notorious pressure upon judges to find as the king wished. Selden, the greatest lawyer in the country, commented, "Now the judges they interpret the law, & what judges can be made to doe wee all knowe." With respect for the law courts dwindling and Parliament unsummoned, the base of the government's active supporters was being narrowed.

Archbishop Laud. The king also gave himself to his other great enterprise: to make the Anglican church universal and unrivaled in his lands. In practice, however, it was only Puritans and other Protestant dissenters who felt the weight of repression; Roman Catholics had lapsed into quiesence and ceased to call attention to themselves, except when they attended mass at the chapels of the queen or Catholic envoys.

William Laud, promoted archbishop of Canterbury in 1633, directed the campaign against Puritan clergymen with tenacious energy and efficiency. He barred them from pulpits and press and punished their transgressions by every means short of hanging and the stake. His use of the ecclesiastical court of High Commission for these disciplinary measures drew the fire of the common-law courts; the practice of bishops sitting in cases involving their own interests profoundly offended the principle of law that no man should be judge in his own case. Laud did not succeed in rooting out the Puritans, for they had defenders in plenty among the gentry, nobility, and merchants. The archbishop did complete the alienation of the Puritans from the Anglican church; they gave up all hope of achieving their purposes within its framework and became its open enemies.

There was no way, however, for either Puritans or erstwhile Parliamentarians to thwart the king. Their rancor seemed futile. Parliament did not meet, and would not so long as the king could live within his means, as he managed to do; and without Parliament, united resistance was impossible. The law courts were more and more tractable to the royal will. Individual resistance, like Hampden's, led only to defeat. No one contemplated such wild folly as general rebellion. The slow implacable grinding down of opposition made it seem certain that the king would achieve his purposes.

Rebellion in Scotland. Their very success in England prompted the king and the archbishop to undertake the selfsame work in Scotland. They assumed, and were much deceived, that because the Scots had been quiet during the English troubles, they were tame. In their Calvinist convictions and their devotion to their ministers the people remained unshaken. As for the nobility, they had turned against the crown and made common cause with the Calvinist divines when Charles I, in the first year of his reign, ordered the recapture of all crown and church lands given away since 1542. Laud's decision to complete transformation of the Scottish kirk on the Anglican model set the spark to the tinder. In 1637 the Scottish bishops, till then barely tolerated, attempted to introduce a new Book of Common Prayer and uniform services patterned on the Anglican liturgy.

Rioting broke out in Edinburgh. Throughout the land obedience was refused to the royal authorities. When the king commanded his council at Edinburgh to repress the disorders, the councilors replied that they were powerless. In 1638 the character of the Scots' purposes was made clear in a Solemn League and Covenant signed by most of the population; in it they promised to resist innovation in religion even at the cost of life, but reaffirmed their loyalty to the monarchy and its laws and liberties. Charles refused to accept the Covenant: it would reduce him, he said, to the impotence of the doge of Venice.

He soon discovered that he had no power over the unwilling Scots, who defiantly took up reform of church and state in spite of his ban. To safeguard their work, they were willing to fight with arms. While Charles assembled a force in England, the Scots organized their own under experienced officers who had seen service on the continent. When the two armies met at last in June 1639, it was the king's which withdrew ignominiously without risking battle. The treaty of Berwick which ended this First Bishop's War was a royal capitulation; the Scots were authorized to elect a new Parliament and a new general assembly of their kirk.

Strafford. Charles I had driven himself into a corner. If he continued his efforts to reduce the Scots to obedience, he would need an army; to raise and pay it, expedients would clearly not suffice. The English Parliament would have to be summoned again; but this was to risk pulling down the whole system of government by prerogative which Charles had slowly and carefully erected during the previous eleven years. If he permitted the Scots to preserve the self-rule they had won with such swift ease, he would have to swallow an open insult to his royal majesty; nor would his English system be safe any longer, for the example of the Scots was contagious. He would have to do something, but what?

Temperamentally, Charles I was drawn to a solution by force. It was embodied for him in the person of Sir Thomas Wentworth, lord deputy of

Ireland. A former leader of the parliamentary opposition who had gone over to the crown when he glimpsed danger to the social and political order, Wentworth had governed the English North and then Ireland in a harsh, despotic and effective manner he called "Thorough." Charles called Wentworth back from Ireland to become his supreme councilor; to enhance his authority, the king named him earl of Strafford.

The Short Parliament. At the same time, the king attempted to gain the advantages of a policy of conciliation. Hoping by sweet promises to wheedle funds, Charles summoned another Parliament to meet on April 13, 1640. When the members assembled at Westminster, they displayed no willingness to play the king's game; instead, they reflected the great disquietude and hostility aroused in the country by eleven years of rule by prerogative. Commons threw down the gauntlet to the king by taking its leadership from John Pym, who had been imprisoned for his part in earlier parliamentary resistance.

When Charles asked it for funds, promising to consider grievances once they were granted, Commons replied with its own version of first things first. Pym put together all the scattered demands for parliamentary right and privilege into a comprehensive program; if all these demands were conceded, essential sovereignty in England would pass from monarch to the representatives of the nation. Charles, angered at having his game balked, dissolved Parliament on May 5. It had sat for three weeks, well meriting the name of Short Parliament.

"Thorough"—Trial and Failure. Strafford now had the opportunity to act on his own strategy of "Thorough." He told the council he could reduce the Scots even without funds to pay for troops. In that case, the government would be released from "all rules," since in an emergency everything was to be done "that power might admit." The army in Ireland, his strong keen sword which had cut down rebellion there, could be brought "here to reduce this kingdom."

The Scots' victory in the Second Bishops' War turned this Machiavellian boast to ashes. In the treaty of Ripon (October 1640), Charles was compelled to promise pay of £850 daily to the Scots forces encamped on English territory; until it was paid off, the army would maintain its position, ready to act. Even worse, the Scots were hailed by many Englishmen as friends and allies, not invaders! It was essential to divide these two causes by sending the Scots back to their own land. Seeing no way to obtain the money, Charles summoned another Parliament. He hoped it would be a lesser evil, and a brief one.

When it assembled on November 3, 1640, his hope was dashed. Half of the members of Commons had sat in the Short Parliament. Strafford prepared to decapitate the opposition by accusing its leaders of plotting treason with the Scots against the king. Pym and his friends attacked first. Six days after Parliament opened, Commons began an impeachment of Strafford, charging him with treason. When the evidence against Strafford proved legally inadequate, the Commons abandoned the trial and took the more certain step of passing a bill of attainder (a statutory declaration of guilt) against him; the House of Lords passed it in turn and sent it to the king. In a final gesture of self-sacrifice, Charles's councilor urged him to sign the bill, lest outright rebellion ensue. The monarch, in tears, fearful for the safety of his queen and children, signed. On May 12, 1641, Strafford mounted the scaffold, not fearing death now that his world was crumbling. "I . . . doe as cheerfully put off my doublet at this time, as ever I did when I went to bed," he said. The axe fell. The author of "Thorough" was the first victim of its failure.

Parliament followed up its advantage by striking from the king's hand the oft-used weapon of dissolution. The Triennial Act provided that Parliament must be summoned not later than three years after a dissolution, and created machinery to summon the assembly if the monarchy failed to do so. Another act forbade royal adjournment or dissolution of the existing Parliament without its own approval. Other bills abolished the two courts of the Star Chamber and High Commission. Unnerved and almost deserted, Charles gave his assent. When it came to going beyond reform of government to remaking the church, the parliamentarians were divided: a bill to abolish the episcopacy (the "Root and Branch Bill") received the support of only the extreme Puritans.

The Grand Remonstrance. With Strafford gone and Laud in the Tower under parliamentary impeachment, Charles was thrown upon his own resources of mind and will. The outbursts of Catholic rebellion in Ireland, where many thousands of Protestants were slain, especially in Ulster, began the final ruin of the king's cause in England. The Parliament at Westminster dared not trust Charles with the army that had to be raised for defeating the Irish insurgency; the members feared, with reason, that he would prefer to use these troops against his English subjects. It voted therefore an army bill reserving to itself the appointment of army officers. Then in a Grand Remonstrance (December 1, 1641), it summarized all its grievances. Concession on these issues would reduce the king's power to nil.

In a stab of desperation to redeem his position, Charles attempted to carry through Strafford's plan of arresting and punishing the leaders of Parliament. He marched in person to the Parliament building to seize Pym, Hampden and three other leaders of Commons; when he arrived, the "birds had flown" to the City of London, which stood ready to defend them with arms (January 20, 1642). Charles thereupon fled from his rebellious capital to York, closer to the Scots in the North. There he refused his assent to bills establishing Parliamentary control over the church, the army, and the king's ministers, requiring its approval for creation of new peers, and giving it guardianship over the royal family—the supreme indignity.

III. The Civil War

The struggle of arms for control of England began, while the Scots looked on, ready to throw in their weight as their interests dictated, and the Irish Catholics spread their rebellion with impunity.

Cavaliers and Roundheads. The Cavaliers included two distinct groups: noblemen personally devoted to Charles I, dashing, gallant courtiers contemptuous of the common folk; and more sober men, usually country gentlemen like Sir Edward Hyde, who wished to preserve the traditional monarchy and constitution as the essential foundation of the entire civil and social order, and therefore urged reconciliation between the king and all temperate elements among his people.

The contrary party was equally diverse. It numbered in its ranks probably a majority of the merchants and lower classes in the country, but also a substantial minority of the nobles and squires. It drew support from Anglicans moved to opposition by the king's attempts to rule by prerogative, and from Puritans (called Roundheads because of their close-shorn hair) moved at least equally by questions of religion. It included a moderate wing of those who believed they were defending the existing order in society and the state against royal innovation, and an extreme wing of ardent reformers who combined religious separatism and enthusiasm with sharp hostility to the existing social and economic system.

The geographical base of the two parties reflected this disparity: although both had adherents throughout the land, the Cavaliers were strongest in the western and northern parts of the country, where there were fewer trading towns, the Parliamentarians in the east and south, where commerce and its attendant, a more capitalistic agriculture, were dominant.

A substantial majority of Englishmen belonged to neither camp, however. They watched most great events with detached interest, except for their antipathy to Roman Catholicism and their distaste for whatever disturbed the even tenor of their lives. In 1642 this preference for calm removed them from the royalist camp; their allegiance to the Parliamentary side depended immediately upon the success of its arms and ultimately upon its policy.

Victory of the "New Model Army." The decision now lay not with the debaters and lawmakers, but with those upon whom they called in the final fearful case to enforce their wills—the warmakers. In the organization of armies for civil war which followed the escape of the king from London, both sides had advantages. Many of the Cavalier gentlemen and nobles who took the royal "commissions of array" to raise companies had been schooled in the craft of war in continental campaigns; but there was no money in the royal treasury to pay the troops. The parliamentary army, organized under the Ordinance of Militia (March 3, 1642) did not possess as many skilled commanders, but its paymasters had filled coffers, thanks to Parliament's ability to collect taxes and make loans.

The first two years of fighting were indecisive. It was not until a Puritan country gentleman, Oliver Cromwell of Huntingdonshire, took leadership in the parliamentary camp that a break came in the strategic stalemate. From the victorious Swedes in Germany (see ch. 14, p. 331), Cromwell learned the value of hard drill, strict discipline, and devotion to a cause in the establishment of an effective fighting force. Cromwell's regiment of "Ironsides" proved the success of this system in the defeat of the royal army at Marston Moor (July 2, 1644), which gave Parliament control of the North. During the next year, Cromwell built a larger "New Model Army" of 22,000 men on the pattern of the "Ironsides." At Naseby (June 15, 1645), it cut down the last effective force on Charles's side. Fighting continued on a small scale until Sir Jacob Astley surrendered to the parliamentary forces at Stow-on-the-Wold (March 26, 1646). The royalist commander told his captors, "You have now done your work and may go play, unless you will fall out amongst yourselves."

The Solemn League and Covenant. Astley's compliment was slily barbed. Military victory had been easier to achieve than political concord among the Parliamentarians. The very breadth of the opposition which Charles I had called into being was a cause of dissension and weakness. Among the king's opponents were Anglican royalists who wanted only to persuade him to accept loyally the legislation of 1641 assuring Parliament a share in the power of the state. Their Puritan allies wanted more and, thanks to the aid of the Scots, were able to achieve it. In September 1643, 25 Puritan members of the House of Lords and 288 members of Commons put their signatures to a Solemn League and Covenant like that made in Scotland five years before; it placed upon them the obligation to unify the religion of the British kingdoms "according to the word of God, and the examples of the best reformed churches"; it also pledged preservation of the Church of Scotland.

The conflict of purposes between the Anglicans and Puritans, between the moderates and the bold spirits, came into the open after Marston Moor. The commander of the parliamentary army, the earl of Manchester, told his lieutenant-general, Oliver Cromwell, "If we beat the king ninety and nine times, yet he is king still and so will his posterity be after him; but if the king beat us once we shall all be hanged, and our posterity made slaves."

"If this be so," Cromwell retorted, "why did we take up arms at first? If so, let us make peace, be it never so base."

Presbyterians and Puritans. It was not surrender but more resolute war which Cromwell favored. He seized the initiative for stronger actions against the crown with the aid of the Scots. The Covenant of 1643 had changed them from passive onlookers, though far from disinterested, to active participants again in English events. In January 1644 a Scottish army had crossed the Tweed again to bring its assistance to the Parliamentarians. The alliance of English Puritans and Scottish Presbyterians bore fruit a year later, when Archbishop Laud, their common archenemy, was executed under act of attainder (January 1645) and Parliament established Presbyterianism as the state religion of England; but there was a worm in the apple, a proviso permitting rights of toleration to Independents.

Unlike Scottish Presbyterianism, a sternly disciplined and strictly organized church since its formation by John Knox, English Puritanism had always remained a loose and informal alliance of more or less like-minded religious reformers; the factions within it began to break apart in the moment of their common triumph, and the separatist moods generated by a decade of Laudianism took the form of advocacy of self-rule by independent congregations. This was highly offensive to the Scots, for whom their own system of tight ecclesiastical discipline, with presbyteries of individual congregations subordinated to an elaborate series of higher authorities, was the only form of church organization authorized and permitted by Scripture. Since mid-1643 they had argued this position with tenacious fervor in the Westminster Assembly, a conference of English Puritans and Scots ministers called together to seek agreement on religious questions between the two countries.

The ability of the Scots to impose their practice upon the English declined abruptly after the parliamentary victory at Naseby. Cromwell's regiments, predominantly Independent in religion, were in no mood to knuckle to Presbyterian intolerance, English or Scots. They knew that their blood and weapons had won the victory over the king, they knew for what they fought and loved what they knew, and would not obey Parliament merely because it supplied their pay.

The Breach between Parliament and Army. For Charles I, who gave himself up to the Scots (May 5, 1646), the wrangling among his foes gave cause for hope. An opportunity to make his peace with the English Parliament and regain his liberty was given the king in the Newcastle proposals (July 1646); but to sign the Covenant, accept Presbyterianism as the state religion, and concede Parliament control of the army for two decades was too great a price to pay when army and Parliament seemed ready to fall out. Once again the overwily monarch misplayed his hand. In return for £400,000, half the sum due them for the back pay of their army, the Scots handed over

Charles I to the control of the English Parliament (January 1647). As Charles had anticipated, the dispute between the representative assembly and the army became a breach; but he was no longer a free agent, able to seek his own advantage.

Parliament moved to quell the insubordination of its instrument of victory. It passed over Cromwell, the lieutenant-general, in reappointing Thomas Fairfax, a moderate, as commander-in-chief; it re-enacted the Self-Denying Ordinance of 1645, preventing generals from holding seats in Parliament; and ordered all soldiers unwilling to serve in Ireland against the Catholic rebels to be discharged with a puny portion of the back pay due them. At the same time, it reopened negotiations with the king in the hope of achieving an agreement with him by which its need of the army within England would be eliminated.

The King Seized and Deposed. Cromwell and his colleagues struck with their customary speed and sharpness. A detachment of troops seized Charles I. Meanwhile the army encamped at Triptow Heath proclaimed its intention of resisting disbandment until its purposes had been achieved, and elected delegates to debate issues of moment. Efforts of the army to strike an agreement with either the king or Parliament failed. In August it entered London and compelled the assembly to permit the members favorable to its cause to retake their seats.

The escape of the king to the Isle of Wight, off the south coast, in November, gave Parliament its chance to regain the upper hand by reaching an agreement with the monarch in its turn. But Charles, though made a prisoner by the military commander on the island, rejected four bills by which he would accept parliamentary control of the army for twenty years and the legitimacy of all parliamentary activity during the civil war. The king made a secret engagement with representatives of the Scottish nobility (December 1647); in return for his promise to establish Presbyterianism as the state religion in England, suppressing both Independents and Anglicans, the Scots agreed to invade England in order to re-establish his power. As soon as Parliament realized what was afoot, it at last abandoned the pretext that it was against the king's evil ministers, not himself, that it was acting, and declared that he had forfeited his kingship (January 1648).

Civil war began again. The course of battle ran swiftly and surely in favor of the parliamentary forces of England. The English royalists were defeated in Cornwall, in Wales, and near London. The downfall of the Scots at Preston Pans in August was the last battle of the war. The fighting done, the victors turned to the contest among themselves.

The Execution of Charles I. When Parliament reassembled in March, the moderate Puritans, now called Presbyterians like their Scots brethren, were in a large majority. They reopened negotiations with the captive king and made a treaty with him in December; the army retaliated by seizing Charles once more and by sending Colonel Thomas Pride to eject another 140 members. "Pride's Purge" left no more than 60 Independents out of more than 500 original members of the House of Commons; but the remnant of that assembly continued to claim the rights and play the part of the sovereign representative of the English nation.

The first action of the Rump Parliament was to cease negotiations with the king and bring him to trial. A special court of high justice, with 135 members, was entrusted with the task. Charles defended himself with vigor and courage. He denied the legality of the trial, since all authority in the state derived from him, and warned that the freedom of all Englishmen, not merely his own life, was at stake. Harsh warnings from Cromwell were necessary to bring a majority of the 67 judges present to condemn the king to death (February 4, 1649); the ancient tradition of the sacredness of kings had not been violated for almost two centuries, and then in the heat of battle by rivals for the throne, but never before in such cold deliberation by subjects. Yet Charles I, by persistent ineptness, by callous contempt for the opinions of lesser men, by repeated duplicity, had undermined his own rule and called forth from within his subjects forces and passions which destroyed him.

After his sentence, the monarch conducted himself with honesty and dignity. He believed that God was punishing him for his cowardice in accepting Strafford's sacrifice. When he walked out from his palace at Whitehall on February 9, 1649, onto the scaffold, it was of the fate of the peoples of Britain and not of himself that he spoke; then he put his head upon the block and calmly gave up his life to the axe.

IV. The Commonwealth

The abolition of the title and office of king transformed England into a "Commonwealth," as a state without a monarch at its head was called.

The Dissimilar Victors. England—the land and the rule over it—belonged no longer to the king as his inherited estate, but to the nation. The nation, at the moment, meant the victors, the bold and dedicated men in and out of Parliament who had waged the supreme struggle against the king. They all held, to a greater or lesser degree, an image of a better life, more permeated with religion and more sedate in its habits than the England of yore.

But their unity was fragile. One group among them numbered the revolutionaries for whom the revolution had come to an end with the execution of Charles I. They were men of wealth and standing who wished to keep

England a complex society of classes set one above another, in which property in land and commerce was linked to political and social privilege and power.

In the other group were the revolutionaries for whom the revolution continued. They represented the new forces which had emerged during the crisis of the 1640's. They were principally shopkeepers or artisans, men of little or no wealth, of the kind who hitherto had obeyed, not commanded. For them "Commonwealth" meant more than a republic; it also signified a more even distribution of property, an austere and sober way of life. However sedate in private life, they acted and spoke on public matters with vigor and asperity. They had found a forum for their ideas in the debates conducted in the army during the mid-1640's. In religion they advocated total independence of church congregations and voluntarism in membership, and frequently they practiced an intensely mystical religious life.

Levelers and Diggers. The most important among them were the Levelers, who advocated universal suffrage, religious tolerance and social reform. Their leader was John Lilburne, who had resigned an army commission because he felt that Parliament was defending aristocracy. Even more drastic than the Levelers were the Diggers, led by Gerrard Winstanley; redistribution of ownership of land was the center of their economic program, but Winstanley himself was a mystic for whom economic equality followed from the fraternity of men under God. When the Diggers began to plow up the untilled heathlands near London, the government suppressed them. Had power been transferred from king to Parliament by debates and votes instead of by the argument of arms, such visionaries would never have come to the fore of public life. But, because they furnished the bulk of the soldiery for Cromwell's "New Model Army," they found themselves thrust into the center of politics, where they could exert influence upon the character of the state.

It was the conservative revolutionaries who kept control of England. They repressed the most violent of the democratic reformers and moved to reorganize the state. They did not reshape the whole system of government but merely adapted the old royal pattern to the conditions of republicanism. The source of authority was in theory the Rump Parliament, in which only half a hundred members still sat. A council of state of 41 members, almost three-quarters of them members of Parliament, exercised the executive functions like the privy council of which it was the lineal descendant. In law the council was the supreme executive; in fact, it accepted the leadership of Oliver Cromwell, who was named commander-in-chief of the army.

Oliver Cromwell. Cromwell, more than any other single man, was the personification of the English revolution in all its multiplicity and inner tensions. The army accorded him a personal loyalty such as the professional soldiery of the continent gave their captains, but he was more than the *condottiere* of the revolution. He was the indispensable go-between and arbiter among its numerous elements, who were torn between their increasing mistrust and even hatred for each other and their need to co-operate for their common defense. A country gentleman with a keen business sense and an intense Puritanism of an Independent kind, he had grown with the crisis of England into a master of politics as well as of war. In the midst of perils and problems, he remained self-possessed and self-assured. He used men royally, for his own purposes. He was devoted to the cause which had made him great and powerful, and he was ready to employ blunt strength and cunning trickery to keep that cause safe and strong.

The English victors' action in abolishing the monarchy and establishing the Commonwealth brought war with both Scotland and Ireland. Both proclaimed the eldest son of the late king as Charles II. Scottish Presbyterianism had never taken on a republican character; it did not seek to shake the order of the state, but only to make the king an honest and faithful Calvinist. For the Irish, fidelity to Charles II was more of a pretext, for it was against the English and their Protestant religion, rather than for the king, that they rose. Cromwell, the successful rebel, now faced defenders of the fallen dynasty; in his eyes, however, it was they who were "rebels" against legitimate authority, for God by granting his arms victory had demonstrated the righteousness of his cause.

Defeat of the Irish and Scots. Cromwell first took his army to Ireland, where it had refused to go at the command of Charles I. It defeated the Irish forces in the open field and cut down or enslaved the defenders of Drogheda and Wexford (1649), as barbarians fighting against civilization and God's cause; harshness towards them would discourage other Irish from revolting. The massacre of Drogheda became fixed in Irish memories as proof of English savagery, an Irish Guy Fawkes' Day as it were, which embittered them against their conquerors for centuries. The last of Irish resistance was put down by 1652. Englishmen of the triumphant party were rewarded with grants of "plantations," formed by lands seized from the native Irish who remained to till on rackrents the soil they had once held as personal or tribal property.

The Scottish resistance to the English developments lasted longer. The young Charles, more supple than his father, swore loyalty to the Covenant and gained the support of the Scottish divines as well as of the nobility. Cromwell, once back from Ireland, carried the war to the Scots. He defeated them at Dunbar in September, 1650, but they kept an army in the field which Charles led in an invasion of England a year later. Cromwell swung back from the Scottish port of Perth, which he had just captured, and crushed the Scots at Worcester, far to the south, on September 3, 1651. Charles II fled to France in disguise, after hairbreadth escapes and harrowing difficulties; the repeated assistance he received during his flight from those who stayed behind and faced grim penalties indicated the persistence of powerful, though repressed, royalist sympathies in England.

The Protectorate.   Victory won, the republicans turned again to the dissensions among themselves. The Rump Parliament claimed sovereignty according to the doctrines evolved during the struggle with Charles I. Its pretensions proved hollow when it attempted to lay down the law to the army. In April 1653 Cromwell, acting on behalf of the military, dismissed the Parliament and the council of state which had taken its side.

Four years after the formation of the Commonwealth, its constitutional character was again in suspense. Cromwell would not yield to the dictates of the Rump, but neither did he desire to rule by the naked sword, like the tyrants of fifteenth-century Italy. Thus he did not set himself up as a military dictator but endeavored to rebuild a parliamentary basis for his government. A nominated Parliament of 140 members ("Barebone's Parliament," so-called after one of its most vocal members, a London merchant and Baptist preacher named Praisegod Barbon or Barebon) assembled briefly to establish a new system of government.

The Instrument of Government was the first and only written constitution in the history of England. It instituted Cromwell "Lord Protector of the Commonwealth of England, Scotland, and Ireland" (December, 1653). Cromwell put on many of the trappings of kingship: he held court in the royal palaces and he signed papers with his first name and the initial of his title, "Oliver P," as the late king had signed "Charles R(ex)"; his office, most significantly, was made hereditary. The council of state was reorganized with 21 members and a triennial Parliament established with 460 members, including 30 each from Scotland and Ireland, sitting in a single house of commons. Voters were limited to those who held at least £200 in property; this was a more narrow electorate than that which chose the Tudor and Stuart Parliaments. Parliament retained the right to vote taxes and grant revenues to the lord protector. The protectorate was therefore essentially a reconstitution of the monarchy, without a king but with the protector playing the king's part.

Military Dictatorship.   The elections to the new Parliament brought in a majority of moderate Presbyterians who were appalled by the upsurge of separatist religion and democratic political movements, especially in the army and the towns. They soon entered into direct conflict with the protector. When they tried to use their power of the purse strings to control him, he struck back; to accept fiscal subserviency was to undergo political subordination, and he possessed as strong a sense of his rights, and of the righteousness of his policy, as the king whom he had sent to death. In 1654 Cromwell attempted to expel recalcitrant members from Parliament, but it responded by declaring his office elective, not hereditary. Angry at its independence, he dissolved it in January 1655. The quasi-king was employing the very method of dissolution which had brought to issue the contest between Parliament and the Stuart kings!

For the next twenty months, Cromwell governed as a military dictator. He did not summon Parliament and he pushed the direct authority of the central government down into the counties and towns. Local government was taken from the control of justices of the peace and sheriffs, where it had remained through all the earlier changes, and entrusted to eleven major generals. Their rule brought home to all Englishmen the moral and social code of conduct which the Puritans had developed for themselves and now attempted by the persuasion of arms to enforce upon their countrymen. The traditional "merrie England" gave way to an ascetic "Zion." Characteristic of the new sobriety and religiosity was stringent sabbatarianism. Sunday ceased to be a day when men relaxed with games, songs, and dances after church services; it became a day of long sermons and longer silences, from which both play and work were barred.

Most Englishmen soon hated this new tyranny of compulsory righteousness, especially after it began to exact unprecedentedly high taxes with rigor and efficiency. They began to yearn for the return of the "good old days" of monarchy, so slipshod and easygoing in its control and its moral purpose compared to the rule of the generals, who sought victory not over the visible enemy on the battlefield but rather over the frailties and laxities of ordinary men.

In September 1656 Cromwell summoned a new Parliament in an effort to bolster the base of his regime. His efforts to control the election of members failed and the assembly began an attempt to limit the protector's authority. A group of his supporters urged Cromwell to take the title of king and establish a new dynasty as a means of consolidating his power and making it permanent beyond his own lifetime. Cromwell declined the offer, partly because of his own lingering antipathy to royalty, partly also because of his concern not to alienate the army, the last stronghold of republicanism, at the very moment of his contest with Parliament. The proposal, even though rejected, was a confession of the failure of the English revolution to breathe life into its form of government. It developed a permanent crisis of authority and gained neither the willing adherence nor the passive acceptance of the majority of the people.

The Mirror of Theory.   The faltering of the revolution in its practice did not hamper political debate. The analysis of society and government rose above the level of pamphleteering to sustained theoretical discussion of extraordinary penetration and vigor. Lilburne put forward his democratic and republican ideas in *The Agreement of the People* (1648); Winstanley continued to expound his doctrines of economic equality in *The Law of Freedom* (1652).

The leading defender of the Commonwealth and Protectorate was the poet John Milton, who served Cromwell as secretary for Latin correspondence. For Milton the republic was the embodiment of the cause of virtue, wisdom, and true religion. He gave voice to his convictions in prose of great color and strength, but his work achieved greater effect in future generations than in his own; his *Eikonoklastes* (1649), a treatise defending the execution of Charles I, had little effect on the continent, where the regicide caused horror. John Harrington, in his *The Commonwealth of Oceana* (1656), a political analysis of an ideal republic, emphasized the economic basis of political power.

Most profound and provocative of all was a controversial figure, Thomas Hobbes. A royalist by conviction, he offended his fellow-royalists by his materialist philosophy and by his paradoxical arguments on behalf of absolute monarchy. He rejected the divine-right theory current among royalist thinkers, and advanced instead the doctrine of the political or social contract. Although he maintained that the grant of power to the king by the people was irrevocable and that disobedience to the state was utterly heinous, he argued that a state which was in practice incapable of affording protection to its subjects lost the right to their proper obedience. In other words, Hobbes defended only strong monarchies, which presumably did not need his succor, and vindicated successful revolution. The new regime benefited by his arguments because defeated Cavaliers found in them justification for making their peace with the usurpers.

Foreign Triumphs. The uncertainty of its domestic affairs did not handicap the government of the Commonwealth in its relations with foreign powers. It took up and maintained, without distraction by interests of dynastic connection, the ancient precepts of English policy: to control the sea by a strong and active fleet; to favor English trade and shipping; to keep a port of entry to the continent on the coast of the Low Countries or France; to hold high the dignity of England by establishing its precedence in diplomatic and naval ceremony. Despite the outcries in Europe over the beheading of Charles I, the European states recognized the new regime; indeed, the monarchies of France and Spain were far less hesitant than the republicans of the United Provinces.

The Dutch were the first people to feel the power of the Commonwealth. Neither their republicanism nor their stalwart Calvinism protected them when they refused to cower before English threats. Three questions merged in arousing hostility between the English Commonwealth and the Dutch Republic. The English demanded that the Dutch permanently exclude from public life the Orange family, which had been connected with the Stuart dynasty since the marriage of William of Orange (later William II) to Mary Stuart, daughter of Charles I, in 1641; but the Dutch rebuffed this pretension as undue interference in their internal affairs. Neither would the Dutch accede to the English claim of the right of first flag salute from Dutch warships. Fierce economic competition also antagonized the two states. In 1651 Parliament enacted the first Navigation Act, a mercantilist measure which permitted goods to be imported into England only in ships belonging either to England or the exporting nation; though the law had little immediate effect, since the English and their suppliers together did not have enough shipping to carry their products, it made clear the English intention of displacing the Dutch as the foremost shippers and merchants of Europe.

Naval fighting broke out in 1652. In this first Anglo-Dutch war, the English had two crucial advantages. The Dutch continued to use converted merchantmen for the bulk of their war fleet, while the English began to employ primarily ships built as men-of-war, which were therefore heavier and carried larger and more numerous cannon. The English economy remained predominantly agrarian, despite the great progress of trade and industry; it sufficed for the needs of the country and thus enabled it to survive naval defeat, unlike the Dutch economy, which depended for its very existence upon the maintenance of seaborne trade and fishing. After the English won a series of naval victories, the Dutch signed a peace upon English terms in 1654.

Two years later, in 1656, the Commonwealth took up the fight against Spain, a power which the English were more accustomed to hate and fight. This war proved profitable when one admiral captured the Spanish treasure fleet off Cadiz and another the Caribbean island of Jamaica. France joined in the war against Spain in 1657; the fruit of the alliance for England was the capture of Dunkirk in 1658, which remained under English sovereignty when peace was made in the treaty of the Pyrenees the next year (see ch. 9, p. 210).

Richard, Monck, and Restoration. Meanwhile the crisis of domestic politics had boiled up again. In February 1658 Cromwell dismissed Parliament. Before he was able to establish his regime more solidly upon the basis of his sole authority, he died in September, 1658.

Oliver's son Richard followed him as lord protector. He was peaceable and conciliatory, but when his free spending did not keep the army friendly, he abdicated in May 1659.

The initiative passed to George Monck, the commander of the army of occupation in Scotland, which was the most effective military force in the Commonwealth. While in England officers and officials squabbled endlessly, unwilling to abandon any of their particular advantages and aims for the sake of the common cause, Monck recognized that the large majority of the population in England and Scotland was ready and eager to return to the old accustomed ways of legitimate monarchy; its misdeeds and mistakes were forgotten after the tyrannies of usurpers and upstarts.

Monck marched his troops to London, where he assumed control as captain-general. Then he summoned the Long Parliament, which by the provisions of the Triennial Act of 1641 was still legally in existence. The members who had been excluded during Pride's Purge were called back as well as those who had sat during the Commonwealth. In agreement with Monck, Parliament entered into negotiations with Charles II, who was in exile in the Spanish Low Countries.

After friendly discussion, a basis of agreement was reached: restoration of the conditions of 1641, that is, the participation of Parliament in the sovereign powers of the state; recognition of all voluntary property transfers during the interregnum (as the period from the death of Charles I was called); freedom of religious conscience; payment of the back pay due to the troops; and amnesty. Charles II accepted these principles, but set them forth in a declaration made at Breda (April 1660) on a voluntary basis, rather than as a formal treaty with his people. The Long Parliament had meanwhile dissolved in March, its last work accomplished. A new convention Parliament was elected in the following month, and proclaimed Charles as king on May 8 upon the basis of the declaration of Breda.

Three weeks later, Charles II returned to his capital, nine years after he had fled England for his life. All the people rejoiced but the irreconcilable and inconsolable Puritans. Republican government had failed in England; dynastic monarchy had a new start.

12

Spain in Greatness and Decline

1474 - 1664

THE SIXTEENTH CENTURY was the golden age of Spain, the *siglo de oro*. When Queen Isabella seized the scepter of Castile in 1474, Spain was divided, weak, and backward. Under Isabella, her husband Ferdinand, and their successors, Spain became united and strong, until by the later sixteenth century it commanded an immense overseas empire and dominated the political and cultural life of Europe.

There were flaws in that greatness, however. Unity had been thrust upon Spain from above; it remained incomplete in the life of the people. Spain's dominance in Europe, furthermore, derived largely from its position as the center of Hapsburg dynastic power. The Hapsburg connection, it turned out, imposed tasks upon Spain beyond its capacity to sustain. When the European states combined to resist Hapsburg "universal monarchy," Spain became their principal target.

Thus the country's age of glory was brief. When Philip IV died in 1664, Spain was an exhausted and depleted giant, ready to become the victim of those who had replaced it as the masters of Europe.

I. Ferdinand and Isabella

The modern history of Spain begins with a royal elopement. In 1469 Princess Isabella of Castile, a girl of eighteen, defied the command of her

266

stepbrother, King Henry IV, to marry Alfonso V of Portugal, who was almost thirty-eight. She fled, pursued by the king's riders, to give her hand to the seventeen-year-old Ferdinand, heir to the throne of Aragon.

The Union of Castile and Aragon. Within five years Isabella was queen of Castile, succeeding Henry IV after defeating an armed faction which supported the candidacy of his daughter. Five years later Ferdinand ascended his own throne of Aragon. *Los reyes* (the kings) were equal partners in the rule of their lands. A popular couplet put it neatly:

> *Tanto monta, monta tanto,*
> *Isabel como Fernando.*
> (Man and wife alike in rule
> Are Ferdinand and Isabel.)

It was only the monarchs who were wedded, however, not their realms. Castile and Aragon remained separate states, each with its own forms of government, its own codes of law, and even its own ruler. In Castile Ferdinand was legally no more than Isabella's consort, without independent authority; loyal and loving spouse though she was, Isabella insisted upon her own dignity and power as "queen proprietress." In Aragon, their positions were reversed. There was as yet no single country "Spain," but only the plural "Spains" of popular speech.

The Land. Division was natural to Spain. Geography cut it into numerous distinct regions. Its economic strength was concentrated in the narrow coastal plains, especially on the southern shoreline, where the warm sun and the rain-laden southern winds favored a lush agriculture. Communication between the seaboard regions was limited by the absence of coastwise roads and the paucity of bays, which hampered interregional shipping. None of these coastal regions had been able therefore to establish its domination either over its neighbors or over the entire peninsula.

The political heart of Spain lay instead in the *meseta*, the inland plateau separated from the seaboard by a series of mountain ranges. The *meseta* was a region of sparse people and wealth, for its thin soils and continental climate favored the herdsman and not the tiller of the soil, and hence supported little trade. Though the *meseta* was cut into compartments by low mountains and fast rivers, communication between the regions on the plateau was easier than along the coast.

The Peoples. The cultural variety within the people was equally great, but with more flowing over of one pattern into another. The peoples used several distinct languages and many dialects. Castilian had become the most common form of literary and official Spanish, but Galician, a dialect resembling Portuguese, was spoken in the northwest, while the Aragonese spoke their own variety of Spanish. The peoples of Catalonia and Valencia, under the crown of Aragon, spoke closely related languages more similar to the Provençal of southern France than to any form of Spanish.

The various Spanish tongues were strongly influenced in vocabulary, though not in structure, by Arabic, the language of the Moorish population who had resided in Iberia since the eighth century. The Jews used the languages of their neighbors for everyday purposes but reserved their ancient Hebrew for religious writing and for scholarship. The Basques of northeastern Spain spoke a language unlike any other in Europe, or indeed in the world.

These linguistic differences were matched by other dissimilarities in garb, social customs, and characteristic habits and attitudes, to which Spaniards were keenly sensitive. The Castilians and the Basques were dry and harsh in demands upon themselves and their fellow men. By treating trade as dishonorable and menial work as worse, the Castilians gave all Spaniards a bad name among thoughtful Europeans. The Florentine observer Guicciardini accused the Castilians of "claiming to be all *hidalgos* (noblemen)." Workmen in the towns and peasants in the fields, he observed, "toil so long as need drives them and then they remain idle until they have spent their earnings."

Other Spaniards did not merit such blame. The Andalusian, living in fertile plains, was readier for both toil and play, and more open and gentle in his ways; the Catalan was even more diligent, a purposeful tradesman, craftsman, or artisan. Unlike as they were among themselves, the various kinds of Spaniards merged for other Europeans into a single type, intense and passionate, with an invincible pride, which was inured to hardship and stoic in the face of perils.

Religion set off all Spaniards from their Moorish and Jewish neighbors, but economic traits and other customs reinforced the differences. The Moors, who were Moslem in religion, and the Jews, who formed the Sephardic group in European Jewry, usually dwelt in distinct communities but maintained frequent and close contact with the Christians by trade, intermarriage, and cultural interchanges. The principal occupation of the Moors was tilling the land in prosperous Andalusia and Valencia. The Jews were active in trades and crafts and as professionals, especially medical doctors and scholars; but the minority among them who earned their livelihood as bankers and tax collectors drew the fierce hatred of the ordinary Spaniard upon the whole people.

Particularism and Nationality.   Carried over into political attitudes and practices, Spanish particularism presented to Ferdinand and Isabella the most permanent and pressing problem of their rule. The long campaign to regain the country from the Moors, beginning in the eleventh century, had strengthened an awareness of single nationality which dated back to the West Gothic state of the sixth to eighth centuries; but the sense of common

Hispanic destiny and the readiness to serve any but the narrowest local interests had dwindled away almost to nothingness after the *reconquista* (the Christian reconquest of Spain from the Moors) came to a standstill in 1349. The historic liberties of Spaniards belonged to them not individually, but as members of localities and provinces. These rights were set down in the *fueros*, or codes of privilege, which their possessors stubbornly defended against any infraction by royal authority.

Ferdinand and Isabella undertook to bring their kingdoms under tighter control and to build an effective common policy. Despite the stubborn particularism of Spain, they possessed substantial advantages in this endeavor. The nobility by constant civil war had displayed their inability to develop stable government. The vigorous initiative of *los reyes* rapidly revived the slumbering tradition of royal leadership. Large-scale feudalism and manorialism, creating little states within the state, did not exist, except to a limited extent in Aragon. The nobility in most of Spain owned their lands outright, but had no right of government over the peasantry, who were usually personally free or subject only to a mild form of serfdom.

Cortes and Fueros. In Castile the Cortes, or representative assembly, was more the crown's tool than its rival. Only the towns continued to send deputies to its meetings; the absence of clergy and nobility deprived it of the potential support of these numerous and powerful groups. The functions of the Cortes were to grant extraordinary taxation (the *servicios*) and to present grievances for the consideration of the crown; but the tradition that the *servicio* was voted before grievances were presented to the king prevented the Cortes from easily using its power of the purse to limit royal policy.

The Cortes of Aragon was, on the contrary, a stronghold of aristocratic power, for in it the nobility sat in two estates, along with the clergy and the burghers. A rebellion against the crown had been put down shortly before Ferdinand became king, and the assembly dared not assert any boldly independent policy. But the limitations upon the power of the Aragonese crown remained large and effective. The most important of these was the institution of the *justicia*, an official empowered to safeguard the rights of subjects to fair trial and personal security. Ferdinand did not touch the powers of the *justicia*, though he did restrain some of the most exaggerated privileges embodied in the *fueros*, such as the right of a lord to slay a vassal accused of felony without trial or defense of any kind. Aragon remained constitutionally a limited monarchy of the medieval type, where the oath of allegiance proclaimed the people's readiness to obey the king if he obeyed the laws and usages of the realm, but not otherwise.

During the decade of the 1480's, Ferdinand and Isabella rooted out lawlessness and disorder, which had infested Spain. The royal government, not yet strong or efficient enough for the task, used the *hermandades* ("brotherhoods," or leagues, of the towns) to put down brigandage by their own armed forces and courts. Criminals condemned by the *hermandades* were executed by squads of archers; the bodies of the slain, hanging from the stake and bristling with arrows, were warnings to evildoers. By the end of the decade, the work of the *hermandades* was done: Spain was peaceful and safe as it had not been within the memory of living men.

In the long run, however, it was not safe for the monarchs to entrust the preservation of law and order to groups of armed subjects. Ferdinand therefore undertook the reform and strengthening of the royal administration.

The Power of the Kings. Appointed councils became the principal instrument of government. The most important of these were the councils of Castile and Aragon. These were omnicompetent bodies which advised the kings, executed their specific orders as well as their general policy, and supervised the rest of the royal administration. The appointment of two members who sat on both the Castilian and the Aragonese councils facilitated the unification of their policies. The council of the Indies, formed in 1509, took over from the council of Castile the government of the new territories conquered in America. Royal control of local and provincial affairs was also made more effective. The traditional local officials were not displaced or removed, but came under the supervision of royal inspectors and controllers. Ferdinand also reduced corruption in the royal courts and speeded their proceedings. He brought the tax collectors under closer supervision and cut the loss of revenues between the taxpayer and the treasury.

The ambitious policies pursued by the king and queen made their financial demands grow constantly larger; the customary taxes no longer sufficed, and they shied off from constant dependence upon the *servicios,* lest the Cortes assert its own power. New taxes were therefore introduced, and old ones extended; and every device that could produce revenue was adopted. One of the most lucrative was the assumption by the crown of the grand-masterships of the three great orders of religious chivalry, Santiago, Calatreva, and Alcantara. The Mesta, or guild of sheepherders, was favored by the crown in exchange for a share in its profits as well as frequent special grants from its coffers. Later, the overseas conquests of Spain furnished new resources, notably the crown's *quinto* (fifth) and customs dues (see ch. 6, p. 134).

Ferdinand also created a professional standing army, especially during the wars in Italy around the turn of the century (see ch. 7, pp. 158-159). Gonzalo de Córdoba, the "Great Captain," and his successor, Gonzalo de Ayala, adopted the innovations of the Swiss and the German *Landsknechte,* particularly the use of the pike formation which made the foot soldier the key figure in battle; but they carried further than the Swiss the utilization of both the older cavalry arm and the new weapons of firearms.

The regiments of Spain became feared for their skill and leadership, as well as for the endurance and stoicism of the soldiery. Sea power fared less well under Ferdinand; his Catalan forces were declining, and the Basque sailors of the northern coast, though resolute and skillful, especially in the use of ship-borne artillery, were not a major force on the western ocean.

The Fall of Granada. The decade of the 1490's was the time of greatest accomplishment for *los reyes*. Their first achievement was the subjugation of the emirate of Granada, the last remnant of Moorish power on the peninsula. It was primarily a Castilian enterprise, dear to the heart of the pious Isabella; but Ferdinand, whose thoughts ran rather to Aragonese aspirations in Italy, nonetheless gave his talents as an organizer to the campaign.

In November, 1491, the king and queen promised to the Moors the safety of their persons and property and the right to practice their religion unmolested; this was in line with the tradition of the medieval *reconquista*, in which religious fanaticism had been characteristic not of the Spaniards but of the crusading foreign volunteers. Not long after, on January 2, 1492, the last Moorish stronghold, the city of Granada, surrendered.

Baptism or Exile: the Jews and the Moors. On the same day a Castilian royal edict was issued from Granada ordering the Jews, who had no arms to wield in their own defense, to accept baptism or be expelled from the country. Those who would not abandon their religion sold their goods for pittances and fled abroad; some went to nearby Portugal, whence they were expelled after a few years; others sailed to Africa and eventually made their way to the Levant, where they formed colonies of Sephardic Jewry. Those who remained in Spain as forced converts, or Marranos, continued to suffer from popular hatred.

Despite her promise of toleration for the Moors, Isabella did not intend to permit any of her subjects to adhere to hostile faiths. Immediately after the fall of Granada, she entrusted to the bishop of Talavera, Pedro González de Mendoza, the task of converting the Moors. Mendoza, who believed in love and persuasion as the tools of the missionary, did not achieve results quickly enough for the impatient Isabella. In 1499, she placed at his side the more imperious archbishop of Toledo, Francisco Jiménez de Cisneros, who took the work of conversion into his own hands.

Pressure upon the Moors to be baptized became more flagrant and violent. In 1502 the bitter option of baptism or exile, which had been given to the Jews ten years before, was placed before the Moors of Castile and Leon; Ferdinand, who disapproved such violence against industrious subjects who paid substantial taxes, would not allow the edict to be introduced into his own kingdom of Aragon. The Moors who fled to North Africa carried with them a revived hatred for the Spaniard. Most of those who remained in

Castile and Leon accepted outwardly the Christian faith, but many of these Moriscos practiced Moslem rites in secret.

"Purity of Blood." Moriscos and Marranos alike came under the implacable scrutiny of the Inquisition, for, having accepted baptism, they were subject to the penalties for heresy and relapse. The "New Christians" remained under a pall of suspicion and disabilities. They were barred from many public offices on the doctrine, unprecedented in Christianity, that they were inferior because their ancestors had not been Christian. "Purity of blood" became a criterion of racial distinctiveness and integrity, novel to Spain and contrary to the facts of the formation of the Hispanic peoples and of their historic development. Nonetheless it evolved into one of the strongest motive forces in Spanish popular belief and national practice.

The religious unification of Spain, thus begun, gratified the piety of the queen and the wide mass of her people, but it did not add to the strength of the country. Economically the departure of an industrious and many-skilled population meant inevitable loss in national productivity; only the availability of foreign artisans and traders to fill the gap prevented it from being a disaster. Isabella, however, had no regrets. In 1494, Pope Alexander VI bestowed upon her and her husband the honorary title of "the Catholic kings." This was for her reward aplenty for deeds conceived in righteousness and carried out with heartless passion and power.

Foreign Ventures. The year 1492 was one of new beginnings for Spain, not only in its religious life but also in the world of power and politics.

Not long after the victory at Granada, Isabella authorized Columbus to venture forth into the western Atlantic in the journey of exploration which brought immense territories under the crown of Castile. The lands of the Americas provided little of the coveted gold and silver in the first decades after their discovery. Nonetheless they began to draw Spanish energies across the sea.

The first venture of *los reyes* into grand policy in Europe was made at Ferdinand's behest. He preserved the Aragonese rule over Sicily, brought the neighboring kingdom of Naples under his control (1504), and laid the basis for further gains in northern Italy. It was no easy victory, for powerful potentates, notably the king of France, had their own ambitions in Italy. But Ferdinand played the game of diplomacy and war with vigor and verve. His trickery was admired by Machiavelli: when Louis XII of France complained that Ferdinand had lied to him, the Aragonese king laughed that it was not the first time that he had done so.

The army built by Gonzalo de Córdoba and Ayala provided Ferdinand with the brute strength needed to back up his guile on the field of battle. The principal weakness of Ferdinand's position in Italy was lack of control of the sea; the Genoese fleet, which dominated the waters between Italy and

Spain, was generally hostile to the Aragonese. Maritime communications with northern Italy remained difficult and precarious, but were easier with Sicily, where Ferdinand had adequate naval bases at his disposal.

Royal Weddings and Deaths. Ferdinand and Isabella, who had made so much political capital out of their own marriage, built a large part of their foreign policy upon the marriages of their children. The first such marriage, between their eldest daughter and the heir to the Portuguese throne, ended when the princely pair died childless.

Marriages were also arranged with the royal family of England and the ducal family of Burgundy. Their immediate purpose was to provide Spain with allies against France. The *infanta* Catherine (known in England as Catherine of Aragon) was given as bride first to Prince Arthur, heir to the throne of England, and then, after he died, to his younger brother, Henry (see ch. 10, p. 257). A double wedding was arranged with Burgundy in 1496: Prince Juan of Spain with Margaret of Burgundy, and his sister Joanna with Margaret's brother Philip. Ferdinand and Isabella hoped thereby to safeguard their realms for their own progeny, and to acquire a possible claim on the rich Burgundian possessions. Mortality played them false. Juan died not long after, and the Spanish inheritance fell to Joanna, who thus brought to her husband an unexpected and rich dowry.

The consequences of this shift in expectations soon appeared. Isabella died in 1504, leaving her crowns of Castile and Leon not to her husband but to her daughter Joanna, with Duke Philip as her consort. Ferdinand retained his own crown of Aragon. Duke Philip came to Spain with his wife and contested with Ferdinand for the government of Castile. Their quarrel threatened to destroy the unity of the Spanish kingdoms so laboriously built up by Isabella and Ferdinand over almost three decades of rule. The sudden death of Philip in 1506 removed that peril and at the same time gave Ferdinand his coveted control of Castile, thanks to the insanity which attacked Joanna in her bereavement. Ferdinand governed all Spain for another decade, until his death in 1516.

II. Charles the First and Fifth

For more than forty years "the Spains" had been half-united under the system of parallel rule instituted by Ferdinand and Isabella. Now their grandson, Joanna's eldest son Charles, proclaimed king of the Spanish realms at Brussels, inherited all their lands. But he was already titular duke of Burgundy, ruler of the rich and powerful Low Countries, and heir to the possessions of the Austrian dynasty of the Hapsburgs, with the expectation of following his grandfather Maximilian I upon the throne of the Holy Roman Empire.

The Flemish King. The question therefore arose: Which interests would Charles pursue—those of his homeland, the Netherlands; or those of the Hapsburg lands he was about to inherit; or those of Spain, the country he had never seen? There was reason to anticipate the worst. Charles accepted his Spanish inheritance as a birthright for which he was not in any way obligated to his new subjects. Despite the pleas of Cardinal Jiménez de Cisneros, who governed Spain in his absence, Charles lingered on in the Low Countries for eighteen months before he sailed for Spain.

Charles did not win at once the respect or the affection of the Spaniards. They saw in him an ungainly youth of seventeen, whose dangling jaw, too big for his face, made him slobber when he ate and mumble when he spoke. He knew no Spanish, only French and a little Flemish. His shy sad look troubled them; they did not know what went on within his mind. One called him "a man of sixty years, as grave as he is old." His outward aspect revealed his inner self as it was, however—a boy outgrowing his boyhood and unready for the independence of manhood.

He allowed the Flemings, the friends and mentors of his childhood who accompanied him to Spain, to run the government of Spain as they saw fit. They looted the royal treasuries and bestowed the most lucrative posts upon themselves.

The Spaniards reacted wrathfully. The Cortes of Castile and Aragon both spoke out against the Flemish spoilers. They demanded that the king obey the laws of the land, reserve its administration to natives, and withdraw the taxes imposed to pay for the costs of Charles's candidacy in the fiercely fought election for the Holy Roman emperor in 1519.

The Rebellion. Their protests were desperate and vain. Charles became Emperor Charles V (see ch. 13, p. 300), and sailed north in 1520 to sit upon the most honored throne in Christendom. When he reached the Low Countries, he told the States-General in Brussels that his heart had always been there. Then he went on to Germany, to confront the crisis of the Lutheran rebellion against the Roman Catholic church, to which, like the Spaniards, he gave his unshaken allegiance.

Back in Spain, the resentment against the king flared up in rebellion. The cities took the lead in an armed struggle against the Flemings; all the other classes of Spanish society—nobles, churchmen and common folk— joined in resistance. The rebels were called *comuneros* after the "communities" (*comunidades*) which took over government of the cities.

Toledo became the center of the uprising. Under the leadership of a nobleman, Juan de Padilla, it fought off the troops sent by Charles's vice-

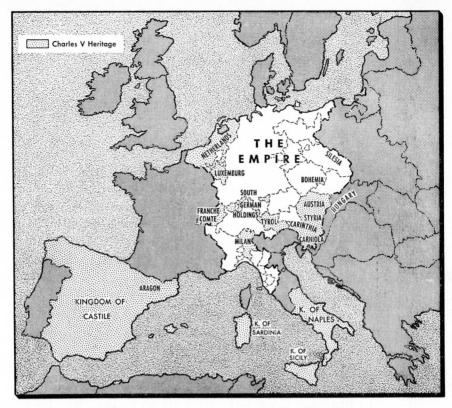

Realms of Charles V, 1519

regent, Cardinal Adrian of Utrecht. Deputies of fifteen towns formed a Holy Committee (*Santa Junta*) to lead them. Some of its demands were directed toward defense of Spanish interests against foreign exploitation, others aimed at reform of government within Spain, including improvement of the courts, autonomy for the *comunidades,* and their right to name deputies to the Cortes without hindrance.

From Worms in Germany Charles issued a decree charging the *comuneros* with high treason; but at the same time he suspended the collection of the most oppressive taxes and named two Castilian grandees to serve as coregents with Adrian. An upsurge of attacks upon the privileges of the nobility and Adrian's offer of amnesty for those who laid down their arms shattered the front of the insurrection. In April 1521, the rebels were routed at Villalar; Padilla and other leaders were taken and executed. The collapse of the rebellion followed quickly.

A parallel insurgency in Valencia and Majorca lasted somewhat longer. Organized by the *germanías* (brotherhoods) of the guilds, it was almost from the beginning an assault upon the existing economic and political order. The *germanías* ordered abolition of all rents, dues, and taxes, and destroyed all effective government. Thus the class character of the rebellion at once

275

lost it the sympathy of the propertied groups, which supported the repression by the king's troops.

A Spaniard, and a Master. In July 1522 Charles V (for the Spaniards henceforth called him by his imperial title, though legally as king of Spain he remained Charles I) returned to Spain. He was a youth no longer but a man, confident and competent. He displayed new skill in the art of rule. He took pains to win the loyalty of the Spaniards. While abroad, he had learned the Spanish language. He treated his Spanish subjects with consideration, taking their desires and needs into account whenever possible. In particular, he brought no more Flemings to Spain to displace the native leaders in its administration and exploitation. He made the strict impartiality of justice the supreme principle of his government. He ceased to be a thoroughgoing Fleming and took on the spirit and interests of Spain more than of any other of his realms.

Nonetheless he was the master who slipped a halter of obedience about the Spanish necks. In 1523 he called on the Cortes of Castile, meeting at Valladolid, for a *servicio* to be spent outside Spain. Discuss our grievances first, they asked. He replied: "Yesterday I asked you for funds. Today I want your advice. . . . You know that it has been the custom to make the grant first; thus it was under my royal predecessor. Why try to innovate with me?" They dared not deny the king who had crushed the towns for which they spoke the 40,000 ducats he demanded.

The character of Spanish government changed. Charles governed with the same instrument of state Ferdinand and Isabella had employed—the great councils, with the council of Castile at the head—but he used them with a difference. His grandparents, seeing no conflict of interests between themselves and their realms, had encouraged the councils to exercise broad initiative. Charles, on the contrary, dared not permit his Spanish councils any leeway for their individual judgments. He did not do so anywhere in his wide empire, lest he turn it into a political shambles. In each of his realms the local officials, if left to their own devisings, tended to act according to the traditional interests and the immediate needs of their provinces. Only the will of their common master could enforce a single policy upon them. Absolutism was therefore the inevitable form of the government of Charles V.

Dynastic War. Dynasticism—the interest of Charles in the hereditary rule of his family in its various possessions—was the most pervasive force in Charles's policy. In 1543 he told his eldest son and heir, Philip, that his purpose was "to leave you no less than the inheritance which fell to me." Because he contemplated no additional acquisitions of territory, Charles was sure in his mind that he pursued the plainest policy of defense. The lesser princes of Europe, on the other hand, looked upon his far-flung empire as a colossus threatening to crush them. Thus Charles, who wanted peace but inherited the quarrels of many lands, was constantly involved in war.

Charles V was the enemy of France, at war or preparing for war, throughout his reign. He was unwilling to abandon his inherited claim to the duchy of Burgundy, which the French crown had seized from his ancestors by forfeiture in the fifteenth century; he was reluctant to declare himself a vassal of France for the fiefs of Flanders, Artois, and Hainaut in the Low Countries; and he was the rival of Francis I for control of Italy. Only in the last of these quarrels was any specifically Spanish interest involved; Castile relied heavily on grain imported from Sicily, while Aragon had a historic claim to Sicily and Naples. But northern Italy, which became the principal point of contention, held no direct importance for Spain; it was essential, however, for the movement of troops and supplies from Spain to the emperor's forces in central and northern Europe.

Charles's victory over the French at Pavia in 1525 brought the French king, Francis I, to Madrid as a captive, but proved a hollow triumph so far as Charles's ambitions outside of Italy were concerned (see ch. 8, p. 171). In Italy, however, it gave him control of Lombardy, the keystone in the land connections between Spain and Austria. The defection of the Genoese Admiral Andrea Doria from the French to the imperial side in 1528 (see ch. 7, p. 156) gave Charles a port in North Italy immediately adjacent to Lombardy; it also provided him with easy access to the valuable credit resources of the wealthy bankers of Genoa, and assured him safer maritime communications in the western Mediterranean. Spanish command of North Italy was not seriously troubled thereafter.

Against the Infidel. Charles also revived the campaign against the infidel, partly for its own sake and partly in order to strike at an ally of Francis I (see ch. 8, p. 172). After the victory at Pavia, Charles commanded the conversion of the Moors still remaining in Spain as an expression of his gratitude to God. The large majority were baptized; isolated rebellions among the resistors were easily put down with the aid of several thousand German mercenary soldiers.

Charles's campaigns against the Moslems in North Africa were less successful. He could not and would not maintain the costly sustained effort required to capture and to hold the ports from which Moslem pirates sailed out to raid Christian shipping in the Mediterranean. The ultimate consequence of his intermittent attacks was to spur the corsair potentate, Kheireddin Barbarossa, to place himself under the suzerainty of the Turkish sultan, and thus to extend considerably the Ottoman power in North Africa. By the end of Charles's reign, Spain faced a greater Moslem power than it had ever known, more united and readier for action.

The Price of Pride. The Spaniards, once unhappy at their connection with the realms of the Burgundians and the Hapsburgs, now basked in the glory of their king's imperial title and his universal mission. They were flattered by the thought that they were the spiritual and political center of his monarchy, that they were no longer almost outsiders in European affairs but more and more the leaders and masters.

They paid a high price for their pride, however, for they had to meet the largest part of the immense costs of Charles's wars. An economic council, the council of the *hacienda*, formed in 1523 (though confirmed in its title only under Philip II), increased the revenues of the crown two- to threefold.

Nonetheless the king was compelled several times to suspend payments of the *juros*, or state annuity bonds. He became more and more dependent upon foreign bankers, first the Germans and then, after 1528 especially, the Genoese. The debt rose from 18 million maravedis in 1504, at the death of Isabella, to 99 million in 1534, midway through Charles's reign, and continued to swell thereafter. The interest the emperor-king was forced to pay rose as the perils involved in lending him money increased. By 1540 it was 14 per cent of the face amount, but discounting increased the true rate.

American treasure seemed the only solution, but it was usually signed away as security for a loan before it was received. In any case, it did not reach very large figures until the opening of the Potosí mines in Upper Peru (Bolivia) in 1545, and even then remained smaller than the taxes paid by the Low Countries. Despite all the efforts of the government to retain American gold and silver in Spain for its own use, the metals slipped across the borders, sometimes by smuggling, sometimes by official channels, to pay for imported goods and for the wars abroad.

Abdication. The impoverishment of Spain was symbolized in the physical and moral exhaustion of the monarch himself. By the beginning of the 1550's, only his rigid sense of duty enabled him to continue with the tasks of government. The failure of his campaign to crush the Lutherans in Germany was the final blow (see ch. 13, p. 313) in a series of defeats which sapped his strength. The combined Spanish-Burgundian-Hapsburg inheritance, with its dependencies in Italy and the New World, was too much for the government of one man.

Charles therefore resorted to a division of his empire. He transferred his Hapsburg possessions in central Europe to his younger brother Ferdinand and his rule in the Low Countries, Spain, Italy, and the Indies to his son Philip. He abdicated his Spanish throne at Brussels on January 16, 1556, and returned to Spain to spend the two remaining years of his life in the monastery of Yuste, in Estremadura, meditating upon the mysteries of God's providence for men.

III. Philip the Prudent

The reign of Philip II began well. For the first time in a century, a new monarch ascended the throne in both Aragon and Castile without an outbreak of civil war. Not even the continued absence of the king in the Netherlands, where he was detained by the needs of the war against France, caused any breach of civil peace in Spain. When Philip returned to Spain in 1559, he was greeted as the country's own king.

The Reticent Autocrat. Philip II was indeed a Spaniard through and through, by birth and upbringing. He spoke only Spanish, and shared the habits and attitudes of his countrymen. Philip II ruled Spain as an absolute monarch. He accepted without reservation the doctrine that kings existed for the people and not the people for the kings, but added the corollary that it belonged to him and not to the people to determine and defend their interests. His right to rule came from God; subjects could not tamper with it except upon pain of treason.

Yet Spaniards did not complain against this complete autocracy; their desire for self-government seemed to have burned out with the failure of the revolt of the *comuneros* and the *germanías*. They bewailed instead the reticence of a king who lived in their midst but seldom appeared among them. They wanted him to be, in the words of one report, "the public and open oracle to whom all subjects come for aid in their toils and consolation in their difficulties." Philip believed, on the contrary, that subjects gave most respect to a monarch whom they admired and obeyed from afar, without discovering his human frailties by too close scrutiny. Furthermore, his system of government was one which made Spaniards feel the effects of his decisions, without the sense of his personal presence and participation.

The Crowned Bureaucrat. The complaint was a reaction at once partly false and partly true to the facts. Philip II was a diligent king who gave the most detailed personal attention to the government of Spain, but he trusted his subordinates even less than his father had. Nonetheless he did not go out into the country to see for himself the state of affairs, but governed first from his capital at Valladolid, then from Madrid, and after 1584 from the monastery-castle of the Escorial, which he built twenty-seven miles from Madrid. He read a multitude of written reports from every nook of his several kingdoms, and reserved to himself all important decisions as well as a host of minor ones; even documents settling minor issues in small towns bore the signature *Yo el rey* (I, the king).

Yet he disliked making decisions. He delayed interminably the orders which he would permit no one else to make and without which the machinery of government remained motionless. "The original sin of our Court," wrote Luis de Requesens, an able Spanish statesman and general, "is never to decide anything in time and opportunely." Spanish diplomats in foreign capitals received replies to their dispatches so tardily that they expressed the sardonic hope that death would come to them by way of Spain, for then they would live to a gray old age.

Subjugation of Aragon. Philip continued the unification of Spain which had begun with the marriage of Ferdinand and Isabella. Above all the separate councils of the individual kingdoms he placed a single private council, the council of state, to discuss all important questions of internal and foreign policy. He encouraged the intermarriage of the nobility of the lands of Aragon and Castile, so that a common Spanish aristocracy began to be formed. He granted to the Aragonese the same rights of trade and settlement in the Indies which previously had been reserved to the Castilians. The institution of the *justicia* in Aragon, who assured subjects of that kingdom of the right of fair trial, was the sole breach in the edifice of absolute government.

Philip tolerated it, however, until 1592, when his secretary, Antonio Perez, implicated in a murder scandal, fled from Madrid to Saragossa, the Aragonese capital, and placed himself under the protection of the *justicia*. The king ordered Perez seized in spite of the Aragonese *fueros*. The ensuing rebellion was crushed by Philip's troops; the *justicia* who had defied him was captured and hanged without trial; but Perez himself escaped from the country, to remain a thorn in the side of Spain by his propaganda against the tyranny of his former master. Philip did not abolish the post of *justicia*, but made him removable by the king and hence amenable to the king's orders.

The rebellion in Aragon was not the first during Philip's reign. Among the half million Moriscos who remained in Andalusia, many continued to practice Moslem rites in secret despite their public profession of Roman Catholicism. The Inquisition, by its incessant heretic hunt, caused an outbreak of rebellion among the desperate Moriscos in 1568. For two years they held out against a powerful royal army commanded by the king's half-brother, Don John of Austria. After the defeat of the insurgency, the Moriscos returned to their plows, but the hatred of the Spanish populace against them was more violent than ever.

The Spanish Dynast. Preservation of his imperial inheritance of states and lands was a primary purpose of Philip II. It was a task he shared with Spain. On the one hand, he called upon his homeland for the major part of the forces with which to resist attacks upon his empire; on the other hand, the Spaniards enthusiastically accepted Philip's cause as their own. The relationship of most of the other portions of the Spanish empire to the rule of Philip II was more passive. His subjects outside Spain did not feel toward him as did the Spaniards. A Venetian ambassador reported early in the reign that Philip was "disliked by the Italians and hated by the Flemings."

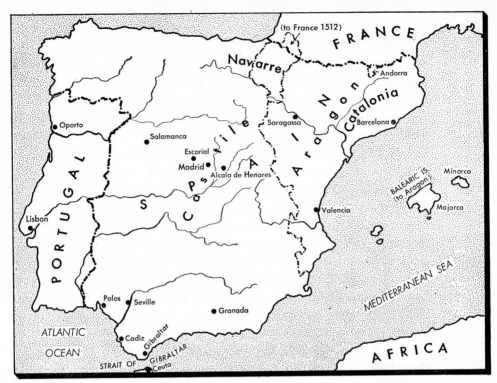

Spain in the Sixteenth Century

Nonetheless the Spanish colonies in America and the Philippines, the king's subject lands in Italy, and the Burgundian province of Franche-Comté paid for the expenses of their own government and defense without open hostility. Thus they did not drain the Spanish treasury; indeed, they contributed taxes and soldiers to the common enterprises in which Spain's interests weighed most heavily.

When Philip attempted to reduce the Low Countries to the docility and subservience of these other portions of his empire, he met a resistance for which he was unprepared both in policy and in resources. Unlike his Burgundian ancestors, Philip treated the provinces of the Netherlands not as their common sovereign, whom they happened to share with Spain, but as a conqueror—Spanish and accordingly foreign. He refused to accept their traditions of popular participation in government by means of their Estates, and endeavored to impose upon them the same kind of central bureaucratic institutions by which he governed Spain. He also wished to extirpate in these provinces the Protestant heresies he successfully destroyed everywhere else in his dominions.

Revolt of the Low Countries. The rebellion which broke out in the Low Countries in 1568 became a running sore in the side of the Spanish imperial power. Neither the policy of brute force followed by the duke of Alva, nor the more supple policy of combining force and persuasion employed by his successors, first Requesens and then Alexander Farnese, prince of Parma, was able to bring all the rebellious provinces to their knees. The best that Parma could achieve, and he was the most gifted military commander in Europe in his day, was to retain the southern provinces for Philip; but he could not bring down the Dutch rebels who held out north of the Rhine river line. Yet Parma's successes aroused Philip's jealousy, and his independence of judgment the king's distrust. Only Parma's death from a battlefield injury in France in 1592 saved him from peremptory dismissal.

Without Parma's genius, the hope for total reconquest of the Low Countries seemed doomed, but Philip doggedly continued his struggle against the hated Dutch. (See ch. 15, p. 128.) The revolt of the Netherlands deprived him of the resources of his wealthiest provinces; it also drained away a huge portion of all his revenues from his other European realms and from America. It furnished his foes with an ally whose dogged resistance hampered Spanish operations against them. It was the supreme defeat of Philip's policy.

Portugal before 1580. By comparison with a mishap of such proportions, Philip's success in bringing the kingdom of Portugal into his empire in 1580 was of modest magnitude. The Portuguese power had declined greatly from its height at the end of the fifteenth and early sixteenth century; it was a weakened land, already largely living on memories of past glories, which Philip acquired. The exploits of Dias, Da Gama, and their successors in creating the Portuguese empire had briefly given great wealth to the small land but had overtaxed its strength. The physical geography of the frontier facing Castile had made it easily subject to Spanish pressure.

Nonetheless the Portuguese remained a proudly independent people. They preserved the identity of their language against the competition of Castilian, and considered themselves to be a people separate from other Iberians. In Luis de Camoens' epic, the *Lusiads*, they acquired a work of genius which magnified their pride in their own culture and in their triumphs in the Indies. During the sixteenth century, the kings of Portugal consolidated their absolutist and centralized government along lines similar to that of Castile. They unified their land in religion by expelling the Jews, both native and refugees from Spain, in 1496; while those who accepted baptism fell under the same popular mistrust and the same scrutiny by the Inquisition which the Spanish Marranos met.

Union with Spain. The crusading spirit led, however, to the loss of Portuguese independence. It drove Sebastian I, who came to the throne, to undertake in 1578, over the dissuasions of the pope and Philip II, a campaign against the Moors in North Africa. Sebastian, his army, and his native allies were all destroyed at the battle of Al Kasr Al-kabir (August 4). The aged Cardinal Henry, uncle of the fallen crusader, reigned for two years until his death in 1580.

Philip II, as grandson of Manoel I, who had reigned from 1495 to 1521, put forward his claim to the vacant throne. He was opposed by his cousin Antonio, prior of Prato, whose candidacy was pushed by wide sections of the populace despite his illegitimate birth. The duke of Alva drove into Portugal with a powerful army, defeated Antonio's forces, and set the Spanish monarch on the Portuguese throne as Philip I. The king attempted no innovations in Portuguese government, and linked the country to Spain only by personal union; he employed Portuguese officials to govern the country and respected the local laws. The country, if hostile, would have provided the enemies of Spain a valuable foothold on the peninsula; but thanks to Philip's prudence it remained quiet under his reign.

War with France. The maintenance and expansion of his empire constituted the supreme purpose of Philip's foreign policy. He did not singly pursue this aim, however, but also undertook the championship of the Catholic Reformation by the sword and the defense of the specific interests of the Spanish state and people. The result was much the same kind of dispersal of efforts and lack of persistence in any single endeavor as that which had lamed Charles V's policy.

Toward his imperial cousins in the Holy Roman Empire, Philip felt more jealousy (as having been deprived by them of part of his just inheritance) than friendship; but the general peace which prevailed in Germany after the Peace of Augsburg (1555) kept this internecine rivalry from appearing too prominently before the world.

For Philip II, as for his father, France was the hereditary enemy. The victory over France embodied in the treaty of Cateau-Cambrésis (1559), almost at the start of his reign, encouraged Philip to continue his endeavors to complete the overthrow of French power. The French wars of religion offered him his great opportunity. He offered his aid in money and troops to the Catholic party, but his minimum price was their acceptance of his leadership, and his maximum objective was to win the French crown for his own dynasty. His intervention, however, which culminated in war in 1589, only served to bring together the Catholic and Huguenot opponents of Spanish domination, and thus to enable his relentless foe, Henry IV, to maintain himself as king of France. The treaty of Vervins (1598) marked the failure of Philip's attempt to control France for his own advantage. (See ch. 19, pp. 189-190).

The "Great Armada." England was Spain's other great opponent under the reign of Philip. In the first decade of his rule, he avoided open hostility toward Elizabeth, his sister-in-law, who succeeded his first wife Mary I on the English throne. After the outbreak of rebellion in the Netherlands, peace with England became an even more important interest for Spain: there could be no more dangerous ally for the rebels than the island kingdom, with its sea power and its growing economic prowess. Despite her prudent policy, Elizabeth dared not permit Spanish reconquest of the whole of the Low Countries, and intervened in their assistance. For his part, Philip was drawn into overt antagonism to Elizabeth: she permitted Sir Francis Drake and other English "sea dogs" to wage a piratical war upon Spanish ports and shipping in Europe and America; she lent aid to the Dutch rebels in their most critical hours; and she sent (or permitted to be sent) to the block her Catholic rival and prisoner, Mary Queen of Scots, whose cause had been publicly taken up by Philip.

The "Great Armada" of 1588 was his reply. It failed; England did not fall; the Dutch continued their resistance. Philip accepted with stoic resignation the defeat of his fleet, and set about the reorganization of Spain's naval power, which reached new efficiency during the following decade. The war with England still continued, engaging small forces but sapping the energies of both sides, when Philip died in 1598.

The only clear-cut success achieved by Philip was won against the Turks in 1571 when a combined Spanish-Venetian fleet smashed an Ottoman naval force at Lepanto in the Adriatic. Politically this proved an empty victory, however, for Turkish power in North Africa—whence it sustained constant piratical attacks upon Spanish shipping as well as European shipping in general—remained undiminished.

Bankruptcy. The immense Spanish effort over the four decades of Philip's reign consumed all the resources which he could pump from his vast empire. At the end his peoples were weakened and exhausted. Even though the American treasure brought in annually increased almost fourfold from 1554 to 1598, it was impossible to finance the huge Spanish military effort by these means only. It was Spain, and within Spain principally Castile, which carried the main burden of taxes.

Philip was able to see only the needs of his state; how they were met did not interest him, and he had no understanding of the economic consequences of his policy for Spain. He called repeatedly on the Cortes of Castile and Aragon for *servicios,* which they dared not refuse him although they repeatedly pointed to the impoverished state of the nation. Philip relied particularly on the *alcabala,* a sales tax of 10 per cent imposed on each transfer of goods, not merely on the final sale. The state thus extracted revenue repeatedly in the movement of commodities from producer to consumer, but caused a disastrous increase in their cost over and above that resulting from the monetary inflation.

All the increases in taxation, however, failed to suffice. The king made loans from bankers, especially the Genoese, at rates as high as 20 per cent;

PHILIP II OF SPAIN. Engraving by an anonymous artist, probably Flemish, published at Rome by Marcellus Clodius, 1588.

This is part of a large print published at Rome in the year of the Armada. The simultaneous resolution and resignation of Philip the Prudent in his year of fate are well portrayed. (Achenbach Foundation)

but his revenues failed to cover even the interest. The inevitable result was repeated bankruptcy (1557-1560, 1574).

The consequences in the life of the Spanish nation were not long delayed. Idleness and beggary increased. Poverty among the common people was not unusual in Europe, but the raggedness of great numbers of Spanish *hidalgos* revealed widespread inability in the ruling classes to "live nobly." Only the upper nobility maintained its wealth by combining with its rentals from immense estates the gifts and salaries it drew from the monarchy.

IV. Philip III and Philip IV

Spanish power had derived from the combination of the energies of the people with the leadership of the crown. From Ferdinand and Isabella down through Philip II, the ruling monarchs had been intelligent and industrious, giving themselves completely to the tasks of their offices. Charles V and Philip II had led Spain into the trap of an exaggerated imperialism, and the country had weakened under the strain thus imposed; nonetheless no Spaniard had sacrificed more of himself in the task than did these kings.

285

The "Validos." Under their successors, however, Spain continued to be a bureaucratic monarchy, administered from above by royal authority—but without bureaucratic kings. Philip III (1598-1621) and Philip IV (1621-1665) devoted themselves to the life of court and chapel, not to the duties of state; they entrusted government to *validos*, or favorites, who ruled as chief ministers.

The government of the *validos* differed from the firm, often harsh, but usually just rule of the sixteenth-century kings. The first concern of the *validos* was to enrich themselves, their families, and their friends at the expense of the state. Being dependent upon the caprices of the kings, they had to concern themselves with defense of their positions against rival cliques even more than with questions of general policy. The honesty in reporting conditions which Charles V and Philip II had required of their officials and diplomats came to an end; dispatches had to correspond not to reality but to the picture of his success which the chief minister painted to his master. Policy came more than ever to depend upon the caprices of a person rather than upon realistic evaluation of the interests of the state and people of Spain.

Lerma. The first of the *validos* was Francisco de Sandoval, duke of Lerma. His domestic administration was distinguished chiefly by the final expulsion of the remaining Moriscos from Spain. The protection of the nobility, who valued them as rent payers, was insufficient to withstand the combined hatred of the people and the government. Between 1609 and 1611, close to half a million Moriscos, permitted to take only what they could carry of their belongings, were driven from every part of the country and shipped to North Africa. As during the past century, the place of the expelled Moriscos in the Spanish economy was only partly made up by the foreigners, especially Frenchmen and Italians, who came to Spain to work but seldom to settle.

In foreign policy, Lerma recognized that Spain did not have the strength to maintain the great efforts of the previous reigns. An attempted invasion of Ireland failed in 1602 and peace was made with England two years later. In the Low Countries, the Spanish General Ambrosio Spinola continued to win victories against the Dutch without ever striking a mortal blow. In 1609 a truce was negotiated with the Dutch Republic for a period of twelve years. Enmity with France was likewise abandoned after the death of Henry IV (1610); a treaty of peace was signed in 1612, and was soon followed by the betrothal of Princess Anne to Louis XIII. This pacific policy did not meet wide approval in Spain, for it meant admitting defeat in the great enterprises inherited from Charles V and Philip II. Lerma was forced to retire in 1618.

Control of foreign affairs passed to a trio of Spanish administrators who were not even resident in Spain, the governors of Milan and Naples in

The Spanish Empire in the Sixteenth Century

Italy and the ambassador to Vienna. At their behest, Spain fought brief wars with Venice, Savoy, and the "Gray Leagues" controlling the Valtelline passes in southeastern Switzerland (see ch. 9, p. 204). Then, after the outbreak of the Thirty Years' War in Germany, Spain entered the conflict on the imperial side. The price of this renewed boldness was the continuation of Spanish military expenditures at a high level, and the worsening of the economic and financial condition of the country. The opportunity to husband its resources was neglected; the mirage of power and prestige still entranced the Spaniards.

The "Count-Duke" Olivares. Under Philip IV, who succeeded to the throne in 1621, Spain experienced a final feverish burst of endeavor, which brought initial successes and ultimate defeat. Philip himself was unwilling and unfit to rule in person. His best side was his sponsorship of artists, not least Diego Velásquez, who painted him with uncanny truth, showing his grave solemnity which became utter boredom. His worst side was his ability to combine debauched morals with devout religion. His most important act

287

of policy, so far as the public life of Spain was concerned, was to select as his all-powerful chief minister, Gaspar de Guzmán, count of Olivares and duke of Sanlucar.

The "count-duke," as Olivares was usually called, was a paradoxical figure. He was no mere adventurer, bringing to politics nothing but cunning, ambition, and ruthlessness; a member of one of the greatest aristocratic families of Spain, he had earned the doctor's degree at the university of Salamanca; he often suffered the pangs of self-doubt, but fought his weakness to maintain his self-command and his control of the Spanish government for twenty-two years.

Olivares's government was harsh and authoritative. He reduced the bloated ranks of government officials and halted the policy of giving gifts to courtiers with a free hand (although he arranged a very lucrative revenue for himself). He took up the work of unifying and centralizing the government of Spain, but brought to it unaccustomed energy and persistence. He did not discard the basic system of administration through the great councils of state, but placed over them secretaries of state, such as were assuming increasingly important roles in the government of France and England. He slashed the few remaining privileges of the Cortes in the various kingdoms, and enforced uniformity not only of policy but also of methods and organization through Spain.

Such a policy of eliminating the remnants of Spanish particularism in the government of the peninsula required the strictest frugality for its success, so that the resentment of the population would not be further aroused by the imposition of new taxes.

The Contest with Richelieu. But Olivares did not hesitate to call upon Spain to undertake a bold and costly foreign policy. The opportunity to recoup Spain's power against the Dutch, the German Protestants, and the French was too great for him to let pass. The Dutch war had resumed after 1621, on the expiration of the truce; Spinola, by winning continued military triumphs culminating in the capture of Breda in 1625, gave hope that the rebels could be crushed by small continued effort. In Germany the victories of the Catholics, led by the Hapsburg emperor, encouraged increased participation in the Thirty Years' War. France, which came under the guidance of Cardinal Richelieu in 1624, did not seem a major threat to Spain at the moment; civil war deprived Richelieu of the possibility of intervening directly against Spain.

Nonetheless it was Richelieu, not Olivares, whose policy succeeded. The Dutch held out, the German Protestants seized the initiative in Germany during the late 1630's, and France, pacified internally, turned at Richelieu's command to open war against Spain and the emperor. In Spain, on the other hand, Olivares's policy aroused a series of revolts. The first, in 1631 in

THE DUKE OF OLIVARES. Painting by Diego Velásquez, about 1631–1635. The Prado, Madrid.

The self-image of the great statesman and great aristocrat—here the "Count-Duke" Olivares—is captured by the Spanish baroque realist, Velásquez. Olivares rides a prancing mount, symbolic of action; holds out his baton in a gesture of command; and looks upon the world with that calm confidence he desired but did not have. Velásquez takes the scene and makes it, by masterly strokes of color and form, at once an unending delight to the eye and a glimpse into the human spirit. (Metropolitan Museum of Art, New York)

Viscaya (the Basque country), was directed against a new salt tax; it was put down by military force, but the government deemed it wise to withdraw the tax.

Revolts in Catalonia and Portugal.　The year 1640 was one of trial for Olivares's policy of centralization and increased efforts. Two aristocratic conspiracies in Aragon and Andalusia were detected before they endangered the government. The movements which broke out against Spanish authority in Catalonia and Portugal were wider and deeper. In these lands particularist feeling was always strongest and resentment against the Spanish administrators and their taxes most violent.

The Catalonian rebels proclaimed the deposition of Philip IV and received the assistance of France. They organized their own government and defended themselves against the assaults of Spain until 1652, after the Fronde in France had forced Mazarin to withdraw French troops. Even then, though they again recognized Philip as their count, they negotiated the terms of peace with his government. By the settlement of 1659, the king acknowledged their traditional privileges and exemptions.

The rebellion in Portugal resulted from the failure of Philip II's successors to continue his policy of respecting the autonomy of the country, and from their inability to prevent the Dutch from seizing most of the Portuguese colonies in Indonesia and Brazil. Lisbon took the lead in the insurrection, with the encouragement of its archbishop and a majority of the Portuguese nobility. Early in 1641, Duke John of Braganza, who had been sent into Portugal as governor by Olivares, was proclaimed King John IV of Portugal by its Cortes. With aid from the French, who had supported the conspiracy, from the English, and from the Dutch, the Portuguese were able to defeat Spain in a series of battles, but it was not until the decisive victory of Villaviciosa in 1665 that Spain recognized its inability to regain Portugal and accepted its independence (February 13, 1668).

The End of Glory. Olivares did not live to see the debacle of his policy. He was dismissed in disgrace in 1643 and died insane two years later. His successor was his nephew, Luis de Haro. The goal sought by Haro was not to win, but to hold on and make peace on the best possible terms. His most brilliant stroke was to negotiate a separate peace with the Dutch at Münster in 1648; Spain acknowledged the independence of the republic of the United Provinces, but broke the French-Dutch alliance of 1635 and enabled the Spanish forces in the Low Countries to continue the struggle against France for another decade. He also terminated the rebellions in Catalonia and in southern Italy (see ch. 6, pp. 155-156). After the entry of England in the war as an ally of France, and the combined Anglo-French victory at Dunkirk (1657), Haro entered into peace negotiations. A treaty ending the war was signed in 1569 on the Isle of Pheasants in the Bidassoa river, the French-Spanish frontier in the Pyrenees.

The Peace of the Pyrenees gave France a strip of Spanish territory along the southern boundary of the Low Countries, as well as the county of Roussillon, on the northern side of the Pyrenees; but it recognized Spanish sovereignty over Catalonia. The treaty also gave the *infanta* Maria Theresa as a bride to the French king, Louis XIV. Haro permitted the principal French negotiator to incorporate into the treaty a proviso that Maria Theresa's renunciation of her rights to the succession to the Spanish mon-

archy would depend on the payment of her dowry. The sum was beyond Spain's ability to find, so that the danger that the king of France might have a claim on the Spanish monarchy in the name of his queen when Philip IV died was very real. The birth of a son to Philip in 1661 seemed to obviate the peril, but Prince Charles's chronic ill health even as an infant presaged renewed problems as he grew up.

Spain's age of glory had come to an ignominious end. The strength of Spain was exhausted, her pride abased. The center of power among the nations had shifted northward to France, England, and the Dutch Republic, all of which had preserved their independence against Spanish attack. Now Spain lay supine before Europe. The question was no longer what she would do in Europe, but what Europe would do with her and to her.

13

Germany: The Balancing of Faiths and States

1493 - 1555

"Of the riches of Germany none can doubt, for it abounds in men, riches, and arms. . . . But it is such as cannot be used."* Thus wrote the observant and thoughtful Florentine, Niccolò Machiavelli, at the dawn of the modern era. The fault lay not in the people of Germany, for they were able, energetic and numerous; nor in the land they dwelt on, for it was varied and productive.

Germany was weak because, in a world where large and unified states were taking shape, it remained a conglomeration of middling and minute territorial states—the ill-named and ill-starred Holy Roman Empire. Germany was weak because its political life was a baffling confusion of cross-currents: the interest of the Hapsburgs in their non-German lands; the cleavage of the Protestant Reformation; the narrow territorial policy of the German princes. Until, somehow, clarity and unity were brought out of this confusion, Germany would continue to be weak in fact, though a giant in potential strength.

* N. Machiavelli, *Ritratto delle cose della magna*, quoted in *New Cambridge Modern History*, I (Cambridge, Eng., 1957), 194.

I. Maximilian I

In 1493 the reigning king of Germany, the Holy Roman Emperor Frederick III, died at Linz, in his native Austria, after a reign of fifty-three years. Although the throne of Germany was elective, Frederick's son Maximilian succeeded him at once; seven years before, he had been named emperor-elect or "king of the Romans."

The Strength in Germany. Germany was in turmoil as Maximilian began his reign. The authority of the imperial crown was widely flouted. Noblemen waged private wars among themselves. Impecunious knights often eked out their thinning revenues by banditry. Only by alliances known as "public peaces" (*Landfrieden*) could the towns and states of Germany assure themselves an uncertain safety.

Nonetheless the elements of national strength were not absent. The twenty million Germans were, despite wide diversity, a single people. They had a common, though not wholly uniform, language and a broadly shared cultural life. They inhabited mainly the central belt of Europe, extending from the Baltic on the north to the Adriatic on the south, and from the Rhine valley on the west to beyond the Elbe in the east. Further east, along the Baltic coast, and in Poland, Bohemia, and Hungary, there were large nests of German population.

The economic life of Germany was generally prosperous. The productivity and diversity of the soil enabled the country to meet all its need for foodstuffs, and to export grain from its northeastern regions. The subsoil, especially in the mountainous areas, was rich in copper, iron, and other minerals. Industrially Germany was less advanced. Her handicraftsmen, though equal to any in skill, supplied chiefly local markets. The textile industries were falling behind in the competition with the Low Countries, but a vigorous metalworking industry was developing in the valley of the Ruhr, a tributary of the lower Rhine. The position of the country in commerce was confused, a mixture of a favorable past and an uncertain future. The Hansa, a league of German towns on and near the northern shores of the country, was losing its control of the trade in the North and Baltic Seas to new competitors, particularly the Dutch. No such weakness beset the merchants of southern Germany. They learned the most modern techniques of business from the Italians with whom they traded, and spread their activities beyond trade to mining and banking. By the beginning of the sixteenth century, the powerful merchant families of Augsburg in particular were taking from the Italians the lead as the bankers of Europe.

The System of Power. The political constitution of Germany made it difficult, however, for Maximilian to put to use the immense resources of the German land and nation. In name, the German state was the Holy Roman

Empire. German legists and choniclers considered it to be the descendant of the Roman empire of antiquity. In 1486 the phrase "of the German Nation" had been added to its name to indicate that the empire was German, rather than universal, in character. In form, it was a feudal elective monarchy; its king was chosen by seven electors (the archbishops of Mainz, Trier, and Cologne, the elector Palatine, the king of Bohemia, and the electors of Saxony and Brandenburg). Until crowned as emperor, traditionally by the pope, the monarch continued to be known as "king of the Romans." Maximilian abandoned this custom when he proclaimed himself "elected Holy Roman Emperor" in 1503, without papal coronation.

Though the emperor was the fount of all authority in Germany, he shared his powers of legislation and taxation with the Reichstag (imperial diet, or parliament). It included six of the seven electors (not the king of Bohemia); the other leading vassals, almost three hundred in number; and eighty-five free cities.

Some of the vassals, or Reichsstände (imperial estates) were noblemen holding hereditary fiefs; others were ecclesiastical princes—archbishops, bishops and abbots—whose fiefs belonged not to them but to their benefices. The "estates" also included the free cities, self-governing municipalities directly under the suzerainty of the imperial crown. These were most numerous in western and southern Germany; among them were centers of trade and commerce like Frankfurt on the Main, Nuremberg, and Augsburg. There were also a large number of "immediate knights," especially in western and southwestern Germany, who owed allegiance only to the emperor. Their tiny fiefs did not suffice in most cases to maintain a noble style of life. Many of these knights therefore became *Raubritter* (robber knights), whose depredations ravaged wide areas of the country.

Even agreement between emperor and Reichstag did not enable the central government to operate effectively. There was no adequate imperial machinery for the administration of the common business of state: no imperial treasury and no national army. The vassals collected taxes voted by the diet, and enforced imperial laws and ordinances. They had transferred the reality of power to themselves and away from the emperor. Though nominally subordinate to him, they were almost sovereign. This status was recognized in the title "prince" customarily given to them. Elsewhere the term was ordinarily restricted to fully sovereign rulers, but in Germany it was used for the great vassals of the emperor.

Within their lands in turn, the princes were not absolute but usually faced assemblies of their own estates, in which their subvassals sat. The consent of these estates was essential to taxation. The princes sought to dominate rather than to destroy their territorial diets, which enabled them to advance the unification of their lands. The princes used the diets, as well

THE BOOKPLATE OF A HUMANIST.
Woodcut by Albrecht Dürer, c. 1500.

This bookplate by the great German artist who introduced Renaissance themes and techniques from Italy into his native country was made for Willibald Pirckheimer, a wealthy merchant and humanist. The three mottoes at the top acknowledge in Hebrew, Greek, and Latin that "The fear of God is the beginning of wisdom." The figures of children, or *putti*, are an Italian device derived by Dürer from his experience in Venice. *(Achenbach Foundation)*

as their professional administrators, to weld into single territorial states the conglomeration of lands which they held by a variety of titles and rights.

Although Maximilian lacked real power as king and emperor, he was first among the princes of Germany in his position as archduke of Austria, ruling the hereditary lands of the house of Hapsburg. These lands lay principally in the southeastern part of the empire, on the easterly and southerly slopes of the Alpine range.

Programs of Reform.   Reform that strengthened his authority was Maximilian's answer to the country's need for peace and order. A national treasury with national taxes collected by national officials, a national appellate court, a national army trained and paid on a professional basis—these were the goals of reform as envisioned by Maximilian.

His vassals looked upon such powers as constituting not reform but enslavement, not "German freedom" but the "French servitude" of obedience to a powerful king. One of their leaders, Berthold von Henneberg, archbishop-elector of Mainz, developed his own program for a reform in which the princes would be supreme in Germany, and the king-emperor, under their control, would be no more than their agent.

A compromise was reached at the diet of Worms in 1495. The imperial council was not organized; but an annual Reichstag with considerable powers of control was established. A supreme appellate court, the Reichskammergericht (imperial chamber court), was formed. A "perpetual public peace" was proclaimed, ending all private wars and feuds throughout Germany.

The compromise was hollow, however. The laws could be enforced only by the old method, the delegation of authority to the princes. Violators of the public peace were to be punished by the closest imperial estate. The danger of civil war continued, since the estates themselves retained their freedom of judgment and decision. The chamber court did not exalt the crown's authority; of its seventeen judges, only the presiding member was to be named by the emperor, the others at the nomination and with the approval of the princes.

The need for public peace had still to be met. In the absence of a powerful central monarchy, some larger public body was required to punish violators of the perpetual public peace. This was devised in the system of six "imperial circles" created in 1500, and expanded to ten in 1512 with the inclusion of the electorates and the Hapsburg hereditary lands. The members of a circle elected an executive authority with powers of enforcement; the system was purely formal in the circles encompassing the territory of a single ruler, but elsewhere it reduced the private wars. It was the only lasting constitutional reform of Maximilian's reign.

Dynastic Ambitions. For all of Maximilian's concern about imperial reform, it was not the heart of his purposes. His supreme goal was the grandeur of his family. To it he subordinated his strong sense of German nationhood and his program of imperial reform. Because it could be achieved only by the acquisition of new territories, foreign policy became his primary interest.

The basic fact of Maximilian's diplomacy was his marriage in 1477 to Mary of Burgundy, daughter of Duke Charles the Bold, who had just been slain by the Swiss at Nancy. Maximilian, especially after Mary's death in 1482, took upon himself the defense of the interests of their son Philip as duke of Burgundy at the age of four. The aspirations and enmities of the house of Burgundy—notably the reconquest of the duchy of Burgundy which had been declared escheated (fallen back) to the French crown in 1477*— became part and parcel of Hapsburg policy. It was a momentous change, for until then the rulers of Austria had been increasingly concerned with expand-

---

* The duchy was occupied by the forces of the French monarchy and governed as an integral part of the French state. Not only the claim to the duchy but also the title "duke of Burgundy" was retained by the descendants of Charles the Bold, who continued to rule in the imperial fief of Franche-Comté, the adjacent "county of Burgundy," until 1678.

ing their domains in eastern Europe rather than involving themselves with the affairs of western Europe. But the strength of the Low Countries, combined with that of the Hapsburg dominions, made the house of Hapsburg a power of the first rank, greater than any in the Holy Roman Empire and perhaps equal even to France. It was a strength compounded of the resources of many lands, and depended for its preservation and extension upon the unity of the dynasty.

Modesty and caution were not the characteristics of Maximilian's personality nor of his foreign policy. With restless persistence, but little continuity or coherence of purpose, he continued his quest for glory and advantage. In 1493 he married Bianca Sforza, niece of Duke Ludovico il Moro, to whom he granted Milan as an imperial fief. Nonetheless he stood aside while Charles VIII invaded Italy in 1494. In the next year Ferdinand of Aragon, with a promise of a double marriage between their houses—the hand of his heir Juan for Maximilian's daughter Margaret and the hand of his daughter Joanna for Maximilian's son Philip—tempted the German king into the anti-French camp. In 1496 he sent a puny expeditionary force—the empire granted him no aid, and he accepted aid from the Fugger bankers and the Venetians —into Italy, where it became a laughingstock for its ineffectual siege of the Florentine port of Livorno (Leghorn). Nonetheless Ferdinand stood by his promise, and Margaret and Juan were wed in October 1496, Philip and Joanna in the spring of 1497. But Maximilian did not achieve the subordination of Spain to his policies; Ferdinand was too clear-eyed and realistic to take his lead from the bombastic king of Germany, while Philip began to take charge of his own policy.

The advent of Louis XII in France in 1498 brought a resurgence of Maximilian's bellicosity. It seemed an opportunity to regain the duchy of Burgundy and to assist Ludovico il Moro against the threat from Louis, who was a rival claimant to Milan (see ch. 7, p. 170). But the princes of the empire did not wish to join his campaign. He railed against them for deserting him: "I must and will make war. . . . This must I say, even should I have to throw the crown at my feet and stamp upon it." The French king easily thwarted Maximilian's attack, severing the German's allies from him, winning Duke Philip for a treaty of friendship, and stirring up the Swiss against their imperial overlord.

The Swiss Confederation. A series of disputes between the Swiss and the imperial authorities over the jurisdiction of the latter in Switzerland broke into armed conflict in 1499. The ultimate issue, however, was the independence of the Alpine cantons from any effective control by the empire, of which they were nominally a part.

Switzerland was a confederation of cantons (provinces) with even looser constitutional bonds than those of the Holy Roman Empire. Their will to co-operate, based upon recognition that their safety and independence depended upon their unity, was far greater than that of the Reichsstände, however. The twelve principal cantons shared equally in the determination and execution of foreign policy, which was their only common business; domestic affairs were completely their individual concerns. There were in addition allied cantons, which retained control over their internal affairs but did not participate in the decisions of the confederation; and dependent cantons, which had no say in either their domestic or foreign affairs.

The safety of the Swiss depended upon the valor of their infantry. The pike square of the Switzers had destroyed the heavy cavalry armies of Charles the Bold of Burgundy during the 1470's. Swiss mercenary soldiers were an essential part of the economic life of the country. Only a few Swiss towns on the trade routes between Italy and northern Europe enjoyed a moderate prosperity; the forest cantons, limited to herding for their principal livelihood, were unable to sustain their whole populations. The sturdy mountain lads gladly accepted the harsh discipline and training required for effective combat as pikemen. Their wages in foreign service were not the only addition to the revenues of their cantons; the princes who hired them were compelled to pay pensions to the officials of the home districts.

The Swiss overwhelmed Maximilian's army in July, 1499. He made peace with them at Basel two months later. They retained their territory intact and were implicitly exempted from the jurisdiction of the imperial courts. Though Maximilian called them his "obedient kinsmen," they were independent in fact.

Hungarian Connection. For the next eighteen years, Maximilian continued to take an active part in the Italian wars. His only clear purpose was to regain Milan for the Sforzas, but he did not scruple against granting the duchy to Louis XII as a fief when it was necessary to make a temporary peace with France. In 1518, Maximilian finally accepted a five years' truce with France, which maintained its acquisitions while Maximilian gained only a small corner of land from Venice.

Maximilian's policy displayed no such ineptness and inefficiency when turned eastward. It was concerned with the constant threat of the further expansion to the northwest of the Ottoman empire, and with acquisition of new realms for the Hapsburgs. Austria itself was safe from the attack of the Ottoman Turks only as long as Hungary stood fast. Under King Matthias Corvinus (the Raven), who ruled it with firm authority from 1458, Hungary not only held back the Turks but even invaded Austria during the 1480s, holding Vienna and Lower Austria. The Hungarian conquests ended with the death of Matthias in 1490. With the withdrawal of Matthias' forces, the Austrian lands returned to Hapsburg rule.

Maximilian revived the hereditary claim of the Hapsburgs upon the

Hungarian throne, established in the treaty of Sopron (Ödenburg) of 1463 but held in abeyance during Matthias' reign. The Magyar nobility of Hungary, fearful of German domination, elected as their king Wladyslaw (Ladislas) Jagiello, the eldest son of the reigning king of Poland and himself king of Bohemia since 1471. Maximilian thereupon invaded Hungary in 1491. He could not upset Wladyslaw's election but did obtain his agreement that the Hapsburg claim would be recognized whenever Wladyslaw's line failed of sons to inherit the throne. The Hungarian diet accepted the agreement in 1492, but it had to be reinforced by a series of marriage accords, culminating in the treaty of Vienna of 1515. It resulted in the double marriage of Wladyslaw's son Louis (Lajos) to Maximilian's granddaughter Mary and of his daughter Anna to the emperor's grandson Ferdinand.

Maximilian's dream of Hapsburg greatness was materializing. One grandson, Charles, was already king of Spain, ruler of the Low Countries and titular duke of Burgundy (see ch. 12, p. 273), and the emperor, at the lad's beseeching, sought to have him named king of the Romans, that is, acknowledged successor. He had overcome the endeavors of Francis I, king of France, to obtain his own election by means of promises and bribery; but papal opposition to Charles prevented his receiving the title in 1518. Ferdinand, Maximilian's other grandson, had the inheritance of Hungary—his future brother-in-law, Louis Jagiello, alone stood between him and Hungary's crown of St. Stephen; but Louis was an ailing youth, who might not live to bar his way.

While the emperor thus doted on his dynastic ambitions, a small event at Wittenberg—the posting by Luther of his theses on the indulgence— marked the opening of a new phase of German history. But Maximilian did not live to see it grow from a "monk's quarrel" within the confines of the church into the storm of the Protestant Reformation. In January, 1519, the Holy Roman emperor died, penniless, in his childhood home at Wiener Neustadt.

II. Charles V

The contest between the kings of France and Spain for the throne of Germany became open and bitter. Theirs were not the only names put before the electors: even Henry VIII of England was a candidate, without supporters; and the Elector Frederick the Wise of Saxony, although he had the respect of his fellow princes and the advocacy of Pope Leo X, refused their support and threw his own vote and influence to Charles. Popular opinion, too, believing Charles to be a German in character and aspirations, gave him its enthusiastic voice.

The Electoral Contest. Assured of Saxony and Bohemia, Charles needed the votes of the other five electors. The envoys of Francis I promised them huge sums of cash for their support; the Hapsburg representatives countered with letters of credit upon the banking house of Fugger, to be paid after Charles's election. Only Frederick of Saxony remained publicly aloof from the haggling negotiations. Since the arguments to the electors' purses thus balanced out, the decisive factor became the desire of the imperial princes to maintain their autonomy and their influence in the central government. In Francis they saw a king who ruled his own country imperiously, permitting no challenge to his authority from the great nobles of France. Charles, on the other hand, was younger, less self-assured, and accustomed to the substantial liberties of his subjects in the Low Countries. When Charles agreed to accept an "electoral capitulation," or treaty, confirming the privileges of the princes, the electors thereupon gave him their unanimous vote on June 28, 1519.

Charles, who had remained in Spain all during the contest, sailed for Germany in 1520. He was crowned King Charles V at Aachen (coronation by the pope as emperor was ten years away) but first signed the electoral capitulation as promised. In it he agreed not to use foreigners in governing Germany, nor to bring in foreign troops, nor to call a meeting of the diet outside the country. He assured the electors increased powers in a regency council (*Reichsregiment*) and agreed not to put any one under the ban of the empire—a decree of outlawry—without his being heard first.

The Germans found Charles V much as the Spaniards had on his first arrival—unimpressive in personal appearance, and anything but a patriot king devoted to the interests of a single country. He was a born Fleming ruling in his native Low Countries, in Spain, and now in Germany, who in all his lands felt himself to be the paramount champion of the Roman Catholic faith.

Luther at Worms. It was this last characteristic which first shattered the delight of the Germans in their young king. Charles V quickly showed himself to be a rigid Catholic, not the leader of "the nine-tenths of Germany who raise the battle cry 'Luther'" (as the papal nuncio described the situation). He had no special sympathy for the specifically German grievances against the papacy, although he accepted the need for reform of the church within the framework of the Roman Catholic communion. Martin Luther, who had refused to bow to the authority of the papacy, appeared before the diet at Worms to be heard, as was required by Charles's electoral capitulation, before the ban of the empire was pronounced upon him.

Though Charles firmly intended to outlaw the Wittenberg professor, he did not at once issue the edict banning Luther. He needed the help of the imperial princes for the war which was beginning against France, and dared

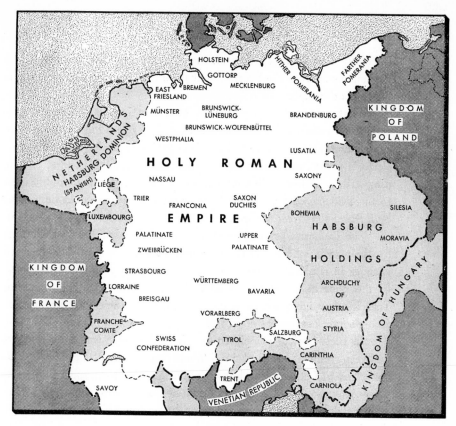

The Holy Roman Empire in 1519

not offend Luther's protector, Elector Frederick of Saxony. The diet accorded Charles an army of 20,000 infantry and 4,000 cavalry for a period of six months. To maintain the control of the imperial estates over the army, the diet gave Charles the troops after they had been raised by the princes, instead of the money to enable him to form an army in his own pay.

Charles and the imperial estates also argued vehemently over the form and powers of the regency council he had promised in his electoral capitulation. They wanted a body under their control sharing permanently and effectively in the government of the empire. He wanted to restrict it to being an advisory body, while effective power of decision and execution remained with him. A compromise was reached providing that the council would govern Germany only during the king's absence, confining itself to advice at other times. It could concern itself only with the internal business of the empire, but not with its foreign affairs nor with the granting of fiefs.

The Reformer Banned. These matters settled, Charles closed the diet and issued the edict putting Luther under the ban of the empire. He acted upon his own authority, without the assent of the full diet, after the Wittenberger's supporters had departed from Worms. It was a bold gesture. It showed forcefully that Charles's capitulatory compromise with the imperial estates did not come from the heart, and that he intended to rule Germany according to his own lights.

What mattered, however, was less intention than performance. The action of Frederick the Wise in spiriting Luther into hiding at the Wartburg, in defiance of the ban, put Charles's capabilities to the acid test. Under the elector's protection, Luther stayed safe. Charles could thunder, but no lightning struck. Power in Germany belonged not only to the king, but even more to the princes, who governed in their territories and could be swayed only by force or the threat of force.

The Lutheran princes began to reform the churches in their territories by their own authority. In so doing, they did not confine themselves to changes in ritual, doctrine, or organization. They also seized the possessions of the church—usually revenue-producing lands—for their own domains. Thereby they increased their income at a time when other groups were suffering severe economic difficulties.

In ecclesiastical principalities, where the ruler was a bishop or abbot, Lutheran reform occurred in different ways. Sometimes the chapter was converted to Lutheranism, but maintained itself in existence as the source of political authority; a Lutheran "administrator" was named to perform the temporal duties of the bishop and enjoy the benefit of his revenues. An even more drastic procedure of secularization was followed by the grand master of the Teutonic Order in Prussia, who upon Luther's advice converted the lands of the order into his permanent hereditary possession.

The Government of Ferdinand. Charles V, lord of many lands, could not remain in Germany to give his whole attention to its affairs. Spain, stirred by revolt, needed his personal governance even more than the empire. Charles therefore sailed for Spain in 1522, leaving the administration of Germany to his brother Ferdinand and to the regency council, which had been set up the year before.

Ferdinand, formally only his brother's lieutenant in Germany, was actually more. In April, 1521, Charles had secretly granted him the five duchies of Upper Austria, for himself and his posterity, and later added the provinces of Hither Austria. Ferdinand thereby re-founded the specifically German dynasty of Hapsburg, with its traditional interest in eastern Europe reinforced by his aspirations to the crowns of Hungary and Bohemia. The Hapsburgs now formed a general European dynasty, however, with the Austrian branch, under a younger brother, subordinate to the Burgundian-Spanish branch under the elder. Nonetheless Ferdinand developed a distinct personal policy in the government of Austria and in the exercise of his brother's authority as king of Germany during his absence. He became first and foremost a German prince. He followed reluctantly his brother's policy of using the Empire for the sake of Spain and the Low Countries. He was readier than Charles to work with the princes as partners in the government of Germany, and to make concessions to the Lutherans.

The Failure of Regency Rule. The regency council set up at the diet of Worms represented an effort to channel the energies and purposes of the imperial princes into an effective organ for Germany's central government. It began its activity vigorously in 1522, but soon faltered when neither the king nor the princes were willing to give up any of their own powers to it.

The weakness of the regency council was demonstrated when Franz von Sickingen, the greatest and ablest of the robber knights of western Germany, launched a campaign against the archbishop-elector of Trier. The council of regency issued a ban against Sickingen, but had to call upon three princes in the neighborhood—the elector of Trier himself, the elector Palatine, and Landgrave Philip of Hesse—to put down the overmighty knight. They captured and killed Sickingen in 1523 at his castle of Landstuhl. All through western and southern Germany, other imperial knights were forced to accept the destruction of their castle strongholds. It was the doom of their independence, and another victory for the German princes in their competition for power over their rivals.

The failure of the regency council to attain vigor and permanence reflected the shift in German public life from emphasis on reform of the constitution to reform of the church. The relationship between the new Lutheran faith and the old Roman Catholic merged into the older question of the relationship between the emperor and his great vassals. Religion became, and remained for a century, the paramount problem in German history.

It was the paradoxical achievement of Charles V that his policy first enabled Lutheranism to survive in its difficult early years and later halted its spread over all Germany. The cause of this contradictory result was simple in the extreme. Charles would not sacrifice his other aims—the defense of his dynastic ambitions, especially against France; the struggle against the onmoving Turks; the aspiration toward universal monarchy—for the sake of the Roman Catholic religion in Germany. Thus he was not able to concentrate his efforts upon the single task of championing the Roman church in Germany. Because he would not take the lead of the religious revolt, it came under the domination of the territorial princes, and its survival became bound up with their success in maintaining their aristocratic liberty against royal centralization.

The Peasants' War. The princes enhanced their political preponderance when they met successfully the challenge of the Peasants' War of 1524-1525. This was a violent rebellion of the peasantry which began in the southern Black Forest in the summer of 1524 and spread through Swabia, Franconia, Thuringia, and Alsace—the same area of tiny states where the robber knights had flourished. An acute sense of injustice had long prevailed among the peasants in the area, breaking out frequently in flurries of violence. Their conditions did not worsen to any important extent in the quarter-century immediately before the rebellion; they obtained increased personal freedom from the bonds of serfdom, but were compelled to pay larger rents for the land they tilled.

Their resentment was sparked into open armed protests by the ideas and the example of the Lutherans and the Anabaptists. They took Luther's proclamation of the spiritual freedom and equality of all Christians and applied it, as he did not, to the outer world of society; Luther's advocacy of resistance to the established authority of Rome encouraged them to turn upon their landlords and princes, who took so large a portion of their earnings in oppressive rents and taxes. They had near at hand the model of a peasant people—the Swiss—who had successfully defended their rights and their independence by arms against the duke of Burgundy in the 1470's and against Emperor Maximilian himself in 1499.

The peasants put forward their demands in various programs, the most widely adopted being the Twelve Articles drawn up by Sebastian Lotzer of Memmingen. In it radical religious ideas, like election of priests by their parishioners, were combined with economic demands, like abolition of serfdom, increased peasant rights in the village communities, elimination of new obligations, and reduction of rents.

In the beginning, the rebellion went well. The peasants won some allies: town workmen who joined them because of their own hatred for the oligarchies which ruled the guilds and the municipalities; and knights, led by the fearsome Götz von Berlichingen, who despaired of finding a way for themselves in the harsh new times of princely domination. A few *Landsknechte*, or professional infantrymen, brought their skill to the peasant bands. But the rebels lacked any enterprising leaders able to lead them against the formations of trained troops organized by the princes, particularly with infantry and cavalry brought back from Italy after the imperial victory at Pavia (1525). Most of the knights backed the princes, not the peasants. Both Catholic and Lutheran rulers collaborated against the peasantry. The turn in the fighting began in April, 1525. By June the rebellion had been put down, with savagery and bloodshed on the part of the princes exceeding that of the peasants, who mingled good-heartedness with their bloody deeds.

Territorial Religion. The defeat of the peasants did not lead to a sharp worsening of their conditions. The result in most places was to shatter the readiness of the peasantry to take up arms; they remained in economic and political stagnation, the forgotten majority of the nation, unhappy with their subjection but unheard. They did not forget, however, that they had looked upon Luther as a voice for their aspirations, and that he had failed them.

The Lutheran movement lost its impetus among the common folk of Germany, and became increasingly an affair of the states and upper classes—an indirect but not unimportant consequence of the Peasants' War. (See ch. 4, p. 86.)

The question of Lutheranism came before the Reichstag which met at Speyer in 1526, the first assembly of the imperial estates since the end of the Peasants' War. Charles V, off in Spain, ordered his brother Ferdinand to permit no tampering with Christian belief or tradition, and to proceed at once with the enforcement of the edict of Worms. The diet asked that Charles reconsider and join with it in pressing for a general or national council to settle the controversy in religion. Until then the diet ordered that the estates of the empire should "live with, rule over, and direct their subjects . . . in such fashion as each of them hopes and expects to give answer for to God and to Your Majesty." This "order" was not a decision, but an agreement to avoid one. It acknowledged the fact that the churches of Germany were becoming territorial churches, protected and governed by the princes.

War in Italy. The king's foreign involvements prevented him from following the policy of his own instructions to Ferdinand. The League of Cognac, formed in 1526 between Pope Clement VIII, Venice, Milan, and France, with Florence as a secret member, threatened Charles's position in Italy. He needed the assistance of his German vassals, and accepted the compromise at Speyer. He received in recompense a force of 11,000 *Landsknechte* who crossed the Alps into Italy, where they joined Spanish forces under the command of the fugitive French duke, the Constable of Bourbon.

The *Landsknechte* were mainly Lutherans who considered that they were fighting a war for their faith against the pope; the Spaniards were staunch Catholics, who fought Clement only as a temporal ruler. For all their clashing faiths, they did effective work on the battlefields. The storming and sack of Rome in 1527 removed the pope from the list of Charles's enemies. It was two more years before Francis I accepted his defeat. In the treaty of Cambrai (see ch. 8, p. 171), the two rulers accepted the territorial status quo: Charles abandoned his claim to the duchy of Burgundy, Francis his to Italy, a far larger spoil of war.

The reconciliation between Charles and Clement led to the German king's coronation as emperor by the pope on February 14, 1530. The ceremony was held not at Rome, but further north at Bologna: Charles was impatient to return to Germany to take over the task of crushing the Lutheran heretics, who had used the years of his absence from the country to consolidate their position.

The Speyer "Protestation." The division between the princes of the two faiths, which had been obscured during the Speyer Reichstag of 1526, came into the open at the diet which met in the same city three years later. The Catholics were in absolute majority. The Catholic princes proposed, and the emperor embodied in an "imperial recess," measures to halt the spread of Lutheranism: no action was to be taken by any estate for reform of religion until a church council met; Catholics were to be tolerated in Lutheran territories; and Lutherans were to cease interfering with the "authority, properties, and taxes" of the Catholic church in their lands.

Landgrave Philip of Hesse took the lead of the Lutherans in opposing the decision of the majority of the Reichstag. A Protestation was drawn up declaring that the Speyer decision of 1526, having been adopted unanimously, could not be withdrawn by a simple majority. When God's honor and the soul's salvation were affected, it asserted, princes could appeal to their consciences. (The name "Protestants" for the religious reformers, which became general in subsequent years, derived from this Protestation of Speyer.) The constitutional principle of the Protestation, that majority decisions of the imperial diet did not bind in questions of religion, was novel. Henceforth the religious unity of the Holy Roman Empire could not be re-established by constitutional means but only by force, actual or implied. The split of Germany into two hostile camps, Lutheran and Catholic, was now a matter of politics as well as of religion.

The Lutherans were in a difficult position. To defend their religious convictions against the combined authority of emperor and a majority of the Reichstag was an act of near-rebellion. Some Lutheran jurists and theologians argued that such resistance to the emperor was permissible, that princes could take up arms in such a cause. When the leading Lutheran princes, led by Elector John of Saxony and Philip of Hesse, and many imperial cities formed a league for mutual assistance at Schmalkalden on December 31, 1530, Luther modified his earlier stand against resistance to the established powers by endorsing the right of the princes to defend themselves.

III. Charles and Ferdinand

The emperor did not undertake a military campaign against the Lutherans, as he had originally intended. Instead he concentrated his efforts for the election of his brother Ferdinand as king of the Romans. Over the opposition of Saxony, Ferdinand was elected Charles's successor on January 5, 1531. The emperor thereupon turned the government of Germany over to Ferdinand; but he reserved to himself the right to take charge of policy in case of need.

The Turks in Hungary. Despite his new title and authority, Ferdinand was unable to concentrate his attention upon the business of the empire. The resurgence of Turkish power under the command of Sultan Suleiman the Magnificent endangered Ferdinand in his eastern lands, where his chief interests lay. Suleiman had overwhelmed Louis II of Hungary in 1526 at the battle of Mohacs. Louis's death while in flight left empty the thrones of Hungary and Bohemia. Ferdinand quickly declared himself the king of the two countries. He was elected in both, but met armed resistance in Hungary, where a native Magyar party held its own election and declared John Zapolya to be king. Ferdinand defeated Zapolya in battle with an army brought in from Austria, but the Magyar turned for support to the Ottoman sultan. Suleiman recognized Zapolya as king of Hungary under Turkish suzerainty, and then launched his own attack upon Ferdinand in his home country. On September 27, 1529, after an easy passage through Hungary, Suleiman stood with a huge army before Vienna. Ferdinand beat off the siege in a few weeks with the aid of 5,000 imperial troops.

It was a victory which saved Austria for the moment, but did not strike at the far-off sources of Turkish power. Suleiman returned to the attack in 1532. To ward off the new attack, the emperor and the king of the Romans combined to seek more substantial aid from the German princes. Charles negotiated an armistice in the religious disputes, assuring the Lutherans peace until a general council. The Reichstag voted a "Turkish help" and sent a substantial force to Vienna. It did not fight any large battles, for Suleiman, slowed down by the siege of the small fortress of Guns, turned aside from Vienna to attack Graz and then withdrew from Austria with no gains.

Ferdinand then made his own private peace with Zapolya. The Hungarian chieftain retained his title of king, but agreed that Ferdinand should succeed him. When Zapolya died in 1540, however, some of the Hungarian nobles refused to accept Ferdinand. Instead they recognized a son of Zapolya as monarch. Suleiman came to their support in 1541, defeated an Austrian force, captured the Hungarian capital of Buda, and then declared Hungary to be a province of the Ottoman empire. The Reichstag of 1542, asked for aid in the defense of Austria, sent a force of almost 50,000 men; but it was comprised mainly of contingents sent by the princes individually. It failed to recapture Pest, across the Danube from Buda, and retreated westward. During the following years, Suleiman's troops pushed his control of Hungarian territory until only a strip at the western edge of the country remained under Hapsburg domination. Throughout the rest of the country, the Magyar nobility continued to govern the land under Turkish overlordship.

The Schmalkaldic Alliance. Meanwhile the maneuvering for position between the religious parties continued in Germany. The Protestant princes worked constantly to buttress the alliance they had formed at Schmalkalden. The dukes of Bavaria, after the Hapsburgs, the most powerful Catholic princes in the empire, were moved by fear and jealousy of the Austrian archdukes to form a parallel alliance at Saalfeld in 1531 with Saxony, Hesse, and other Lutheran rulers. The failure of the Zwinglian reform movement in Switzerland (see ch. 4, p. 91) impelled the cities of Upper Germany, no longer able to find support from the Swiss Protestants, to draw closer to the Schmalkaldic league.

Collaboration between the Protestant alliance and the king of France, negotiated in 1534 by Philip of Hesse and Francis I, indicated the shape of a new pattern of power relationships in Germany—the alliance between the German Protestants and the king of France, the "eldest son" of the Catholic church, to thwart the aspirations of the Catholic emperor to crush his foes in the Holy Roman Empire. The alliance reconquered the duchy of Württemberg for its Lutheran ruler, who had lost it to the Hapsburgs. Philip, as well as John of Saxony, refused to march against the Hapsburg hereditary lands, as desired by Francis. The sense of a common German unity had not yet been completely destroyed by the passions of religious war.

For another decade the Schmalkaldic league safeguarded the interests of the Protestant princes of Germany, while Charles V moved in and out of war with France. The emperor held his acquired positions of strength in Italy, the French king thwarted an imperial invasion of France, and the fighting achieved little by way of shifting the balance of forces. The formation of a counterleague of Catholic princes at Nuremberg in 1539, with Bavaria as its leader, marked the break-up of the earlier collaboration of the Schmalkaldic league with the Wittelsbach dukes of Bavaria. King Ferdinand stood firm for reconciliation between Catholics and Lutherans. An agreement at Frankfurt in 1539, suspending trials in the imperial chamber court against Lutheran princes who had secularized church estates and assuring peace between the religious parties for at least fifteen months, was Ferdinand's work. Charles was not happy with the agreement; it was accompanied by two important acquisitions for the Lutheran side, the electorate of Brandenburg and ducal Saxony. North Germany was almost completely won over to the new faith.

The Bigamy of Philip of Hesse. The strength of the Schmalkaldic league lay in large part in the political skill of its leader, Philip of Hesse. He possessed a keen sense of realities and possibilities, the ability to negotiate and to guide, and the personal attractiveness which enabled him to hold together the diffuse and often hostile forces of German Protestantism. A mischance in his personal life therefore imperiled the whole Protestant cause. His first marriage turned out unhappily, and in the late 1530's he fell passionately in love with another woman. He insisted on making her his lawful wife, but lacked adequate grounds under existing law for dissolving his marriage. He appealed to Luther and Melanchthon in 1539 to approve a second marriage; they gave him their permission, partly out of fear of losing a needed champion, partly upon the basis of the examples of polygamy in the Old Testament. The marriage was performed in 1540 in Melanchthon's presence. Philip's bigamy could not be kept secret, and he would not lie in his own defense. The emperor received grounds for legal proceedings against Philip, and the Lutheran princes turned away from him. The Schmalkaldic league had to face the coming test of strength without the wise guidance of its creator.

The crisis took four years to develop. Charles V decided by 1541 that the time to exterminate the Lutheran heresy was fast approaching. His anger was sharpened by the continued spread of Protestantism. In 1542 the Schmalkaldic allies drove Henry of Brunswick, the last influential Catholic prince in northern Germany, from his duchy. In the same year Herman von Wied, the archbishop-elector of Cologne, openly joined the Protestants with whom he had long sympathized. His drive to secularize the principality of Cologne met immediate resistance from the chapter of the cathedral and the city council of Cologne. Charles, fearing the establishment of a Protestant state on the borders of his own lands in the Low Countries, gave them support. The conversion of Frederick II, the elector Palatine, to the Reform in January 1546 was the culmination of the threat to the position of Roman Catholicism in Germany, for his vote gave the Protestants a majority in the electoral college.

War with France. Only the pressures of foreign war delayed the start of Charles's campaign to suppress the Lutherans. In 1542 Francis I, in alliance with the count of Jülich, in the lower Rhineland, opened another phase of his recurrent combat with the emperor. Charles conciliated the Protestants for the moment in order to obtain their aid for the war. In 1544, a Reichstag meeting accorded him help for the war against the French; at the same time, he won the alliance of England. An invasion of France by Charles's soldiers, driving from the Low Countries close to Paris, compelled Francis to make peace at Crépy (September 18) upon the basis of a return to the prewar situation. The war which had flared up again with the Turks continued until 1545, when Ferdinand obtained an armistice from Suleiman by agreeing to pay him tribute for the towns held by the archduke in Hungary. It was a blow to Hapsburg pride, but Ferdinand's forces were released for the campaign against the Lutherans within Germany.

The last steps of preparation were taken when an alliance was concluded with the pope in 1545 and the duke of Bavaria in 1546. Pope Paul III dropped his long-standing quarrel with the emperor in 1545, made an alliance with him for the war of suppression, and promised him valuable financial assistance. In the next year the duke of Bavaria withdrew from his association with the Schmalkaldic princes and formed an alliance with Charles. Then the emperor won over a number of Protestant princes by assuring them that he was not planning a war of religion, but one against rebellious subjects. One of those who followed Charles was Duke Maurice of Saxony, whose political gifts were as great as his Protestant faith was mild; in him the Schmalkaldic league lost a potential leader to take the place of Philip of Hesse. Philip and Elector John Frederick of Saxony were put under the ban of the empire. All was ready for the emperor's war. Not long after the death of Martin Luther on February 18, 1546, the fighting began: the fate of his reform now belonged to the decision of the sword.

The Schmalkaldic War. The first advantage lay with the Schmalkaldic forces. They had more troops than the emperor, and the publication of the pope's alliance with him belied his contention that he was not fighting a war to destroy their religion. But they paid the penalty of inept leadership and inadequate funds. They failed to cut Charles's communications with Italy, whence he could draw upon the troops and supplies maintained with Spanish treasure; they attacked the Bavarian fortress of Ingolstadt in September in desultory manner, and then gave way before an imperial counteroffensive. Maurice of Saxony invaded electoral Saxony, where his cousin the elector John Frederick, ruled. Imperial forces crushed resistance in Upper Germany. The Palatinate (the territory belonging to the elector Palatine), Württemberg, Ulm, Augsburg, and Strassburg all had to pay heavy ransom to save themselves from devastation.

The next year brought even greater successes. Charles V defeated Herman von Wied in Cologne, and compelled him to resign his electorship in favor of his Catholic coadjutor. Imperial troops aided Maurice in maintaining the conquest of electoral Saxony. A Bohemian rising against King Ferdinand failed to save John Frederick. Spanish troops under the duke of Alva crushed the electoral and the Bohemian forces at the battle of Mühlberg. John Frederick was taken prisoner and a sentence of death passed against him; but the emperor was content to hold it over him while he kept him prisoner under harsh conditions. John Frederick ordered the Saxons to cease resistance and abandoned the electorate, which was given to Maurice. He refused to capitulate on the question of religion, however; he remained the emperor's prisoner, but became a hero of the Lutherans for his firmness. Philip of Hesse, discouraged by the downfall of Saxony, decided to make the best of a bad position by surrendering to the emperor. His expectation of lenient treatment proved wrong; Charles kept him in close confinement.

The Interim of Augsburg. By the time a new Reichstag assembled at Augsburg, at Charles V's call in September 1547, his military victory was complete. Now he could put through the policy towards which he had worked for almost thirty years: to end, at last and for all time: the Protestant heresy in Germany; to revise the constitution of the Holy Roman Empire upon the basis of more effective monarchical institutions; and to compel

Paul III to accept his leadership in the reform of the Catholic church, which had been entrusted to the general council just convened at Trent. He issued a declaration on the religious unification of Germany "until the determination of the general council shall have been made." The Interim, as it was called, was made imperial law by the "recess" of June 30, 1548. In southern Germany, where his power was concentrated, Charles was able to enforce the Interim, although Strassburg in particular accepted it only formally. Brandenburg and Hesse, too, made only outward subjection to it, but John Frederick, in prison still, refused it, while Maurice, the new Saxon elector, accepted it in December in weakened form.

Charles's triumph led to his downfall. He failed in his efforts to compel the church council at Trent to reach a theological compromise with the Protestants—for it was not so much the specific doctrines of the Roman church as its universality which Charles defended. His vigor against the Lutherans within Germany was more eloquent, however, than his defense of their right to present their views at Trent. The princes who had accepted his leadership in the years since 1546 came to fear that they had given themselves a hard master. He kept Spanish troops in the Empire in spite of the promise made in his electoral capitulation not to bring in foreign soldiers; and the Spaniards made themselves hated for their violent behavior. The emperor's action in keeping John Frederick and Philip of Hesse imprisoned further envenomed the German princes against him.

The Princes' Rebellion. Charles V's dynastic ambition for his own son, Philip, led to the collapse of his edifice of victories. He decided to ask Ferdinand, who was king of the Romans, to step down in favor of Philip as emperor-elect and successor to Charles. Ferdinand refused, but finally, agreed that Philip should become Ferdinand's successor, with Ferdinand's son Maximilian to follow him in turn. Maximilian, although unhappy with the plan, agreed not to oppose it; both Catholic and Protestant princes in Germany protested, however, that it would perpetuate foreign rule. The Reichstag which met at Augsburg in 1551-1552 refused to accept the Hapsburg agreement on the imperial succession.

The immediate consequence of the princes' fears lest the emperor impose the "brutish Spanish servitude" of absolute monarchy upon them was a conspiracy formed in 1551. It found its leader in Maurice of Saxony, who had done so much to achieve the triumph of Charles V to date. Maurice was deeply perturbed by Charles's action in keeping John Frederick and Philip of Hesse imprisoned, and wished to consolidate his own position as a territorial prince.

Once again the emperor's foreign commitments undid his German policy. On Charles's initiative, the war against the Ottoman Turk was revived in the Mediterranean, leading to Turkish counterattacks not only in the southern sea but also in Hungary. Ferdinand found himself under pressure in Hungary and therefore with reduced forces available to assist his brother in Germany. France made peace with England in 1551 and turned at once to renewed war with the emperor, a conflict over Piacenza in Italy serving as the pretext. Thus the conspirators were assured that Charles would not be able to concentrate his forces against them, while they would find an ally and subsidies in France.

The emperor's conduct began to reflect his lassitudes and near-exhaustion after more than thirty years of ceaseless activity which never proved complete. He heard rumors of Maurice's treachery but could not bring himself to disbelieve the Saxon's guileful assurances. After capturing Magdeburg on behalf of the emperor in November, 1551, Maurice threw off the mask of obedience and struck at his imperial master. He almost caught Charles at Innsbruck, in Austria, but the forlorn emperor escaped in haste. As Maurice pursued him into Tirol, he drove at the same time toward Trent, where the general council of the Catholic church was being held. It quickly disbanded and fled, like the emperor, to Italy for safety.

Talks of Peace. Peace negotiations began at Passau in June, 1552. Ferdinand acted as his brother's chief negotiator; he had not approved Charles V's policy of enforcing religious unity and political absolutism by force. He worked out terms for a settlement, by which the imprisoned princes would be released, the Interim abolished, and peace would be re-established whether or not a general council, at which the Protestants would be represented, should be held. Even though Ferdinand pleaded with him in person to accept these as the best that could be attempted, Charles refused. He would accept them provisionally, until the next Reichstag, but the idea of a permanent religious division of Germany, admitting heresy to a legal status upon the ground of principle as well as of expediency, was more than he could swallow. He did not wish to abandon all he had gained over the Lutherans in 1546-1547. He was somewhat more confident because he had made an armistice with France in May. The Lutherans, knowing that they could no longer count upon the French for support and lapsing into quarrels among themselves, accepted the emperor's terms. They were free to follow their religion, but only until the next imperial diet.

The war against the Turks continued, and that with France was resumed. The Lutherans aided the Hapsburgs in both struggles. Maurice supported Ferdinand in Hungary and Albert Alcibiades of Brandenburg joined Charles in the fight against France. But when the emperor's siege of Metz failed ignominiously against the resistance led by the duke of Guise, he withdrew on January 1, 1553. Albert Alcibiades turned to marauding on his own behalf, and Maurice of Saxony joined battle against him. Maurice, who had undone the emperor when he was at the height of his victory, was killed in the fighting. The Brandenburger was banned and fled in 1554 to France. The Empire regained its calm and peace after many long years of turbulence. A Reichstag to make a settlement was possible. Charles, worn by his long struggles and torn between the need for peace and the desire not to give heresy a permanent place of right in his Empire, turned over to his brother the direction of the negotiations at the Reichstag, which convened in Augsburg in 1555. The princes of both religions were tired, too, and ready to come to terms, though some retained ambitions for further gains in the future.

The Peace of Augsburg. The terms of peace were embodied in the "imperial recess" of September 25, 1555. The Lutherans attained full legal freedom within the empire: they had defended with success their doctrines, their states, and their right to existence. All temporal princes in the empire had the right to choose between the two legal faiths; Calvinists, who were beginning to win adherents in Germany, were excluded from the privileges of the Peace. The right of choice belonged only to princes, not to subjects; these had to accept their ruler's faith, according to the principle *cujus regio, ejus religio* (whose the region, his the religion), or go into exile. Only the inhabitants of the Hapsburg lands were excepted from the right of voluntary exile. An ecclesiastical reservation inserted in the Peace at the insistence of the Catholic majority, and reluctantly accepted by the Lutherans, provided that Catholic prelates who converted had to abandon their office and their territory. Thereby the three ecclesiastical electorates of Mainz, Trier, and Cologne were permanently assured for the Catholic side; since the Hapsburgs commanded the vote of Bohemia, they were assured a majority against any Protestant candidate for the imperial throne. Ferdinand would grant only secretly, and not within the treaty, a promise to give Lutheran knights, towns, and communes a tolerated position in the ecclesiastical principalities. This *"Declaratio Ferdinandeo,"* as well as the ecclesiastical reservation, held ill-concealed seeds of future discord. But for the time being, they remained beneath the surface.

Peace had come back to Germany. The price included acceptance of the novel idea that two faiths could co-exist within a single state, and hence that heresy was to be permitted. The price also included abandonment of the earlier attempts, by both Berthold von Henneberg and the Emperor Maximilian, to reform the constitution of the Holy Roman Empire. The effort to unify and strengthen Germany as a coherent political organism had failed. The empire was becoming increasingly a thing of theories, less and less part of the world of political realities. Effective political power in Germany stayed, more than ever before, in the hands of the princes, or great vassals. To them passed the opportunities and the responsibilities for the fate of their country in the uncertain period which lay before.

14

Germany in the Age of the Thirty Years' War

1555 - 1648

GERMANY WAS at peace again. The contending parties—Lutherans and Catholics; the emperor and the estates of the Empire—had tried their strength and found themselves equally matched. At Augsburg this balance of forces had been recognized and accepted, but only for the time being. The belligerents were exhausted, not reconciled. They hoped to return to the fray once their vigor returned. The peace that had been given Germany remained precarious.

I. An Interim of Equilibrium (1555-1600)

In the mid-sixteenth century the advantage of numbers belonged to the Protestants. The Venetian ambassador to Germany estimated in 1557 that seven out of every ten Germans were Lutherans, another two belonged to other Protestant creeds, and only one was still a Catholic.

Protestant Gains. Nor was the shift of allegiances at an end. In southern Germany, where the rulers of Bavaria and Austria remained faithful to Rome, almost the entire nobility, as well as much of the peasantry and the

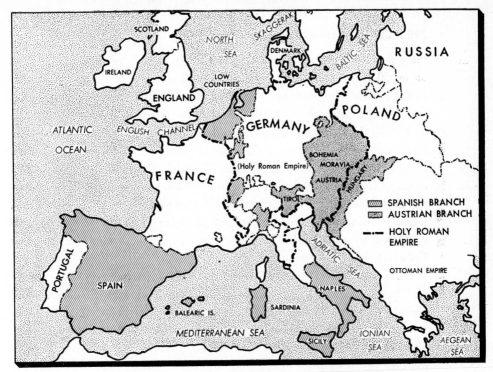

The Division of the Hapsburg Lands, 1555

urban population, passed over to the Lutherans. In northern Germany, a number of ecclesiastical principalities also became Lutheran. The cathedral chapters, which elected the bishops, were the preserve of the younger sons of the nobility, who were already overwhelmingly Lutheran. Since a Protestant could scarcely obtain ecclesiastical confirmation by Rome, as required by canon law, the Protestant bishops-elect confined themselves to receiving feudal investiture from the emperor and governed their territories as "administrators." This evasion of the spirit, if not the letter, of the "ecclesiastical reservation" of the Peace of Augsburg became one of the first objects of Catholic attack.

Nonetheless the pace of Protestant progress was slowed. Divisions within their camp kept the Protestants from using their numerical advantage effectively. The Lutherans were split into followers of the ironbound doctrinaire, Flacius Illyricus, and the soft conciliator, Philip Melanchthon; both resisted the growth of Calvinism, the new and more active form of Protestantism (see ch. 4, p. 96). The religious quarrels were repeated in politics. The Lutherans, led by the elector of Saxony, were not eager to overturn the settlement of Augsburg; but the Calvinists, who gained the adherence of the electors Palatine, were ready for a resort to arms.

Catholic Revival. The Catholics, on the other hand, ceased to retreat. The squabbles among the Protestants gave them renewed confidence, while the definition of doctrine at the council of Trent reduced their own debates on questions of dogma and permissible concessions. The Catholic Reformation moved into Germany and took up the battle for men's minds.

It was a battle almost lost before it was well begun. It depended in large part upon the favor and protection of the Hapsburg emperors, and the dynastic succession nearly gave the imperial office to a Protestant. To be sure, Ferdinand I, who succeeded Charles V on his abdication in 1556, was a steadfast Catholic even though it was he who had made peace with the Lutherans at Augsburg. He was devoted to the cause of reform of the church and hoped to bring the Lutherans back into its fold; but he knew that this aim could not be accomplished with the force available to him and the other Catholic princes in Germany.

The tradition of alliance between the house of Hapsburg and the church of Rome was strained almost to the point of breaking when Ferdinand's son, Maximilian II, succeeded him as Holy Roman emperor. Maximilian had been won over to much or possibly all of the Lutheran creed or at least to the hope of rebuilding the church on largely Lutheran lines. His Protestant leanings had been so evident during his father's lifetime that Ferdinand put forward his son's candidacy as king of the Romans only after he solemnly swore fidelity to the Catholic religion. After his accession, Maximilian still did not dare to break with Rome. He was a mild man, a kind of crowned Melanchthon who saw the good in contrary causes and wished to reconcile them by fair words, without a fight. His brothers, on the other hand, were fervent Catholics who dinned into him the necessity to stand by his oath or face their resistance. Maximilian was also deterred from conversion by the possibility that he might become heir to his cousin, Philip II, since a Protestant could scarcely expect to rule in Spain. Thus the Lutherans lost the near chance of winning an emperor to their side and thereby achieving such a political preponderance in Germany that their total and final victory could hardly have been prevented.

Bavarian Gains.   Instead it was the Catholic Reformation which gained time to recoup its spiritual energies and slowly to resume the initiative. Bavaria became the model land of Catholic reconquest. Duke Albert V came under the influence of the Jesuits in the 1560's and moved with determination to extirpate the Lutheran heresy in his duchy.

Other Catholic princes followed his example. The bishop of Fulda put down the Lutherans in his diocese; the nearby Protestant rulers were dissuaded from coming to their aid by warnings from the emperor and the duke of Bavaria. The Protestant princes complained that the Catholic counteroffensive was a violation of the *Declaratio Ferdinandeo* (see ch. 13, p. 313). In 1575, when Maxmilian's son Rudolph was elected king of the

Romans, the Protestant electors sought to include the *Declaratio* in his electoral capitulation. He rejected the demand, knowing that the personal and political conflict between the elector of Saxony and the elector Palatine was too sharp to permit them to act effectively. The death of Maximilian the following year removed from the Protestants the thin but real shield of his resistance to the militancy of the Catholic Counter Reformation. His deathbed gesture of refusing the Catholic sacrament of extreme unction showed his inner sympathy for the Protestants, but did not guard them against the Catholic fervor of Rudolph II.

Rudolph II. Under the new emperor, the momentum of the Catholic drive to regain the ascendancy increased rapidly. Its primary purpose was to enforce in the territories of the Catholic princes the rule of Augsburg, *cujus regio, ejus religio*, but to limit its application elsewhere in the Empire.

The importance of the change in emperors soon became visible. Aachen, the ancient city in northwestern Germany, had become the scene of a sharp struggle between a population which became predominantly Protestant during the 1560's, and the dwindling Catholic group which attempted to maintain its grip upon the municipal government. In 1580 the Protestants won a majority in the town council and voted to permit Lutherans and Calvinists to practice their religion openly. The attempt of the Catholic group to prevent the innovation failed when the emperor found he had to conciliate the Protestant princes in order to obtain their aid against the Turks. But in 1598, the city was put under the imperial ban. Troops from the Spanish Low Countries and the duchy of Jülich enforced the decree. The Protestants' resistance was soon crushed; they lost their political domination, their right of public worship and their freedom of conscience.

In Magdeburg, the issue was the right of a Lutheran majority in the cathedral chapter to elect Joachim Frederick, nephew of the elector of Brandenburg, as bishop in 1566. Although refused investiture by the emperor as a non-Catholic, Joachim Frederick continued to govern the bishopric as administrator. His appearance in person at the Reichstag of 1582 brought the struggle to a head. The Catholic members threatened to quit the meeting if he or his deputy remained. When Saxon mediation failed to achieve a compromise, Joachim Frederick withdrew. Thus his position in Magdeburg remained uncertain, for the charge of illegality lay publicly upon it. But the Catholics did not attempt to expel him from his post.

In Cologne the struggle continued between Catholic and Protestant for control of the crucial ecclesiastical principality. If the Protestants could gain it for their side, they would hold a majority in the electoral college and hence control the choice of future emperors. Despite the expulsion of Herman von Wied (see ch. 13, p. 309), the Lutherans remained strong. They sought to persuade a series of archbishops of the advantage of turning Protestant and making the principality a dynastic possession. They came closest to success with Gebhard Truchsess von Waldburg, a Catholic who was elected with the support of the Protestant members of the cathedral chapter. He became a Protestant in 1582 in order to marry, but lost his principality to the Catholics after the emperor brought in Spanish troops and the pope deprived him of his see. Bavarian forces took over in 1583-1584; Prince Ernest of Bavaria was elected the new archbishop, receiving papal confirmation; and the victory of Catholicism was complete.

A similar contest between Catholic and Protestant groups in the cathedral chapter brought an intermittent "Bishops' War" to Strassburg, where imperial support had helped to give Catholicism a new foothold. The attempt of the Catholics to exclude the Protestants led to the formation of rival chapters and then, upon the death of Bishop John of Manderscheid in 1592, to the election of a Catholic bishop and a Protestant administrator. Fighting ensued, resulting in a compromise partition of the territory, and then in 1604 to the withdrawal of the Protestant candidate upon payment of a large sum of money.

Foreign Wars. Throughout this period, the Protestants failed to press their advantage when the emperors found themselves in difficulties in foreign affairs. In 1562 Ferdinand I made a truce with the Turks, but it was broken four years later when the sultan supported John II Zapolya, prince of Transylvania, in resisting Austrian conquest. The death of Suleiman I and the accession of a pacific sultan in the person of Suleiman II enabled Maximilian II to obtain a treaty of peace in 1568. It was repeatedly extended until 1593. In that year a party of war hawks won influence in Constantinople and brought about renewal of the fighting. The struggle continued with victories and defeats for both sides. For a while, the elector Palatine and his supporters, who now were chiefly Calvinist in religion, refused to approve "Turkish help" to the emperor, but in 1600 they conceded the point when Kanisza, the key to Styria, fell to the Turks. In the West the civil wars in France and the Low Countries enlisted the sympathies of both sides in Germany for the contending parties, but occasional expeditions of Protestant forces to aid the Huguenots in France, and the use of the Rhineland as a corridor for the movement of Spanish troops, proved the limit of German involvement.

The four and a half decades between the Peace of Augsburg and the end of the century thus passed without any fundamental alteration in the settlement. The equilibriums of strength between the estates and the emperor and between the Protestants and the Catholics remained the essential facts of public life.

II. New Alliances (1600-1618)

The beginning of the new century marked a turning point. The initiative passed to those who were utterly dissatisfied with the Augsburg arrangements and wished to overturn them for their own advantage. On the one side was the Catholic Reformation, with the houses of Hapsburg and Bavaria as its bulwarks; on the other the Calvinist Reform, based on the Palatinate. Between them lay a third party of Lutheran princes, led by Saxony, who were disturbed by the rise of aggressive Catholicism but were equally reluctant to offend the emperor or to aid the hated rivals who took their creed from Geneva, not Wittenberg.

Protestant Union and Catholic League. The prospect of continued peace paled when the opposing parties began to form alliances. There had been talk of such leagues since the period of 1559-1560, but nothing came of them until the sharp increase of political and religious tension after 1600. In 1608 the elector Palatine, under the influence of an ardent Calvinist, Christian of Anhalt, formed a Union with the Protestant cities and princes of southern Germany. Its purpose was proclaimed to be defense against illegal and violent attacks upon its members. Electoral Brandenburg joined two years later, but the elector of Saxony, the most influential of the Lutherans, remained outside and openly hostile. The Catholic princes responded by forming their own League in 1609 under the leadership of Duke Maximilian of Bavaria.

The Jülich Succession. The immediate occasion for the formation of the Protestant Union and the Catholic League was the dispute over the succession to the duchy of Jülich and its associated lands of Cleves, Mark, and Berg. Together these formed a wealthy principality whose value was enhanced by its strategic location in the lower Rhine valley, dominating the main route between Germany and the United Provinces. The death of Duke John William in 1609 brought on a series of claims upon all or part of the succession. The two principal contenders were the elector of Brandenburg and the count palatine of Neuburg; Saxony claimed Jülich and Berg, and the emperor, Rudolph II, declared that the entire succession had escheated to him by default of true heirs. The threat of imperial seizure prompted the Brandenburg and Neuburg claimants to agree to a compromise whereby they shared in government of the disputed lands pending a decision by Protestant arbiters as to their rightful ownership. Rudolph responded by sending Archduke Leopold of Styria with troops to rule as commissioner. The Protestants negotiated a treaty of support with Henry IV of France. After his assassination in 1610, the French army he had gathered moved into Jülich and expelled the Spaniards, but it refrained from any further aid to the Protestants.

The rivalry between the two chief claimants, held down but not removed by the agreement on common government, resulted in their both changing religion in the hope of gaining the whole succession. John Sigismund, the elector of Brandenburg, renounced Lutheranism and proclaimed publicly his conversion to Calvinism, with which he had been secretly sympathetic; this made him more acceptable to the Protestants in Cleves-Jülich, who were predominantly Calvinist, as well as to the elector Palatine and the Dutch republicans. On the other hand, the count palatine, Wolfgang William, turned Catholic and married a Bavarian princess. Their allies enforced on them a treaty of partition in 1614. By it Cleves and Mark, together with some lesser territories, went to Brandenburg; while Jülich and Berg went to the count palatine. There was no war, but the lines of battle were being drawn between Catholics and Calvinists, with the Lutherans inclining toward the former in their sympathies.

Hapsburg Dissensions. While the fate of Jülich was being debated and decided the attention of the Hapsburg dynasty—emperors and archdukes alike—was distracted by quarrels among themselves. The emperor and head of the house, Rudolph II, was a fantastic spirit, devoted to astrology and magic, irresponsible and careless in the conduct of the business of state when he bothered with it at all. Furthermore, he was not married, so that his successor could not be chosen by the simple rule of filial inheritance. His brothers, led by the vigorous and rough-spirited Matthias, decided to take the decision out of his hands. They agreed upon Matthias as heir to the various Hapsburg lands and the imperial office, then attempted to impose him upon Rudolph as administrator during the remainder of his lifetime. Rudolph, though half mad, wanted no guardian and resisted their demands.

The archdukes were spurred to more resolute action by a threat to Hapsburg power in Hungary. In 1604 Stephen Bocskay, prince of Transylvania, rose in rebellion, brought the Magyar nobility into his camp, and obtained the assistance of his Turkish overlord. When Rudolph sat idly by, the archdukes threatened to rebel against his slothful government. Matthias received conduct of the war in Hungary and brought it to an end by vigorous negotiations as well as military operations. He made peace with the Hungarians upon the basis of religious freedom and confirmation of the rights of the Hungarian estates; he left Bocskay in control of Transylvania and several Hungarian counties, but took for himself the government of Hungary, though without the royal title still held by his brother. Matthias also made peace with the Turks upon the basis of the status quo, including continued payments of tribute to the sultan. It was scarcely a glorious peace, and Rudolph, who would neither fight nor concede, opposed it; but it achieved Matthias' purpose, to free Hapsburg power for use elsewhere. For the better part of the century, the Turks remained passive while the Hapburgs battled first for predominance and then for very existence in the Holy Roman Empire.

The tension between Rudolph and Matthias led to war between them.

Rudolph found himself alone against his house, which formally though secretly took Matthias as its head. Matthias won the backing of the estates of Austria and Hungary by measures of conciliation; they granted him funds to form an army with which he conquered Moravia and threatened Bohemia. In 1608, the hard-pressed emperor granted the crowns of Moravia and Hungary to his brother, but kept Bohemia for himself, although Matthias would receive it too upon his death.

Bohemian Liberties. The fraternal rift gave a respite to the Protestants of Bohemia, who had been threatened with a Catholic Counter Reformation such as Rudolph and Matthias had undertaken in Austria with considerable success. To hold the Protestant estates of Bohemia loyal to his cause, Rudolph issued in 1609 a "Letter of Majesty" granting them extraordinarily wide freedom of religious belief and practice. They were permitted to build churches and maintain schools not only on the lands of Protestant noblemen but also in cities owing direct allegiance to the crown (royal cities). Furthermore, a committee of Protestant leaders, the Defensors, was established to protect these rights; it was later granted the right to call an assembly of the Protestant estates of the kingdom in case of need. Despite these concessions, Rudolph lost the estates of Bohemia when Matthias invaded the country to force his brother's withdrawal from power. Rudolph abdicated in May 1611 and Matthias was elected king of Bohemia at once. Next he undertook to win his election as king of the Romans, but Rudolph died in 1612 before it could be arranged. Matthias was thereupon elected without debate.

The vigor of Hapsburg government returned with Matthias, but not a solution to the problem of succession. Neither he nor his younger brothers Maximilian and Albert had children. Matthias, though well past fifty, retained hopes of fatherhood, but his more realistic brothers successfully insisted that Ferdinand of Styria be made the single universal heir of all the Austrian Hapsburg lands and offices. Ferdinand was elected king of Bohemia in 1617 and king of Hungary the next year.

III. The Bohemian War (1618-1620)

With Ferdinand, the Catholic Reformation obtained at last a ruling Hapsburg prince devoted to its principles and ready to seek its goals without timidity or reservation. Educated by the Jesuits, he took as his principal task the extirpation of heresy wherever he ruled.

The "Defenestration" of Prague. This at once brought him into conflict with the Protestants in Bohemia, whose privileges had been confirmed and extended in the "Letter of Majesty" of 1609. A conflict developed over the status of Protestant churches newly built in lands held by the Roman church as fiefs under the crown. The Catholic local authorities in several towns, denying that church-owned territory was "royal land," began to tear down these rival establishments. The Defensors called on Ferdinand to sustain their rights under the "Letter of Majesty," and called a meeting of the Protestant estates for March 1618. Ferdinand rejected their appeals and forbade their meeting. The Defensors persisted and the assembly met in May, the king's ban notwithstanding.

The leaders of the estates, under the influence of the theories of Huguenot writers (see ch. 7, p. 182), and fearing that Ferdinand would crush the Bohemian Protestants as he had their Austrian coreligionists, decided to carry their nation into a complete and final break with Hapsburg kingship. They initiated their rebellion in the classic manner of Bohemian revolutionaries, by pitching the imperial lieutenants in Prague from the high windows of Hradčany palace. The officials survived thanks to the piled-up muck below, and escaped. Nonetheless the "defenestration of Prague" served its purpose. The Bohemian Protestants gave their immediate assent and support to what had been the isolated act of a few desperate leaders.

Not since the start of the Dutch war of independence against Philip II of Spain half a century before had such defiance been made to the combined forces of Catholic Counter Reformation and monarchical absolutism. In Bohemia as in the Netherlands, the Protestant Reformation and the system of government by and with estates merged their interests and their fortunes. Whether the Bohemians could achieve the success of the Dutch—who in the same year of 1618 won virtual recognition of their independence by the Spaniards in the Twelve Years' Truce—depended upon their ability to maintain their own unity, to carry on the struggle with energy and intelligence, and not least to obtain foreign allies.

The first requirement, unity, was most easily met. All of Bohemia, with the exception of the mainly German-inhabited cities of Budweis and Pilsen, joined the uprising. The second requirement, energy and intelligence, proved more difficult to meet. A Directory of thirty members took over leadership and set about forming an army; it evolved no positive program of action and failed to create an effective executive. The Bohemians who were opposed to paying taxes to Ferdinand were almost equally unwilling to pay them to their own government.

As for allies, these came to the Bohemians slowly and in small numbers. Silesia, a dependency of the Bohemian crown, joined the rebellion, but Moravia, most closely linked ethnically to Bohemia, refused to follow her lead. Hungary and the estates of Austria gave sympathy and no more. It was even more difficult to obtain help from the Protestants of Germany. Bohemia was no longer felt to be a part of the Holy Roman Empire, and the rebellion appeared to be in part a struggle by Czechs, a Slavic people, against the German dynasty which ruled them.

The "Winter King." Nonetheless the Protestant Union finally decided in October, 1618, under the leadership of Christian of Anhalt, to accept the Bohemian cause as its own; but its assistance was confined to forbidding recruitment in its territories for armies to serve against Bohemia, and preventing the passage of such troops. Christian of Anhalt, a fervent Calvinist and foe of the Hapsburgs, conceived the idea of linking the cause of the German and Bohemian Protestants more closely by proposing the candidacy of Frederick V of the Palatinate for the throne of Bohemia, which was declared vacant on the grounds that the election of Ferdinand had been made under compulsion and hence was invalid.

Matthias, who had let the leadership of Hapsburg interests pass into the hands of Ferdinand, died in March 1619, and Ferdinand was elected Holy Roman emperor in August. At almost the same time, the Bohemian estates elected Frederick of the Palatinate as king of Bohemia. Despite the opposition of a majority of his own councilors in the Palatinate, as well as of his father-in-law, James I of England, Frederick accepted the throne. He was moved by the desire to aid the Bohemian Protestants, to expand his power, and not least to gratify his beauteous wife Elizabeth's desire to reign as a queen, as befitted a princess of England. Frederick, by taking a crown which Ferdinand considered to be rightfully his own, threw down a gauntlet which the emperor took up at once. The war which began between them lasted for thirty years, long past their lifetimes, and spread outward from Bohemia and Austria until it encompassed all Germany and involved most of the powers in western and central Europe.

The first operation of this Thirty Years' War was an invasion of Austria by the Bohemians. They reached Vienna, but lacked the strength to take the city. Not even a Hungarian uprising against Ferdinand enabled the Bohemians to utilize their initiative effectively. Yet the rebellion of Bethlen Gábor (Gabriel Bethlen), prince of Transylvania since 1613, was a major threat to the Hapsburgs. Bethlen, fighting under the banner of defense of Magyar religious freedom, captured most of Hungary by the early winter of 1619 and then drove against Vienna.

In October 1619 Frederick V went to Prague to be crowned. The crowds cheered him wildly, seeing in him the savior of Protestantism and freedom. His advisers, however, were dismayed by the political ineptitude and indiscipline of the Bohemians, who did not permit Frederick to form a strong executive; for it had not been their intention to exchange Ferdinand of Hapsburg for a Protestant absolute ruler. Nor would they grant their king the money he needed to form an army able to defend them against the coming assault from Austria. Christian of Anhalt, named Bohemian commander-in-chief, was able to bring together 20,000 men under the colors by June of 1620, including 8,000 soldiers from the Palatinate, but they were an ill-paid, badly trained force which he found too weak for any use but defense.

If the new regime were to last, it needed foreign allies. The most important potential assistance was lost when John George of Saxony turned on the Bohemians because of the election of Frederick and the strong Calvinism of the Bohemian leaders. Without the Saxon elector, the Protestant Union remained loose and ineffective. Bethlen played his own game. First he made an armistice with Ferdinand in January 1620, which he kept until he arranged his own election as king of Hungary in Ferdinand's stead in August. Even then he was ready to aid the Bohemians only at their expense, which meant little since Christian of Anhalt lacked funds for his own troops.

The Battle of White Mountain. Ferdinand did not hasten into action, but carefully built up a hedge of hostile alliances around the Bohemians. He obtained the alliance of the Catholic League, which agreed to form an army under the command of the duke of Bavaria, Maximilian I, to whom the emperor promised Frederick V's position as elector once he had been banned as a rebel. It was not difficult to keep the elector of Saxony and other Lutheran princes out of the Bohemian camp. Concessions on the issue of the Protestant administrators, and promises of territorial gains from lands to be conquered from the Bohemians, won over John George to an active part on the emperor's side. Spain agreed to furnish Ferdinand 12,000 troops from Italy, Spain, and the Low Countries. Pope Paul V promised him substantial financial assistance. The Catholic king of Poland gave his alliance. Even France, the ancient foe of the Hapsburgs, did not have to be feared: the queen mother, Marie de Médicis, was still in control, and she remained benevolently neutral to Ferdinand's crusade against the Calvinist heretics.

Ferdinand's meticulous preparations paid off when a combined army of League and imperial troops invaded Bohemia during the late summer of 1620. After devastating the countryside, the Catholic army appeared before Prague early in November. The defenders met them at White Mountain, not far from the capital, on November 6. Within two hours the army under Christian of Anhalt was broken, dead, or in flight. The monarchy of Frederick V, its shield shattered, vanished in an instant. The king fled to Breslau, in Silesia, and then made his way across Germany to The Hague, the sardonic sobriquet of "the winter King" already given to him as one who had ruled but a year.

Five days after White Mountain, the Bohemian diet docilely accepted Ferdinand as legitimate king. The emperor was not to be satisfied with an ounce of repentance; he insisted upon his full pound of punishment for the rebels. Many of the principal leaders of the Bohemians fled abroad; those captured were given long prison terms or executed. The estates of the Bohemian Protestant nobility were confiscated in large numbers for the benefit of the imperial treasury, and resold or given as gifts to Catholic leaders in Ferdinand's service. Thus the native aristocracy of Bohemia, predominantly Protestant in religion and resistant to absolute government, gave way to a new Catholic nobility which was wholly beholden to the Hapsburg monarchy for its fortunes. A vigorous Catholic campaign to extirpate Protestantism followed in the lands of the crown of Bohemia. Only Lusatia, which had been conquered and retained by John George of Saxony, and Silesia, were spared the rod of the Counter Reformation.

IV. War in Germany (1620-1625)

His success in re-Catholicizing Bohemia persuaded Ferdinand to proceed with increased vigor in his endeavor to remove the taint of Protestantism from his own Austrian hereditary lands. Compulsory conversion, which had played so great a role in unifying Spain as a Catholic country in the previous century, was now employed on a large scale. It led to a furious peasant war in Upper Austria in 1626. Once more Ferdinand, short of troops to fight his battles, was compelled to call upon Maximilian of Bavaria for aid. The Bavarian general Pappenheim slowly but steadily crushed the rebels. Ferdinand thereupon resumed the interrupted work of Counter Reformation. At the same time he swept out of existence the estates of Upper Austria, which had been a nest of resistance both to his absolutist methods of government and to his religious policy.

His triumphs in Bohemia and his hereditary lands did not satisfy Ferdinand. Frederick V managed to keep an army in the field in Germany under the hireling general, Ernst von Mansfeld. Until Frederick was destroyed, and his patrimony of the Palatinate was taken from him, Ferdinand would not rest. He put Frederick under the ban of the empire and called into Germany an army of Spanish troops under the command of Ambrosio Spinola to enforce the decree of outlawry. The war had ended in Bohemia, after one swift campaign. It began anew in Germany, though no one suspected how long it would be before the guns were still again.

Spinola. Spinola's 16,000 infantry and 3,000 cavalry were matched in number by the forces of the Protestant Union, but not in quality; the Spaniards were battle-hardened veterans against whom the native German soldiers, once the best in Europe, could not stand. In April 1621, fearing Spinola's guns and pikes, the Protestant Union obeyed Ferdinand's command to disband.

Spinola's success was due not only to the quality of his troops, but also to his ability to maintain them without pay from the impecunious Ferdinand.

He proceeded to make the war pay for itself. The right of an army in the field to compel the local population to furnish it food, fodder, and shelter was well recognized, but it was customary that the troops pay for such supplies and services. Lacking funds from Ferdinand, Spinola imposed upon the populace an emergency tax for the troops' supplies. Neutral territory was not spared this system of compulsory contribution. The old problem that had oppressed rulers engaged in warfare—how to meet the constantly expanding need for soldiers from a fixed revenue—seemed to have been met. As a result, there was no longer the same need to stop fighting when money ran out which had terminated so many wars during the sixteenth century.

The "Condottieri": Mansfeld and Brunswick. With the Union dissolved, only the small forces serving Frederick V continued to resist the overwhelming might of the emperor and the League. From The Hague, where he had taken refuge, Frederick played upon the desire of the States-General, which had resumed war with Spain in 1621, to distract Spanish attention from their own frontiers to more distant regions. His mercenary Mansfeld showed himself an agile and ruthless general who adopted and extended Spinola's method of compulsory contributions to make good the inadequate funds received from Frederick. Two additional armies were formed on Frederick's behalf by Margrave George of Baden-Durlach and Duke Christian of Brunswick-Wolfenbüttel; like Mansfeld, they used the elector Palatine's commission as a basis for living off the country. They failed to combine their forces and their operations, however, and the League general Tilly—in sole command after Spinola returned to the Low Countries—defeated them individually in turn. His victory over Christian at Höchst in June 1622 led to the capture of the Palatinate. The next year, having recruited a new army, Mansfeld and Christian of Brunswick undertook to redeem the defeats of 1622. Their failure was even worse. Tilly crushed Christian at Stadtlohn in August; the conquest of the Palatinate was safe.

Transfer of the Electorate. Once again Ferdinand had won a campaign. The spoils of victory remained to be distributed. Maximilian of Bavaria demanded for himself and his heirs Frederick's seat in the electoral college, as the emperor had promised. The other electors resisted such a transfer; they found the idea of dispossession of an elector, even one guilty of rebellion, distasteful in the extreme. Not till 1623 was a compromise arranged by which Frederick lost the electoral title to Maximilian, but the Palatine family retained its claim, to be determined in the future by the other electors. Ferdinand's hesitations in making good his word estranged Maximilian and made him seek for a position of independent strength in the Empire, apart from and if need be against the emperor.

By 1624 not a single enemy force remained in the field to oppose Ferdinand. The question therefore presented itself whether he should rest satisfied with this victory, or seek to extend it from his own lands to the entirety of the Holy Roman Empire. For Ferdinand II, the dutiful scholar of the Jesuits and the proud head of the house of the Hapsburgs, the answer was clear: it was his opportunity and his obligation to put his sword at the service of the Catholic Reformation, at least by undoing the gains made by Protestantism in Germany since the Peace of Augsburg; to strengthen the institutions of imperial power in the Empire and bring the princes to a proper subservience; and to expand the territorial possessions of his dynasty. It was an ambitious program he undertook—so ambitious that it roused up fear and resistance at once not only within the Empire but in foreign capitals as well.

The first and ultimately the most formidable foe which appeared in the way of Ferdinand's goal was France. Cardinal Richelieu, who took over leadership of the French government in 1624, made the crux of his policy the overthrowing of the Hapsburg might before it grew beyond defeat. His first substantial achievement was to cut off the movement of Spanish forces to Germany by way of the Valtelline passes in the eastern Swiss Alps. It was an initial step toward separating the two branches of the house of Hapsburg, preventing them from aiding each other, and breaking their encirclement of France. He could do no more at the moment, however; for the domestic broils of France—the risings of the Huguenots and the nobility—demanded his attention.

V. Danish Intervention (1625-1627)

The struggle against Hapsburg dominion in Germany was taken up again by Frederick V, the deposed elector Palatine; he found allies not only in a small number of German Protestant princes, but also in England, the United Provinces, and Denmark. Christian IV, the Danish king, took command of the Protestant army in Germany. The war ceased to be primarily an affair of the Germans themselves and came to be a struggle between the Hapsburg emperor and foreign powers, fought on German soil with largely German soldiery and almost totally at the expense of the German people.

Facing Christian IV in Germany were two Catholic armies. One, under the command of Count Tilly, who had won his spurs in the Low Countries, served the Catholic League; it was inferior in numbers to the Protestant forces. The other was a new army, commissioned by Ferdinand himself, which had been organized and was under the command of a Bohemian nobleman, Count Albert von Wallenstein.

Wallenstein Emerges. Till this time Ferdinand's battles in the empire had been fought by troops either belonging to the League or lent by Spain;

he lacked funds to raise his own army for service outside his own territories. He had therefore seized upon the offer of Wallenstein early in 1625 to give him without cost a force of 15,000 infantry and 5,000 cavalry. This Bohemian noble was a new figure upon the political scene, but already an extraordinarily successful one. He had served on the imperial side in the Bohemian rebellion, had garnered huge estates for himself at little expense from the confiscated lands of the Protestants, and had organized their administration with great efficiency.

The wealth accumulated from his estates provided Wallenstein with the initial funds for recruiting his soldiers. To maintain them he expanded the system of compulsory contributions which Spinola had introduced into Germany and Tilly had adopted in 1623-1624. He made local officials whether in friendly, hostile, or neutral territory, collect the requisition tax, and increased it to include the cost not only of the troops' supplies, but also of their complete pay as well as that of the officers. He also compelled the populace to serve without compensation in building fortifications, transporting supplies, and other tasks ordinarily done by civilians for pay. Wallenstein directed the whole system with the cool and ruthless efficiency he had used in making his Bohemian estates profitable.

Wallenstein prevented the Protestant army, at last stronger than Tilly's force, from turning the scales of war against the Catholics. He defeated Mansfeld in April 1626, and enabled Tilly to follow up this victory by one over King Christian of Denmark four months later. Bethlen Gábor, who had used the opportunity to return to his sporadic endeavor to expel the Hapsburgs from Hungary, withdrew from the fighting in December; he died three years later, before another chance to take up arms offered itself.

War on the Baltic. Wallenstein continued his campaign against Christian of Denmark in 1627. Christian had lost his foreign allies, but attempted to continue the struggle. Wallenstein, his army increased to 70,000 men—an immense figure for the time—destroyed Christian's army piecemeal, principally on the territory of the neutral elector of Brandenburg. Then, after combining with Tilly, he drove into Denmark until he had occupied all of the peninsula of Jutland except a few stubborn fortresses.

A new phase of the war began. The emperor's army had reached the North and Baltic Seas. The Spaniards proposed that direct trade be re-established between the Hansa cities and Spain, by-passing the ports of the Dutch rebels. Ferdinand accepted the Spanish plans. He named Wallenstein "General of the Baltic and Ocean Seas" and granted him the duchy of Mecklenburg in north Germany, which had been seized from the Protestant dukes. Thereby Wallenstein became a full-fledged prince of the empire; but the ire of the great vassals was aroused against his elevation to their class. Wallenstein went on to lay siege to the Pomeranian port of Stralsund, which he intended to use as a naval base. The garrison received the aid of the Danish and Swedish fleets, united for the first time in defense of the Protestant cause despite the sharp antipathy between the two crowns. After the Danes landed relief troops, Wallenstein decided in July to break off the siege, and made peace with Denmark the following May. Christian received back his territories of Holstein, Schleswig, and Jutland, but agreed to abandon his German allies and to refrain from interfering in the affairs of the Empire.

VI. Catholic Triumph and Disunity (1627-1630)

The settlement with Denmark was the prelude to a sharp rise in the desire for internal peace in Germany. Wallenstein, with his legalized plundering, was bleeding the country white. It was becoming even more disastrous for the general population to sustain the systematic exploitation of the armies than to face the fierce but brief bursts of actual warfare.

Opposition to Wallenstein. The Catholic elector of Mainz and the Lutheran elector of Saxony joined in an attack upon Wallenstein's methods at a meeting of the electoral college in October 1627, but the reluctance of Duke Maximilian of Bavaria to join them deprived their assault of any effect. Only after Ferdinand promised to make the electorate hereditary in Maximilian's family in February 1628 did the Bavarian turn his fire upon Wallenstein, and then he took the leadership of the Bohemian's foes within the empire. The electors demanded Wallenstein's dismissal, and the conflict between the emperor and the League approached the breaking point when the Catholic princes agreed to maintain an army of 27,000 infantry and forty cavalry squadrons to use not against the Protestants but against Wallenstein.

The opposition to the victorious general was not limited to the princes, but extended into the imperial court. The ultra-Catholic party, with the exception of the Spanish ambassador, turned upon him because his Catholic convictions were only skin-deep. Other officials protested that his use of the Hapsburg lands to quarter troops endangered the prosperity of the emperor's home country.

The Edict of Restitution. The general's lukewarm attitude toward the Edict of Restitution issued by Ferdinand on March 6, 1629, proved the final blow to the emperor's confidence in him. He was dismissed in 1630 and sent in exile to his estates in Bohemia.

The edict was Ferdinand's response to the opportunity given him by Wallenstein's triumphs. It ordered the return to the Catholic church of all bishoprics and abbeys secularized by the Protestants after 1552, if in territories belonging to vassals, and after 1555 if directly under the imperial crown. Many long-lost lands were thereupon restored to Catholic control, especially in central and northern Germany. Since the Catholic prelates re-established in their powers possessed the right to enforce a reconversion of their subjects, the danger to Protestantism increased. The Protestant princes also suffered in their purses, for the restitutions meant fewer places in which to place their younger sons. Even the Protestant rulers who had been subservient to the emperor broke away from him in anger and desperation. Nonetheless it seemed no more than a matter of time before they too should be forced to disgorge and be reduced to supine obedience to their imperial master.

VII. Gustavus Adolphus (1630-1632)

They were rescued from such "Spanish servitude" by the sudden intervention of the young king of Sweden, Gustavus II Adolphus. On July 6, 1630, the Swede landed at Peenemünde with 12,500 troops. He had brought his long-festering war with the Poles to an end by a six-year truce in 1629 in order to act in Germany and prevent a total Hapsburg victory. Wallenstein's conquests in northern Germany raised a grave threat to Swedish control of the Baltic Sea; while the strict Lutheranism of the Swedish nation would be imperiled by the destruction of their brethren in faith in Germany.

Reluctant Allies. The expedition was, on first sight, a foolhardy venture. Gustavus Adolphus had no allies in Germany to lend him assistance, for the Protestant princes held aloof. His army was only a handful compared to the forces under Tilly, who held a combined command over all the Catholic forces. If the German princes joined him and lost, their fate would be far worse than before. If he won, they feared he would be a new master—and they wanted no overmighty savior to rule them, not even a staunch Lutheran. Gustavus Adolphus still did not give up the battle before it was fought. He compelled the duke of Pomerania, in whose territory he had landed, to join him, and then made the alliance of Bärwalde with France (January 1631), which assured him 400,000 talers annually for five years to aid in maintaining a force of 30,000 foot and 6,000 horse. In return he promised to avoid combat with the League if they stayed neutral, and to tolerate Catholicism where it was practiced in the regions he conquered.

Despite these provisos, Maximilian of Bavaria decided to take up the challenge of Gustavus Adolphus, and he sent Tilly with the League army to co-operate with the imperial army. Tilly first went to the aid of his subordinate Pappenheim, who had been besieging the Protestant stronghold of Magdeburg, one of the last north German free cities to hold out against the

Catholic Counter Reformation. Gustavus Adolphus was unable to rush aid in time, and Magdeburg was stormed in May. During the sack, which was conducted with usual ferocity, fire broke out and consumed the city. Protestants blamed Tilly for the holocaust, though it was to his disadvantage, and coined the bitter phrase "Magdeburg justice" for pitiless and systematic enforcement of Catholic order in Germany.

Nonetheless the Protestant princes refused to accept Gustavus Adolphus' alliance, for those who had come in with him had had to accept a quasi-vassalic subordination. Not till Ferdinand demanded that John George of Saxony send his army to co-operate with the imperial forces, or dissolve it, did the elector join with the Swede. This gave Gustavus Adolphus a force of nearly 40,000 men, almost half of them Saxons. With them he met Tilly's force of 36,000 advantageously posted at Breitenfeld, near Leipzig. Victory came to the Swedish arms (September 17, 1631).

Swedish Military Methods. A military revolution as great as that of the Swiss and the Spaniards more than a century before had been wrought. The Swedes were a close-knit force of devoutly Lutheran peasants, who fought for their faith and their king rather than just for pay, or for their colonel and their comrades, as did the German mercenaries. Gustavus Adolphus had developed a new tactic in Poland, using more mobile units, arranged in files rather than squares, and employing lighter guns capable of more rapid fire; his cavalry were used for shock action rather than to guard the flanks. The Spanish tactics employed by the German forces, using larger masses arranged in squares, proved inadequate by comparison. The experienced commanders of other European armies rapidly adopted the new Swedish system, but until their troops became experienced and skilled in its use the inventors retained a valuable advantage on the battlefield.

Politically the effect was equally great. Tilly lost his reputation of invincibility. Protestant courage revived. The re-Catholicization of Germany came to a halt; the question arose, instead, of the renewal of Protestant gains. Ferdinand had brought down the edifice of his own victory by demanding too much of it. Pride and blind purpose had exacted their price.

Accompanied by the adoration of the Protestant populace and the tremulous respect of the potentates of Europe, Gustavus Adolphus marched across Germany to the Rhineland in order to attack the Catholic League in its home country. The French, troubled by his disregard for their policy of separating the League from the emperor and by the growth of a power they could not control, attempted to persuade him to make a settlement with Maximilian of Bavaria. His demands, particularly for the right to quarter his troops upon the territories of the League, were too much for them. They had no desire to suffer from the Swede what they had from Wallenstein, and decided to entrust their fate to battle. Late in March 1632 Gustavus Adolphus marched his army into Bavaria, engaged Tilly at Lech in mid-April, and defeated him. The League commander received severe wounds and died a few days after the battle.

Death of Gustavus Adolphus. The war was not over, however. Gustavus Adolphus at last met Wallenstein on the battlefield. Wallenstein had sulked in his estates in Bohemia even while John George of Saxony invaded the country and captured Prague in November 1631. He had listened while Gustavus Adolphus offered to feed his revenge by aiding him to overthrow the ungrateful Ferdinand. When the emperor accepted his own terms for coming back, Wallenstein preferred to resume his old command in December 1631. In April he was made supreme commander, though without full control of the forces of Spain and the League. His old officers and soldiers, attracted by the magic of his name and the gleam of high pay and possible booty, hastened to sign up for service. By May he had between 30,000 and 40,000 troops under arms.

The war rapidly rose to a climax. Wallenstein drove the Saxons out of Bohemia into their home country. Even though the Protestants of Austria, after a decade of harsh repression, were ready to attempt revolt again with the aid of the Swede, Gustavus Adolphus did not move into Ferdinand's crown lands. Instead he hurried up from Bavaria to the support of John George, in order to keep him from leaving the fray and to protect his own route to Sweden. In an effort to prevent the union of the Swedes and the Saxons, Maximilian rushed the forces of the League, under the command of Tilly's lieutenant Pappenheim, to join Wallenstein and intercept Gustavus Adolphus. The armies met at Lützen on November 16, 1632. The first advantage went to the Catholics in fighting of extraordinary ferocity. Pappenheim and Gustavus Adolphus fell. The Swedes, held together in the critical moment by Bernard of Weimar, a German commander in Gustavus Adolphus' service, at last beat down Wallenstein's forces. The Catholic armies drew off the field of battle, leaving the Swedes the victors.

Gustavus Adolphus had died before his program had been completely won, however. He had rescued German Protestantism in its hour of danger and had destroyed the Hapsburg threat to the liberty of the German princes and to Swedish domination of the Baltic. But Swedish leadership was still not willingly accepted by the princes of Protestant Germany, who resisted the status of quasi-vassals within a *"corpus evangelicorum"* (Protestant union), which the late monarch had sought to impose upon them. Nor had the "satisfaction" he had demanded as payment for his expenses in Germany—the acquisition of territories in the Holy Roman Empire for the crown of Sweden—been given him. Therefore the Swedish chancellor Axel Oxenstierna, who took the policy of Sweden in hand during the minority of

Queen Christina, Gustavus Adolphus' six-year-old daughter, decided that Sweden should not withdraw from the war in Germany until all these objectives had been achieved.

VIII. Wallenstein's Fall (1633-1634)

The next great victim of the war fell not on the field of battle but in a frontier inn, slain by assassins. The fall of Wallenstein came quickly. His crime was in acting as a free agent, not as a docile servant of Ferdinand II. During 1633 he carried on the war in a desultory fashion; his true purpose was to achieve somehow, in secretive and disjointed negotiations with the emperor's foes, a peace settlement which preserved his own interests, if need be at the expense of the emperor's. Ferdinand decided to dismiss Wallenstein, but could not do so by the mere issuance of an order, for although emperor, he possessed no military force capable of enforcing his will upon the general. The army's paymaster was not the emperor, whom it nominally served, but Wallenstein, whose requisitioning officers brought it the funds to maintain itself.

Wallenstein Slain. Ferdinand resorted to the revolutionary's weapons of conspiracy and assassination against his too-powerful subject. He secretly won over three of Wallenstein's highest officers, including his second-in-command, Gallas. Wallenstein, aware of machinations against him, tried to hold his officers' fidelity on a personal basis, but failed against the bland deception and sly recruitment of the three conspirators, who gained the support of a majority of the army. The emperor thereupon issued decrees dismissing and outlawing Wallenstein, and entrusting his arrest and punishment to Gallas and his two fellow-plotters. Wallenstein thereupon fled from Prague to Eger, on the Bohemian frontier, to be near the support of Bernard of Weimar, the Protestant general. At Eger the commandant, a Scot named Gordon, and two aides from Britain, when asked to go over to the Swedes with Wallenstein, decided to slay him instead. On February 25, 1634, they murdered the forlorn leader. The great *condottiere* died at the hands of lesser mercenaries from the distant island. The control of war and policy again became the business primarily of statesmen, not of generals.

The Beginning of Peace. Without the balky Wallenstein in command, the campaign against the Protestants went forward with vigor, as the emperor desired. Gallas took charge of the imperial army. After joining forces first with Maximilian of Bavaria and then with a Spanish expeditionary unit, he met and crushed the Protestants at Nördlingen, September 5-6, 1634.

Nördlingen virtually ended the war as a struggle between the princes of Germany. Saxony was the first to make peace with the emperor at Prague, on May 30, 1635; Brandenburg followed suit in September, and all but a few of the Protestant and Catholic princes accepted the peace in turn. The Protestants received equal representation in the imperial chamber court and the Edict of Restitution was abolished for lands secularized before 1627 but further secularization of church property was forbidden and the lands already restored to the Catholic proprietors were not given back to the Protestant claimants. The transfer of the Palatine electorate to the duke of Bavaria was accepted by the Protestants. All special alliances within the Empire were to be dissolved, and it was agreed to form an imperial army to expel the foreigners from the Holy Roman Empire.

The hatred of the foreign participants in the war explained why both Protestants and Catholics, weary of the devastation of their country and feeling that they were serving interests other than their own, accepted the compromise of the Peace of Prague. For all the concessions to the Protestants, however, the main advantage went to the emperor. But he had calculated without the great power that stood, alert and watching, on the western frontier of the empire—France.

IX. French Intervention (1634-1644)

Richelieu had defeated the Huguenots and the nobles in France, and was at last able, as he had always been ready, to undertake the supreme struggle to prevent Hapsburg preponderance in the empire and throughout Europe.

Richelieu's War. The cardinal took the lead from the Swedes, with whom he renewed the French alliance; to aid them in continuing the war in Germany, he arranged an extension of the Swedish-Polish armistice for another twenty-six years. After occupying the duchy of Lorraine in 1634, which gave him a means of easy entry into Germany, Richelieu sent a French army across the Rhine at the end of December, 1634, to support Bernard of Weimar, the lone important German Protestant commander in the field against the emperor. It was an undeclared war until the emperor formally declared a state of hostilities in 1636. The Swedes henceforth operated chiefly in the east of Germany. They turned upon the Saxons for their betrayal, battling them back and forth across helpless Brandenburg, until the Swedish victory at Wittstock in 1636. This purely Protestant victory was followed by the successes in the West of the forces of Bernard of Weimar, a Protestant, and France, a Catholic power. Bernard won a brilliant series of successes in Alsace in 1637, and began planning to form his own principality out of his conquests. The French, reluctant to have him rise higher than the status of a vassal, held back on their aid to him. Before open struggle ensued between them, he died in 1639. The French brought his army, which desired a generous paymaster, into their service. Henceforth, the burden of war against the Hapsburgs in the West rested almost wholly on their shoulders.

Ferdinand III. In the meantime a new emperor put on the imperial crown. He was Ferdinand III, elected king of the Romans in 1636 and reigning since 1637, on his father's death. Ferdinand III, though educated by the Jesuits, was not dominated by reasons of religion. Skilled in the administration of the state and its finances, he knew the exhaustion of the Austrian lands and the Empire and the need to re-establish order and peace. He began negotiations for ending the war, but found that the foreign participants were not ready to end a struggle fought principally on other soil and —thanks to the system of enforced contributions—at the expense of others.

The emperor's position continued to worsen. In 1642 the Swedes defeated his forces in the second battle of Breitenfeld and captured the great city of Leipzig. The next year brought the French victory over the Spaniards at Rocroi, in the Low Countries; the main French forces were released for the offensive in Germany. The Hapsburg position in Hungary was again attacked by a prince of Transylvania, George Rakoczy; but the imperial troops, improved by the long campaigning in Germany, threw him back and compelled him to make a compromise peace in 1645. Elsewhere Ferdinand continued to meet new difficulties in holding the worn and battered German princes to his alliance. Brandenburg, under the new elector, Frederick William, who began to reign in 1640, was the first to make an armistice with the Swedes in 1641. It was followed by Saxony in 1645 and Bavaria in 1647. The last loss was the greatest, for Bavaria was the emperor's most important ally.

X. The Peace of Westphalia (1644-1648)

While the soldiers had been fighting the diplomats had been talking. The desire for peace had been rising in the empire since the early 1630's, but only since the Peace of Prague in 1636 had serious feelers gone out preliminary to a formal peace conference. In 1642 the emperor had agreed to negotiate at Osnabrück, in Westphalia, with the Swedes, and at nearby Münster with the French.

Talk of Peace. Actual meetings began in 1644. At first they were concerned more with ceremony and procedure than with matters of substance; but as the decision of battle turned more and more strongly against him, the emperor steeled himself to greater and greater concessions. By 1646 he was ready to abandon Alsace to the French, but would not give up the war against them as long as they were at war with his Spanish cousin. Not till 1648 did he give up this last point of honor. Other difficulties arose over the religious settlement. Some strict Lutherans opposed the inclusion of the Calvinists, while Catholic extremists denounced the impending peace as a betrayal of the faith.

Nonetheless the need for peace within Germany was too great to be stayed. The pattern was set when Spain and the United Provinces made a separate peace at Münster on January 30, 1648. The general peace was signed on October 24.

The Terms of Peace. The gainers were the foreign powers who had entered the war late and stayed to the end—Sweden and France—and the territorial princes of Germany. Sweden received Pomerania and Rügen on the southern shore of the Baltic, including the mouth of the Oder river, and the bishoprics of Bremen and Verden in western Germany, as imperial fiefs, with a seat in the Reichstag. She also received five million talers to pay off her troops in Germany and prevent their threatened mutiny. France received the possessions and the rights of the house of Hapsburg in Alsace, though the exact character of these rights remained unstated; unlike Sweden, she did not enter the empire as an estate with a seat in the Reichstag. Switzerland, which had stood aside during the war, and the United Netherlands, which had championed the Protestants, received explicit recognition of their total sovereignty, independent of the Holy Roman Empire to which they had once belonged.

The domestic provisions were based on a wide compromise. A general amnesty was proclaimed back to the year 1618. Bavaria retained the electoral seat it had wrested from the elector Palatine, and continued to hold the Upper Palatinate as a war indemnity. Charles Louis, the son of Frederick V, who had died sixteen years before, was granted a new, eighth electoral seat, which was created for him by the emperor, and retained the Rhenish Palatinate.

The principles of the religious settlements of Passau and Augsburg were confirmed and extended to the Calvinists. The Protestants were permitted to retain bishoprics and lands, together with the attached right to sit and vote in the Reichstag, if they had been in possession by January 1, 1624; but the restitutions made before that date, principally in Bohemia and Austria, remained in effect. The emperor maintained his right to enforce religious uniformity within his own lands with great stubbornness; his only concession was to permit Silesian Protestants a small amount of toleration. All subjects elsewhere in the empire were to retain whatever rights of religious practice and conscience they possessed as of January 1, 1624; if they converted thereafter, they were subject to expulsion. By these provisions the period of the religious transformation of Germany, which had brought repeated trouble and turbulence to the population, came to an end.

Germany after the Peace of Westphalia, 1648

For the future, religious equality between the three recognized faiths was to be maintained. The rule of the majority on questions affecting religion ceased; each side, Protestant and Catholic, formed a "corpus" or chamber, with a right of veto. The princes and the Reichstag, which was their voice in central affairs, received controlling powers: the emperor could neither make laws, nor wage war, nor make peace or alliances, nor raise taxes, nor do almost any other significant deed of state, without the assent of the Reichstag. The princes received, on the contrary, the right to make alliances among themselves and with foreign states; the proviso that such leagues must not be directed against the emperor or the Empire was an empty restriction. The imperial cities were raised in status in the Reichstag, where their college received equal powers with the electors and the other princes.

The powerlessness and degradation of Germany as a state was demonstrated painfully by the provision of the treaty naming France and Sweden as guarantors, with a right to intervene. "German liberty" thereafter meant the pre-eminence and virtual independence of the princes of Germany, who conducted their government within and without their territories as they pleased. It meant also the loss of leadership in European affairs to the states in the West, the ancient power of France, the new power of the United Provinces, and the rising power of England.

Nonetheless the bells that rang out the news of peace throughout Germany brought joy and contentment to the population. They looked back at thirty years of war—thirty years filled with great aspirations and shattered dreams, with pride and humbling, but most of all with death and devastation for the participants and the innocents alike—and were glad that it was over. The population had declined in numbers, some thought as much as half. The peasantry had suffered most, and many villages and farmsteads had been abandoned. Landlords tightened their control over the peasants to make up their own losses. The cities had been taxed and sacked too, so that their position was not much better. The trade decline which had begun in the sixteenth century continued. Nonetheless the basic strength of the land and the people remained, to be used for rebuilding as soon as quiet and order returned. That was the task which now, in the Germany shaped by the Peace of Westphalia, fell to the territorial princes.

15

The Netherlands United and Divided

1477 - 1648

A LAND WITHOUT a traditional name or natural frontiers, a people speaking two different languages, a state that was a conglomeration of semi-independent provinces—this was the Netherlands at the end of the fifteenth century. Yet this almost formless mass was already being shaped by the great impersonal forces of geography, economics, and culture, as well as by the deliberate action of its rulers, the dukes of Burgundy, into a single state, one of the most powerful in Europe, with a people who shared a growing sense of common destiny.

The artisan of that unity—the house of Burgundy—was also its destroyer. When the dukes merged their dynasty into the triple house of Hapsburg-Burgundy-Spain, they grew away from the country in spirit and policy until in the fifteen-sixties a rebellion broke out against Philip II as a foreign oppressor. The insurgency half succeeded: an independent Dutch Republic rose up north of the Rhine, while provinces south of the river fell back under the dominion of Spain. North and South developed separately thereafter along contrary lines of religion, culture, and politics. The united nation of the "Low Lands by the Sea" became, in the words of a modern Dutch historian, "a life cut short, a historical opportunity that failed." *

* Johan Huizinga, *Verzamelde Werken* (Haarlem, 1948–1953), II, 162.

I. Land and People

A traveler journeying from France to Germany by way of the coastal plain observes no important line of geographic demarcation. Nonetheless a distinct region—the Low Countries—lies between the two.

The Low Lands by the Sea. Three primary features set this region apart from its neighbors. One is its situation in the narrow waist of the north European plain, where the foothills of the central European ranges approach the western sea most closely. The other is its position where three rivers— the Rhine, the Scheldt (Escaut) and the Meuse (Maas)—meet, join and flow together into the North Sea. The Netherlands at the beginning of our period extended beyond this great delta. To the south, it took in the generally navigable stretches of the Scheldt, the Meuse, and their tributaries; to the north, the provinces around the shores of the Zuyder Zee, an inlet of the North Sea.

The most striking characteristic of the region, however, is its lowness, especially in the western coastal area which has been its historic heartland. Most of Flanders and Brabant, the most important provinces south of the Rhine, is barely above sea level; while much of Zeeland and Holland, to the north, lies below the level of the surrounding water and must be kept open by means of dikes and pumps. Further inland, the country rises to an average level of a few hundred feet, reaching an elevation of more than a thousand feet only in the extreme southeast. The earliest generally used name for the region was "the low lands by the sea," without either political or ethnic implications; in the form of "the Netherlands" or "the Low Countries," this geographical name later came to designate both a state and a people.

Language and Culture. The Netherlands was inhabited by branches of the two great adjacent peoples, the French and the Germans. South of a line running roughly west-east from Dunkirk through Brussels to the German boundary between Liége and Maastricht, the common folk spoke Walloon, a dialect of French; to the North, Flemish-Dutch, a variety of Low German which had developed in the later middle ages into a virtually independent language. The aristocracy throughout the country spoke and wrote standard French as their primary tongue, although most knew the popular speech of their areas as well, particularly in the North.

The linguistic separation was only partly reflected in the culture of the peoples, which was blended of French and German elements into a distinct pattern. The breadth of literacy in the country astounded foreigners. "Almost everyone, even the peasants and countryfolk, can at least read and write," wrote the Florentine observer Francesco Guicciardini, "while the use and knowledge of foreign languages among them are marvelously widespread."

Emporium of the World. The Netherlands was the principal center of trade in northern Europe. To Antwerp, the great emporium near the mouth of the Scheldt, came ships from almost every land in Europe, bringing wares for exchange in a huge and varied commercial enterprise. Among the principal products were wool, both as fiber and cloth, from England; spice from the Indies, especially after the discovery of an ocean route to the East at the end of the fifteenth century; wines from France; grain from the Baltic countries; and textiles and hardware from the Low Countries. Few of the ships that sailed up the Scheldt to moor at the wharves of Antwerp belonged to Antwerpers; most belonged to foreign shippers, though an increasing number were owned and manned by Zeelanders and Hollanders, who had long been active in the fishing and carrying trade.

Although the economic life of the Low Countries was channeled largely through Antwerp, the prosperity of the region rested upon a wide foundation of intensive industry and agriculture. Handicraft industries serving an international market furnished the livelihood of the population in a multitude of towns, each usually with its own specialty. Guicciardini, for all his familiarity with urbanized North Italy, marveled at the clustering towns of the Netherlands: "One can leave Utrecht in the morning, travel to any one of twenty-six towns as one pleases, have the noonday meal there and enjoy good cheer, and be home in the evening in time for supper."

The countryside, too, was thickly populated, for the cities required huge quantities of foodstuffs for their sustenance, as well as industrial raw materials like flax for their looms. Except in the outlying provinces like Hainaut and Luxemburg, which were little affected by the changes in Brabant and Flanders, the manorial system had long since given way to production for the market and personal freedom for the peasantry. The plentiful supply of investment capital from the towns found an important outlet in the creation of new farmlands from the sea by diking (the polders of Zeeland, Holland and, to lesser extent, the Flemish coast).

The total wealth of the Low Countries was enormous by the standards of the age and astounding when compared to the size of the land—about a tenth of the area of France. There was an opulent class of great landowners and merchants, and a numerous class of well-to-do which thrived on trade and manufactures.

Along with affluence went poverty. The lesser nobility, limited to the fixed revenues of their small estates in an age of rising prices, found themselves unable to live "nobly" and were threatened with decline into the ranks of the outright needy. A huge class of propertyless wage workers had grown up: in the towns, journeymen with no hope of taking a place in the oligarchic guilds; in the countryside, laborers without their own patch of land and hence without a place in the village communities. Thus the huge riches of the

Netherlands were accompanied by uncommonly vigorous social discontents, which during the centuries just past had frequently exploded into armed rebellion.

II. The Burgundian State

Politically the Low Countries presented a unique combination of particularism and power. Actually there was no Netherlandish state, but only a series of separate provinces in the region of the Low Countries which by result of wars and marriages had come into the possession of a single dynasty, the dukes of Burgundy, during the late fourteenth and fifteenth centuries. Most of the provinces nominally formed part of the Holy Roman Empire, but this connection had loosened as a result of their independent economic and cultural life; Brabant, Holland, and Zeeland were the most important of these provinces. Several of the provinces, notably Flanders and Artois, were nominal fiefs of the French crown, but it exerted no effective power within them.

Liberties and Power.   Within each province, the duke of Burgundy ruled as its particular duke, count, or lord, according to its special institutions. On his accession, he usually swore solemn loyalty to its individual charters. The most famous of these compacts between duke and province, the *Joyeuse Entrée* (joyous entry) of Brabant, formed the model for many of the others. These charters safeguarded the traditional juridical liberties of the provinces and towns and made all extraordinary taxation dependent upon the grant of the duke's petition by the assembled Estates (or States—see footnote, p. 17) of the province.

Despite these limitations, the duke of Burgundy matched the greatest kings in strength. He could put the resources accumulated from all his provinces to the service of a single policy. In this sense a state was being created, and the name "Burgundy" came to be applied to it as well as to the duke's original possessions of ducal Burgundy in eastern France and the adjacent "free county" (Franche-Comté) of Burgundy in the Holy Roman Empire. In governmental documents, however, the Low Countries as an entity remained the vague "Hither Land" (*les pays de deçà*).

To what use would the duke of Burgundy put the immense power drawn by him from the Low Countries? To defend the interests of its people—the peace which was the precondition of the safe and steady trade by which they lived, their favored position in the exchange of goods and movement of ships? Or to seek the aggrandizement of the dynasty whose roots in the Burgundian mountains remained vigorous still, at the expense of the Low Countries?

Charles the Bold. The extent of his power tempted Duke Charles the Bold, who had come to the throne in 1467, to undertake a policy along the latter lines. His goal was to establish a kingdom based on the Low Countries, but extending across Lorraine and his ancestral Burgundian lands possibly as far as the Mediterranean. His invasion of Lorraine brought into action against him a new military force, the Swiss. Twice during 1476, their pike squares defeated Charles's professional soldiery of mounted knights in heavy armor; then, in 1477, they destroyed the Burgundians completely at Nancy, leaving the duke among the fallen.

Mary of Burgundy. The duke's defeat was an unearned victory for his subjects in the Low Countries. They had chafed under his stern control while he used their wealth for adventures from which they reaped no benefit. They took their revenge upon his daughter Mary, who succeeded him as duchess at the age of twenty, and had no strength but their loyalty. They defended her against the attempts of Louis XI of France to wrest away the counties of Flanders and Artois, the duchy of Burgundy, and Franche-Comté. But they made her pay a heavy price: the abandonment of the centralized institutions of government created by her father. In the "Great Privilege" signed at Ghent, she confirmed the traditional rights and exemptions of the provinces and accepted their veto upon her power to declare war. She also permitted the provincial States to come together in a States-General by their own initiative, thus creating a potential rival for leadership of the common fatherland of "Hither Burgundy."

The humiliation inflicted upon the proud duchess made her take a champion without delay. In August, half a year after her father's death, she married Maximilian of Austria, son and heir of Emperor Frederick III (see ch. 13, p. 296). With his help she regained the initiative in domestic affairs and limited the loss of powers involved in the "Great Privilege." Meanwhile Maximilian reorganized her armies and carried on the war against France. Death as the result of a fall from horseback in 1482 ended the duchess's enterprise of re-establishment far short of accomplishment.

Philip the Fair. Without Mary's personal authority, Maximilian could do no more than preserve the Burgundian heritage for their young son, Philip, the new duke. Maximilian ended the war with France by a compromise peace at Arras (1484) and put down an insurgency of Flemish cities which did not wish to accept his authority. Philip remained in the Low Countries to be trained by a Flemish nobleman, William de Croy, sieur de Chièvres.

When Philip took over the government from Maximilian at the age of fifteen, he was a Fleming, not a German, and saw the world with the eyes of a Netherlands nobleman, haughty and chivalrous but attuned to the needs of trade. He resisted his father's attempts to use the Low Countries for his chimerical wars in Italy. Instead he assured the country peace. In 1496 he made a trade treaty with the English (the *Magnus Intercursus*), assuring the continued supply of the wool upon which depended in such large degree the prosperity of the Netherlands.

Only in the matter of a bride did the handsome young man—called Philip the Fair—accept his father's choice. He married Joanna of Spain in 1496 and went with her to Spain ten years later when she succeeded Isabella upon the throne of Castile. Less than a year after his arrival, he died in Spain. His heritage of Burgundy and the Netherlands passed to his eldest son, Charles, born at Ghent in 1500.

III. Charles V

Maximilian again took upon himself the regency of the Low Countries. He did not return to Brussels, however, but named Charles's aunt, Margaret of Austria, as his guardian and as governor. A worldly-wise and self-reliant woman, Margaret ruled the Netherlands with a strong hand, and turned over to her nephew a peaceable and prosperous country when he began his personal government at the age of fifteen. The next year the youth began to reap the remainder of his harvest of inheritances. The death of Ferdinand of Aragon (1516) brought him the kingdoms of Spain (see ch. 12, pp. 273-274); that of Maximilian I, the Austrian lands of the Hapsburgs and election as Holy Roman emperor (see ch. 13, p. 299).

Margaret of Austria. From a Burgundian and a Fleming, Charles V became a man of many nations. With him, dynastic aggrandizement reached beyond the limits of state-formation to a supranational dualism of dynasticism and universalism. What the change boded for the Netherlands began to emerge in 1516 when he sailed for Spain to take up his heritage there. He entrusted the government of the Low Countries, as Maximilian had done, to his aunt Margaret, though under his close supervision. In domestic affairs he generally accepted her decisions; but he took for granted, as she did, that the Netherlands would contribute their treasure to his many wars.

Under Margaret's administration, the territorial unification of the Low Countries was completed (with the single exception of Liége, which remained an ecclesiastical principality under its bishop). Friesland, Utrecht, and Gelderland, which had broken away from the dominion of Burgundy on the death of Charles the Bold, were brought back by purchase, negotiation, and war. Charles V held the Low Countries after 1528 by seventeen feudal titles: duke of Brabant, Gelderland, Limburg, and Luxemburg; count of Flanders, Holland, Zeeland, Artois, Hainaut, Namur, and Zutphen; margrave of the Holy Roman Empire (in Antwerp); and lord of Friesland, Mechlin (Malines), Utrecht, Overijssel, and Groningen. These became known as "the seventeen provinces" of the Low Countries, although not all were full-fledged provinces with regular administrations.

Mary of Hungary. A year after Margaret's death in 1530, Charles replaced her in the governorship by his own sister, Mary of Hungary, widow of King Louis (Lajos). At the same time, he reorganized the more or less haphazard system of common institutions for governing the seventeen provinces into a coherent centralized system of government based on three "collateral councils": the council of state, in which six members of the high nobility named for life discussed major questions of policy and made proposals to the governor; the council of finances, a technical body; and the privy council, which supervised the judicial and political administration of the country and served the governor as her trusted advisors and agents.

Despite his predilection for autocratic government, which was strengthened by the steady obedience of the Spaniards after the defeat of the *comuneros*, Charles did not cast aside the institutions by which his Netherlands subjects shared in government. His need for funds to wage war was too great to permit undertaking a major struggle with the provincial States, which were able therefore to continue collecting taxes by their own means. The result was the rise of permanent provincial institutions, separate from and not directly controlled by the central government. Charles V also convened the States-General, a joint meeting of the provincial States, almost annually. The States-General eased Mary's task in obtaining funds from the provinces, but it also brought their leaders closer to each other and encouraged the growth of a sentiment of common interest and responsibility.

The one issue on which Mary sharply disagreed with Charles was that of religious persecution. In her youth drawn toward Lutheran ideas and thereafter staunchly Erasmian, she was like most Netherlanders in disliking the use of the sword to enforce religious uniformity. Charles had less and less patience for heretics, who were successfully defying him in Germany. He issued repeated edicts (called "placards" because they were posted for the information of the people) for the extirpation of heresy. Mary obediently enforced the edicts to the best of her ability, but it was impossible to cut off the Netherlands, with all its trade and shipping, from the influence of the new beliefs. Lutherans, Anabaptists, and especially the Calvinists, who were vigorous latecomers, organized secret churches in the hope of a better day.

Abdication of Charles V. Having spent most of the years of his manhood in compliant Spain and rebellious Germany, Charles V returned to his native Netherlands to abdicate (October 24, 1555; the formal act was dated 1556) his crowns in Spain and the Low Countries in favor of his son Philip.

The reign of Charles V had been a time of uncertainties for the Netherlands. The basic questions—whose interests the country would serve and what its governmental organization would be—remained unsolved. He had permitted Margaret and Mary a large degree of autonomy, and they had kept intact the coalition of the nobility with the Burgundians. He had tightened the central institutions of government without abolishing those of the provinces. The country had laid out its wealth in vast amounts for his wars, but its rapidly increasing prosperity had enabled it to carry the burdens with grumbling but little violent resistance. During all the years of his absence, he remained for the Netherlanders "Charles of Ghent," their own prince, from whom they would suffer much.

IV. Philip II and William the Silent

The Netherlanders soon sensed that they could expect a clarification of the problems bequeathed by Charles V in a way wholly to their dislike. Their new sovereign, Philip II of Spain, spoke neither French nor Flemish; he looked upon the Low Countries as a possession, not as a fatherland shared with his own people. Not even the two great victories of Saint-Quentin (1557) and Gravelines (1558), won by the most eminent Netherlands nobleman, Lamoral, count of Egmont, though they terminated the costly war with France by the favorable peace of Cateau-Cambrésis (1559), won Philip the favor of the people. When he sailed for Spain in August, they were, according to a contemporary report, "universally happy, the great and the small alike."

Margaret of Parma and Cardinal Granvelle. Philip attempted to govern the Netherlands, as he did the rest of his dominions, from Spain. To represent him as governor-general or regent, he chose a gifted and energetic woman: his half-sister Margaret, duchess of Parma, who was the offspring of an illegitimate union between Charles V and a Flemish woman. But he did not entrust her with the reality of power. Though Charles's three collateral councils were maintained, she was actually under the thumb of a committee of three: two Netherlanders and the Burgundian Antoine Perrenot, Cardinal Granvelle, the most powerful of the group.

Hanging over Margaret's government from the beginning was the determination of Philip to use the Low Countries as a treasurehouse for his policy, which was primarily Spanish in character. The Netherlanders had no wish to be his financiers. Burdened with a debt of 9,000,000 guilders, they demanded that the king withdraw the Spanish garrisons and cavalry regiments, which cost them almost half a million guilders a year. In order to obtain "petitions" (money grants) from the provincial States, Margaret and Granvelle sent the *tercios* (Spanish regiments) home in 1561, without Philip's prior approval.

With the bulk of his army gone from the country, Philip nonetheless insisted on stirring up a hornet's question with a program for ecclesiastical reorganization of the Netherlands. The three dioceses of Tournai, Arras, and Utrecht, unchanged in size since the days of Roman rule, were too unwieldy for the immensely enlarged population of the region. Philip's proposal to replace them by fifteen dioceses under three local archbishops struck at the interests of the nobility and aroused popular fear of an Inquisition.

Recalcitrance of the Nobles. The issue of the bishoprics led directly into a challenge from the high nobility to Philip II's political system in the Netherlands. The blame for the hated decision was placed on ambitious Granvelle, who actually had sought to dissuade Philip, largely because the nobles saw in him the moving spirit of the king's new absolutism. Three members of the council of state—William, count of Nassau and prince of Orange, Philip of Montmorency, count of Hoorn, and the count of Egmont—took the lead against Granvelle. In 1561 they demanded that the king dismiss Granvelle, and two years later, when Philip refused to accept their resignation from the council, they defied him by ceasing to appear at its meetings.

Their departure demonstrated the fragility of absolute government in the Netherlands. The government possessed few troops of its own; enforcement of the law was mainly in the hands of the municipalities and the nobility. It did not even possess its own staff of tax collectors. Against the opposition of the great nobles, it was difficult to obtain taxes from the provincial States. Margaret, herself at odds with the dictatorial Granvelle, again took the initiative. She persuaded her brother to send the cardinal home to Besançon—to see his mother "at his own request," according to the king's instructions.

Egmont, Hoorn, and Orange resumed their places in the council of state. A period of collaboration between them and Margaret ensued. It was an unhappy experiment, not so much for lack of good will between the nobles and the regent as for the king's unwillingness to accept the policy they saw as necessary. He insisted upon introducing the edicts of the council of Trent, with their rigid definitions of Catholic doctrine, and would not withdraw the "placards" against the heretics. He was ready to make concessions on ordinary matters, he informed his sister, but would rather die a thousand times than permit heresy to go unpursued and unpunished in his dominions. When Philip's command to act was placed before the council of state, William of Orange, as he left the chamber, muttered, "We shall now see the beginning of a great tragedy."

Rebellion of the Nation. The whole political class of the country, still predominantly Catholic in the older Erasmian tradition rejected by the council of Trent, combined to oppose Philip II's policy and to resist its application. Judges frequently declined to pass sentence on heretics, and when they did, the town officials likewise refused to execute sentence.

The impasse in government released the controls over the populace. The spread of Calvinist beliefs among them had been hastened by the economic hardships of an unusually frigid winter in 1564-1565 and a decline in trade and work as a result of commercial conflicts with England. On August 10, 1566, a rampage against the "idols" in the churches began in the textile town of Steenvoorde and spread rapidly to many parts of the country. Precious statuary and stained glass were destroyed by mobs of "Iconoclasts" (picture breakers), against whom the local governments were usually either unwilling or unable to act.

The crisis which had begun within the narrow confines of the council of state, though on issues of general import, now became a civil war encompassing every class and every corner of the country. Calvinists and a league of rebellious small nobles joined to seize a number of towns, notably Antwerp and 's-Hertogenbosch (Bois-le-Duc). Egmont and Hoorn, loyal still at heart to the king and to the old church, stood aloof, but Orange moved to take the lead of the insurgents, hoping to keep their movement broadly national instead of purely religious. Margaret broke with the nobility, whom she held responsible for the breakdown of authority and order, and recruited troops which recaptured Antwerp and other rebel-held towns. Nonetheless she continued to pursue a policy of reconciliation, limiting punishment to the leaders of the rebels, permitting non-Catholics a modicum of toleration, and accepting the participation of the nobility and the provincial States in the government of the land.

The Iron Duke. The decision was no longer hers to make, however. Philip II decided that the time for conciliation and dissembling had passed, and the time for force had come. He sent a man of action to the Netherlands —the "Iron Duke" of Alva, his most trusted commander—to take over military and political leadership of the campaign against the rebels. Less than half a year after Alva arrived at Brussels with a force of 10,000 soldiers— Spaniards, Italians, and Albanians—Margaret had laid down her office and withdrawn to Italy.

The duke proceeded to act with speed and determination against the hostile Netherlanders. His soldiers stormed rebellious cities one after another, trampling on their own promises of safety to those who surrendered. The rebels called the Spaniards by the mocking name "Angels," and sang with rueful hate:

> A Spanish pardon holds no better
> Than open fingers full of flies.
>
> (*Een Spaens pardoen dat houdt so vast,*
> *Als een open handt vol vlieghen.*)

Alva also established a special tribunal, the council of troubles, to hunt down and condemn heretics and rebels alike. Its ruthless efficiency soon won it the popular name of "council of blood." The council did not restrict its victims to the poor and the weak. It arrested Egmont and Hoorn and tried them as traitors, although they had refused to join the rebellion: it was enough that they had resisted the king's will in the council of state and thus brought on the crisis. They were beheaded on the great public square in Brussels before an immense and awestruck crowd—a warning to the land that none, however high in rank or esteem, could stand against the monarch and live.

William of Orange. The duke, in striking down Hoorn and Egmont, only strengthened the rebellion. Egmont, in particular, though beloved of the people, was incapable of leading a revolution. William of Orange, who had slipped into Germany beyond the duke's reach, was a man of different stripe. Honored rather than loved by the populace, firm in his resolution and flexible in his policy, and utterly dedicated to the defense of his country's liberties and rights, he took up Alva's challenge. Granvelle had admired and feared the subtlety and strength of this great nobleman, who spoke fluently and yet did not reveal his inmost purposes, and so had ironically dubbed him "William the Silent."

In Germany William raised a force of soldiers with the aid of his German relatives and struck into the Netherlands. He proved no match for Alva on the battlefield, and withdrew across the border to prepare for a new round of fighting.

Alva meanwhile found a foe whom he could not defeat by headlong assault: an empty treasury. Sixteenth-century mercenary soldiers, ardent Spaniards no less than politically indifferent *Landsknechte*, would not fight without pay. Philip had no funds to spare for Alva, who thereupon demanded that the States-General introduce the Spanish system of taxes (10 per cent on sales, 2 per cent on real-estate transfers), in addition to granting him an immediate tax of 1 per cent on all capital. All that the duke could obtain, after long pleading and threatening, was a "petition" of 2,000,000 guilders for two years. But once he consolidated his grip upon the provinces, he planned to bring in obedient administrators and ultimately to rule the Low Countries on behalf of Philip as autocratically as the king ruled in Spain itself.

"The Sea Beggars." By the beginning of 1572, Alva seemed to hold final triumph in his hand. Suddenly it was snatched from him because he commanded the land but not the sea, and hence not the seacoast either. Alva had seen no reason to waste garrisons on most of the ports in Zeeland and Holland when they were needed to fight the prince of Orange, who continued to make incursions in the southern and western provinces. Thus when a force of privateers, the "Sea Beggars," operating under letters of marque from

William the Silent (issued by him as sovereign prince of Orange, a little landlocked state inside southern France), were expelled from England by Elizabeth as hardly better than pirate desperadoes, they fell upon Brill, a little port at the mouth of the Meuse, as a port of refuge.

Once Brill was theirs, they decided to try their strength upon the other towns of Zeeland and Holland. By the beginning of summer, most of the provinces north of the Rhine—Holland, Zeeland, Gelderland, Utrecht, and Friesland—were in their control. The Calvinist minority joined with them in overthrowing unfriendly municipal administrations. Thousands of Calvinists and other non-Catholics flooded north to escape Alva, bringing with them the determination and ruthlessness of exiles.

When William's second campaign met the same overwhelming defeat as the first, he withdrew to the North instead of to Germany. Now he had a base of operations within the Low Countries, in the northern provinces protected from the easy onslaught of the *tercios* by the huge ditch of the Rhine and the low, easily flooded countryside. The task of crushing the Netherlands now became too much even for the Iron Duke. In December 1573 he withdrew from the country.

The "Pacification of Ghent." A period of confusion, political and military, followed. Attempts at peace and reconciliation failed. The first was made by Luis de Requesens, Alva's successor. His armies could not take Leiden, a key city in southern Holland, despite a long siege (1574). William marked its relief by founding there a new university with the basic task of training ministers for the Reformed Church, a clear indication of the strong Calvinist tide that was running in the North. When Requesens entered peace talks with William, they failed because the Spanish commander could not grant toleration to non-Catholics.

After Requesens' death in March 1576, the unpaid Spanish forces mutinied, captured Antwerp and sacked the wealth-laden city on the Scheldt in a "Spanish Fury" of murder and looting. William of Orange won an agreement from all the provinces, north and south, to combine to drive out the Spanish forces and settle the fate of the country by the decision of their own States-General. This "Pacification of Ghent" provided for religious toleration, approved the supreme command which William had assumed in Holland and Zeeland, but acknowledged Philip II still as lawful sovereign of all the provinces.

Meanwhile a new governor-general appointed by Philip reached the Netherlands. This was Don John of Austria, his half-brother and the famed victor of Lepanto. John was able to enter the country only after he accepted the Pacification of Ghent. He soon discovered that he had a title but no power; effective control was shared by the States-General and the prince of Orange. Don John lost patience and decided to make the country "absolutely obedient." With a force of German mercenaries, he seized the citadel of Namur. The entire country turned against him, and Philip refused him further assistance. The thwarted hero died in October 1578. A new commander and governor—Margaret of Parma's son Alexander Farnese—was already in the Netherlands, ready to take Don John's place.

Farnese and the Union of Arras. Farnese came to the provinces—which had become a graveyard of Spanish reputations—with the intention of redeeming the situation and thereby achieving the glory and fame which were his highest aspiration. He brought to the endeavor of rewinning the Netherlands a methodical and resolute military talent, but he did not rely upon arms alone. He was also an astute, flexible, and humane statesman who knew that he could never reconquer the North unless he first won the South by persuasion as well as by compulsion. In this persuasion he was aided by the religious divisions within the common Netherlands camp organized by William of Orange. The Calvinists insisted on toleration for themselves in the other provinces, but would not grant it to Catholics in those they controlled, especially Holland and Zeeland; the Catholics in the South, though opposed to the rigors of the Inquisition, wished to maintain their religion and demanded freedom of conscience and worship for their fellow-Catholics in the North.

In an effort to rescue the traditional government without capitulating to Philip II, the Catholic nobility persuaded the States-General to offer the sovereignty of the Low Countries to Archduke Matthias of Austria, Philip's cousin. Matthias, the future emperor, remained a nonentity and left the Netherlands after three years.

A minority of Catholic nobles moved closer to reconciliation with Philip. On January 5, 1579, a group of deputies from the districts of Tournai, Artois, and Douai formed a Union at Arras for the defense of Catholicism and the maintenance of the king's sovereignty providing he abandoned his absolutist projects in government. This Union gave Farnese a basis for winning back all the Catholic nobility south of the Rhine to the allegiance. His armies recaptured one town after another below the Rhine river line. Farnese offered terms of mercy not only to the Catholic inhabitants but also to the Calvinists, who were allowed to emigrate peaceably with most of their property. Alva's work was bit by bit undone. A Catholic Netherlands came back into existence, its people loyal to its duke and count, who was also the king of Spain, but sharing in the government of their country and maintaining its religious unity without the inhumanities of the Inquisition.

The Union of Utrecht. Farnese's program could not regain the North. There the grip of Calvinism and the distrust of Philip were too strong. The northern provinces united into a loose state, midway between a perpetual alliance and a federation, in the Union of Utrecht (January 29, 1579). They agreed to act as one in foreign affairs and defense while maintaining their separate identities and powers in internal affairs. The Union also gave Calvinism a favored status. The prince of Orange, still clinging to his ideal of a common Netherlands fatherland, did not favor the Union, but could not prevent its conclusion. Present strength and advantage mattered more to the majority of the rebels in the northern provinces than the possible salvaging of the Pacification of Ghent.

The unity of the Netherlands, shattered by the formation of the two Unions of Arras and Utrecht, could be reconstructed only by a change of heart on both sides, or by the military triumph of one over the other.

Philip II confirmed the choice of war and force in 1581 by issuing an edict of outlawry against William the Silent. He proclaimed the prince of Orange a traitor and public plague and promised 25,000 gold ducats and noble rank to anyone who slew him.

The Abjuration. The provinces of Holland, Zeeland, Utrecht, and Gelderland, as well as the two southern provinces of Brabant and Flanders, where Farnese had not regained control, replied by an Act of Abjuration (July 22, 1581), casting off the sovereignty of Philip II as forefeited by his tyranny. They justified their action by the doctrine that the ruler's power was held by him as a hereditary office, not an indefeasible possession: a prince was responsible not only to God but to his subjects, who in the person of the intermediate magistrates (the nobles and the town governments) could deprive him of his office when he acted persistently and violently against the interests of his people. The influence of Huguenot monarchomach theoreticians was felt in the Act of Abjuration, but it arose primarily from the long tradition of provincial and town autonomy in the Netherlands.

To maintain the liberty of the Low Countries against the military genius of Farnese was more than the provinces could achieve by themselves. William the Silent was indefatigable as a statesman, steady in his purposes and adept at expedients, but he had no gift as a general. He persuaded Duke Francis of Anjou, brother of the French King Henry II, to accept the sovereignty of the Netherlands (with the exception of Holland and Zeeland, which beseeched William to become their count). The prince hoped thereby to obtain French aid, but his attempt misfired. The vain and light-minded Anjou thought to accomplish by one stroke of violence what Alva, Requesens, and Don John had failed to do: to place the Low Countries under monarchical absolutism without their assent. His garrison in the citadel of Antwerp made a surprise assault upon the city, but this "French Fury" was soon defeated and the duke and his troops withdrew from the Netherlands.

William himself meanwhile lived under the threat of assassins who wished to earn Philip's 25,000 ducats and the glory of killing the heretic leader. He was badly wounded in 1582 but recovered. Then on July 10,

THE ASSASSINATION OF WILLIAM THE SILENT, 1584. Etching by an unknown seventeenth-century Dutch artist. The dark line in the center results from the folding of the original print for binding in a book of Dutch historical prints put together late in the seventeenth century.

The murder of the Prince of Orange by Balthasar Gérard at Delft is portrayed with melodramatic force and detail, though dubious artistry and erroneous date. The paper held by Gérard is a petition which he pretended to be bringing to the Prince. *(Achenbach Foundation)*

1584, Balthasar Gérard, a young Burgundian, shot him down in his home at Delft. The prince, dying, gasped, "My God, have pity upon my soul and upon this poor people!"

V. The Netherlands Divided

The dead leader and his people had built better than he knew. The improvised revolutionary state, with only the Union of Utrecht and the Act of Abjuration as its charters of establishment, survived, preserved its independence against the press of Spanish armies, and became for a century one of the great powers of Europe.

353

The Rise of Amsterdam. In the very midst of war, and partly as a result of it, the seacoast provinces, Zeeland and particularly Holland, developed their economic activity at an extraordinary rate. Their ships continued to ply the waters of the Atlantic and its adjacent seas, carrying the goods of Europe and bringing life-giving trade to Holland. The competitive advantage of the Dutch lay in the efficiency and cheapness of their shipping. They "run their ships better and pay their crews less, so that it is said that a Holland ship can be handled with six men where a Hansa ship of the same size would need more than ten," according to a contemporary report. After the formation of the East India and the West India companies in the early seventeenth century, Dutch shipping sailed all the seas of the world. Though the Baltic trade remained Holland's "mother commerce," long-distance trade to the Indies provided some of the most impressive profits to Dutch investors.

Amsterdam, a port on the Zuyder Zee, took over the role of Antwerp as the emporium and banker to all Europe. Its growth was particularly rapid after Farnese's capture of Antwerp in 1585 (see below, p. 356); for the Dutch fleets blockaded the Scheldt river and cut the city from the sea by which it lived. As once the whole Low Countries had been, in the phrase of a modern historian, the economic suburbs of Antwerp, so now the entire republic of the United Provinces became the suburbs of Amsterdam: and their common prosperity rested in large degree (or so they believed) upon the economic death of Antwerp.

Thus the consequence of war and political separation was to deepen the chasm between the peoples of the northern and southern Low Countries, by putting between them not only the differences of religion and politics but also those of the purse. But the expansion of the North provided a broad and sturdy base for the enormous exertions of the war of independence, which continued, with one interlude of twelve years, for another six and a half decades.

Republican Government. The death of William the Silent impelled the United Provinces (or United Netherlands), as the Dutch republic came to be called, to consolidate its governmental arrangements. In the first phase of the rebellion, the fiction had been maintained that the prince of Orange exercised authority in the provinces as stadholder (lieutenant) for Philip II; but William of Orange had shared his powers with the provincial States. These bodies became the sole inheritors of the sovereignty wrested from Philip II. They were in turn no more than delegations from the various orders, primarily the towns and the nobility (which had one member in Holland and Zeeland but was more numerous and influential in the inland provinces). In military matters and in relations with foreign states, the States-General acted as sovereign on behalf of its member provinces; but its authority was strictly limited by the rule that all basic decisions had to be unanimous. The voice of Holland, which paid 58 per cent of the expenses of the Union, nonetheless carried the greatest weight; and the "land's advocate" of Holland, its permanent legal representative who functioned as a kind of executive political secretary, came to play a similar role as the permanent leader of the States-General.

The princes of Orange became another focus of leadership in the republic, sometimes collaborating with Holland and sometimes combating it. The death of William the Silent had prevented his accepting the countship of Holland and Zeeland and replacing Philip as their sovereign. His son Maurice of Nassau did not take these titles, but accepted appointment as stadholder of Zeeland and Holland from the provincial States; he further received from the States-General, the common authority in the Union, command of their armed forces as captain and admiral-general. Thus he was a servant of the sovereign provinces; but at the same time, as stadholder, he retained the privilege of nominating numerous officials within the provinces, which made him to some extent their master.

The Earl of Leicester. This paradoxical arrangement did not seem adequate for sustaining the demands of a war of independence still to be fought and won. The leaders of the Republic continued William the Silent's policy of seeking a sovereign from abroad, strong enough to defend the new state and willing to share authority with his subjects. The dominion of the provinces was offered first to Henry III of France, who declined in 1585, and then to Elizabeth I of England. She too declined, but sent her favorite, the earl of Leicester, with an expeditionary force to aid the Dutch against their common enemy, Spain. The vain Leicester, to her dismay, accepted the title of governor-general (1586). Like Anjou before him, he mistook his quasi-sovereignty for the full measure of absolute power. He attempted to govern the provinces autocratically, ordered a halt to the profitable trade with Spain and the southern Low Countries, and fomented an unsuccessful popular rebellion in Utrecht against the governing party. Faced by the implacable hostility of the province of Holland and discredited by his own ineptness and the treason of several English officers in his command, he left for home in 1587. The Republic would have to stand by itself, with sovereignty resting in the "people" (or, more precisely, in the provincial States which had earlier claimed no more than a right to grant and collect extraordinary taxation).

Maurice and Parma. The Republic passed under the dual leadership of Maurice, who grew into manhood in the years immediately after his appointment, and John of Oldenbarnevelt, the advocate of Holland. The task they faced was formidable.

Farnese, who had become duke of Parma on his father's death in 1586, was methodically recapturing the towns south of the Rhine: Bruges, Ghent, Brussels, and after a tremendous siege in which he cut off the port from the sea by means of a fortified dike across the Scheldt, Antwerp. Brabant and Flanders ceased to be part of the Union of Utrecht and returned to the allegiance of the king. With these victories achieved, Parma prepared to cross the Rhine and beat down the rebels in their strongholds.

But Philip II, seeking other goals, twice distracted Parma from this objective. First he ordered him to use his forces for an attack upon England in 1588 in conjunction with the Invincible Armada. The fleet of the Dutch, by assisting the English in dispersing that threat, thereby gave succor to the hard-pressed armies of the Republic on the land. (See ch. 10, pp. 234-235, and ch. 12, p. 284.) The accession of Henry IV to the throne of France in the next year prompted Philip to order Parma, over his protests, to assist the Catholic League there. (See ch. 9, p. 187.) The duke delayed, but did not prevent, Henry's conquest of his kingdom. Parma's death in 1592 was a victory not only for the French king, but for the United Provinces as well.

Maurice combined the results of his studies of warfare in Roman antiquity with the lessons of Parma's campaigns to create a new strategy, based on an elaborate and systematic siegecraft, defensive and offensive, which exploited to the full the soggy ditch-divided terrain of the Netherlands, and attained numerous successes during 1597. Oldenbarnevelt meanwhile conducted a deft foreign policy for the States-General. He negotiated a triple alliance with France and England in 1596, which constituted the first recognition by major European states of the virtual sovereignty of the new Dutch Republic.

The Archdukes. In the southern Netherlands, Parma's policy began to succeed after his death. In 1598, Philip II decided to bestow a kind of semi-independence on the provinces in the Low Countries still faithful to him. He granted the provinces to his daughter Isabel and her bridegroom-to-be, the Archduke Albert of Austria (who was released from clerical orders and a cardinalate to become her husband), as their independent possession, subject to return to the Spanish crown if they bore no children. They promised secretly to accept the policies dictated by Madrid. The practice turned out otherwise. Isabel and Albert, called "the archdukes," were clearer minds and stronger personalities than Philip III, who succeeded to the Spanish throne in 1598. They administered their state as they saw fit. They furthered the reconciliation of their subjects to Catholicism but avoided the trouble-causing rigors of a harsh Inquisition. They conducted their court with regal pomp but avoided absolutist methods in dealing with their subjects, and accepted gracefully the participation of the States in the government.

In the crucial business of the war with the rebel North, the archdukes took the lead for Spain rather than from it. In Ambrosio Spinola, a Genoese nobleman, they acquired in 1603 a military commander almost of Parma's

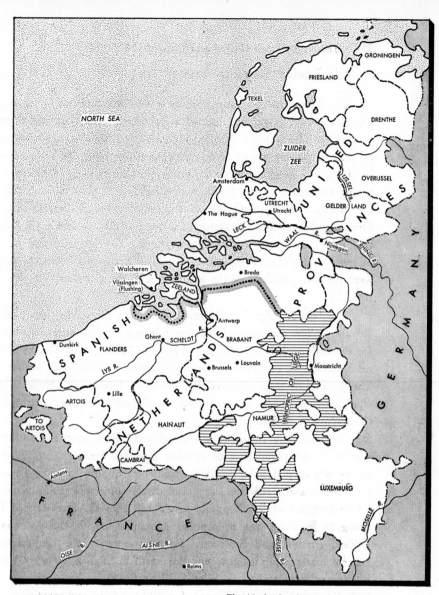

The Netherlands Divided, 1609

stature. His successes in 1606 and 1607 did not deceive Albert into expecting a recovery of the North by arms. He persuaded Philip III to accept a compromise half-peace, a Twelve Years' Truce signed in 1609. The Spaniards finally abandoned their demand for religious liberty for Catholics in the United Provinces, the Dutch their demand for free trade with the Spanish overseas empire. The Spaniards did not recognize outright the independence of the Republic, but acknowledged the United Provinces as having the quality of "free States over which the archdukes make no claim."

357

VI. Twelve Years of Truce

The Truce enabled the archdukes to continue their policy of moderation. The southern Netherlands gained a breathing spell, but not their former prosperity. The Dutch controlled both sides of the Meuse-Scheldt estuary as a result of the capture of Sluis, on the southern bank, by Maurice of Nassau in 1604. The blockade against Antwerp remained as strict as ever. The lingering commerce of the South was compelled to pass through the ports of the North. The cultural life of the country became exclusively French; Flemish relapsed into the status of a popular dialect, lacking its own literature and increasingly distinct from Dutch. The intensity and braggadocio of the baroque style captured the world of art in the South, replacing as it were the lost grandeur of the actuality with the grandiosity of the imaginative life.

The "Golden Age." The armistice began the golden age of the Dutch Republic. The cessation of fighting released the full energies of the Dutch for expansion of their trade and shipping. Their vessels, thanks to their low rates for cargo, carried an ever-larger amount of Europe's seaborne goods. The growth of trade fostered the increase of industry. Holland, the principal province where the economic development was concentrated, became the beehive of all Europe.

A specifically Dutch culture developed, based upon the ability of wide groups in the population to sponsor painters, builders, and poets. Their works carried a double, subtly contradictory quality: a note of realism, full of sobriety, and a subdued but proud display of new wealth and power. The intellectual life of the Republic brought it into the forefront of European thought; learning was widespread, enhanced by the new universities of Leiden, Utrecht, and Franeker. Scholars came to the Netherlands—as it became increasingly usual to call the North in English, as against the South, which was more and more called the Low Countries—as once they had gone to Italy, and still went to France, for study, debate, and creative work.

Less than Theocracy. Despite the leading role of the Calvinists in the revolution against Philip II, they had never achieved their aim of making the United Provinces into another Geneva. The Reformed religion became the preferred religion, but not the only one permitted. Mennonites and Catholics alike were allowed to worship in peace, though not in public, as were the Jews who began to come into the country, especially from Portugal.

Too many Dutchmen and too many refugees from the South had suffered and bled for "the cause of liberty" rather than "the sake of religion," for a new uniformity to be clamped upon the country. The native religious strain was Erasmian and undogmatic, or as it came to be called by its enemies, "libertine." The Calvinist grip, furthermore, was weakest upon the most influential class in the country—the merchants and patricians—and strongest among the poor. Indeed, many of the wealthy ("the soundest and richest part" of the nation, Oldenbarnevelt admitted) remained Catholic, for they were best able to resist conversion against the dictates of conscience.

The Calvinist advantages consisted chiefly in the favored status of the Reformed church, in its use of the public churches, and in the revenues given it by the state from the properties confiscated from the old hierarchy. It was decreed that all officeholders in the state must be members of the Reformed church; the measure accelerated the conversion of the political class, but did not wholly achieve it, for many of the regents were willing, for the sake of principle or less praiseworthy reasons, to wink at violations. Reformed preachers were trained in the state-supported universities, Leiden becoming an international center of Calvinist learning second only to Geneva if to any. The price for this assistance was a heavy one: dependence upon a government which was not wholly or willingly under the control of the orthodox and strict Calvinists.

The Fall of Oldenbarnevelt. As long as the ruling groups remained united, the Reformed clergy had to confine their indignation to petulant complaining. Their opportunity for action came after the Truce, when Maurice of Orange broke with Oldenbarnevelt and the dominant party in the States of Holland primarily over the refusal of the Hollanders to subordinate themselves to the general authority of the Union, that is, to the States-General and the captain-general-stadholder. The occasion for the rupture was the struggle in the Reformed church between the Remonstrants, followers of the theologian Arminius, and the Contra-Remonstrants, adherents of his adversary Gomarus. The Arminians weakened the Calvinist doctrine of predestination, making it less terrible and difficult of comprehension; the Gomarians, on the contrary, stiffened the doctrine as they defended it. The Arminian strength was greatest among the governing class, the Gomarian among the preachers and populace.

The Contra-Remonstrants, who dominated most of the provinces outside Holland, persuaded the States-General (1618) to convoke a national synod at Dordrecht (Dort). The States of Holland refused to go along, and ordered the raising of town militia to maintain order against Contra-Remonstrant rioters. "It would be better to live among the Turks than in a land where the rabble has a free hand!" cried one Remonstrant preacher.

Maurice, already offended with the Hollanders because of their opposition to a resumption of the war against Spain on the expiry of the Truce, was stirred to violent anger by this establishment of an armed force not under his command. He obtained a commission from the States-General to re-establish its authority and arrested Oldenbarnevelt and several of his closest colleagues, including the young pensionary (legal secretary) of Rotterdam, the already famed scholar Hugo Grotius. They were tried by a special court on charges of treason and sentenced to death. The 72-year-old Oldenbarnevelt would not admit guilt or seek pardon, and gave up his life beneath the executioner's great sword in 1619. The other sentences were commuted to life imprisonment. Grotius escaped from his prison cell, thanks to the ingenuity of his wife, who secreted him in a trunk supposedly filled with books; he fled abroad, to remain a prince among scholars, the darling of kings, and an exile from his homeland.

At the synod of Dordrecht (1618-1619), the Gomarians drove the Arminians out of the church. But their victory proved largely hollow. Open Remonstrants were banned, but the governing powers refused to hunt down those who did not make public resistance. Maurice himself, never interested in the theological controversy as such, relented once Oldenbarnevelt had been destroyed and the province of Holland became amenable to his policy. It did not stand in the way of renewal of the fighting in 1621.

VII. To the Peace of Münster

Maurice's touch as a soldier had been lost, however. He failed to prevent Spinola from besieging the city of Breda, south of the Meuse estuary, and died in 1625, shortly before it fell.

Frederick Henry. Maurice's work was taken up at once by his brother Frederick Henry, who assumed his offices. Frederick Henry resumed Maurice's old strategy of systematic siegecraft, capturing 's-Hertogenbosch in 1629, Maastricht in 1632, and Breda in 1637; only Antwerp, the supreme prize, escaped him, and Amsterdam held back in the grant of supplies in fear that its prostrate rival would recover if once admitted into the northern Union. Frederick Henry's diplomacy was more astute and supple than his brother's had been. He judiciously supported the Protestant enemies of Spain in the parallel Thirty Years' War under way in Germany (see ch. 14, pp. 327-336), brought France into open alliance (1635), and maintained the league despite the tensions of Richelieu's wars against the Huguenots (see ch. 9, pp. 198-199). His last big achievement was a personal one: to win a royal bride for his son William, who in 1641 married Princess Mary, daughter of Charles I of England.

The Spanish Netherlands. The southern provinces, during the same years, fell back under the rule of Spain and became for another century "the Spanish Netherlands," as distinct from the "United Netherlands" of the North. Albert died in 1621, just before the Truce ended. Isabel followed him twelve years later, leaving the land to her nephew, Philip IV.

The new sovereign did not greatly change the system of government, with its combination of Catholicism and tolerance, but the country suffered more and more as the years passed without peace. Spain retained its hold not because it drew any revenues from the Low Countries to make good its own deficits, but as a favorable base for waging the war which began with France in 1635. The country remained generally quiet, although feelers put out to the Dutch by some noblemen for assistance if they rebelled against Spain indicated an undercurrent of discontent.

The last success of the Spaniards in the war against the Dutch was the capture of Breda in 1625, whose surrender Velásquez depicted in his painting "Las Lanzas." The next year the slow steady decline of Spanish power began. Isabella and Spinola combined in 1628 to urge peace negotiations upon Madrid. Olivares, who guided the Spanish government, persuaded Philip IV not to make peace without victory; but the United Provinces scorned the very notion of accepting the Spanish king as their public protector, to whom they would pay an annual tribute; or permitting Catholics freedom of worship; or opening the Scheldt to trade with Antwerp; or refraining from trading with the Spanish possessions in the Indies. Spinola went to Spain to demand 3,000,000 crowns annually for the needs of the war, but treated Philip's acceptance as meaningless, since the king's total revenue was no more than 4,500,000 crowns for all his expenses. He therefore resigned in 1530 without returning to the Low Countries, lest his good name as a military captain be damaged. Without him, Spanish power gave way. In 1637 the Dutch recaptured Breda, and in 1643 the French defeated the Spanish *tercios* in a battle on the open field at Rocroi.

The Peace Treaty. The obstacles in the way of peace grew fewer. In Spain Olivares was dismissed from office in 1643, and his successor, Luis de Haro, took as his task the ending of Spain's wars. (See ch. 12, p. 290). In the Dutch Republic, the very success of the French-Dutch alliance in beating down Spanish power in the southern Netherlands raised a new bogey to haunt many. This was the fear that once the Spanish Netherlands were divided between the United Provinces and France, the erstwhile French ally would become a peril. A Latin motto, *Gallus amicus non vicinus* (The Frenchman for a friend, not a neighbor), summed up this attitude succinctly, but a pamphlet, *The Holland Sybil*, put it more vividly: "It is better to live among adders and serpents than with a bad wife; but better with a bad wife than next to such neighbors." The province of Holland, where the interests of trade were paramount and the desire to wage a costly war for the sake of glory was absent, was the seat of the movement for peace.

Frederick Henry set himself against it. Peace meant reducing his powers and prerogatives within the state, which rested on his command of the armed forces. He died in 1647, leaving his offices but not his influence to his son,

William II. The young stadholder was unable to prevent the conclusion of a peace between the United Provinces and Spain at Münster in 1648.

For the sake of separating the Dutch from the French, the Spaniards conceded almost every point the triumphant rebels asked. Philip IV recognized "their lordships, the States-General of the United Netherlands" as "free and sovereign States, Provinces, and Lands." The Dutch retained all their conquests south of the Rhine; the Scheldt remained closed to seagoing traffic, assuring the continued subordination of the southern Netherlands to the economy of the North.

Two Netherlands. The Burgundian state, once so full of promise, was dead. There was no longer one Netherlands, but two.

The descendants of the dukes of Burgundy, now the kings of Spain, retained only the southern provinces. The Spanish Netherlands was a pallid, tattered remnant of a state. It became, nonetheless, a separate land, and its people had the opportunity of separate growth.

The earlier glory and power of the Burgundians passed to the Republic on the north side of the Rhine. There the Dutch, all the while fighting a war for survival, had built their country into a great state. It was wealthy, sturdy, and, more than any other European land, a haven for freedom.

16

North and East Europe

1453 - 1650

THE LANDS ALONG the northern and eastern edges of Europe—Scandinavia, Poland, Russia, and the Balkan possessions of the Ottoman empire—were distinct parts of the continent at the beginning of the sixteenth century, not only in their geographical location but also in many other aspects of their life. They differed widely from the countries of western and southern Europe in many of their economic, social, and political ways.

During the early modern period these outlying regions came to be more and more intimately involved in the life of the rest of Europe. In the process, they began—except for the Ottoman state—to resemble it more closely.

I. Scandinavia

In 1500 the kingdoms of Scandinavia—Denmark, Sweden, and Norway —were joined in personal union under a single monarch. It was a conjunction which fell far short of merger: the facts of geography as well as of economic and political interest both united and severed the peoples and states.

Each of the three Scandinavian countries had a distinct geographical situation, to which it responded by its own pattern of life and policy.

Despite geographic and economic differences, the Scandinavian nations had a sense of general identity. They were descended from the same ethnic stocks and shared many elements of common civilization. Although distinct administrative and literary languages had begun to take form in Denmark and Sweden, the speech of the common folk in all three countries shared the likenesses and differences of dialects within a common language.

Denmark. Denmark, the most southerly, lay astraddle the waterways connecting the North and Baltic Seas. To the east of the Kattegat and the Sound it included the southernmost part of the Scandinavian peninsula, notably the fertile farming district of Skåne (Scania). West across the straits it took in the peninsula of Jutland, whose sandy soils supported a sparse population. Most of the half million Danes tilled the richer soils of the islands in the Danish archipelago. The sea, at no point more than twenty-five miles distant, encouraged internal communications and the formation of a commercial class. The German merchants of the Hansa, particularly of Lübeck, still dominated Danish commerce, however, and directed its profits principally to their own pockets.

Thus the revenues available to the Danish monarch from taxes upon his own people were limited. During the fifteenth century Erik VII devised a valuable new source of income. He built fortresses on either side of the narrow waist of the Sound, at Helsingør (the "Elsinore" of *Hamlet*) on Zealand, the main island, and Helsingborg, in Skåne. He then collected dues from foreign shipping for the ostensible purpose of maintaining a navy to put down piracy; but the bulk of payments went in fact to Erik's coffers, and the military forces he hired with these funds enabled him and his successors to assert their pre-eminence within the Scandinavian union.

Sweden and Norway. Sweden and Norway were favored and limited by nature in different ways. Between them they occupied the bulk of the Scandinavian peninsula, with the range of mountains known as the Keel (Kölen) separating them. Sweden on the east faced the Baltic, Norway on the west the Atlantic. A broad agricultural life flourished on the rolling plain of southern Sweden. In Norway, on the other hand, the mountains reached to the sea, so that tillage was confined to narrow strips near the fjords and to individual farms hewn out of the forest. A large proportion of the Norwegian population fished for a livelihood. The extensive forests of both Norway and Sweden provided the lumber, pitch, and tar exported in huge quantities, especially to the Netherlands and other comparatively treeless lands. The invention of a water-powered saw in the early sixteenth century permitted the rapid development of the lumbering industry in Norway. Sweden possessed another important asset in its large deposits of iron and copper ore; the famed Copper Mountain (Kopparberg) was intensively mined.

The Union of Kalmar. The Union of Kalmar in 1397 had recorded agreement among the three countries to accept the same monarch upon their separate thrones, but it had also provided for the preservation of their individual statehood and governments. It had not removed the two crucial difficulties in the way of preserving the Union: the conflicts of interest between its member peoples, and their continuing right separately to elect their kings.

There was general discontent in Norway with the petty tyrannies of the officials; most of them were Danes over whom the king—a resident of Denmark—had little control. Nonetheless the country accepted Danish domination without major resistance. There was no native class able to take up the challenge of the Danes. The burghers and the nobility were few in numbers and small in wealth, while the peasantry and fisherfolk lived in widely scattered farms and settlements with little tradition of sustained collaboration over large areas.

The Swedes, on the other hand, resisted Danish control almost from the beginning of the Union. They had a powerful sense of nationhood. Neither the peasantry, tightly knit into vigorous village communities, nor the nobility, proud and accustomed to leadership, took kindly to rule by foreign kings and foreign officials. The Swedes did not consider their right of electing their kings a mere formality, and repeatedly rejected the Danish choice, especially after the advent of the Oldenburg dynasty in Denmark in 1448. Time and again the Danish kings reconquered Sweden; but the Swedes did not stay on their knees.

Breakup of the Union. Christian II, who was elected to the Danish and Norwegian thrones in 1513, came close to final triumph over the Swedes. A skilled administrator and eager reformer, he was also avid for absolute power and did not scorn any means for achieving it. His philosophy of government was set forth in a conversation with Erasmus, who criticized Luther's violent attacks upon the church. "Weak medicines do no good," he told the great Christian humanist. "The best and most effective remedies are those which make the whole body shake and tremble."

When in 1516 the Swedish regent, Sten Sture, attacked the Archbishop Gustav Trolle, the leader of the pro-Danish party, Christian applied these principles. He defeated Sture's peasant armies in 1518 and then two years later, in Stockholm, executed more than 600 of Sture's followers—among them the flower of the Swedish nobility and burghers—despite a promise of amnesty. Armed resistance flared up again under the command of Gustavus Erikson Vasa, son of one of the victims of the "Stockholm massacre." Disguised as a cowherd, Vasa escaped from captivity in Denmark and organized an army to liberate Sweden; the peasants and miners of Dalarna (Dalecarlia) formed the main body of his troops. By 1523, with the aid of loans from

Lübeck, Vasa drove the Danes from all Sweden except the Scanian provinces. In the same year the Swedes elected him king as Gustavus I Vasa.

Downfall of Christian II. The year 1523 was also that of Christian's downfall in his native land. He had pressed the royal power beyond his ability to maintain it. He made an enemy of the Catholic church by depriving it of the right to receive gifts and forbidding it to appeal to Rome against his decisions. He offended the nobility by limiting its rights of local government and by attempting to prevent the continued decline of the once-free peasantry into serfdom. Yet neither the bourgeoisie nor the peasantry was willing to pay in heavily increased taxation for the benefits they received from him.

The nobles, acting upon the right granted them in Christian's electoral charter to throw off their allegiance if he violated its provisions, rose in rebellion and in 1523 placed his cousin the duke of Holstein upon the throne as Frederick I. Christian fled to the Netherlands, where his brother-in-law Charles V ruled. Henceforth a Machiavellian without weapons, Christian beseeched the assistance of others to aid his restoration. Not till the death of Frederick I a decade later did Charles agree to help; then he gave Christian enough assistance in ships and troops to enable him to launch an invasion of Norway, whence he hoped to reconquer Denmark itself. But Frederick's son and successor, Christian III, defeated and captured Christian, his cousin, and kept him prisoner until his death in 1559.

The chief accomplishment of Frederick I's reign was to facilitate the spread of Lutheran beliefs; the new faith became the religion of state under Christian III. Christian deprived the bishops of their jurisdiction, both temporal and spiritual, and confiscated the property of the church. This new wealth tripled the king's annual revenue. It enabled him to build a more efficient and obedient administration, to place a fleet of some thirty ships upon the adjacent seas, and thus to make Denmark the strongest of Baltic states.

The Internal Changes in Denmark. In spite of these gains, the Danish monarchy became increasingly dependent on the aristocracy, its principal domestic rival for power. To maintain himself, Christian III had to abandon his predecessor's policy of relying upon the middle and lower classes. The kingship remained elective, and the practice of enforcing an electoral capitulation upon a new monarch eroded the royal power. The nobility expanded their estates and took an increasing role in the government of the country as appointed officials. In their self-esteem and confidence, they began to prevent the entry of new families into their ranks by either ennoblement or marriage, and became a closed caste, with narrow interests and loyalties.

The bourgeoisie, though barred from movement up the social scale, benefited by the prosperity of the country. The Hanseatic merchants lost their privileges, particularly after the unsuccessful effort of Lübeck, under

The Expansion of Sweden, to 1660

its mayor, Jürgen Wullenwever, to impose its candidate for the Danish throne against Christian III in 1533. The profits from the increasing Danish exports of cattle, wheat, and butter thereafter went to Danes instead of to Germans. The peasantry got no such recompense. Their conditions grew worse, the grip of serfdom tighter, and the hope of justice at the hands of a strong and friendly king less and less.

Christian IV. Christian IV, who came to the throne in 1588, began his administration by vigorous measures of improvement. He enlarged the har-

367

bors of Copenhagen and other ports, abolished the privileges of the Hansa, encouraged Dutch immigrants to bring their skills to build up the Danish economy, and chartered companies for overseas trade. Nonetheless the net effect of his rule upon Denmark was one of woes and burdens.

The rivalry with Sweden over the issue of Skåne, which Gustavus Vasa had not been able to wrest from Denmark, resulted in two wars during the reign of Christian. The first (1611-1613) was inconclusive. The common Protestant interest of Denmark and Sweden in the Thirty Years' War dampened their ardor for resuming the struggle for three decades. Christian's intervention in the German war ended in his utter defeat in 1629, and a war which began with Sweden four years later turned out no more successfully. The Swedish army, tested and toughened in Germany, was a foe of unanticipated prowess. The Danes, badly defeated, gave up to the Swedes one of the Scanian provinces, Halland, as well as territory in Norway, which had remained within the personal union with Denmark; Swedish ships were also exempted from payment of the Sound dues. The Dutch, by this time the principal carriers in the Baltic trade, thereupon compelled the Danes to grant them similar exemption. Although the Dutch paid a blanket sum in lieu of dues, the Danish revenues from this source fell almost two-thirds. When Christian IV died in 1648, he bequeathed to his son Frederick III an impoverished country, a weakened crown, and a thirst for revenge.

Gustavus Vasa. Sweden's freedom had been won by the efforts and sacrifices of all classes in the population under the leadership of a chosen king. The problem for Gustavus Vasa was whether he could wield these same forces in the work of peace as well.

Before Gustavus could make much progress with consolidating the power of the state as well as his own power within the state, he found it necessary to affirm his control over the church. He needed the clergy in order to influence the people in his favor, and the wealth it controlled as the richest landowner in the nation, holding more than 20 per cent of the land in the country as compared to the crown's 5 per cent. (The nobility held another 20 per cent, and the tax paying peasantry the rest.) Since the war of independence had also been directed against the pro-Danish archbishop Gustav Trolle, the king asked the papacy to confirm his own candidate John Magnusson in Trolle's place. Rome, expecting that his power would soon collapse, refused, and ordered Trolle's reinstatement. To make matters worse, the Swedish clergy rejected Gustavus's request for a subsidy to help cover the indebtedness accumulated during the war. These two rebuffs outraged the king and led him to break with the papacy and introduce the Lutheran Reformation. In 1527 the diet of Västerås severed the church of Sweden from Rome and placed it under the control of the king. It gave the bishops' palaces and lands to the crown, together with their tithes, and ordered the restitution to the nobility of gifts received from them since the mid-fifteenth century.

The changeover to the new faith did not proceed peaceably, particularly since it came at the same time as high taxes required to pay off Gustavus's debt to Lübeck. A half-dozen peasant rebellions between 1525 and 1543 kept the new dynasty on the edge of disaster. The most dangerous was that of the peasants of Dalarna, who had fought so well for him in the war of independence that they boasted that they had "put King Gus in the high seat." The king crushed the insurrections by force.

Nonetheless he adopted a peaceful foreign policy in order to avoid additional impositions upon the population. He did not take up arms to attempt to overturn the continued Danish preponderance of strength in the Baltic, but was satisfied to remove the heavy hand of the Lübeckers from Swedish trade by abolishing their special privileges in 1537. At the same time, he proceeded with modernization of the state. He established a systematic centralized administration with adequate regular finances, and a regular army under his direct command, instead of levies from the peasantry and the nobility. He did not tamper with the traditional constitution of the country, which provided for a share in government for the parliament (Riksdag) in which sat representatives of the peasantry as well as of the nobility, clergy, and townsmen.

By the time of the king's death in 1560, he had largely carried through his great work of reorganization. He had kept the nobility friendly, but strictly controlled. Less than one-third of the country remained outside the direct administration of the crown. The exploitation of the country's resources was being encouraged by protective measures as well as by exemplary operation of the crown's estates and by royal supervision of the mines, which improved their equipment on the latest German lines. Finally, the crown had been made hereditary in the king's male line, ending the hazards of the elective principle.

The Sons of Gustavus Vasa. The three sons who followed Gustavus Vasa upon the throne—Erik XIV, John III, and Charles IX—did not understand the necessity for the prudent foreign policy which their father had followed. They took the strength of the Swedish monarchy for granted, not having struggled as he had to build it up. Like their fellow kings in other lands, they wished to earn glory in the proper way, by wars of conquest. During his lifetime, Gustavus had prevented them from carrying out their plans; after his death, they became openly bold and even reckless.

The principal Swedish effort was directed across the Baltic Sea, toward the conquest and control of the eastern shores. In 1561 much of Estonia was captured, together with its principal port Tallinn (Reval). Swedish interest in maintaining this acquisition led to the termination of a seven-years' war with Denmark in 1570, and the waging of a war with Russia from 1571 to 1577; only the alliance of the Polish king, Stephen Báthory, enabled the Swedes to maintain their hold in Estonia.

These friendly relations with Poland had been tightened when John III replaced his brother Erik XIV in 1568 after a fierce civil war. John married Catherine Jagiello, of the Polish royal dynasty; their son Sigismund became heir to the Polish as well as to the Swedish crown. The Articles of Kalmar of 1587 provided for a personal union fated for an even swifter failure than the union made almost two centuries earlier at the same place between the Scandinavian lands. John was a quasi-Catholic, and his son an outright adherent of the Roman faith. To prevent Sigismund's accession in 1592, on his father's death, his uncle Charles, last of Gustavus Vasa's sons and leader of the Protestant party, turned his arms against his Catholic nephew and finally defeated him in 1598. Six years later Sigismund and his line were declared to have forfeited the crown of Sweden; Charles, who had governed the country as regent, was proclaimed as king in his stead. The Protestant Reformation in Sweden was confirmed by a law barring Catholics from succession to the throne and from all offices in the state; those who remained steadfast in the old faith were ordered deprived of their wealth and exiled from the country.

Charles IX, who came to power by war, continued to be a man of war during the seven years of his reign. His one important innovation in domestic policy was to introduce a form of conscription; the country was divided into districts which were required to furnish the royal army with a fixed number of recruits. Charles intervened in Russia during the Time of Troubles (see p. 381 later in this chapter) in an unsuccessful effort to place a Swedish tsar upon the Muscovite throne. He also shattered the forty years of peace with Denmark by claiming Norwegian territory in the Northland, at the upper end of the Scandinavian peninsula. The war, which began in 1611, the year of his death, was brief; but in two years the cruelty and depredations of both sides turned into hatred the earlier mistrust between the Danes and the Norwegians on the one side and the Swedes on the other.

Gustavus Adolphus. Gustavus II Adolphus, who succeeded his father in 1611, just short of his seventeenth birthday, began his reign as a man of peace. He brought the wars with Denmark and Muscovy to an end, and devoted himself for ten years to tasks of internal consolidation. He reorganized the administrative system upon the basis of specialized councils (or "colleges") with particular tasks; he made the Riksråd (national council) the supreme instrument of his authority. He did not attempt to throw over the Riksdag (parliament) but instead reorganized it upon a firm basis, with fixed rules and regular representation from the nobility, the clergy, the townsmen, and the peasantry, each sitting in its own chamber. By keeping the initiative of legislation and taxation in his own hands, but seeking the approval of the Riksdag for his own projects, Gustavus Adolphus was able to be master of his policy and at the same time to win for it the approval of the nation.

In 1621 Gustavus Adolphus at last took up the challenge to his throne from his Catholic cousin, Sigismund III, who reigned in Poland and claimed Sweden as his birthright. Gustavus's concern for his crown and his faith was reinforced by a desire to consolidate the Baltic conquests of Sweden. He conquered Livonia, the province south of Estonia, but made little progress against the Poles in Prussia. In 1629, appalled by the drain of the war upon his finances, he made a truce confirming temporarily his possession of Livonia and other parts of the Baltic shoreline. He also obtained the right to levy tolls in the ports under his control; these dues gave him in 1629 a half-million rixdollars, as much all told as the Swedish parliament had granted him in extraordinary taxation in support of the war. The Baltic port tolls thereafter became one of the essential pillars of the Swedish fiscal structure, and hence of the increasing power of the Swedish state.

These resources were strained to the utmost when Gustavus Adolphus intervened in 1632 in the Thirty Years' War (see ch. 14, p. 330). He began, and Axel Oxenstierna continued after his death in 1534, the system of making the Germans pay for the Swedish expenses of war. Nonetheless the Swedish government was compelled also to summon up all the home strength it could manage. The Dutch were called in to assist in exploitation of Sweden's forest and mineral wealth, and the export of copper became one of the principal sources of the government's revenue. The Dutch established their control over most of the country's commerce and mining, at the very same time when Gustavus Adolphus sought to make Sweden economically more independent by measures of mercantilism. (See ch. 26, pp. 586-587, for a discussion of mercantilism.)

Oxenstierna, who governed Sweden during the minority of Gustavus Adolphus's daughter Christina, was unable to maintain the Swedish position in Germany at the high point to which the warrior king had brought it. He salvaged much, however, in the Westphalia peace negotiations, so that Sweden obtained 5,000,000 rixdollars for her expenses, and gained possession of Hither Pomerania, Wismar, and the secularized bishoprics of Verden and Bremen, with a seat in the Reichstag and a status as guarantor of the treaty, along with France. Sweden thus became the great power in the North and the pre-eminent Scandinavian state.

II. The Slav States

During the early modern period, both the large independent Slav countries—Poland and Russia—underwent major internal changes and entered more and more closely into the general system of European politics.

Poland: Republic and Monarchy. Poland was a country of the plains. The very name *Polska* meant "(the land) of the field (or plain) dwellers." Occupying, together with its associated state the grand duchy of Lithuania, the breadth of the European continent between the Baltic and the Black seas, Poland lacked natural barriers both on the west facing Germany and on the east facing Russia. The Silesian hills to the south gave some protection, but the Baltic Sea was another avenue for possible invaders. Thus open to attack from several directions, Poland had greater need of a strong state to guard it than any other land in Europe.

This need was magnified because the inhabitants lacked that cohesion which arose from a common language and religion. Poles, the most numerous element in a population of perhaps 6,000,000, were a Slavic people. In speech, therefore, they were related to the Little Russians (the present-day Ukrainians) of the southeast and the White Russians of the northeast. But the Poles were Roman Catholic and the Little and White Russians Greek Orthodox. The Lithuanians, who spoke a language of the Baltic family, were divided between Catholicism and Orthodoxy. Germans formed a large part of the population of the cities, especially in the west. Though Catholic in religion like the Poles at the beginning of the sixteenth century, they remained strongly attached to the civilization and language of Germany. The Jews, who formed another large segment of the urban population, spoke a German dialect. Their continued adherence to their ancient religion, as well as the frequently exploitative character of the few occupations they were permitted to follow, brought upon them the hostility of the general population.

Despite the perils from foreign incursions and internal disruption, the Polish state evolved a pattern which gave liberty and power to a few and security to none. It was a monarchy imbued with the spirit and furnished with the institutions of a republic; a republic, however, in which a single class, the gentry, pre-empted the name of "the people" to the exclusion of all others born in the land.

The Gentlemen of Poland. The pre-eminence of the gentry (*szlachta*) arose from a combination of economic and political advantages. As the landowning class, they had reaped the benefits of the economic prosperity which came to Poland during the fifteenth and sixteenth centuries from supplying grain and other products of field and forest to western Europe. The peasants lost by the changes. The Constitution of Piotrków (1497) deprived them of their personal freedom and bound them to the estates on

East Central Europe
in 1559

which they had been born. Whether or not they had been the owners of
their lands or rent-paying tenants, they were compelled to give labor service
of from one to three days a week to the landlords. After centuries of freedom,
the peasantry were again forced back into complete serfdom; in 1518, they
were placed under the sole jurisdiction of the gentry, without a right of
appeal to the royal courts.

The *szlachta* took pride in the fact that it was a "noble" (or "gentle")
class without a hierarchy of ranks; indeed, a law adopted during the sixteenth century barred the use of titles imitated from abroad, like "duke" or
"count." The *szlachta* defended with vigor the privileged legal status of its
members, the "poor gentlemen" who lived little better than the peasants as
well as the estate-owners of moderate means and the wealthy magnates.

When the Renaissance brought in the political doctrines of Greek and
Roman antiquity, the thinkers of the *szlachta* developed a doctrine of republican liberties and popular rule as bold as any in Europe. In practice this
republicanism meant that the gentry was able to enforce its will upon the
king, or at least to prevent him from enforcing his will upon them, without
at the same time taking upon itself the responsibility of central government.

Since the extinction of the native founding dynasty, the Piasts, in 1370, the *szlachta* had expanded its powers at the expense of the crown's. The Jagiello kings, who had followed the Piasts, had not ruled by hereditary right but had been elected by the nobility. Whenever a weak monarch or one beset by difficulties came to the throne, the gentry extracted from him concessions which by the beginning of the sixteenth century made them the only class in the country with political rights.

The Diet (Sejm) and "little Diets" (Sejmiki) were the instruments of the *szlachta's* power. The Diet comprised a Senate in which sat the bishops and the principal holders of state office, and a Chamber of Deputies elected by the Sejmiki and bound by their instructions. The towns had no representation in the Diet, with the single exception of a deputy from Cracow, the capital. The Constitution of Radom, adopted in 1505, established the principle that no new law could be made without the assent of the Diet. At the same time, the rule began to be followed that unanimity of the deputies was required for acceptance of a law, and that a single negative vote brought the meeting of a Diet to an end ("exploded" it, in the vivid technical term). The right of *liberum veto* ("free veto") was used infrequently during the sixteenth century, but came into practice during the following century. There were parallels to the *liberum veto* in other countries, but nothing like another Polish institution, the *rokosz*, or legalized insurrection, employed as an instrument of ordinary politics instead of as the ultimate argument in cases involving the very structure or existence of the state.

The base of the *szlachta's* power lay in the "little Diets," where the magnates had less influence. Most taxes were collected by the Sejmiki, who retained them for their own use. They also recruited and paid for the troops of the Republic at the request of the Diet.

The King of Poland. The king's only standing army was a bodyguard of a few thousand soldiers. He could afford no more. The crown revenues were confined to the income from the crown lands and were inadequate even to pay the wages of a professional administration. High officials held their posts by inheritance and could be removed by the ruler only with the consent of the Senate.

The throne of Poland nonetheless remained a coveted office. It gave its occupant the title and dignity of king in an age that placed rank high and often first in its standards of value. Limited though the royal power was, it could be used effectively. A monarch like Stephen Báthory, who reigned from 1575 to 1586, was able by guile and charm to carry the *szlachta* along with him in an active foreign policy. At the worst, a king could thwart his opponents even if he could not attain his own positive purposes.

The kings made repeated efforts to make Poland bigger and more powerful. Their major success was the consolidation of the union with Lithuania, begun with the advent of the Jagiellos in 1370 and completed in 1569 with the Union of Lublin. By the Lublin accord, Poland and Lithuania agreed to elect their sovereign—king in the former state, grand duke in the latter—in common, and to have one diet and one currency; but the administrative systems and officers of state remained separate, as before. Lithuania transferred to Poland its possessions in the Little Russian area in the southeast, involving thereafter the Polish crown and gentry directly in the conflict with the Muscovite state over the fertile although thinly peopled region.

Polish efforts at territorial and political aggrandizement sooner or later fell short, whenever the *szlachta* began to feel the pinch of increased taxes. They were more willing to risk their lives in gallant cavalry charges than to spend their money. Alexander I, who lost control of the region east of the Dnieper river to Muscovy, summed up in a single sentence the story of his ill-fated reign: "It is vain to labor for the welfare of those who do not care a jot about it themselves." The gentry, indeed, looked to the king to give them money, and not the reverse. They were pleased with Wladyslaw IV (1632-1648), a free-handed monarch, because he was "a king bee who will give us nothing but honey"; but when he attempted a bold and active foreign policy, they left him in the lurch. As a result of the uncertain and usually inadequate support of the *szlachta*, the kings were not able to prevent Sweden from establishing its control over the Baltic provinces, thereby cutting Poland from its own seacoast. Sigismund III could not make good his claim to the Swedish crown, nor was he able to make his son Wladyslaw tsar of Russia. An even more momentous failure was the loss of most of the Ukraine (Little Russia) to Tsar Alexei as the result of the revolt of the Cossacks under Bogdan Khmelnitsky (Chmielnicki) in 1648-1657.

Muscovy. At the start of the early modern period, the least well-known of all the European states was Muscovy, the land of the Russians. It was a distant, landlocked, and inaccessible principality whose strongest historical ties linked it to the Byzantine empire, now conquered by the Ottoman Turks. Yet it was an essentially European state and society, though in most respects at an earlier stage of development than the countries to the west.

Muscovy was then neither very large nor thickly peopled. It occupied a wide band of forested plain—"flat as a maple leaf, made by God for man to use," according to the peasant proverb—to the east of Poland-Lithuania, between the Arctic Ocean to the north and the treeless semiarid steppe to the south. The most useful system of communications was a network of rivers, some running north and northwest, others south and southeast, which arose in the neighborhood of Moscow. In the spring, after the passage of the thaw floods, these streams provided a route for shallow-draft vessels; in the winter, frozen hard, they were natural roads for sleds.

The population of Muscovy was principally Russians, the easternmost of the Slavic peoples. Mingled with the Russians, especially in the north and to the east, were many indigenous peoples. They spoke a variety of languages, many of the Finnish linguistic family, and most of them were still in a tribal stage of life.

The population was small because Russia remained economically backward. The Russian still retained much of the woodsman in his life. Although most persons by the fifteenth century earned their livelihood from agriculture, there were many who continued to gather objects of use and export, like furs and honey, from the forest. It was not long since the primitive slash-and-burn system of clearing temporary farmlands out of the forest had been in wide use, and it still had not come to an end everywhere. In general, however, tillage land was permanently cleared and was maintained according to the three-field system (see ch. 2, pp. 29-30). Some peasants rented land from landowners, others from the state. The presence of nearby uncultivated land in the forest and the shortage of labor kept the conditions of the peasantry at a higher level of prosperity than it had been during the previous centuries. There were signs, however, of increasing pressure to fix the peasant upon the soil and compel him to labor for the landowners at higher rentals or lower pay.

The landlords were a gentry much like the Polish *szlachta*, owning their estates by freehold (the *votchina*, or "father's land," as it was called). At the end of the fifteenth century, they still remained legally equal, with the common name of "boyars." The only exceptions were the princes and the "little princes" (*kniazhata*). The princes, as descendants of Rurik, the Scandinavian founder of the Russian state, shared in the possessions of the reigning dynasty, while the "little princes" were so named because they, or their ancestors, had once ruled independent principalities which had been incorporated into the grand principality of Moscow.

The Muscovite Principality. The Russian state, like the Russian economy, was forest-born. The grand princes of Moscow had built the principality of Moscow in the wooded country just north of the steppe. There they, and their subjects, found escape from the constant threat of the Mongols (Tatars) of the Golden Horde, who commanded the open treeless plain from their capital at Sarai, on the lower Volga. The princes of Moscow had grown strong by serving the khans of the Horde as their tribute collectors, but in the late fifteenth century had thrown off the Mongol overlordship. Thereafter Muscovy had a unique position among European states: its neighbors on the north and east were not highly organized states but primitive tribal communities of small numbers. Thus there remained an outlet for Russian population growth by colonial expansion into the adjacent territories of Asiatic Siberia. Furthermore, if and when Russia began a political

East Central Europe
after 1660

Habsburg Domains

expansion westward, it had no need to fear the assaults of powerful and unfriendly states on its other borders.

The Muscovite state was based on a strong dynastic conception. The country was considered to be the patrimony (*votchina*) of the ruling family, which they ruled by right of ownership. The individual princes received lifetime grants of apanages for their support. This system did not exclude, however, the notion of private property in land. The peasants bought and sold "the prince's land in our possession," so that dual rights of ownership, the prince's and the peasants', existed in practice. The state revenues included both rents from the crown lands, and taxes, paid by the peasants, from all other estates.

Ivan III, "Autocrat." The creation of a single Russian state was principally the work of Ivan III, who reigned as grand prince of Muscovy from 1462 to 1505. His first big achievement was to halt payment of tribute to the Golden Horde after the khan avoided battle with him in 1480. To indicate his absolute sovereignty, Ivan took the title of "autocrat." His ambitions swelled to include the heritage of Byzantium's imperial status and political pre-eminence. In line with this image of himself, Ivan took as his second

377

wife Zoë Paleologus, niece of the last Byzantine emperor. After the fall of Constantinople, she had been brought up in Italy as a Catholic, and had been approved as Ivan's bride by the Vatican. Zoë, renamed Sophia, disappointed the papacy's hope that she would convert her husband and his realm to Catholicism, but she favored the development of the theory that Moscow was the "third Rome."

This doctrine was proclaimed in 1492 by the monk Philotheus. "Two Romes have fallen," he wrote. "The third Rome will be Moscow, and there will never be a fourth." According to this conception, the Muscovite prince derived his powers from God. As God's vicar, he was beyond control by human beings. But he was obligated to use his autocratic powers in defense of God's "true church"—Orthodoxy—and on behalf of the people. Thus two notions of the state—the proprietary, emphasizing the prince's powers, and the divine, emphasizing his duties—took their place alongside each other. At the moment, they reinforced each other, but events could drive them into conflict.

Boyars and "Service Men." The theory of autocracy was accompanied by practice, and the semi-independent boyars were its first victims. Hitherto they had served the prince in his armies and government on a voluntary basis, maintaining the right to withdraw and even to transfer their allegiance to another prince. Ivan III began to enforce the system of obligatory service by all subjects. Instead of depending on the recalcitrant boyars, he promoted lesser men to positions of authority, and provided for their maintenance—for salaries were nearly meaningless in the absence of a widespread commodity system—by means of estates granted for the duration of their duty (*pomiestie*). With these "service men," Ivan began the establishment of permanent administrative bureaus (*prikazi*), some for the government of territorial districts and others for general tasks like the maintenance of the army. Rudimentary as the *prikazi* were, they made it possible for the Muscovite state to rule effectively over a wide territory.

Ivan's work of expansion and consolidation was continued under his eldest son Vassili III, who reigned until 1533. The apanaged princes lost all political powers, as did the boyars and "little princes." In recompense, however, they received a system of ranks, the *chin*, assigning to each a place of precedence according to the post held by his fathers, and guaranteeing to him tasks of the same honorific level. Without obtaining the hereditary titles of the Western European nobility, the Russian aristocracy was approaching it in structure and aspirations.

Ivan IV, "Tsar." When Vassili died in 1533, his son Ivan IV was only three years old. His mother Helen, serving as regent, fought off the attempts of the boyars and princes to regain their political influence. When she died five years later, the young prince fell under the control of the Shuisky faction. Andrei Shuisky, who prided himself on being descended from Rurik, like Ivan, treated the boy with insolent scorn. When Ivan reached the age of thirteen, he threw off this tyranny. The pikemen of his bodyguard slew Shuisky at the prince's command. Shuisky gone, Ivan aspired to play the part of autocrat. He possessed the will but not yet the knowledge and the skill. He depended upon advisers and resented the dependency. In order to place himself on a rank with the kings of Europe and with the Holy Roman emperor himself, Ivan in 1547 took the title of "tsar" (meaning "caesar"), the Russian appellation for the Byzantine emperor.

A period of calm government followed for thirteen years. Ivan took as his advisors the archpriest Silvester and the minor nobleman Alexei Adashov, who combined unusual intelligence with deep human sympathy. Under their inspiration, Ivan introduced a series of reforms designed to tie the tsardom closer to the nation. A legal code (the *Sudebnik* of 1550) established courts with elected judges sitting beside appointed ones. The peasant village community, the *mir*, was given increased responsibilities and a measure of self-government, although the right of the peasant to move about in search of better conditions was restricted. The service obligation of the nobility was extended, and they received *pomiestie* for purposes of revenue only and not of administration.

The Rule of Terror. The boyars stirred restlessly as they saw the strengthening of the state and the direction of its policy. Their mutterings convinced Ivan that enemies were everywhere around him, plotting to kill him. He began to feel that Silvester's and Adashov's policy was too gentle, and in 1560 he dismissed them, sending the archpriest to a monastery and Adashov to exile in the frigid north.

Ruled by his fears, often veering over into apparent insanity, Ivan imposed fourteen years of public terror upon Russia. His instrument of frightfulness was the *oprichnina*, which was at once a parallel government, a bodyguard, and a secret police, provided with its own estates. The *oprichniki*, who shared the violent debaucheries of Ivan's personal life, ranged over the countryside killing without trial or explanation. Their victims were mainly the boyars and lesser princes. By the time Ivan died in 1584, many of the boyars were gone. Only a single Shuisky survived—but not the tsar's eldest son, slain by his father in a fit of rage. The epithet *Grozny* ("stern" or "fear-inspiring"—"terrible" in its sixteenth-century meaning) was given to Ivan.

In his endeavor to expand his state and prove his greatness by an aggressive foreign policy, Ivan IV met both success and failure. Against the declining khanates of the southeastern plain he did well. In 1551 he took Kazan, the key to the valley of the lower Volga, and five years later Astrakhan, near its mouth. When he shifted his armies to the Baltic, in an effort to take the Livonian provinces, the Swedes and Poles were too much for him. In 1582 he abandoned his claims to Livonia. The closing of the Russian trade route on the Baltic was compensated in some part by the opening of the White Sea route by the Englishman Chancellor. In the same year, however, a Cossack captain named Ermak, acting on behalf of the trading family of the Stroganovs, conquered the basin of the Ob and Irtysh rivers and began Russian penetration into Siberia, the forested plain of Asia north of the steppe. It was a movement little noted abroad, and apparently unimportant compared to the loss of Livonia; but it was a sustained, relatively peaceful conquest which after several centuries gave the tsars an immense continental empire.

Half-senseless savagery did not make the Russian state strong, as Ivan had hoped. On his death, it slipped into a decline, and then into a headlong fall, from which it was rescued by the resurgence of the nation, acting of its own will and on its own behalf.

Boris Godunov. Fedor (Theodore), a younger son who succeeded Ivan in 1584, was a living mockery of his father's ambitions. He was weak of mind and purpose, and would have been helpless before the remnants of the boyar nobility had it not been for his brother-in-law, Boris Godunov. Boris, who had managed to survive the reign of Ivan without being stamped with the *oprichnik* terror, became regent and ruled wisely and skillfully for fourteen years. He sought to heal the wounds of the past and to reconcile the principal groups in the nation. The service men, or new nobility, supported him in this purpose, but he could win few of the old boyars to his side. They were jealous of his power and accused him of personal ambition. When the tsar's half-brother and heir, Dmitri, died of a slashed throat in 1591 in a mysterious playtime accident, the charge was placed upon Boris. The finding of a court that Dmitri had cut himself during an epileptic fit was rejected by his enemies as rigged.

On Fedor's death in 1598, his widow Irene abdicated, and for the first time it became necessary to elect a tsar. Boris was named by the Zemski Sobor (assembly of the land)—a quasi diet comprising leading nobles, churchmen, officials, and townsmen—over the rival candidacy of Fedor Romanov, a cousin of the late monarch. Boris was able to continue his policy of mildness for several years, and sought to relieve as best he could the hardships of famine and plague which struck the country from 1601 to 1604.

Out of the intrigues of Boris's opponents arose in 1603 a new foe, a youth who claimed to be the heir Dmitri, miraculously escaped from death twelve years before. The "False Dmitri" crossed into Poland, where he won the support of the court, and with the aid of Polish troops invaded Russia to seize the throne. Boris accused the boyars: "This is the work of your

hands." He defeated the impostor in 1604, and died the next year. His son
Fedor ascended the throne, but was soon overturned by the army and slain.

The Time of Troubles. Eight years of political and social upheaval followed, known in Russian history as the Time of Troubles. The Russian state
and Russian society were pushed to the verge of destruction and disintegration.

The False Dmitri, recognized by the boyars as tsar in 1605, undid his rule
by his own flightiness and ineptness. He permitted his Polish followers to lord
it over the Russians and allowed his wife, the Polish noblewoman Marina
Mniszech, to practice her Roman Catholic faith in Moscow, to the indignation
of the Orthodox. In 1606 he was overthrown and killed in a revolt led by
Vassili Shuiski, who was elected tsar by a crowd assembled on the Red Square
before the Kremlin in Moscow.

A new threat rose up out of the depths of Russian society, bringing to
bear against Vassili all the accumulated hatreds and aspirations of the various groups in the nation. In the southwest both the peasantry and the
nobility took up arms against the tsar. For a while they fought together, but
when the peasants began to kill landlords and the rich generally, Vassili was
able to defeat them separately. One peril passed, another came up at once.
Another False Dmitri, combining the character of a peasant rebel, a common
bandit, and a political adventurer, organized another revolt against Vassili.
Known as "the thief of Tushino" from his encampment outside Moscow,
this impostor ravaged the countryside far and wide. Swedish troops entered
the country to aid Shuiski at his request (1608), followed by Poles a year
later acting on their own account. The Poles seized Moscow and attempted
to put a Polish candidate on the throne as tsar.

Shuiski, his hopes dashed and his power lost, fled to a monastery in
1610. The nation was left to its own resources. The first call to lay down
the old quarrels and combine against the Poles came from the clergy, led
by the monks of Troitsko-Sergievo east of Moscow, and by the patriarch.
A Zemski Sobor was formed, which took upon itself the organization of
resistance. It was more than a year before Moscow was taken and months
longer before the Polish garrison in the Kremlin capitulated.

The Romanov Dynasty. In 1613 the Zemski Sobor met again in Moscow
to elect a tsar. Foreign candidates were swept aside without consideration.
Michael Romanov, too young to have chosen sides in the war and linked to
the extinct Rurik dynasty by marriage, was named tsar. Order was quickly
re-established throughout the country. The Peace of Stolbovo was patched up
with the Swedes in 1617, at the price of losing the shoreline of the gulf of
Finland to them. Soon afterward, an armistice was made with the Poles, who
held the White Russian territories west of a line running through Kiev and
Smolensk.

Michael reigned, but his father Fedor, who had become a monk under the name of Filaret, and then patriarch, governed. He acted with energy and boldness, especially in foreign affairs, but the Zemski Sobor resisted his costly enterprises. On Michael's death in 1645, he was followed by his son Alexei. There was no election, for the late tsar's death-bed designation was accepted without question although no law of succession had been enacted.

Alexei's reign was soon marked by renewed popular insurrections. Though himself a gentle monarch, with a taste for art, his government put heavy burdens on the people. The worst of these was the quadrupling of the salt tax. In some cities millions of pounds of fresh fish from the rivers were allowed to spoil because the population would not or could not pay the increased cost of salt. Rioting broke out in 1648 in Moscow and spread to other cities. The next year the salt and tax monopolies were abolished. The next major riot took place in Moscow in 1663 when the silver coinage was replaced by copper money of less value; the *streltsi* (musketeers) of the tsar's bodyguard put down this disorder, but the silver currency was brought back. A Cossack revolt led by the legendary Stenka Razin broke out five years later, and held large areas of the southeast under its control before it was crushed by regular troops.

The Cossacks, Poland, and Russia. The most important event of Alexei's reign was the incorporation of Little Russia into the Muscovite state. This was the steppeland south of the forest, known in Russian as the "frontier country," or *Ukraine*. It had been absorbed into Lithuania during the period when the princes of Moscow had been active "gathering in" the Great Russian lands. After the Union of Lublin of 1569 it had been incorporated into Polish crown territory. The Poles attempted to introduce their own social and economic arrangements into the Ukraine, but met sharp resistance from the local population.

The leaders of the Ukrainian people were a conglomerate group known as the Cossacks, semisoldiers, semibandits. They had been recruited over the decades, especially after the withdrawal of the Tatars in the early sixteenth century, from persons fleeing the increasing oppression of the peasantry in Russia and Poland alike. Orthodox in religion, they resisted especially the efforts of the Poles to bring in Roman Catholicism. The Poles had endeavored to make use of the Cossacks' military prowess, and at the same time to limit their numbers by "registering" them. The Poles were unable, however, to bring under their control the Cossacks who held the region beyond the rapids on the Dnieper river.

It was from these Zaporozhe ("beyond the rapids") Cossacks that a rebellion against Poland broke out in 1648, under the leadership of the hetman (commander) Khmelnitsky. The Polish nobility, along with the

Russia in 1682

Catholic clergy and the Jews who had served as their estate managers, fled to Poland. A treaty of peace with the Poles was short-lived, and in 1654 Khmelnitsky accepted the overlordship of Russia. A war between Russia and Poland began which lasted until 1667, when they signed the armistice of Andrusovo, by which Russia retained the territory east of the Dnieper river, along with Kiev and a small region west of the river. The Ukraine remained a mainly self-governing Cossack state under Russian rule, but tension arose between the peasants, who had made themselves free proprietors under Khmelnitsky, and the Cossack leaders, who adopted the habits and attitude of a class of landowners.

Changing Russia. With the southern frontier closed off and the Ukraine no longer a refuge from oppression, the long efforts of the government and the nobility to prevent the peasants from moving about freely succeeded. The position of the peasantry within Russia rapidly became more difficult. Serfdom of a rigorous kind began to be enforced.

At the same time, the status of the nobility began to improve. The distinction between the old boyar aristocracy and the new service nobility became thin. The service nobility won the right to keep their estates as hereditary possessions, while the owners of patrimonial estates were compelled to do military service and forbidden to transfer their allegiance to other states.

During the period of Michael's and Alexei's reigns (1613-1676), there was growing interest on the part of the government and the nobility in the civilization and intellectual life of western Europe. Those who had contact with foreign lands realized their superior technology and skill in adminis-

383

tration. At the same time, Russian national pride and hatred of the foreigner and all things foreign remained strong.

This conflict between admiration and distaste for the outside world came to a head when Patriarch Nikon, with the encouragement of Tsar Alexei, attempted to revise the liturgy of the Russian church to conform with the earliest practices of Greek Orthodoxy. At a national council meeting in 1656, Nikon declared that "though a Russian and son of a Russian, [I have] the faith and the ideas of a Greek." His reforms consisted not only in issuing carefully collated editions of the sacred books, but also in such details as increasing from two to three the number of "Halleluias" chanted and the number of fingers used in making the sign of the cross. Among the common clergy and in widespread sections of the population, who did not usually understand the Old Slavonic of the services, horror was the response to these changes. A movement of "Old Believers" broke away from the Orthodox church, despite rigorous government repression. Some, seeking refuge in the northern forest lands, committed mass suicide when punitive expeditions came upon them. The schismatics reflected in their opposition to the reforms not only a rigid literalism in religion, but also fear and hatred for the many changes that were taking place in the life of the Russian people generally.

III. The Ottoman Empire

The Ottoman empire belonged geographically to Europe as well as to Asia and Africa, but it remained essentially outside the European system. It was a different kind of society and state, following a different religion and organized in a different way. Nonetheless it concerned Europeans a great deal. To some, it was a military threat, and the memory of the fall of Constantinople in 1453 remained alive. To others, it was a model of military and governmental efficiency, to be studied and when possible imitated.

Military Empire. The Ottoman empire strongly retained the marks of its origin in the military conquest of the Byzantine dominions by a nomadic people out of central Asia. During the fourteenth and fifteenth centuries, they had followed up their earlier conquest of Anatolian Turkey, in Asia Minor, by seizing the whole of the Balkan peninsula, with the capture of Constantinople in 1453 as the capstone of their achievement. The Turkish system of rule, especially in the Balkans, rested upon the traditional methods of the Mongol and Turkic nomads of Asia combined with the similar practices prescribed by the Moslem religion, to which they had been converted. They neither adapted themselves to the civilization of those they conquered, nor required the defeated peoples to adopt the ways of their conquerors. Instead, they permitted the indigenous population, mainly Christians in the

Balkans, to maintain their own communities under the rule of their own clergy or chiefs, so long as they paid tribute to the Ottoman sultan.

A novel method of recruiting the government and the army—without parallel in Europe—was adopted. Those born Turks and Moslems were no longer usually employed in these functions; instead these were entrusted to persons who, though born Christians, had been seized from their parents before they reached manhood. They became slaves of the sultan, but slaves converted and educated as Moslems, to whom the administration of Ottoman power was given. Some were made soldiers, called Janissaries, who distinguished themselves by their ardor and skill on the battlefield. Others became civil administrators, rising even to the lofty post of grand vizier, or chief adviser and executive for the sultan. As long as these slaves were prevented from raising families (some were castrated, others forbidden to take wives), the system worked with extraordinary success; but when, during the sixteenth and especially the seventeenth centuries, they began to marry, they formed a troublesome class which sought to escape its slavery and transform its political role into a position within, rather than over, Turkish society.

Greatness and Decline. The Ottoman state remained in the ascendant from Mohammed II (1451-1481), who destroyed the Byzantine emperor, to Suleiman I (1520-1566), whom the Turks called "the Law Giver" because of his work of consolidation and the Europeans called "the Magnificent" because of his military victories. Under Suleiman's successors, particularly after the loss of the naval battle of Lepanto to a Venetian-Spanish coalition in 1571, the decline in Ottoman power began. The Ottoman state, well adapted to tasks of conquest, proved less fitted for the government of a stable state with a fixed territory.

The pressure upon the European states continued, however, especially along the borders of the Hapsburg realms in Hungary and Austria. It slackened, however, during the period of the Thirty Years' War, permitting the Hapsburgs to concentrate their efforts against their foes in Germany. (See ch. 14.) The main effort of the Sultan during this period was directed toward the conquest of the Venetian-held island of Crete, begun in 1645 and completed in 1664.

The European powers, even those who knew the sting still possessed by the Turk, nonetheless ceased to fear him or to admire him as a master of war and government. The Ottoman empire continued on its way, however, heedless of its decline and scornful of the Christian Europeans.

PART TWO

The Old Regime and
the Revolution

Europe in 1660

LEGEND:
- ▬▬▬ HOLY ROMAN EMPIRE
- HAPSBURG LANDS
  - /// (AUSTRIAN BRANCH)
  - ▓▓ (SPANISH BRANCH)

RUSSIA

LIVONIA (to Sweden)

• Reval

E. PRUSSIA (to Brandenburg)

POLAND

• Warsaw

• Cracow

Moldavia

Transylvania

Wallachia

Constantinople •

OTTOMAN EMPIRE

CYPRUS

BLACK SEA

Stockholm •

SWEDEN

BALTIC SEA

Christiania

NORWAY (to Denmark)

Copenhagen •

DENMARK

Brandenburg

Berlin •

SAXONY

• Prague

AUSTRIA

• Vienna

Budapest •

• Munich

Venice

ADRIATIC SEA

K. Naples

Naples •

SICILY

NORTH SEA

United Provinces

Amsterdam •

Spanish Netherlands

Brussels •

Cologne •

Frankfurt •

Mainz •

SWITZ.

Savoy

Genoa

Milan •

Papal State

Rome •

Florence •

Edinburgh •

SCOTLAND

ENGLAND

London •

ENGLISH CHANNEL

FRANCE

• Rouen

• Paris

Franche Comté

Lyons •

Comtat Venaissin

Orange •

Marseilles •

CORSICA (to Genoa)

SARDINIA (to Spain)

Dublin •

IRELAND

• Bordeaux

Barcelona •

BALEARIC IS. (to Spain)

MEDITERRANEAN SEA

ATLANTIC OCEAN

SPAIN

• Madrid

PORTUGAL

Lisbon •

17

France under the Grand Monarch

1661 - 1715

WITH LOUIS XIV the ancient monarchy of France attained the zenith of its development. The king, as the hereditary, absolute, and personal ruler, became the complete embodiment of both state and nation. The Grand Monarch was the be-all and the end-all of France.

The total priority of monarchy thus claimed was realized only in the externals of public life. Nation and state were more than mere extensions of the royal will. The people, forming a rich, vigorous, and varied society, did not owe their existence to the king. The state, too, existed prior to him and in a sense independently of him, for he held power only because it was transmitted to him through the political institutions of the country. This tension of beliefs and practices gave rise to the central question of the reign —whether the king of France existed for the people or the people for him. This question in turn involved another—whether Louis XIV, strong with the strength of his country, could make himself master of Europe, creating, as the Hapsburgs had failed to do, a "universal monarchy."

I. Rule Personal and Absolute

In 1661, when Cardinal Mazarin died, Louis XIV announced that he himself would give all commands in matters of government. Despite the predictions of the worldly-wise that he would soon tire of the chore, he governed France in person for fifty-four years. Never, even in illness or discouragement, did he give any subject that general and supreme control of the state which Richelieu and Mazarin had held.

The Grand Monarch. This imperious and majestic monarch was nonetheless a slave through all his reign. His master was offended pride. He never forgot that he, whom God and right of birth had set upon the throne, had suffered indignity at the hands of his subjects during the Fronde. He was not satisfied to hold the reality of power but had to make the world about him acknowledge his pre-eminence. He took as his emblem the sun, the source of all energy, the supreme power. He lusted for an everlasting place in the memory of men; and to glory and fame the Sun King gladly sacrificed his own labors, his country's wealth, its peace, and the peace of Europe.

He did not mind the toil of seeking glory. A "do-nothing king" (*roi fainéant*, the description given to the later Merovingian kings) failed, he believed, in a monarch's first duty, which was to govern. He told his son that "the profession of a king is great and noble, a thing of delight." He enjoyed, in fact, the drudgery of reports and dispatches and the harder work of thinking and deciding. Though he spent much of his day in ceremonies and entertainments, especially in the first quarter-century of his rule, he turned without complaint to spend many additional hours daily with his ministers of state.

This extraordinary diligence and purposefulness made up in some measure for the limitations of his mind. To be sure, he was methodical, patient, and prudent; willing to learn from those with special competence, he acquired an immense knowledge of the affairs of the European states. But he was headstrong and arrogant and, sly rather than wise, did not think deeply or far ahead. Since he was vain and held power, he blamed others for his failures, not himself.

"God's Lieutenant." Louis XIV believed implicitly in the doctrines of the divine right of kings and their absolute authority. "He who gave kings to men wished them to be respected as His lieutenants, and He kept for Himself the right to examine their conduct," he told his son. "His (God's) will is that all who are born subjects obey without question." He was lord and proprietor of the kingdom: he had "by nature the full and free disposition of all the wealth in the country, whether it is owned by churchmen or laymen." He was aware that he was responsible to God to rule well and in the interests of his subjects. He could not distinguish, however, between their interests and what he himself happened to desire. "There is no body of the nation in France; it resides entirely within the person of the king," he declared. Bishop Bossuet, the king's preacher and the foremost exponent of divine-right theory, proclaimed that "the will of the whole people is embodied

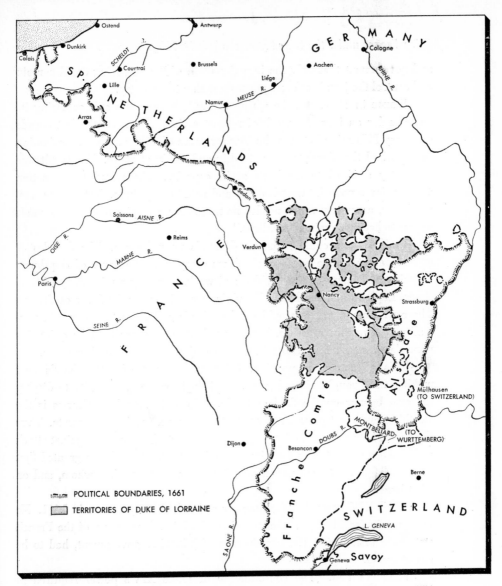

The Expansion of France under Louis XIV

within his will." Such doctrines were not at all original with Louis XIV; James I of England and Philip II of Spain had proclaimed almost identical principles. The difference was that Louis XIV practiced them with unprecedented success.

Indeed, as ruler of France, Louis was more absolute than the institutions by which he ruled. He was able to have his way because he was implacable with the powers he did have. It became dangerous for those who had held privilege to stand on their rights, although privilege was so built into society and government that only the imperious will of the Sun King could contain and control the jungle of cross-purposes within the country.

France in 1661. In the spring of 1661, France was still gathering its energies for an immense work of reconstruction. Not since the last decade of Henry IV's reign between the Vervins peace of 1598 and his assassination in 1610 had the kingdom been steadily and safely at peace. The result was a country strained to the limit of its capacity. There was, the Venetian ambassador reported, "wretchedness and ruin" everywhere. Yet France was, as always, a country which needed no more than a respite from the demands of war to become again a "fair land."

In 1661 war could make no demands upon France. The decades of exertion and struggle had brought down every foe. The house of Hapsburg, Austrian and Spanish, was divided and weak, Germany a miscellany of little states, England and the Dutch Republic competitors for the favor of France. Those who could not or would not be friends and allies took cover in neutrality. To remain at peace, France needed do no more than be quiet, for none dared attack her. Her military pre-eminence was beyond question.

This advantageous position, however, was not of Louis XIV's own making and brought him no glory. He itched for the opportunity to display his own banner on the field of battle. "To add to one's territories is the worthiest and most pleasant of occupations for a sovereign," he wrote. Thus the choice between war and peace, between guarding the nation against attack and seeking combat, was for him no choice at all. He took for granted that he would fight. The only open questions were when, against whom, and on what issue.

Louis XIV knew that the time for action had not yet come in 1661. He had to gain familiarity in the direction of affairs. The power of the French state, still brittle after the two decades of Mazarin's government, had to be strengthened.

Fouquet's Fall. The consolidation of Louis XIV's power required in the first instance the elimination of rivals. The traditional competitors with the king—the princes of the blood, the great nobility, the *parlements*—were quiescent. Condé had come back to France with a pardon for his treason given by the king as part of the Peace of the Pyrenees; but all his surly independence of spirit was vanished. Where Louis XIV saw danger was within his government, among those who had served him and Mazarin with constant faithfulness during the Fronde.

Nicholas Fouquet, the superintendant of finances, held in his hands the control of the royal treasury. He had grown rich by peculation, formed a coterie which included not only poets, architects, and noble mistresses, but also soldiers and officials. His motto, *Quo non ascendam?* (Where will he not climb?) hinted at unspoken ambitions.

Fouquet's undoing came after he played lavish host to the king at his sumptuous estate of Val-de-Vaux. The monarch, envious of Fouquet's wealth and afraid of his power, arranged for his arrest and trial on charges of embezzlement and conspiring against the crown. A special, hand-picked court, under Louis' prodding, convicted Fouquet and sentenced him to banishment. The king, exercising his personal authority as supreme judge of France, changed the sentence to perpetual imprisonment (he had with difficulty been dissuaded from sending Fouquet to the block). It was a warning to the great ones of France neither to rival the king in magnificence and display, nor to build cliques available for rebellion against his throne.

Taming of Courts and Nobles. Louis XIV also compelled the courts of justice to give up their independent habits. In 1665 he deprived the *parlements* of their title of "sovereign courts," and permitted them only the name of "superior courts," lest he appear to share his sovereignty with them. In a *lit de justice* he commanded the *parlements* to register his laws without debate or vote. In 1673 he relented so far as to permit them a "humble remonstrance," but only after registration of the laws in question.

The lesser nobility received their warning in the stern punishment given to aristocratic brigands in Auvergne and Forez. These were poor upcountry provinces in central France where royal justice had come seldom and stayed briefly. During 1665-1666 special courts made up of members of the Parlement of Paris were sent to Clermont to bring to trial miscreants who had defied or dominated the local authorities. Hundreds were convicted, many sentenced to hanging, during these *grands jours* (great days).

The order thus established was thereafter maintained throughout the country by a rural mounted police, the *maréchausée*, which not only hunted down offenders but tried and punished them. Its speed and ruthlessness were indicated in the motto ascribed to it: *Pris, pendu* (No sooner taken than hanged).

The Court. Louis XIV was not content to cow the nobility. His purpose was to make them useful as well as tame. A relatively small number, gifted with intelligence, assiduity, and high-placed friends, found posts in the government. Most served in a different way, by paying attendance upon the king's person. The nobility were expected to reside at the royal palace, near the king and away from their ancestral provinces. Those who came were rewarded with favors—appointments to office in the state or church, "pensions," or outright gifts of money—and such revenues in the king's gift became more and more important to the aristocracy of France, for the income from their estates continued to decline. Those who did not come, those of whom the monarch remarked, "He is one of those who keeps out of sight," could expect no favors.

An elaborate organization of etiquette and ceremony controlled life at court. There were balls, operas, and ballets, as well as constant attendance upon the king and queen. At first glance, the court was like a fairyland. Beneath the surface of gaiety and abandon, however, there were depths of boredom and impoverishment. The necessity to flatter, to dissimulate honest feeling, to intrigue and deceive, corrupted the soul of the nobility of France. They lost the sturdy independence of spirit which had accompanied their rebelliousness and disorderliness during the past centuries; instead they became idlers, hangers-on, coddled by the king while the real work of the nation and the state was done by others.

The very palace which he had built as his favorite residence—Versailles —incorporated the spirit of the court. The vagaries of nature were disregarded in its planning. The buildings were balanced and orderly, with no trace of fancy. Showplaces to impress the eye and mind, they were poor places in which to live, badly heated, with inadequate sanitary facilities, thick with filth and odors.

Patron of the Arts. The literary and artistic talents of Frenchmen and foreigners were also put at the service of the king. Until his death in 1683, Jean Baptiste Colbert, Louis' leading minister, acted as virtual "controller general of arts and letters." The poet-critic Boileau summed up Colbert's aim in the phrase, "An Augustus may easily call Vergils into being" (*un Auguste peut aisément faire des Virgiles*). Colbert attempted to make the king the principal, indeed almost the sole, patron of the arts and sciences in France, even though his budget for these purposes (apart from architectural and similar large-scale expenditures) was never more than 100,000 livres a year.

In exchange, artists and writers had to obey Colbert's simple instruction, "The king must be praised everywhere." The fable-writer La Fontaine amplified with the observation that "There are only three sorts of persons whom one cannot overpraise: one's gods, one's mistress, and one's king."

The principal instruments of royal support were a series of academies, which provided stipends for their members and means of control over the expressive life of France. The most important of these academies was the French Academy, previously a private club of men of letters sponsored by Cardinal Richelieu; Colbert took it over for the king and made it into a public academy of forty members. It was entrusted with the task of preserving the purity of the French language by preparing a dictionary from which all crude and vulgar words were barred. Academies were created for the other arts as well, principally during the first decade of the king's rule, when there was most money to spend for things other than war.

Intendants, Secretaries, and Ministers. Louis XIV was able to rule everywhere in France because he made over the haphazard and incomplete machinery of government into an effective instrument for his purposes. His

COLONNADE OF THE LOUVRE. East façade, after design by Le Vau, Le Brun, and Claude Perrault, begun 1665.

This is a masterpiece of French neoclassical architecture, built by Perrault according to the design of a group under his leadership. Their conception was adopted instead of a baroque proposal by Bernini. The stately majesty of this colonnade is imposing but wholly balanced and harmonious. The columns are slender and well spaced, adding lightness to the massive construction. However, as with the earlier Renaissance architecture, the classical elements are merely laid upon the exterior of a modern building.

basic reform consisted in using the "intendants" on a permanent and general basis, as neither Richelieu nor Mazarin had done. In their districts, called "generalities," these "intendants of justice, police, and finance" were virtual viceroys, supervising and controlling the regular administration of the state: the judges and their subordinates, the tax collectors, and the troops. The intendants were wholly at the king's disposal because they held their positions by "commission," subject to dismissal at his command. They had no vested interest in their offices, which were not "venal" (purchased and held as property).

The king found less to change in the uppermost agencies of government. The tasks of giving advice and executing orders continued to be distributed among the chancellor, four secretaries of state, and the controller-general of finances (the superintendancy of finances, abolished in 1661, was recreated under this new title in 1665). The chancellor retained his position as the chief judge of the country but lost his broader influence over the general administration. Direction of the intendants as well as of the specialized branches of administration (foreign affairs, army, navy, the king's household, and Protestant affairs) passed fully into the hands of the secretaries of state. The controller-generalship reached a height of importance under Colbert, who made it a virtual ministry of finance, colonies, and economic affairs.

The king also named three to five ministers of state to advise him on

395

LOUIS XIV. Line engraving by Robert Nanteuil, 1672.

This portrait is called "aux pattes de lion" (with lion's paws), a device aptly symbolic of the power of the Grand Monarch in the year when he began his war upon the Dutch Republic. (Achenbach Foundation)

matters of general policy. Once appointed to the *conseil d'en haut* (upper council), they held the title of minister of state for life; but they had no property right in the office and could be dismissed from the actual function at the king's desire. The secretaries of state were frequently also ministers of state; in that case, the distinction between their functions was more formal than real. Otherwise, the secretary functioned under the direction of the corresponding minister.

The King His Own First Minister. Louis XIV excluded from active political life everyone but his ministers and secretaries of state, and a very few others, notably Turenne, who served him as a tutor and elder statesman during the 1660's, and the members of his "council of conscience," which guided him in religious matters. The princes of the blood, the dukes and peers, the royal mistresses, and all their varied horde of associates and hangers-on, lost their age-old prerogative of influencing policy. The monarch lived among them in his court, dancing and romancing, receiving their flattery and doling out favors, but he did not permit them to interfere with the work of government. Many who complained much about arbitrary absolutism referred less to the king than to his ministers, and their complaints meant that they had less hope of gaining their aims by intrigue and influence than ever before; but others, especially later in the reign, aimed at Louis himself.

Though the king relied strongly on his ministers for information, judgment, and proposals, he kept the final authority and the basic decisions in

COLBERT. Line engraving by Robert Nanteuil, 1676.

Jean Baptiste Colbert, the great minister of Louis XIV. His elaborate dress and the intertwined initials under the coronets indicate, perhaps more clearly than any words, the pride of nobility assumed by the one-time cloth-merchant's son of Reims. (Achenbach Foundation)

his own hands, particularly in foreign relations and religious matters. Yet he could not be a master of every problem which came before him. On many matters, particularly of lesser importance, he trusted the minister in charge and approved whatever he proposed.

The history of France during the reign of Louis XIV, therefore, became largely the story of the work of the great ministers of state. Many of them, especially in the first half of the reign, were men of skill and will, fit agents for a grand monarch. They had been trained under his predecessors in a period of struggles against open enemies; they possessed not merely knowledge but also resiliency of method and purpose. Their successors knew as much as they, but found their tasks harder. The fault lay partly in the increased complexity and difficulty of the situation, but also partly in the habit they absorbed from the king of commanding, not persuading.

Louis XIV was in general a faithful and kind master. Most of his ministers retained their posts for long periods, many until their deaths. Some, Colbert and Louvois for instances, served him for more than two decades. In more than half a century, he appointed only sixteen ministers of state. He rewarded them richly. They received grants of noble title, munificent remuneration, favors and offices for their families. With the king's encouragement, their children married into the highest nobility below the royal family: Colbert's daughters, whose grandfather had sold cloth, became duchesses. The ministerial families became a new element in the aristocracy

397

of France, a nobility of high government service. Although some of the older nobility of the sword and robe sniffed at them as upstarts, others eagerly contracted marriage alliances with them, hoping thereby to gain the royal favor.

Colbert. The key minister in the decade after 1661 was Colbert, who replaced Fouquet in the administration of the royal finances. Mazarin had "bequeathed" Colbert to Louis XIV as a particular treasure: he was a master of that most intricate and delicate art, getting and keeping money. The monarch, who did not understand the art—*his* specialty was spending—but knew his need for one who did, gave his confidence to Colbert. He approved whatever the minister proposed in his own field of action, so long as it did not interfere with the king's wider purposes, and so long as he provided the funds called for.

Colbert became a minister of state in 1661, immediately after Fouquet's fall from office; in 1665 he received the new title of controller-general of finances, and four years later became secretary of state for the navy.

Finances were his first and foremost responsibility. "We do not have little things to do in this reign," he wrote in 1664, and great things cost money. Some were wars, which became larger and more expensive; others were vast works of construction, of which the magnificent palace of Versailles was most important. The situation Colbert faced was not easy. In 1661 the crown received 22,800,000 livres in revenues and spent 32,000,000. Colbert's task was to make income cover expenditures.

Financial Reforms. His first reform was to bring clarity out of the confusion of Fouquet's fiscal administration. He introduced a clear system of bookkeeping and a rudimentary budget. The hole in the system, however, was the monarch himself. Louis XIV did not feel bound by any budget. He freely issued orders for payment upon the treasury whether or not provision had been made for such expenditure, and never took fiscal considerations into account when making decisions of grand policy. He learned slowly that war is a beast ravenous for money as well as men.

The tax system, with its imbalance and its inefficiency, was also faulty. Colbert did what he could to make taxes fall less heavily on those with least wealth. In the first years of his administration, he reduced the taille, which produced the largest revenue and was paid only by commoners. Almost at once, however, he found himself compelled to increase the rates of the gabelle, which was even more oppressive to collect than the taille.

He was more successful in cutting the share of income paid to the creditors of the state. He called in state loans for conversions to lower rates of interest or reduction of the principal: those who rejected these terms (which constituted a kind of repetitive partial bankruptcy) faced long delays in the payment of both interest and principal. The tax farmers also felt Colbert's heavy hand. He had their accounts examined and made them disgorge huge sums improperly collected or retained. He also compelled them to accept terms for the lease of the indirect taxes more favorable to the state.

He could do not without the tax farmers, however, or make fundamental reforms in the tax system as a whole. The pressure of the king for funds was too great to permit any reduction, even temporary, in the amount collected from the general population. At the same time, it was too dangerous to strike at the tax exemptions of the nobility at the very time when they were being persuaded to accept a less independent status as a court nobility.

Instead Colbert had recourse to old devices of fiscal policy which had given no permanent solutions to the same problems under previous administrations. He borrowed against future revenues, thereby worsening the long-term credit of the state, and manipulated the currency, at the expense of its stability and reliability. Even more harmful was the wholesale creation of new and unneeded venal offices (including such posts as fresh-butter inspectors and wig controllers) for the sake of their initial price.

Mercantilism. Colbert saw clearly the inadequacy of all such expedients. "All the great things which Your Majesty has already done and may still do during his whole life are dependent upon this increase in the amount of currency," he told the king in 1670.

To increase the amount of currency within France—the liquid cash which could be tapped by taxes—Colbert used the methods already sketched by his predecessors and proposed by mercantilist tracts. By increasing the production of goods, especially those for export, by decreasing imports and by shifting transport of French goods from foreign to native ships, a favorable balance of trade—that is, one which increased the quantity of money within the country—would be created. A moderate import tariff of 1664 was doubled and tripled in 1667, making a wall few foreign goods could cross. Industrial and commercial companies were favored by the grant of royal monopolies and subsidies. These included companies for the East Indies and West Indies (1664), a Northern Company trading to the Baltic (1669), and a Levant Company (1670). Of these, only the East India company survived long after Colbert's passing. The manufacturing companies likewise remained in existence only when they filled a genuine need with some adequacy. To favor French shipping, which was only a tiny fraction of the Dutch (Colbert estimated that it was much less than 10 per cent), he continued in effect a duty established by Fouquet on foreign ships taking on cargos in French ports, amounting to 50 sous per ton. French colonization in America and in the East Indies was expanded and protected. The colonies were placed under the rule of the *"Exclusif"*—they were permitted to trade exclusively with the motherland. Their primary purpose was to make France wealthier and stronger.

Many of these measures met sharp resistance from established merchants and manufacturers. They did not want the direction and control which the controller-general imposed on them. They were satisfied to continue to produce, to buy and sell as they had been doing, rather than to take on the risks and expenses of expansion and new activities. Merchants, for instance, preferred to continue working with the Dutch; they had no confidence that they could match the Dutchmen in costs or skill. Nonetheless, after almost two and a half decades of work, Colbert achieved a considerable increase in the volume of both trade and industry. Had the demands made upon him, and by him upon the country, been more moderate, he might well have succeeded in making ends meet.

To the Verge of Bankruptcy. Louis XIV's requirements, however, were anything but moderate. During the 1670's, he fought the Dutch war and continued the construction of Versailles at the same time. In 1680, the deficit amounted to 22,000,000 livres, more than double that of 1661; furthermore, more than 50,000,000 of the following year's revenues were already obligated. Colbert, faced by the debacle of his plans, wrote despairingly to the king: "With regard to expenditures, although they are no concern of mine, I merely beg Your Majesty to permit me to tell him that in war and peace he has never considered his finances in deciding his expenditures, which is a thing so extraordinary that surely it is without example." The gesture was bold and vain. Colbert, who died in 1683, spent the final years of his life somehow finding money for the king, but neither changing the monarch's habits nor seeing any hope of achieving his own aim of a prosperous France and a balanced budget.

What Colbert had not been able to do, none of his successors as controllers-general, men of lesser ability faced with even worse problems, could do either. They continued to use his methods, but their only important achievements were two new taxes, the *capitation* (head tax, actually a modified income tax) and the *dixième* (tenth, a uniform tax of 10 per cent of all personal income including that of the privileged classes.) When Colbert died, the revenue of the state had mounted to 93,000,000 livres and expenditures to 109,000,000, leaving a deficit of 16,000,000; in 1715, when Louis XIV died, income had fallen to 69,000,000 while expenditures had risen to 132,000,000. The French state, at the end of the glorious reign of the Grand Monarch, was on the verge of bankruptcy.

Le Tellier and Louvois. Within a decade after Louis XIV began his personal rule, Colbert's place as the leading minister had been taken by the secretary of state for war, François le Tellier, marquis de Louvois. This post had been held since 1643 by Michel le Tellier, Louvois' father, and the two held it conjointly from 1666 to 1677. During this period, Louvois took on an increasing part of the burden of office, so that by the time Le Tellier became chancellor in 1677, his son had long since become the sole minister of war. From 1677 almost until his death in 1691, Louvois remained Louis's most intimate adviser.

Although Le Tellier and Louvois were unlike in character—the father was a quiet-spoken man given to persuasion, the son a bully—they followed the same fundamental policies. Between them they made the French army into the most powerful single military force in Europe.

They increased the size of the army steadily. Comprising only seven regiments with between 15,000 and 20,000 men in 1661, it had 72,000 six years later, at the beginning of the War of Devolution; 120,000 in 1672, at the start of the Dutch war; 290,000 in 1688, before the War of the League of Augsburg; and almost 400,000 in 1703, just after the start of the War of the Spanish Succession. The soldiers were recruited from volunteers within the country and increasingly from foreign countries; by the end of the reign, more than half the soldiers of the king of France were not Frenchmen.

Le Tellier and Louvois also reorganized the military system. The hierarchy of command was brought under more effective royal control. Venality was abolished for all grades except captain and colonel; the money needed to pay off the proprietors of companies and regiments was never available. Strict discipline was enforced for all ranks, including generals and marshals. Arsenals and storehouses were built. The work of supply was taken from the regimental commanders and given to civilian officials of the war ministry. The French army became the first large field force in Europe able to subsist on its supply train without living off the land.

Innovations in the equipment and tactics of the field armies came slowly. Louvois was hesitant about accepting the suggestions of such gifted commanders as Turenne and Condé, lest he weaken his own influence over the king. On the other hand, he encouraged Vauban, who had no important rank by birth, to employ his genius as a military engineer in fortification and siegecraft. Vauban constructed a belt of fortifications along the French frontiers so strong and tight that the country was able to withstand the immense blows of the allied coalition during the War of the Spanish Succession.

The Navy. Similar work in reorganizing the French fleet was undertaken by Colbert, his son Seignelay, and their successors. New ports and shipyards were constructed; many additional warships were sent to sea; discipline unprecedented aboard ship was introduced. Nonetheless the fleet always remained a second thought with Louis XIV, for it could not conquer territory, which was the visible sign of successful campaigning. When funds ran short during the wars of 1688-1697 and 1701-1713, he abandoned the attempt to maintain a battle fleet, relied on privateers to harass the English and the Dutch, and concentrated his resources on maintaining the largest possible land army.

II. War and Glory

War—the preparation for it and the waging of it—dominated the policy of Louis XIV. Of the fifty-four years during which he governed France, exactly half were spent in actual fighting.

The King as Diplomat. In 1661, the king eagerly anticipated the resumption of active campaigning, which had ended with the Peace of the Pyrenees only two years before. War was his opportunity to prove his merit and win his glory in proper royal fashion. Yet he did not rush into every quarrel that came his way but used the wiles of diplomacy to ease the task of the soldiers.

The French diplomatic service was by and large the best in Europe. It was the most numerous, with envoys in every capital except Moscow. French diplomats were in the main men of experience, skill, and judgment. Even more important was the quality of the foreign minister, who co-ordinated their activities into a single comprehensive program. All the four foreign ministers who served Louis XIV between 1661 and 1675 were men of great ability. Nonetheless they always remained the king's servants. Not they but the king made the ultimate decisions as to the general character and often the detailed execution of French policy.

As a diplomat, Louis XIV revealed himself to be a pupil of the subtle Mazarin. At his best in judging those who were without honor and integrity or were, like himself, self-centered and vain, he did not understand those who defended principles he did not himself hold or continued to fight when reason seemed to dictate surrender.

The War of Devolution. During the first five years of his government, while he was strengthening his hold on France itself, Louis XIV sought only facile successes which magnified his prestige but not his territories. He was satisfied to compel the king of Spain and the pope in Rome to make humble public apologies to him; to send a contingent of troops to aid the emperor against the Turks besieging Vienna in 1664; and to come to the aid of his Dutch allies against the English during the second Anglo-Dutch war (1664-1667). But he did not commit himself to any large enterprises.

His attitude changed after the death of his father-in-law, Philip IV of Spain, in 1665. Though Philip left an infant son, Charles II, on the throne, the French king brought into the open the claim on the Spanish monarchy which Mazarin and his foreign minister, Hugues de Lionne—who still served Louis XIV in the same capacity—had so carefully prepared (see ch. 9, p. 210). The dowry of his Spanish queen, Maria Teresa (known in history by her French name Marie Thérèse) had never been paid, and it was asserted therefore that her renunciation of her rights of inheritance in Spain had been nullified. For the moment, however, Louis did not claim for his wife the entire heritage of Spain but only a part of the Low Countries where a local law (the "law of devolution") was cited as a pretext because it provided for the transmission of property to children of a first marriage in the event of remarriage by a surviving parent: Marie Thérèse was the eldest child of Philip's first marriage and Charles the offspring of his last.

The Spanish government refused even to discuss the issue. In 1667 Louis XIV therefore turned to the decision of arms. His troops invaded the Low Countries in the War of Devolution. Commanded by Turenne and Condé, with Vauban directing the siege of the Belgian fortresses, the French moved forward against the weak Spanish forces.

To the indignation of the French, the English and the Dutch combined to oppose further French progress in the Spanish Netherlands. The Triple Alliance of January 23, 1668 (so-called because it was later joined by Sweden) gave Louis XIV pause. He did not wish to oppose both sea powers at the same time. He therefore contented himself with making peace at Aix-la-Chapelle (Aachen) on May 31, 1668, receiving a group of towns along the frontier as the reward for not continuing the war.

The Dutch War. Louis then prepared to punish the Dutch, who had been his allies since 1662, for barring his conquest of the entire Spanish Netherlands. A "little war" of tariffs and counter-tariffs, as Colbert called it, touched off by Colbert's high protective tariff of 1667, further embittered French-Dutch relations. Lionne set to work to break up the Triple Alliance. In the treaty of Dover of 1670, Charles II entered an alliance with France against the States-General in exchange for French subsidies. Sweden too was extracted from the Triple Alliance by the same pecuniary argument. Münster and Cologne, which bordered on the United Provinces to the east, were made French allies, while most other German princes agreed to remain neutral.

The assault upon the United Provinces began in the spring of 1672. The French route of march passed alongside the Spanish Netherlands, through the territories of the archbishop of Cologne. Within less than two months, the French army had penetrated to the heart of the Dutch Republic. Only the Dutch action in opening the dikes and flooding the polder country between the Zuyder Zee and the Rhine halted the French advance.

Facing the simultaneous naval assault of the English, the States-General offered terms for peace which included the cession of their "Generality" lands south of the Rhine. Louis XIV preferred to make even harsher demands, which would have created a French protectorate over their provinces. Rather than abandon their independence, the Dutch decided to fight on. The war continued for six years. The French retained the military advantage, although the theater of operations moved to the Spanish Netherlands and the Rhineland. The diplomatic advantage passed to William III, the prince of Orange, who became the leader of the Dutch in 1672. He created a Grand Alliance of the United Provinces, the Holy Roman emperor, Spain, and Brandenburg. Charles II of England made a separate peace in 1674 and four years later had to promise to become an ally of the Republic unless France made peace. To prevent such a combination of the maritime powers against him, Louis XIV accepted a treaty of peace at Nijmegen in 1678. The Dutch came off scot-free, retaining all their territory and compelling France to abandon Colbert's protective tariff of 1667. Spain, militarily weak, paid the price of peace by ceding Franche-Comté and several Belgian cities to France.

"Grandeur and Force." The Peace of Nijmegen was in practice a confession that the French military force could hold off the armies of half Europe, but not destroy them. Louis XIV had proved, indeed, that he was *nec pluribus impar* (not unequal even to many), as he had boasted in the motto he had adopted during the war. But he had not been "more than equal," and he could not bring himself to confess that Nijmegen had been anything less than a ringing triumph. He dismissed Pomponne, a cautious and moderate diplomat who had succeeded Lionne as foreign minister in 1671, because he "lacked the grandeur and force one should have in executing the orders of a king of France who is not unfortunate."

The next decade was spent in actions of bravado which would justify, he hoped, the name "Louis the Great," which the municipality of Paris bestowed upon him. The first was the transformation of the province of Alsace from a territory under his feudal suzerainty (according to the terms by which the emperor had ceded it to him in 1648) into a region under his full sovereignty. The method employed at the suggestion of Croissy, Colbert's brother who succeeded Pomponne as foreign minister, was to "reunite" the various feudal dependencies in Alsace under the jurisdiction of the French courts. These "reunions" caused indignation and protest among the many German princes who held Alsatian fiefs, which now became effectively part of France instead of the Holy Roman Empire. The French seizure of Strassburg in 1681 made the Germans angrier still. In 1683 Louis launched a peacetime campaign to take Luxemburg, in the southeastern Low Countries, from Spain; the government of Madrid, oblivious of its military weakness, declared war, but had to cede the province the following year. Genoa, which had continued to act as banker for Spain, was punished by bombardment from a French fleet.

The War of the League of Augsburg. The year 1685 brought the beginning of a change. James II, an open Catholic, came to the throne in England. Louis XIV fed subsidies to him, as he had to his brother, to encourage his defiance of Parliament, but Protestant resistance to James was coupled with ever-widening hostility to France. The revocation of the Edict of Nantes (see below, p. 408), withdrawing the toleration which it had assured to the

Huguenots in France, intensified anti-French feeling in England and broke up the French alliances with the Protestant princes of Germany. In 1686 a group of princes in western and southern Germany combined at Augsburg in a league for mutual protection against France. William III, the Dutch stadholder, was active wherever resistance to France was rising, urging the reorganization of the Grand Alliance which had halted Louis XIV during the Dutch war. Such an alliance was the bane of Louis's diplomacy and he sought desperately to prevent it. In 1688 a French army installed Cardinal William Egon von Fürstenberg, the French candidate, as archbishop of Cologne over the papal designate, Prince Clement of Bavaria. At the same time Louis sent an army to occupy the Palatinate, in the name of the rights of inheritance asserted for the duchess of Orléans, a daughter of the late elector.

While the French were moving into Germany, William III was sailing to England to take leadership of the rebellion against James II (see ch. 19, p. 445). In the expectation that the Dutch would be tied up in England, Louis XIV did not divert his army to attack the Netherlands. The quick success of the English revolution undid his plans. William brought both England and the Dutch Republic into war with France, and formed a coalition the next year with Spain, the emperor, Savoy, and Brandenburg. The Grand Alliance had been recreated.

The French fleet carefully built by Colbert and his son Seignelay was destroyed off the roadstead of La Hougue, in Normandy, in 1692. French effort at sea thereafter was limited to the action of privateers who hurt the enemy's trade but did not touch his fleet. On land the war went better, with numerous French victories in the Low Countries, Germany and Italy, but as in the Dutch war they were inadequate to bring total triumph. The strain of war began to tell very heavily upon the French; the outbreak of tax and hunger rebellions was a sign of exhaustion.

Again a compromise peace was made. By the treaty of Ryswick (Rijswijk) in 1697, France kept Strassburg but ceded several Alpine fortresses to Savoy and returned Luxemburg to Spain. The most bitter pill for Louis XIV was recognizing William III as king of England, with a promise not to support the exiled James II, who had taken refuge in France.

The Treaties of Partition. Louis XIV had learned the lesson of caution, that he could not attain his purposes against the opposition of the other European states, in particular the sea powers. He held to this principle even when the imminence of the death of Charles II of Spain reopened the question of the succession to the Spanish monarch. In order to avert another war, which France was unprepared to wage, French diplomats negotiated a treaty of partition in 1698, not with the rival candidates but with the Dutch and English, who had the power to permit or prevent. This treaty took the young son of the elector of Bavaria as the agreed-upon heir to Charles II. When the child died in 1700, Louis XIV even agreed to another treaty of partition, with Archduke Charles of Austria as the principal beneficiary.

This treaty, like the first, was a compromise which reckoned without the hosts—the king of Spain and the Spaniards themselves, for whom the integrity of the Spanish monarchy and its possessions was the paramount consideration. Charles II, shortly before his death in November, 1700, foiled the treaty makers by naming the grandson of Louis XIV, Philip of Anjou, as his universal heir; failing acceptance by Philip or other French candidate, Charles of Austria; and failing him, the duke of Savoy.

The French monarch and his advisers were confronted with a situation of puzzling uncertainty. If the duke of Anjou did not accept the unexpected inheritance, it would pass to his principal rival. That the sea powers would fight Spain and Austria to enforce the treaty of partition seemed unlikely. Louis therefore decided to have Philip accept the bequest. When Philip V, as the duke of Anjou was now called, was presented to the Spanish ambassador, the envoy expressed pleasure that his sovereign's journey to Madrid would be easier because "the Pyrenees have melted away." His remark summed up the problem for the sea powers—the danger that a Bourbon monarch ruling in Spain would mean French domination of the Iberian peninsula and hence of the Mediterranean sea. Nonetheless they did not stand in the way but recognized Philip.

The War of the Spanish Succession. Just when peace seemed assured, Louis XIV reverted to the old habit of acting brusquely even in seeking a prudent purpose. He reaffirmed Philip's right to inherit the French throne, thus creating a danger of personal union between France and Spain. When he recognized the son of James II as king of England and sent French troops into the Spanish Netherlands to expel the Dutch garrisons in the "barrier" fortresses (see ch. 24, p. 544), the scales were tipped to war.

England and France opened the hostilities. They were soon joined by the emperor and other German princes in the Grand Alliance of 1701. Louis XIV had as allies Bavaria and, briefly, Cologne, Savoy, and Portugal. The fighting went badly for the French. Their year of misfortune was 1709; military reverses were combined with a winter of unusual harshness and the worst famine France had known in centuries. The question became not to hold Spain for the Bourbon dynasty but to protect France itself from invasion.

The Peace of Utrecht. Louis XIV took the initiative for peace. He sent his foreign minister, Torcy, to The Hague to negotiate with Anthony Heinsius, the grand pensionary of Holland and leader of the Dutch since the death of William III in 1702. Louis agreed to recall Philip from Spain, to cease aiding him, and even to support the Allies with funds if his grandson

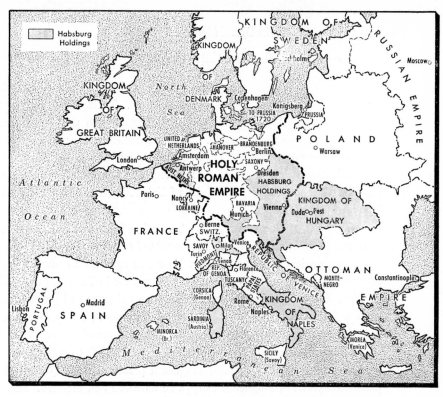

Europe after the Peace of Utrecht (1713-1714)

remained. But he would not swallow the Allies' demand that a French army join in driving Philip from Spain. "I prefer to wage war upon my enemies rather than my children," the French king told his people in a manifesto asking renewed exertions. Despite the immense hardships they had already suffered, they responded with their last energies. These were barely enough. France had only a single army left in the field when the fall of the duke of Marlborough, the leader of the war party in England, made peace negotiations possible.

A peace congress assembled at Utrecht, in the Netherlands, and prepared a treaty ending the twelve years' war. France ceded Acadia and Hudson Bay in Canada and the Caribbean island of Saint Christopher (Saint Kitts) to England, recognized the Hanoverian succession to the English throne (see ch. 19, p. 450), and approved a Spanish grant of the valuable *asiento* (the contract to deliver Negro slaves from Africa to Spanish America) to an English company. The Dutch regained their "barrier" fortresses in the southern Low Countries, facing the French frontier. But Philip V remained king of Spain, together with its American possessions. Archduke Charles, who had meanwhile become Holy Roman emperor as Charles VI, received the Spanish Netherlands, Milan, and Naples as his share of the inheritance.

407

III. "His Most Christian Majesty"

Along with foreign wars, Louis XIV fought another series of struggles for dominion over the souls of his subjects. Taking literally his title of "Most Christian Majesty," he saw as his first duty to God the assurance of "true religion" within the state. As to the identity and nature of true religion, he was not troubled. He was a Roman Catholic for whom his faith was little more than a belief in hell and the efficacy of certain rituals in warding off that danger; the duke of Saint-Simon said the king had only "the husk of religion."

The Edict of Nantes Revoked. To such a king and such a believer, the existence of more than a million Huguenots in France as a tolerated sect was an offense against God and himself. He encouraged their conversion, particularly after Turenne, the most eminent Huguenot in France, turned Catholic in 1668. Converts were exempted from personal taxes and granted six livres from a "conversion fund." The mass of Huguenots, prosperous merchants, manufacturers and farmers, spurned the fund's pieces of silver.

Losing patience, the king began during the 1670's to cut away the rights granted in the Edict of Nantes. Huguenot places of worship were closed on fabricated pretexts, Huguenot clergymen harassed and arrested. These measures left French Calvinism hurt but alive. Louvois, at the peak of his influence after 1680, characteristically tried another and more direct way to make converts—military terror. He ordered mounted infantrymen—the dreaded dragoons—to be quartered upon Protestant families, with the privilege of plundering, raping, and torturing at their pleasure. Scores of thousands of Huguenots accepted public conversion (usually remaining adherents of their previous faith in private), in order to escape the horror of the *dragonnades*.

Louis XIV took the reports of this massive change of faith at face value and decided that there was no longer any need for half measures. In 1685 he issued the Edict of Fontainebleau revoking the Edict of Nantes. The Huguenot religion ceased to be legal in France. The revocation was widely hailed in Catholic countries, although the pope soon came to be troubled by the impiety of simulated conversions at sword's point. Protestant Europe protested angrily and welcomed the several hundred thousand Huguenots who fled from France in search of freedom and safety.

Those who remained in France, especially the peasantry who so loved the land they tilled that they could not bear to leave it, passed under a reign of oppression. Hanging and the galleys were the fate of some, kidnaping of their children to be brought up as Catholics that of others, and a legal status often near to outlawry left them at the mercy of their Catholic neighbors. But they endured. In some places, as in the mountainous area of the

Cévennes, they took up arms against the tyrant in the "war of the shirt-wearers" (*guerre des camisards*). Within fifteen years of the revocation, Louis XIV admitted that he had largely failed. For the rest of his reign, he followed a mixed policy, sometimes reverting to oppression and sometimes ordering his officials not to enforce all the laws against the Huguenots. But he had shaken the fidelity to the crown of a large and prosperous segment of the nation; he had made Protestant Europe hostile; while Catholic potentates applauded, they would not accept his domination any the more gladly.

Gallicanism: National Catholicism. Toward his own Catholic church, Louis XIV faced the problem of maintaining, without at the same time falling into schism from Rome, his control over the French clergy despite the papacy's assertion of its authority. As a rigidly orthodox Catholic, the king looked on the supreme pontiff as his ally against all variations within the church; yet his efforts to bring the revenues and offices under royal control led Louis XIV to enter into frequent and bitter controversy with Rome and many French churchmen.

This struggle came to a head in the conflict over the *régale*. This was the right of the French crown to collect the revenues of vacant bishoprics and abbacies in northern France. The extension of the practice to southern France in 1673-1675 led to a clash between pope Innocent XI, the "stubborn saint," and the church of France, supported by Louis XIV. In 1682 a Gallican council adopted four articles reviving doctrines of the supremacy of general councils over the pope and affirming the autonomy of the Gallican church.

Innocent refused to confirm French bishops for vacant sees as long as these quasi-schismatic doctrines were maintained in France. Louis XIV was no less stubborn, for his absolute rule over all Frenchmen was at stake. By the end of the 1680's the vacancy of numerous bishoprics began to create a difficult problem in church administration. When Innocent XII became pope in 1689, his conciliatory attitude made a compromise possible. A settlement was negotiated in 1693 by which Rome confirmed the nominated bishops and accepted the principle of the *régale*, while the Gallican church retracted the four articles and the king agreed to forgo the revenues at dispute. Even though French theological seminaries continued to teach the four articles, Louis shifted to an otherwise almost completely ultramontane policy. Deeply anxious about his salvation, he felt safest when his confessors and the pope approved his conduct. At the same time, the struggle against variant movements within the French Catholic church impelled him to seek the support of Rome.

Jansenism and Quietism. The most important of these Catholic groups which dared to defy both king and pope was the Jansenists. They took their name from Cornelius Jansenius, late bishop of Ypres in the Spanish Netherlands. In a huge theological tome, the *Augustinus* (1640), he had argued in favor of doctrines emphasizing the inscrutability of divine purpose, as expressed in the election of those souls to whom grace was given and the damnation of all others. Jansenius' followers, led by the erudite Antoine Arnauld, doctor of theology at the Sorbonne, added an emphasis upon moral rigorism which brought them into conflict with the Jesuits, whose casuistic teachings stressed the variety and complexity of specific moral judgments. The Jansenist position obtained even wider attention with the publication of Blaise Pascal's *Provincial Letters* in 1661. The effectiveness of this attack by a mathematician of genius upon the Jesuits as moral teachers without honor or Christian principle was increased by Pascal's wit, fervor, and transparent prose.

The Jansenists were denounced by Rome as near-Calvinists, while Louis XIV attempted to force them to admit the accusations and recant their views. They indignantly replied that they were only teaching what the church had always taught and so could not have been guilty of heresy. Left to themselves, the Jansenist churchmen would not have been numerous or influential enough to have fought off the combined assault of papacy and crown. They found valuable allies, however, in the magistracy of the *parlements*, traditional foes of papal authority and Jesuit influence within France. They found friends, too, within the government. Lionne, the foreign minister, negotiated an agreement known as "the Peace of the Church" with the papal nuncio in 1668. This was an apparent acceptance by the Jansenists of the papal condemnation of the book *Augustinus*, although they continued to deny that it in fact contained any heretical propositions.

The "Peace" endured for about a decade. The conflict over the Jansenists was resumed with full harshness in the mid-1690's, when their leadership passed from Arnauld to an Oratorian, Father Quesnel. They then abandoned the tactic of verbal maneuvers and became forthrightly aggressive. In 1702 the Jansenists took the initiative in seeking withdrawal of the old condemnation of Jansenius' propositions. The king angrily obtained bulls from the pope (*Vineam Domini*, 1705, and *Unigenitus*, 1713) explicitly condemning the Jansenists as heretics. He acted to destroy the roots of Jansenism by ordering the evacuation and destruction of the convent of Port-Royal, the center of Jansenist activities, in 1709-1711.

Despite the repression, Jansenist views continued to be widely held, especially among the lower clergy, for whom they were a way of expressing resistance to both royal and pontifical domination of the church. The lay public took an increasing part, while the great magistrates who had defended the Jansenists in earlier years began to turn away from them as a source of turbulence in the state.

Another movement within Catholicism which drew the fire of the government was Quietism. This was a mystical doctrine which emphasized the loss of all individuality and activity of the human soul in the encompassing love of God. It won support within the royal family, for a while including Madame de Maintenon, the king's second wife. It did not engage the loyalties of wide groups, however, and its condemnation by the church was soon followed by its repression and disappearance.

IV. King and Nation

The glory of the Grand Monarch was reflected on the French people. His victories in war and diplomacy were theirs too. They boasted of their prowess against the massed nations of Europe. The feeling of shared accomplishments strengthened support for the royal absolutism among the people, as did the ending of the turmoil and pain of the civil wars.

There resulted an increased willingness to accept the limitless authority of the king, even in the ranks of the classes—the nobility and the town patricians—which traditionally held a share of political power in France. This docile, even joyous, acceptance of divine-right absolute monarchy became the public image of the political character of the French people.

Moods of reluctance and resistance continued within the French nation, however. On the eve of the Dutch war in 1672, a high-placed Frenchman secretly visited the ambassador of the States-General to tell him that many subjects of the king wished the Dutch success in repelling the "servitude" of absolute monarchy which had already been imposed on them. This was only a harbinger of wider, less furtive opposition during the last fifteen or twenty years of the reign. The anonymous pamphlet *Soupirs de la France esclave* (*The Sighs of France Enslaved*, 1690), attributed to Huguenot exiles, expressed in vivid language doctrines of anti-absolutism seldom heard since the wars of religion a century before. Similar ideas were given less blatant but no less persuasive voice in the work of influential Catholic thinkers and critics within France. One, La Bruyère, wondered whether the tillers of the French soil were truly men or, as they appeared, only talking beasts of burden. Bishop Fénelon, in his *Telemachus* (1699), a novel of instruction for his pupil the duke of Burgundy, inveighed against the narrow selfishness of the monarch and drew a picture of a better rule in a limited and decentralized monarchy, under the domination of the aristocracy not as it was but as it should be. The great military engineer Vauban put forward proposals showing even deeper sympathy with the common people. These reforming tracts resulted only in Vauban's disgrace.

Vauban met mishap because he touched with ideas of practical reform the problem which La Bruyère had stated in general terms: "Was the flock made for the shepherd, or the shepherd for the flock?" Louis XIV had always believed and acted upon the principle that it was the nation which served him, and not vice versa. He had rejected in annoyance Colbert's notion of a budget, which would restrict his expenditures, and had serenely entered into repeated wars with little or no thought for the people whose labors paid for his campaigns and his glory.

The cost to the French people of the king's wars and magnificence increased almost beyond endurance. The life of the ordinary people, in particular, was difficult in the extreme. Men earned between three and thirty sous a day while the cost of a pound of bread, the staple of the French diet, had increased from a sou to three or four times as much. In the countryside the peasantry constantly rioted against the exactions of the tax collectors. The widespread rural violence caused a general fear of "banditry."

With the Peace of Utrecht in 1713, France at last drew breath. There was a respite from decades of exhausting fighting and labor. The time for recuperation of energies had come. Louis XIV died two years later, before the work of recovery had more than barely begun. On his death bed, he whispered to the great-grandson who was to succeed him the tragic admission, "I loved war too much." It was the most accurate and devastating of all the judgments made, then and later, upon the reign of the Grand Monarch.

18

France: Throes of the Grand Monarchy

1715 - 1787

THE GRAND MONARCHY of France, in the year 1715, was a thing half-finished. Louis XIV had built a state wherein all power belonged to the king alone. He had not, however, reduced the French nation and the French state to mere extensions of his authority, lacking their own character and their own purposes. The people still needed the protection of government and provided its wherewithal—but what would happen, should the monarch continue to rule more in his interest than in theirs, remained uncertain. Upon the answer ultimately depended the permanence of Louis XIV's achievement, the welfare of France, of Europe, and of the world.

I. The Regency of Orléans

With Louis XV, the kingdom passed from old age to youth. Louis XIV died in the final days of his seventy-sixth year; his great-grandson came to the throne aged five years and six months. There was no queen mother, however, to take the tutelage of her son and the governance of the realm, as Marie de Médicis had done in 1610 and Anne of Austria in 1643. Nearest in blood to Louis was his uncle, Philip of Anjou; but as Philip V of Spain, the duke had renounced his claims in France. Next in line was Louis's father's cousin, another Philip, the duke of Orléans.

Single Regency. Barring the way to Orléans' sole regency was the late king's testament of July 1714. Disliking and distrusting the duke for his scoffing independence, Louis XIV had decreed the creation of a regency council. Orléans, as nominal regent, would preside over it, but effective power would be held by its members, a majority of whom were his opponents; the duke of Maine, a legitimized bastard of the late king, would be Louis XV's personal governor.

Orléans acted at once to make good his own power. He had secretly won the adherence of the regiment of French Guards even before Louis XIV's death. The very next day, placing the Guards before the doors to the palace of justice, the duke read the testament to the Parlement of Paris, declared it null and void, and proclaimed himself regent of France with full and exclusive power. The Parlement, delighted to defy the monarch who had kept it mute for half a century, gave solemn approval. The duke thereupon returned to it its lost right to remonstrate upon legislation presented for registration upon its books. This act was more than political give-and-take: by reviving the political powers of the great court of justice, the regent tore the first slow rip in the fabric of French absolutism as created and bequeathed by Louis XIV.

Government by Councils. In the duke of Orléans private vices dwelt with public virtues. A libertine in morals, he continued his private debaucheries and made no effort to enforce good conduct upon others. After the often hypocritical piety of the previous reign came a time of rollicking orgies and carousals, though in provincial towns and in the countryside life went on more evenly and sedately. In his public capacity Orléans was a different man. He desired the general welfare as well as his personal advantage, and was ready to seek them in bold new ways.

The regent turned first upon Louis XIV's system of government by professional officials. He dismissed the secretaries of state and gave their duties to six (later seven) councils of ten members each, with the princes of the blood and the great dukes in the majority. Government by multiple councils (dubbed with the Greek name of Polysynodie) took the edge off absolutism but gave the wider nation no share in power. The Fronde of the princes, put down by Mazarin some six decades earlier, had achieved a delayed triumph.

The high-born lords bungled their chance. They had little skill in the business of state apart from military and naval affairs. They talked much, decided little, and worked less. Soon, preferring gambling and boudoir gallantry, many stayed away from council meetings altogether. In the summer of 1718, the regent swept away Polysynodie by a *lit de justice*, abolishing the councils and re-established the secretaries of state. Government went back to the methods of Louis XIV, and there was no new Fronde; no one stirred.

The "Mississippi System." Polysynodie looked to the past for its ideas and purposes: the other great event of Orléans' regency—the "Mississippi System" of John Law—looked to the future. Law was a Scotsman who had learned business practice and the theories of mercantilism while a young man working in the banks of Britain and Holland. After slaying a man in a duel, he fled to France for safety. Living as a gambler, he devised a quick and easy way for France to extinguish its immense public debt and to acquire greater wealth and power. The heart of his system was the use of paper money not only as a means of exchange but also as a creator of credit. The principle itself was sound and rested upon Law's perception of an essential element of the capitalist economic order, but he counted on obtaining within a few years results that were to take more than a century to develop.

The regent came under Law's influence and made him the master of France's economic and financial life. Law established a private bank in 1716 which received the right to issue bank notes acceptable in payment of taxes. It was converted into a Royal Bank in 1718, and became the core of Law's complex "Mississippi System." The single bank combined many functions: the acceptance of deposits, the issuance of paper currency, the organization and financing of business enterprise, the collection of taxes. It established a privileged Western Company which took over all French overseas trade, eventually changing its name to the older title of "India Company."

Law painted a pretty picture of the profits to be made in Louisiana, the vast valley-land of the Mississippi which was granted to the company by the regent. The imagination of France—that is, of those with money to invest—was bedazzled. Hectic speculation in the company's stock ensued, with aristocrats and common folk jostling each other to buy. The price of the stock was driven far above what any prospective earnings warranted. Meanwhile paper money came off the presses, at first relatively slowly but rising from 180,000,000 livres in circulation in December 1718 to 640,000,000 the following October and 1,100,000,000 in January, 1720. It was in that month that the Mississippi Bubble (like the contemporaneous "South Sea Bubble" in England; see ch. 20, pp. 456-457) was pricked with doubts. A rush to sell brought down the price of the stocks. The Royal Bank failed and its notes were called in by the government at a small fraction of their face value. Law's whole system fell. Its inventor, penniless, fled and died soon after. France turned back to the traditional methods of public finance and their accompanying problems.

New Friends Abroad. Orléans broke no less sharply with tradition in foreign affairs, and with more success. His fundamental purpose was to keep France at peace. To achieve it he abandoned the notion of revenge against

England. He sent his former tutor, the dissolute, self-seeking, and able Abbé Dubois, to negotiate secretly a treaty of alliance and friendship with England and Holland, and the next year accepted Austria, making the Triple into a Quadruple Alliance. With Spain the Bourbon dynastic connection bred antagonism rather than amity. Philip of Spain denounced his renunciation of the French throne as invalid and plotted against the regent's authority in France. Philip of Orléans, seeing in his cousin a competitor for the crown should Louis XV die before becoming a father, treated him as a foe. He did not scruple to use French arms against Spain when Philip V attacked Sicily in 1718-1719 in an attempt to overturn the peace settlement of Utrecht.

II. The Administration of Fleury

Death, thwarting the uncles' calculations, came first to age. The duke of Orléans died in 1723, no longer regent because the king had passed the age of thirteen.

The Bourbon Ministry. Louis XV was still too much a boy to govern and gave his powers to his namesake, Duke Louis of Bourbon, whose sole claim to the post of prime minister was his royal descent. Too wispy-minded to think out his own policy, Bourbon deferred to the judgment of his mistress, Madame de Prie. She was the first of the political paramours who brought their dubious "other talents" into play during the reign of Louis XV. Her main purpose was to defend her position of power and the good things it brought her.

At her behest, Bourbon scuttled the alliance with Spain, which had been re-established. Although an *infanta* had been sent from Madrid to Paris as royal bride-to-be, de Prie decided to find the king a queen who would be beholden to her. She found such an unprepossessing princess in Marie Leszczyńska, dowdy daughter of the exiled former king of Poland. The *infanta* was sent home; Marie came to France from Germany and exchanged a French pension for a French crown.

The next year, 1726, the king dismissed Bourbon and chose in his place his tutor, Bishop Fleury, soon elevated to the cardinalate. His age of seventy-three years did not daunt Fleury. Though to the king he was mild, even indulgent, to France he was both strict and kind. He was an obdurate traveler of the middle way, rude and ruthless toward those who demanded clear solutions which set men at each other's throats.

Jansenist Troubles. Jansenism, which had come back into the open during the Orléans regency, soon felt the blast of Fleury's opposition. It had lost support among the bishops but had spread among the lower clergy and the populace. Their turbulent enthusiasm led to disorders. The most scandalous, in Fleury's eyes, was the enactment of "miracles" in the cemetery of Saint Médard upon the grave of a Jansenist deacon named Pâris. When the cemetery was closed, the Jansenists replied with a couplet:

> *De par le roi, défense à Dieu*
> *De faire miracle en ce lieu.*

(The king's command prohibits God
From working wonders on this sod.)

A more effective weapon than such quips was a secret journal established by the Jansenists, *Les nouvelles ecclésiastiques* (*Ecclesiastical News*). It continued a drumfire upon the Jesuits and their friends in government. Its arguments ran less to questions of grace and more to those of church organization. Speaking for the poor churchmen, like the parish priests subsisting on a few hundred livres a year while bishops collected hundreds of thousands, it favored what were known as "Richerist" doctrines (after Edmond Richer, an early seventeenth-century rector of the Sorbonne). These minimized the sacramental importance of the bishops in favor of the common priesthood acting through national councils.

Peace and Peacemaker's War. In most of his foreign policy the cardinal-minister was a man of peace. He opposed a return to Louis XIV's assertive policy, lest war cause the French finances to buckle. He continued the regent's policy of friendship with England, which Walpole's equivalent attitude toward France made possible. Yet Fleury steered clear of the shoal of French subordination to Britain. He revived the alliance with Spain as a balance to the English connection. When the English quarrel with Spain over American trade flared into the War of Jenkins' Ear (see ch. 20, p. 461), he prepared to contest with Britain for rule of the seas and the lands beyond the seas.

He avoided war on the land. The only large war of his administration before 1740 was the War of the Polish Succession. Fleury waged it almost from the start as a peacemaker's war, with an eye on the final settlement rather than on victory.

In 1733, on the death of Augustus II, king of Poland, Stanislas Leszczyński, now father-in-law to the king of France, again put forward his candidacy to the Polish throne. He was opposed by the Saxon elector Frederick Augustus. When both were declared elected by rival Diets, the War of the Polish Succession ensued. A tiny French expeditionary force to Danzig did not prevent Stanislas' defeat by an overwhelming Russian force supporting Augustus.

The flight of Stanislas did not end the fighting. It became a conflict between France, Spain, and Sardinia on the one side, and Austria on the other. French troops occupied the free duchy of Lorraine, whose sovereign was betrothed to the Archduchess Maria Theresa. After 1735 the fighting slackened off and the diplomats became active. The peace signed at Vienna in 1738 repeated most of the terms negotiated three years before. The duchies of Lorraine and Bar went to Stanislas as a kind of consolation prize, with provision for their incorporation into the French monarchy on his death. The dispossessed duke of Lorraine received in compensation the grand duchy of Tuscany, which had come vacant.

Prosperity: Royal and National. Fleury's peaceable policy enabled him to replenish the royal treasury without too great strain upon the people. His controllers-general reduced the use of the expedients that had made the people and the king poor and the financiers and tax farmers rich. He gave his steady support to Orry, controller-general after 1730, whose blunt energy won him the description of "a bull loose in the park of Versailles." Orry was harsh not only to moneyed men but, if need be, to the poor. He introduced a royal *corvée* which compelled the peasantry to spend from eight to forty days a year in building and repairing the highways. But he refused to permit the *corvée* to be converted into just another money tax, which would be spent for "more urgent" needs. Though the peasantry complained of the burden, their labors gave France a matchless system of highways within a few decades. Orry's success was clear in 1739, when the revenues of the crown covered its expenditures. It was the first time in untold decades that the royal accounts balanced.

The economy of France thrived on this sober political diet. The stabilization of the currency in 1726 was the first and not the least of the acts of government favorable to trade and industry. Orry, a mercantilist in the tradition of Colbert, gave special encouragement to commerce with France's colonies. The French islands of the Antilles shipped sugar to France for refining and re-export and bought their supplies from the homeland. By the end of Fleury's administration in 1743, colonial trade had increased two and a half times since the end of the reign of Louis XIV. Exports to European countries grew too, though not as strikingly. Industrial production responded to the incentive of large demand. Agriculture, too, prospered more modestly in a period of generally good crops and increasing prices.

Fleury in Ebb. Under Fleury's restraining hand absolutism worked, but at the price of risking its character. The monarchy ceased to be ambitious. Foreign statesmen began to discount the power of France because it was so seldom seen on the battlefield. Within the country the aristocracy was restive. Peace, or a halfpenny war like the brawl over the Polish succession, gave them little or no chance to show their merit and win the king's favor by deeds of heroism. Nor was Louis XV himself ready to accept the loss of prestige that resulted from too persistent avoidance of war. It took, too, more patience and courage than he had to stand aside when great events with possible grave consequences for France were in the making.

The war party in France gots its chance when Frederick II of Prussia pounced upon Austria Silesia at the end of 1740 (see ch. 22, pp. 496-497). They clamored that the time had come to strike down the Hapsburg power. The king, abandoning at last his old tutor's caution, joined in the war. Fleury kept his office but not his influence. For three years he watched the wreckage of his hopes and work. Then, in 1743, a broken man, he died.

III. The Rule of Louis XV

For the next twenty-nine years, till the end of his reign, Louis XV served as his own "prime minister," in conscious imitation of his predecessor, "Louis the Great." As a man and a ruler, however, he was made of a different stuff.

Intriguer-in-Chief. King almost since he could remember, he was bored, proud, and lazy. He took refuge from languor of spirit not in the detail and the frenzy of governing his country, but in hunting—for he so loved his dogs that his generals wished he would give his armies the same care—and in ceaseless lechery, beginning with women of the court and ending with harlots brought to his private brothel.

His pride concealed timidity, and worse. Fleury had unwittingly killed the moral manhood of the king, leaving him unsure of himself, superficially pious but without any true sense of kingly obligation to his people and his land. Nonetheless his intellectual powers, though hardly matching those of the philosopher upon the Prussian throne, were excellent. He understood what went on about him and even what might be done. But for most of his life he was too dispirited, too disinterested, too devious to act with vigor. His long view and short concern were well summed up in the phrase attributed to him, "After me, the flood" (*Après moi, le déluge*).

As head of government, Louis XV was more ruled than ruler. He named the ministers and dismissed them, but seldom gave them a policy to follow. France was ruled in fact by a succession of quarreling ministers who owed their office to the intrigues of court cabals and royal mistresses. To make things worse, Louis looked upon his ministers as rivals and competitors, not servants; he went behind their backs, until he became "the intriguer-in-chief." The policy of France became a shambles of cross-purposes, and absolutism a mockery of itself.

Quixotic War and Stupid Peace. Yet the times required leadership of a far different kind. The war into which Louis XV had taken France in 1741 was going badly. French diplomacy helped elect Charles Albert of

Bavaria as Emperor Charles VII and French forces aided the conquest of Upper Austria and Bohemia. Frederick of Prussia became a French ally too. Nonetheless their strategy and operations remained separate, and the Franco-Bavarians lost their conquests. The fighting shifted to the West.

In Germany the French held on against a coalition which now included Britain and the United Provinces as well as Austria. In the Austrian Netherlands, Louis XV gave command of his forces to a German-born marshal, Maurice de Saxe, illegitimate half-brother of the elector of Saxony. Saxe, a dashing, sly, and persistent commander, began the conquest of the Austrian Low Countries in 1745; three years later he stood in Dutch territory, waiting the opportunity to complete the victory which Louis XIV had lost in 1672. The French advantage in the continental fighting was balanced by the British superiority in naval and colonial warfare, which began in earnest in 1744 with the declaration of war. The French fleet was defeated and driven to refuge in its home ports; in North America the British colonists of New England captured Louisbourg, the French fortress on Cape Breton Island commanding the mouth of the Saint Lawrence river, and thus imperiled the whole French position in Canada.

To make matters worse, the French war aims, always uncertain, became quixotic. France could not hope for any important acquisition of territories even from victory, for the king was fully aware that to retain the Austrian Netherlands was to make perpetual the conflict with Britain and the Dutch Republic. He was satisfied, therefore, to make peace in 1748 at Aix-la-Chapelle (Aachen). Though boasting that he would "treat not as a merchant but as a king," he used Maurice's conquests in the Low Countries to regain the French territories lost in America and India. The armies went home; the frontiers stayed unchanged.

France seethed with indignation at seven years of war fought to so little purpose. They coined the witty phrase "stupid as the peace" (*bête comme la paix*); its companion expression, "to work for the king of Prussia," that is, for nothing, was a bitter comment on the fact that only Frederick II, who kept Silesia, gained by the war.

Reversal of Alliances. The peace of Aix-la-Chapelle was, as its negotiators foresaw, only a truce. No one was satisfied but Frederick of Prussia; the rulers of Austria, Britain, Russia, and not least France, hoped for vengeance or to make good aspirations not quite reached.

France, for all Louis XV's magnanimity in the Peace of Aix-la-Chapelle, found herself without a single strong ally. An opportunity came in 1750 to break out of this isolation. Maria Theresa made overtures for an end to the enmity between France and Austria, but Louis rebuffed her, for he did not wish to make an enemy of Prussia. This reluctance faded when Prussia and Britain formed an alliance in 1756. Louis XV feared that there was more

"THE ALLIANCE OF AUSTRIA AND FRANCE." Engraving by Madame de Pompadour, after a drawing by François Boucher. (Size reduced.) From *Suite d'estampes gravées par Madame la marquise de Pompadour d'après les pierres gravées de Guay, graveur du Roy* (n.d.).

This print by the mistress of Louis XV, Madame de Pompadour, illustrates not only her pride in bringing about the French-Austrian alliance of 1756, the key element in the Diplomatic Revolution, but also her interest and ability in the arts. *(Achenbach Foundation)*

to it than its ostensible purpose of mutual defense in Germany, and so took up the repeated Austrian initiative. The first treaty of Versailles, of May 1756, was likewise an agreement for defensive neutrality between France and Austria; Frederick's invasion of Saxony later that year, an effort to forestall what he feared was a coalition forming against him, caused the Bourbon and Hapsburg rulers to make their new connection a full alliance.

This "reversal of alliances," as the French called it, or "Diplomatic Revolution of 1756," as it is usually called in modern historical works, transformed the general pattern of relations between the continental states of Europe. Instead of the antagonism between Hapsburg and Bourbon as its pivot, the hostility between Austria and Prussia, both central European powers, became the fixed factor around which other arrangements were made.

Stupid War and Inglorious Peace. French policy in the Seven Years' War, which followed Frederick's invasion of Saxony, remained confused and uncertain. On the one side it was tied to action on the mainland, in conformity with ancient tradition, but with little hope of direct gain; on the other, with a struggle at sea and overseas against Britain, which had resumed in 1754 without a declaration of war and now became intense and general. It swung from one emphasis to another, never totally abandoning either, with dire effects upon the solidity and persistency of French war efforts.

Overseas the French suffered a series of disastrous defeats, losing Canada and most of French India to the English. This time, however, there were no major victories, no triumphant Marshal Saxe, to make good the ground lost in the colonies. The French armies were badly led, badly supported from home, where the financial straits of the government became acute, and pursued no clear strategic aim. Louis's foreign minister after 1758, the duke of Choiseul, had to seek peace. The peace settlement made at Paris in 1763 recognized the loss of most of France's colonial empires. England retained Canada and India, while France transferred the part of Louisiana beyond the Mississippi to Spain, to recompense its partner for its losses. That England did not dictate even harsher terms was due not to any accomplishment of France, but to the fall of the implacable Pitt as prime minister in London (see ch. 20, p. 465).

Resurgence of the Parlements. Within France the monarchy of Louis XV, after two decades of the king's own government, stood in no better posture. Fleury had not so much solved the difficulties of absolutism as lived with them; his royal pupil rushed headlong into problems, and then backed away or wandered about uncertainly when energy, tenacity, and audacity were required.

The first of these problems, as always, was the impoverishment of the state while the nation grew richer. For a while, to be sure, there was a glimpse of betterment. A vigorous controller-general, Machault, struck at the tax exemptions of the nobility and the clergy as the fundamental obstacle to an effective fiscal system. After peace was made in 1748, he persuaded the king to introduce a new income tax at the rate of 5 per cent, the "twentieth." No group in the population was exempted. The Parlement of Paris led the wails of those whose privileges were thus assaulted. Louis, jealous of his prerogatives, overrode its objections and enforced registration of the edict. When the tax, ineffectually collected, brought in meager revenues, when the assembly of the clergy of France in 1750 contested the principle of the "twentieth" as a violation of its liberties, when riots against the tax broke out in Paris, the king's resolution wilted. He withdrew the edict in exchange for an annual grant from the clergy of ten million livres.

In April 1753 the Parlement of Paris presented to the king a Grand Remonstrance in which it claimed the right to resist even him in defense of the fundamental laws of the realm. The very name "Grand Remonstrance" was an overt reminder of the protest of the English Parliament of 1641, at the start of civil war; it was also an expression of the Parlement's claim to share in the sovereign power, like its English namesake. Louis XV replied to this demi-Fronde by exiling 193 magistrates to the provincial city of Bourges. The remaining courts in the capital halted the administration of justice; in the streets the populace, particularly the numerous hangers-on of the legal profession, rioted for a return of those who assured their livelihood. The king meanwhile ran short of money and recalled the magistrates after little more than a year (1754) ; but he commanded them to register his laws without discussion.

The Shrinkage of Authority. The judges did not fear the king who had so often given in to resistance. They continued their remonstrances. Louis attempted to put down their recalcitrance again in 1755 and 1756. He assigned many of their duties to the grand council, an appointive body, and established another "twentieth" tax over their protests. When, in December 1756, he abolished two chambers of the Parlement, Paris broke out in turmoil again. Early the next month the king was the victim of a stabbing attack. The icy unconcern of the Parisians—only six masses were said for his recovery—frightened the monarch. He dismissed Machault and his colleague, D'Argenson, the originators of the strong policy against the Parlements, who were even more emboldened.

The price of renewed capitulation was paid during the Seven Years' War, then just beginning. The proposal of the controller-general Silhouette in 1759 for a "territorial subvention" (a twentieth of income in kind, or of capital in cash) was defeated; taxes on luxuries like coffee, furs, and lackeys were enacted instead. The emptiness of this substitution was so obvious that wits gave the controller-general's name to the new shadow-pictures, all outline and no content. Silhouette's successor Bertin was more ruthless, and no more successful. The protests of the *parlements* of Rouen, Toulouse and Rennes brought down Bertin and his taxes. The Parlement of Paris, unapprehensive of the king's disapproval, decreed the dissolution of the Jesuit order in France in 1762, as a body hostile to the laws of the kingdom, and persuaded him to accept its decree the following year. They had avenged a century of persecution of the Jansenists.

Maupeou: The Reassertion of Authority. The remaining years of the 1760's were filled with royal attempts to introduce increased taxation and successful resistance by the aristocracy, under the leadership of the *parlements*, in Paris and the provinces alike. The struggle between crown and courts was becoming a permanent and bitter enmity. In 1770 the Parlement of Paris again refused to continue the administration of justice when the king attempted to prevent the conviction of the duke of Aiguillon, who had contested the authority of the *parlement* of Rennes. Louis turned to his chancellor, Maupeou, to form a new government and enforce a new policy. Maupeou brought into office as part of his "triumvirate" the duke of Aiguillon as foreign minister and Abbé Terray as controller-general.

When the Parlement of Paris objected to Terray's moderate reform decrees, Maupeou struck at the very source of its power in 1771. The magistrates were not only exiled but were also deprived of their venal offices; a new Parlement (the so-called "Maupeou Parlement") was established with appointive judges, paid by the king instead of by gifts from suitors; and much of its jurisdiction was assigned to five new provincial "superior councils."

Fury greeted Maupeou's stroke of state. The new Parlement was denounced as a vile instrument of royal oppression, while the exiled magistrates were painted as paragons of civic virtue, devoted not to their own private advantages but only to the public good. Maupeou stood firm and the king backed him with a new-found tenacity. Terray eased the consolidation of the new Parlement by returning to fiscal expedients rather than attempting to introduce new taxes. Slowly the new court began to do the work of the old: cases came before it, for the law could not stand perpetually still. By 1774, it was being generally accepted, though still widely loathed. At this moment of turnabout, when absolutism was returning to its native way after two decades of irresolution and relinquishment, the king died of smallpox, execrated and despised.

IV. The Reign of Louis XVI

As Louis XVI, nineteen-year-old grandson of the departed king, began his reign, the Grand Monarchy was in the grip of its greatest crisis. Whether it would be a crisis of growth, leading to new health and recovered strength, or the mortal crisis, consuming the last energies before death, only the years would show.

The Instrument of Authority. The monarchy was still able to undertake, if it would, the creation of effective order and true strength in the state. Its essential instrument of control—the royal authority, the national habit of obedience to the king's command—had been battered during the struggles of the recent reign. The final battle over the Maupeou Parlement, in which it was used with determination and grim purpose, proved that this instrument was not broken.

The establishment of a supreme judicial court of a new type was the key to the restoration of that authority. The institution of appointed magistrates, if maintained in Paris, could be extended to the whole country. The abolition of venal office in the law courts, its stronghold, could then be carried to every part of the royal administration. The king and his ministers would be able to regain effective control of the machinery of government, which they had sold piecemeal to the officeholders over the past two to three centuries. The king's power would become monarchical in fact as well as name.

Yet for the king to have the highest power wholly in hand would not be enough. He would have to use it to solve the problems confronting the state, or Maupeou's triumph would be empty.

Taxes and Tax Exemptions. These problems had now resolved themselves into two major questions, whose component elements constantly crossed and interwove almost beyond the possibility of separation.

The more immediately urgent problem was that of the state's finances. While the riches of France grew greater during the century, the monarchy grew steadily poorer. For untold decades it had spent more than it received. It had performed this miracle by occasional bankruptcy and perpetual borrowing. But as the interest paid upon the loans rapidly approached half of all revenues, the instrument of credit began to twist dangerously, bringing bankruptcy, its very opposite, closer and closer.

Somehow the government had to tap the national wealth more effectively. To do so was becoming more and more difficult. The steady growth of tax exemptions had narrowed the tax base until it became a virtual sign of poverty to pay most imposts. The privileged groups doggedly defended their exemptions, partly for the sake of enhanced social status but even more to protect the family fortunes. Furthermore, French taxes fell most heavily on agriculture, which grew slowly and intermittently in eighteenth-century France, and most lightly on overseas trade and industry, which expanded rapidly.

The Maupeou courts, lacking the prerogatives of their predecessors, could not bar tax reforms. The monarchy now had the means to make all Frenchmen subject to the call of the state upon their funds.

Revolution from Above? Such a change could not stand by itself. According to widespread belief, it meant beginning a social transformation of much wider scope—the abolition of the division of French society into distinct orders. It meant emphasizing the unity of the French nation, the inhabitants of all the lands between the Alps and the Pyrenees, between the Atlantic and the Mediterranean. It meant advancing toward a society under uniform laws, equal for all subjects. It meant, in a word, the ultimate replacement of the Old Regime of liberties and privileges by a New Regime of equality before the law.

Within the Old Regime, however, there was one supreme, towering privilege—the king's own rule, inherited, absolute, personal. Because he commanded the wealth and the persons of all his subjects, he was rich and powerful beyond the possible attainment of any of them. It was this exalted status which made kingship a glorious thing.

Arguments against particular privileges of subjects tended to strike upward to the larger general privilege of the king himself. Thus the crown was loath, in rebuffing the attacks of the aristocratic opponents of royal authority, to destroy their prerogatives lest it at the same time undermine its own. On the other hand, if it undertook to make the king the general servant of the people, it would be possible to crush these privileged recalcitrants, to widen immensely the range of those whose interests committed them to upholding the royal power, and to open up the channels for bringing the wealth of the nation into the coffers of the state. Such a king would be a monarch of a new kind: strong insofar as he served the people—but his personal, hereditary claim would lose force, and royal absolutism would give way to a state wherein the people participated in rule.

The king therefore had a hard option: preserve the Old Regime and imperil his own authority, or save his power by presiding over the transformation of the Old Regime into the New. It was much to ask of any French monarch who prided himself on being the "first gentleman" of France. It was much to ask of any king, to save his state and status by being a revolutionary, even if one who made his revolution "from above."

The New Forces. Yet France was not the mere creature of her king, and French society was being transformed all during the century at a pace without precedent. Agriculture remained the livelihood of nine-tenths of all Frenchmen, but wealth was being created more swiftly in trade and finance. Talents, too, were building careers which led to fame, sometimes to wealth, sometimes to influence.

At the same time the political structure of France was becoming steadily less responsive to these upsurging forces within. The channels of political and social ascent were almost completely closed off to new riches. It was less and less possible to buy one's way into the venal officialdom. The state established few new offices compared to the massive creations of the reign of Louis XIV; and the offices in being remained for the most part in the hands of the same families. The nobility of the sword and robe were drawing close to each other, by intermarriage, by common desire to hold off the new men, commoners without rank but with wealth or talent.

The New Thinkers. Political thought, too, was escaping the service of the crown. Leadership of opinion was boldly taken by the *philosophes* (philosophers; see ch. 27, pp. 607-609). They became one of the powers outside the state, wielding the sharp swords of intelligence and fashion.

Although the *philosophes* probably did not command the active beliefs of a majority of literate Frenchmen, their doctrines, summed up in the name "Enlightenment," had the compensating advantage of being the vogue. Only a Voltaire could deny, without losing face, having read an anonymous pamphlet whose witty scurrility and incisiveness proclaimed him its author; and his smile gave away the game. The *Encyclopédie*, that compendium of knowledge with its half-concealed cargo of critical analysis of the institutions of church and state, was to be found on the shelves of leaders of both church and state, including those most violent against the *philosophes*.

Indeed the *philosophes*, who were seldom democrats and even less often revolutionaries, did not directly imperil the monarchy. Their purpose was to make it enlightened, not to destroy it. Yet the assumptions on which their ideas rested—confident reliance upon human reason; belief that it was right and proper to apply the critical and creative powers of reason to all institutions, especially those which ruled over men's minds and bodies—were corrosive forces in a society and a state which rested so much upon tradition and authority. If the monarchy did not make use of the *philosophes* (and it was no more efficient or persistent in suppressing them than any other group which stood up manfully for itself in eighteenth-century France), it would have to face them, sooner or later, as outright opponents of uncertain but quite real strength.

The New King. "The young king of France will need strength and genius." In these words the aging king of Prussia, Frederick II, summed up the situation of Louis XVI. Needing more than anything else vigor of character and mind, the king lacked vigor most of all. Otherwise he was a "good man" for the everyday world of pious, kind little people. Fearful of his own impulses, he complained that he had never been taught his profession of king. His indolence and self-indulgence kept him from trying to make good the omission; he was satisfied to learn, and learn well, the common trades of locksmith and clockmaker. Yet he knew that something was amiss in the state and was ready to let a remedy be sought. He was concerned about the poor: they must be able to buy bread at two sous, he told the police chief of Paris. But he did not have a streak of wilfulness to give him courage; he flinched before opposition, especially from within the royal family. He was the least despotic of kings; yet he felt the burden of history upon him to maintain the prerogatives of monarchy and imitate the grandeurs of Louis XIV.

His first act of state was to dismiss Maupeou and Terray, whose program of economy had won them the hostility of the royal family and the courtiers. Maupeou warned the king that his safety required the maintenance of the new nonvenal courts, but Louis could not withstand the clamor against them. He reinstated the old Parlement of Paris, warning it not to remonstrate against laws before registering them, or to suspend the operations of the courts, or to resign in unison. Such chidings, unless backed by an unrelenting will for obedience, had long since ceased to carry weight with the magistrates, and remonstrances issued forth from their chambers in undiminished number.

Turgot: Toward a New Regime. Having struck from his own hand the best weapon against balky privilege, Louis XVI proceeded to accept from his mentor, the count of Maurepas, the appointment of the thoroughgoing reformer Turgot as controller-general. As thinker and as man of action, Turgot was dedicated to making France into an "enlightened despotism," an absolute monarchy dedicated to the general interest by means of both public improvement and self-improvement. Turgot accepted the economic teachings of Gournay, who favored freedom of enterprise against state regulation. As intendant of Limoges, however, he had been anything but a passive looker-on; he encouraged industry and trade to develop on their own, and in his new post he adapted this policy to the whole kingdom.

The *philosophes* acclaimed Turgot's appointment as a victory of their cause. D'Alembert, co-editor of the *Encyclopédie*, was both jubilant and worried. "If good does not come of this," he declared, "it must then mean that good cannot be."

The first, immediate problem was the finances. The state collected a little more than 275,000,000 livres annually in revenue but spent some 50,000,000 more than this figure. Turgot promised the king to close the gap without bankruptcy, additional loans, or new taxes. Expedients like reducing the profits of the tax farmers helped somewhat, but permanent improvement required both expanding the taxpaying wealth of the country and practicing severe economies. His introduction of free trade in grain, designed to increase agricultural production, brought him into the first difficulties. Speculators worsened the shortage caused by a poor crop in 1774; bread rose rapidly in price, leading to riots in Paris and elsewhere. Turgot put down the disorders without compunction or pity.

When he began to apply his general program, he ran into more dangerous opposition. "Since the expenditures of government are aimed at the interest of everyone," he declared, "everyone should pay his share." In addition to spreading the tax base over the entire population, he also favored gradual abolition of manorial land tenures, full freedom for Protestants, the development of education and public charity outside the control of the Catholic church, and the establishment of provincial consultative assemblies elected by all landowners. Such a program, carried into practice in its entirety, would go far toward transforming the Old Regime into the New.

The Fall of Turgot. Turgot's attempt to reduce the expenditures of the royal court brought upon him the hatred of the queen. His plea to the king, "You must employ your kindness against your kindness itself, remembering the source of the money which you can distribute to your courtiers," was to Marie Antoinette at best mere silliness and at worst arrogant intrusion upon her most precious rights.

The queen personified the Old Regime in all its pretty glamor and its stubborn resistance to facing unpleasant realities. An archduchess of Austria, she had become the bride of the dauphin of France in 1770, their wedlock sealing the Diplomatic Revolution. As frivolous as her husband was sedate, she looked upon the kingdom of France as no more than the provider of good things that were hers by right. It did not offend her that her mother, Empress Maria Theresa, and the Austrian ambassador to France, Mercy-Argenteau, plied her with political instructions; she felt no bond to her husband's homeland and too much deserved the name of "Austrian woman" (*l'Autrichienne*) by which she came to be called. The queen's purposes might be small, but her will was strong. She was, said one sly observer, "the only man" in the royal family.

Turgot's political edifice tumbled in 1776 when he introduced two major reform edicts. One replaced the royal *corvée* (see p. 418) with a money tax upon all landowners; the other abolished the guilds and established freedom to engage in commerce and industry, with a few minor exceptions. Tumult ensued. The noblemen complained at being made to pay a commoner's tax, and a leading member of the Parlement of Paris justified their resistance because commoners were "born subject to the taille." The Parlement as a whole, attacking the edict on the guilds, proclaimed that the privilege of the masters, "as a right of personal property," was inviolable. On such a principle, no reform whatever was possible, for every privilege and exemption could thus be equated to private property.

The king was aghast at what Turgot seemed to be doing. "It is not my purpose to mingle the orders of society," he announced. Prodded by his still angry wife, he dismissed Turgot on May 12, 1776. The controller-general, in his final interview with the king, gave him a warning as far-seeing as it was courageous: "Never forget that weakness put Charles I's head upon the block." Among the advocates of enlightenment outside, there was consternation and despair. Mademoiselle de l'Espinasse, at whose salon foregathered the élite of the *philosophes*, shuddered: "We have lost hope itself."

Necker: The Miracle that Failed. The royal *corvée* was reintroduced, many guilds were re-established, but the state of the king's finances became no better. The famed banker Necker, who had published pamphlets in condemnation of Turgot, was named in his place; because he was a Genevan by citizenship and a Protestant by religion, he could not be named controller-general, but received instead the title of director of finances. Necker had a reputation as a financial wonder worker, thanks to his success in amassing a fortune as a speculator and banker. He was confident that he could restore the financial health of France where Turgot had failed, and without arousing the antagonism of the court.

His miracle consisted in his ability to make immense loans from the bankers of Europe; he floated more than 500,000,000 livres in new borrowings in five years. Nonetheless his failure to attempt any fundamental reforms brought sharp criticism against him. He defended himself by publishing an *Account (Compte rendu)* of his administration. His figures were distorted in order to show a surplus of 10,000,000 livres in ordinary accounts when there was actually a deficit of about 46,000,000; nonetheless they revealed to some extent the inner workings of the royal treasury, as had never been done before. His disclosure of the huge sums being spent on the royal court and courtiers turned them against him, and he was dismissed in May 1781, a victim of the same forces that had brought down Turgot.

The War of American Independence.   The court, for all its extravagances, was not the major immediate cause of the desperate financial situation. That was rather French participation in the War of American Independence. The rebellion of the North American colonists against their British motherland was an opportunity long awaited for revenging the defeat of 1763. Vergennes, who had become foreign minister at the beginning of the reign, had carefully avoided entanglements in continental European wars; he had drawn the lesson of the two previous reigns that no conquests lay open to France on the mainland of Europe which would not arouse the powers against her. Nonetheless he waited for the American victory at Saratoga, in December 1777, before he moved beyond surreptitious assistance to overt alliance. French naval and military might swung the balance to the American side. In 1781 Cornwallis, the British commander, capitulated at Yorktown to the American Washington, and the Frenchman Rochambeau.

Two years later the treaty of peace was signed at Versailles. The Americans gained recognition of their independence and sovereignty. France obtained as her meager material gains the return of two West Indian islands and an African trading station. But Albion, her fleet, and her army had all been humbled, and that revenge sufficed.

Vergennes then turned to amity with Britain, in order to make the peace permanent. He joined the English in defeating a Russian-sponsored proposal to partition the Turkish empire and establish a "Greek empire" in 1782-1783. He also concluded a trade treaty (called the Eden Treaty after the principal English negotiator) which opened the French market to English manufactures by sharp tariff reductions.

Calonne: The Inevitability of Reform.   The financial difficulties of the state grew alarmingly. The American war had cost many millions, which Necker had obtained chiefly by loans. By 1786 the interest on the outstanding debt took more than half the revenues of the state. A reform could not be evaded.

Even Calonne, the controller-general who had followed Necker in 1783, for all his promises of painless improvement, admitted his failure three years later and proposed a program to Louis XVI which was little more than Turgot's of a decade earlier. Now the king, at Calonne's plea, agreed to call an assembly of notables for 1787 to consider means of improvement. The monarch, by accepting the counsel of subjects in his need, admitted the incompetency of absolutism. The times were dangerous for such a confession of weakness.

Hardship and hunger stalked the fair land of France. After some seven

The Provinces of France in 1789

decades of steady, often spectacular, growth, French prosperity had wilted in the late 1780's. A succession of disastrous harvests in the grain fields and the vineyards caused havoc to trade and industry, which the Eden Treaty, by bringing in English competition, made infuriatingly worse. The "little folk," for whom this economic adversity meant misery and famine, became increasingly restive and turbulent. "Banditry" became widespread; it was often only a beggary which looted and stole crops in the field.

At the same time, the prestige of the king and queen suffered a dangerous blow in the notorious affair of the necklace. The cardinal of Rohan had been swindled into paying an enormous sum for a diamond necklace for Marie Antoinette. A public trial of Rohan, along with the swindlers, brought the cardinal's acquittal, to the dismay of the king and queen. Apparently the prince of the church had desired only to extinguish the queen's hostility to him, but public opinion thought he wished to buy her most intimate favors and that she had taken the jewels and refused herself. There was contempt for the royal couple—in the troubled conditions, contempt that was even more dangerous than hatred.

Personal monarchy was on the verge of disaster, though few at court knew what was happening. The political doctrines of the *philosophes* had been only theories for long decades, setting the paramountcy of the public interest against the argument of divine right. The war of American Independence proved that such ideas could be embodied in effective public institutions. It also reminded Frenchmen of the revolutionary belief that the

431

people might rightfully resort to force to overthrow tyranny. With personal respect for the monarch shattered, with an empty treasury depriving the monarchy of the "sinews of peace," the American example gave hope of a new start.

For the moment, however, Frenchmen remained without exception monarchists; violent revolution was an eventuality they all wished to avoid. For the moment, too, the initiative in public affairs remained in the king and his ministers. Upon them rested, as the notables assembled in 1787, an immense and fearful responsibility.

19

Britain under the Later Stuarts

1660 - 1714

IN 1660 ENGLAND set to work to restore the old order in the state, in society, and in men's conduct and character. Thus the way of life which the Commonwealth had interrupted could be made permanent, proof against human misjudgment and misconduct. This was, at its best, the dream of Restoration.

It was already a fantasy, untrue to life. The England—and even more the Britain—of before 1642 had not been Eden, nor was Britain in the years that followed 1660. Men, with high hopes and low ambitions, struggled then and did still. The system of state, which looked so stable after the turmoil of two decades, was uncertain, haphazard, and incomplete. Monarchy, Parliament, and people overlapped in powers and purposes.

Nonetheless the attempt to recreate the past became a shaping force in the future. The memory of the past, admired or execrated, limited and directed the activity of Britons for long decades, till the problems posed were at last roughly solved and new vexations rose.

I. Charles II

On May 29, 1660, Charles II, dapper and graceful, rode back into London. This was the town where he had been born thirty years before to the very day, the town, too, where his father had died on the block some eleven years before. Now all was joy and affection. Charles's subjects lined the streets to cheer him, and he responded with an easy smile.

England in 1660. Merriment and abandon were the signs of England's return to the "good old times." The restraints of the Puritan Commonwealth were thrown off. The ancient sports and dances, forbidden for a decade, were practiced again. Once again Sundays were marked by games and bearbaiting as well as by churchgoing.

The re-establishment of the theater was characteristic of the new times. It had been abolished by the Puritans as the teacher of iniquity; under the Restoration it mocked their ostensible virtuousness by tales of vice triumphant, or at least delightful. The women's roles were given not to boys, as before, but to actresses whose easy virtue was notorious. The life of the court duplicated the tales of the stage, with the king himself the master of the revels and orgies. He did not disdain, indeed, to take Nell Gwynn, half-actress and half-harlot, for one of his bevy of mistresses.

Yet any who saw England only in the image of the licentious court mistook her strength. The navy was the pet of the new regime. It received notable commanders, including Monck, who became duke of Albemarle, and the king's brother James, duke of York. Both were bold and resourceful commanders, though Albemarle was a landlubber who made his crews laugh by giving orders in the language of the drill field. Even more important was the work of professional officials who took increasing charge of the administration of the fleet. Most influential of these new administrators was Samuel Pepys, who won a place in literature for his shrewd and candid secret diary. He was more than a diarist; he was also a model official, informed, capable, and persistent, though no more honest than was expected in an age of widespread corruption.

The land forces fared less well because of the fear of a standing army after the experience with Cromwell's "New Model." Charles II was able to retain only a few regiments as his guards, including Monck's own Coldstream Guards.

The economic strength of England was considerably greater in 1660 than it had been in 1642, at the start of the Civil War. Commerce had expanded under the impetus of naval victories over the Dutch and the new opportunities in the West Indies. Within the country industrial and agrarian activity responded to the spur of new markets. Many traders and artisans had been involved in the political-religious movements of the revolution and now were excluded from public life; but they were permitted to continue their livelihoods, to which they devoted themselves with increased diligence and ultimately greater profits.

Convention and Cavalier Parliament. Whether England could maintain her strength depended upon the preservation of the civil accord which marked the Stuart Restoration.

The first signs were favorable. A Convention Parliament was already meeting when Charles II came to England. Although it had been assembled at Monck's initiative without royal writs and included a majority of Presbyterians, the king permitted it to continue, together with the restored House of Lords.

It granted the king the revenues of the customs and excise for life. These barely sufficed for the everyday needs of government; they did not permit him to maintain his court above a parsimonious level to which he did not, after the penury of his exile, attempt to accustom himself. From the beginning, Charles II resented and resisted the paucity of his income.

The Convention Parliament also began to make into law the principles of the king's declaration at Breda, before his return: amnesty for all but a small number of regicides, and re-establishment of Anglicanism, together with safeguards for "tender consciences."

The Convention Parliament nullified the legislation of the Long Parliament and the Commonwealth which had never received the royal assent. Purchasers of crown and church lands during the interregnum were evicted without compunction; otherwise, the general principle was maintained that private transactions were valid. Thus many Cavaliers who had been forced to sell all or part of their estates to pay fines imposed upon them by the revolutionary authorities found themselves unable to recapture their lands. Their bitterness was made all the harsher because "private bills" were passed restoring estates to friends of the king and his ministers, despite the principle.

The "Clarendon Code." The Cavaliers took their vengeance upon the Presbyterians when the Convention was dissolved at the end of 1660 and a new, regular Parliament was convened. As the most forthright adherents of the Stuarts, the Cavaliers won a huge majority in the House of Commons.

They proceeded to enact a series of laws between 1661 and 1665 reaffirming and reinforcing Anglicanism as the established and favored church of England. Christians who accepted the doctrine of the Trinity were permitted a bare tolerance, without freedom of worship or equality of rights. Only Anglicans were permitted to hold office in state or church, to teach (with minor exceptions for a few purely utilitarian subjects), or to hold religious services; clergymen expelled from their livings for rejecting the Book of Common Prayer were forbidden to come within five miles of organized towns ("corporate boroughs").

The name of "Clarendon code" given to this repressive legislation symbolized the still-concealed cleavage within the Restoration monarchy. Edward Hyde, earl of Clarendon, who had been Charles's chief adviser in exile and was now lord chancellor of England and the leading minister of state, had not come out against the bills, but he had not favored them. Like the great mass of the Cavaliers, he wished to re-establish the traditional monarchy, in which he saw the God-given basis of the existing social order. He accepted the legislation of 1642, which left the monarchy dynastic but confirmed its limited and constitutional character. On the matter of religion, however, he differed with the Cavalier majority. Though as pious an Anglican as any of them, he favored either "comprehending" the major Protestant dissenters within the Anglican church, or, if this endeavor failed, at least permitting the Presbyterians an adequate toleration.

The "Un-Cavalier" King. The king was even less a friend to the Clarendon code. The Cavaliers who saw him as another Charles I did not see him as he was. He did not share their fervent Anglicanism, although he maintained the outward forms of its observance. He inclined towards his mother's Catholicism, which he admired for its support of absolute monarchy. He did not attempt to prevent the duke of York from adopting Catholicism; brought Catholics into his personal service; and began secret discussions with the papacy about the possibility of his own eventual conversion and that of his realm.

As concerned the character of the state, however, Charles II was utterly his father's son. He had little knowledge and less understanding of the traditional English monarchy, with its ill-defined combination of government by king, Parliament and common-law courts; and what he knew and understood, he did not like. His goal was to rule by prerogative, which he equated with absolute monarchy as it was being practiced by Louis XIV in France; he was willing to accept the collaboration of Parliament and courts provided they took their policy from him.

Yet his passive acceptance of the Clarendon code was also characteristic of this king of many aspects. Charles II did not wish ever again "to go upon his travels," as he sardonically called his exile; he wished to enjoy the pleasures, so long missed, of kingship, which were for him chiefly indolence, lechery, and patronage of the arts, sciences, and race track. In exile he had learned to distrust big words, big beliefs, and strong feelings. He had become a master politician, cynically ready to use the worst and the best in men in the achievement of his own aims. He was both supple and stubborn: when he met resistance which could not be easily crushed, he seemed to accept what he could not alter. When the situation changed, he returned to his purpose.

For all their doctrines of nonresistance to the monarch, the Cavaliers opposed Charles when he proved an "un-Cavalier" king. Their clamor compelled him to withdraw a declaration of indulgence to dissenters in 1662. Their hostility became even sharper and more open when he went his own way in foreign affairs, disregarding the desires of Parliament. His sale of

Dunkirk, the solitary English foothold on the continent, to Louis XIV in 1662, for the sum of £290,000, aroused new tirades against his policy.

The Second Dutch War. Attention was soon distracted toward the rivalry with the Dutch Republic. Parliament had re-enacted into law, with stricter provisions, the Navigation Act of 1653. The law of 1662, like its predecessor, was the prelude to war. Dutch and English merchants competed sharply in both the West and the East Indies; and soon warships fought "beyond the line" (in colonial waters) on behalf of the merchantmen. Open war was declared in 1665, explicitly over the issue of Dutch refusal to acknowledge British dominion over the nearby seas. Charles II had in addition his own family interest in the conflict. His nephew, William III, prince of Orange, had been excluded from all offices in the Dutch Republic by the treaty of peace with Cromwell and the accompanying Dutch legislation (see ch. 24, p. 544). Charles expected that part of the fruits of victory would be the re-establishment of young William, who would be duly grateful to his royal uncle.

This second Anglo-Dutch war did not go as planned. Early British triumphs at sea were soon counteracted by the vigorous measures of John de Witt and the dominant republican party in Holland. Louis XIV, linked to the Dutch by the alliance of 1662, could not avoid entering the conflict on their side; but he was, as he explained to Charles, a reluctant participant. His troops aided the Dutch to drive off the forces of the bishop of Münster, who had become the sole English ally; and his fleet came up from the Mediterranean to the Channel, where it avoided actual combat but nonetheless hampered English naval operations.

The Peace of Breda. The English will to war was worn thin by two holocausts of nature. One was an attack of the bubonic plague in 1665, which killed some 60,000 Londoners—more than a tenth of the city's people—and left the country trembling. Less than a year later an immense fire devastated the capital. It destroyed more than 13,000 houses, though it caused few deaths.

The final stroke was the successful Dutch naval raid into the mouth of the Thames in the early summer of 1667. They raided the naval shipyard at Chatham, burning docks and ships and towing off the flagship, the *Royal Charles*—a personal insult to the king.

Meanwhile Louis XIV contributed doubly toward the making of peace. He invaded the Spanish Netherlands in the War of Devolution, arousing the old English fear of French control over these strategic provinces; and he offered his mediation to the English and Dutch in their war. A peace was quickly patched up (July 31, 1667) at Breda, in the United Provinces. All conquests were mutually restored, with the exception of the New Netherlands, which remained in English hands as New York, and Surinam, on the Guiana coast, which the Dutch retained. Nonetheless it was "a snarling peace," as Sir William Temple, one of the British negotiators, wrote—one resting more upon the two sides' common anxiety over French aggrandizement than on the triumph of either, or on their reconciliation.

The Cabal Ministry. Within England the honeymoon harmony of Restoration was shattered. Parliament, angry over the signs of subordination to France, turned upon Clarendon, the supposed author of this policy. When impeachment proceedings were begun against him in 1666, the king ordered him into exile to save him from Strafford's fate—at the hands of a Cavalier parliament!

In Clarendon's place as his principal adviser, Charles II named not a single man, but a group of five ministers. They were artfully selected to represent different segments of the nation: Clifford, an avowed Roman Catholic; Ashley Cooper, a Presbyterian during the Civil War and Commonwealth; the duke of Buckingham, an Anglican of immense wealth and great personal influence; the earl of Arlington, Charles's own man, a veteran of the Cavalier army who was ready to take his policy from the king; and Lauderdale, a Scot who gave over his erstwhile Presbyterianism to become the agent of the king's effort to implant episcopalian Anglicanism in Scotland. From the secrecy of their meetings and the accident of their initials, public opinion applied the hostile name of "Cabal" (faction) to them. But Charles was satisfied with them, for by contending among themselves they left him safely dominant over them all; and their varied policies afforded him different possible courses of action according to circumstances. Yet their squabbling and mutual distrust deprived him of orderly counsel and administration, a weakness which came to the surface only when renewed war put the king's system to the hard test.

The Triple Alliance. After the Peace of Breda, Charles indicated to Louis XIV his willingness to go into an alliance with France directed against the Netherlands, provided the price in a French subsidy grant was large enough to enable him to do without asking Parliament for additional funds. When the French monarch rejected the proposal as too high in cost, Charles turned toward the Dutch. He sent Temple, who had become friendly with De Witt, to The Hague in January 1668 with a proposal for an alliance to halt the French conquest of the Low Countries. A treaty was signed which became known as the "Triple Alliance" by reason of the inclusion of Sweden a few months later.

It was a bold and subtle stroke of policy. The English Parliament, with fear of France paramount in its mind, rejoiced at the alliance with the former enemies and gave the king new taxes, over and beyond the customs and excise duties which had been granted him for life at the beginning of the reign. At the same time, Charles destroyed the Dutch-French alliance of

1662, which had contributed to his defeat in the recent war. Furthermore, within the Netherlands, he weakened De Witt's position and gave new spirit to the Orangists.

Yet friendship with the French king remained the heart of Charles's policy. Louis XIV, confronted with the Triple Alliance as a barrier to his aggrandizement, became readier to meet English terms. With the aid of Charles's sister, Henrietta, who was married to the duke of Orléans, a secret treaty was negotiated at Dover in May 1670. Charles promised to turn Catholic and to begin conversion of his kingdoms; in the probable event of rebellion, France would send 6,000 troops to aid in repression. In the meanwhile a French subsidy of £200,000 annually would enable him to prepare for conversion and for war against the Dutch. Because the king did not dare to reveal the religious clauses of the treaty to his Protestant ministers, a spurious negotiation was entrusted to Buckingham, which culminated at the end of 1670 in a duplicate treaty, differing from the Dover pact only in that the subsidies provided for conversion were assigned toward war preparations.

The Third Dutch War. In January 1672 Charles unexpectedly halted payment of government obligations held by the goldsmiths of London, who did the major banking business of England. This "Stop of the Exchequer" puzzled and enraged the business community, for it violated the government's pledged credit and caused a number of banking houses to fail. Its purpose became clear only in March when an English force waylaid the Dutch merchant fleet returning from Smyrna, in the Levant; though the attack was beaten off, Charles declared war on the Dutch the next month. It was to wage this war that the drastic and dangerous measure of the "Stop" had been taken.

Even in combination with the French, the English navy was unable to wrest command of the narrow seas from the Dutch. In the great battle of the Texel, off the entrance to the Zuyder Zee, the Dutch admiral De Ruyter thwarted the best efforts of his opponents to close off Amsterdam from the sea. Subsequent English naval action was no more successful.

Charles II's political difficulties were not eliminated by the war although the government appealed to the nation's sense of commercial rivalry with the Dutch with the cry of ancient Rome, *Delenda est Carthago!* (Carthage must be destroyed!). English reluctance to fight alongside France was sharpened by a declaration of indulgence which the king issued two days before the declaration of war. By according the right to exercise their worship not only to Protestant dissenters but also to Roman Catholics, it aroused a fervor of antipapist agitation. The opposition denied that the king had the constitutional power to revoke, by an act of prerogative, what statute had set down as national policy. The king resisted their importunities until 1673 when his need for funds to wage war compelled him not only to withdraw the declaration of indulgence, but to accept a Test Act permitting only those who took the Anglican sacrament of communion and explicitly renounced the doctrine of transubstantiation to hold office. The duke of York, who was lord admiral, and two other high officials, resigned their posts, but the king received a grant of £1,200,000 from Parliament.

Furthermore, Charles discovered that he had no tool of his policy in his nephew, William III, who had received power in the Netherlands as a result of the Anglo-French assault (see ch. 24, p. 544). William, ungrateful for promotion by such means, devoted all his efforts to the defense of his fatherland. He sent agents to England to play upon the fears that Charles was leading that country into Catholicism and subjugation to France. The outcry in the nation and in Parliament against the French alliance became so strong that Charles, fearing to lose all control, bowed to necessity and made peace with the Dutch in the treaty of Westminster in 1674.

Parties and Party Strife. The Cabal fell victim to the king's failure in the third Dutch war, as Clarendon had succumbed to the debacle of the second. Clifford, the unhappy Catholic, committed suicide, while Ashley Cooper, meanwhile raised to the peerage as earl of Shaftesbury, gave his skill as an orator, thinker, and organizer to the formation and leadership of an opposition to the royal policy. Charles called upon a new man, Sir Thomas Osborne, now named earl of Danby, to lead his government.

Danby, a firm Anglican, was opposed to giving friendship to France or concessions to Catholics. But he was also a convinced royalist who was willing to do his master's bidding. He enabled Charles to rule more easily by making him less dependent on Parliament. He restricted expenses, brought new efficiency into the fiscal organization of the government, and increased the income from taxation. At Charles's behest, he steered a shifting course between Parliament, which offered financial assistance only at the price of aiding the Dutch against France, and Louis XIV, who now offered subsidies to the English king provided he kept his country from joining the hostile coalition.

The Protestant and anti-French party, confronted by a king who did not share their hates and likes, turned toward William of Orange as their hope and often their secret guide. His position was strengthened by his marriage in 1677 to Mary Stuart, elder daughter of the duke of York.

The second success won by the opponents of France was a treaty of alliance with the Dutch the next summer. It provided for English entry into the war on the Dutch side if France did not make peace with them at the Nijmegen conference by August 10, 1678. This ultimatum compelled Louis XIV to order his negotiators to accept terms of peace at the eleventh hour before its expiry.

The next triumph of the anti-French party was the institution of impeachment proceedings against Danby in 1679 after a disgruntled ambassador revealed the character of negotiations with Louis XIV for subsidies. To protect him, the king not only dissolved Parliament, which had been sitting since 1661, but also placed Danby in the Tower, beyond the reach of ordinary judicial proceedings.

In the hope of recovering national support, or at least of dividing his opponents, Charles inaugurated a new experiment in government. Temple, who had a high reputation for his part in the Triple Alliance and for aiding the Dutch at Nijmegen, was the leading spirit in the new council. Shaftesbury, the leader of the opposition, was named its president. The innovation soon failed, partly because the council was too big and clumsy, partly because Shaftesbury would not play the king's servant.

Popish Plot and Whig Conspiracy. Tension, political and religious, grew worse until it burst with the revelation of the so-called "Popish Plot." One Titus Oates, who had been born an Anglican, studied at Salmanca in Spain, and become a Jesuit, ostentatiously returned to his first faith. He disclosed to a judge that he had taken part in a conspiracy by Catholics, under Jesuit leadership, to slay Charles II and place James, his papist brother, on the throne. The mysterious murder of the judge led to a furor of fear and terror. Those implicated by Oates were brought to trial and many, including the duke of York's secretary, were executed.

The king, though aware that Oates was a perjurer linked to Shaftesbury's party, permitted the judicial murders of those he had once protected. His one interest, besides protecting himself, was to safeguard the hereditary transmission of the crown. This was not easy to do, for the "country" (opposition) party introduced bills into three successive Parliaments to exclude Roman Catholics from succession to the throne. Charles was willing to permit deprivation of most of a Catholic monarch's prerogatives, but stood fast against invasion of the rule of succession. He also signed a tightened Test Act. But Parliament was not to be halted, and dissolution was the means the king was forced to employ to bar enactment of the successive exclusion bills.

Shaftesbury and his followers held the initiative from 1679 until 1681, when, as Charles II had expected, the excesses of Oates' perjuries spawned disbelief and revulsion among more sober Englishmen. Then came the turn of the king to use the same weapon of falsified or distorted accusations.

During the meeting of the third Parliament at Oxford in 1681, a band of Shaftesbury supporters rode armed into the city, arousing fears of civil war. The government announced that it had detected a conspiracy to overthrow the king on behalf of his bastard son, the Protestant duke of Monmouth. This plot, like its popish predecessor, was a mixture of fact and fable. It was utilized nonetheless by the monarch to strike down Shaftesbury, who fled to Holland.

For the next four years Charles ruled by means of his prerogative without Parliament, over a restless, fearful, deeply divided but still obedient country. The opposition lost its stronghold in the organized towns when "quo warranto" proceedings were instituted to deprive numerous corporate boroughs of their charters on grounds of exceeding their powers. When the king died in 1685, he had maintained himself but solved no problems.

Tories and Whigs. Two distinct parties among the English people rose out of the welter of the two contrary conspiracies and the struggles over exclusion. One, the king's supporters or "court" party, were dubbed by their opponents as "Tories," a jeering name for Irish rebel bandits. The "country" party in turn received from its foes its appellation of "Whigs," a slurring name for Scots Presbyterian covenanters. Each side rejected its name as libelous and denied that it was a party, or faction; and insofar as they lacked formal organization and membership, this denial was true. But in a loose way they were parties, bound together by fundamentally differing sets of beliefs on crucial points of state and religion.

The Tories, the descendants of the Cavaliers of the Civil War days, affirmed the divine right of the monarchy, which subjects could not legitimately resist by force of arms. Yet they did not favor absolute monarchy; rather, like the departed and now dead Clarendon, they supported the crown as the leading force within a framework of parliamentary constitutionalism. This emphasis upon the representative assembly arose out of their experience in resisting Charles's near-Catholicism and the Romanism of the duke of York; for the Tories were staunch Anglicans whose antipathy for Presbyterians and other Protestant dissenters seldom toned down their plain hatred for Roman Catholics. For both dissenter and recusant they favored a policy of strict repression and exclusion from public life. The Tories, though drawing from every group in the nation, represented primarily the most numerous political class, the squirearchy of country gentlemen.

The Whigs were a more heterogeneous party. They received the support of a majority of the urban men of business, as well as of many great aristocrats whose immense wealth and local leadership enabled them to flout the royal will. Though very largely members of the established church, they did not share the Tories' intense and narrow Anglicanism; instead they advocated toleration of Protestants, though not of Catholics. In political doctrine the Whigs stressed the importance of Parliament and sometimes ventured the notion that it possessed ultimate supremacy.

II. James II

James II ascended the throne in 1685 without open resistance. He lacked flexibility and adroitness and was insensitive to the world about him. He was, too, endlessly persistent in the endeavor to do what he thought right. Where his late brother had looked to his advantages, James stood upon his principles. Despite all the clamor for exclusion, he had neither abandoned his Roman Catholic faith nor lost any of the powers of his prerogative.

The Royal Resources. At his first meeting with the privy council after his accession, James declared with unrehearsed vehemence: "I have often heretofore ventured my life in defense of this nation; and I shall go as far as any man in preserving it in all its just rights and liberties." He interpreted these rights and freedoms to mean, however, little more than to live under his benevolent absolutism. He retained the old Stuart ambition to rule by prerogative, without restraint or with a docile Parliament.

He had a better opportunity to achieve this ambition than any of his forebears. The keys to his success lay in keeping his expenditures within the limits of the fixed revenues of the crown, which were given him for life; in consolidating royal control over the machinery of state; and in calming the nation in matters of religion.

The first key lay easily within James's hands. England had grown steadily in prosperity during the quarter century since the Restoration. Despite the defeats in the last two wars against the Dutch, English merchants and shippers handled an increasing portion of Europe's trade. India, the West Indian islands, and the colonies on the North American shoreline all contributed to this development. Within England industry responded to the expanding market for its goods by producing a greater variety of manufactures in greater quantities than ever before. The crown's revenues had increased in steady proportion, even more rapidly than prices. Thus the king was able to live on his permanent revenues as long as he avoided bold and expensive enterprises.

Tightening of the royal grip upon the machinery of state was made easier by the first great crisis of the reign, the rebellion of the duke of Monmouth.

Monmouth's Rebellion. During the exclusion struggle, Monmouth had become the hope of many Whigs. They accepted rumors that Charles had secretly married Monmouth's mother, Lucy Walters, despite the king's denials; in such an event, Monmouth, not James, was the rightful king of England. Monmouth, a vain and shallow man, had shared their belief, but his interposition of his candidacy for succession to the crown had brought upon him his father's wrath and exile from the country.

Soon after James's enthronement, Monmouth decided to assert his claim. Despite the discouragement of his cousin, the prince of Orange, he set sail with a small force from the Netherlands, where he had fled, and landed on the southwest coast of England to raise the standard of rebellion against his uncle. He won recruits from the "small people," especially in the countryside, but most of the gentry and aristocracy stood aside, deaf and cold to his appeals. James's small army, commanded by a veteran of the continental wars, Sir John Churchill, crushed Monmouth's troops of rustics.

The gentlemen of England watched silently and thoughtfully as Monmouth was rushed to execution, and as Judge Jeffreys, in his "Bloody Assizes," sat in savage judgment upon the forlorn rebels. Jeffrey's rank partisanship, his contempt for the forms of the common law, his assertion of absolute royal authority—these were, they realized, the quality of the rule which James II wished to impose upon the whole nation.

They dared not stir, however. The could only wait for the monarchy to pass from James to his Protestant daughters: Mary, wife of William of Orange, and Anne, married to Prince George of Denmark. Both were rigid Protestants who refused to follow their father in his return to Rome. Though the widowed James had been married in 1673 to Mary d'Este, daughter of the duke of Modena and a Catholic, none of their children had lived past infancy. As the king was now more than fifty years of age, they could hope he would not become a father again. Patience therefore enabled them to remain safely loyal to the monarch while inwardly opposed to his policy of absolutism and Catholicism.

Scotland was the scene of similar and almost simultaneous events. In the northern kingdom James ruled in a frankly absolutist spirit, according to the suggestion of an official who wrote: "Scotland is not England. Measures need not be too nicely kept with this people." The Latin mottos on the muzzles of the king's cannon—*Haec est vox regia; Non sine fulmina regnat* ("This is the king's voice"; "There is no ruling without lightning striking") —spoke loudly. A rebellion, led by the earl of Argyll, was defeated as easily as Monmouth's, and the repression was no less harsh.

Prerogative and Papism. James, seeing the field cleared of open resistance, swept away the remnants of Whigs among the officeholders in the state. Lukewarm Tories too suffered the same fate. The courts were brought under tight control by summary dismissals of judges who would not take their orders from the crown, unlike Jeffreys, the new lord chief justice. The rule was enforced that they held their judgeships not during good behavior, but at the king's pleasure. As during the reign of Charles I, the subservience of the courts began to shake the popular faith in the justice and rightness of their findings.

James, ever more confident in his strength, did not consider it right or necessary to refrain from his attempt to restore Catholicism in England because of the opposition of an immense majority of his subjects. Despite his coronation oath to defend the church of England, he set to work to break the monopoly of the Anglicans in church, state, armed forces, and education. He compelled the colleges of Oxford and Cambridge, the training places for Anglican clergymen, to accept Catholics as fellows and rectors, in defiance of the Test Act. The king maintained, as Charles had done before him, that he had the power to suspend the application of laws; thus there was danger that all parliamentary statutes could be discarded at his whim. Elsewhere in the state, Catholics were appointed in like manner. Open Catholic worship was resumed in the capital, and a nuncio from the pope came to London and was publicly welcomed.

Fear that the king would go beyond these measures arose when he called troops from Ireland and established them in a training camp on Hounslow Heath, near London. He appointed to their command Catholic officers, who boasted that before they finished their work England would return to the obedience of Rome.

In 1687 James issued a declaration of indulgence to both Catholics and Protestant dissenters. Parliament refused its approval, but James did not budge. The next year, indeed, he commanded all parish clergymen to read a reiterated declaration of indulgence in their churches. This strained the patience of Anglican ecclesiastics, torn between their duty to obey and their loathing of what they were commanded to do. Seven bishops petitioned the king to relieve them from enforcing the order. James angrily denounced their plea as rebellious and ordered their trial. The jury refused to find them guilty of sedition and set them free.

William of Orange. The hostility of the vast majority of Englishmen to the royal policy was sparked into open flame when a son, James Edward, was born to James and Mary of Modena on June 20, 1688. The hope that their tribulations would end with the reign of James was doomed, for the young prince would be raised a Catholic. The rumor swiftly spread that the infant was an impostor smuggled into the lying-in room in a warming-pan. It found acceptance even among the less credulous Protestants, while many of those who did not believe such a tale of slander nonetheless went along with it for expediency's sake.

Within less than a month from the birth of the infant prince, a letter crossed the North Sea bringing to the prince of Orange an invitation to come with an army to England to rescue the country's religion and its laws. Seven leading figures in church and politics, some Whig and other Tory, put their signatures—the assurance of death if they failed or were betrayed—on the letter. They were not making a stab in the dark, however. William had previously indicated his willingness to make the expedition provided the English leaders committed themselves unequivocally and irrevocably. Till the birth of James Edward, he had urged patience and caution upon his English friends while emphasizing the paramount importance of preserving the established religious and political order.

William received from Louis XIV a warning that an expedition to England would bring an immediate declaration of war by France upon the

States-General; but the French king's simultaneous action in sending his army to the Palatinate (see ch. 17, p. 405) reassured the prince that immediate danger was small. He accepted the invitation, obtained the support of the States-General, and landed in November with 15,000 troops at Torbay. He had been favored by a "Protestant wind" which had carried his fleet safely down the Channel while it held James's ships in Portsmouth harbor.

The Fall of James II. It was a strange invasion, welcomed as a liberation rather than as a conquest. William's banners proclaimed his purpose: "I will maintain" (*Je maintiendrai*, the motto of the house of Orange) and "The laws and religion of England." His manifesto to the people of England proclaimed that he had come to aid them in their time of need; precisely how, it did not say. He joined in denouncing the birth of Mary of Modena's son as fraudulent, though his wife had previously congratulated her father on the event. William's ultimate aims remained uncertain; he did not press a decision, but improvised, slowly and boldly, as events unfolded.

As William's army marched slowly across England toward London, the leaders of state and army one by one quit the king and joined the prince. The final blow to James's hope of resistance was the defection of Sir John Churchill, the commander of his army; the general owed his rapid advancement to the monarch's favor and friendship, but quit his allegiance under the spur of his strong Protestantism and his realization that the king's cause was lost. James lost his nerve. He sent Mary and her son in disguise to France, then fled himself. Captured by fishermen and taken ashore, he remained under guard until William, who refused to meet him, deliberately left the way open for another, unimpeded escape.

James II had fallen victim to his own misconception of his powers even more than to his political ineptness. He did not realize that a king of England could rule only within the grand lines of his people's beliefs and affections: inside those circumscribing limits, he was powerful, but when he strayed beyond and would not return, his strength drained away.

III. William and Mary

A revolution had been waged and won, though without the shedding of blood. The task of a new establishment of authority remained.

The Gift of the Crown. The members of the House of Lords in London took control in the absence of the king, in order to prevent the onset of anarchy. A Convention was called together to take the place of James's Parliament. Meanwhile negotiations began with William as to the nature of his future position in England. Leaving the initiative of proposals to the English, William refused to be either a regent exercising the kingship for the absent James, or a king consort for his wife Mary as reigning queen. Finally it was agreed early in 1689 that William and Mary should reign together as king and queen, with the powers of the throne in him alone.

The transfer of the crown was incorporated in a Declaration of Rights. It asserted that James, by his flight, had virtually abdicated, and thus his daughter Mary, as his rightful heir (Mary of Modena's son being deemed supposititious), succeeded him; but it also made the accession of William and Mary conditional upon their acceptance of the rights of Englishmen as set forth in the statute. A rule of succession was established: Mary's own children, if any; if none, then her sister Anne and her offspring; lastly, any children of William in event of a second marriage.

The Declaration proclaimed as the "true, ancient, and indubitable rights of the people of this realm" various principles which Charles and James had trampled. The king was shorn of his power to suspend the operation of laws or to dispense from their penalties; the ecclesiastical high court, drawing its powers from the royal prerogative, was forbidden; jury trials were required in all cases; it was declared illegal to collect taxes without parliamentary grant, to prevent freedom of debate in Parliament, and to require excessive bail; the rights to petition the sovereign and to keep arms were reaffirmed.

William and Mary at once assented to the Declaration of Rights and on the same day, February 13, 1689, were proclaimed the sovereign rulers, as William III and Mary II.

Theories of Power. The "Glorious Revolution," as the events of 1688-1689 were called, was the accomplishment of both the great parties in English political life. This rare collaboration was not accompanied by similar agreement upon the meaning of what had been done.

The Whigs had ready-made a theory of sovereignty which fitted the facts of the revolution. It was embodied in a tract against divine-right monarchy probably written around 1681, during the exclusion controversy, by the secretary of the earl of Shaftesbury, the physician and philosopher John Locke. He updated his manuscript *Treatises on Civil Government* by adding a reference to King William, "who now rules," and giving as his purpose "to justify to the world the people of England." He argued that a king who persistently violated the rights and interests of his people was a tyrant who broke the contract by which the people, in whom ultimate sovereignty lay, granted him authority. Rebellion against tyranny was not illegal but rightful and proper; it was not the breakdown but the re-establishment of the reign of law, by which the liberty and property of subjects were preserved.

The Tories lacked any such neat explanation. They had taken a leading part in overthrowing James because he was the one kind of king they had not anticipated in their divine-right theorizing—a Roman Catholic. As fervent Anglicans, they had assumed that the monarch would always be of their own faith, so that obedience to his commands would be little more than compliance with their own purposes. When a choice had been thrust upon them from which they could not escape, they had put their faith before their political doctrines; but now they were in deep embarrassment. Since their own theories made rebellion indefensible, these reluctant revolutionaries preferred to avoid theoretical controversy. They continued to feed the hope that James or his son (for few intelligent people continued to believe the tale of the warming-pan baby) would embrace the Anglican religion and enable them to re-establish the monarchy on its old basis.

The Method of Government. In governing his new kingdom, William had to cope with the fact that both parties had given him the throne. In doctrine he inclined more to the Tories, for he did not wish to abandon the prerogatives of the crown. On the other hand, they disputed his general policy of religious tolerance and war with France; and worse, he knew that many of them had not cast off all sympathy for James II, who was in exile in France and continued to claim the throne. The Whigs, who had no such Jacobite (from the Latin *Jacobus* for James) tendencies, held doctrines of parliamentary supremacy which were not to William's taste, and more important, they did not control a majority in the Parliament which replaced the Convention Parliament in 1690. William therefore ruled with the support of whatever party dominated the House of the Commons: the Tories until 1693, when their majority broke up; the Whigs, who obtained a majority in the Parliaments elected in 1695 and 1698; the Tories again when they gained control of the fifth Parliament elected in 1701; and the Whigs in the last year of the reign, 1702.

The ministers became dual agents, responsible primarily to the king but mediating between him and the broad nation as represented in Parliament. William was familiar with the methods of such mixed government, for that was the pattern of his rule in the United Provinces, despite the great differences in details. Having governed by means of a strongly entrenched system of Estates, he had learned to persuade before he tried to compel, to compromise on lesser business in order to have his way on larger matters, to play the game of politics as a participant and yet to remain above it as "eminent head"—and it was in these ways that he governed England.

He was not willing to accept a lesser role. When the English began to reduce his prerogatives after the death of Queen Mary in 1694 and especially after the Peace of Ryswick (see below, p. 449), interfering with his conduct of foreign affairs and railing against the Dutchmen in his entourage as foreigners, he threatened to resign the throne and return to the Netherlands. Only the action of Louis XIV in proclaiming James Edward as "James III" in 1701, on the death of his father, rallied almost the whole nation behind the Protestant king.

The Bank of England.   The Whigs were responsible for the most important innovation of the reign, a national bank. The war against France (see below) placed great strains upon the financial resources of the state. Even taxes did not tap the wealth of the nation quickly and effectively enough. In 1694 the Whigs obtained a charter for a joint-stock company called the Bank of England. In return for lending the government £1,200,000 at 8 per cent interest, it was authorized to discount commercial bills, to issue banknotes, and to conduct general banking business. Thus the credit of the treasury and of the business community of England were tightly linked, to their great mutual advantage. William enunciated the rule of the new policy in one of his last messages to Commons in January 1702: "Take care of the public credit, which cannot be preserved but by keeping sacred that maxim, that they shall never be losers who trust to a parliamentary security."

The linkage of the credit of the state and of the nation became one of the great weapons of English policy, enabling more of the national strength to be brought to bear in war than any other state except the Dutch Republic could achieve.

King William's War.   William's primary interest was to hold Britain firmly in the Grand Alliance which waged a war against Louis XIV from 1689 to 1697. The English, while sharing his concern for reducing the greatness of France and preventing a Bourbon "universal monarchy," were more interested in utilizing the conflict for their own advantage. They wished to push open the gates to trade with the Spanish empire for themselves, not for the Dutch (whom William also governed). They were troubled too by William's plodding generalship. John Churchill, promoted earl of Marlborough, had not done well in the Low Countries campaigning, and his continued contacts with the court of James II at Saint Germain led to his dismissal as commander. William, taking over leadership, was like his great-grandfather, William the Silent, more gifted in fighting undiscouraged by defeats than in winning victories. By diplomatic means, however, he held the Grand Alliance together until its bulk and weight wore down the strength of France. William was able to conclude a peace at Ryswick in 1697 which deprived Louis XIV of the advantages won in the field by his armies' superior military excellence.

William remained distrustful but not vindictive toward France. When Louis showed willingness to be satisfied with a share of the disputed Spanish succession, the English king made two successive partition treaties with his French cousin. William was indignant at French acceptance of the Spanish inheritance as bequeathed by Charles II of Spain to Philip V, and negotiated another Grand Alliance. The English people, however, feared to be, as they felt they had been in the recent war, "the Fight Alls, the Pay Alls, and the Lose Alls" of Europe. They did not accept entry into the war until Louis XIV angered them by his proclamation of "James III" and by his seizure of the "barrier" forts in the Spanish Low Countries (see ch. 17, p. 406), But the artisan of the Grand Alliance, William III, died of a fall from horseback in March 1702, before war had been officially declared.

Ireland Reconquered. Scotland accepted William III as its king in 1689 without difficulty. The Presbyterian church was re-established, and the powers of the Scottish Parliament were greatly increased by the abolition of the Lords of the Articles, its "steering committee" which had been dominated by the crown.

Ireland, on the other hand, was the scene of a bitter struggle. The Stuart restoration had brought some improvement in the conditions of the Catholics but a worsening in those of the Ulster Presbyterians. Both Charles II and James II, however, continued to treat Ireland as a subject dominion. Even James, though he gave Catholics a virtual monopoly in Irish offices, shared the common English contempt for both the native Irish and the Anglo-Irish; his primary purpose lay in using the Irish for his ambitions in England.

When James, after his flight to France, regained his courage and decided to fight for his kingdom against his usurping nephew, Ireland appeared as the obvious base for a campaign of reconquest. Louis XIV gave him a small force with which he landed in Ireland in 1690; the Catholics rallied to his cause and pressed the Protestants back upon their Ulster fortresses. William thereupon embarked his own army, with his Dutch regiments as its backbone, for Ireland and defeated James at the battle on the river Boyne. James fled, calling the Irish cowards while they named him *Shaemas-na-cacagh* (James the Dirty).

Ireland continued to be a subordinate and dependent state, ruled not only by a foreigner but by a "heretic." Most of its land, too, was in the hands of the foreign heretics and not of the native peasantry who tilled it.

IV. Queen Anne

A new reign began in March 1702 with Anne, second daughter of James II, as queen. Her right of succession, as a Protestant, against her Catholic half-brother "James III" had been assured in the previous year by an Act of Settlement which forbade inheritance of the throne by a Roman Catholic. The Act also stiffened the laws on religion and established the succession after Anne on the dowager electress Sophia of Hanover, who was the nearest Protestant descendant of James I, and her heirs.

The Queen, the Duchess, and the Duke. Anne, though retaining a sense of guilt at the dispossession of her father and now of her half-brother, hung grimly to the queenship. The dominant figure in her government became

Marlborough, who was the husband of her closest friend, Sarah Churchill. Marlborough became the leader of England's military and political effort in the War of the Spanish Succession. In 1704 he expelled the French from Germany by the victory of Blenheim. Two years later he cleared the Low Countries by the triumph of Ramillies. England's naval forces won a victory of even more lasting importance when Admiral Rooke captured the Spanish fort at Gibraltar, controlling the straits between the Mediterranean and the Atlantic.

Marlborough's political leadership was directed mainly to obtaining support for his military endeavors. He was not closely committed to either Tories or Whigs, and drew his strength from his fame as a general, which won him promotion to a dukedom, and from his wife's personal domination over the queen. Anne was not neutral in the party conflict, however. She was a fervent Anglican and bitter against the Whigs, who advocated greater toleration for Protestant dissenters. She was deeply unhappy when Marlborough, finding that the Whigs would support him only if he ruled with them, established an all-Whig ministry in 1708. Marlborough continued to win military victories, defeating the French first at Oudenaarde in 1708 and then at Malplaquet in 1709.

The Whigs showed themselves greedy in the moment of success. They refused to accept Louis XIV's terms for peace because he would not join the allies in expelling Philip V from Spain. The belief rose up in England that the country was fighting not for its safety and advantage, which were now assured, but for the selfish interests of Marlborough and the Whigs.

The Whig position was further weakened by an upsurge of religious controversy. In 1709 a fanatical Tory clergyman, Dr. Henry Sacheverell, preached a sermon denouncing the Whig doctrines of toleration and the right of resistance to the throne. Impeached by the Whig House of Commons, he was given a sentence by the Lords so mild that it was hailed by Sacheverell's supporters as a victory.

The next year Anne dismissed the Whig ministry and dissolved Parliament. A new election brought a Tory victory in the House of Commons. In 1711 the queen quarreled openly with Sarah Churchill and dismissed Marlborough from all his offices. The new Tory government entered into the peace negotiations at Utrecht with the intention of ending the war, and succeeded in reaching an agreement favorable to England's interest. Nonetheless the government was able to win the assent of the House of Lords to the treaty of peace only by having the queen create twelve new Tory peers pledged to vote for it.

The Scottish Union. While the war was at its height, the personal union between England and Scotland was replaced by their unification into a single state. Scotland's interest lay primarily in overcoming her economic backwardness by incorporation into the great market of England and the English overseas dominions. That of England consisted in maintaining the dynastic connection, since there was no assurance that after Anne's death the Scots would choose the same king as the English. The question could not be put off: not one of the eleven children the queen had borne to Prince George was still alive, and she was past the age of bearing.

The final union came in 1707 after elaborate and detailed negotiations. It provided for the inclusion of Scotland politically within a single state, the United Kingdom of Great Britain. Scotland would elect 45 members directly to the House of Commons, while the native Scottish peers would be represented by sixteen of their number whom they would elect to sit in the House of Lords. The distinctive Scottish system of law, based on the Roman written law, was to be maintained, together with the existing Scottish courts; final appeals from Scottish courts would not go to an English court but to the House of Lords.

End of the Dynasty. With the Scottish union accomplished and the victory over France won, the only work done in the one year that remained of the reign, 1713-1714, was to arrange the transition to a new ruler.

At the very last moment the Tory leaders divided on the question of maintaining the Act of Settlement, which fixed the succession on the Hanoverian line. The Earl of Oxford, who was the principal figure in the government, favored adherence to the Act. Viscount Bolingbroke, the other leading Tory, had been dropped from the ministry and began intrigues for return of the Old Pretender. Late in July 1714, the queen, ill and remorseful over her ill-treatment of her half-brother, dismissed Oxford. In his stead, on July 29, she named Bolingbroke.

Two days later she was dead. The most prominent Tory leaders consulted on their course of action. One, the Jacobite bishop of Rochester, Atterbury, urged proclamation of "James III" as king. Bolingbroke, despite his flirtations with the Pretender, thought it a hopeless gesture. "England would as soon have a Turk as a Roman Catholic for king," he warned.

The Whig leaders had no mixed feelings. They were totally committed to the Hanoverian succession, which the moderate Tories behind Oxford accepted without enthusiasm. The Whig lords on the privy council proclaimed the elector of Hanover as George I, king of Great Britain and Ireland.

20

Britain: Consolidation and Change

1714 - 1789

THE EIGHTEENTH CENTURY was Britain's time of consolidation and growth after long ages of turbulence. Slowly, unevenly, and almost invisibly, the consequences of the Revolution of 1688 were worked out. The theory of politics remained simple and clear but practice was complex and difficult to define. Still, the quarrels of politics did not boil into the conflicts of armies, except for two Jacobite rebellions which made more noise than damage. It was a time of peace within the boundaries of the island kingdom and of expanding national power beyond them.

Behind the shields of civil peace and might abroad, Britons worked steadily and effectively at their tasks of ordinary life. The country remained fundamentally agrarian but trade and industry developed at an accelerating pace. By the last decade of the century it could be seen that a quiet and immense transformation of Great Britain was in the making—an economic and social change besides which the Revolution of 1688 would pale almost into insignificance.

I. George I

In 1714 a new dynasty came upon the throne of Great Britain, raising once more, as in 1603, the difficult and disturbing problems of personal union.

The King. The king, George I, dawdled for two months in his electorate of Hanover before setting out for his greater realm across the North Sea; it was September before he reached London. He came to England a stranger, and a stranger he remained during the thirteen years of his reign. Great-grandson of James I, son and grandson of German princes, he was by habit and attitude all German. He neither spoke nor understood English and did not attempt to learn it; he was content to converse with his ministers in French and "dog" Latin. Even to an England accustomed to raw ways of life, he was shockingly gross in his manners, too often drunk, and streaked with vicious cruelty.

The king remained Hanoverian at heart in his politics, but adapted himself as best he could to the character of his British subjects. He looked upon his Hanoverians as "children" who owed him absolute and unquestioning obedience, with no share in government. He did not dare to treat Englishmen in the same way, but was determined to use the substantial powers given him by the British constitution to advance his purposes as a German princeling. The provisions in the Act of Settlement designed to prevent the subordination of British to Hanoverian interests did not hamper him; some, particularly the requirement that he could not leave the kingdom without parliamentary assent, were repealed; others were simply disregarded.

The Whig Triumph. For all the king's Hanoverian bent, Britain did not become a stepchild within the personal union. The island kingdom far excelled the German principality not only in strength of numbers and wealth but also in political self-assertiveness. Indeed, for Englishmen the accession of George I meant first and foremost the triumph of one political party, the Whigs.

George knew that the Whigs alone were totally committed to his dynasty, to the exclusion of the Stuarts. The Whigs had no hesitation in taking advantage of the monarch's gratitude and dependence upon them. Though they were now the "court" rather than the "country" party, they did not abandon the principles of the Revolution of 1688. Locke's doctrine that the "people" —meaning men of property as represented in Parliament—possessed ultimate sovereignty became for them a commonplace beyond debate. Representing both nation and throne, they ruled by bringing these two forces into collaboration and did not trouble themselves with the theoretical problem of possible conflict between the king and his subjects.

They spoke for most of the great noblemen as well as for the bulk of the business classes; the country gentry, to be sure, remained predominantly in the Tory camp, but Whig policy carefully catered to their economic interests, though not their religious or political predilections. The Whigs maintained intact the religious settlement of the Revolution of 1688. Anglicanism remained the single established church in England (as did Presbyterianism in Scotland) but the penalties upon the Protestant dissenters were lightened. The recusancy laws against Roman Catholics were kept upon the statute books, but were mildly enforced if at all.

Tory Discomfiture. For the Tories the world had gone awry. They were monarchists to their marrow, yet the reigning king looked upon them as the most dangerous opponents of his throne and gave them no trust whatsoever. He realized—and the Whig leaders were at his elbows to remind him if need be—that the Tories considered only "James III" to be in the rightful line of succession. But religion divided the Anglican Tories from their Catholic "king over the water." James would not change his faith to win over their support: he did not think London, or all Britain, to be worth the loss of the mass. He was confident that when he called to them, the Tories would still troop to his colors.

Yet the staunch Anglicanism of the Tories was confounded by the changes that were occurring within their own church. The bishoprics were no longer peopled by High Churchmen, spiritual descendants of Laud bent on preserving every last jot of Anglican doctrine, discipline, and predominance. Instead, the official leaders of the church were latitudinarians, who held open the doors of the state religion as wide as possible, and rationalists, who interpreted its tenets in the light of reason and common experience. Only in the local parishes did the alliance of Tory and High Church maintain itself: for the gentry controlled these lesser appointments and bestowed them on clerics of their own spirit.

The unhappy confusion of the Tories was worse confounded by their loss of effective leadership. Oxford and Bolingbroke were impeached on charges of treasonable misconduct in the negotiation of the Utrecht peace treaty. Bolingbroke, convicted by an act of attainder, fled to France, where he became disconsolate adviser of the pretender, without confidence in the Jacobite cause he served. Oxford stayed in England and went to the Tower for two years. The lesser chieftains of the Tory party took refuge either in exile or quiescence.

"The 'Fifteen." The banishment of the Tories from political influence was completed by the outbreak of a Jacobite rebellion in 1715 (whence its name of "The 'Fifteen"). "James III," proclaimed at Aberdeen in September, landed in Scotland three months later to lead a legitimist counterrevolution against the Hanoverian "usurper." He hoped that his personal appearance would release the pent-up loyalism of both Scots and English. To his dismay, adherents came only from the Scottish Highlands, where Catholicism remained strong among the clans. Neither the Lowland Scots, for all their discontent with the small benefit they had derived from the union with England, nor the English Tories, who could not stomach a Catholic king, rallied to the pretender's banners. Nonetheless he sent an army south to invade England.

It reached Preston, a Lancashire town some two hundred miles from London, where it was met and crushed by a government force. Less than two months after his arrival, in February 1716, "James III" sailed back across the water to exile.

In Britain the repression was comparatively mild. Two Scottish lords and twenty-six lesser Jacobites were executed. Others were given lighter sentences or pardoned outright.

The Tories subsided into a "country party" without influence over the government, penalized for a Jacobitism it distrusted but preserving intact its domination over wide stretches of the counties of England. In Parliament they formed a perennial opposition with no visible prospect of returning to power.

The Victors Fall Out. The danger past, the Whigs fell to quarreling among themselves. The first issue of dispute was the king's insistence that Britain support his Hanoverian ambitions. The Great Northern War (see especially ch. 24, p. 548) was coming to an end, with Sweden about to lose her mainland possessions. George I hankered for his share of the spoils, in particular the bishoprics of Bremen and Verden. Sir Robert Walpole, the principal minister, resisted the royal pressure to bring Britain into the Baltic war. James Stanhope, a secretary of state and Walpole's rival, displaced him in the king's confidence by supporting an actively Hanoverian policy. Walpole resigned his office in 1717 and went into opposition. Stanhope took over the leadership of the government.

War and the threat of war marked the first years of Stanhope's ministry. He joined with France, an enemy only four years since, to defeat by arms a Spanish attempt in 1718-1719 to overthrow the peace settlement of Utrecht. Meanwhile the British fleet supported the Hanoverian ambitions by bold expeditions to the Baltic. The results were gratifying to the king-elector: he received Bremen and Verden from Sweden for Hanover.

Stanhope obtained the reward of the good servant. George I permitted him to determine policy for England. The inner "cabinet" of the most influential ministers began to meet separately from the king. The monarch thus retained his ultimate power of decision but gave away the hardly less essential powers of day-by-day discussion and control of affairs. The German king reigned; the English ministers ruled.

The South Sea Bubble. The biggest domestic problem was to reduce the huge burden of public debt inherited from the wars against Louis XIV. Some £50 million was outstanding, at interest rates as high as 9 per cent. The nation was richer than ever, but the state did not draw upon that wealth proportionately. In 1719 an experiment was made in national finance similar to John Law's "Mississippi Company" in France (see ch. 17, p. 415).

The debt was transferred to the eight-year-old South Sea Company, which had received the monopoly of British trade to Spanish America and the Pacific islands, as well as the *asiento* contract for supplying African slaves to the Spanish colonies. Intensive publicity blared the great expectations of the company's profits. The price of the stock soared from 128½ in January 1720 to 1000 in July.

Hundreds of similar joint-stock companies were hastily formed to reap the harvest of public confidence, though their prospects were much vaguer. Most announced some specific industrial or trading activity, but even one which advertised a "design which will hereafter be promulgated" found takers for its promise of a promise. Government action against the worst of these speculative monstrosities pricked the "South Sea Bubble," as they were collectively called. Prices collapsed as confidence vanished: South Sea shares dropped to their January prices.

The government bailed out the South Sea Company with the aid of the Bank of England and the East India Company. Those who had exchanged government annuities for South Sea Shares received about half the original value of their holdings.

The crisis was painful but did not stay the vigorous activity of English traders and manufacturers. Their prosperity rested not upon the fragile basis of speculation but on the solid foundations of efficient and enterprising production and a commerce which encompassed ever-larger sections of the world.

Investigation revealed that prominent members of the government had been corruptly involved in the promotion of the South Sea Company, and others were negligent if not culpable. Stanhope died in disgrace in 1721; his colleague Sunderland was saved from impeachment by the endeavors of his Whig foe Walpole. Sunderland resigned, and Walpole returned to the direction of affairs.

Prime Minister Walpole. For the next two decades Walpole served as "prime minister." He was the first great minister in the history of his country whom the title fitted in its modern sense. He was not the king's do-all, like Wolsey to Henry VIII, or the monarch's most influential servant, like Burghley to Elizabeth I. His formal powers as first lord of the treasury and chancellor of the exchequer were those of a finance minister; but he was also the immediate master over all his colleagues, whom he selected and for whom he laid down general policy. Together they formed Walpole's "administration," rather than the king's, as during previous reigns.

Walpole held this position of virtual "head of government" because he was more than the servant of the king and of Parliament, in particular of the House of Commons. Both the monarch and the legislature, sharing power in the half-defined constitutional settlement of 1689, depended upon the prime minister to maintain accord between them. George I, and after 1727

George II, could not safely or easily direct British policy into paths favorable to their Hanoverian interests; but a strong and agile English chief minister could. Such dependence enabled Walpole to take the initiative in matters of British policy, acting on the monarch's authority but to his own purposes. It was more difficult for Walpole to control the legislature. He remained in Commons throughout his ministerial career in order to keep direct personal control over the lower House, which was more numerous and acquiring greater importance than the Lords.

The "Connections" of England. Walpole's problem was not the hide-bound Tories, who seldom numbered more than one-fifth of the House of Commons, but the Whigs, his own party. He could count for sure support only upon the Scottish members and upon those who sat for "treasury" boroughs. These were towns where shipyards or similar state establishments provided the government with large numbers of docile voters. Most seats in Commons were controlled by "connections," local cliques based on ties of family and friendship.

The mastery of these connections over the counties, which sent eighty "knights of the shire" to sit in Commons, was almost always complete and unquestioned. The forty-shilling-freehold requirement for the suffrage was loosely interpreted to include tenants on lifetime leases and others with a modicum of revenue and status. The total number of voters in the forty counties was about 160,000. By force of habit and fear of retribution, the voters usually accepted the candidates put before them by the great families of the county. The absence of a secret ballot made it simple to enforce obedience at the polls.

The boroughs, which provided the majority of members, likewise customarily took their candidates from the notable families nearby. Large number of seats in Commons were held by sons of titled noblemen who sat in the House of Lords, or by their relations and dependents. "Pocket" boroughs, where only a tiny electorate subsisted, simply accepted the candidates put up by their proprietors. "Rotten" (corrupt) and "close" (having an electorate restricted to municipal officials) boroughs were for the most part more independent; but their freedom consisted rather in selling their votes to the highest bidder than in selecting nominees on the basis of their policy. These boroughs were the most open to men of talent and wealth, though with limited connections, who wished to sit in Commons. Thus, though Commons took the lead in affairs during the century, it seldom met direct opposition from the Lords, for it spoke predominantly for the same class of landed wealth and titled rank; the borough representation, however, gave voice also to the class of commercial and industrial wealth.

The Newcastle System. Walpole nonetheless managed usually to keep a tight rein over the unwieldy Whig party. This was the achievement of constant, laborious management of the multitudinous connections. In 1724, Walpole gave these managerial duties to Thomas Pelham, duke of Newcastle, who held the office of secretary of state but devoted his time chiefly to aligning the connections behind the government.

Newcastle drew upon the treasurehouse of rewards in the government's grant—offices, honors, pensions (to a very limited extent taken from the "secret service" funds at the king's disposal)—to construct a majority for the government. But since the amount of these favors was limited, the majority was fragile and required constant rebuilding, toward which Newcastle gladly employed himself.

Walpole's Policy. Walpole was interested in more than power itself. His fundamental aim was to keep things as they were. The Revolution of 1688, he held, had brought the constitution of England to such perfection that any change would be only harmful tampering. "I am no Saint, no Spartan, no Reformer!" he boasted. But he sought the welfare of England as he saw it.

He emphasized as the first requirement for national prosperity the improved management of the finances of the state. He acted on the principle that the public debt was the responsibility of the nation, as represented in Parliament, rather than of the monarch aided by parliamentary grants. In order to reduce the burden of interest payments, he established a "sinking fund" to pay off at least a portion of the outstanding obligations, which were mainly in life annuities with no fixed expiration debt. The "fund" received the revenues of specific taxes; it was not to be touched for current expenses, but the principal would be reinvested until a sufficient sum for repayment had been accumulated.

When Walpole reduced the land tax, which had expanded greatly during the wars, revenues fell behind expenditures. To make up the deficit by a tax which would fall widely on the population, he increased the excise (internal revenue) duties on alcoholic beverages and tobacco in 1733 and at the same time took measures to repress smuggling. Widespread rioting ensued; not alone because of fear that prices would go up, particularly of the cheap gin with which the poor soaked away their miseries, but also because the liberties of Englishmen were in peril, for revenue officers were authorized to raid homes and to impose fines on their own authority. Always one to skirt difficulties rather than to ride them down, Walpole withdrew the excise increase. The continued expansion of British trade added meanwhile to the customs revenues, while the minister did not scruple, despite his promises, to dip into the sinking fund for current needs.

Peace and Prosperity. Walpole also saw a pacific foreign policy as another requirement for British national prosperity. In his view, war was expensive and needlessly dangerous. In 1734, during the War of the Polish

Succession, he boasted to the queen that of the fifty thousand men who had died that year in Europe, not a single one was English.

He built his policy upon maintaining friendship with France and the United Provinces. The States-General, their prowess grievously fallen off since their golden age in the seventeenth century, no longer even considered the possibility of waging war against the English (see ch. 24, p. 545). The French, under a succession of peace-minded ministers, found agreement with Britain to their own advantage. Thus covered against attack by the other sea powers, Walpole was able to ward off a Spanish assault upon Gibraltar in 1727 and to compel Austria to disband the Ostend Company, in which the English and Dutch saw an unwanted new competitor (see ch. 24, p. 547).

The benefits of a long period of consolidation were soon to be seen in the expansion of British commerce and manufactures. The English colonies in the Caribbean and on the shoreline of North America developed rapidly in both trade and shipping (see ch. 25, pp. 568-569). Within Britain, the spur to enterprise was even sharper, and the response easily visible in growing cities and population.

II. George II

The accession of George II in 1727 brought little change. Walpole held a firm grip on affairs for another decade.

Walpole's Last Decade. The new king had at first no liking for Walpole, who during the late reign had stood behind George I in his quarrels with the heir to the throne. He soon discovered that he had the same need as his father for the prime minister's deft hand to administer English affairs, and did not turn him out of office. Walpole for his part was able to persuade the king, who had been born and educated a Hanoverian, by means of his queen, Caroline of Anspach. The queen's death in 1737 deprived him of a steadfast friend and supporter and hastened the crumpling of his power.

His influence over Parliament meanwhile was eroded by increasing discontent with his policies. Discontented Whigs joined the Tories in opposition, and found in Frederick, prince of Wales, a rallying point within the royal family. This new party of "Patriots" turned the weapon of the press against the government. Newspapers and pamphlets became a force such as the printed word had not been since the days of the Commonwealth.

Dissatisfaction was sharpest in the centers of trade. The *asiento* had been a will-o'-the-wisp: the trade in Negro slaves, though profitable, never reached a volume to make it an El Dorado. The "permission ship" to Mexico covered a persistent and increasing smuggling trade to Spanish America, but the English appetite was whetted by what it fed on. Englishmen felt that unhampered trade would yield the greater profits for which they yearned. They resented the searches of their ships made by the Spanish coast guards in the Caribbean, which created some danger and more difficulties for their half-illicit commerce. The attitude of many Englishmen was pithily expressed in 1733 by a still obscure young man of twenty-five, William Pitt: "When Trade is at stake it is your last Retrenchment; you must defend it or perish."

The War of Jenkins' Ear. Resentment took the shape of patriotic outcries against Spanish cruelties. The best publicized of these outrages was that said to have been committed upon a merchant-ship captain, Robert Jenkins. He testified to the House of Commons about the search of his ship by Spanish coast guards and held up to their gaze a detached ear which they had lopped off. Asked what he had done then, he replied that he had committed his soul to God and his cause to his country. In commemoration of such eloquent patriotism, the conflict with Spain which broke out in 1739 received the name of the "War of Jenkins' Ear."

Walpole was unable to deter the nation from its appeal to the vindication of arms. Newcastle, veering with the wind of opinion, favored war. When it came, Walpole told him, "It is your war, and I wish you joy of it." Nonetheless Walpole retained his nominal premiership at the king's insistence, though without control of affairs, until 1742, when he became earl of Orford.

The war with Spain soon became part of the general European conflict loosed by Frederick of Prussia's invasion of Austrian Silesia in 1740 (see ch. 22, p. 495). Britain entered on the side of Maria Theresa, combining English enmity to France, in full blast after Walpole's withdrawal to the House of Lords, with Hanoverian hostility toward Prussia, France's ally. British troops fought as Hanoverian auxiliaries; not until 1744 was there an official declaration of war by Louis XV against Britain.

The War against France. The government was under the formal leadership of Newcastle's younger brother, Henry Pelham, but the dominating force was Lord Carteret, the secretary of state. Carteret wielded British prowess with arrogant vigor. He would "knock the heads of the kings of Europe together," he boasted; Frederick of Prussia said that he treated kings "like little boys." The strength of Britain proved greater in untapped reserves than in actual force available: the army was small, and the navy—Britain's special weapon—had been allowed to go slack during the long interval of peace. When Marshal Saxe, the French commander, invaded the Low Countries in 1744, English armies were unable to prevent his steady advance. The failure of Carteret's arrogant policy resulted in his dismissal in 1744.

The Pelhams decided to strengthen their administration by bringing into it William Pitt, a vigorous critic of Carteret. The king refused to accept a man who called his beloved Hanover "that despicable electorate." Only the threat of mass resignation by the entire government compelled him to name Pitt to a subsidiary post as paymaster general: the rule that the ministry was primarily the representative of the nation, rather than of the king, was slowly emerging from the practice of politics.

On the continent British policy went from bad to worse. Saxe continued his conquest of the Low Countries: the French forces occupied the whole of the Austrian Netherlands and penetrated into the United Provinces. The British diplomats negotiating peace at Aix-la-Chapelle (Aachen) were given important bargaining counters by the British colonists in America, acting on their own initiative. A force from New England captured the French fortress of Louisbourg, on Cape Breton Island at the mouth of the St. Lawrence river. The peace concluded in 1748 ended the fighting. The prewar territorial position was restored; but England had entered the war with voracious ambitions and the stand-off peace left her unsated and angry.

The " 'Forty-five." War between France and England led to a second Jacobite rebellion in 1745, known therefore as "the 'Forty-five." Charles Edward, son of "James III" and called "the Young Pretender," counting on the favorable opportunity, landed with a small force in northwestern Scotland in July.

Wider support came to him than his father had received three decades before, reflecting the fact that many Scots were still not reconciled to the union with England. Some Anglicans joined his cause as well as the Catholics, but the Presbyterians looked on; Calvinist antipathy to the idea of a Catholic monarch was greater than their dislike of the English. The pretender captured Edinburgh and invaded England, reaching Derby, in the English Midlands, in early December. When the expected rebellion of English Jacobites failed to develop, the counselors of Charles Edward compelled him to order a retreat to Scotland. After a period of hesitancy and defeats, the government forces, led by the duke of Cumberland, crushed the Jacobite troops at Culloden Moor in the Highlands on April 16, 1746.

Cumberland earned himself the name of "Butcher" by the severity of his repression, which included almost 3,500 arrests and 120 executions. He built military roads into the Highlands, defended by blockhouses, which for the first time enabled the crown to control and disarm the clans. The semi-feudal clan system, with its obligation of military service at the call of the chieftain, was destroyed by giving outright ownership of the land to the chieftains who had not been disloyal. A series of expulsions of farmers from their holdings, to make possible the creation of huge sheep runs, followed; the consequence was a wave of emigration of poor Scots to the American colonies.

At the same time the reconciliation of the majority of Scots was aided by the beginning of a policy of mildness and assistance. The income from forfeited estates seized from rebels was used to aid the population, on the principle enunciated by one commentator: "Feed the clans and they will obey; starve them and they must rebel." The Lowland Scots at the same time began to benefit by the trade as they made fuller and more effective use of their equal rights to trade. The economic reorganization of Scotland on the model of England began.

The Seven Years' War. The years after the Peace of Aix-la-Chapelle were years not of peace but of uneasy and irresolute preparations for war. The king went off to Hanover in 1755 nonetheless and refused to return till he was ready. "There are kings enough in England," he replied to pleas that he was needed. He did not want "to be plagued and teased there about that D—d House of Commons." Fighting began again in 1756, with the conflict between France and Britain over their overseas colonies merging into the Seven Years' War on the continent.

Mutual recriminations between London and Vienna over their infidelities and shortcomings in the last war contributed to the "reversal of alliances" in 1756. The astonished and reluctant British found themselves with Frederick of Prussia as their ally and facing them a monster coalition of France, Austria, and Russia. The demands of war quickly proved too much for the talents of Newcastle, who had become prime minister in 1754 on the death of his brother. The duke was better able to manage the multifarious connections of English party politics than to crush foes by the weapons of war. In India Calcutta was lost to the French, while the loss of the Balearic island of Minorca, off the southern coast of Spain, deprived Britain of a first-rate strategic base held since the War of the Spanish Succession. Pitt turned on Newcastle with a savage phrase, calling the duke "a child driving a go-cart on the edge of a precipice."

Newcastle had to step down from power in 1756 to make way for a government under the nominal leadership of the duke of Devonshire but actually directed by Pitt. George II hated Pitt more than ever, however, and peremptorily dismissed him from office in April 1757.

Pitt: The Minister of Victory. Newcastle, who returned to head the government, discovered that Pitt had sources of power excelling those of connection. He had independent wealth inherited from his grandfather Thomas Pitt, famed as "Diamond" Pitt for the gems he had brought back from India. He had his own family connection with the influential Whig clan of the Grenvilles. He had his recognized skill as a government administrator. Last of all, he had his talent for oratory, by which he brought the House of Commons to his side, and beyond Commons rallied wide circles of the nation.

The king had the undoubted privilege under the constitution of choosing his ministers, but Commons had theirs, more recent but no less solid, of refusing to do business with a ministry of which it disapproved. As the war faltered on, legislature and crown remained deadlocked. Finally, in June 1757, Newcastle, accepting the inevitable, persuaded the monarch to overcome his loathing and name Pitt again as secretary of state, under Newcastle's nominal prime ministry. The duke now put his skills at party management to Pitt's service.

For the next four years Pitt took charge of every major branch of affairs: the army, the navy, diplomacy, and finance. He directed their movements with an imperious resolution and self-confidence hardly known in England since the days of Cromwell. He put together a complex war strategy, with British wealth and sea power as its essential elements. The British fleet, by taking command of the seas, gave Pitt the initiative in the overseas fighting and in the continent of Europe as well. The Canadian, Caribbean and Indian possessions of France fell to English arms. On the continent of Europe, Frederick II, ruling a small and straitened Prussia, was able to sustain the blows of the great triple alliance in large part thanks to the aid given in the form of British subsidies.

III. George III

In George III, who succeeded his grandfather George II in 1760, Britain at last won her victory over Hanover for the soul of their shared monarch. Before long, it proved to be a hollow and costly triumph.

"A Patriot King." The third king of the Hanoverian line was the first to be born in England. He prided himself on his true English birth and upbringing, despised Hanover, and took the tasks of his office with utmost seriousness. It was his purpose to be "a good king," according to his mother's repeated injunctions to him during his youth, to be "a patriot king" in the terms of Bolingbroke's treatise on *The Idea of a Patriot King* (1749). This meant a monarch singly devoted to the interests of his people and employing the powers of the throne to further them. George III understood those powers not in the absolute sense of James I, but constitutionally within the framework of the settlement of 1688-1689. He accepted the "Glorious Revolution" without any reservations and did not seek to wrest from Parliament any of the prerogatives embodied in it. On the other hand, he did not accept as legitimate the transformations in the arrangements of British political life since 1689, least of all those which had occurred since 1714.

In theory, executive power—the right to propose policy, subject to the assent of the legislature, to choose the ministers, and to conduct affairs—still belonged to the monarch. In practice, however, the executive functions had passed to the cabinet, the inner royal council, during the reigns of the first two Georges. The cabinet in turn was subordinate to a prime minister; he had to win and hold the support of Parliament, particularly the House of Commons, for his government, and it was also felt that he ought to have the confidence of the king. The ministry for its part worked to control Parliament by the party system as it existed in the eighteenth century: combinations of connections whose votes in Parliament were obtained partly by persuasion, but no less by the devices of patronage. The Tories had been excluded from influence; major political struggles were waged within the Whig party. This party system received no more formal recognition in common constitutional theories than did the cabinet and the prime ministry, but was as much a part of the constitutional reality.

The Fall of Pitt. George III, rejecting the innovations of the past half century, dreamed of being his own chief minister, a king who ruled as well as reigned. But to undo Walpole's silent work in creating effective government by a prime minister was more than the king could manage. He was unfitted for the task of governing. He had been slow to grow to manhood, especially in character. His father had died when George was thirteen, and the young prince of Wales had bestowed an immature affection and confidence upon his tutor, the serenely self-confident Scotsman, Lord Bute. This dependence upon Bute had large consequences when George III came to the throne at the age of twenty-two. Bute aspired to Pitt's place, never doubting that he could do better than the domineering minister.

A dispute over English war policy enabled Bute to achieve his aim. Pitt demanded that Britain declare war upon Spain, which had remained neutral though friendly to France. Only arms, he held, could remove the barriers to British trade in Spanish America. The king and Bute saw a chance for easy popularity by coddling the popular complaints against Pitt's "bloody and expensive" war (as the monarch wished to call it in his speech from the throne, until prevented by the minister). Thwarted and angry, refusing to be responsible where he could not direct, Pitt finally resigned in October 1761. Bute at first took Pitt's place only as secretary of state in Newcastle's cabinet. Three months later war was declared upon Spain, which refused to compromise the issues at dispute. In May 1762 Bute became prime minister.

"The King's Friends." Bute proceeded to smash the existing party arrangements. He ended the political exile of the Tories, whose last lingering Jacobite sympathies had been dispelled by the defeat of "the 'Forty-five." He used the factions into which the Whig party was divided in order to destroy its dominance. He attempted to make the crown the controlling force within the British political system by using its unquestioned prerogatives to the full. He turned Newcastle's system to the service of the throne, manipulating patronage and, to a much lesser extent, bribery in order to create a new party of "king's friends."

The net effect of his efforts was to re-establish politics along lines reminiscent of the reigns of Charles II and James II. The Tories again combined rigid Anglicanism with stalwart royalism and became the "court party." The Whigs concerned themselves with maintaining the principles of 1688 by emphasizing the limited and constitutional aspects of the monarchy, and moved back toward the status of "country party."

Bute meanwhile brought the war to a close by the treaty of Paris in 1763. The triumphs won under Pitt enabled the British to obtain highly favorable peace terms. Britain received all of French Canada, the land between the Appalachians and the Mississippi, and most of French India. France retained only shreds of her colonial possessions: the islands of Guadeloupe and Martinique in the Caribbean were returned to her, and she kept her fishing rights off Newfoundland. Britain returned Cuba and the Philippines, which had been conquered during the war, to Spain, which also received the part of Louisiana across the Mississippi, together with New Orleans, from France.

Meanwhile the arrogant Bute had worn out the king's love and confidence, won the hatred of the country, and lost the support of Commons. In April 1763, less than two months after the signature of the peace, he was dismissed.

"The King's War." For the next two decades, British policy was dominated by the problem of relations with the American colonies (see ch. 25, pp. 569-570). During this trying period, the command of affairs in Britain passed through the hands of a succession of proud and self-satisfied ministers, most of whom had small abilities with which to confront a great crisis.

The first of the "small men" who came after Pitt was George Grenville. His ministry, from 1763 to 1765, was marked by the beginning of an effort to impose more effectually upon the Americans the sovereign supremacy of the British state. Grenville's attempt to impose taxes upon the Americans without their assent, and to stiffen their subordination to the British "mercantile system" (see ch. 25, p. 569, and ch. 26, pp. 586-587) began to work them loose from their hitherto firm attachment to the British "motherland."

Under the marquess of Rockingham, who succeeded Grenville in 1765 for a year, the pressure upon the Americans became sharper. Rockingham, an aristocratic Whig, fell because he could not retain the support of the king. He was followed by Pitt, who now sat in the House of Lords as the earl of Chatham, though the king loathed him as "that perfidious man"; but the one-time master of events was now an ill man, dispirited at the turn of affairs and unable to achieve a conciliation with the "little Englands" over the seas.

The duke of Grafton, who followed Pitt in 1768, attempted to whip the Americans into docility, but failed.

Lord North, who became prime minister in 1770, remained in office for the next dozen years. He effectively combined the support of the king's friends and beneficiaries with that of his own Whig coteries. North's endeavor to subdue American recalcitrance by force of arms received the support of the monarch and a majority in the British Parliament, but was resisted by Chatham and many of the Whigs, including Rockingham's secretary, the Dublin-born Edmund Burke, who was becoming well-known as a political theorist. The onset of armed American resistance in 1775, and the Declaration of Independence a year later, involved Britain in a war she had not anticipated and did not relish. The Whigs denounced the policy which had led to "the King's war." Whig commanders fought indifferently, reflecting the reluctance of their party.

Defeat. The conflict led to Britain's loss of the initiative in diplomatic affairs to her great defeated rival, France. The French king became the ally of the American rebels in 1778; what had been a surreptitious trickle of aid became a growing flood as Rochambeau, with a fleet and an army, followed the individual volunteers like Lafayette. At the same time, British command of the seas was challenged not only by France but by the neutrals, who at the suggestion of the Russian empress, Catherine II, leagued together to defend neutral shipping. The surrender of Cornwallis at Yorktown in 1781 marked the end of the fighting on land; a British naval victory in the Caribbean the next year took the edge off defeat and improved the bargaining position of the British negotiators in the peace talks which now got under way.

It was not Lord North, however, who directed the work of peacemaking. He fell victim to British dismay over the defeat which had undone the achievement of Pitt and the country in the Seven Years' War. The pace of economic expansion had been slowed, and the expenses of war caused a rapid increase in taxation and the national debt. North stepped down in 1782, and Rockingham returned to office.

British diplomats began the work of peace, seeking not only to end the conflict of arms but to weaken the ties between France and the new American republic. These efforts largely succeeded in the preliminary peace treaty made at Paris in 1782. The sovereign independence of the United States was recognized, and it received the territory extending to the Mississippi river. France, for its efforts, received only the small Caribbean island of Tobago and the tropical African colony of Senegal; Spain kept Minorca and the peninsula of Florida in America, but did not regain Gibraltar.

The Younger Pitt. Rockingham repeatedly incurred the king's hatred. His responsibility for making an ignominious peace was one "misdeed" in the king's eyes. His Irish policy was another. Rockingham worked to settle the long struggle with the Irish by a compromise. He obtained repeal of the laws subjecting Ireland to the control of the British Parliament and privy council, and made concessions to the Irish Catholics easing their status as tenants and landowners. For George III, who believed any improvement of the Catholic position incompatible with his coronation oath, such a policy was a personal offense. Rockingham's sponsorship of a series of measures, Burke's "Economical Reform," which reduced the royal patronage and brought the king's expenditures under closer parliamentary scrutiny, further aroused his anger. Before the monarch's wrath could break him, however, Rockingham died at the end of 1782.

Lord North and the Whig chieftain, Charles James Fox, though political foes, patched up a coalition ministry which lasted long enough to sign the final treaty of peace in 1783 and then make way for William Pitt, namesake and second son of the earl of Chatham.

The "younger Pitt," as the new prime minister was known, was only twenty-four years of age. Yet he was ready for the exacting tasks of governing a great nation. From childhood he had taken the career of a statesman as his goal and had become an orator, debater, and administrator of consummate skill. He shared his father's principles, a devotion to country, impeccable honesty, a concern for reform of abuses; but unlike Chatham he accepted the role of "king's servant" in a personal as well as a political sense. He drew his strength from the common support of the nation, which elected a new Parliament in which he had a large majority, and the crown; yet was less independent and self-willed than his father had been.

Tory, Whig, and Radical. Pitt became a party leader. He reorganized the Tories, the "king's friends," and his own supporters into a new and somewhat more cohesive Tory party; but it had a strongly conservative bent that inhibited Pitt's own reformist tendencies, and he did not have the spirit to smash opposition from his own side.

Set against Pitt and the Tories were two political groups. The larger and more influential by far was the Whigs, now under the leadership of Charles James Fox. Their principles were little changed from those of Walpole's day, except for a greater willingness to propose reforms and a more voluble concern for political freedom.

Much of the support that had earlier been given to the Whigs by business circles and by dissenters (who somewhat overlapped) now went, however, to the Radicals. Relatively few in numbers and without links to the dominant connections of English public life, they lacked any substantial representation in Parliament and were even less organized than the Whigs and Tories. They drew upon middle-class circles that were strongly attracted by the developing reform ideas of Enlightenment (see ch. 27, pp. 607-

609), and found support in segments of the urban poor, notably the literate clerks and artisans, who combined eagerness for betterment with a virulent hatred of the rich who ruled the land—a hatred that easily spilled over into rioting. The great achievement of the Radicals had been to impose the adventurous publicist, John Wilkes, upon the House of Commons from which he had been repeatedly expelled for printed attacks upon the king.

Pitt at Work. Pitt set himself the tasks of re-establishing the health, the might, and the prestige of Great Britain after the debacle of the American war.

The vigor of the island kingdom depended in the first place upon the soundness of her economic life and the national finances. His economic policy was based upon the ideas of Adam Smith, whose *Wealth of Nations* (1776) Pitt studied closely. He favored the expansion of trade and manufactures, particularly by negotiating trade treaties which opened foreign markets wider for British merchants. The Eden Treaty of 1786 with France was the most important of these commercial pacts. Pitt's fiscal policy was even more successful. The sinking fund was re-established and £11,000,000 of the debt was paid off within eight years. Taxes were increased, yet the elimination of many sinecures in the treasury and other measures of economy made the collection of taxes more efficient and often less burdensome.

Pitt was less successful in efforts at political reform. He proposed the abolition of 36 "rotten" and "pocket" boroughs, with compensation to their electors and proprietors; their 72 seats would be assigned to London and the underrepresented counties of the Midlands and Yorkshire, where recent industrialization and urban development had greatly expanded the population. He also proposed to extend the right of vote to copyholders (customary tenants) in the counties and to householders in the boroughs. These measures were rejected in 1785; Pitt followed Walpole's example in the face of resolute opposition rather than his father's: he backed away, in the expectation of returning to the question at some more favorable time.

Pitt Victorious. On two crucial issues, however, Pitt defeated Fox and the Whigs. One was that of the government of British India. Fox brought in a bill to place the East India company under the control of parliamentary nominees. The measure was defeated with the assistance of a warning from the king that he would treat those who voted for it as his personal enemies. Pitt's own subsequent bill which reorganized the company under royal control was passed; it permitted the trade and most of the local government in India to remain in the hands of company officials.

The other crisis came in 1788 when George III suffered an attack of insanity. Fox and his party proclaimed that full powers of regency automatically belonged to the prince of Wales, their personal friend and political ally. Pitt, taking the side of parliamentary supremacy which was the usual

Whig doctrine, brought in a regency bill which gave the prince only limited powers, insufficient to enable him to overturn the political balance in favor of the Whigs. Before the bill came to a vote, the king recovered in April 1789 and resumed his functions in person.

In foreign affairs, Pitt concentrated on regaining the initiative from France and using British power efficaciously on behalf of British trade and command of the seas. In conjunction with Prussia, he supported the stadholder in the United Provinces in his conflict with the French-supported "Patriots" in 1788 (see ch. 24, p. 545). He used armed force to counter Spanish territorial claims on the Falkland Islands in the South Atlantic and to the Nootka Bay region on the Pacific shore of North America (present-day Vancouver). France, the great rival, was gripped by growing political difficulties and social turmoil, to which the Estates-General meeting in 1789 might bring a solution or new fuel; for the moment, however, Britain had recovered her primacy among the powers of Europe.

IV. Britain in Change

Britain was all the while undergoing a transformation in economic and social life, though without the accompaniment of such political upheaval as was developing in France.

A Changing Land. England approached the end of the eighteenth century with a rapidly increasing population. Wales included, she had numbered little more than five million when the Revolution of 1688 occurred; in 1760, the population was a little under seven million; and now the nine-million point was close. The first regular census, taken in 1801, showed a population of 9,168,000.

Such expansion of population reflected the changing character of English society. For all the continued harshness of life for common men, existence grew somewhat easier for many of them. Prices remained stable while wages rose slowly. More people than before ate white bread, rather than loaves of coarser flour. Improvement arose from the continuous economic growth of Britain during the eighteenth century.

Agriculture remained the main activity of a majority of Englishmen, yet the proportion of the nation involved in work on the land was growing smaller. The enclosure movement drove many people off the land; but the soil became more productive. The nation became constantly more urban. Trade and especially manufacturing gave work to an ever-larger number of people. This change in economic emphasis was reflected in the shift of population from the southern counties to the Midlands and Yorkshire; London alone of the southern towns continued its growth at a pace equal to that of the new manufacturing centers to the North. (See ch. 26, pp. 576-578.)

The Wealthy and the Poor. Britain remained a land where wealth ruled, all the more since wealth had increased so rapidly during the century. Wealth in land was still foremost: the nobility and the gentry remained overwhelmingly a class of landowners. Their estates and houses matched those of the wealthiest aristocrats on the continent in luxury and size.

Yet the British aristocracy was less closed off from other forms of wealth than ever before. New wealth might come into existence with signs of its origins in trade and manufactures clearly marked upon it. These signs soon wore off; where religion did not bar the way, the ancient process of the merger of the wealthy classes continued so vigorously that the quantity rather than the kind of possessions became increasingly the key to status. Snobbery was rife, but it often reflected the attitudes of upstarts more than of ancient ranks. Merchant princes ceased to cast off their connections with commerce and lose themselves in the country gentry, as once they had done; instead, landed gentlemen and nobility invested more and more of their funds in commerce and manufactures.

As Britain changed character, so did the poor. The rural populace split asunder as the yeomanry, who were relatively independent and prosperous small farmers, often on copyhold tenancy, declined in numbers. The proportion of propertyless farm laborers increased, widening the cleavage of rural society according to wealth. In the cities, the increase of commercial and industrial enterprise resulted in a rapid expansion of the working classes. On the one hand, the numbers of those who worked in factories, under desperate conditions, grew steadily; but so did the numbers of literate clerks and skilled workers, who were already sensitive to disparities between the common theories of political liberty and their own limited resources and rights. A new kind of "common folk" was emerging.

The Older Religions. The eighteenth century was a period of significant religious development in England, less productive of innovation and less turbulent than the previous two centuries but creating a new balance in the religious life of Britain. The formal structure of religious institutions remained the same, but new kinds of belief and practice rose up within them.

The established religion in England, Wales, and Ireland remained Anglicanism. The power of the state over the church continued strong. Appointments remained in the hands of the crown and were given chiefly for political reasons, as part of the system of patronage and connections. The ancient parish system remained untouched and untouchable, despite major shifts in population, because of the revenues attached to these "livings." Doctrines were not changed but interest in them declined. Deism and rationalism took hold of many, but even more apparent was an intense dislike for "enthusiasm," for fervid preaching and the quest of men's souls.

Protestant dissent, after its ages of success and repression, developed along lines similar to those in the state church. Dissenters suffered mildly for their differences: exclusion from the English universities and ecclesiastical appointments, although their own academies were generally superior in quality; dependence upon parliamentary acts of indemnity to spare them the penalities of violating the Test Act when they held government office. Dissenters devoted themselves to economic activity with a greater persistence and steadiness than Anglicans; and generally their reputation for honesty and sobriety helped their businesses to prosper.

The situation of Roman Catholics and Jews remained unchanged in theory. It proved impossible to remove or even to modify legislation against the Catholics, owing to fears of papist revival; but the laws were enforced mildly if at all. Jews settled in England without difficulty; but the government was unable to pass laws to ease their naturalization as subjects.

Methodism. From within Anglicanism arose a new religious force. This was Methodism, the creation of John Wesley and his brother Charles. As Oxford students, the Wesleys underwent "conversion" as an intensely emotional religious experience. Remaining Anglicans in doctrine, they undertook preaching to the "unconverted," that is, those who did not participate in the religious life of the land.

The Wesleys and their adherents at first endeavored to do their work within the framework of the Anglican church, but their "enthusiasm" barred most church doors to them, and they found themselves increasingly preaching in the open, evangelizing in the fields where their appeal to live a "methodically" religious and moral life appealed to many, especially in the new urban classes, who were stirred and fearful in the new society with its novel dangers and burdens. Finally the Wesleys and their followers, who became known as "Methodists," were forced to set up their own church organization because of the necessity to maintain the flow of ministers when Anglican bishops would not ordain their converts. Methodism, by giving hope and comfort, eased for many the difficulties of the new industrialism.

Reform. Another novel force in eighteenth-century Britain was that of "reform." The word ceased to have its old meaning, primarily religious, and came to cover the range of activities designed to improve man's life in this world. It drew its force partly from religion, encompassing most of the faiths held by Britons, and partly from the new movement of the Enlightenment.

Educational reform was confined to endeavors to expand the system of primary education, which had become almost utterly dependent upon private initiative since the religious changes of the sixteenth century. Elementary instruction was expanded, often in connection with Sunday schools. Higher scholarship was little touched by the efforts of reformers; Oxford and Cambridge remained somnolent seminaries for training Anglican clergymen, mildly concerned with the new intellectual ferment all about them. The Scottish universities were in the forefront of new thought, however, with professors whose erudition, judgment, and creative thought made them widely known; one, Adam Smith, achieved the first level of fame as an economic thinker.

Reform of the prisons was a more individual enterprise. The jails were half-public, half-private affairs, where the prisoners, many indigent debtors, were expected to pay their own expenses. Filth, illness, and corruption were prevalent. The reformer John Howard investigated the evils in person, described them to an increasingly interested world, and obtained some limited improvements. But the whole system of justice continued to be built upon public vengeance and harsh punishments tempered by elaborate provisions for protecting the rights of prisoners who could afford the advice of lawyers.

Another form of humanitarian reform was the drive to end the slave trade, or at least to limit its atrocious conditions. This was a movement to which the younger Pitt gave his support; his friend William Wilberforce led the agitation for abolition, but Pitt could not persuade Commons to pass legislation which would hurt the prosperity of the thriving ports of Bristol and Liverpool. The best that Pitt could achieve was legislation providing for improved conditions aboard the slave ships.

Life in the new cities—some legally still villages, others vastly expanded towns—was difficult because of the inadequacy of measures of public health and safety. Where traditional agencies of government failed to act, groups of individuals obtained from Parliament charters permitting them to operate necessary social services. These commissions were known under a number of names, some much narrower than their total functions, like "Paving Commissioners." They created a shared interest between the growing class of administrative officials and the new industrial magnates, which was reflected in the theories of Jeremy Bentham and his utilitarianism, which stressed the test of practical usefulness to which all institutions and legislation should be put.

Thus, though Britain remained a land of triumphant wealth, a rapidly changing country beset with numerous problems, there existed alongside the creators of the new power those who were concerned with adapting it to the needs of men.

21

Germany: The Rise of Prussia and Austria

1648 - 1740

PEACE RETURNED to Germany in 1648. The nation, though burdened with desolations, had the opportunity to recover old riches and rebuild old strength. The need of the nation, therefore, was for public order and for encouragement to the people's efforts. The responsibilities of the new time fell upon the princes, who alone held effective power in the Holy Roman Empire. How well they met this challenge depended upon the character of the states they ruled and upon their own abilities. Yet there were narrow limits to what they could do. The near-extinction of Germany as a political entity exposed it, like Italy, to subjection to decisions taken elsewhere.

I. Germany after Westphalia

Germany in mid-seventeenth century was a giant defeated and fallen, but in energies and resources—the wherewithal of future strength—still a giant among the peoples of Europe.

The People and Their Livelihood. War had worked its first result, depopulation, upon a large scale. Burned villages and cities and deserted farms marked where the armies had marched, camped, and fought. The

Germans, whose twenty millions a half-century before had made them the only nation in Europe to outnumber the French, were reduced to about the same population of sixteen million.

The loss of population resulted not only from the direct ravages of military operations but also from the distortion and destruction of economic life. The balance of productive activity shifted from commerce and industry to agriculture. The land had been despoiled and partly depeopled but it had not been destroyed. The peasants returned to the fields, resuming the eternal round of plowing, planting, and harvesting. Within a few decades, the disruptions of wartime had been largely mended.

Other forms of economic activity, requiring more accumulated funds and a larger and more fragile organization than agriculture, recuperated less quickly. Trade fell off in the cities, most of which became no more than market towns serving small environs. The more profitable long-distance trade was concentrated in a few cities: Hamburg on the North Sea and Frankfort on the Main linked Germany with the West, Leipzig in Saxony with the East. There were more and more foreigners among the merchants. The Dutch were at first the principal beneficiaries of the decline and disappearance of the Hanseatic League, which held its last meeting in 1669; but by the end of the century Englishmen appeared in ever larger numbers in the marts of Germany.

Industrial activity declined, if anything, even more than trade. The once flourishing towns of the Rhineland and southern Germany lost many of their customers. Handicraftsmen, to protect their narrowing markets, tightened the guild monopolies, but to little avail, for the earlier prosperity did not come back.

Nor did many Germans concern themselves with the economic retrogression of their country. The philosopher Leibniz, who did not neglect the affairs of this world, complained of the dangers resulting from this inattention. Economics, he said, was "the most important of the political sciences, yet Germany, because of her ignorance and neglect of it, is falling into further decline."

Culture in the French Manner. In their cultural life, the Germans similarly passed under foreign domination. Dutch and English influences were at work but did not match the breadth and intensity of the French. In the century after the Peace of Westphalia, Germany became a cultural colony of France.

In intellectual and esthetic discourse as well as in government writings, French vocabulary was preferred to the native German. Sometimes French words and phrases were used intact. The printed pages of German books showed the result in the profusion of the italic type used for foreign words in the midst of the Gothic print used for the German. Frequently, however,

French terms were adapted by simply tacking on German endings which did not conceal the foreign character of the roots. Latin, too, continued to be a part of the normal writing pattern. This intermixture may be seen in a famous comment made by King Frederick William I of Prussia on the margin of a protest by a subordinate against a new tax:

> *Tout le pays sera ruiné? Nihil kredo*, aber das *kredo*, dass der Junkers ihre Autorität *nic pro volam* wird ruiniert werden. Ich stabilier die *Souveraineté* wie ein *Rocher de bronce*.

> (Literally: "The whole land will be ruined? I do not believe it, but do believe that the veto authority of the Junkers will be ruined. I am establishing sovereignty like a rock of bronze.")

The arts reflected similar processes of imitation. Architecture adopted the Italian baroque and the French classical styles, creating a sometimes ludicrous and sometimes charming combination. Johann Sebastian Bach, the outstanding composer of the first half of the eighteenth century, wrote string concertos in the Italian style and dance suites after the French manner; but he also continued to compose in the older German forms, especially the chorales derived from the Lutheran hymns.

Religious Quiescence. The ending of religious wars ended the era of heroism and suffering for the cause of faith. In most areas of Germany, the wild swings of conversion and reconversion halted. Religious affiliation remained steady, for even where subjects differed in faith from their rulers, harsh oppression became less frequent. Popular piety recast the elaborate definitions of the theologians into the mold of comfortable and familiar rituals. Theologians taught their own kind of Christianity, despising rival forms but usually avoiding direct controversy with them.

Calvinism, beginning its second century in Germany, lost the boldness of its revolutionary past. It was now one of the legal religions, recognized in the Peace of Westphalia as permissible for rulers and hence for their subjects; but it remained inferior in strength to both Catholicism and Lutheranism.

Official Lutheranism remained sedate and self-satisfied. Beneath its formalism fermented a different kind of religious life, directed toward the emotions rather than the mind. It came to the surface in the teachings of Philip Jacob Spener, born in Alsace in 1635. His Pietism emphasized the worship of the simple humble Christian, at the expense of the formulation and preservation of orthodox doctrines. Spener's teachings won many earnest souls within Lutheranism, even stirring some of its officials from the mere performance of their administrative duties to a more heartfelt religion. The orthodox responded by condemning Pietism as a heresy, but they were unable to expel its influence.

Like Lutheranism, German Roman Catholicism came more completely than ever under the domination of the princes—although Catholics had fought to maintain the dogma of papal overlordship in the church. The princes of the Empire enforced their rights of nomination as vigorously as did the kings of France and Spain. The church, with its lucrative benefices, continued to serve the rulers as a means of endowing family, friends, and servitors with revenues.

The Princes' Empire. The settlement of Westphalia consolidated the balance of political forces which had been emerging in Germany for a century and a half. Nominal legal supremacy still lay in the Holy Roman Empire, but almost every effective means of power had passed into the hands of the princes. In name vassals, they were acknowledged in the treaties of Westphalia to be virtually sovereign.

The princes received the powers of independent monarchs over their own subjects and in their relations with other states. The reservation that they could not make treaties or wage war against the Empire or the emperor was a parchment barrier against princes who commanded their own armies and collected their own taxes. Imperial princes did form such alliances and wage such war, repeatedly. Yet the habits of centuries were deeply ingrained; the princes paid the emperor and Empire a respect greater than that to which actual power entitled them, and acknowledged that only the emperor could grant the vassals the loftier ranks which they coveted.

Within their own territories the princes erased the remaining rights of the representative assemblies to share in government by granting and collecting special taxation. The work of these estates was taken over by an expanding officialdom. The professional government servants were generally recruited from outside the provinces in which they served, and were often subjects of other rulers, to whom they continued to owe primary allegiance. Standing armies were established at the same time. Government thus became absolute, with the powers of decision and enforcement wholly in the hands of the prince and his agents. The tone of government nonetheless remained patriarchal; the princes continued to look upon their territories as inherited "entailed estates," with themselves as the paternal landlord-governors.

The Debate on the Empire. German thinkers differed in describing and judging the political character of their country after the Peace of Westphalia. Germany was a country and a nation, but was it a state? The Holy Roman Empire was neither monarchy, aristocracy, nor democracy, so that it fitted none of the Aristotelian categories of political organization accepted by theorists. Nor was it a federation of semi-independent provinces, like Switzerland or the Dutch Republic, for it did not present a single sovereign face to the outside world as they did.

Some observers were satisfied with the new situation. The interests of the princes were expounded in the work of B. P. von Chemnitz, writing under the pen name of Hippolytus a Lapide. In his *De ratione statu in imperio nostro Romano-Germanico* (*On Reason of State in Our Roman-German Empire*, 1647), he defended the primacy of the princes and called the Holy Roman emperor no more than their servant. Two decades later the jurist and historian Samuel von Pufendorf, though like Chemnitz opposed to the Hapsburg claims to sovereign power, was less easily satisfied in describing the nature of the Empire. Pufendorf, in his *De statu Imperii Germanici* (*On the State of the German Empire*, 1667), gave the problem a paradoxical solution by denying that any definition was possible; the Empire, he said, was "an irregular body, much like a monster."

Not all princes nor princely servants accepted the newfangled theories of absolute power for the great imperial vassals. Veit von Seckendorff, chancellor of the duke of Saxony-Gotha, in his *Teutsche Fürstenstaat* (*The German Princely State*, 1650), thanked God that the Germans gave to "no individual, calling himself, rightly or not, a sovereign, that kind of power which enables him to command others, according to his will and pleasure, to provide him with what he wants, when and where he wants it." Leibniz, too, who served first the elector of Mainz and then the dukes of Brunswick-Hanover, defended the imperial constitution against the criticism of Pufendorf. Its mixed elements did not clash but supported each other, Leibniz said; they were like separate musical tones uniting in one harmonious chord. Absolutism was wrong, he asserted, for it assigned God's powers to a man and equated the state with a person.

Leibniz's loyalty, however, went to the human race rather than to any single nation, even his own. "I am not one of those," he wrote to Peter the Great of Russia, "who are smitten with their own fatherland or any particular country, but am rather concerned for the welfare of the entire human race. For I hold Heaven to be my fatherland and all persons of good will to be my fellow-citizens, and I should prefer to do much good to Russians than little to Germans or other Europeans. . . ." This cosmopolitanism remained strong among German thinkers throughout the eighteenth century; their boast was that Germany increasingly ruled the empire of the spirit, not things of the world like political power.

Foreign Relations. Foreign affairs in Germany included not only the relations with foreign powers but also those among the German princes. Germany had become a microcosm of Europe, a little system of states within the larger system, rather than a true political entity. The Holy Roman Empire did not function in any significant sense as a state. The term "imperial" came to be a name of prestige indicating the forces and policies of the house of Hapsburg rather than those of the Empire as such.

The bonds of membership in the Empire did not fetter the independence of the princes. They used to the full their cherished liberty, guaranteed by the treaty of Westphalia, to conduct their own foreign policies as virtually independent states. Sovereignty, however, did not of itself lend them the strength needed to participate in the European states system as equals. They were lesser pieces on the European chessboard; only Austria counted as a major power.

As the comparative strength of the German princes declined, the problems facing them became more complex and more difficult. The powers on the west came to include not only France but also the ascendant kingdom of Great Britain. When these two states were hostile, the princes of the Empire were able to barter their alliances for substantial subsidies as well as support of their political aspirations, but when France and Britain were on good terms, the German rulers found that they were not valued at their own estimation. The Scandinavian states lost their earlier influence over German affairs, but the emergence of Russia as a major power under Peter I and his successors replaced them with an ever weightier threat on the eastern flank of Germany. The Turks continued as an intermittent foe to the southeast, but were the direct concern only of Austria.

In 1648, Austria alone among all the German principalities held a position among the major powers of Europe. All the rest, some two hundred in number, ranged in size and strength from moderate to the most minute. Yet the large majority of Germans lived within these lesser territorial states. Only a handful of these states were sufficiently large and distinctive to warrant even brief separate description here; the rest are best treated according to their types.

The "Priests' Alley." The ecclesiastical principalities strung along the Rhineland in western Germany—the "Priests' Alley" (*Pfaffengasse*) in the popular nickname—maintained their autonomous existence. Most of them remained under Catholic control and were ruled by bishops and abbots in their secular function. The remnants of Protestantism in these territories were cut down by persistent pressure. The usual measures were deprivation of privileges and excessive taxation but little outright violence.

Otherwise, the government of these principalities was less efficient but also less oppressive than that in the secular states. The absence of dynastic house interests spared the ecclesiastical states territorial ambitions. On the other hand, the various Catholic ruling houses waged bitter contests within the cathedral chapters and abbeys whenever an election was held. To gain one of these principalities meant not only to bestow its revenues upon junior members of the family, but also to align its policy with that of the elder prince of the house.

Imperial Cities and Knights. Their direct subordination to the emperor constituted the most essential safeguard for the free cities and the imperial knights, the tiniest "princes" in Germany. While their territories were coveted by their larger neighbors, their safety came not from their puny armies but from the counterbalancing rivalries of the would-be aggressors, who had, furthermore, a lingering reluctance to seize territories outright and without any semblance of legal claim.

The independence of these toy states meant neither strength nor progress but rather somnolence. The lethargy of German life after Westphalia reached its extreme in them. The cities preserved some tradition of effective local government, although economic retrogression stifled boldness of spirit, political or otherwise.

The knights, however, could not make their diminutive possessions into true states, equipped with a full-scale army and administration. Some pressed the last drop of taxes and rentals out of their subjects in the effort to live like great nobles. Others, kinder or more ambitious, sought their careers elsewhere and put themselves at the service of the greater princes. Among the "foreigners" who swarmed in the military and civil services of Germany, these knights of fortune gained an extra fillip of rank from their "imperial immediacy." Being the most important beneficiaries of imperial overlordship, the knights held more vigorously than most other Germans to the ideas and spirit of German imperial patriotism.

The Middling Territories. Greater than these toy potentates were the territorial princes, who possessed sufficient land and resources to build up true, if small, states. Most of these principalities were artificial creations, scattered territories brought together under one scepter by the accidents of dynastic inheritance. The historic sense of common origins, shared life, and like interests resided in the individual provinces rather than in the conglomerate dynastic state. These territorial states were seldom sufficiently large to permit the establishment of administrative organisms like those of France. The effort to maintain a full complement of judicial, fiscal, and other officials tended to make government more costly, often without any increase in efficiency.

The aspirations of the princes rose above the narrow confines of their actual condition. They wished to live like kings and took as their model Louis XIV of France. This imitation extended beyond methods of government to the luxuries and vices of the French monarch. Small-scale editions of the palace of Versailles were erected in many parts of Germany, and courts established within them according to the etiquette in force at Versailles. Acceptance of the French model was carried to the point where some of the princes established "official mistresses" (*maîtresses en titre*), publicly recognized and honored. Mimicry became ludicrous, however, when Frederick I of Prussia named an "official mistress" for public purposes, without requiring that she actually perform the private duties of the office.

The resources for such enterprises could not be extracted wholly from the impoverished regions ruled by the princes. Even extortionate taxation would not suffice. The incessant demands for money could be met, however, by putting the policy and the armed force of these little states at the service of the great and wealthy powers. In the seventeenth century France was the principal paymaster of the German electors, landgraves, and their kind; in the eighteenth century, England, emerging as a first-rate power, competed with France for the services of the German princes.

The Larger Principalities. The largest of these middling principalities assumed sufficient importance to play a persistent, if secondary, role in European affairs. Notable among these were Bavaria, Saxony, Brunswick-Hanover, and Brandenburg-Prussia.

Bavaria, barring only Austria, was the largest of the Catholic principalities. It was not wealthy, for it occupied a largely mountainous area in southern Germany. It had grown in territory and influence during the Thirty Years' War by taking the lead of the non-Austrian Catholic party, and by its acquisition of the Upper Palatinate and the electoral rank of the elector Palatine. These successes tempted the dukes of Bavaria to undertake an even bolder policy during the century after the Peace of Westphalia, contesting directly with the Hapsburgs for leadership of Catholic and princely Germany.

This policy was attainable only with the assistance of France, which the dukes did not shrink from accepting. The French alliance brought Bavaria into hostility with most of the other German states during the wars of the League of Augsburg and of the Spanish Succession. For a short time during the 1690's, the Bavarians even hoped to put a son of the duke upon the throne of Spain. Thereafter, during the eighteenth century, Bavaria remained steadfastly on the French side; it suffered grievously when France was weak and met defeat, but always regained what it lost when France re-established its advantage.

Saxony, once the leading Protestant principality in Germany, declined steadily from that eminence. In 1697 Elector Frederick Augustus I abandoned the Lutheran faith of his forebears and became a Catholic in order to gain election as king of Poland, under the name of Augustus II. Thereafter Poland dominated Augustus's policy toward Saxony. He treated the electorate as an adjunct to the Polish realm, drawing from the Saxons fiscal and military resources he could not obtain from the Poles. (See ch. 24, pp. 553-554).

Even after his conversion, Augustus continued to enforce his leadership upon the *corpus evangelicorum,* the grouping of German Protestant princes, holding it to be a prerogative of the Saxon dynasty since the days of the Reformation.

The ducal house of Brunswick likewise acquired royal rank. This great fortune was not the result of its own work but was the chance consequence of its Protestantism, a dynastic marriage, and events in Britain. In 1692, in compensation for Brunswick's support in the War of the League of Augsburg, Emperor Leopold I elevated it to the status of the ninth electorate under the name of Hanover. Its second elector, George Louis, was the great-grandson of James I of England, and as George I received the heritage of the United Kingdom of Great Britain in 1714 under the terms of the Act of Succession of 1701 (see ch. 20, p. 453). Both George I and George II remained Hanoverians and utilized their influence in England to the advantage of their electorate. The acquisition in 1719 of the former bishoprics of Bremen and Verden, lying at the mouth of the Elbe river, was Hanover's concrete gain from British support in the Great Northern War.

II. Brandenburg-Prussia

The emergence of Brandenburg from its contemptible position during the Thirty Years' War to a place of strength only behind Austria was the most startling development in Germany during the century after the Peace of Westphalia. It was the work neither of geography nor of events occurring elsewhere, but was primarily the achievement of several gifted members of the ruling house of Hohenzollern.

The Patchwork State. Brandenburg embodied to the extreme the diversity of origins and character typical of the principalities of Germany. The very name Brandenburg was used to indicate both the electorate itself, in the center, and the totality of the Hohenzollern possessions extending from Cleves in the west to Prussia in the east. The electorate was an economically backward, sparsely inhabited, and overwhelmingly agrarian country in the flatlands north of Saxony. Further Pomerania, between Brandenburg and the Baltic Sea, which was even poorer, also belonged to the Hohenzollerns, but Swedish-held Hither Pomerania controlled the mouth of the Oder river, the principal stream in Brandenburg, and thus enabled the Swedes to collect the valuable port tolls. The duchy of Cleves and the county of Mark, in the Rhineland, were more prosperous but much smaller in size. Ravensberg and Minden, to the northeast, formed stepping stones to Brandenburg itself. The duchy of Prussia, an area of marshes and pinelands, lay outside the boundaries of the Holy Roman Empire, across the Polish region of Pomerelia (Pomorze), or West Prussia (in contradistinction to East, or ducal, Prussia). The poverty of agricultural Prussia was in part balanced by the hinterland trade which passed through the Prussian ports of Königsberg and Memel.

Brandenburg was thus more widely dispersed than any other German principality. Its discontinuity made it difficult for its rulers to protect the scattered parts against attacks and to unite them under a single government.

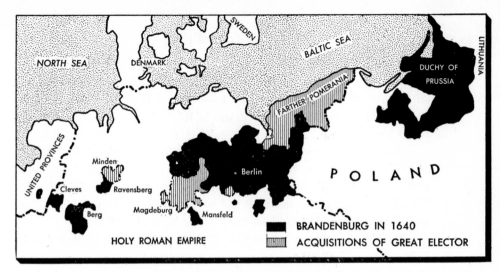

Brandenburg in the Period of the Great Elector, 1640-1688

On the other hand, these very perils spurred the Hohenzollerns to seek to acquire the intervening regions, with the goal of making the principality compact and more defensible. Thus their policy became essentially unstable, hovering between disaster and triumph.

The Great Elector. The transformation of Brandenburg into a modern state began with the accession of Frederick William as elector in 1640, at the age of twenty. He soon proved that in the harsh and trying business of state he was no youth. The abject weakness into which Brandenburg had fallen appalled but did not unnerve him. Even before peace was made eight years later, he set to work to rebuild his principality and make it "formidable." His aim became to maintain himself "at all times in a good posture," so that whenever war or the threat of war recurred, his lands would not be the "theater upon which the tragedy is played." He was absolutely clear about the means for attaining this purpose: to establish his own authority over his subjects beyond debate or resistance, to put on foot a permanent army, and to govern by means of professional officials responsible only to him. He also possessed the character needed for this task: a good intelligence reinforced by wide knowledge of European affairs, wisdom in deliberation, and unhesitating boldness when the time came to act.

The first task which confronted him was to subdue his principal rivals within the various provinces under his rule. These competitors for authority were the estates (*Landtage*), which possessed by tradition the right to consent to taxation and to collect sums so granted. The estates in the electorate came to heel quickly, but in the outlying provinces resistance to taxation imposed by the elector without their approval was bitter and sustained. Cleves and Mark did not go beyond vocal protests, but Prussia put up a stiffer fight in 1661. Rather than continue to pay to the elector the taxes which the Swedes

483

had extorted during their occupation during the recent war, many Prussians proposed to return their duchy to Polish sovereignty, which had been cast off in 1657. Frederick William put down the resistance by a show of force in 1662. The leader of the recalcitrants in Königsberg was sentenced to perpetual imprisonment. Another rebel stalwart, a nobleman named Kalckstein, was kidnaped in Warsaw, where he had taken refuge, brought back to Prussia, and executed. Accused of violating natural law, Frederick William replied with a characteristic phrase: "I did not intend to commit any injustice, but I wanted to be master and they had to be subjects." But if his subjects obeyed then he would love them "as a father loves his children."

The Means of Power. As master of his land, Frederick William steadily built up its strength. He reorganized the government on the pattern common to all the larger German states, with central councils set over the local estates, but he pursued his absolutist measures with greater system and deliberateness than most of his fellow princes. He also emphasized the use of army administrators without local affiliations for purposes of civil administration. A "general war commissary" was named in 1660 to take over from provincial officials the collection of taxes for the army. The army, established on a permanent basis, was both expanded and reorganized. It increased in size from 8,000 in 1646 to 25,000 nine years later, and twice that number at the end of the reign in 1688. The elector's powers of command were enhanced by abolition of the traditional system of treating the regiments as the personal property of their commanders.

The resources for maintaining this apparatus of power came from the domain (the lands owned by the prince as direct proprietor) and from two new taxes, the excise and the "contribution." The domain was administered with close attention to increasing its revenues and preventing fraud and misuse. The excise was an indirect tax which fell upon townsmen in particular, while the "contribution" was a tax upon the rural population, including the nobility. Frederick William also encouraged the economic growth of the country. He fostered commerce and to a lesser degree industry by protectionist measures, built a canal between the Spree and the Oder rivers which linked the capital at Berlin with the sea, and after the revocation of the Edict of Nantes in 1685 brought in industrious Huguenots, who gave many new and valuable skills to their adopted land.

The Use of Power. It was one thing for Frederick William to prevail over his subjects, another to make good his purposes at the expense of other states. Though his central principle was that "alliances are good, but to be strong by oneself is better," he never escaped dependence upon alliance with stronger states. In order to avoid doing the work of his more powerful friends without benefit to himself, he had to employ all the wiles of an open-eyed and usually dispassionate "reason of state," overriding his predilections whenever they conflicted with concrete advantage. But such a nimble policy succeeded only because his command within Brandenburg was complete, and provided him with military resources sufficient to make his friendship valuable.

His two leading aims were to throw off Polish suzerainty over his duchy of Prussia and, by expelling the Swedes from Pomerania, to open Brandenburg proper to the sea. He lacked the power during the first part of the reign to gain these purposes singlehandedly against either prospective foe. He therefore first joined with the Swedes in 1656 to defeat the Poles, achieving his first major victory at Warsaw in July. In the treaty of Wehlau the next year, Poland acknowledged Prussia as an independent duchy. Frederick William then turned upon his erstwhile ally, but French support of the Swedes prevented him from making his expected gains in Pomerania at the Peace of Oliva in 1660.

Thereafter relations with France became crucial. Frederick William swung between amity and enmity as the needs and the possibilities of the moment dictated, without concern for abstract principle. The one exception to the rule of safety and advantage which he otherwise followed was to rush to the aid of the invaded Dutch in 1672, under the prompting particularly of his fear that the stronghold of Calvinism would be overwhelmed by the overmighty Catholic power of France. The French armies defeated his forces, and he made peace in 1673. The next year, he joined the alliance against France and shook off the Swedish attack which followed, by his victory at Fehrbellin in 1675. To contemporaries this was a triumph of David over Goliath, and the title "Great Elector" was bestowed upon Frederick William. Nonetheless, at the peace of Nijmegen in 1679, France was able once again to deprive him of the fruits of victory over Sweden. Recognizing where power lay, the elector again turned French ally. But the aggressiveness of French policy, and especially the revocation of the Edict of Nantes, caused him to change sides again. When he died in 1688, he was preparing to join the Grand Alliance being formed by his nephew, William III, against France.

Frederick I, King in Prussia. The Great Elector sought the hard core of power; his son and successor, Elector Frederick III, gave himself to the externalities of princely office. In the words of his grandson and namesake, Frederick the Great, Frederick III was great in small things and small in great. His vanity and pompousness found their outlet partly in regally lavish display, and partly in seeking a royal title to cap his dignities.

His capital at Berlin was the center not only of an elaborate court modeled on Versailles but also of an expanding intellectual and artistic life. The elector gave his support to Leibniz, founded an academy of sciences in Berlin, and established a university at Halle in 1694. The expenditures thus incurred were met by increased taxation and by subsidies from wealthier powers, to which he easily gave subservience of policy.

The acquisition of royal rank was Frederick's "grand project." He was jealous of the new honor of his neighbor, Elector Frederick Augustus of Saxony, who became king of Poland in 1697. Frederick proposed to match Augustus rank for rank by elevating the duchy of Prussia, which lay outside the Empire, to the status of a kingdom. Frederick took for granted that he could not assume royal rank without the emperor's permission, and therefore subordinated his policy to that of Austria. His reward came in 1700 when Leopold I granted him permission to entitle himself "king in Prussia." The phrase, "*in* Prussia," was a concession to Polish feelings, since West Prussia was a part of the Polish kingdom. For the next dozen years of his reign, King Frederick I, as he was called after his coronation in 1701, gratefully and loyally supported Hapsburg interests in the great war against France. His payment had been given in advance, as it turned out, for Prussia —the name henceforth given to the Hohenzollern state—gained no significant advantage in the peace settlement of 1713-1714.

Frederick William I. With Frederick William I, who succeeded his father Frederick I in 1713, the pendulum of Hohenzollern character swung violently to the opposite extreme. The new monarch was coarse, blunt, disdainful of thinkers and artists; he was utterly single-minded in his concern for power and the instrumentalities of power. Yet the hinge of his policy continued to be the grandeur and the strength of the house of Hohenzollern. He maintained his sovereignty within his dominions "like a rock of bronze," in his famous phrase, and insisted upon being able "to have his say among the powers."

Frederick William began his reign by enforcing the strictest measures of economy. He permitted the academy of sciences to lapse, sent the artists and writers elsewhere to seek more open-pursed patrons, and discarded the elaborate and expensive court. He met with his cronies and councilors in a "tobacco cabinet," where all the major and most minor decisions of state were made amid thick smoke and heavy drinking.

Nonetheless the Prussian administration began to emerge as the most efficient in Europe. Frederick William did not bother to abolish formally the old system of estates government in the provinces, but simply let it dangle uselessly, without functions or power. Its work was completely taken over by royal officials, who were stingily paid and strictly supervised. The lower ranks were recruited largely from retired subaltern officers, the upper from educated burghers and increasingly from the class of higher officers. Unity of control was created in 1722 by merging the superior councils in charge of the three main branches of administration into a single board of government. Its full name, the *Generaloberfinanzkriegsunddomänendirektorium*

(General Superior Directory for Finances, War, and Domains), accurately described its function; but even Germans in love with ponderous titles soon abbreviated it to the "General Directory." The members of the General Directory divided the tasks of administration by provinces instead of by functions. Its ironbound rule was the practice of economy. The king refused to approve any but the most necessary of expenditures for civil government.

The "Sergeant King." Yet Frederick William was not a miser, devoted to the mere accumulation of treasure. His constant aim was readiness for war, and he considered money only as its sinews. The hoard of coin he amassed, nine million talers by 1740, was designed to provide the wherewithal for several campaigns, safe from the difficulties of increasing taxation, borrowing, or negotiating subsidies.

The army was the darling of his life. He increased it from 38,000 to 81,000 men during his reign, and personally directed its training and development. His concern for detail won him the sobriquet of "sergeant king." Actually, it was Prince Leopold of Anhalt-Dessau who originated and organized the reform of the Prussian army, introducing such innovations as formal drill. But the drive behind the work of the "Old Dessauer," as he was affectionately called by the soldiers, came from Frederick William. The king's particular vanity consisted in a regiment of grenadier guards, composed of *langen Kerls* (tall fellows, over six feet in height). The recruitment of the regular regiments was strengthened by the "canton" system, first introduced in 1665 by the Great Elector but made general by Frederick William in 1733. Under this arrangement specific districts were assigned to provide recruits to each regiment. Prussia thereby became the first state in Europe to introduce a form of conscription.

The king so loved his army, however, that he was loath to use it. He was sensitive to the unpredictable dangers of actual war, and to the rapidity with which even the best armies were worn down and destroyed in combat. He preferred therefore to evade such risks by following in practice a peaceable foreign policy. He continued in the path of his father's subservience to the Hapsburg emperors, and did not seek out an independent and forthright role for Prussia. Bit by bit foreign statesmen came to lose their respect for the well-trained, well-manned, well-directed regiments of Prussia, since they were sure that they would not appear on the battlefield except in direct defense of Prussian territory. By 1740, when Frederick William died, for all his expenditure and devotion to the military, Prussia had gained little in the way of territory, no more than Hither Pomerania to the Oder mouths. The Prussian monarchy was still a scattered state strung across the whole extent of North Germany, but a stronger state than it had been a century before, strong indeed beyond its size.

III. Austria

The Peace of Westphalia dealt a death blow to Hapsburg ambitions to make the imperial power effective, but Hapsburg strength, rooted in the hereditary lands, remained sufficient to make Austria the one great power within Germany.

Leopold I. Ferdinand III, who had presided over the destinies of the house of Hapsburg in the final decade of the Thirty Years' War, died a decade after the Peace of Westphalia, in April 1657. The Hapsburg cause, battered and weakened, was put under a new stress. Ferdinand's son and heir, Leopold, had not been named king of the Romans during his father's lifetime, so an imperial election was necessary. Leopold was not the only candidate; the French prime minister, Cardinal Mazarin, unofficially offered to the electors the name of the young king of France, Louis XIV. They were not eager to place a French monarch, commanding the immense resources of the French state, above them, thereby exchanging Hapsburgs in decline for Bourbons in ascendancy. Instead, in 1658, after an interregnum of 16 months, they unanimously chose the Hapsburg archduke, a youth of eighteen, as Leopold I, after forcing upon him an electoral capitulation which barred imperial aid to Spain and definitively made the Holy Roman Empire a "state of princes" (*Fürstenstaat*), proof against the rivalries of both emperor and their own subjects.

During the next half century, Leopold accepted the new state of affairs; he was satisfied to reign over the Empire, so long as he ruled over Austria, his own dominions. Under his guidance, Austria turned back more and more strongly to the path of seeking power in its own lands, not in the Empire. Austrian resurgence was a double feat, for neither the personality of the ruler nor the structure of the Hapsburg state seemed favorable to such an enterprise.

In almost everything but his staunch dynastic purposes and his love of literature and music, Leopold was the opposite of his great rival, Louis XIV. He neither governed well himself, nor permitted anyone else to do so for him as prime minister. He hated to make up his mind. "O God," he once wrote—in Italian—to his confessor, "how I hate to come to decisions." He depended upon subordinates for ideas, but detested bold new conceptions; instead he responded to the pressures of the moment, and could not be held to a single steady policy. One foreign envoy despairingly compared him to a clock which needed constant rewinding. Yet he had a strict sense of duty and an unvarying desire to extend the possessions of the house of Hapsburg.

The Hapsburg State. The Austrian state was equally unpromising as the instrument of Hapsburg power. Austria, like Brandenburg-Prussia, was a multiple state, but one considerably larger and quite different in character.

It was a ramshackle assemblage of provinces and kingdoms, including the German archduchies of Austria and the kingdoms of Bohemia and Hungary. The divergencies between the constituent elements of the Austrian state were therefore greater than in Prussia, but the Hapsburg rulers provided the element of cohesion which knit the scattered lands into a single "power" so far as other states were concerned.

Hapsburg central administration was set above the local and provincial authorities without replacing them. The regions continued to be autonomous within themselves. Local and national diets collected taxes, nominated most local officials, directed the work of administration, and controlled the lower courts of justice. Their major obligation to the reigning Hapsburg prince was to turn over a portion of the tax revenue to him; they had no longer any right to refuse that grant. Over each of the main regions of the Hapsburg state was a council to direct its affairs as part of the common policy of the monarchy.

Turks and Magyars. Yet the integrity of the Hapsburg territories was under threat almost at its center for half the reign. Magyar magnates under Turkish overlordship controlled almost all of Hungary; only a narrow band of Hungary, along the Austrian frontier close to Vienna, remained under Hapsburg control. The Hungarians and the Turks were encouraged and supported in their hostility to Austria by France; rebellion and war in the East distracted Austrian attention from events in the West, where French influence persistently penetrated into the Empire.

Twice during a single generation the Turks carried war to Austria. In 1663 an enterprising grand vizier, Mohammed Köprülü, led an assault which reached all the way to the Raab river, southeast of Vienna, before it was halted by combined Austrian and imperial forces at the battle of St. Gotthardt in the summer of 1664. Leopold's concern over the extension of French influence in Germany, embodied in the Rhine League, led him to make a twenty years' truce with the Turks at Vasvar, which left the territorial frontiers unchanged.

Exactly twenty years later, in 1683, the Turkish onslaught reached to Vienna itself. The immediate spur to the invasion was a rebellion of Magyar nobles in Austrian-ruled Hungary against Leopold's efforts to enforce tighter royal control and to restrict the liberties of the Protestants. At the instigation of Emeric Tököly, the Magyar rebel leader, the Turks took the field with 200,000 troops. A siege of Vienna ensued for two months, while the garrison and burghers held out manfully. A relief force of imperial troops and an army of Poles led by their king, John Sobieski, marched to the support of the Viennese. Their arrival in September 1683 led to the collapse of the siege, the defeat of the Turks, and their inglorious retreat. The Hapsburg forces were inadequate to follow up the victory at once, but after reorganization continued the campaign against the Turks and their Magyar allies. In 1686 Budapest, the principal Hungarian city, fell to the Austrian armies; the next year the Turks were defeated at Mohács, the very place where their armies had conquered Hungary a century and a half before.

The immediate consequence was a fundamental change in the character of the Hungarian monarchy. Hapsburg control was re-established over almost all of Hungary, with the important exception of Transylvania. A diet was convened at Bratislava which made the crown of St. Stephen hereditary in the male Hapsburg line. Archduke Joseph, Leopold's son and heir, was crowned king. The nobility preserved their social rights and their system of government but lost their centuries-old privilege of resisting misrule by force of arms. The war with the Turks continued with intermittent successes and defeats until 1699. Austrian victory at Zenta in 1697 compelled the Ottoman rulers to accept peace. The treaty of Karlowitz in 1699 gave Leopold all of Hungary, including Transylvania, except one district (the banat of Temesvár) in the south.

Prince Eugene and Joseph I. The battle of Zenta also marked the emergence of Prince Eugene of Savoy, who commanded the triumphant imperial forces, as a figure of pre-eminent leadership in the Austrian state. A member of the ducal dynasty of Savoy and a grandnephew of Cardinal Mazarin, he had fled France in anger at his neglect by Louis XIV and taken service under the emperor. His forthrightness, enterprise, and devotion to the Hapsburg dynasty and the general Austrian cause set him off from the common run of Hapsburg servants. His value to Leopold was again demonstrated in 1704 when he combined with the English general Marlborough to win the decisive battle of Blenheim during the War of the Spanish Succession. It was on this note of victory, confirming Austria's place among the great powers of Europe, that the reign of Leopold I ended in 1705.

Prince Eugene, Paris-born and a Frenchman by language and culture, became the dominant personality in the Hapsburg monarchy under the next two emperors, Joseph I (1705-1711) and Charles VI (1711-1740). Joseph was an eager, warlike ruler, who delighted in the victories brought him by Eugene. Eugene retained his post as president of the war council, to which he had been named by Leopold I. From this vantage point he directed the military administration of Austria, while as commander-in-chief he led the armies in the field. He did his best to shake Austrian administration from its sloth. "Even when the worst news comes, nobody worries or thinks of remedies," he complained during one wartime crisis. "The calm is amazing; everything is allowed to take its course." Despite his constant and almost singlehanded exertions, Eugene could not overcome this lethargy.

Charles VI. In 1711 Joseph I was succeeded by his brother Charles VI as ruler of Austria and Holy Roman Empire. He retained Prince Eugene

in a place of leadership, but did not accept his counsel as easily as had Joseph. He permitted Eugene to negotiate the treaties of Rastatt and Baden, which brought to a close the German side of the War of the Spanish Succession. Eugene could not regain by his diplomacy the Spanish monarchy which Charles himself, during his spell as claimant king of Spain, had been unable to hold (see ch. 24, p. 539); but the southern Netherlands were transferred from Spanish to Austrian rule. Charles would not abandon his Spanish dream, however, for almost a decade. The combination of France and Britain to maintain the Utrecht settlement in 1719 thwarted him of attaining his ambition; he responded by making a brief league with Spain; it resulted, however, only in the discomfiture of both Philip V and his Austrian cousin.

Eugene meanwhile redeemed the prestige of Austria by a series of victories over the Turks. In 1716 he defeated them at Peterwardein (Petrovaradin), in Serbia, and captured the key river port of Belgrade. By the Peace of Passarowitz in 1718, the Turks abandoned to Austria the banat of Temesvár, the northern part of Serbia including Belgrade, and part of the Rumanian province of Wallachia; but the Venetians, on whose behalf the Austrians had entered the war, did not regain the Morea (the peninsula of ancient Peloponnesus), which the Turks had captured from them. Eugene, at the peak of his prestige, urged Charles to continue to press the campaign against the Ottoman empire in order to expel it completely from the Balkans. Charles, unwilling to sacrifice any one of his purposes for the sake of another, rejected this idea of a predominantly eastern direction of growth for Austria.

The Pragmatic Sanction.   Instead Charles VI concentrated on maintaining the dynastic unity of his lands. The Pragmatic Sanction of 1713 was his instrument for achieving this purpose. It provided that in the event that there was no direct male heir, his own daughters should inherit, followed by the female line of Joseph I. By abolishing the rule of exclusively masculine descent which prevailed in Bohemia and Milan, the Pragmatic Sanction assured that the realms of the Hapsburgs would not be sundered by dynastic mischance. During the years 1720-1723, Charles obtained the assent of the principal estates to the Pragmatic Sanction, and thereafter gained one by one the promise of the principal powers of Europe to accept it, thereby abandoning whatever claim they might have by collateral male inheritance. Eugene was skeptical of these promises, which required major concessions from Austria. The time and energy would be better spent on building an army to defend the unity of Austria, he pleaded.

But to no avail. The aging Eugene could not stiffen the administration of army and state with his flagging labors. The penalty was soon visible. Charles's effort to bolster the economic edifice of his states by re-opening the Austrian Netherlands to seagoing traffic failed when Britain and the Dutch Republic united to compel him to abandon the Ostend Company, established in 1722. (See ch. 24, p. 547.) During the War of the Polish Succession (1733-1735), Austria was unable to prevent France from seizing the duchy of Lorraine, which belonged to the bridegroom of the Austrian heiress Maria Theresa; the peace treaty took Lorraine from Duke Francis, recompensing him with the grand duchy of Tuscany. In the next year Austria found herself allied with Russia in war against the Turks. This time all went badly, for Eugene died early in the year. Ottoman triumphs on the battlefield, reinforced by French mediation in the chambers of diplomacy, led to the treaty of Belgrade of 1739, by which the Austrians lost Belgrade and the part of northern Serbia seized two decades before. It was on this note of failure that the reign ended, in 1740, with the death of Charles VI.

22

Germany:
The Rivalry of Prussia and Austria
1740 - 1790

IN 1740, the deaths of the Emperor Charles VI and of the Prussian King Frederick William I destroyed the unstable German political equilibrium. Germany dropped into another long period of wars and desolation.

I. Germany in 1740

At mid-point in the eighteenth century, the multiplicity of political units into which Germany was divided imperiled not only the prosperity of the nation but also its cohesion.

In 1740, the German nation was earning the rewards of many decades of hard and diligent work. The devastation of the Thirty Years' War and the smaller destruction wrought by the briefer conflicts of the following period were only memories. The farms were under the plow; the workshops and the merchant houses were busy. The villages and the towns had been repeopled. The population was increasing steadily toward the old figure of twenty million.

Nonetheless, the recovery was limited in scope and character. The country remained overwhelmingly agrarian, while trade and industry did not regain the importance they had had in the late medieval period. German merchants did not participate to any noteworthy extent in the swift development of oceanic commerce. Mining, in which the Germans had once excelled, had declined; the famous silver mines of an earlier age could not compete with the mines of Mexico and Bolivia, while the large-scale extraction of iron ore and coal—the mark of a new economic order based on industrialization —was still absent. Compared to the surging economic expansion of Britain, and to lesser degree of France, Germany was falling behind.

German economic enterprise continued to be hampered by the splitting of the country into a multitude of narrow markets created by the boundaries of the petty states. The burden of the customs barriers at each frontier was made even heavier by the many toll stations on the rivers, which were the principal transport routes.

The fantastic compartmentation of the German economy was exaggerated by the effort of each principality to become self-sufficient. The German princes, encouraged in their own mercantilist ambitions by Colbert's successes in France, erected high protective tariffs, or forbade all imports. They usually managed thereby only to keep abreast of each other in taxable resources, but fell behind the economic titans of western Europe.

The Resurgence of German Culture.   German cultural life, long dependent upon foreign nations, began to take on independence and equality during the second half of the eighteenth century. This result grew out of several developments. The German artists and writers themselves had acquired competence in the styles, methods, and ideas brought in from abroad and so were able to venture confidently upon their own. Furthermore, they received the necessary patronage thanks to the increased prosperity and political self-confidence of the country.

Literature and the arts moved into the first rank in Europe. The language was purged of excessive foreign vocabulary and developed a clear prose style which blended the pithy vigor of Luther's German with the balance and control learned from the French and English neoclassicists. Poets, too, began to write in their native language, abandoning their schoolboyish imitations of French neoclassical verse. The drama reflected these achievements with the composition of plays in both prose and verse. The novel developed rapidly and attained high level, and so did critical writing. In all those forms, the supreme figure was Johann Wolfgang Goethe, whose literary genius equaled or surpassed that of any contemporary anywhere.

German thought, however, took on the characteristic pedantry of the university professors who dominated it. It emphasized systematic and detailed exposition, erudition, and frequently a turgidity that called itself "profundity." "Amateur" thinkers after the French and English fashion, men who did not earn their living in the universities but wrote and talked for the interest of their subject matter, and for the fun of it, were rare in Germany.

The Princes' State. Politically Germany in 1740 was the "princes' state" of 1648, spelled out in detail and consolidated by nine decades of princely predominance. The great vassals were more effectively sovereign than ever, and a number among them had become reigning monarchs in foreign lands.

In their little realms the princes were generally still absolute monarchs. Some were petty tyrants, others "enlightened despots," concerned for the welfare of their subjects. One of the worst of the former was Duke Charles Eugene of Württemberg. In 1759 the celebrated political theorist John Jacob Moser, who had criticized the duke's misrule, was arrested and kept imprisoned without trial for five years. On the other hand, princes like Charles William Ferdinand of Brunswick and Charles Augustus of Weimar, Goethe's patron, won praise for their work in sage, moderate government.

Germany as an entity—the Holy Roman Empire—was neither tyrannical nor benevolent, but rather a thing of words. The imperial office had ceased to have any significant function or powers save those of ceremony. Yet the Hapsburgs did not dream of abandoning it to any rival. Austria continued to play the leader among the German states, not because the elected emperor was always the head of the house of Hapsburg, but because Austria was stronger than any of the other German states and had been able to keep them divided. Yet Austrian power was uncertain because the Hapsburg state was itself half in and half out of the Empire. The preservation of this precarious balance between Austria and the princes depended therefore both on the maintenance of Austria's internal cohesion and on the absence within Germany of any rival who could effectively contest Vienna's leadership.

II. Three Silesian Wars

This balance broke in 1740, when the deaths of King Frederick William I of Prussia and Emperor Charles VI gave control of affairs to their successors.

The Philosopher-King. May 31, 1740—the day of Frederick William's death and the accession of Frederick II—was a "day of dupes" in German history. Crown Prince Frederick had once been the living refutation of all for which his father had stood. Where Frederick William had been an enthroned sergeant, practical, powerful and uncouth, his son was a devotee of philosophy and the arts, who played the flute and wrote French verses, and was therefore presumably inapt for power. Those who expected a change in the character of government remembered the high tragedy of 1730, when the eighteen-year-old Frederick, despondent at his father's contempt and harshness, attempted to flee to England; his companion in flight, Lieutenant

Katte, had been executed while the crown prince was compelled to look on; then Frederick had been broken from his military rank and sent in disgrace to Küstrin. What had been overlooked or was not known was the young man's subsequent experience: his dutiful and then eager interest in the business of government and military command in which he was drilled; his re-establishment in a colonelcy; his return to a free life, with an estate of his own, whence he had corresponded with Voltaire and other notables of the Enlightenment; all capped by the reconciliation of son and father, thanks to their new awareness of each other's dedication to the power and the glory of the house of Hohenzollern. Frederick II, when he ascended the throne, was therefore no pale aesthete lost to reality, but a toughened and ambitious man of twenty-eight who grasped power with greedy expectancy.

On the throne, Frederick was a crowned philosopher, though only the years would tell whether he was more king than sage. He took his stand as a political thinker in a book published anonymously in Holland the year of his accession: the soon-celebrated *Anti-Machiavel* (*Anti-Machiavelli*), a refutation of the Florentine's analysis of the self-interest of the prince in taking and maintaining power. The *Anti-Machiavel* was a book at once deceptive and revealing. On the one hand, Frederick affirmed the classical political doctrine that the ruler held power for and on behalf of his people; his only duty was to make them happy. "The prince is not absolute master but only the first servant of his people," Frederick declared. Cardinal Fleury, guessing who had written the *Anti-Machiavel*, commented, "If the author is a prince, he is accepting a solemn obligation toward the public." Yet in practice the driving purpose of the new king, as he admitted in a letter to a friend, was for action to meet the demands of his "youth, the fire of passion, the longing for fame, curiosity and, in the last instance, a secret instinct." On the other hand, Frederick justified in the *Anti-Machiavel* not only wars of defense but also offensive wars to maintain one's rights and to prevent universal monarchy. Such definitions, wielded by so adept a manipulator of ideas as the new king of Prussia, opened the door to bold and ruthless policy. His quest for fame would not be thwarted by an inconveniently rigorous morality.

The Gamble for Silesia. War and conquest, not the gentler works of peace, were the means by which Frederick intended to create his fame. For some months after his accession, he prepared to use the army and war treasury prepared by his father to seize the Rhineland territory of Berg, which was claimed by both Prussia and the count palatine of Neuburg. He suddenly shifted his goal when Emperor Charles VI died on October 20, 1740. The very day the news arrived, the Prussian king wrote to Voltaire that he planned "the boldest, most rapid, and grandest undertaking in which a prince of my house has ever been engaged," "a means of acquiring reputation and increasing the power of the state." Not little Berg but the wealthy and populous Austrian province of Silesia, up the Oder river from Brandenburg, upon which the Hohenzollerns held some dubious claims, was Frederick's target. The conquest of Silesia would go far to transform Prussia from a state always in danger of slipping back into weakness and defeat into one able to maintain itself among the powers of Europe. Silesia equaled all of Brandenburg-Prussia in population and wealth. It also commanded a strong strategic position on the flanks of both Bohemia, to the west, and Poland, to the east.

Frederick foresaw no grave danger in this enterprise. The archduchess Maria Theresa, who succeeded her father Charles VI, according to the provisions of the Pragmatic Sanction, could not conceivably cross him. She was no more—or so it seemed—than the dutiful and affectionate wife of Grand Duke Francis of Tuscany, who had lost his native duchy of Lorraine in the War of the Polish Succession. She had displayed no qualities of command, no sharp intelligence, no implacable purposefulness. She faced, furthermore, claims to all or part of her realms from rivals who asserted that the Pragmatic Sanction was null and void; the Spanish Bourbon demands could be written off, but not that of Duke Charles Albert of Bavaria, after Austria the most influential Catholic state in Germany. The feebleness of Hapsburg government was notorious. Frederick therefore called upon Maria Theresa to cede him Silesia, or at least its principal districts; in return he would stand by his father's acknowledgment of the Pragmatic Sanction and guarantee the remainder of the Austrian monarchy. To his surprise, Maria Theresa refused to discuss the offer. Silesia was hers by right and she would not yield it to the threat of force. Frederick had met an antagonist of mettle equal to his own, a woman of courage and competence in public affairs, with a keen sense of the right and readiness to defend it.

There remained to Frederick the choice between backing away from his demands, which he could do only at the cost of Europe's laughter and the loss of his self-respect, or acting upon his threat.

The First Silesian War. On December 16, 1740, Frederick II led 30,000 Prussian troops into Silesia. The invasion of a lightly defended province on the fringe of the Austrian possessions went quickly enough, but it was another matter to hold it. The Prussian and Austrian armies met at Mollwitz on April 10, 1741. The Prussian cavalry fought badly; Frederick, unnerved, fled the field; but the infantry, commanded by Field Marshal Schwerin, held firm and at last drove off the Austrians. The king's shame became a lesson in future bravery; never again, even when total disaster threatened, did he play the poltroon.

The victory of Mollwitz did not end the war. Maria Theresa refused to accept defeat. In order to gain the support of the restless Hungarians, she went in person to Bratislava to have her infant son Joseph acknowledged as king. Hard negotiations with the Magyar magnates led to a bargain; the

Parliament granted her troops and taxes, and she confirmed the traditional constitution of Hungary, abandoning the half-century-old endeavor of the Hapsburgs to rule the country by absolute authority.

The next year nonetheless went from one difficulty to another for the archduchess. France and Bavaria became the allies of Prussia in mid-1741, and a Franco-Bavarian army invaded Bohemia, capturing Prague in November. Charles Albert was proclaimed king of Bohemia and, with the encouragement of Frederick II, won election as Holy Roman Emperor Charles VII the next January—the first non-Hapsburg to reign over Germany since mid-fifteenth century. Maria Theresa, in order to concentrate her efforts on regaining Bohemia, left recovery of Silesia for a later time. She made an armistice with Frederick II at Klein-Schellendorf in October 1741, then drove out the Bavarians from Bohemia, although the proud French continued to cling to Prague. Then she made peace with Frederick, who feared the entry of Russia into the war against him. By the treaty of Berlin (July 28, 1742), Maria Theresa ceded to Frederick all of Silesia except three counties. But she was free to wage war upon Charles VII, whose election as emperor she refused to acknowledge as valid or rightful.

The Second Silesian War. Maria Theresa at once sharpened her attack upon her remaining foes. Austrian armies compelled the French to flee from Prague in a disastrous mid-winter retreat (see ch. 18, p. 420), and invaded Bavaria. A "Pragmatic Army" of Dutch, English, and Austrian forces, reinforced by German mercenary troops on hire from lesser imperial princes, marched from the Low Countries up the Rhine and defeated the French and Bavarian armies at Dettingen in June, 1743. All the while Frederick II stood upon the sidelines, an increasingly troubled neutral. His one-time protégé, Charles VII, was floundering; the emperor's downfall would, he feared, enable Maria Theresa to resume her deferred but not abandoned purpose of recapturing Silesia. Frederick thereupon decided to forestall her; while the Austrian forces were engaged in an invasion of French Alsace, Frederick struck hard in a sudden invasion of Bohemia in mid-August of 1744. The War of the Austrian Succession, as the duel for Silesia came to be called, entered its second round.

Maria Theresa now made Silesia the center of her objectives. She called back her troops from Alsace and concentrated upon the campaign against Frederick. The issue of the Bavarian emperor disappeared when Charles VII, his dream of glory shattered, died on January 20, 1745. Three months later Charles's son Maximilian Joseph, accepting the decision of battle, made peace, abandoning all claims to Austria and the imperial throne.

During the remainder of the year 1745, the war seesawed between Prussia and Austria. The Hapsburg cause was worsened by defeats in Italy and the first successes of Marshal Saxe in the Low Countries; but Maria

Theresa hewed to her central purpose and attempted to drive Frederick out of Silesia. He held off her armies, displaying to full advantage his command of the theory and practice of war, from large-scale strategy to resolute and inventive battlefield leadership. Against him Maria Theresa's generals could pit only their persistence and their caution, which enabled them to lose battles with dignity. For all his successes, Frederick remained on the defensive. Politically he had to retreat. He could not prevent the election of Francis of Lorraine as Emperor Francis I. After an attempted invasion of Prussia through Saxony failed, Maria Theresa, war-weary and worried by the continuing victories of Saxe, made peace with Frederick at Dresden on Christmas Day, 1745. She confirmed Prussian ownership of Silesia and Frederick recognized Francis as Holy Roman emperor. The Austrian war with France went on in the Low Countries, with less and less advantage to the Hapsburg defenders. Finally, in 1748, France made peace at Aix-la-Chapelle upon the basis of the situation as it had been before the war.

Interbellum: 1745-1756. The peace was not a stalemate which ended the struggle but a truce in preparation for its resumption. The Prussian and Austrian monarchs worked feverishly to strengthen their states for a new trial of strength. Yet the shape of future war—the pattern of allies and enemies—remained uncertain. Frederick loathed the French, who had proved domineering allies; to be the ally of France, he winced, was to be her slave. Austria felt much the same about its ally Britain, which had fought France for the sake of its own colonies and Prussia for the sake of Hanover, but which had left Austria to wage its own war with Prussia as best it could without direct help. Russia loomed to the east as a giant of unknown but redoubtable strength; its empress, Elizabeth, hated Frederick II and became the ally of Austria in 1746.

The decade that followed belonged to the diplomats, who shuttled back and forth across Europe, seeking to make friends without adding foes. Maria Theresa's inflexible purpose was to build up an alliance which could crush Prussia and liberate Silesia; Frederick's frantic objective was to thwart Maria Theresa. The initiative fell to Austria, and was used with bold imagination by Count Wenzel von Kaunitz, who represented the empress at Paris as ambassador from 1750 to 1753, when he became the director of Hapsburg foreign policy as chancellor. In order to isolate Frederick, he proposed to drop the ancient enmity of Hapsburg and Bourbon for friendship and alliance. France was reluctant to take the step, although it had been considered both by Louis XIV after the Peace of Utrecht and by Cardinal Fleury. Kaunitz patiently waited for events to change Louis XV's mind. Frederick turned the trick for him when, by the Westminster Convention of 1756, he agreed to undertake mutual defensive aid with Britain-Hanover. The French king, who had sent an envoy to Berlin to renew his alliance with

Prussia, shuddered at the thought of isolation and hurriedly took up Kaunitz's proposal. The treaty of Versailles later that year completed the "Diplomatic Revolution" of 1756. Even at this late moment, Kaunitz had not yet won his hand, for France agreed only to mutual defense, not to an aggressive war against Prussia. Only if Frederick attacked would France enter the struggle. Even so, Kaunitz had built his trap.

The Seven Years' War. Frederick, correctly apprehensive that while he waited an immense triple alliance of Austria, France, and Russia was preparing to leap upon him as soon as the spring of 1757 brought good campaigning weather, decided to act first, on the principle that it was "better to surprise than be surprised." On August 29, 1756, he opened a sudden attack upon Saxony, the planned jumping-off ground of the allies.

The trap was sprung. France and Russia both came to the aid of Austria and Saxony, while most of the imperial princes either joined in the war against Prussia, or remained neutral. Only England-Hanover, Hesse-Kassel, Brunswick, and Gotha took the Prussian side. Frederick's attempt to pose as the defender of European Protestantism, though it won some credence in England, was generally laughed at, for, as one writer put it, the Prussian king, "had cried out *religion*, as folks do *fire* when they want assistance."

For three years Frederick's military genius concealed the extent of his difficulties. He began the war with a force of 150,000 troops and a sizable war fund of 11,000,000 talers, but once the fighting became lengthy, he was forced back upon emergency measures—some reminiscent of Wallenstein, like contributions exacted from occupied regions; and others economically harmful, like inflation of the coinage—as well as upon English subsidies. From 1758 until 1761, while Pitt was prime minister in Britain, Frederick received about four million talers yearly, while occupied Saxony paid between five and ten million. Frederick did not plan upon a long war, however. His strategy was to defeat his enemies singly, first the Austrians and then the Russians and the French. Shattered and discouraged, they would presumably capitulate in turn.

The Ordeal of Prussia. The resistance of the Saxons before they were overwhelmed deranged his plans. The battles in Bohemia and Germany which followed, though generally ending in Prussian victory, were costly in lives and drained his resources. In 1757 he suffered two major defeats, one, in person, by the Austrian General Daun at Kolin, which compelled him to evacuate Bohemia, and the other the acceptance of an armistice at Klosterzeven by the duke of Cumberland, the commander of the British forces in western Germany, which deprived him of English support at the very time when his enemies seemed about to overwhelm him. The Russians penetrated into East Prussia; the Swedes, who had joined the hostile alliance, into Pomerania; and an Austrian force reached Berlin. But Frederick redeemed

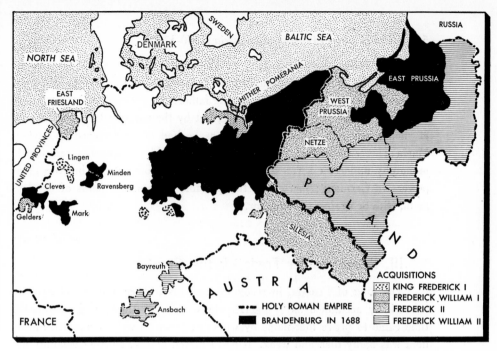

Prussia in the Eighteenth Century

the situation by two victories, the first at Rossbach on November 5, which persuaded Pitt to repudiate the Klosterzeven armistice, and the second at Leuthen a month later, by which he saved Silesia from reconquest.

These were victories which won him the admiration of an astounded Germany and Europe, but they did not bring his enemies to their knees. He failed in an invasion of Moravia during 1758, and then himself faced imminent disaster in 1759. The worst was his defeat by a combined Austrian-Russian army at Kunersdorf in August. During 1760, although he could muster only 100,000 troops against his opponents' 223,000, Frederick's tactical genius enabled him to maintain a strategic stalemate. The next year nothing seemed to avail. His supporter, Pitt, fell from office in Britain, and the allies bit by bit pressed in on his territory. "If fortune continues to treat me so unmercifully," Frederick wrote as the year ended, "I shall undoubtedly succumb. Only she can deliver me from my present situation."

Succor came from "Her Majesty Accident," as Frederick called fortune. On January 5, 1762, Elizabeth of Russia, a foe more implacable even than Maria Theresa, died; her successor was her nephew Peter III, an ardent admirer of Frederick's. Peter signed peace on May 5 and even entered into alliance with Frederick; but in July the new tsar was overthrown by his wife Catherine and assassinated. Catherine withdrew into neutrality; but without Russian assistance, the Austrians could not continue the war. On February 15, 1763, they made peace with the hated Prussian at Hubertusburg. Frederick retained Silesia, returned Saxony to its elector, and promised his vote for the election of archduke Joseph, Maria Theresa's heir, as king of the Romans, successor as emperor to his still reigning father.

Frederick II had won his gamble, but by the narrowest of margins and at such a price in lives and treasure as he had never dreamed of paying. Maria Theresa had lost Silesia, but she had held together her ramshackle monarchy under the severest strain. There were now not one but two great powers in Germany; there were two possible leaders, two paths of development, with or against the emperor.

III. Prussia under Frederick the Great

The king of Prussia, in recognition of his feats as warlord of Prussia, was widely acclaimed as "Frederick the Great." With the end of war, the time came to prove that name by works of peace as well. Frederick's kingdom was badly torn and weak. It had suffered about 180,000 casualties and the population had fallen half a million. The misery and the poverty of the people recalled the dread Thirty Years' War.

The Misanthropic Reformer. Frederick set to work at once to repair the damage of war by the varied devices of government. He became the foremost of the "enlightened despots"—the absolute monarchs of later eighteenth-century Europe who decked out their rule in the fashionable garb of the Enlightenment (see ch. 27, pp. 607-609). Frederick accepted without question the social-contract doctrine and dismissed the divine-right theories of the preceding century. The ruler of the state, he declared, is "obliged to act with honesty, wisdom, and complete unselfishness, as if he might be called upon at any moment to render account for his administration to its citizens." He had, however, no intentions of being taken literally in such magnanimous words. He governed autocratically, permitted his subjects to speak or print no word of criticism of his rule, and never considered granting to them that kind of control over the monarch which Locke made the ultimate safeguard against tyranny.

For the benevolent core of Enlightenment political theory—the welfare of the subjects—was only an affair of the intellect to Frederick II. He had been soured in spirit by the exertions and perils of the Seven Years' War; in 1762 he had described himself as "gray, furrowed with grief, bowed with bodily ills—only fit, in short, to be thrown to the dogs." Nor did the coming of peace soften his soul. He had learned to despise the people he ruled, because even in wartime they retained their own hopes and purposes. He continued to serve them, out of a sense of duty and vanity mixed, but with cynical antipathy.

The Army after Victory. The primacy of his concern for power over all other considerations was most clearly indicated by Frederick's continued emphasis upon the army, the instrument of his victory. It became, in the blunt phrase of a French visitor, the national industry of Prussia, so that the Prussian state existed to serve the interests of its army rather than the other way about. Under the rule of Frederick II, militarism—the subordination of civil to military interests—became rooted in the Prussian pattern of government, and increasingly in the habits of the population.

The king kept the army in a constant state of preparedness for war. The first requirement was numbers. By 1786, when his reign ended, there were 181,000 troops in the army, although Prussia was at peace. This was for the period an immense force even for a great state, and Prussia was no more than the bottommost of the great powers in resources.

To train new officers in the command of troops and in the tactics and strategy of warfare, he established cadet schools. These were restricted to the sons of the nobility, for he thought that they alone brought the proper traditions of honor and valor to the military service. He rigorously excluded the burgher youth who had become officers during the repeated wars, when casualties had thinned the commanding ranks to a dangerous degree. "I prefer to have no commoner scum in the army," he declared. Noble rank by itself did not suffice to make good officers, and cadet training was only the beginning. Frederick introduced frequent maneuvers, to equip the commanders with the skills of their trade and at the same time to drill the troops, who were increasingly recruited by conscription within the regimental "cantons," to absolute obedience. For the king the common soldiers were hardly better than brutes with the power of speech; he did not trust their fidelity nor their steadfastness in battle, but enforced a discipline so severe that the soldiers feared their sergeants more than the enemy.

Nor did Frederick forget that an army in wartime lived on money in great quantities. He kept at hand a "little treasure" of 4,300,000 talers, instantly available, as well as a "great treasure" which rose to more than 55,000,000 talers by the end of the reign. This war treasure was the largest cash reserve held by any prince in Europe.

Good Government. Frederick's method of government served this ideal of strength. He did not attempt to reform the institutions of state but continued to use those which he had inherited from Frederick William I. His single modification was to tighten control over the General Directory by making the responsibility of its members individual and personal, rather than resting upon the entire board. Autocracy, efficiency, and economy remained the bywords of his rule, as they had been his father's.

He achieved these aims by taking upon himself the burden of personal direction of the entire machinery of state. Although he insisted upon a considerable level of training and competence in his officials, he denied them all important rights of initiative and decision. High or low, they were errand boys at the king's disposal. Over subjects, however, their authority was complete. A discipline reminiscent of the barracks and the drill ground was clamped upon the civilian population.

The striking distinction between Frederick's reign and his father's in respect to government lay in their attitude toward justice. Frederick II sincerely looked upon himself as "the poor man's lawyer," and endeavored to assure equality and fairness of treatment of all by the courts of the kingdom, insofar as the established social and economic order were not thereby endangered. He laid down the principle that the operation of the courts would be free of royal interference. "In the courts, the laws must speak and the ruler must be silent," he directed the jurist Samuel von Cocceji, whom he named chancellor and entrusted with the reform of the judiciary and the codification of the laws of the various Prussian provinces which had begun under Frederick William I. Only when he suspected that judges were biased against commoners did he infringe this rule.

Cocceji drew up a preliminary general law code in the Codex Fridericianus of 1747, which placed all Prussian subjects under a single court system. In practice, however, the peasants of east and central Prussia were restricted to the manorial courts dominated by the Junkers (squires); the rule that the judges of these courts had to pass examinations in the law was a safeguard of limited efficacy for the peasantry. Cocceji also persuaded Frederick to introduce other legal reforms, the most important being the abolition of torture in legal proceedings. Such measures were typical of Frederick's "enlightened despotism," which was an absolutism tempered only by the king's self-denying rule.

An Overflowing Treasury. The welfare of the people and the strength of the state required, in addition to good government, recuperation from the damage of war. Frederick II undertook this task from a vantage point of strength, for while the Prussian "people" (the subjects of the state) had been stripped of their resources during the fighting, the Prussian state had managed to emerge without debt.

To avoid borrowing remained the first principle of Frederick's policy during the twenty-three years that remained of his reign. Excessive indebtedness, he knew, could bring down even the most powerful of states, while an overflowing treasury enabled even small states to play a part in affairs far beyond their inherent capabilities. Therefore the maintenance of the crown's revenues came before all other considerations. He brought in French fiscal experts to organize and run the collection of indirect taxes; this new fiscal system even retained the French name of *Régie* and became thoroughly hated by the population for its efficiency and its ruthlessness. But the king was not disturbed, for the indirect taxes soon brought in more revenue than direct taxation upon individuals.

Economic and Social Policy. Frederick also worked with vigor to help the people repair the destruction of the war. His success was evident within a decade after 1763. Virtually every ruined village was rebuilt, and some 900 new ones were created. Almost 300,000 colonists were brought into Prussia; many of the foreign soldiers in Prussian service were persuaded to remain as settlers. Much of the territory for the expanded agriculture consisted of marshlands drained and diked with the aid of grants from the crown. In order to favor agriculture still more, the king attempted to discourage serfdom. In 1763 he even ordered that "all serfdom be totally abolished, absolutely and without discussion, from this hour forward." But Frederick, looking upon the nobility as the backbone of his army and state, was easily persuaded by their argument that the peasants, because they held and inherited property, were not serfs. The Junkers therefore were able to continue to exact forced labor service and manorial rents from their peasants.

Other measures were taken to encourage trade and industry. Perhaps the most essential was the replacement of the debased coinage issued during the war with sound money. Soon after its foundation the Bank of Berlin began to make credit more easily available within the country. New canals were built, linking the Oder to the Havel and Elbe rivers and the Netze to the Vistula (which after the first partition of Poland flowed through Prussian territory). Protective tariffs encouraged the development of industry, which the king admitted was "still in the cradle." Annual grants of about 2,000,000 talers were poured into the infant manufactures until they were well established. At the end of the reign, the factories of Prussia were producing goods worth 30,000,000 talers a year, and the balance of trade in favor of Prussia was between 3,000,000 and 4,000,000 talers.

But in all that he did, Frederick II endeavored to preserve and strengthen the existing social order. He kept the division of society into clearly separated classes, each with its particular task in service to the state. The nobility were his favorites, although he insisted on their absolute obedience and tried to restrain the worst excesses of their dominion over their peasantry. The burghers, though in his opinion unfitted for the honorable duties of war, were useful in providing the economic sinews of war. The peasants, because they fed the nation and fought as common soldiers, had to be protected, too, but in their subordinate situation, without any right to obtain greater freedom as a class or to climb individually up the ladder of social rank.

Culture and Religion. As crown prince, Frederick II had suffered the scorn and ill usage of his father for his love of music and literature. On the throne, he gladly played the part of a patron of arts and letters. The Academy of Sciences in Berlin, abandoned by the late king, was resuscitated in 1743. Frederick did not see fit to place a Prussian, or indeed any German, at its head, but selected the French mathematician and astronomer Mauper-tuis. The academy, in accordance with the king's contempt for his native German language, conducted its affairs entirely in French and many of its members were foreigners, particularly French and Swiss. The royal patronage slackened after 1763, when Frederick became more and more satisfied to play his beloved flute in solitude, and save his money.

Frederick also broadened the educational facilities available to the youth of Prussia. He declared elementary education to be obligatory in 1763, but did not risk large funds on establishing new schools or paying teachers more than a pittance. His "enlightened" ideas appeared particularly in the curriculum laid down for a "modern school" (*Realschule*, school of things), which emphasized modern languages, economics, and natural science instead of the classical humanism to which the traditional gymnasium confined itself.

The king's "Enlightenment" was also evident in his religious policy. His personal views were wholly deist, but like his mentor and friend Voltaire he considered the traditional revealed religion useful in maintaining social discipline. As between Rome and Geneva, he was neutral, and he kept the Lutheran Pietists quiet. He permitted the Catholics to build their own church, St. Hedwig's, in Berlin in 1747. When the Jesuit order was dissolved in 1773, he invited Jesuits expelled from Catholic countries to settle and work in Silesia. Only the Jews remained outside the pale of his toleration, despite the appeal of the dramatist Lessing for humane treatment.

The Barracks State. For all the veneer of culture and "Enlightenment," the kingdom of Prussia was and remained a despotism, ruled with a hard hand, where free spirits felt constrained and strange. The press was free, but not to comment upon political matters. Goethe, who had been enthusiastically *"Fritzisch"* as a youth, visited Berlin in 1778. He observed morosely, "saying not a word in the Prussian states which they could print," as he wrote afterwards, and returned to the mild rule of Weimar. Lessing was more outspoken: "Let anyone speak up in Berlin who is for the rights of subjects and against exploitation and despotism, as some do now even in France and Denmark, and he will soon discover what is to this very day the most slavish country in Europe." The liberty-loving Italian playwright Count Alfieri was even more to the point. After a visit in 1769, he called Frederick's kingdom "the great barracks Prussia." All of the king's devotion to the arts, all his "enlightened" political doctrine, ceased to blind perceptive and thoughtful men to the inner quality of Prussia under Frederick the Great. And the king himself made the tragic complaint, "I am tired of ruling over slaves!"

New Hands: Frederick William II. In 1786, Frederick II died. He had no children, and the kingdom passed to his nephew Frederick William II.

VOLTAIRE AND FREDERICK THE GREAT.
Line engraving by Pierre-Louis Baquoy after a drawing by Nicolas Monsiaux, about 1795.

Voltaire is shown in the royal Prussian palace at Potsdam, receiving King Frederick II. The caption repeats the legend of the great friendship: Voltaire "is heaped high with honors and benefactions, his only burden being to spend some hours with the King, correcting his works and instructing him in the secrets of the art of writing." (Achenbach Foundation)

Prussia had grown to a territory of 75,000 square miles with a population of 5,500,000. The crown took in a revenue of about 20,000,000 talers annually, of which more than half was spent on the army. There was no debt and the treasury held between 60,000,000 and 70,000,000 talers. The army numbered 200,000 men.

The new monarch, proud of such power, was nonetheless hostile to the principles of his predecessors and lacked the force of character and mind to set Prussia clearly on a new path. In any case, his ideal was the re-establishment of the "good old times." He abolished the *Régie*, with its hated monopolies, and re-organized the General Directory upon the basis of shared ("collegial") responsibility. An edict on religion in 1788 re-establishing the Protestant church in its "original purity" was a declaration of battle against the Enlightenment. The king himself was under the influence of the Rosicrucians, a mystical sect of Protestant enthusiasts.

Otherwise, the Frederician state remained as it was, a rigid, heavy machine of government. But, as Frederick II had anticipated, it began to creak and slow down as the hand in control weakened. Prussia, as the three outstanding Hohenzollerns—the "Great Elector" Frederick William; Fred-

507

erick William I; and Frederick II—had made it, was strong beyond its
means because it had strong monarchs. It entered the new time of trial that
began in the 1790's under a king who lacked all his forebears' qualities of
greatness.

IV. Austria: a Time of Reform

The wars for Silesia tested the powers of endurance of the ramshackle
Hapsburg state. The half century that followed the invasion of Silesia saw
the attempt of its rulers to make it a sound and stable political organism.
This was the endeavor of two rulers, a mother and son of strikingly disparate
personalities seeking fundamentally similar objectives.

Maria Theresa. Maria Theresa reigned as hereditary archduchess of
Austria and queen of Hungary and Bohemia until her death in 1780. She
did not share her powers of government with her beloved but unintelligent
husband, Francis of Lorraine and Tuscany, even after his election as emperor
in 1745.

Maria Theresa appeared a simple woman by comparison with such vivid
and complex contemporaries as Frederick of Prussia and Catherine of Russia.
Yet beneath her placid appearance there were cross-currents of personality
and purpose which escaped most observers. She was a devout Roman Catholic, who unhesitatingly put her own judgment as to the welfare of the church
ahead of the pope's. She had a keen sense of right and believed that the
same morality held in public and private life; yet she practiced "reason of
state" so well that, except for the loss of Silesia, she did not fall behind in
the contest for territory and advantage. She governed her lands with a steady
eye to the preservation of her absolute powers, yet with so light a hand that
men thought of her as the kind "mother of the country."

Tightening the Ties of State. Her failure twice to recapture Silesia from
the once-scorned Prussians impressed Maria Theresa with a hard truth. Only
by making the multiple lands beneath her scepter function more and more
like a single state could she bring the scattered resources of the Hapsburg
lands into effective use for sustaining Austria's stature as a great
power. In 1748, therefore, she named Count Frederick William von Haugwitz, a Silesian nobleman, as chancellor with the mission of "bringing the
government out of confusion into order." A conservative official called this
less flatteringly an attempt to "turn topsy-turvy a form of government which
has come into being through many centuries, from the beginning of the
Most Serene Archducal House." Maria Theresa, who did not care to make
changes for their own sake, knew that she could not afford such immobile
traditionalism and backed Haugwitz with the full weight of her authority.

Haugwitz took as his model the upstart monarchy of Brandenburg-Prussia. The very means by which Prussia had risen from debility to vigor in a century could also redeem Austria. Haugwitz, like his royal and imperial mistress, worked quietly and effectively. He permitted the estates (diets) of the Austrian provinces and Bohemia to continue in existence, leaving them their judicial rights, but stripping from them their considerable powers to grant and levy taxes, to raise and pay troops, and to nominate officials. These functions were given in 1749 to a central board in Vienna, the *Directorium in publicis et cameralibus* (Directory for public and fiscal affairs), which despite its Latin name conducted its business in German. Such a seizure of powers from the diets was not attempted in recently pacified Hungary, or in the outlying Hapsburg lands, Lombardy and the Austrian Netherlands.

Reform at Slow Speed. Haugwitz began as well the reform of the fiscal structure of the monarchy, and with it measures to assist the economic development of the country.

The subjects of the queen paid taxes according to very unequal rates, differing according to their economic and social status, their historical relationship to the house of Hapsburg, and the ease with which the collectors could reach into their purses. Direct taxes, as was usual in other countries, fell lightly on the wealth of merchants and manufacturers but heavily on the peasantry. The Austro-Bohemian nobility, virtually exempt at the beginning of the reign, were placed on tax rolls by Haugwitz, but they managed to shift the principal burden to the peasantry on their estates. Maria Theresa recognized that the fiscal needs of the state could not be safely met by spreading the net of taxation more widely and drawing it more tightly, lest untoward resistance be encouraged. Instead, once the period of war was over, she avoided great expenditures, improved the efficiency of government, and was able to avoid bankruptcy and even to bring the revenues and expenditures of state into balance during the 1770's.

The economic policy followed by Maria Theresa reflected her moderate approach. A general tariff was set around the Austrian and Bohemian lands but its rates were kept low on the luxury goods imported by the nobility. A more vital problem, and one less easily settled, was that of serfdom in the German, Bohemian, and Hungarian regions of the Hapsburg state. Noble estate owners held their peasantry in a tight grip, requiring from them both the payment of dues and the performance of labor service and controlling them by the manorial courts. Crown officials deplored this system, recognizing that it held back the economic growth of Austria and also that it limited the amount of taxes that could be taken from the peasants. Maria Theresa set an example by relieving the peasants on the crown domains from many of their servile obligations, notably the labor service. The landowners, especially in Bohemia, did not indulge in the flattery of imitating her, and she did not dare to shake their fidelity by imposing reform upon them.

Joseph II. Maria Theresa's policy of circumspect reform came to an end with her death in 1780. It gave way, as she foresaw and feared, to her son Joseph II's attempt to reform his lands so impetuously and systematically that the reform amounted to a revolution from above. During the last fifteen years of Maria Theresa's reign, after the death of Emperor Francis, she had brought Joseph into the government of Austria as co-regent, although he reigned in Germany as emperor. There had been constant tension between them, for although she did not make light of his opinions she frequently rejected them and kept the ultimate power of decision for herself.

Joseph was the very opposite of his mother in personality. He wore his heart on his sleeve, but his feeling for his fellow-man was abstract and impersonal. Unlike Frederick of Prussia, on whom he modeled himself, he did not despise mankind; he simply did not understand people as living individual human beings. Joseph's general goals were those his mother had sought, but he pursued them brutally and directly. He was at one and the same time an "enlightened despot" who swallowed whole the teachings of eighteenth-century philosophy, unsalted by the cynical worldliness of his Prussian and Russian counterparts, a pious Catholic, an imperious absolutist, and a practitioner of the flintiest "reason of state." He was driven to action not only by the requirements of theory but also by an insatiable lust for achievement and fame. With his mother's guiding and restraining hand removed, Joseph set to work at once to make over the Hapsburg monarchy according to his vision of the strong state and the good society.

The "Peasant Emperor." The revolutionary emperor did not fear to tread upon the dangerous ground of economic change. The boldest measure came first. In 1781-1782 he proclaimed the emancipation of the peasantry from serfdom. The personal servitude of the peasants to the estate owner was abolished, as distinct from their economic obligations. Though the manorial courts were permitted to continue, the state undertook to provide defense for the peasants who came before them. The peasant also received a right of hereditary possession, subject to payment of a rent. Compulsory labor service was reduced to a fixed amount and provisions made for it to be paid off. The other dues, payable in kind, were converted in 1783 to money payments at an established rate.

These measures were in themselves only a limited reform but were obviously intended to improve the conditions of the subject class in the countryside, the peasantry, at the expense of their overlords. They therefore constituted the beginnings of a social revolution to be conducted by the authority of the monarchical state. The peasantry responded to this news of hope by undertaking a revolution from below. Believing that the emperor had liberated them from all obligations to their lords, they refused to pay dues or perform labor services. The effort of the estate owners and local officials to enforce these obligations was met by a series of peasant rebellions, especially in Bohemia and Hungary, where conditions had been worst.

Joseph II used armed force to put down these risings, for he had no intention of countenancing the action of subjects in taking the law into their own hands. But he refused to drop the whole program of agrarian reform, as the nobles and most officials requested. He insisted that the countryside increase its tax payments to the state; the increase was possible only if the manorial obligations of the peasants were reduced and the nobles themselves began to pay taxes according to the measure of their wealth, as the nobles did in Britain and Holland. He therefore ordered the beginning of a land register in 1786. In 1789 he followed with an edict placing equal tax obligations on peasant and noble land. The nobles therefore pinned the scornful name of "peasant emperor" upon him. It was deserved, for the peasants, thankful for a ruler who tried to help them, gave him their love.

State over Church. Personal rule, unhampered by his mother's caution, enabled Joseph II to undertake another enterprise to which she would have given even less approval. This was to reorganize the religious life of the Hapsburg dominions according to the notions of the Enlightenment. Insofar as he endeavored to make the Catholic church subservient to the institutions and interests of the Austrian state, he was merely continuing her own policy. In particular she had favored the establishment of educational institutions under state rather than church sponsorship. Neither had she been loath to reduce papal control over Catholicism in Austria, or to reform ecclesiastical practices and reduce the number of holy days by her own authority. But she would not concede religious toleration, holding it to be the prelude to "ruin and total revolution."

After his accession, Joseph II went his own way. A toleration edict issued in 1781 reduced Roman Catholicism to the status of a "dominant religion," not the sole legal religion; Protestant sects, however, were not allowed to have public churches or to worship except in private homes. Jews were not included in the edict, but their situation was somewhat eased. The emperor also struck at the monastic orders, which had been particularly numerous in the Austrian lands, as idle and useless "fakirs." His control over the Catholic church was stiffened by ordinances forbidding the clergy to send or receive communications from Rome except by way of the government in Vienna, and compelling bishops and other high ecclesiastics to swear to obey the prince in all things, without reservation or exception, before they accepted papal confirmation.

Reform and Rebellion. All of Joseph II's measures of "enlightenment" ultimately rested upon the adequacy of his "despotism" to carry them into practice. He was not satisfied to place a few institutions of central government over the disparate realms under his scepter, for their persistent particularism continued to thwart his reforms. He therefore discarded all the vestiges of local autonomy which Maria Theresa had permitted to remain, and imposed a coherent system of direct central government over all the Hapsburg states. The various lands were divided into "governments" (*Gubernien*), relatively equal in population, with deliberate disregard for the boundaries of historical provinces. Administration was taken out of local hands completely and bureaucrats appointed by the central authorities were brought in. In 1787 Joseph ordered that officials must possess university degrees and be selected on the basis of their abilities; he thus opened careers in government service to the lesser nobility and the bourgeosie, although the higher posts continued to be held principally by great aristocrats. As a further measure of political unification, Joseph ordered the introduction of German as the language of government and education in all his realms except Lombardy and the Austrian Netherlands. The Hungarian university of Bratislava even established a course in *Amtsstil*, the official German style, since the Hungarians had used Latin for government affairs.

The German and Bohemian territories under the Hapsburg rule, where the power of the estates had been broken early in the seventeenth century, accepted Joseph's changes quietly; such resistance as occurred was passive and hardly to be told from the usual sloth of officialdom. In Hungary and the Austrian Netherlands, on the other hand, the emperor's measures violated still lively feeling of national separateness and historical methods of government. In Hungary the diet refused to send supplies and recruits to the Vienna government, and contacts were secretly made with Prussia should the conflict worsen. In the Low Countries, Joseph II's edict of June 18, 1789, abolishing the historic charter of Brabant liberties, the *Joyeuse Entrée*, sparked an armed uprising which expelled the Austrian authorities. Meanwhile the beginning of revolution in France sharpened the concern of all monarchical governments for the preservation of their authority. Early in 1790 the emperor withdrew some of his reforms, but he died in February before Hapsburg control could be re-established in the rebellious provinces. The dying monarch wrote his own epitaph: "Here lies a prince whose intentions were pure but who had the misfortune to see all his endeavors fail." It was an epitaph as well upon the "enlightened despotism" of which he was indeed the purest representative, for it sought the good of the people not only without consulting the people but also by refusing their participation and even throttling the expression of their own desires. A revolution from above had failed; it fell to Joseph's successor, his brother Leopold II, to guide Austrian destinies at a time when in France revolution surged up from below.

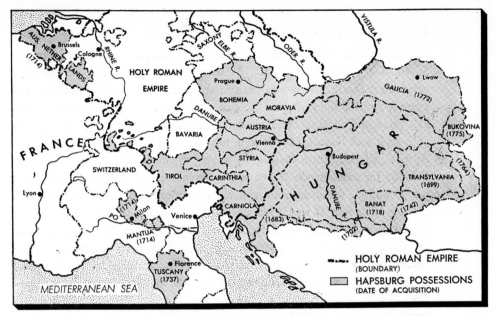

Austria as a Great Power (1789)

V. The Unsteady Peace

The peace which returned to Germany in 1763 resembled the war which it followed. Two great powers faced each other in Germany, distrustful of each other, neither able to outdo the other by its own forces, while the weight of decision passed increasingly to foreign states.

Partners in Plunder. Until 1780, the relationships between Prussia and Austria were dominated by the bad blood between Maria Theresa and Frederick II. The Prussian king, content with the conquest of Silesia, sought no new gains from Austria and was willing to let the recent war be bygones. The empress, who had been the loser, would neither forget nor forgive, but she knew that a war of revenge and reconquest would be foolhardy unless she built an overwhelming alliance against an isolated Prussia. France was at best an ally of uncertain value due to her domestic troubles; Russia under Catherine II might be won, but only at the fearful price of permitting Russian territorial expansion in Poland and the Balkans. The possibility that Maria Theresa might succeed in turning Catherine against him was the bane of Frederick's plans. To keep the empress of Russia friendly to him became his first concern as well.

The victory of Russia over Turkey in the war of 1768 led to friendlier relations between Prussia and Austria, as they did not want Catherine to act independently in Poland. Joseph II paid two personal visits to Frederick II in 1769 and 1770; they agreed that Turkey should be maintained against further Russian attack. Frederick then slily turned to Catherine and won her assent to a partition of Poland; Austrian resistance would be overcome by persuading Maria Theresa to become the third partner in spoliation. The empress resisted the invitation "to risk our honor and reputation for a miserable piece of Poland or Moldavia and Wallachia." But the combined pressure of Joseph and Kaunitz, her foreign minister, was too much. For one thing, Austria had just shown the way by seizing the disputed region of Zips from Poland; for another, she feared to see the increase of Prussian and Russian power without commensurate Austrian expansion, and if she were to suffer the loss of honor, it would not be for small gains. She therefore gave her approval; as Frederick said later, she wept but she took. On August 5, 1772, the three powers signed a treaty with Poland by which Austria received Galicia and Prussia Ermeland and West Prussia. (See ch. 24, pp. 555-556.)

The "Potato War." Though, unlike his mother, Joseph II admired Frederick II, it was he who led Austria into renewed war with Prussia. The particular stake at conflict was the succession to the Bavarian electorate, which came open in 1777 with the death of Elector Maximilian III. The deeper issue involved was whether or not Austria would recapture her pre-eminence in Germany, thereby humbling and endangering Prussia.

Joseph was eager to gain Bavaria for the Hapsburg monarchy, for it would extend Austria into the heart of Germany. He persuaded the heir to Maximilian, the Elector Palatine Charles Theodore, to accept an Austrian claim upon Bavaria in exchange for honors and advantages to himself and his bastard children. Frederick II denounced this treaty before the Reichstag, and war followed in the summer of 1778. There was little fighting. Because the soldiers, ill-supplied, spent much of their time seizing crops in the field, the name "Potato War" was given to the conflict. From the beginning there were negotiations between the belligerents, for Maria Theresa considered that her son had blundered again. France urged the conclusion of peace and Catherine II, by a threat to join Prussia, compelled Austria to accept terms at Teschen in 1779; Austria received as her sole acquisition the small Bavarian region known as the "Inn Quarter."

Balkan War. Five years later Joseph, now ruling in his own name, tried again to acquire Bavaria. He persuaded Elector Charles Theodore to agree to an exchange of Bavaria and the Austrian Netherlands. He was thwarted by a Princes' League organized by Frederick in 1785 to prevent such a shift of forces within the Empire. The abandonment of the Bavarian project followed.

Defeated in his German policy, Joseph turned to support of Catherine II in her struggle with the Ottoman sultan. He formed an alliance with her by which Catherine would re-establish a Greek empire, including the Balkans to the Danube river, for her grandson Constantine, while Austria would receive the rest of the western Balkans. A personal visit by Joseph to Catherine at Kherson, in the Crimea, in 1788 stirred Turkish apprehensions, and the sultan declared war upon Russia the same year. Austria was drawn in, and in 1789 retook Belgrade, which had been lost for half a century. But before any new attacks could be organized, Joseph was forced to withdraw his forces to cope with the rebellion in the Low Countries.

23

Russia as a Great Power

1676 - 1796

WHEN TSAR ALEXEI died in 1676 old Muscovy, a land largely set apart from Europe, was slowly giving way to a new Russia involved with the affairs, concerns, and influences of the West.

The West exerted its pull upon Russia partly by the vigor of its spiritual and economic life, but even more by military and political power. From the Time of Troubles, the threat that they would come under the rule of their neighbors to the west continued to hang over the Russians. However, there was no agreement in Russia on how to ward off that danger. Some advocated learning from the West the techniques of knowledge and might, somehow fusing spiritual imitation and political independence. Others did not wish to see their land remade on the model of Europe and believed that its safety lay in preserving their ancient institutions intact. The struggle between the alternatives—aloofness from the West or integration with it—became the central theme of Russian history.

I. Russia in 1676

Confusion, uncertainty, and inefficiency were the hallmarks of Russian social and governmental life in 1676.

516

Foreign Influences. Russia was both a giver and a receiver in the interplay of influences. Expansion of Russian territory brought the tsar increased numbers of subjects; a population of perhaps ten million made Russia the third most numerous country in Europe, after France and Germany. The Great Russians continued to be in the majority, but there were now many White Russians in the region facing Poland and many Little Russians in the Ukraine. Siberia held uncounted numbers of native tribesmen within its immensities. The very name "Russia" became something of a misnomer as more and more "native" (non-Russian) peoples came into the Russian state. Yet the Russian conquerors brought to them the civilization of the West.

The Russian form of that civilization was itself changing. The inclusion of the Ukrainians sharpened the struggle within Russian religion and culture. The Russian faith was the Greek Orthodoxy inherited from Byzantium, but shorn of the control and direction of the patriarch of Constantinople. Toward Latin Christendom, whether Roman Catholic or Protestant, the Russian church felt scorn and antipathy, mingled with fear for the power held by these schismatics. The seat of Russian Orthodox learning was Kiev, the ancient capital of the Ukraine which had long been under Polish—and hence Roman Catholic—rule. There Orthodox scholars met Catholic thought directly, and while most rejected it utterly, some adopted one or another of its doctrines; others turned to Lutheran Protestantism for a way of warding them off. In Kiev, too, a few Orthodox churchmen began to learn Latin as well as the Greek of the Byzantine tradition. Such scholars, brought to Moscow by the tsarist authorities in the struggle against the "Old Believers," sharpened interest in the West and furnished the key to the sources of western learning. They also aroused the loathing and hatred of those who saw the purity of their church befouled by the influence of heretics.

The influence of the West was concentrated in the capital, Moscow. There a colony of foreign merchants and artisans provided services to the tsar's court and to wealthy Russians. The foreigners dwelt within their own district, the "German Quarter" (the name "German" was used for many western Europeans). However, the Muscovites usually saw western life in the pattern of the Poles, for they were the nearest people formed in the Latin tradition, while their Slavic language made their works more accessible. Polish modes in furniture and clothing were adopted by venturesome Muscovites like the rich and influential Vassili Golitsyn, who amassed western books and manuscripts in his western-style palace. Natalia Naryshkina, the widow of the late Tsar Alexei, was another center of western influence.

The Peasantry and Nobility. The persistent instability of both society and government showed that the conditions out of which the Troubles of the early seventeenth century had arisen had not been remedied.

Russia remained almost completely an agrarian land. Tillage was done in the age-old fashion, within the framework of the village community (*mir*), with primitive tools, and in generally thin soils. Increase in the total agricultural productivity therefore depended primarily upon bringing new land into cultivation. Such internal colonization had been almost completely halted, however, by the spread of serfdom.

Legally and economically there were many kinds of peasants, some "free" (that is, obligated only to the state), particularly in the forested regions of the north and east, while others were bound to individual masters or to monasteries. In the Cossack communities of the Ukraine, though freer conditions prevailed, the powerful "elders" sought to subjugate their lesser brothers. Everywhere the movement was toward imposing a stringent serfdom upon all peasants. This was a servitude harsher than the serfdom that had been known in medieval Europe in the West, for the will of Russian masters was seldom effectively restrained by either custom or law. Indeed, serfs could be sold, individually or in families, away from their native villages; they were not "slaves," however, for they had to pay taxes, unlike those supposedly "inferior" beings, who did not.

The nobility, too, were in a state of fluid change. The ancient landed aristocracy, the boyars who owned their estates as freehold (*votchina*), had no obligation of service to the state. The new service nobility (*pomieshchiki*), contrariwise, held their lands by grant from the tsar in payment for service in the army or government. In practice, however, the boyars found themselves increasingly reduced to the status of subjects, wealthy and socially pre-eminent to be sure, but nonetheless bound by the tsar's command to serve; while the *pomieshchiki* used all their wiles to have their estates treated as hereditary property, and to lighten the burden of compulsory service. Each group was influenced by the ideas and aspirations of the other. The example of the nobility in the West was also at work; there was envy for the independence of the Polish *szlachta* (gentry) toward the crown, and the Polish word was adopted for a while as a name for "nobility" in Russian.

The Government. The Russian system of government resembled that of the western absolutist monarchies. All legal power rested in the tsar, particularly since the Zemski Sobor (assembly of the land), which had exercised some of the functions of sovereignty during and for a while after the Time of Troubles, was less relied upon. The principal agencies of central government were the *boyar duma* (boyar council) and the *prikazi* (literally, "orders," and hence "offices of state"). The *boyar duma* included both government officials and boyar nobles; it acted as a royal council with legislative and advisory functions, and as a supreme court of appeals. Most of the work of government was done by the *prikazi*; there were some forty to fifty of these, each assigned to a specific function, like the "ambassador's

The Expansion of Russia, 1689-1796

prikaz," which was in charge of Russian diplomacy, or the "Siberian *prikaz*," which administered the huge Asiatic possessions of the tsar. The *prikazi* had no clear differentiation of their respective responsibilities. Government away from the capital was in the hands of *voievods* (governors), but elected "elders" collected taxes and maintained order; in the thinly populated north local officials had broad autonomy.

The army of the tsars comprised a variety of forces. The majority of troops were *pomieshchik* nobles serving as infantry together with peasant volunteers; poorly trained and equipped, their inferiority to the armies of the West had been repeatedly demonstrated on the battlefield. The Cossacks provided a loosely disciplined but rough and ready cavalry. In Moscow, the task of guards troops were entrusted to quasi-hereditary regiments of musketeers (*streltsi*, literally "marksmen"). The military training of the *streltsi* was particularly wanting, although the permanence of their station developed a strong sense of common loyalty among them.

II. Peter the Great

Russia remained in a state of weakness and vacillation for twenty years after Alexei's death in 1676. Then, under his youngest son Peter, it entered a period of stormy change which strained its physical and spiritual resources but made it a power of the first rank in Europe.

Brother Tsars. Alexei was succeeded by his eldest surviving son, the fourteen-year-old Theodore III. The new tsar had been a lifelong invalid but nonetheless had received what was for a Muscovite an excellent European education. Theodore knew Polish well and even a little Latin. Vassili Golitsyn, who could orate fluently in the Roman tongue, found in the tsar a ready ear for his plans of reform according to the western pattern. A Slavonic-Greco-Latin Academy, whose purpose was indicated in its title, was founded; improvements in the army were undertaken. The most drastic measure of change was the abolition in 1682 of the *mestnichestvo* (system of places), the elaborate organization of inherited rank which provided for appointment to positions of command in army and state according to the level reached by one's ancestors rather than one's own service or talent. The only opportunity for display of energy in foreign affairs came in the war with the Turks, which had been under way intermittently in the Ukraine since 1672. The conflict ended in 1679 with the Turks retaining their hold on the Dnieper river.

Theodore's death in 1682 brought on a struggle over the succession. The Naryshkins put Natalia's son, nine-year-old Peter, on the throne; the *streltsi*, at the instigation of the rival clique of the Miloslavskis, replied by seizing the Kremlin palace and murdering all the Naryshkins and their partisans whom they could find. Sophia, Peter's elder half-sister by Alexei's first wife, led the insurrection. At her call, the *boyar duma* and the patriarch of Moscow proclaimed as co-tsar with Peter I his fifteen-year-old brother Ivan V; but Sophia took command of the government as regent. She found her major problem to be control of the *streltsi*. Their success as tsar makers encouraged them to flout orders and to demand concessions to their private interests. When they mutinied again, they were put down by regular troops.

Under Sophia's regency, Russia continued to hover between accepting and resisting the trend to westernizing. In religion she was a vigorous supporter of Orthodoxy against the Latin heresies. When she fell in love with Golitsyn, however, she permitted him to spin out his plans for remodeling Russia on the pattern of the West. He did nothing about them in practice, for Sophia compelled him to take command of an army attacking the Turks, against whom a "Holy Alliance" had been formed with Poland. Golitsyn's failure to capture the peninsula of the Crimea, on the Black Sea, led to Sophia's downfall in 1689.

The Titan of Russia. During the years of Sophia's regency, young Tsar Peter had been living in the village of Preobrazhenskoe not far from Moscow, but nonetheless away from the seat of political power in the Kremlin. He had grown up almost helter-skelter, with a brief formal education; but he had turned his play into preparation for his life's work. He organized his companions into regiments of childish troops who fought sieges and battles, and introduced himself to the art of navigation with an abandoned English sailboat that he found on a nearby lake. As he began to grow into manhood, he took to frequenting the German Quarter of Moscow, where he was enthralled by the glimpse of western technical mastery in the arts of war and industry which he discovered among the German, Dutch, and other residents.

While Peter was young Sophia had neglected him, but in 1689, when Golitsyn met defeat in the Crimea, Peter was seventeen and a danger to her regency. Before she could bring her half-brother into her power, a rumor of impending attack led Peter to escape from Preobrazhenskoe. Several regular army regiments responded to his call for aid and he overthrew the regent. Sophia was confined to a nunnery; Ivan, the co-tsar, passive throughout the dispute, continued to reign with Peter until his death in 1696. The work of government was entrusted by Peter to his mother Natalia until 1694, when she died; it was only then that he took on with confident readiness personal command of Russia.

By this time the personality of the tsar had taken firm shape. He was possessed of fantastic energy, which he expended not only in orgies but also in relentless activity as ruler of Russia. With the sword and the whip he enforced equal exertions upon his companions and upon the entire Russian nation. He shared the coarseness and earthiness of the simple Russian; the snobbery of the boyar was no part of him. Neither was sympathy for the modest purposes of ordinary men, who desired safety and comfort. The tsar aspired to glory and fame, which he enshrined in the phrase "service to the state."

However, Peter I was more than a brawler and a bully at the head of the state; he was also a man with a vision of strength and vigor for Russia based on the methods of the West. He was an eager learner, but chose his subjects. He was ready to accept the maritime skills of the Dutch and the English, the military and political accomplishments of the Swedes, and the resourcefulness of the French in inventing and collecting taxes, but did less to borrow from the art, literature, science and philosophy of these nations.

Journey into Europe. Peter initiated his personal government by a campaign in 1695 to capture the ice-free port of Azov, on the Don river, from the Turks. To the tsar the attack on the Turks was only a continuation of the war games of his youth. "We've had fun at Koshukhovo and now we're on our way to play some more at Azov," he wrote one friend. The Turks refused to play their assigned parts and fought off the attackers, who were poorly trained and ineptly led. The tsar learned his lesson. He returned to Azov the next year with a naval force—the first in modern Russian history—and captured the city.

On his return to Moscow Peter suppressed a conspiracy by the *streltsi* guards to restore Sophia to her power, and then in 1697 went abroad to see the West with his own eyes. His first extended stay was in Holland, where he studied shipbuilding in the yards at Zaandam, doing the work of a carpenter for perhaps a week, and visited various Dutch military and commercial establishments. He then went to England where he was received by William III and by Parliament (whose obvious power and orderly debates puzzled him), and visited the shipyards at Deptford. He resided in the admiral's house at Deptford, but reduced it from a mansion to a shambles. This was symbolic of the meeting between the tsar and Europe: he was blind to the culture of the West, not to its tools of war.

"A Window Opened upon Europe." In 1698 the tsar's journey was cut short. While at Vienna en route to Venice he received news that the *streltsi* had risen again and proclaimed his son Alexei as tsar in his place. Although the new-style regiments organized and led by his Scottish friend and military mentor from the German Quarter, Patrick Gordon, defeated the *streltsi*, Peter rushed back to Moscow and vented his wrath and fears upon the defeated guardsmen. They were tortured in an effort to discover if his sister Sophia was implicated, and then hundreds were beheaded upon the Red Square in front of the Kremlin.

Peter then turned back to the task he had set himself during his stay in Europe. This was to resume Ivan the Terrible's conquests upon the Baltic, where Sweden barred Russian access to the sea. He had won the alliance of Poland and Denmark while in Europe and freed himself in the south by making peace with the Turks in 1700. On November 30, 1700, the tsar's dream of glory collapsed at Narva when the young Swedish king, Charles XII, commanding 8,400 Swedes, defeated a Russian army of 40,000. Peter fled the battlefield but soon recovered his calm and set about rebuilding his forces. While Charles, contemptuous of the humiliated braggart tsar, busied himself elsewhere, Peter won a series of small battles that finally brought much of eastern Finland and Estonia under his control.

In 1703 Peter began the construction of a new city in the marshes at the mouth of the Neva river, at the head of the Gulf of Finland. He named it St. Petersburg and planned it as a "new town" free of the retarding influences of old slumbering Russia still so strong in Moscow; it would be Russia's port to the West, her base for expansion of Russian power in the entire Baltic region, in the phrase of the poet Pushkin a century later "a window opened upon Europe."

Poltava and After. To defend St. Petersburg against conquest by the triumphant Charles XII became the tsar's obsessing purpose. His Polish ally, Augustus I, was driven out of Poland by the Swedes, and Peter faced Charles alone. The Swedish king was diverted from an assault upon Moscow in order to join forces with the Ukrainian Cossack commander Mazeppa, who threw off his allegiance to Peter. The Russian forces withdrew slowly, destroying the villages from which the invaders hoped to draw sustenance. Then, on July 8, 1709, the two armies met at Poltava, in the Ukraine. The Russians outmaneuvered and outfought the Swedes, most of whom were slain, wounded or captured; Charles XII fled to nearby Turkey for refuge. The victory was sweet for Peter: his personal foe had been humbled, and St. Petersburg was safe. The building of the new city continued; the marshes were drained and filled; and imposing edifices in the neoclassical style of the West rose in the midst of the bare countryside. In 1715 Peter declared St. Petersburg his capital and moved the government from Moscow.

The duel with Charles was not over. The Swede persuaded his anxious Turkish hosts to declare war upon Russia in 1710, and Peter moved toward the Danube and the Balkans. He was met and held by the Turks on the Prut river, and made peace the next year at the price of foregoing Asov. But Turkey stayed neutral while the fighting continued along the Baltic, where it became known as the "Great Northern War." Russian forces completed the occupation of Estonia and Livonia, including the ports of Riga, Reval (Tallinn), and Viborg (Viipuri). In 1713 a Russian fleet, the mighty descendant of the English sailboat on the lake near Preobrazhenskoe, captured Helsinki, Turku (Åbo), and Hangö from the Swedes. Russian prestige was at a height. Charles asked for peace but Peter did not hasten to accord it. He went abroad again in 1716 and now found the West not only more respectful but also less willing to help build up Russian strength. A visit to France in 1717 enabled him to see the sights of Versailles and Paris but not to gain the alliance of the French king.

After Charles XII's death in 1718, the new government in Sweden decided to continue the war. Russian expeditions replied by ravaging the Swedish coast. Peace was made at Nystadt in 1721. Sweden ceded Livonia,

Estonia, and Ingria (the region around St. Petersburg), as well as Viborg and its hinterland, Karelia. The Senate (see below) celebrated the triumph by proclaiming Peter as "Emperor" (*Imperator*) and "the Great."

A new war began in the southeast, with the possessions of Persia on the Caspian Sea as the tsar's objective. A campaign begun in 1722 failed to reach the distant khanate of Khiva, but the southern and western shores of the Caspian were captured, including the ports of Derbent and Baku. In 1724 both Persia and Turkey recognized the new conquests.

Reform of the State. The colossal demands put by Peter I upon the Russian state to wage the wars of his reign could not be met by the old form of government. He therefore became a bold and energetic reformer, the creator of a politically "modernized" Russia, modeled upon the states of western Europe.

The first of the great changes was the abolition of the *boyar duma* in 1700; it was clumsy and infested with the spirit of resistance to Peter's "western" interests. An "intimate chancery" of close friends and counselors took its place. Nine years later the *prikazi* were abolished in turn; their functions were given to eight (later eleven) territorial governors. In 1711 the major measure of reorganization was taken. A Senate of nine members was established to control the collection and expenditure of revenues, to supervise the officialdom, and to direct the general policy of the governors. The Senate was also empowered to make decisions of policy in the tsar's absence. Further steps of reorganization were taken in 1718, with the advice of foreign consultants who took the government of Sweden as their model. The eleven "governments" (regions under governors) were divided into provinces, which were in turn subdivided into districts, with provision for partial self-government by the nobility and townsmen. The work of tax collection was separated from that of the judiciary and the police. Central administration, which proved beyond the capacity of the Senate and its clerks, was given to "colleges" (boards) of thirteen members.

Fiscal needs were met without recourse to loans, foreign or internal, solely by taxation and by currency inflation. The old taxation could not be expanded to meet the new needs. At first a series of improvisations were introduced, many patterned on western excise taxes and others suggested by "profit finders," as those who proposed them were called. A census taken in 1710 showed a decline in "hearths" (taxable families) from 812,000 in 1680 to 637,000; though the cause of depopulation was patently the constantly increased demands upon the people, the tsar did not dream of abandoning his plans of aggrandizement. Instead the general tax was adapted to the new situation. A "poll" tax was established on individuals (or "souls"), actually upon all males, rather than on "hearths"; but the villages and towns were made responsible for the collection of the total amount due. The result was satisfactory from the point of view of the tsar: an increase from 1,800,000 rubles in direct taxes in 1718 to 4,600,000 rubles four years later. This total amount went to the needs of the army; the naval requirements were met by various indirect taxes. At the end of the reign, the government was collecting almost 10,000,000 rubles in taxes every year, but its expenses were running still higher.

Nobles, Serfs, and Townsmen. Russian society, no less than the state, had to adapt itself to the demands of the impetuous warrior tsar. In his measures towards the various classes, Peter was moved by no higher principle than to make the population serve him well, in one or another way.

The tsar's demands for an adequate class of administrators and soldiers began the transformation of the nobility. The old boyar aristocracy was compelled to accept the yoke of obligatory service or be destroyed; the majority complained but obeyed, giving their sons at least a smattering of the required elementary education and sending them to serve in the tsar's regiments, often as common soldiers. The higher officialdom gradually became a new aristocracy. Peter recruited his civil and military servants with utter disregard for their social origins, but he bestowed noble rank upon them together with state lands and serfs for their maintenance. A table of ranks established in 1722 created three parallel paths of government service —the armed forces, the civil service, the court—with fourteen equivalent levels, the eight uppermost carrying a grant of nobility. These fresh-baked aristocrats did not lag in putting on a coating of family pride, and gradually merged with the boyars to form a single nobility of service.

The peasantry paid the price for the creation of this new upper class as well as for the tsar's wars. The various types of peasant obligations were made heavier and tighter; the control of the nobility became harsher and serfdom ever-nearer to actual slavery.

Though Russia remained overwhelmingly an agrarian land, the tsar neglected neither towns nor industry. His interest in the former lay mainly in taxing them effectively, but he was assiduous in sponsoring the creation and expansion of military production. Under the direction of a "college of mines," which was a kind of primitive ministry of economics, iron mines and mills were organized in the Urals and began to furnish the raw materials for Russian weapons. By 1725 Russia was producing more iron than England, and much of it compared in excellence to that of Sweden. Textile production was less successful. In the absence of a large supply of free labor, industry was permitted to acquire serfs for factory work, a form of bondage which became especially hated.

Trade was also favored, particularly by the abolition of most monopolies. The requirement that imports and exports pass through St. Petersburg, rather than the old port of Archangel on the White Sea, proved only a temporary disturbance. A network of canals, completed in 1725, linked the Neva river to the Volga, and eased transport between St. Petersburg and inner Russia.

The Holy Synod. The Russian Orthodox church followed the same path of service and obedience to the state. The tsar himself was anything but devout. He delighted in orgiastic ceremonies with his companions in blasphemous imitation of the church's rituals. But he knew that the immense majority of Russians were pious and that a movement of resistance to his authority would have some hope of success if it recruited the support of the clergy. His policy therefore was to deprive the church of its own leader, the patriarch. When Patriarch Adrian died in 1700, Peter declined to name a successor. Instead he imposed upon the Russian clergy a small but energetic group of Ukrainian bishops and abbots who had come under Protestant influence and strongly supported the doctrine of ecclesiastical subordination to the state.

In 1721 Peter tightened his control on the church and its wealth. He established a Holy Synod of nine members to exercise the historical functions of the patriarchate. Over the synod he placed an official of the state, a procurator-general, who permitted no dissent or disobedience. At the same time a "college of economy," composed of laymen, was set up to administer the estates belonging to the church; most of the revenues went into the tsar's treasury instead of to the monasteries. Many convents of regular clergy were abolished or limited in membership.

The Westernizing of Culture. The most obvious imitation of the West occurred in cultural activity. On his return from Europe in 1698 Peter was determined to make at least upper-class Russians look like Europeans of the same station in the West. He ordered all but clergy and peasantry to cut their beards, which were dear to the pious because Orthodox doctrine taught that only a bearded man remained "in the image of God," while without a beard one was "like a cat and not a man." Such arguments weighed little with Peter, and he personally used the scissors upon recalcitrant boyars. Peter also required his subjects (again with the exception of the peasantry, an enormous majority) to adopt clothing in the pattern of France, Hungary, or Germany.

Reform of the calendar was a similar measure. Instead of the Byzantine calendar in use, which began the year on September 1 and dated it from an assumed time of creation in 5508 B.C., Peter ordered the introduction of the Julian calendar, which began the year on January 1 and dated it from the birth of Christ, as in the West. The astronomical corrections adopted in the Gregorian calendar, tainted because they had been introduced by a Roman Catholic pope, were rejected, and the calendar when adopted was ten days behind the Gregorian.

Peter also carried through a partial westernization of the Russian alphabet. He replaced the forty-three ancient Slavonic letters with thirty-six letters largely derived from the Greek but typographically influenced by the Roman. Printing plants were established to issue translations of Western texts in geometry, mechanics, ballistics and anatomy, as well as religious materials. The Russian language came under the same influences. A new official and literary language evolved; it was laden with foreign words sometimes used in direct transliteration, sometimes adapted to the sound patterns of Russian, like *ratusha* for the German *Rathaus* (town hall) ; Russian words for new ideas were created on the pattern of foreign words. Foreign turns of phrase came into use.

To increase literacy the tsar ordered the establishment of provincial elementary and secondary schools, but made attendance obligatory only for the sons of priests and government officials. A shortage of teachers and pupils slowed the growth of these schools, and complaints about such "un-Russian" innovations were frequent; but gradually attendance improved.

The Crisis of Succession. This vast enterprise of westernization and modernization was imposed upon a reluctant and suffering people. Revolts broke out repeatedly during the tsar's reign, especially along the southern and southeastern edges of the empire, where traditions of local self-rule remained strong. Astrakhan was held during much of 1705 and 1706 by a group of insurgents opposing "German garb, the loss of beards, and the changed faith." Even more dangerous was a rebellion of the Don Cossacks in 1707 directed against the "princes, the boyars, the profit finders, and the Germans."

The hopes of old Russia centered in Peter's son, Alexei, who grew up loathing all that his father loved—the army, innovation, hard work, and danger. Peter's utmost efforts to train Alexei in these values by dragging him to battle only increased the young man's antipathy. Alexei listened to the wild talk of would-be rebels but did not dare to take their lead. Peter warned him not to count upon the fact that he was his father's only son, for "a capable stranger would be better than my own good-for-nothing." In 1718 Alexei fled abroad to take refuge with the Holy Roman emperor, but the tsar's agents tracked down the fugitive and enticed him to return home. He was tried as a criminal and died while under torture, in which, according to some accounts, Peter himself participated.

The succession to the crown—traditionally confined to the eldest son— lay open. Peter decreed that the reigning tsar should have the right to name his successor. An indication of his choice came in 1724 when he had his wife Catherine crowned as empress. The unprecedented action in sharing the throne with a woman was all the more surprising because Catherine had begun life as a Latvian peasant girl whom the tsar took for his mistress during the Baltic campaign of 1703. The sturdy Latvian lass had accompanied Peter thereafter, comforting and calming him in his fits of wrath, and he had married her in 1712. After Catherine's coronation, a rumor of a love affair between her and a courtier turned Peter against her. Weary and ill beyond recovery, the tsar died the next year. On his death bed, he began to write a note selecting a successor, but his hand fell lifeless before he could put down a name. The future of Russia and of Peter the Great's achievement lay beyond his power to entrust, and fell into lesser hands.

III. The Era of Palace Revolutions

Struggle over possession of the throne became the pattern for Russian history throughout the eighteenth century. The social, economic and political transformation of the country was essentially affected by the contest of candidates for power and by the intervention of the noble guards regiments as the decisive tsar makers.

The Guards, the Germans, and the Throne. In 1725 the choice for Peter I's successor lay between his grandson Peter and his widow, Catherine. The late tsar's friends, led by Catherine's mentor Alexander Menshikov, persuaded the guards regiments to support her proclamation as empress in her own right. During the two years of Catherine I's reign, Menshikov governed with a drunken sense of power and shameless self-enrichment. When she died in 1727, he arranged the accession of eleven-year-old Peter II. After four months, Menshikov was overthrown by a faction led by the Dolgorukis, an old boyar family that had not been reconciled to the changes introduced by Peter the Great. They did little toward bringing back the old order before the death of Peter II from smallpox in 1730 ended their domination.

A different kind of reform was attempted by Prince Dmitri Golitsyn, who took the initiative in the crisis caused by the absence of any established successor. Dmitri was a "westernizer" like his late cousin Vassili, but his particular ambition was to transform Russia from an autocracy into a limited monarchy, with the aristocracy holding the essential power of state, as in contemporary Poland or Sweden. He therefore proposed the candidacy of the impecunious niece of Peter I, Ivan V's daughter Anna, who was the widowed duchess of Courland (a Baltic fief of Poland). At Golitsyn's suggestion, the crown was offered to Anna on condition that she transfer actual power to a council dominated by the greater nobility. Anna accepted these terms, but on arrival in Moscow shook off the shackle of the "Conditions," as they were called, with the aid of the lesser nobility represented in the guards regiments.

During the ten-year reign of Anna, Russia was governed and ruth-

The Expansion of Russia, 1725-1801

lessly exploited by the Germans who accompanied the empress from Courland. Their leader was Anna's lover, Baron Bühren, whom the Russians called "Biron." Anna gave the duchy of Courland to Biron, placed the army under the control of the competent Munnich and foreign relations under the direction of Ostermann.

Return of the Russians. Anna, at Biron's suggestion, named as her successor Ivan, son of the duke of Brunswick-Bevern and grandson of her sister Catherine. Ivan VI, still a babe less than a year old, came to the throne in 1740. Biron ruled as regent for three weeks and then was overthrown by the guards regiments on behalf of Ivan's mother Anna Leopoldovna, who became regent in turn. Anna Leopoldovna's public envy and hatred for Peter I's surviving daughter, Elizabeth, led to another palace revolution on December 6, 1741. This insurrection was organized by the French and Swedish ambassadors in order to thwart the influence of Austria. Their hopes of dominating the new empress were soon disappointed. Elizabeth governed Russia until 1762 by and on behalf of the native Russian nobility, and in the interests of the Russian state.

The Nobility and the Serfs. The recurrent brawls for the throne made the rulers more and more dependent upon the support of the nobility. The result was a reduction in the nobles' obligations to the state and an increase in their control over the peasants upon their estates.

Under Anna, despite the constant terror against the older aristocratic families, the fidelity of the mass of smaller noblemen was assured by various concessions. The distinction between the freeholder status of the boyars and the conditional possession of the service nobles was largely disregarded, though its retention in law dangled a threat over the latter. Obligatory service was reduced from twenty to five years, and one son in each family was entirely exempted so that he might look after the family estates. A special cadet school was established for the military training of young noblemen. The rights of the peasantry to free movement and to judgment in the tsar's courts were further limited; at the same time the estate owners were entrusted with the collection of the poll tax.

Elizabeth's policy toward the nobility was a continuation of the same pattern. She permitted only noblemen to own land and gave them the right to sentence serfs to exile in Siberia. Peasants were compelled to attach themselves as serfs to one or another landlord. Elizabeth also reduced the taxes upon the serfs in order to permit the nobles to increase the dues paid to them by the same amount.

Changing Russia. The development of a stronger Russia, one more like the West in many ways, proceeded in spite of the political disturbances. The number of inhabitants increased to about 25,000,000 in 1762, partly by the inclusion of additional provinces but principally by growth of population, especially in the Ukraine and the southeastern steppeland.

The industrial development of the country, though still small, was continuous. The number of factories increased from fewer than 200 in 1725 to almost 700 in 1762. The Urals continued to be a center of iron production while textile manufacture was concentrated in Moscow.

Cultural life also developed at an increasing pace. The Russian language began to emerge as an effective literary tool. Writers employed the various forms of western literature, such as satire, history, and novels; relatively crude and inexperienced though their works were, they were the material for steady improvement in taste and skill. One author, the fisherman's son Michael Lomonosov, was Russia's Goethe, achieving fame as a historian, poet, grammarian, and physicist. An Academy of Sciences, planned by Peter the Great, was founded immediately after his death, and was followed in 1755 by the establishment of the University of Moscow. Theaters were built and magazines published. The use of the French language became increasingly frequent among the educated aristocracy. Indeed, the French model was usual in everything fashionable, including dress, manners, and ideas.

Russia among the Powers. The strength of the new Russia was made evident by the appearance of Russian troops in the West and by the increasing importance of Russian diplomacy.

The principal direction of Russian effort until the accession of Empress

Elizabeth lay in the south against the Turks and the Persians. Here in the beginning there were few successes and more failures. A war against the Turks in 1726, in alliance with Austria, gained a strip of steppeland but did not retake Azov. In 1732 the Caspian ports were lost to Persia.

Elizabeth's reign, however, was marked by major triumphs. The Swedes, who declared war upon her in 1742 in retaliation for her refusal to pay for their help in putting her on the throne by a cession of territory, were badly defeated in Finland; 17,000 Swedish soldiers were captured at Helsinki. The treaty of peace made at Åbo in 1743 gave Russia more of the Karelian area to the northwest of St. Petersburg. At the beginning of the wars for Silesia, Elizabeth maintained a neutrality favorable to Austria, and became an outright ally of Maria Theresa in 1746; the Russian empress feared Frederick II of Prussia for his prowess and hated him for his sarcastic remarks about the laxity of her morals. The entry of a Russian corps into Germany in 1748 helped bring the War of the Austrian Succession to an end on terms not too unfavorable to Austria. During the Seven Years' War, the repeated blows of the Russian army brought Frederick to the brink of disaster (see ch. 22, pp. 500-501). Never before had the prestige of Russian weapons been so high.

IV. Catherine the Great

The new Russia which had been taking shape since the days of Peter I was consolidated during the last third of the eighteenth century, under the last empress to reign in Russia in her own right, Catherine II (the "Great").

Peter III. When Empress Elizabeth died on January 5, 1762, she was succeeded by the heir whom she had designated, her nephew Peter. The new tsar was a strangely distorted and diminished reflection of his namesake Peter I. Like him he wished to be a warrior and a reformer; but his character was formed of sand, not steel. Born Duke Ulrich of Holstein-Gottorp and educated as a German, he had been rebaptized after his selection as heir to Russia and received for his bride a German princess, Sophia of Anhalt-Zerbst, who took the Russian name of Ekaterina—Catherine. The duke and duchess separated after a few years, for Catherine was a woman of learning without patience for the childish games of her spouse. Both remained in Russia.

Peter III's policy was dominated by his admiration for Frederick of Prussia. His first act on coming to the throne was to make peace with Frederick and then become his ally against Austria. His only interests were the army and the duchy of Holstein: the one he attempted to reorganize and reclothe in the Prussian manner; to the other he subordinated the interests of the Russian state and nation. On other matters, favorites were able to shape policy. The one significant act of legislation to which Peter III put his name was the manifesto of March 1, 1762, which released the Russian nobility from the obligation to serve the state. The peasants took the news to mean that they too had been freed from bondage, and rose in widespread rebellions against their noble masters. The army quickly put down these disturbances.

Peter sparked the hostility against him into open rebellion when he ordered the guards regiments to march west to fight for Holstein against Denmark. One of the guards officers, Gregory Orlov, lover of the tsar's estranged wife Catherine, took the lead with his brother Alexei in organizing the overthrow of the ruler. Catherine joined the rebels, who proclaimed her empress in her own right, and marched with them against Peter. He abdicated on July 10 and was strangled a week later by Alexei Orlov during a convenient fit of anger.

The Enigmatic Empress. Catherine II was one of the most striking and yet most enigmatic personalities of her age. She combined irreconcilable qualities with no apparent difficulty or embarrassment. She was German by birth, French by education, and Russian by adoption. A devotee of the Enlightenment (see ch. 27, pp. 607-609); an admirer and sponsor of such bold *philosophes* as the deist Voltaire and the materialist Diderot, she was also assiduous in the practice of the Russian Orthodox faith. An intellectual who for years had found in literature and philosophy escape from the perils and boredoms of her situation, she was obsessed with holding and using political power at any price. A crowned libertine who took one lover after another for more than three decades, she bore her discarded paramours no hatred but rewarded them with wealth, honors, and office. She was willful to the extreme ("I terribly want what I want," she wrote once), yet was patient and self-controlled when the times required, and was capable of the most devious plans. Eager for the flattery of the world, particularly from the leaders of intellectual fashions, she nonetheless usually saw herself with greater honesty than they. Perhaps her greatest self-deception was to think herself an original thinker rather than merely an intelligent reader.

Enlightenment . . . No monarch of eighteenth-century Europe was more publicly devoted to the persons and principles of the Enlightenment than Catherine II. Montesquieu, perhaps the most gentle of the *philosophes*, was her particular favorite. *The Spirit of the Laws* was her handbook of political philosophy; she quoted it easily and to the point, and with equal ease and purpose subtly kept its tone while changing its argument when to do so was to her advantage. She was also an avid participant in the contemporary doings of the intellectual world; she corresponded with such eminences of the Enlightenment as Voltaire and Diderot, and also with lesser figures like

Baron Grimm, her principal newsgatherer in Paris. Voltaire was fulsome in his praise: *"Te Catharinam laudamus, te confitemur"* (To thee, Catherine, we give praise and confession), he wrote, parodying the *Te Deum* hymn of the Roman church.

The artistic and intellectual life of Russia reflected the empress's intensely western interests without losing contact with its native Russian origins. The leading tendencies of western opinion won a public within Russia: not only the Voltairean deism of the Enlightenment, but also Free Masonry, with its blend of rationalism and ritualism, and the frankly mystical movement of the Rosicrucians. In 1784 Catherine permitted the establishment of private presses in addition to the governmental presses. Although the use of French in conversation and writing increased among the educated classes, the Russian language was not neglected, and the first dictionary of Russian was published by the Russian Academy. Interest in Russian antiquities resulted in a hunt for ancient manuscripts reminiscent of the Renaissance in the West. The most valuable find was the single known surviving copy of the Russian epic, *The Song of the Host of Igor.*

. . . **Despotism.** For all her fondness for the Enlightenment, Catherine did not allow herself to be led into the application of its principles if these might endanger her power over Russia. She knew the might of the tsar makers—the guards regiments—and of the nobility from whom they were recruited. Her first principle of action therefore was to preserve their fidelity; she coddled the guards and protected the interests of the nobility, making their obedience facile and profitable. Within the limits of this rule, however, she worked with the diligence of a Peter the Great and the clockwork regularity of a Louis XIV to make the Russian state more efficient.

Catherine's first need was to know better the country she ruled. Her long residence at court under Elizabeth had been a period of isolation from practical affairs. In order to fill the gap of her knowledge, she decided to call upon the nation for information and suggestions. In late 1766 she ordered election of a legislative commission with the task of drawing up a new code of law. Deputies were elected by all classes of the population except serfs in full bondage and the clergy; they brought with them statements of grievances and proposed reforms which painted the social situation of Russia with wealth and precision of detail, as well as with vigor of feeling that the empress had not anticipated. She had drawn up for the commission an "instruction" based upon the principles of Montesquieu's *Spirit of the Laws,* but modified so as to leave untouched the autocratic system of Russian government. Her intent was to simplify the structure of the state and to soften the harshness of its rule, but not to give away her power. The debates in the commission revealed to the empress the intensity of the hatred among the merchants, the nobles, and the peasantry, and the difficulty of reconciling them. At the end of 1768, she disbanded the assembly on the grounds that war was beginning with Turkey, but in fact because she had learned "what is necessary and what requires attention."

Catherine's first reforms strengthened the Senate as the principal instrument of central government. She divided it into six "chambers" to speed its work and abolished the parallel administrative colleges. Provincial governors were placed under the authority of the Senate. Local administration was later reorganized upon the basis of fifty provinces instead of the eleven huge governments; these provinces were further divided. The nobility retained a measure of self-government, including the right to elect their own marshal (a kind of sheriff) and judges; townsmen received similar rights, but the peasantry were placed under the complete control of their landlords.

The Pugachev Rebellion. The empress did not hesitate to sacrifice the peasantry to the nobility. When Diderot, during a visit to St. Petersburg in 1773, urged measures of reform, she dismissed his proposals as unfitted to Russia, because of its immense territory and its backwardness. She extended serfdom to the Ukraine and abolished the last surviving privileges of the Don Cossacks. Although she transferred a million church peasants to the ownership of the state, which was a relatively more favorable status, she gave almost two million "free" peasants as serfs to her favorites. She also retained the emancipation of the nobility from the obligation of service. Most of the advantages thus granted went to the relatively small number of "great" nobles, who more and more adopted a French pattern of life alien to the people; the more numerous "small" nobles were hard pressed to maintain their standard of living, and a few intellectuals rose from their ranks to give voice to their restlessness and their aspirations.

The subjugation of the peasantry and the Cossacks met fierce resistance. Desperate rebellions had recurred constantly throughout the century, but with limited and brief success. In 1773 a Don Cossack named Emelyan Pugachev presented himself to his fellow-Cossacks as Catherine's husband, the Tsar Peter III, who had miraculously escaped assassination. The revolt led by this "false Peter" started on the Ural river, spread westward almost to the gates of Moscow, and down across the southeastern steppe. Cossacks, serfs, and native Bashkirs and Kirghiz all responded in droves to Pugachev's promise of "land and liberty." Rebel victories over the poorly led government troops were followed by the massacre of landlords, government officials, and factory owners. Not until 1775 did regular troops, led by the hard-bitten and efficient General Suvorov, put down the insurrection. Pugachev, turned over to Suvorov by his own followers, was taken to Moscow in an iron cage and executed. The empress, badly frightened, ceased even to play at being a follower of the *philosophes*.

Triumphs of War and Diplomacy. For Catherine II it was not enough to have established her own rule within Russia. It was also necessary to consolidate her power and to feed her vanity by victories abroad. Her first action in European affairs, after she came to the throne in 1762, was to take Russia out of the Seven Years' War, but she kept her hand in the tangled diplomacy of Europe. Her policy was dominated by two closely related problems: first, how to make use of the continuing antagonism between Prussia and Austria; second, how to expand the territory and influence of Russia west and south of its borders. In 1764 she returned to the alliance with Prussia, abandoning the league with Austria which had been maintained since 1726 except for the brief interlude of Peter III's reign. Frederick II, she knew, was readier than Maria Theresa to join her in maintaining the existing political regime in Poland and, when the occasion should arise, in carving up that hapless kingdom. From 1767 until 1772 Catherine and Frederick negotiated the terms of a Polish partition.

In an attempt to prevent the dismantling of the Polish state, France instigated a Turkish war against Russia in 1768. Catherine took up the challenge and concentrated upon defeating the sultan. A Russian army penetrated the Balkans to Bucharest, while a Russian fleet sailed from the Baltic base of Kronstadt through the Atlantic and the Mediterranean to burn the Ottoman naval forces at Chesme (Çesme), on the western coast of Turkey (1770). In 1771 the Russians captured the Crimea. Although Turkish resistance continued, Catherine turned her attention westward, where a partition treaty with Frederick II in 1772 brought Russia the easternmost portion of Poland, with a population of 1,600,000, mainly White Russians.

Renewed operations against the Turks finally brought a peace treaty at Kuchuk Kainardji, a village in Bulgaria, in 1774. Turkey recognized the independence of the Tatars of the Crimea and the adjacent steppeland, which was an obvious prelude to their incorporation into the Russia state, while Azov was ceded outright to Russia. The Straits between the Black and the Aegean Seas were opened to Russian merchant shipping. Russia restored to Turkey her conquests in Moldavia and Wallachia, as well as in the islands of the Aegean archipelago.

Further Triumphs. Catherine's grandiose objective after 1774 was to drive the Ottoman sultan out of Europe and to build out of his reconquered territories a new Greek empire for her grandson Constantine. Austria's support in the contemplated war against the Turks was so essential that Catherine bought it by abandoning the Prussian alliance in 1780. The leadership of the campaign fell to her former lover, Potemkin, who was her principal minister for fourteen years. Potemkin encouraged settlement of colonists in the empty lands of the southern steppe and led in the conquest of the Black Sea ports of Kherson, Sebastopol, and Nikolaev. In 1783 Catherine proclaimed formal annexation of the Crimea and visited her new territory. Her rebuff of the sultan's demand for evacuation of the Crimea led to a Turkish declaration of war in 1787.

Joseph II of Austria, who had visited the empress in the Crimea, entered the war as promised, but gave slim assistance. Sweden at the same time took the opportunity to redeem its losses to Russia and launched an attack toward St. Petersburg; this assault was defeated, and peace was made in 1790. Suvorov defeated the Turks in 1789 at the battle of Rymnik in Rumania. The Turks made peace at Jassy in 1792 by recognizing the Crimean annexation and ceding the region of Bessarabia, between the Bug and Dniester rivers, to Russia. Meanwhile resistance in Poland to Russian control boiled over into open war, but Catherine and Frederick William II of Prussia combined to impose a new partition upon King Stanislaus in 1793; Russia took most of the remaining White Russian territories of Poland as well as the old Lithuanian capital of Vilnius (Vilna). A renewed rebellion of Polish patriots led by Kościuszko was crushed by Suvorov and the peace treaty of 1795 brought the extinction of the Polish state with its third and complete partition. Catherine received the territories of Courland, Lithuania, and Volhynia to the Bug river. This was the last diplomatic triumph of Catherine II before her death on November 17, 1796.

The empress had fully earned, by the standards of her age, the title of "the Great." She had taken the strength of Russia, which was largely the work of her predecessors, and used it to make the empire larger and more respected among the powers of Europe. Russia itself she left essentially unchanged to face a new and revolutionary age.

24

The Lesser States in Decline

1650 - 1789

DURING THE century and a half after the Peace of Westphalia, nations once great and strong declined to the status of lesser powers. Some of these states turned their attention inward, away from the temptations and perils of grand policy to the problems and opportunities of domestic development. Achieving a good measure of internal stability and strength, they were usually able to protect their independence. Those states, however, which suffered material and spiritual degradation often became the prey of voracious and powerful neighbors. For the weakling nations of Europe, the eighteenth century was a time of loss and even total disaster.

I. Iberia

Nowhere except in Poland was the fall from greatness more visible or painful than in Spain and Portugal. After the grandeur of the sixteenth century came poverty, torpor, and weakness.

The Sickly King and Kingdom. In 1665 Spain received a king fitting for a time of degradation. The five-year-old Charles II was feeble of body, wracked by illness, irresolute and shy. Yet he grew to be proud of his royal rank and race and could be unexpectedly stubborn in defending his rights.

From the moment of Charles's accession, the boy king's various royal cousins began to plan for the event of his death. They burnished their claims to the Spanish throne—taking for granted that he would die before reaching manhood, or, if he lived, would be too frail to father a successor. In 1667, Louis XIV became impatient of delay and undertook the War of Devolution, the first of his campaigns to seize Spanish territories in the Low Countries. Spain replied haughtily to each of Louis's demands but was too weak to defend herself; only the combination of the powers prevented the French monarch from completing his conquests. (See ch. 17, pp. 402-403.)

The nerveless incoherence of Spanish public life became even greater under Charles II. Trade, industry, and agriculture all languished. The finances of the state were in perpetual crisis; the government found brief respite by replacing copper coinage with an even cheaper money, but the resulting inflation only worsened the situation. Government was in the hands of a succession of avid incompetents: first the queen-mother, Maria Anna, who sacrificed Spanish interests to those of her own Austrian Hapsburgs; then the king's illegitimate half-brother, Don Juan of Austria, a proud and inept blusterer; and after him, under the nominal personal rule of the king, various dukes, counts, and ecclesiastics with pretensions but not the ability to pull Spain out of its ruin.

The War of the Spanish Succession. The personal crisis of Charles II and the political crisis of Spain came to a head after the conclusion of the Peace of Ryswick in 1697. The king's health steadily deteriorated while the intrigues of prospective claimants to the crown became more open and energetic. At the same time France negotiated with its erstwhile foes, Britain and the United Provinces, for a peaceful partition of the Spanish monarchy. The news of these treaties, which disposed of Spain's territories and destinies without her participation or consent, infuriated both Charles and his subjects.

Rather than accept such dictation, the king took a measure of desperate boldness. He would split the would-be despoilers by offering all his realms as an indivisible bequest to the strongest of the claimants, France. Charles signed a testament bequeathing his crown to Louis XIV's grandson, Duke Philip of Anjou; however, if Philip refused it, it would go to Archduke Charles of Austria on the same terms of preserving the integrity of the monarchy. This last stroke of state accomplished, Charles II, last of the Spanish Hapsburgs, died on November 1, 1700. Louis XIV, after some hard debate in his council, accepted the testament for his grandson, who became Philip V of Spain.

What the Hapsburgs lost, Spain in a sense won. She had chosen her own king instead of receiving one at the hands of others. Throughout the bitter War of the Spanish Succession (1701-1713), the Spaniards stood steadfastly beside the Bourbon monarch, whose family name they Hispanized as Borbón. The Catalans, characteristically rejecting what the Spaniards favored, supported with equal fervor the Austrian archduke, who proclaimed himself "Charles III." Nonetheless the fundamental decisions on Spain's future were made elsewhere, on the battlefields of the Low Countries, Germany, and Italy, and in the parley rooms of Utrecht, where peace was signed in 1713. Spain kept its possessions beyond the oceans in America and the Philippines, as well as the kingdom of Naples; Sicily went to the duke of Savoy, Milan (Lombardy) and the southern Netherlands to the Austrian Hapsburgs. But Archduke Charles, by then emperor, refused to abandon his claimed Spanish heritage and continued intermittent war with Philip V until 1720.

Bourbon Spain. The Bourbon dynasty brought fresh energy and new methods to the decaying Spanish kingdom. The French ministers who accompanied Philip V to Madrid imported French techniques of government. Centralization under the crown was enhanced by means of a reduction of the government councils to four. Intendants provided Madrid with more reliable agents in the localities. The vestiges of provincial autonomy were eliminated; Catalonia in particular paid for its rebellion between 1705 and 1714 by the loss of its coveted code of privileges.

The French ministers returned home at the end of the war, but under Philip V and his sons, Ferdinand VI (1746-1758) and Charles III (1758-1788), a succession of Spanish ministers carried on with attempts to reform the Spanish economic edifice. Their models were mostly foreign, Colbertian mercantilism in the first half of the century and then, increasingly, physiocratic doctrines. Charles III held a special position among the "enlightened despots" of the second half of the century. He was more moderate in words than most of them, but acted with vigor when the occasion arose; he did not fear to expel the Jesuit order from Spain in 1767 when it seemed to interfere with his absolute power. It was a sign of the changes wrought by the first Bourbons in Spain that the wars against Great Britain (1718-1720, 1727-1729, 1739-1741, 1762-1763, 1779-1783) progressed from initial defeats to substantial gains.

Nonetheless the transformation was the work of the state, not of the people. The mass of the population—nobles, clergy, and common folk— resisted the changes and clung to the old order, with its pride, sloth, and infirmities. The continuation of even limited reform depended upon the impetus given by a king possessing a modicum of courage and purpose: but the Bourbons, no less than the Hapsburgs before them, faced the danger of loss of character and intelligence in the kings they gave to the land. Spain entered the revolutionary age not wholly restored in health.

Portugal, Free and Dependent. Spain's sister nation upon the Iberian peninsula, Portugal, passed through a similar development after establishing her independence. Her glories were memories and her strength was just enough to enable her to select a protector to defend her against reconquest. The first protector was Louis XIV, with whose assistance the war of independence was carried to a conclusion in 1668, when Spain acknowledged Portuguese sovereignty. When a French king ascended the throne of Spain in 1700, Portugal reacted by seeking safety with Britain. Portuguese soil furnished the base for British forces operating against Philip V, and Portuguese armies fought alongside the English. The Methuen treaty of 1703 consolidated the military-political alliance by tying the two countries commercially; it opened the markets of Portugal to British goods, while Portuguese wine ("port," from Oporto), largely replaced French claret on English tables. Thereafter Portugal remained linked to English policy, though avoiding outright war with Spain.

The somnolence of Portugal was shattered during the reign of Joseph I (1750-1777). The king, himself a frivolous weakling, gave control of government to a Portuguese nobleman, Sebastian José Carvalho e Mello, who became marquis of Pombal in 1770. Pombal attempted to wrench Portugal from its weakness by combining the doctrines of "enlightened despotism" with ferocious energy and cruelty. On the one hand, he strove to restore the vigor of Portuguese economic life; he favored the cultivation of grain instead of grapes, aided trade with the Portuguese colonies, and encouraged emigration of colonists. After Lisbon was destroyed by an earthquake on November 1, 1755, he displayed his talents as an organizer to the best, bringing aid to the victims and directing rebuilding of the city. On the other hand, he governed tyrannically, employing police spies and torture unscrupulously against all who stood in his way.

Pombal's policy toward the Catholic church was similarly mixed. An edict abolished the distinction between "old" and "new" Christians, by which penalties had continued to be inflicted on descendants of converted Jews and Moors. Other measures were directed to encouraging teaching and charitable religious orders, while those devoted primarily to prayers and rituals were discouraged; but all had to accept state control without a murmur, and those like the Jesuits who maintained a semblance of independence and international connections were limited in their activity or expelled.

Pombal's power rested solely on the confidence of the king. Joseph's daughter Maria, who became queen in 1777, was a defender of the old order. She dismissed Pombal and put him on trial for his life. He was convicted in 1780, but the queen pardoned him and he died two years later. Portugal was almost unchanged by the nearly three decades of Pombal's ceaseless activity.

II. Italy

Italy remained politically a "geographical expression," a jumble of more or less "independent" states and principalities belonging outright to foreign potentates. The eighteenth century brought a period of frequent shifts of ownership in the dependent lands. Naples passed into the hands of Austria for two decades (1713-1735) before returning to Spain. Sicily was given to Savoy, and Sardinia to Austria, in 1713; in 1720 the islands exchanged owners, and the duke of Savoy exchanged the royal title of Sicily for that of Sardinia. Lombardy, with its capital of Milan, passed from the possession of Spain to that of the Austrian Hapsburgs in 1713. The Medici dynasty of Tuscany died out in 1737, and the once-glorious land of the Florentines was assigned to the dispossessed duke of Lorraine, Francis Stephen, as a consolation prize after the War of the Polish Succession.

In all these transfers, only Savoy (or Sardinia, as it was called after 1720) acted as a genuinely independent power; but its freedom consisted in the ability to choose sides in the wars between the major powers. Deft application of the principle of "reason of state" enabled the dukes to expand their territories in all (save the Polish Succession conflict) of the wars in which they took part.

Venice and the Papal State likewise remained free, but at the price of absolute neutrality in Europe. Venice undertook wars against the Ottoman empire with varying success; it lost Crete at the end of the long Candian war (1645-1669) but held the Morea (the modern name of the Peloponnesus) in Greece from 1685 until 1718. Thereafter Venice remained a passive onlooker in the great events of the century.

Yet the life of Italy escaped the lethargy which gripped Spain in the same period. In many of the Italian states, vigorous and intelligent political leadership helped to maintain the level of economic activity: although Italy did not grow spectacularly rich like England, it did not decline into helpless misery (except for areas like the islands of Sicily and Sardinia, which had been backward for many centuries).

III. Switzerland

The recognition given to Switzerland as an independent sovereign state in the Peace of Westphalia did not tighten the ties of unity among the cantons. They continued to form the loosest of political entities conceivable, lacking even the nominal leadership of a single person such as was present in the Holy Roman Empire. The clash of Catholic and Protestant cantons abated but did not disappear, and broke out in violent war in the two Vilmergen wars (1655, 1712). Nonetheless neither side wished to lose the cherished independence of the country, so that peace without victors was negotiated both times. Although Swiss mercenaries continued to serve in foreign campaigns, the cantons themselves remained neutral amid the repeated wars of the European powers.

The life of the people changed, more rapidly in the valleys and foot-hills than in the mountain cantons. Agriculture steadily improved, with the introduction of new crops and methods of tillage. Fodder crops for livestock made possible the expansion of the dairy industry; but more immediately vital was the cultivation of potatoes, which reduced dependence on imported grain. Textiles, particularly cotton, were the principal manufactures, although clockmaking became important during the latter part of the eighteenth century. Genevan banking took a leading position among the financial powers of Europe, and in the person of Jacques Necker contributed one of the most important ministers of state to the French monarchy just before the revolution. Government power within the towns and cantons remained in the hands of men of inherited citizenship and wealth; yet revolts by peasants and the voteless townsmen achieved some relaxation of the oligarchic monopoly upon the state. The Swiss also began to take a full part in the intellectual and cultural life of Europe.

IV. The Low Countries

The Peace of Westphalia confirmed the division of the Low Countries into the independent North and the dependent South. For a while the United Provinces preserved their status as a leader among the nations of Europe in power, wealth, and civilization, but the eighteenth century saw a steady decline from pre-eminence. The southern Netherlands, however, remained in doldrums, passing from Spanish to Austrian sovereignty, yet with signs of restive self-assertion.

The "True Freedom." Peace brought into the open the clash between the interests of the mercantile classes of Holland, whose wealth had paid for the victory over Spain, and the prince of Orange, whose forebears had given military and political leadership to the Republic. Holland wanted peace and neutrality so that she could give her full efforts to profitable trade; William II desired the resumption of war with Spain as well as armed intervention on behalf of his father-in-law, Charles I of England. Though unable to save Charles's life, William struck against his Dutch rivals for authority in 1650. When the province of Holland attempted to dismiss the regiments in its pay despite a decision of the States-General, the prince seized the leaders of the "republican" (anti-Orangist) party in Holland and laid siege to Amsterdam.

A compromise giving him essential control prevented the outbreak of full-scale civil war. But before he could take advantage of his triumph, William II died on November 6 of smallpox; a week later, on November 14, a son also named William was born to his wife, Princess Mary.

The republicans of Holland jumped to the occasion. The death of the prince of Orange left them predominant in the leadership of the Republic. They used their power and their influence to organize what they proudly called the "True Freedom." At their initiative, the States-General refrained from naming the infant William III to command of the armed forces (with a lieutenant holding effective command until the prince came of age) ; at the same time the provincial States left the office of the stadholder unfilled (except for the two northernmost provinces, where a second cousin of the prince was stadholder). The prerogatives held by the princes of Orange since the foundation of the Republic were taken over by the provincial States and the self-governing towns. The quasi dynasticism of the Orange stadholders, which had introduced a monarchical element into government, was totally eliminated. All power belonged to "the people"; but "the people" were not the total population but only the families of wealth, education, and traditional political eminence. The poorer classes had no say whatever in government, except when they rioted in response to hunger in times of hardship, or in answer to the appeals of their Calvinist preachers and the adherents of "Our Prince," as the common folk continued to call William III. Nonetheless, this Dutch oligarchy was much wider and more open than that which governed Venice, and it gave its subjects greater freedom of conscience, speech, and press than was to be found anywhere else in Europe.

John de Witt. In 1652 the Republic floundered into a fierce naval war with the English Commonwealth, a power far more formidable than Spain had been for half a century. The Dutch were bitter against the English Navigation Act of 1651, which cut into the Dutch carrying trade. Rivalry over colonial possessions, especially in the Indies, worsened feelings between the two republican states. The immediate occasion for war, however, was Dutch refusal to accept English political domination, particularly in measures against the Orangists, whom Cromwell feared as potential supporters of the Stuarts. The war went badly for the Dutch, who lacked effective leadership. In 1653 they entrusted responsibility to a young man of twenty-seven, John de Witt of Dordrecht, who became councilor-pensionary (executive secretary) of the province of Holland.

De Witt was the most illustrious representative of the patricians who governed Holland. A republican wholly dedicated to the "True Freedom," he was a mathematician of note. As grand pensionary (to give him the name used by foreigners), he was only the servant of the provincial States of Holland and of the States-General; but his day-by-day direction of their affairs enabled him to guide them by persuasion. His basic policies were to protect the commercial interests of the Republic against rising competition, to assure its safety against great neighbors, and to prevent the re-establishment of the Orange princes in the places of power. He ended the succession of disasters in the war with England but was unable to compel Cromwell to abandon the Navigation Act, while the English protector enforced upon the States of Holland an Act barring the princes of Orange from the stadholderate for all time.

The restoration of Charles II to the British throne in 1660 revived the threat from the Orangists in the Netherlands, for the king was the uncle of William III. De Witt thereupon assured the safety of the Republic by obtaining the alliance of France in 1662. Renewed Anglo-Dutch warfare in 1665, caused by sharpening colonial competition, ended in a compromise peace two years later. Louis XIV's invasion of the southern Netherlands in 1667 constituted a menace to the interests of the Dutch, who feared to have so mighty a neighbor next to them. De Witt brought the United Provinces into the Triple Alliance of 1668 with Britain and Sweden in order to call a halt to Louis's victories. France responded by organizing a war to punish and destroy the Dutch Republic. Louis XIV purchased the alliance of the English against his former ally and launched an invasion in 1672. French armies penetrated to within a score of miles of Amsterdam and The Hague before they were stopped by the opening of the dikes and the flooding of the land. William III was named captain-general, and De Witt was forced to resign as councilor-pensionary. In August the fallen statesman was lynched by an Orangist mob which falsely accused him of treason on behalf of France.

The Stadholder-King. The regime of the "True Freedom" collapsed. The prince of Orange regained all the offices held by his forefathers, becoming not only admiral and captain-general, but also stadholder of the five principal provinces. William III took up the struggle with Louis XIV with unsurpassed obstinacy. The Dutch fleet held off an English naval onslaught, while the land war was shifted from Dutch to Belgian and German territory with the intervention of Spain, Elector Frederick William of Brandenburg, and the Holy Roman Emperor Leopold I. In 1674 William, effectively playing upon parliamentary hostility to Charles II, compelled England's withdrawal from the war. Four years later, at the Peace of Nijmegen, Dutch negotiators won a favorable peace from Louis XIV. The agreement was made against William's wishes, but the Hollanders, led by Amsterdam, did not share his impassioned desire to continue the war until the power of the French king was destroyed.

During the war William had been granted his several high offices as hereditary in his family, but he was compelled nonetheless to govern the United Provinces as much by persuasion as by compulsion. He obtained the willing assent of the country to his English expedition in 1688, which gave him the throne of Britain the next year. As stadholder-king, William led the Grand Alliance against Louis XIV during the war of 1689-1697. After the Peace of Ryswick, he was willing to settle the controversy over the Spanish Succession by negotiated partition; but when the French monarch seized the Dutch "barrier" forts established by the Ryswick treaty, William III led both England and the Republic into the War of the Spanish Succession in 1701.

A Second-Rate Power. William III died in 1702, leaving no heir to succeed him in his offices. The Dutch decided to appoint no successor to him, but his policies continued to dominate the Republic under the leadership of his friend, Antonie Heinsius, grand pensionary of Holland. Dutch safety depended above all on the English alliance, and to it was sacrificed the traditional emphasis of the Republic upon sea power. During the War of the Spanish Succession, the Dutch effort was directed primarily to maintaining land forces, while the English took the lead at sea; yet it was the Englishman, Marlborough, who held the command of the combined Anglo-Dutch armies. When peace was at last made at Utrecht in 1713, Great Britain had attained pre-eminence among the states of Europe and the United Provinces had declined to a secondary position.

The habit of seeking safety in the English alliance continued until mid-century. The two sea powers joined to enforce the terms of the Utrecht settlement upon Spain and then to compel Austria to abandon the Ostend Company (see below, p. 547). This subordination led Frederick II of Prussia to indulge his taste for sarcasm at the Dutch expense; he called the Republic "a dinghy boat trailing the English man-of-war." English influence was strengthened in 1747 when the populace, outraged by Maurice of Saxe's successes in the Dutch possessions south of the Rhine, compelled the provincial officials to establish William IV, a distant collateral descendant of William III, as admiral, captain-general, and stadholder. Four years later he was succeeded by his son William V. During this period French influence revived. A party of "Patriots" arose to advocate the political ideas of the Enlightenment. In 1788 civil war broke out between the Patriots and William. He was quickly victorious with the aid of Prussian troops.

End of the Golden Age. The golden age of the Republic gradually declined into a silver period of economic and cultural quiescence, below the level of France, Britain, and towards the end of the eighteenth century of Germany as well. The wealth of the United Provinces remained high, but its sources were beginning to run dry. The trade, transport, and fishing which had provided the Dutch with their largest revenues suffered increasingly from the competition of the new sea powers, particularly England and France. Instead Dutch revenues began to depend upon the interest earned upon loans made out of the huge accumulations of liquid capital acquired during the extraordinary prosperity of the previous age. The Bank of Amsterdam remained one of the financial pillars of Europe, alongside the Bank of England.

The life of the spirit underwent a similar development. Smugness took the place of creative vigor. After the painters of supreme genius, notably Rembrandt, came the lesser figures—men of good training, with an eye for charming scenes and color, but lacking psychological penetration and tragic depth. No longer were there writers of general European influence, like Vondel; instead came men of letters of local importance. In the Jewish-born Spinoza, who died in 1677, Holland possessed a philosopher of the very first order; but after him the country's thinkers of importance were not only lesser figures but also for the most part French Huguenot refugees, like Pierre Bayle and Jurieu. As the United Provinces became a backwater, the Dutch language lost its currency among men of learning and became a tongue restricted to natives.

The Southern Netherlands. The ten southern provinces of the Low Countries remained a portion of the Spanish monarchy until 1713. The wars for the Spanish succession were largely fought in this patch of land between France, Germany, and the United Provinces. At the end, the Peace of Utrecht transferred these provinces to Austrian sovereignty. Austria accepted the old restrictions placed upon Spain: the barring from the Scheldt river of all seagoing traffic to Antwerp; the maintenance of Dutch garrisons in the fortresses along the southern border, as a "barrier" against France. Austria also agreed to maintain the traditional liberties of the provincial States, which had been generally observed by Spain since the days of Parma and the archdukes. In practice the Dutch "barrier" fortresses were a thin shield against the assaults of French armies during the wars of the Polish and Austrian successions, so that the southern Netherlands again became a battleground of nations.

Despite their subordination to the Hapsburg dynasts, the people of the southern Netherlands retained a strong sense of their identity. Towards the end of the eighteenth century the Latin name "Belgium," once applied to the whole Netherlands, came to be used only for the Catholic southern province. The feeling of common nationality with the Dutch was washed thin by decades of separation and hostility. Many of the Belgians (to use the name in the restricted sense) spoke Walloon, a French dialect, while the community of language between the Flemings and the Dutch continued only among the ordinary folk; the southern upper classes all spoke and wrote French as their usual language. Toward their successive Spanish and Austrian overlords the Belgians gave obedience without affection; government was relatively mild but it provided little protection again invasion, which weighed heavily upon the population.

Nonetheless the land recovered from its disasters with a resiliency which revealed the inner resources of the people. Agriculture took over economic primacy from trade and industry, but the fertile soil and the farmers' skills combined to make the countryside once more, in the words of an admiring French ambassador, "an enchanted country." The population grew from less than half a million to more than two million. The persistence of business qualities among the Belgians was shown when the Imperial and Royal Company, better known as the Ostend Company, was founded in 1722. It was so successful in trading with China and India that Britain and Holland, outraged at new competition, compelled the Austrians to suspend the company five years later and to abolish it outright in 1731.

In 1787 conflict broke out between the Belgians and the Austrian sovereign, Joseph II, as a result of his attempted reform of the government in their provinces. Austrian troops put down the armed rebellion which began in 1789, and Leopold II, Joseph's successor, adopted a conciliatory policy.

V. Scandinavia

In the Scandinavian countries the decline of political power was marked in the period after 1660. The eighteenth century was, however, an age of incipient economic and social transformation in both Sweden and Denmark-Norway. Political separation of more than a century intensified the distinctness of the Scandinavian nations.

Sweden. *The Debacle of Aristocratic Rule.* In 1660 the conquests of half a century made Sweden an imperial power bestriding the Baltic Sea. Besides the whole eastern slope of the Scandinavian peninsula, the Swedish empire now included all Finland and the eastern shore lands of the Baltic, except for the intervals of Prussian and Polish territory. The whole region had a population of two and a half million, compared to about one million within Sweden itself. The political resources of the Swedish monarchy were drawn largely from the conquered lands, where tolls could be collected on goods brought in and out of almost all of northern Europe.

The defense of this empire against jealous neighbors became a burden upon the Swedish nation. The faction of great nobles which dominated the government during the minority of Charles XI (1660-1672) endeavored to combine spendthrift luxury at home with an adventurous policy abroad. They placed Swedish armies at the service of Louis XIV in return for ample subsidies. This policy led to abandonment of the Triple Alliance of 1668 (see ch. 17, p. 403) and entry into the French-Dutch war in 1674 on the French side. The penalty for years of slapdash administration came in 1675 when Frederick William of Brandenburg won his victory over the Swedes at Fehrbellin. Only the persistent support of Louis XIV enabled the Swedes to avoid the loss of Pomerania to Brandenburg at the Peace of Nijmegen (1678-1679).

Agony of Empire. Charles XI, by now a bitter, hard-bitten man, drew the lesson from this humiliation. He took control of affairs into his own hands and determined to break the hold of the aristocracy over the state. In 1680 the Riksdag (parliament) assembled at his command and enacted legislation (the so-called "Reduction") to recapture from the nobility all the lands they had received from the crown which produced more than a limited revenue. At the same time, the monarch was declared to hold absolute personal power, for which he was responsible only to God. The council of state was transformed into a royal council; its members declined from the status of born collaborators of the king to officials dependent on his will and word. For the remainder of his reign, Charles XI devoted himself not to waging war but to strengthening his kingdom and building up the means of war: the army, the navy, and the state finances.

Charles XII, who succeeded his father in 1697, was a lad of only fifteen when he began to reign, but he was already a man in his intensity and resolution of purpose. He was not reluctant to fight. When Tsar Peter of Russia joined with Denmark and Saxony in 1699 in an attempt to snatch the possessions of Sweden beyond its pre-1660 frontiers, Charles led his armies against them and defeated them in turn. His icy skill and iron will won him the admiration of Europe. His victory over the Russians at Narva in 1700 (see ch. 23, p. 522) destroyed the hopes of the would-be conquerors of Sweden. But now Charles was unwilling to make peace until he had unseated the Elector Frederick Augustus of Saxony from the throne of Poland. Final triumph evaded him, and defeat at Poltava in 1709 forced him to take refuge in Turkey. For five years he remained in the village of Bender, at once the guest and the prisoner of the sultan. But the goal of revenge remained fixed in his soul. In 1714 he was able to return to Sweden to take up personal command of the war. But the gift of victory had left him and he died of a bullet, fired perhaps by one of his own party, while besieging a Danish fortress in nearby Norway in 1718.

Peace then came quickly. The Great Northern War, as the two decades' struggle was called, ended by the treaties of Stockholm, Copenhagen, and Nystad (1719-1721); by the first, Sweden gave up the German bishoprics of Bremen and Verden to Hanover and the port of Stettin to Prussia; by the second, Denmark returned the Swedish possessions on the Baltic shore of Germany; by the last, Sweden abandoned the Baltic provinces and southeastern Finland to Russia.

The "Era of Liberty." The death of Charles XII also resulted in a political transformation of Sweden. His heir was his sister Ulrica Leonora, but she wished her husband, Frederick of Hesse-Cassel, to reign in her stead.

She therefore abdicated in his favor in 1720, but an election by the Riksdag was necessary to legalize the break in the hereditary line. The parliament granted the crown to Frederick after he accepted a new constitution (the "Reform of Government") which took from him all essential powers—the grant of taxation, the voting of laws, control over the ministers and their policy—and gave them to the Riksdag. The explicit model for this reform was the limited and constitutional monarchy of Britain, particularly as it had been reshaped by the Revolution of 1688 and the establishment of the Hanoverian dynasty.

Sweden thereupon developed a political party much like that of Britain, with the "Caps" of Count Arvid Horn set against the "Hats" of Count Carl Gyllenborg. The parties were both led by the resurgent aristocracy, which merged with the lesser nobility or gentry; and both were dedicated to the preservation of the new "Era of Liberty," as it was called. But Horn advocated a cautious policy of rebuilding Sweden; he avoided foreign wars and introduced strong mercantilist measures to protect native industry and shipping. This policy Horn's opponents condemned as timid and cowardly, and they called his party the Night-Caps (subsequently shortened to Caps), while for themselves they kept the name of Hats, which had a ring of martial valor in the Swedish language. The Hats won the support of the Riksdag in 1738 and thrust Sweden into the wars of 1740-1763 as an ally of France. The old prowess of Swedish arms had vanished, however, and by 1765 the result was not only defeat abroad but also economic hardship at home. The Caps returned to power and gave their trust to an alliance with Russia, only to find their country threatened by Russian voracity. The Hats regained office four years later, but lacked the strength to prevent a crisis early in 1770.

Gustavus III. The initiative passed to the crown prince, who came to the throne the next year as Gustavus III. His aim from the first was the restoration of monarchical power, which he achieved by a *coup d'état* on August 19, 1772, when he imposed a new constitution upon the Riksdag by the threat of armed violence. He did not make himself absolute but rather reasserted the royal prerogative in executive matters and in general leadership of the state.

Gustavus did not assemble another Riksdag until 1778, when the legislature discovered that the king intended to use his powers to the full and would swallow no resistance on its part. Cowed by his determination, the members did not attempt to balk him. This servility had disappeared by the time the next Riksdag met in 1786, but Gustavus dismissed it and proceeded to govern by his own prerogative. He declared war on Russia in 1788, despite the constitutional requirement for the parliament's approval. Brought to the brink of disaster by a plot of his principal officers and a Danish invasion in the west of Sweden, he was compelled to convene another Riksdag in

1789. The lower estates rallied to his support and overrode the order of the nobility in granting to the king unlimited powers of command in foreign and military affairs.

When revolution erupted in France later that year, Gustavus became the first of the European monarchs to advocate a crusade in defense of the Bourbon absolutism. He even patched up his quarrel with Catherine II of Russia in order that his forces might be free for the campaign. Gustavus missed seeing his wish accomplished, however, for he died in March, 1792, the victim of an assassin's shot during a masquerade ball. The next month war came between revolutionary France and monarchical Europe (see ch. 28, pp. 626-627).

A Changing Nation. While Sweden's politics swung between absolute and parliamentary monarchy, the nation began to take on a different shape. The old economic isolation had been destroyed by the mid-seventeenth century; but it was not until well into the eighteenth century that commercial dependence upon the Dutch and then upon the English was relieved. The major measure of economic emancipation was a navigation act adopted in 1724; it applied against the English the same techniques for favoring national industry and shipping which they had used on their own behalf. But the English, unable to do without imports of high-grade Swedish iron, overlooked such insolent imitation and continued to do business with the Swedes. Industry, particularly textiles and iron mills, became prosperous. Agriculture also progressed, chiefly as the result of enclosures which brought holdings together into more efficient units rather than because of new techniques.

The cultural life of Sweden reflected general European developments. Literature was influenced by English, French, and to a lesser degree German models; Gustavus III himself was a dramatist of considerable ability. In science, Sweden took a leading position, with the botanist Carl Linnaeus the outstanding figure. Emanuel Swedenborg attained fame as a philosopher and scientist before he turned to the propagation of a mystical theology and philosophy.

Denmark-Norway. *The Era of Absolutism.* In 1660 Denmark had ceased to be a Baltic empire, although it retained its possessions to the west, on the Atlantic, principally Norway, as well as the lesser dominions of Iceland, Greenland, and the Faeroe islands. The defeats met during the recent war with Sweden recoiled upon the Danish nobility, which had controlled the power and the policy of the state. King Frederick III used the opportunity to begin the transformation of the monarchy from an elective and limited form to a hereditary, absolute type. He first directed the discontent of the lower orders against the nobility, who then assented to a law removing from all classes the privilege of exemption from taxation. Then Frederick obtained from the Rigsraad (parliament) a grant of the kingship as the hereditary possession of his dynasty. No longer would his descendants have to turn over their powers bit by bit to the parliament by "capitulations" at the time of their election. Frederick then proceeded to proclaim himself as "absolute sovereign lord." Royal absolutism was consolidated in the King's Law (*Kongelov*) of 1665 (not published until after Frederick's death in 1670), which made the monarch all-powerful, except for the obligations to accept the Lutheran form of Christianity and to preserve the kingdom territorially intact.

Under the new system, the nobility had to share the work of government and the fruits of political influence with the other classes of the nation, particularly the increasingly prosperous businessmen in Copenhagen and other trading towns. The wars of the reigns of Frederick III, Christian V (1670-1699) and Frederick IV (1699-1730) drained much of the strength obtained from expanding trade to the fruitless enterprise of regaining Danish pre-eminence in the Baltic.

The Era of Reform. With the accession of Christian VI in 1730, a period of social and economic transformation began. At first the peasantry took the brunt of the increased need of the state for a stable population able to provide an adequate soldiery. In 1733 a decree forbade the peasants to leave their farms, but criticism of serfdom as inefficient only increased. Trade prospered, however, especially under the mild reforming administration of Frederick V, who came to the throne in 1746.

Reform took on a sterner shape under the next monarch Christian VII, who ascended the throne in 1766. Christian was mentally ill for most of his life and came under the influence of a German physician, Struensee, an adventurer, who became the king's principal minister and the lover of the queen, Mathilda. The boastful Struensee ruled Denmark for a year and a half, attempting in that brief span of time to remake the entire kingdom according to the notions of the Enlightenment and with the methods of the sternest despotism. He reorganized the government finances, enforcing reductions on expenditures except those for himself and the queen; introduced civil and religious liberties for the population; and abolished serfdom and the guilds. But he disdained the Danes themselves and depended upon compulsion rather than persuasion to achieve his aims. His adultery with the queen gave his foes the opportunity to organize his overthrow. In January 1772 he was arrested, tried, and executed; the queen was driven out of the country.

Many of Struensee's reforms were discarded during the next decade. When Crown Prince Frederick assumed leadership of the government in 1784 the spirit of reform returned, but a different spirit, careful, patient, and respectful of public opinion. The abolition of serfdom was made permanent and civil rights were given to the nation. The Danish monarchy came to the forefront of enlightened states. The mad king lived on until 1808, while Frederick governed, monarch in all but name.

Norway. During these decades of Danish turmoil, Norway remained politically a part of the Danish monarchy but began to grow apart from the Danes in spirit and interest. It developed its own merchant fleet, particularly after 1740, when Danish neutrality in the War of the Austrian Succession safeguarded Norwegian ships from the perils of war at sea. The peasantry and timber cutters asserted their demands with new vigor. A revolt of the peasants in 1785 was put down, but the farming folk of Norway remained unsubdued and looked upon themselves as the leaders of the nation. Antipathy to Denmark grew stronger, intensifying the sense of Norwegian nationality. But no effort at separation was attempted; the Norwegians lacked all experience of political organization and leadership and possessed no separate agencies of government by which to acquire it.

VI. Poland

No nation paid more heavily than Poland after 1648 for its internal weakness in an age when its neighbors were gathering strength and appetite. Once the greatest power of eastern Europe, it totally disappeared as a state by the end of the eighteenth century.

The Bubble of Glory. The fate of the Polish nation had come to rest in the hands of a single class, the nobility-gentry (*szlachta*). It held a monopoly of both economic and political power. The wealth of the country lay in its fertile and extensive lands, which were owned in freehold by the nobility and worked by peasant serfs. The nobility were able to prevent the king from establishing himself as an autocrat, for the Polish crown lacked the means for taming its aristocracy: it had neither substantial revenues independent of the grant of the Sejm (Diet), nor a professional standing army worthy of the name, nor a bureaucracy to do the work of state. Instead the *szlachta* made its own power absolute by putting into practice the theoretical principle of the *liberum veto*, by which any single member of the diet could veto legislation and dissolve the assembly.

The Polish nobles keeping the royal power weak, nevertheless did not abandon their dreams of national grandeur and glory. During three reigns —of John Casimir, the last of the Swedish dynasty of the Vasas (1648-1668) ; Michael Korybut (1669-1673), and John Sobieski (1674-1696), both native Poles—the *szlachta* repeatedly fought in vast swarms of volunteer cavalry against Russians and Cossacks, Swedes and Turks. Not even Sobieski, who reconquered part of the Ukraine from Russia and won European fame by leading a Polish army to the relief of Vienna during the Turkish siege of

East Central Europe,
1772

1683, could command in his own country. He summed up his reign in a
sentence: "I won victories now and then but confess that I have no means
to save my country."

The Saxon Kings. The Polish throne, for all its deficiencies, tempted
candidates eager for its honorable title and confident that they could
re-establish the regal powers after centuries of atrophy. When Sobieski died
in 1696, the election in the following year was disputed between the elector
of Saxony, Frederick Augustus, and a Frenchman, Prince Louis of Conti.
The Diet split into two factions, each of which declared its own candidate
elected. The elector, who reached Poland before his rival, consolidated his
victory and compelled Conti to sail home. Augustus II (the elector's name
as king of Poland) joined with his principal foreign supporter, Tsar Peter
of Russia, in the attack upon Sweden in 1700 which opened the Great
Northern War. Charles XII, the Swedish king, followed up his victory over
Peter at Narva in 1700 by defeating Augustus near Cracow two years later.
Then in 1704 Charles arranged the election of a native Pole, Stanislas
Leszczyński, as king in place of Augustus. For five years Stanislas reigned

in Warsaw, until his protector's disaster at Poltava in 1709. Then Augustus returned to preside over the destinies of the Polish state.

The country was weak and desolate after the fierce fighting. The need for a strong state became obvious, but two opposite conceptions about the means to achieve it clashed head-on. Augustus wished to make Poland into a hereditary absolute monarchy after the model of Saxony; he contemplated using his Saxon troops and the assistance of Tsar Peter to enforce the change by a *coup d'état*. The nobility wished to entrust all governmental powers to the Diet and resorted to a "confederation" (a quasi-legal combination) to resist the king by arms. Peter of Russia, to whom both sides appealed, did not want a strong Poland and ordered the existing order preserved.

When Augustus II died in 1733, his son Augustus had to contest for the crown with Leszczyński, who presented himself as the defender of national independence. The War of the Polish Succession which resulted became a general European struggle. The peace settlement of 1735, which gave the Polish throne to Augustus III and the duchy of Lorraine to Leszczyński, was the work of the principal belligerents, France and Austria, with the opinion of the Poles given little consideration.

Under Augustus, Poland floundered in anarchy as king and Diet thwarted each other's efforts to govern. But the country remained neutral in the War of the Austrian Succession (though Russian troops crossed Polish territory at will), and the result was the recuperation of the people from their earlier war-caused hardships. The population grew in numbers; both farmlands and cities became more prosperous; and cultural life began to recover vitality, with France as its model. The preservation and continuation of these gains depended, however, on the good will of Poland's neighbors. After the death of Augustus in 1763 their benevolence could no longer be counted on—for in that same year the Seven Years' War ended, permitting Russia, Austria, and Prussia to give their attention to Poland, which lay between them.

The First Partition. Stanislas Poniatowski, elected as king in 1764, was a representative of the new Poland and the new Polish nobility that were emerging from the welter of confusion. Stanislas II was a charming and well-educated young man, alert to the ideas of the age and desirous to serve his country well in its time of need. His strength lay not in the royal office itself but in the fact that he was the nephew of two of the most powerful magnates in Poland, Michael and August Czartoryski. Empress Catherine II of Russia looked upon him benevolently, for he had been her lover before she came to the throne.

Poniatowski and the Czartoryskis led in the introduction of a whole series of reforms designed to give Poland a more effective central govern-

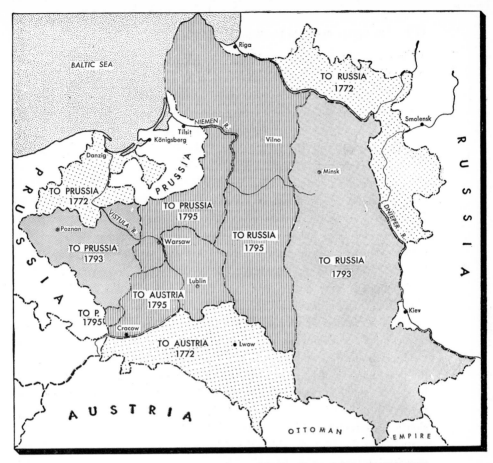

The Partitions of Poland, 1772-1795

ment, with better tax resources, a larger army, and a Diet from which the use of the *liberum veto* was barred. But neither Catherine II nor Frederick II of Prussia wished to see Poland overcome its political anarchy lest it become a strong competitor to themselves. In 1766 the essential reform—the abolition of the *liberum veto*—had to be abandoned at their insistence. They followed up with a demand for political equality with Roman Catholics for the "dissidents," as the Protestants and Orthodox were called. Russia and Prussia declared themselves the defenders of the Polish "cardinal laws"— the guarantees of Poland's weakness—against all change. A movement of resistance known as the "Confederation of Bar for the Faith and for Freedom" broke out in 1768, but was put down by the Russians. King Stanislas first supported the Russians and then attempted to settle the rebellion by compromise; but the preservation of his throne became his very first interest.

The insurgency of the Bar confederation furnished the pretext for the first partition of Poland in 1772. Frederick II took the initiative and Catherine II followed willingly; Maria Theresa took Austria's share reluctantly.

A Diet assembled the next year to approve the cession of West Prussia to Frederick, Galicia to Maria Theresa, and a section of White Russia to Catherine. Stanislas "howled with pain" at the news of Poland's amputation, but accepted the loss when the Russian ambassador threatened him with the loss of his crown.

The Second and Third Partitions. The warning that Poland could not survive without effective government, that she could not, in the contemporary phrase, "stand on nothing," was not lost upon the Poles. The Diet and the king set about the spiritual and political reconstruction of the nation. Six Diets met during the decade after 1776 without being "exploded" by the *liberum veto*. The principal achievement was to expand and improve the system of education in a short period, in order to provide the men, if not the institutions, for the coming trials of strength. The principles of the Enlightenment were taught, and even the delicate question of alleviating or abolishing serfdom was broached.

The beginning of war between Russia and Turkey in 1787 provided the opportunity for bolder action. A "Great Diet" assembled in 1788 and sat until 1792, devoting its efforts to making the eleven million Poles into one of the great nations of Europe instead of the helpless victims of covetous neighbors. A new constitution was prepared with Stanislas's assent and was presented to the Diet on May 3, 1791. It provided for a hereditary monarchy sharing sovereignty with the Diet. The nobility lost its monopoly of representation in the Diet, to which the cities would also send deputies. The new constitution was approved by the "Great Diet" and by the "lesser Diets" in the regions.

Not all the nobility accepted the reformed regime. Three magnates called upon Russia to upset the new constitution. Catherine responded by sending her troops into Poland to re-establish the old order. Two additional partitions, in 1793 and 1795, divided the rest of Polish territory among the victors. Leadership of the resistance was undertaken by General Tadeusz Kościuszko, who had served under George Washington in the American War of Independence. Kościuszko was forced back upon the methods of guerrilla warfare by the Russians and Prussians, who were determined to put down the threat of a free and strong Poland. Stanislas was compelled to abdicate in 1795. Prussian territory was extended to Warsaw, on the Vistula; Austria received the region around Cracow; and what remained of historic Poland was absorbed by Russia.

VII. The Ottoman Empire

The Ottoman empire fell far away from its earlier power and magnificence during the latter part of the seventeenth and the eighteenth centuries, but it avoided the total disaster which befell Poland. Turkey lay on the periphery of Europe, not in the very midst of newly strong states; and it repeatedly managed, when its prospects seemed darkest, to summon up from within itself fresh energies for a short burst of activity.

The governmental system of the sultans, in appearance perfectly rigid, changed subtly but importantly. The army and the political administration gradually ceased to be recruited from the Christian subjects by conversion of selected youth; instead the janissaries and the officials persuaded the sultans to permit them to marry and to pass on their duties to their sons, who were born Moslems. Inefficiency, corruption, and disobedience became rife.

The subject nationalities within the empire began to loosen the grip of Turkish power but were seldom able to throw it off completely except by becoming absorbed into other states. This change was generally the result not of their own decision, however, but of the wars between the Ottoman Turks and the neighboring powers of Europe, particularly the Hapsburgs, Venice, and Russia. The expansion of Ottoman territory was slowed and then halted by the early eighteenth century, but Christian reconquest was sporadic and limited. The Christian nationalities, which had generally maintained a strong sense of identity under the leadership of their priesthoods or their native nobility, began to develop their traditional culture and language and to have vague dreams of emancipation, by their own efforts or with the help of Christian Europe.

25

Europe beyond the Seas

1650 - 1815

IMPERIAL LEADERSHIP passed after 1650 from the Iberian peoples to the Dutch, the French, and the English. These newcomers competed for overseas territories as part of a larger struggle for paramountcy waged primarily in Europe: a world empire was for them a means of achieving strength at home. Nonetheless, like the Spaniards and the Portuguese before them, they carried not only European power but also European civilization beyond the seas. They too were the creators of new societies which applied the technology, the institutions and the ideas of Europe to a wide variety of institutions. Although in 1815 there were still broad stretches in several continents where neither Europe's knowledge nor Europe's power reached, the Europeanization of the world was continuing.

I. Exploration

The fever of exploration subsided in the seventeenth century only to take on new vigor in the eighteenth. Yet none of the new discoveries matched in importance those that had been made in the half-dozen decades beginning in 1492.

558

Discoveries by Sea. Mariners continued to find new lands, sometimes by deliberate search and sometimes—less frequently in the eighteenth century—by being blown off course. The major discoveries lay in the Pacific Ocean.

The finding of Australia and its sister islands to the southeast of Asia began in 1606 when a Portuguese pilot, Pedro Fernandes de Quiéros, led a Spanish fleet of three ships to the New Hebrides. He called them "Australia" (the Southern Land), but the name was soon transferred to the immense island reached by a Dutch ship later in 1606. The Dutch explored the western shores of Australia during the next three or four decades but did not establish themselves. In 1642 a Dutch explorer, Abel Tasman, sailed beyond Australia to an island later named Tasmania after him, and to nearby New Zealand. Other visitors to these lands came later in the century. One, the Englishman William Dampier, described his visits in 1688 and 1699 in widely read books. It was not until the voyages of Captain James Cook in 1769-1770, 1772, and 1777 that the eastern coast of Australia and the neighboring islands were thoroughly explored. The direct result of Cook's voyages was the establishment of an English penal colony on Australia's Botany Bay in 1788.

Scientific curiosity, which was Cook's primary motive, impelled other explorers in the eighteenth century to undertake voyages of discovery. The Frenchman Bougainville came upon the Polynesian islands, particularly Tahiti and Samoa, in 1768 and 1769. Bougainville and his crew suffered severely from scurvy during their long expeditions, but this mariners' curse was lifted by Cook, who introduced the use of citrus fruits (particularly limes) as a preventive. Cook returned several times to explore both the southern and the northern Pacific. He sailed as far south as latitude 60° without finding land, apparently disproving the existence of a southern polar continent. He met death in Hawaii in 1779 after reaching Alaska in a northward voyage. His subordinate, Vancouver, discovered Puget Sound some dozen years later and realized that there was no inland waterway between the Pacific and Hudson Bay.

The Pacific coastal region in America north of the Spanish territories in California came under the control of Russia instead of either Spain or Britain. Vitus Bering, a Dane in the Russian service, proved the existence of a strait between Asia and America in 1728 and returned a decade later to explore the northwestern shore of America. He was followed by other Russian explorers and traders, who established posts from Alaska to the region of present-day Oregon and northern California.

Discoveries by Land. European exploration of unknown inland regions did not wholly cease during this period but was confined mainly to investigation of territories already vaguely known.

Russia had already conquered a vast territory in Asia to which the general name of "Siberia" was given. Beyond the westernmost region of Siberia, adjacent to European Russia, the Russian authorities in the early eighteenth century still had only the sketchiest knowledge and power. In order to ascertain the extent and character of these possessions, the empresses Anna and Catherine II sent out expeditions under both Russian and foreign leadership. The Russian work of exploration and occupation of north-western America was merely a continuation beyond the Bering Straits of that already accomplished in Siberia.

Elsewhere in Asia, Englishmen pushed to and beyond the outer reaches of India. Samuel Turner entered Tibet, on the far side of the Himalayas, in 1783 and met its monk-king-god, the Dalai Lama. The peninsula of Arabia was almost totally closed to Westerners. The combination of desert, heat, and hostility thwarted the curiosity of Christian Europeans. Africa remained little known except for the fringe of coastline. In America the earlier over-land expeditions of Spanish conquistadores were matched in the vastness of their marches by the later explorers of inner North America. The region of the Mississippi and its tributaries was first investigated by Frenchmen from Canada and the Great Lakes. Western and northern Canada was pene-trated by Englishmen in the service of the Hudson's Bay Company.

II. The Battle of the Newcomers

The gigantic struggle for empire which boiled up in the second half of the seventeenth century and continued throughout the eighteenth seldom involved directly either the newly discovered lands in the Pacific or the already established colonies of Spain and Portugal. The contest was waged over the American lands which Spain had not occupied and the trading colonies of southern Asia.

The Rivalry of England and Holland, 1648-1674.   The decline of Spanish power, as attested in her double acceptance of defeat at Münster in 1648 and at the Pyrenees in 1659, whetted the appetites of the victors. The Dutch, the French, and the English all assumed that morsels of the overseas posses-sions of Spain and Portugal were theirs for the taking. Yet only shreds of these empires were lost to the coveters. An English fleet sent out by Crom-well captured Jamaica, a Caribbean island, in 1655. The Dutch seized Ceylon, off the tip of India, from the Portuguese about three years later, while Eng-land received Bombay, on the northwest coast of India, from Portugal as part of the dowry of Catherine of Braganza on her marriage to Charles II in 1661. These Portuguese losses were outbalanced by the success of Portu-guese settlers of Brazil in expelling the Dutch from Pernambuco. Spanish

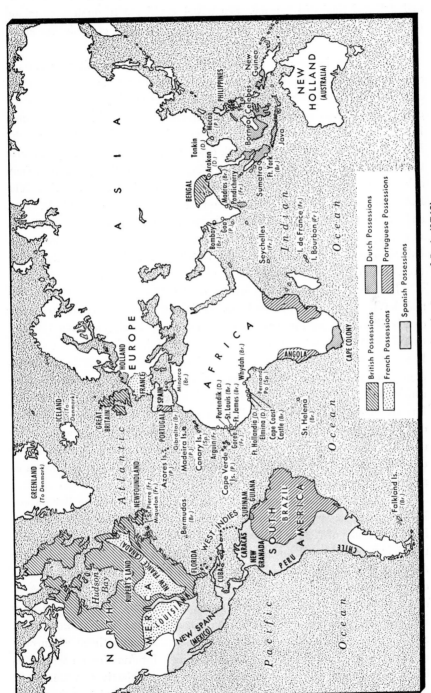

European Overseas Possessions after the Peace of Paris (1763)

mainland possessions in America likewise escaped the clutches of those who had defeated Spain in Europe. Sea power could not triumph over inland colonial empires which did not depend upon the "mother" countries for either minimal defense or prosperity.

The victors in Europe, being unable to sate their appetites on Iberian colonies, turned upon each other. Colonial rivalries were among the principal causes of the three Anglo-Dutch wars. The war of 1652-1654 brought no change in overseas possessions but demonstrated the startling improvement in the English war fleet, which now equaled and perhaps surpassed the Dutch. This increased naval strength enabled the English in 1664 to capture the Dutch colony of New Netherlands, lying between British North American colonies, as well as several Dutch trading stations in western Africa. The Dutch reciprocally captured Surinam, on the Guiana coast of South America, and their naval triumphs in 1667 in home waters led to the peace of Breda (see ch. 19, p. 437), by which England retained the New Netherlands (which became New York), and the Dutch kept Surinam. The third war (1672-1674) left the general equality of the two powers little changed.

The Rivalry of England and France, 1674-1763. The dependence of colonial developments upon the needs and decisions of the mother countries was clearly illustrated by the way in which the sharp rivalry between England and Holland was blunted by their common fear of the rising power of France. It was not in the colonies but on the mainland of Europe and in the immediately adjacent seas that this threat was great enough to override other considerations after 1674. The alliance of Britain and the United Provinces, formed in order to hold back France, continued as the kingpin of their diplomatic policies until 1748, when the Dutch turned toward neutrality for security against French invasion. During these seven decades the Dutch overseas territories were safe from attack by the English, whose naval superiority grew constantly stronger.

During the eighteenth century, the colonial rivalry between Britain and France played a larger part in their policies. The British took from the French as spoils of victory in the War of the Spanish Succession (1701-1713) the right to sell to and buy from the Spaniards on the "Main" and in the Antilles. The *Asiento* of the slave supply and the shipment of manufactures did not provide the English with the anticipated profits. They did not abandon the enterprise of colonial aggrandizement but shifted it to the prospering and competing French colonies in the Caribbean and in North America. Success there was linked to the fate of the wars on the continent of Europe: as the elder Pitt put the matter, England fought for America on the battlefields of Germany. Britain obtained most of these objectives at the end of the Seven Years' War (1756-1763). The English, choosing between the expanses of French Canada and Louisiana east of the Mississippi, on the one hand, and the sugar islands of the Caribbean, on the other, elected the mainland. Thereby they removed a dangerous neighbor from the British colonies on the coastal plain of North America.

The Crisis of the British Empire, 1763-1815. This decision soon proved to be a political miscalculation of the gravest order. After 1763 the British government attempted to compel the American colonists to share the costs of victory by placing new taxes upon them without their consent; in so doing, the home authorities imperiled what the colonists claimed as the rights of "free-born Englishmen." Resistance by the colonials was no longer dampened by dependence upon British arms for protection against France. The dispute over the right of taxation became a contest over sovereignty. A continental congress of the colonists in 1775 met the challenge of British repressive measures by armed resistance. The next year it threw off allegiance to the British crown and made good this declaration of independence by a successful war, with France as a mighty ally. The British admitted defeat in 1783 and acknowledged the sovereign freedom of the United States of America.

British statesmen learned the painful lesson of the war of American independence. Thereafter they treated with gentler courtesy the interests of the residents of the remaining settlement colonies in Canada and the Caribbean. The French Canadians in particular received important concessions: they were permitted to retain their traditional property law, and the British legislation restricting Catholicism was not applied to French Canada, where the Roman church was an integral party of society. Such measures preserved the loyalty of Canada during the war of 1812-1814 between Britain and the United States.

Britain emerged from the long wars against revolutionary and Napoleonic France with her empire intact except for the lost thirteen colonies, and even enlarged. The principal victim was not France, which had little left to lose, but the Dutch. When the French occupied the Netherlands in 1795, the British took the opportunity to seize the Dutch lands overseas. By the peace of Vienna in 1815, Britain kept for itself three valuable possessions: the Cape Colony, in South Africa; Ceylon, a key to India and the Indian Ocean; and the Malay peninsula. It returned the Indonesian archipelago to the Dutch, but with British merchants assured an equal position in the rich commerce of the region.

III. The Americas

In America, Europeans became the creators of new societies rather than the rulers and reshapers of old societies, as in Asia.

Spanish America. Despite the decrepitude of the Spanish monarchy, the colonies won by the *conquistadores* almost everywhere successfully resisted the incursions of the voracious newcomers in colonialism. Jamaica fell to the English in 1655. A century later, in 1762, France gave Louisiana west of the Mississippi to Spain. This vast empty territory was still a land of unexploited potentialities when Napoleon compelled Spain to return it in 1800 and when he sold it to the United States three years later.

The resiliency of the Spanish empire in America was only in small measure the work of Spanish arms or administration. To be sure, there was both military and governmental reform after the arrival of the Bourbon dynasty in Spain in 1700; but the principal strength of Hispanic America lay in itself, in its economic and social organization. The various regions of Spanish America were largely self-sufficient in necessities, produced in plenty by their own ranches and plantations; most luxury goods were imported, but their lack did not weaken defenses. Spanish imperial government was more rigid in form than in fact. The Bourbons could stiffen centralization beyond even the Hapsburgs; but they were no more able than their predecessors to govern lands many thousands of miles distant with clear knowledge, rapidity of command, and certainty of obedience. Below the top level of colonial administration, still entrusted only to those born in Spain, the work of government came almost totally into the hands of Creoles (*criollos*), the numerous class of Spaniards born in America.

This apportionment of function was ultimately disastrous to Spain's control of her American empire. During the eighteenth century the Creoles grew away from the mother country in spirit and purpose. Their prosperity increased rapidly, in some part through evasion of the restrictive channels set by Spanish law for colonial foreign trade. Instead of buying and selling only through Spain (with the exception of the British "permission ship" after 1713), the Creoles connived with British, Dutch and (to a lesser extent) French smugglers. Thus they learned to see Spain's supremacy as a burden not a benefit, and to look with growing scorn on the king's claims of omnipotence. By the end of the century, Creoles called themselves Americans, not Spaniards. Their self-confidence and self-assertiveness increased as they read the tracts and books of the Enlightenment, which penetrated into the Spanish colonies despite the bans of the Inquisition and the Madrid officialdom.

The price of Spanish haughtiness and weakness was demanded after Napoleon displaced the Bourbon dynasty in Spain. A series of revolutionary outbreaks by Creoles seeking independence broke out throughout Spanish America. The rebellions were not all immediately successful, but by 1822 Spanish sovereignty remained intact only in the Caribbean islands of Cuba and Puerto (Porto) Rico. The societies of Spanish America remained largely that of the motherland even after independence: Spain's civilization and culture triumphed as her empire fell apart.

Utopia in Paraguay. Spanish America also witnessed a novel and bold experiment in social engineering during the seventeenth and eighteenth centuries, an attempt to create a "perfect" society in Paraguay under the aegis of the Spanish crown, with the Guaraní Indians as the subjects of the venture and the Jesuits as its directors. In 1607 the Jesuit order was empowered by royal ordinance to administer the region between Brazil and Chile—primarily the upper valley of the La Plata river. The Jesuits brought more than a hundred thousand Guaranís, a people already accustomed to agricultural life, into thirty "reductions," or vast farm communities. These were theocratic Utopias organized on the basis of communal agriculture, with no money in circulation to corrupt the natives' innocence. Nor was there personal freedom for them: the whole round of work and life for the Guaranís was directed by the Jesuits in total detail. The Jesuits were the only Europeans permitted in the communities: indeed, in order to keep the "reductions" safe from European contamination, the Indians were not taught Spanish but their directors instead learned Guaraní.

The experiment was the first in European history to see the ideas of Plato and More on the "ideal" social order applied to a large population, although one wholly foreign to the tradition of Western thought and institutions. Nonetheless—or, it may be, for that very reason—Paraguay prospered. The population increased to 400,000 in the eighteenth century. Prosperity brought the envy and the greed of the Europeans barred from the fertile region. Portuguese from the São Paulo region of Brazil and Spanish ranchers attacked the "reductions," which were defended by Jesuit-trained native armies. In 1750 seven "reductions" were ceded to Portugal; the remainder lasted only until 1766, when Charles III of Spain ordered the expulsion of the Jesuits from America. They quit Paraguay, leaving their charges helpless to take over the management of the "reductions." The Guaranís returned, as best they could, to their former ways. "Utopia" on the La Plata was no more. But Voltaire enshrined its memory in literature in a famous chapter of *Candide*.

Brazil. The relation of the Portuguese colonials in Brazil toward Portugal was stamped from the 1640's with the marks of self-dependence and loyalty at the same time. It was the colonists, not the Portuguese of the homeland, who drove out the Dutch and reasserted the sovereignty of Portugal. The ensuing period was one of increasing wealth and activity. Gold and diamonds were discovered in the Minas Gerais region and produced huge profits for the mineowners and valuable revenues for the Portuguese crown. Agriculture remained the livelihood of most colonists. To work the mines and the plantations, large numbers of Negro slaves were brought in from the Portuguese possessions in Africa. Trade was freer of restraints than in Spanish America, because British merchants were admitted after the expulsion of the Dutch. The fidelity of the Brazilians to Portugal and to the reigning dynasty of the Braganzas continued unimpaired throughout the Napoleonic period despite the political turbulence in the home country.

The Caribbean Colonies. Colonial rivalries were particularly fierce in the Caribbean area. Imperial appetites were whetted by the great profits produced by the plantation economy of the Caribbean. Many of the islands were peopled by colonists from several nations, and wars in Europe were usually (though not always) accompanied by clashes in the colonies: often, indeed, the colonists did not wait for these occasions to fight. Island colonies depended more than mainland possessions upon naval power, but no power established a clear-cut and lasting preponderance at sea until Nelson's triumphs over the French in the early nineteenth century.

The cultivation of commercial crops, especially sugar, developed on a very large scale during the seventeenth and eighteenth centuries. The intense use of the soil caused its rapid depletion, and hence a constant need for new, still fertile land. The Spaniards lost many of their possessions to land-hungry rivals—notably Jamaica to England in 1655 and Hispaniola, Columbus's first establishment, to the French by the treaty of Ryswick (1697)—but they retained their hold on Cuba, largest of the islands. The lesser Antilles were seized by French, English, and Dutch settlers. The English and French interest lay primarily in the establishment of plantations, the Dutch in forming trading stations convenient to their smuggling commerce with Spanish America and to their other, more or less legal, markets in the other colonies.

The immense need for labor on the plantations was met by the massive importation of Negro slaves from Africa. This trade in human beings, already begun in the sixteenth century, expanded enormously during the two following centuries. The Caribbean was one of the principal markets for slaves, the others being Brazil and the southerly colonies of British North America. The Dutch took the lead in this trade, as they did in almost all other seafaring enterprises. After about 1650, however, other nations—particularly France and Britain, but also such lesser powers as Sweden and Brandenburg —attempted to compete with the Dutch as slavers. Most successful were the British, whose slave ships became very numerous in the eighteenth century.

Piracy, sometimes in the legalized form of privateering and sometimes as outright brigandage at sea, took strong hold in the Caribbean. There were valuable cargoes to be plundered, numerous harbors in which to take refuge, and frequent wars to furnish pretexts. Somewhat reduced by the presence of strong naval forces during the eighteenth century, piracy was extinguished in the early 1800's when Britain established its unquestioned maritime preponderance in the area.

French Canada. Canada long remained the stepdaughter of the colonizing powers, but to its own advantage. It was a poor land in a cold climate, at a time when men seeking wealth abroad hunted "El Dorado" in tropical regions. Canada's principal resources were the fur trade and agriculture. Trapping and trading of furs gave occupation to a small number of men, large profits to even fewer, and little revenue to the state. Farming was more important, though it produced only enough taxes to pay for local government, without advantage to the French crown.

Canada was fought for not so much for itself as for the interests of adjacent territories: Newfoundland, with its plentiful fisheries athwart the mouth of the Saint Lawrence; British America, which burgeoned with vitality to the south; and Louisiana, the French territory established in 1682 in the vast empty valley of the Mississippi. In this struggle the advantage of numbers lay easily with the British, who had more than a million inhabitants in their coastal colonies while the French Canadians numbered about 65,000 in 1763. Nonetheless they found it difficult to strike effectively at Canada. The Canadians were a vigorous people who had taken the moribund manorialism of France and given it new life in the valley of the Saint Lawrence. Having no age-old burden of piled-on dues, rents, and banalities, the peasants lived in close connection with their manorial lords, in mutual dependence and affection. A single church, the Roman Catholic, furnished spiritual leadership and tightened Canadian unity and cohesion. The colony was in theory governed autocratically from France but in practice was allowed to live under the mild administration of governors and intendants who served for long periods and identified their interests with those of the colonists. Though there was little immigration, the population increased twenty-fold in little more than a century.

British Canada. Britain nonetheless conquered Canada because it gained command of the seas during the Seven Years' War. However strong-knit the society of French Canada, it had too scant numbers to withstand the combined assault of the British navy and army and the colonial militia. The Peace of Paris in 1763 sealed the passage to Great Britain of sovereignty over Canada.

Desiring little more than to maintain British authority in this area, and unencumbered by the demands of long-established interests, the British government avoided offense to French-Canadian sensibilities. When the new subjects protested the introduction of the English legal code, complaining that it upset their French-derived system of property rights, particularly in land, the old private law was re-established; but English public and criminal law, which provided numerous safeguards absent from the French system, was maintained. Another measure to preserve the obedience of the Canadians was the decision not to introduce into Canada the various English laws against Catholics.

The British grip upon Canada was further tightened when numerous

"Tories," expelled or fleeing from the United States because they had opposed the rebellion, settled in Canada. Some went to the maritime provinces (Nova Scotia, New Brunswick), others opened up the frontier regions west of Montreal and north of Lake Ontario, which became known as Upper Canada (in contrast to Lower, or French, Canada). These emigrants were even more firmly attached to the British cause than the French-Canadians, but both groups spurned the appeals of the "Americans" (as the citizens of the independent United States called themselves, arrogating to their own use the adjectival name of two continents).

British America. Britain's greatest success in transplanting her civilization—and her greatest failure from the standpoint of colonialism—was in British America: the colonies on the Atlantic seaboard from Georgia to Maine. They were a dozen differing "little Englands" and a much-Anglicized "little Holland" (New York): the pattern of life reflected the mother culture in the mirror of a new country.

The various groups of settlers, ranging from gentry through merchants and artisans to impoverished farmers and day laborers, brought over their distinctive manners and attitudes; but once across the sea they and their descendants began to modify their habits and beliefs, sometimes subtly and sometimes with bold strokes. The absence of a class of great aristocrats made the "gentleman" landowners of the South and the merchants of the North the leaders of Society. Beneath them, in North and South alike, the small independent farmers were more self-confident and assertive than their compeers in England, the tenant-farmer yeomanry. In the towns the "mechanics," or skilled workmen, were a proud and often truculent group. A new civilization, basically English and yet significantly different, began to emerge on the shores of North America.

Economic Life. In general, the economic life of the region south of the Potomac differed fundamentally from that of the North, while both were unlike the frontier economy on the fringes of settlement to the West, in the foothills of the Appalachians. The southern economy was based on the production of cash crops, principally tobacco, rice, and later cotton, on large plantations worked mainly by Negro slave labor. It was peculiarly sensitive to the swings of the commodity market, for prices depended not only on the supply in America but also on market conditions in Europe, far beyond the colonials' control; nonetheless they put the blame for difficulties on British merchants who tricked them out of their profits. The northern economy was based on individual farming, with foodstuffs the principal crops; a substantial surplus beyond the farmers' own needs was produced in the more fertile areas for sale in the towns and abroad, principally in the West Indies. The fisheries of New England were another important supplier of food for the export trade of America.

The towns, which formed a thin crust of urban life on the sea edge of the civilization, combined market activities with extensive handicraft enterprise; thus they were linked to the British market. But any tendency to extend productive activity to articles reserved for British manufacturers, like hats and ironware, resulted in sharp conflict with the home authorities. Another source of conflict was smuggling, in defiance of the restrictions of mercantile legislation upon direct trade with the West Indies, especially the Spanish and French colonies. Smuggling was so widespread and so generally accepted as a form of normal commerce that the taint of criminality was usually absent and enforcement of penalties was bitterly resented. Contraband goods supplied a large part of the colonial market.

The frontier economy comprised, almost exclusively, isolated subsistence farming. A minimum of surplus was brought to market. Often transport was so difficult that grain could be transported a distance only in the form of whiskey.

The Loss of British America. Though the British Americans remained "Englishmen" in law and loyalty, they were acquiring in the eighteenth century an independence of character and purpose unbefitting to "colonials." They were accustomed to self-government. Miniature parliaments had been established in the colonies, with powers to legislate and grant taxes. Since executive officers, from the governor down, were paid by the colonial legislatures although appointed by London, the power of the purse—whose potentialities for controlling public policy had been amply demonstrated in England's own history—remained in the colonies. The conflict of authorities which thus lurked beneath the surface of political life did not come into the open before 1763. The mercantilist laws as they were enforced, or rather neglected, claimed more than they obtained. The British Parliament took for granted its ultimate right of control over the colonies but interfered little in practice with their local affairs. The colonists for their part were so dependent upon British arms for safety against the encompassing power of France in Canada and Louisiana that they beseeched the mother country for more aid, not less.

This dependence changed with the downfall of French power on the American continent. The colonies of British America ceased to need the aid of the homeland at the very time when Britain decided to stiffen the framework of mercantilism and to make the colonies share the costs of a war largely fought in their interest. Since the colonial legislatures would not graciously contribute new taxation for this purpose, the British Parliament and Crown enacted a series of such measures, beginning with the Stamp Act of 1765, on their own authority. The colonists replied with sharp resistance. In part, they were reluctant to carry any additional burden of taxes, for they already were deeply in debt to British merchants. In part, they felt that their liberties as "Englishmen" depended upon maintaining control over the state which they could exert only through their own legislature, not through a British Parliament to which they sent no members.

The British government, though it interspersed attempts at conciliation with efforts at enforcement, would concede no inch on the principle of its supremacy. Colonial resistance slipped into illegal violence, British coercion into suppression of colonial political freedom. The appeal to arms came in 1775, when the Continental Congress met as a revolutionary government. The next year the Congress declared the thirteen colonies independent from Great Britain and presented themselves to the world as a new federal state, the United States of America. In 1783 the British acknowledged American sovereignty. For the first time, a European colony had been lost not to a rival power or to a resurgent native populace but to the offspring of the founding nation. The United States represented both the failure of European mercantilist colonialism and a test of the ability of European civilization to survive and grow when politically severed from its roots in Europe.

IV. Africa

Africa, where European overseas expansion had begun in the fifteenth century, held minor interest for colonizers in the subsequent three centuries. Its importance lay in its position across the sea route to the East Indies and in its being a source of slave labor for the plantation economies of America.

Portugal lost its position as the sole European nation with possessions on the west shores of Africa. The Dutch, English, and French, as well as lesser European states like Brandenburg, seized trading and slaving stations from the Portuguese. On the east coast, Portugal retained its hold on several mainland ports. A French colony on Madagascar, an island off the coast of East Africa, lasted only some twenty years (1665-1686) before being destroyed by the native population. The Dutch colony established at the tip of South Africa grew slowly and steadily. The Boers of the Cape Colony adapted Dutch institutions, which had arisen in a land of canals, shipping, and trade, with agriculture mainly truck and dairy farming, to a ranching world, dispersed and lonely. Dutch culture, religion, and language, all carefully preserved by the Boers, nonetheless began to evolve into a distinctive pattern. The easy adaptability and tolerance of the homeland Dutch, characteristic of a trading people, gave way to harsh rigidity of personality and principle.

Inland Africa, both the tropical jungles and the upland plateaus in the center of the continent, long remained impervious to European penetration. The first important explorations were those of the Scottish surgeon, Mungo

Park, up the Gambia and Niger rivers in 1795-1796 and 1805-1806. By the early nineteenth century the dense ignorance of Europeans about the interior of Africa began to be pierced, but there was still no entry of Europe's political and economic influence.

V. Asia

Much of southern Asia, along the Indian Ocean, fell under the control of Europeans. The eastern empires of China and Japan also met the influence of Europe, but examined and rejected it.

India. The subcontinent of India, although the first part of the East reached by Europeans, remained lightly affected by them through the seventeenth century. The Mogul empire, established by Moslem invaders from central Asia, continued to be the preponderant power in India; but its lack of maritime interest or forces, and its willingness to tolerate European traders while it grappled with rival Indian potentates, enabled the newcomers from faraway Europe to maintain their lightly held positions.

Portugal held the ports of Goa and Bombay, on the west shore. Goa became a bit of Portugal in a strange and often hostile land where it rooted its Catholic religion, its culture and architecture and language. Bombay, further north, was given to the English in 1661. The Dutch held Ceylon and several small trading posts, but gave their main attention to the Indonesian archipelago; they did not effectively interfere with the activities of their principal competitors in mainland India, the French and English East India companies.

These two companies operated in similar ways. They confined their activities as much as possible to commercial transactions and courted the favor of the Indian rulers in whose lands they bought and sold. Politics was not their concern: even when the home countries were at war, the companies remained at peace, however uneasily and precariously, because they lacked and did not want to pay for the instruments of war.

British India. The unofficial truce between the English and French East India companies was shattered after 1741 as a result of the initiative of two bold men, the Englishman Robert Clive and the Frenchman Joseph Dupleix, who became the chief resident officials of their respective companies. Confronted by the political chaos in India which had developed after the death of Aurangzeb in 1707, they did not bow to the stiffly commercial policies of their masters back home but struck out on their own. When rulers in whose territories the companies possessed stations demanded military help, previously little wanted or given, Clive and Dupleix furnished them small but well-trained European contingents which braced the large native armies. The companies thereby became entangled in the skein of Indian native politics and found themselves at war with each other. Despite the angry protests of the directors, Clive and Dupleix accepted direct political roles for their companies, first as vassals and later as quasi-sovereign potentates.

In the campaigning, which coincided in time with the period of wars over the Austrian Succession in Europe, Clive had the advantage of superior English naval power, which assured him a steadier and larger supply of reinforcements and supplies. He was finally able to defeat Dupleix and to make India into a reserve for British expansion. The Dutch and the Portuguese, who had remained neutral, were not expelled from India, and the French were permitted to remain in Pondicherry.

India under the rule of the British East India company remained in an anomalous position. The company did not want the political responsibilities with which it was saddled and was unwilling to bear their costs. It became necessary therefore for the officials in India to draw the revenues necessary from the population by means of taxes. The company was thus linked to the system of large-scale landownership and rack-renting which encompassed India. Gift taking and outright corruption became rampant among the company personnel.

In England sharp conflicts arose over the extent of the control to be exercised over the East India company by Crown and Parliament. The trial of Governor-general Warren Hastings on charges of corruption (1788-1795) revealed the weaknesses of the company as an instrument of government. Though Hastings was acquitted, a compromise was patched up by which the company continued to rule India, to its great profit, but itself came under the supervision of royal commissioners in London with particular responsibility for the governing of India.

Indonesia. During this same period the Dutch East India Company expanded and consolidated its rule over the vast Indonesian island group. Where possible it avoided establishing its own direct government; in most cases the native princes, once subdued or bought over, accepted the company's suzerainty and its trading regulations designed to reinforce the Dutch monopoly. The remnants of English trading stations were expelled, notably at Poeloe Run in 1664 and Bantam in 1685. Thereafter, though some English smugglers filtered in, the Dutch maintained their commercial supremacy.

Beneath the surface, however, the company subsided into a slack traditionalism. Its sole concern was to pay out dividends at a rate sufficiently high to keep up the price of company shares. During the eighteenth century dividends ranged from 22 to 40 per cent of par value, though the selling price of shares was much higher. The rate of profit earned began to decline, owing to the competition of the English and French in India and the growing corruption of company employees in Indonesia. The practice of borrowing upon the company's still excellent credit concealed its difficulties but compounded them in the future.

China. No land in the East tempted the Europeans with its wealth and products more than China, but the "Empire of the Middle" did not go the way of India and Indonesia. Its ancient system of government and society remained vigorous and confident, and was easily able to fend off unwanted thrusts of European power. The Portuguese continued to hold their trading station at Macao, near Canton, but were unable to confine all European commerce to this single port. Elsewhere European merchants were few in number and utterly dependent upon the distrustful Chinese authorities. The Europeans' bargaining position was weak, for China wanted few goods from them, while the visitors hungered for a variety of Chinese luxury goods.

Where European merchants were barely tolerated, European intellectuals were welcomed and even lionized for a period of some decades in the seventeenth and early eighteenth centuries. These were Jesuit missionaries whose skills as mathematicians, astronomers and administrators won the admiration of the Emperor K'ang-hsi (1662-1722). During his reign many Jesuits were employed in the government service and thus received the opportunity to present their religious ideas on favorable terms. They deftly discovered numerous similarities or apparent identities between Confucian and Christian beliefs, and adapted Catholic rituals to such Chinese practices as ancestor worship. Numerous conversions demonstrated their missionary prowess and they established twenty-seven residencies in many parts of China.

The whole enterprise toppled in the eighteenth century. At the instigation of the rival Franciscan and Dominican orders, the Jesuits were forbidden to use their "Chinese rites" by Pope Clement XI in 1704 and 1715. Subsequent papal edicts banned the departure of Jesuits for China, where their numbers dwindled rapidly, particularly after the inception of persecution by anti-Christian emperors after the death of K'ang-hsi. The experiment in mutual adaptation between Christianity and a native Eastern religion was relatively brief, but its temporary success was perhaps more remarkable than its eventual failure.

Japan. The problem of Christianity also played a central part in the relations between the Europeans and the Japanese. The fear felt by the Japanese authorities for the conversion activities of Catholic missionaries had already resulted in the repression of the intruding religion by the middle of the seventeenth century. In 1638 an edict closed Japan to foreigners, especially Europeans. The Dutch were permitted to remain on Deshima islet, in Nagasaki harbor, which became the sole window between Japan and the outside world. Through it fragments of European culture continued to reach Japan, which watched with wary curiosity the approach of a power which it little understood and much feared and mistrusted.

26

The Emergence of
Industrialism and Capitalism

1650 - 1815

THE EIGHTEENTH CENTURY saw the beginning of the economic transformation of Europe. From a world of predominantly agrarian activity overlaid with commerce and industry, a world struggling to pull away from the brink of never-distant famine and hardship, it began to grow into a new industrialized society of fabulous productivity. The heart of the change was the invention and the utilization of power-driven machinery in industrial production upon a scale unprecedented in history.

Capitalism triumphed along with industrialism. It brought not only the capacity to meet man's age-old aspiration for plenty but also novel disturbances and increased complexities in the process of economic life. Europeans continued to face grave problems in their efforts to earn a livelihood.

I. Industrialization

So momentous and so gigantic was the transformation of the European economy, which began during the century after 1750 and principally in England, that historians applied to the change the most dramatic description

574

they knew: they called it "the Industrial Revolution." Though in no sense a sudden innovation, the Industrial Revolution was truly an immense quickening of processes already present in European economic life.

Necessity. The two characteristic figures of the Industrial Revolution were the entrepreneur, who organized the new enterprises, and the inventor, who designed the new equipment. Their immediate incentive was the knowledge of growing markets for goods and a confidence in their ability to supply them more cheaply and in larger quantities than ever before.

The first cause of the expansion of demand was the renewal of population expansion in Europe. Most of the seventeenth century had been a period of demographic doldrums, when even the more favored countries did little more than hold their own, while those directly stricken by wars suffered steep declines in numbers. In the eighteenth century, particularly after the Peace of Utrecht, the re-establishment of general peace saw a resurgence of prosperity and population increase. This movement was halted only briefly by the mid-century wars and resumed at a rapid pace after 1763. As a result, the needs of an expanding population began to press upon the relatively fixed supply of products from factory and workshop. The resulting rise in prices encouraged businessmen and inventors to an even more intense effort to develop new devices for expanding production. Thanks to the commercial expansion of the previous two centuries, ample capital was available for investment in manufacturing enterprises.

Invention. The inventive minds of the eighteenth century did not start from scratch, nor were they solitary geniuses working in strange ways on unfamiliar tasks. They built upon the experience of many hundreds of years of mechanical experiment, upon a keen awareness of the problems of invention and a readiness to innovate; the technical conservatism of the guilds had hampered but not stifled inventive creativity, especially in newer fields of production and outside the towns. The inventors came from varied backgrounds. Some were mechanics with skillful hands and inquisitive minds. Others were scientists applying their knowledge of natural laws to practical problems of production; and others were laymen who saw a need and had to learn the elements of the processes of production.

The predominant handicraft method of industry had come close to its limits of productivity. It had developed great ingenuity in making tools, the mechanical devices for transforming the material being worked upon; but it required the skill of an artisan to direct the tool, so that the amount of power that could be exerted was limited by his muscular energy. The expansion of production therefore depended upon use of sources of power able to provide greater and more sustained force than the human muscles; this power was necessarily applied through machines, in which the guidance of the tool was performed by mechanical parts, instead of depending upon the skill of a workman. Though the operations became simple and distinct, in combination they could accomplish complex tasks beyond human strength, at far greater speeds and with complete accuracy.

The various branches of invention spurred each other. The availability of machinery to be driven encouraged the creation of new devices, "prime movers," to provide power; while the availability of power made possible the construction of large-scale machines.

Factories. The introduction of big machinery made necessary the concentration of production into factories, thereby eliminating both the workshop of the artisan and the domestic workroom of the cottage laborer. Only in the factory could the new prime movers—at first water mills and later great steam engines—be linked directly to the machines. Furthermore, the division of labor could be more rationally organized, with little time wasted in the movement of materials. Not least, the supervision of the workpeople was far simpler in a factory, for labor was assembled under a single roof.

Since the "skills" were built into the machines rather than trained into men, it became possible to assign many tasks of supervising the machinery to women and children, who were employed in great numbers. Unskilled and semiskilled hands received less pay than highly trained craftsmen, so that the new cities which grew up around the factories were centers of penury and misery. Life was brief for most. Long hours of toil in dingy, drafty buildings were commonplace; often entire families, adult and child, man and woman, drudged from daybreak to nightfall. Yet labor came as it was needed, from the countryside, where the enclosure movement cut many thousands from the land, and even more from the displaced labor in the towns. The cities continued to grow: the transformation of Europe from a rural to an urban civilization was well under way.

Textiles. The first and largest of the new factory industries was the manufacture of textiles, particularly cotton. Cloth was the most widely used manufactured commodity, for even before the Industrial Revolution handicraft production of cloth in the home—production by the wearers for their own use—had been very largely replaced in Europe by a mixture of handicraft and simple machine production for the market. The primary fabrics had been wool and linen, and their production had been principally in the hands of the guilds. The "putting-out" system of production had already broken the monopoly of the guilds by the beginning of the eighteenth century, and introduced capitalist forms of organization and direction. It was about the same time that cotton fabrics from India were introduced to the European market and caught the fancy of women for their lightness and comfort. Efforts of wool and linen producers to bar the importation or manufacture of printed cloth failed against the insistence of style-conscious women. Because cotton was a new fabric, no guild system had grown up about it, and there was no barrier of custom or authority to halt improvement of the methods of its manufacture.

The principal difficulties in the way of increased cloth production lay in the processes of spinning and weaving. The problem of mechanical spinning was solved by Richard Arkwright and James Hargreaves around 1770. The mechanization of weaving resulted from a series of major inventions, notably John Kay's "flying shuttle" of 1733, which carried the thread across the loom faster and further than was possible by human hand; and Edmund Cartwright's "power loom" of 1785. The first power looms were operated by water power, but from 1803 steam engines were increasingly used to drive them. Cotton thread in sufficient quantities for the new industries became available only after 1793 when the American Eli Whitney invented the "cotton gin" for removing the seeds from raw cotton. Techniques for weaving designs into fabrics originated chiefly with the Frenchmen Vaucanson and Jacquard.

Metallurgy. Large machines required stronger materials for their construction than the traditional wood, with iron (or other metal, especially brass) used mainly on the working parts. A market arose for great quantities of iron in various forms—wrought, cast, and steel in particular—but technical problems made it difficult to supply them adequately. These concerned both fuel and ore. The need to burn charcoal in heating the iron ores was one obstacle to increased production. By the seventeenth century the exhaustion of the forests endangered the iron industry in England and other countries. The only other fuel available was coal; but impurities in coal spoiled any iron it was used to heat. Most small iron foundries had drawn up local supplies of bog iron, which were quickly depleted. Iron ore was often spoiled by excessive amounts of impurities; only the famed Swedish ore was pure enough to be used without difficulties. Increased production therefore required some methods of removing the impurities from the available ores.

These problems were largely, though not completely solved, by the efforts of English metallurgists during the eighteenth century. The fuel difficulty was overcome by Abraham Darby of Coalbrookdale, who developed coke as a fuel in 1709. This was coal heated in the absence of air to drive off impurities, a process essentially similar to that by which wood was converted into charcoal. It was not until late in the century, however, that the prejudices against the use of coal in any form were overcome and coke became the general fuel in ironmaking. In 1784 Henry Cort, who had invented a rolling mill to produce sheet iron, devised the process of "puddling" to make wrought iron. Cort's method was to take pig iron (as the crude bar iron was called) and heat it in a furnace lined with limestone, away from direct contact with the fuel. The molten iron was stirred, permitting the impurities to boil off and be absorbed by the limestone. Puddling permitted the use of most iron ores other than the excessively phosphorous ore of Lorraine.

The use of power-driven machinery was particularly valuable in metal production. At around the time when Cort invented his rolling mill, Isaac Watt devised a steam hammer which delivered 150 blows a minute with a force of 120 pounds. Not long before, John Wilkinson took out a patent on a power drill for boring cannon; it could also bore cylinders for steam engines. Thus the development of devices for military purposes once again served other, peaceful needs: war both hampered and spurred economic growth.

The Steam Engine.   The problem of power supply was not fundamentally solved until the invention of the steam engine in the eighteenth century. Until then relatively large volumes of power could be developed only from water wheels and windmills, which could be placed only where streams flowed and wind blew, and were subject to seasonal and other variations. The need for a steady power supply, available where needed, was particularly acute in the mining industry, where drainage pumps were essential in all but the most shallow mines.

During the seventeenth century, efforts were made to apply scientific principles to the solution of this problem. The Frenchman Denis Papin, among others, constructed primitive devices for the use of steam as a motive force. This work led to the invention of an effective steam engine by the Englishman Thomas Newcomen in 1708. In Newcomen's engine steam was introduced into a cylinder closed off at one end by a piston; when the cylinder was doused with cold water, the steam condensed and atmospheric pressure forced the piston inward. The movement of the piston was transmitted to a mechanical water pump.

The Newcomen engine, though soon put to work in mines, was inefficient. A more effective engine was designed in 1765, and patented four years later, by James Watt, a Scotsman employed at the University of Glasgow as a laboratory assistant. Watt used the expansive force of the steam to drive the piston outward, and permitted the steam to cool outside the cylinder in a separate condenser. In 1782 he built a double-acting engine, in which steam drove the piston alternately from either end. Typical of Watt's further improvements to the steam engine was a centrifugal governor for controlling speed of operation. The construction of Watt engines was undertaken by a company formed by the inventor with a businessman, Matthew Boulton, who provided the necessary capital and entrepreneurial skills. Engines were built for mine pumping, the original use, for driving machinery in mills by means of shafts and belts, and wherever large amounts of power were necessary. By 1800 about 500 steam engines had been built by the firm of Watt and Boulton.

Mining. The extraction of raw materials from the subsoil increased in importance as the demand mounted for ores and fuels. To be sure, the mining of precious metals in Europe declined in the face of the competition of American treasure. But the extraction of ores of the metals used in industry, particularly iron but also copper and tin, became more important.

No less important was the rapid development of coal mining. England, as the heartland of the new industrialization, was favored by the presence of thick seams of coal in South Wales, the Midlands, and the Newcastle area. In Europe the Belgian regions of Liége and Hainaut also rapidly expanded their older mine enterprises. When the mines were sunk to new depths, new difficulties developed, particularly flooding and gas leakage. The utilization of the deeper veins was made possible by the more efficient steam-driven pumps. Another important mining innovation was placing the coal carts upon rails, usually made of wood covered with iron strappings, so that they could be propelled more easily; but human beings still performed the labor of dragging the laden wagons.

Transportation. The pattern of transport changed more slowly. Ships, boats, and barges remained the most economical way of conveying both goods and men any distance. The technique of high-seas sailing changed little, though there were a multitude of detail improvements in the design of vessels. Inland waterways remained of essential importance; rivers continued to be the principal channel of trade, but there was a sharp increase in the number and extent of the canals linking the rivers together in a more efficient network. In canal building, as in so many other things, France and England were the principal rivals. The Languedoc canal across southern France connecting the Mediterranean and the Atlantic was one of the monumental accomplishments of Colbert's administration in France. The English river and canal system, however, particularly after eighteenth-century expansion, excelled the French in general.

Transportation by land depended upon the road network. The French system, previously much inferior to that of the Low Countries, was vastly improved during the eighteenth century. A royal corps of road and bridge engineers was established, with an excellent training school. The establishment of the royal corvée provided them with a supply of local labor to maintain the French highways. But the major technical innovation in road construction was made in Britain. Roadways of dirt packed hard by the hooves of passing animals and the wheels of wagons were seldom able to resist drenching rains and heaving frosts, and soon degenerated into morasses or wheel-breaking ruts. Two Britons, Thomas Telford and John McAdam, devised similar systems of road construction adequate to the new demands. Their method was to build up the roadway in several levels, with large rocks beneath, smaller stones above, topped by gravel; a convex cross-section and parallel ditching assured adequate drainage to keep the roads dry. This system was named "macadamizing," in honor of McAdam, and remained the principal method of road construction for more than a century.

II. The Financial System

The economic growth of Europe, though in the first place an increase in production, also involved an expansion of the financial system. More efficient banks and credit mechanisms and a more stable and usable currency were closely linked to the accumulation of capital for investment on the scale required by the new industrialism.

Banking. The emergence of banks as central institutions in economic life was both effect and cause in the increasing prevalence of capitalist enterprise. The scope and complexity of commercial transactions, especially during the great upsurge of the eighteenth century, were such that the relatively primitive and personal methods of the previous age became inadequate. Banks took over on a year-round basis the fiscal work of the seasonal fairs: the transfer of funds, the balancing of accounts, the conversion of money, and the grant of credit. They also began to make the currency more flexible by the issuance of paper money. A variety of banks appeared which specialized in one or more of these various functions.

A few purely government banks were simply adjuncts of the fiscal system of the state. They simplified the payment of taxes, arranged transfer of funds, accepted deposits for safekeeping, and usually issued paper currency. They generally did not make loans, except to the governments on an emergency basis. The Amsterdam Exchange Bank, established in 1609 by the municipality, was the model bank of this kind. Other similar banks were organized in Hamburg (1609), Stockholm (1656), Vienna (1705), St. Petersburg (1760), Berlin (1765), and Copenhagen (1776).

The Bank of England, founded in 1694, was the most important of the semipublic banks which combined the foregoing functions with those of a central commercial bank. It was not a branch of government but a joint-stock company owned by private persons and operating under a parliamentary charter. Like the French "tax farmers," it enabled the government to anticipate future revenues by means of loans; but tax collecting remained a state function. It issued banknotes upon the basis of its holdings of metal coinage, but avoided the temptation of inflationary overissue. The bank also discounted (bought below face value) commercial paper, i.e., credit instruments issued by business firms in the course of trade. To an increasing extent, however, the Bank of England came to deal with other banks rather than with individuals. Its success in linking the various elements of the business life of England into a single strong and flexible mechanism resulted not only in the extraordinary fiscal strength of the British state during the eighteenth century, but also in the underlying stability of English economic life which was so favorable to the spread of the new industrialism and capitalism.

Private banks, which were common in England, France, Switzerland, and Holland, engaged in commercial banking, particularly in accepting deposits and making loans. They were the usual sources of loan capital for entrepreneurs. The continental private banks did not ordinarily issue banknotes, as did those in England during the earlier part of the eighteenth century. This privilege was taken from the English private banks when they dangerously overextended their issues; the Bank of England then became the sole bank of issue.

Exchanges, Credit, and Companies. The instruments for extending credit changed little during the period between 1650 and 1815, except for greater precision and refinement. More significant was the further development of the system of exchanges, where transactions, often upon a credit basis, were arranged. These transactions covered commodities, money, securities and the underwriting of other transactions. The earliest of these exchanges had been opened at Hamburg in 1558 and London in 1566; others were established at Lyons, the commercial center of France, in 1653, in Paris in 1724, and at Venice in 1771. The development of an exchange for stocks in joint-stock companies began informally in London during the eighteenth century, but the Stock Exchange came into formal existence in 1802. The use of acceptances and endorsements of bills of exchange was greatly extended. In this way certificates acknowledging an obligation entered into the course of exchange instead of remaining with the creditor until due. Their negotiability was improved by stiffening commercial law and making its provisions more precise. A class of professional "bill brokers," specializing in the buying and selling of such credit instruments, came into existence; although at first looked upon as preying upon business, the brokers increased the flow of trade by making bills more instantly and easily salable.

The development of joint-stock companies provided another important means of increasing the entry of capital into business enterprises. The important features of these companies were that they made possible the combination of many relatively small sums of capital into quantities adequate for costly commercial and industrial operations, and that investors were obligated only to the extent of their investment, not to that of their total personal resources, as in personal, family and partnership firms. The "Bubble Act" passed by the British Parliament in 1720, in order to counteract the speculative mania that had followed the establishment of the South Sea Company (see ch. 20, pp. 456-457), restricted the formation of such companies to those granted a charter by special legislative act, but nonetheless they continued to increase steadily in number.

Money and Prices. The change in the character of economic life was facilitated by the increasing stability of currency. The influx of gold from Brazil in the eighteenth century increased the supply of precious metals to meet the expansion of trade. Inflationary recoinages for the purpose of extracting temporary profits from lowering the metal content of currency became less frequent. Britain in particular stabilized its currency during the eighteenth century, and adopted a virtual gold standard in 1774. Bimetallism, with both gold and silver serving for coinage at varying ratios, was more usual. The effective volume of currency was increased beyond the actual holdings of metal by the wider use of credit instrumentalities and by the introduction of paper currency, usually for large denominations and serving principally in making large payments.

Prices responded to the varying pulls of changes in the supply of currency and of commodities. After the great inflation of the sixteenth century, a period of slow shading off began between 1610 and 1620, and continued till about the end of the great war of 1672-1679. A slow rise in prices from about 1680 to 1700 was followed by another period of stagnancy. An upward movement in prices began between 1725 and 1750 and continued till after the end of the Napoleonic wars. The expansion of the currency had been largely balanced by the increase of production.

III. Trade

Commerce continued to be an extremely important producer of wealth in the period after 1650.

Its general character changed little. Retail distribution continued to be performed by small shopkeepers, often the handicraftsmen themselves, in the towns, and by peddlers in the countryside. Wholesale distribution, on the other hand, increasingly came to be the work of chartered and joint-stock companies, although the traditional private firms still played the largest role. Specialization was less common than supply to a general trade.

A large number of colonial products came into the European market. Spices played a less important part in overseas trade than before, though the amount and the variety of spices actually increased. Tobacco, tea, coffee, and cocoa entered the market, while sugar for the first time became available as a product of mass consumption. The fish supply came to consist more of cod taken off the coast of North America than of herring from the North Sea. Cotton became a fabric for common folk to use.

The growth in the volume of foreign trade was especially large during the eighteenth century. The tonnage of goods passing through English ports increased about sixfold during the period; France increased its volume of foreign trade about fourfold between 1716 and 1787. Trade actually grew faster than industrial production. The expansion of commerce was not limited to the Atlantic countries. Hamburg on the North Sea developed largely as a supplier of the Central European lands, while on the Mediterranean Livorno (Leghorn) and Trieste also grew rapidly.

IV. Agriculture

Agriculture also began to change during the same period. More efficient techniques of production were introduced and important changes occurred in the ownership of land. Indeed, the agricultural transformation might well be called an "agrarian revolution" paralleling the better-publicized "Industrial Revolution" of which it was ultimately a part.

Farming Methods. The central problem in improving the output of agriculture concerned the relationship between crops and the fertility of the soil. One difficulty lay in the system of allowing a field to lie fallow every three (or even two) years in order to "rest"—that is, to restore fertility. Another consisted in the heavy dependence upon grain crops to provide bread cereals for the population.

The method of improvement had been devised before the seventeenth century by the farmers of the Low Countries who supplied the crowded urban industrial population of that region. They maintained the fertility of the soil by the use of fertilizers, animal manures in particular, in much larger than previously usual quantities; but this method required livestock to be kept in larger numbers, which in turn required larger quantities of hay for winter fodder. This could only be provided by the cultivation of hay crops, such as alfalfa, on regular fields, instead of dependence upon the natural grasslands of the meadows, and even less upon the leafage of woodlands. The Low Countries farmers also introduced new crops which aided rather than depleted the soil. The most important of these was clover, which fed nitrogen to the soil where it was grown as well as providing a cover crop of livestock fodder. The use of turnips as a food crop for both animals and humans was important because it broke up the soil and did not exhaust it.

The introduction of potatoes from America was another important innovation. Potatoes could be grown on lands which would not sustain most grains, and they produced large quantities of carbohydrate nutrients per acre. The taste for potatoes grew slowly, however; they were first accepted by the peasantry in Ireland, but as late as the reign of Louis XVI in France the king needed to make propaganda against the belief that the plant was poisonous by wearing its flower and eating dishes prepared from the tuber.

English Agricultural Experiments. The principal area of agricultural experimentation in the eighteenth century was England, where the break with tradition was very strong. Charles Viscount Townshend, retiring to his country estates after failing in politics, adapted Netherlandish practices such as rotation of grains with clover and cultivated hays; his insistence upon the use of turnips to break up the soil won him the nickname of "Turnip" Townshend. His disciple, Thomas Coke of Holkham, systematically applied the principle of a four-crop rotation, and achieved impressive results. Jethro Tull concerned himself with problems of tillage practices; he emphasized the clearing of weeds from between the crop plants in order to conserve soil nutrients, and invented a mechanical seed drill to sow on a straight line. Tull's conviction that such practices would obviate the need for fertilizer was soon disproved, but their advantage in combination with other techniques was clear. Robert Bakewell was primarily an innovator in careful selective breeding; he developed sheep lines for their meat rather than wool, as well as dairy and meat cattle and dray horses. In line with his interest in livestock raising, Bakewell emphasized the production of improved grass crops. The improvement achieved by Bakewell was rapidly visible and dramatically effective.

The new agriculture won its most effective propagandist in Arthur Young, who began publication of the *Annals of Agriculture* in 1784, described the results of journeys to France and other European countries a few years later to compare continental agricultural conditions and practices, and was appointed secretary of the newly founded Board of Agriculture in 1793.

Despite the widespread interest in these innovations, they were not all instantly adopted. The large landowners were much more forward than the cautious smaller tillers, who could not take the risk of failure.

Enclosures. It was virtually impossible to introduce the new techniques under the old system of manorial or quasi-manorial agrarian organization. Enclosure in one or another form was requisite. This consisted in replacing the open fields, divided into numerous strips, by compact fields enclosed by fences or hedges.

Two methods of enclosure developed. One was applied in England, where serfdom was totally absent and manorialism had degenerated to a form of landholding with associated rights, rather than remaining in any important sense the medieval system of collaborative agriculture. The enclosure movement of the eighteenth century in England differed fundamentally from that of the sixteenth century, which had been directed towards turning arable land to sheepruns. The new movement was primarily concerned with replacing open fields by unified fields where new principles of tillage and crop rotation could be followed, and with conversion of common lands to tillage. The basic principle followed was that a specific act of parliament was required after the various possessors of rights had come to an agreement.

Landlords often used either wiles or pressure upon the poorer farmers to compel them to accept enclosure; the latter received compact farms of their own, but without the right of access to wood and pasture which had been so available. Cottagers, often technically squatters without rights, were usually dispossessed without recompense. Many large tenants, however, remained in a favorable situation, for they received big unified farms to till; only a relatively small number of the great estate-owners actually tilled all their acres with hired labor. In 1801 a General Act permitted general enclosures under the authority of justices of the peace.

In Eastern Europe enclosure took place on a quite different pattern. There the peasants were forced into outright servile status at the same time that they were largely displaced from ownership (or hereditary tenancy) of the land. The landowners consolidated their holdings into large farms which were generally sown to grain crops and tilled by both compulsory and hired labor.

V. Theories of Wealth and Welfare

The economic expansion of Europe was accompanied by the attempt to develop a theory of the character and proper goals of economic life. Formal economic theorizing dated back to such writers as Jean Bodin in the sixteenth century and Antoine de Montchrétien, whose book, *Traicté de l'oeconomie politique* (*Treatise of Political Economy*), published in 1615, gave to the new science the name of "political economy," which is still current in continental countries.

Political Arithmetic. One of the most important aspects of the new thinking about economic matters was an attempt to go beyond moralizing judgment, essentially over the avoidance of sin in business life, to description of the actuality of economic life. Nonetheless the new economics remained centrally concerned with the choice of proper and effective action.

It was realized that vague generalizations would not suffice for the needs of the new science. Numbers—notably of lands, goods, ships, factories, workshops, consumers, workers, employers, farmers—were required for accurate description and for the calculation of the consequences of economic activity. The associated sciences of vital and economic statistics therefore came into being, especially in England. In 1662-1663 William Petty, a thoughtful English man of business, wrote his *Political Arithmetic, or a Discourse concerning the Extent and Value of Lands, People, Buildings, Husbandry, Manufactures, Commerce, etc. etc.* The book, published in 1691, was used as argument in favor first of mercantilism and later of antimercantilism. Petty's friend John Graunt developed the field of vital statistics and began the calculations which ultimately led into the modern science of demography. He used "bills of mortality," the reports on deaths required by the government, as well as parish records, to calculate the birth and death rate. At the end of the eighteenth century Thomas Malthus, looking upon estimates of population and economic growth, propounded problems of the possible expansion of population at a rate considerably greater than that of the farm production necessary to feed them.

Mercantilism. The dominant economic theory in the seventeenth century is now generally known as "mercantilism," a term adapted by a nineteenth-century German scholar from Adam Smith's phrase "the mercantile system." In its own period it had no specific name, and indeed was not felt to be a body of scientific doctrines and principles akin to those of the natural sciences; it rather was an aspect of the art of good government, and its tenets arose out of practical considerations.

Mercantilist policies were economic means of achieving the welfare of the state more than they were political means of achieving the welfare of economic groups. The particular policies and ideas adopted by the French minister Jean-Baptiste Colbert under the reign of Louis XIV have commonly been taken to be typical of "essential" mercantilism, but the policies adopted elsewhere differed widely from this norm, according to the character and needs of the particular states. Mercantilism did not originate as a clear-cut theoretical system before it was put into practice, but was rather a theoretical clarification of existing practice as well as an argument for specific changes in policy. In the German territorial states, where the ideas enunciated in western Europe during the seventeenth century became a subject of university courses during the eighteenth, the name "cameralism" came to be applied to mercantilist theory, because its concern was with the policies developed in the monarch's "chamber" or office.

Mercantilism reckoned with a number of salient developments in European life: the great expansion of economic activity; the concurrent expansion of currency; the extension of long-distance trade; the acquisition of overseas colonies; and the rise of territorial states as distinct units of welfare and policy. Among its central and basic assumptions was the right of the monarch to exercise control and practice initiative in the economic life of his country, arising partly from his status as proprietor-in-chief and partly from that as principal servant of the state.

Bullionism. The primary purpose of mercantilism was to assure the state an adequate supply of money—the "sinews of war" and in general of political power. It sought not the welfare of the state or its people taken in the abstract and in isolation, but rather competitively; for the strength of one state depended on its position relative to other states; their weakness was equivalent to its own strength. Transposed into economic terms, this strength meant having more of the "sinews of war" than other states, whether by increasing one's holdings of money or by decreasing the holdings of other states: a general increase on an even scale meant no advantage. States therefore endeavored to increase their holdings of precious metals (in the unminted form as bullion and in coinage). Underlying this doctrine was the assumption that with money one could always buy the necessities of war, and that it was more feasible and more economical to stockpile money than men or materials. It was desirable, therefore, to acquire as much bullion as possible. The acquisition might come through mining precious metals within one's own lands, as Spain did from the sixteenth century and Portugal in the eighteenth in America; or from outright capture, as with the privateering and piratical expeditions of Spain's competitors in England, France, and the Dutch Republic; or from exporting more goods than one imported, so that the importing country had to pay in cash for the surplus.

"Treasure by Foreign Trade." Mercantilism had as its basic idea the principle that the state, in order to be able to extract taxes from its subjects for its own needs, had to favor their economic development, especially in such lines as produced taxable wealth. Tariffs were therefore used to protect domestic manufacturers, so that profits and wages remained within the state and hence were available for taxation. Thomas Mun, in his *England's Treasure by Forraign Trade* (1664), urged that export be permitted and even favored when the goods bought in the exchange could be processed and resold within Europe at even higher prices. This principle became general in mercantilist countries. The colonies were mere adjuncts of the colonizing power in mercantilist doctrine and practice: their primary purposes were to supply needed raw materials and to purchase manufactured goods from the "mother" country. The English Navigation Acts required that goods shipped to and from Britain be carried on its own ships (or those of the supplier), thus excluding the Dutch from this profitable trade once the English built enough ships to handle it. Measures were sometimes adopted to eliminate internal barriers to trade and manufacture, such as tolls or the restrictive practices of guilds.

The Dutch, because of the special nature of their economy, favored free trade and free shipping, although they protected domestic industries. Their practice with regard to their colonies contradicted their theory, for in the West they were interested in breaking into the colonial monopolies of other powers, while in the East they endeavored with great vigor to maintain their own exclusive domination, especially of the Indonesian archipelago. The interests of private entrepreneurs had very great weight in the determination of government policy, especially in periods when the control of the House of Orange was absent or weak.

Physiocracy and Laissez-Faire. The very success of mercantilism in aiding the consolidation of commercial capitalism and the development of industrial capitalism created the conditions favorable to new doctrines critical of mercantilism, both in the narrow sense of a system of restrictions and in the wider sense of a system of governmental direction and control of economic life. The entrepreneurial class became wealthier than ever; theoreticians and public officials, impressed with the success of businessmen, more and more thought them able to continue their activity on their own, free of government controls. New economic doctrines began to appear, which culminated in the theory of *laissez-faire* (that is, of government noninterference). These doctrines, like those which they criticized, linked the welfare of the state and the prosperity of the nation, but shifted the emphasis from the state to the citizenry and minimized the desirability and efficacy of government intervention.

Pierre Le Pesant de Boisguilbert, who died in 1714, argued against political interference with economic activity on the grounds that it was controlled by natural laws of universal application. This became the fundamental principle of the new schools of economic thought. His doctrine did not gain attention, however, until it was taken up by François Quesnay later in the century. Quesnay, by profession physician to Madame de Pompadour, the mistress of Louis XV, founded the school of economics known as physiocracy. Quesnay expressed economic laws in mathematical form in his *Economic Table*, published in 1758. The physiocrats maintained that agriculture alone created wealth, while commerce merely changed its place and manufactured its shape. The physiocrats therefore held that only land should pay taxes, that no landowner should be exempt, and that all taxes and burdens upon the land should be reduced to a single tax. They also advocated reform of tillage practice by such means as permitting enclosures and abolishing the right to pasture livestock in a field after harvest.

Adam Smith. In Great Britain the philosopher-moralists David Hume and particularly Adam Smith emphasized the commercial and industrial aspects of the new theories.

In his *Essays* (1752-1753), Hume attacked the central mercantilist doctrine that wealth consisted primarily in money. He denied that a nation was richer when it changed goods for money to obtain a "favorable balance of trade."

Smith, in his *Inquiry into the Nature and Causes of the Wealth of Nations* (1776), went beyond Hume's cursory remarks to a full-scale analysis of economic life. Smith maintained that the source of all wealth lay in labor, a doctrine already put forward by John Locke; but he assigned interest and profits to capital and land rent to the landowner, as well as wages to labor, as just rewards in the economic process. He emphasized unification of the national market and favored low prices to produce large sales. He favored international division of labor and "freedom of trade," with tariff barriers reduced to the minimum required for revenue purposes and for protecting industries vital to national defense. His key doctrine, however, was that an "invisible hand" led men seeking their self-interest to achieve the interest of the nation by increasing production.

Though Smith had in mind the example of the older handicrafts rather than the new machine production, his *Wealth of Nations* became the handbook of the economists of the new industrial age in Great Britain.

27

Arts, Thought, and Science in an Age of Reason

1650 - 1815

THE THOUGHT AND ART of Europe in the period from 1650 to 1815 largely lived under the twin signs of classicism and Enlightenment. Classical antiquity, re-created and modernized in the Renaissance, continued to provide the staple diet of writers and artists, as of education in general. Contrariwise, science, which the Renaissance had hampered no less than assisted, broke loose from the dead weight of Aristotle to achieve magnificent success in understanding the physical world. Emboldened by the triumph of natural science, social and political thinkers subjected age-old institutions to sharp-edged criticism and created the ideas for a revolutionary epoch.

I. The Arts

The delight and inspiration that Renaissance writers and artists had found in the recapture of antiquity was replaced in the seventeenth and eighteenth centuries by an easy familiarity with accepted forms and styles. Even those who proclaimed the virtues of the moderns over the ancients were mainly imitators of antiquity and the Renaissance. Their new styles were for the most part only the old styles refurbished.

590

SANTA MARIA DELLA SALUTE. Church designed by Baldassare Longhena, built 1631–1656. Venice.

The church dedicated to "Saint Mary of Salvation" is an example of Italian baroque architecture. The basic forms are those of Renaissance neoclassicism, but to these have been added a wealth of elaborative detail. The sculptural whorls linking the lower rotunda to the cupola are a characteristic device. Yet the unity and harmony of Renaissance art have not been wholly lost. (Bettmann Archive)

Baroque, Classicism, and Rococo. The dominant style at midpoint in the seventeenth century was baroque. The name was applied in the first instance to a new pattern of architecture, but was used by later historians and art critics to describe the other art forms of the period as well. It was a style easier to describe in a particular art than to analyze in broad esthetic and psychological terms. In general it emphasized complexity over simplicity, decorative detail over the basic line of structure, a striving for immediate impact over the slower but longer-lasting harmony of high Renaissance forms. It was at its best in describing and creating the mood of intensity: the clashing of strongly held beliefs, of passions in equipoise, of incompatible colors, shapes, sounds astonishingly resolved into a unified work of art. The heyday of the baroque was the seventeenth century, especially the first half. In so far as Johann Sebastian Bach is accepted as the supreme composer of baroque music, the style achieved perhaps its greatest height a century later, when it was already long outdated in the other arts.

The Renaissance forms grew more directly into another style quite unlike the baroque except for its impressive manner. This was classicism (more exactly, neoclassicism), so-called because it defined and organized the artistic rules derived from classical antiquity. Harmony, balance, gravity

were its mood; an apparent ease of craftsmanship that concealed the difficulties of working according to a fixed esthetic rule was its method; and the
life of royalty, nobility, and churchmen—the great ones of the land—was its
subject matter. The classical reminiscence characteristic of the high Renaissance was retained: drama, painting, sculpture, and architecture all cast most
of their material into the classical mold. Neoclassicism, which first arose
distinctly in the period just before 1650, triumphed during the reign of
Louis XIV in France and remained the principal form of the arts during the
eighteenth century.

"Storm and Stress." During the eighteenth century the various styles
derived from the Renaissance became formal, pedantic, and dry. The rules
which emphasized the permanent and the typical were obeyed but the effect
sought thereby—to catch nature in a characteristic pose—was lost. For the
emotions, bypassed or suppressed, artists sought an outlet in new style forms.

One new form was the rococo. It was a reversal of the solemnity of
neoclassicism. The rococo style resembled baroque in its love of ornamentation but differed from it in its feeling. It was playful, not impressive; its
colors were light, not deep; its shapes small and whimsical rather than large
and majestical. This gay-hearted style suited the pleasant living, free from
worry and want, such as the aristocracy of Europe lived, or pretended to
live, before the outbreak of revolution in 1789.

Closely linked with the rococo was the school of sentimentalism, which
sought to move the spectator or reader to tears. Its language and forms,
however, resembled those of neoclassicism, emphasizing purity and generality.

Greater success in unifying mood and method was achieved by the
"Sturm und Drang" (Storm and Stress) movement in Germany, and by
similar developments elsewhere, particularly in Great Britain. These movements arose in the latter half of the eighteenth century and were harbingers
of the intense passions of the revolutionary age that was about to break.
The typical gave way to the particular and unique, universal character to
local color, and calm depiction of crisis to all the turbulence of open passion.
The ideal of harmony was abandoned for the sake of what was felt to be a
more lifelike variety. Subject matter changed, too, from the lives of the
great to the careers of ordinary men; if kings and nobles were portrayed,
they shared the qualities of ordinary men. "Ordinary," however, meant the
plain "middle class" or bourgeoisie rather than the numerical majority, who
were usually sunk in poverty and lacked the refining virtues of education
and economic self-dependence.

The Graphic Arts. The vogue of the graphic arts did not diminish
during the period under consideration, but there was a general decline in
vigor and originality. Rembrandt was the last Dutch painter of the very
first rank in Holland's Golden Age, as was Velásquez in Spain's. Craftsman-

RETURN OF THE PRODIGAL. Painting by Rembrandt Harmensz. van **Rijn,** about 1663. The Hermitage, Leningrad.

The tragic sense of the aging Rembrandt is nowhere better seen than in this work, one of his last. Technical mastery has become only a means for creating a world in which human frailty, love, and forgiveness meet. The details are realistic—the half-shod son, the Jewish father drawn from the Dutch Jewry among whom Rembrandt lived—but the total impression is that of a reality sensed, not seen. Perhaps no artist more than Rembrandt rose above the styles of his own age—to say that he is baroque is to remark what is least important in him.

ship did not suffer, but its very successes often lay in the camera-like accuracy of the *trompe-l'oeil* ("fool the eye," meaning the effect of literal reality) school.

Portraiture continued to be an important activity of painters, as all monarchs and most nobles, rich men, and famous men desired to have their

likenesses fixed in oils for future times to admire. The qualities of psychological penetration and honesty as well as sublimity of esthetic creation found
in the best of the Renaissance portraits were seldom present in the works of
the later period. Indeed, the sculptor Houdon achieved such effects with his
taut-nerved marble of the sardonic Voltaire more fully than any painter.

More successful were the other genres of painting. Landscape painters
continued to observe nature, with the subtleties of light perhaps the center of
their interest. The Italians caught the pure intensity of their native sky, the
Dutch repeated on canvas their clouds and their cloud-grayed land and sea,
the English the misty browns and greens of their woods and grasslands. Still-
lifes, using subjects of little inherent interest, came into increasing favor, not
only as examples of *trompe-l'oeil* but also for their qualities of design and
color.

Little change took place in the art of sculpture. It continued to be
largely a form of portraiture for kings and generals, although bas-relief
statuary depicting mythological and classical figures was frequently employed
in architecture. Materials and methods remained virtually the same as had
been used during the Renaissance.

Architecture. As befitted an age of palaces and churches, architecture
continued to be a favored art form. In fact, the successive variations of the
Renaissance style received their names principally from names first given
to architectural innovations. Display remained the principal purpose of great
buildings; they became increasingly magnificent, with an emphasis on
grandeur of dimensions and variety and wealth of decoration. Louis XIV's
own palace, planned and built at his order at Versailles, became the model
both of the neoclassical style and of royal residences elsewhere. In the
eighteenth century, however, rococo became more popular. It was expressed
in the preference for smaller, daintier buildings, many of them virtually life-
size dollhouses for real people. The elements of architecture remained principally the Renaissance classicism, with its mixture of ancient and modern
methods of construction and ornamentation. During the eighteenth century,
Horace Walpole's Gothic revival at his country residence of Strawberry Hill
in England captured the fancy of a public upon which the sedate harmonies
of the Renaissance had palled.

Music. As during the Renaissance, music remained the most independent of the esthetic forms. Its emotional content, particularly when linked
with poetry as in song, paralleled that of the sister arts. In this respect,
music shared the style development of the period: baroque, neoclassicism,
rococo and early romanticism. Yet musical language remained separate, with
a distinct pattern of technical development.

Folk music continued its separate way, furnishing themes and rhythms
to composers but itself little affected by formal music, which was the affair

VOLTAIRE: THE BENIGN SKEPTIC.
Sculpture by Jean-Antoine Houdon,
1781. Vestibule of the Théâtre Fran-
çais, Paris.

Stone here portrays the personality
of the great *philosophe*—the thin smil-
ing lips conveying his sardonicism, the
rest of the face his underlying good
will; the forward-leaning pose suggests
his eagerness for action, and the firm
grip of his hands upon the arms of the
chair his strength of will. Draping the
figure rather than showing it in contemporary clothing was a favorite device of eighteenth-century neoclassicism.
The quality of physical and psychological realism is Houdon's personal contribution. *(French Government Tourist
Office)*

principally of the church, the aristocracy, and the professional musicians who
served them. The family tradition, by which sons learned their craft as
singers and instrumentalists from their fathers and succeeded them in their
employments, remained intact throughout the period. It was from their own
ranks that most composers arose. Musicians often wrote for their own
performances, not for the use of others. However, the grand works—opera and
to a lesser degree church music—began to be composed for sale. The abyss
between professional and amateur musicians remained deep: Frederick the
Great of Prussia might write for and perform upon his beloved flute, but no
man of rank could dream of earning his livelihood by such means.

The period from the late seventeenth to the early nineteenth century was
one of very great creativity both in the development of new musical forms
and in the composition of works of supreme genius as well as of steady,
meritorious talent. Instrumental music saw the emergence both of symphony
orchestras (large assemblages of many and different instruments) and chamber ensembles (small groups, usually of essentially similar instruments), and
of musical forms adapted to them. The primary form was the dance suite,
a series of contrasting movements based on folk dances, with Johann Sebastian Bach's French suites and Brandenburg concerti the outstanding achieve-

595

ments. From the suite, Bach's son Carl Philip Emmanuel developed the sonata, with fewer but more highly formalized movements; the sonata became the basic pattern of most instrumental music throughout the eighteenth century and into the next period. Besides sonatas for solo instruments, there developed from this same form symphonies for large orchestras and chamber music for small groups, with string quartets (for two violins, viola and cello) the most important of these forms. The masters of symphonic and chamber music were Joseph Haydn, who served the Esterhazy magnates in Hungary as resident musician-composer; Wolfgang Amadeus Mozart, whose career was short and, after his childhood success as a pianist prodigy, never economically stable or prosperous, though hardship did not halt his extraordinary productivity; and Ludwig van Beethoven, who built a successful livelihood as a pianist of extraordinary technical power and a composer whose prowess as a musician was matched by the depth and power of his feeling.

The development of opera was affected by changes in literary fashion as well as in musical taste. The Italian opera provided the basic form, upon which Lully, an Italian who settled in France as composer for Louis XIV, developed a true neoclassical style. Italian opera became more and more a medium for singers displaying their talents rather than one for the expression of musical ideas, until late in the eighteenth century Christoph Willibald von Gluck deliberately turned to expressiveness. Mozart followed the various schools of his time but infused them with his own extraordinary gifts.

Church music as such developed little, except for the numerous hymns of the Protestant churches. Music on religious themes, however, continued to be written. Composers set to music the words of the mass and of selected passages from the Bible, in such forms as the Lutheran chorale of Johann Sebastian Bach and the oratorio as practiced particularly by George Friedrich Handel, a German who settled in England.

Poetry. Poetry, most subtle and musical of the verbal arts, lost these very characteristics: the increasing rationalism of the period in its quest for explicitness made poetry more like prose. The French critic Boileau laid down the rules in an *Art of Poetry* (1647) dominated by the spirit of cold reason. In Boileau's own time poets such as La Fontaine, a reteller of fables, and Racine, greatest of France's dramatic poets, obeyed the critic's rules without losing a very subtle music of their own; but after them poetry in France declined for almost a century into an efficient verse that almost never sang. A similar movement dominated English poetry of the late seventeenth and early eighteenth century; its supreme achievements were the spirited satires of Dryden and the didactic works of Pope. The epic poems of John Milton were out of joint with the times and had few followers. Elsewhere in Europe the same aridity was characteristic of most poetic work.

Not until the second half of the eighteenth century did the essential qualities of poetry reassert themselves. The change was most notable in Germany, with the onset of *Sturm und Drang* and early Romanticism, soon reaching a peak of achievement in Goethe and Schiller. In Britain, similar developments began with a revival of ancient ballads, including the spurious "Ossian" works. The Scotsman Robert Burns revived the folk poetry of his Lowlands home and the Englishman William Blake created poetry (and illustrations for it) marked by a mysticism long absent from English verse. With Wordsworth and Coleridge came the creation of an explicitly Romantic poetry, frankly and intensely emotional. In France, the neoclassical tradition remained stronger in poetry, despite the influence of Rousseau and his plea for natural emotion. Poetic drama in France remained stilted and traditional in its imitation of the great masters of the Grand Age of Louis XIV. In Germany, however, it experienced a birth of vigor in the works of Goethe, whose model in his early work was Shakespeare.

Prose Forms.   Prose writing, unlike poetry, flourished.

The principal form of narration became the novel, with the poetic epic almost totally abandoned. A variety of techniques were developed, some directed toward the strong storytelling interest of the earlier picaresque novels which was now represented at its purest in Defoe's *Robinson Crusoe* (1719). Others were directed toward the analysis of emotions and ideas, perhaps most typical of these being *Manon Lescaut* (1731), the Abbé Prévost's sentimental tale of a pair of ill-fated lovers of weak character. Rousseau made the novel into a vehicle for the presentation of his theories in such works as *Émile* (1762), a tract on education according to the rule of natural expression, and *La Nouvelle Héloïse* (1760), which expressed his views upon natural morality.

The essay developed into a form of increased power and variety. It moved in the hands of the Englishmen Addison and Steele beyond exposition and analysis to the uses of entertainment, while Voltaire turned it into an instrument of wit and criticism.

Historical writing moved in two directions. On the one hand, the tradition of history as a purely literary form remained strong, resulting in works of dramatic narration like Voltaire's *History of Charles XII* (of Sweden—1731), or broad philosophical interpretation like Gibbon's *Decline and Fall of the Roman Empire* (1776-1778), or shrewd though often partisan analysis like Hume's *History of England* (1753-1761). The development of historical erudition and historical science, though not always separated from the creation of historical literature, nonetheless was usually a separate activity, pursued by monks carefully editing the works of the early fathers or medieval theologians or compiling saints' lives, or by antiquarians hunting down the simple slippery facts about the past.

II. Science

The purest success achieved by the period that proudly thought of itself as an Age of Reason came in the field of natural science.

The New Physics: Newton.   In the early seventeenth century, Galileo had stated clearly the most significant problem facing those who attempted to understand the physical universe. This was to bring together into a single mathematical explanation the motions of celestial and terrestrial bodies. He had glimpsed, too, the character of the solution, but did not achieve it. The solution was the work of the Englishman Newton. In his masterpiece, *Philosophiae naturalis principia mathematica* (*Mathematical Principles of Natural Philosophy*, 1687), Newton successfully described the motions of bodies on earth and in the heavens by identical general laws. The First Law stated that bodies at rest or in motion continued at rest or in motion at constant speed unless slowed, speeded, or changed in direction by an external force. The Second Law supplied a quantitative relationship between the force and the change of motion. The Third Law stated a principle of balance, that for every motion of a physical body there was an equivalent but opposite motion. Another centrally important Newtonian law related the movement of bodies to their mass and their distance from other bodies, according to the rule that every material body in the universe attracted every other body with a gravitational force directly proportional to the product of their masses and inversely proportional to the square of the distance between them.

Other fundamental work in physics was done in the study of light, notably Newton's experimental demonstration that white light is a mixture of all the colors of the rainbow, rather than a pure form of light which is modified to give the other colors. In 1676 the Dane Olaus Roemer measured the speed of light, using variations in the apparent position of a satellite of Jupiter as the basis for his determination. Robert Hooke and Christian Huyghens developed the notion that light is a wave transmitted through an invisible, intangible, and perfectly elastic "ether"; Newton, in his *Optics* (1704), asserted to the contrary that light was composed of tiny bodies. Newton's corpuscular theory was generally adopted during this period because of his enormous prestige, and because it corresponded more closely with the general atomism accepted by most of the new physicists, but it later gave way to the wave theory.

The New Physics: Mathematics and Experiment.   The key to the Newtonian conception was the principle that physical events were related to each other in an orderly way, describable by mathematical formulae. Like mathematics, the new physics sought by means of deductive analysis to describe particular events in terms of more general rules. Like mathematics, too, it assumed the universality and immutability of its rules and accepted the requirement of "elegance," or preference for simpler proofs with fewer elements. Unlike mathematics, however, the new physics rested firmly on the ground of analysis of data found by "experiment," that is, controlled experience designed to isolate the particular events under study. It accepted the principle that its laws had to be general in form. Where possible it used mathematics as a tool for handling the data it discovered. Thus physics was at one and the same time mathematical and experimental, deductive and inductive.

This duality of rationalism and empiricism, which embodied the threat of an ultimate philosophical conflict, was resolved by most contemporary scientists by assuming that their laws were not merely convenient ways for summing up experience but were actual descriptions of a universe which was rigorously mathematical in structure.

Mathematics. Despite the central importance of mathematics in Newton's system, he did not, in presenting his results in the *Principia*, employ the most recent mathematical innovations, to which he himself greatly contributed, but used only the classical geometry derived from Hellenistic antiquity. He used neither the analytic geometry worked out by Descartes, which made it possible to solve geometric problems by means of algebra, nor the new method of analyzing changing relationships, which he called "fluxions" (flowing quantities) and which has come to be known as the calculus. The calculus, invented almost simultaneously by Newton in England and Leibniz in Germany, was particularly adapted to the new physics, but the systematic application of the calculus to physical problems was initiated only in the eighteenth century by Euler, Legendre, and Lagrange.

Many fields of mathematics were originated or greatly developed. Although much effort went into the development of mathematical physics, mathematics increasingly became a study pursued for its own sake, as a purely independent discipline. During the seventeenth century, Fermat and Pascal in France made fundamental contributions to the theories of numbers and of probabilities as well as to the new analytic geometry. In the next century, numerous special problems in these various areas were propounded and a number of solutions were found.

Chemistry. By mid-seventeenth century chemistry was little advanced beyond the best work of the medieval alchemists; it was able to compound a certain number of materials according to rules which were more the result of accident than the accomplishment of systematic knowledge. A century and a half later it had evolved into a science, with tested principles and an effective method.

In the later seventeenth century Robert Boyle, in Great Britain, vigorously rejecting the Aristotelian-scholastic approach in terms of qualities, elaborated a methodology emphasizing quantitative measurements, precision, and controlled experimentation. Boyle asserted that the ultimate constituents of matter were "atoms," indivisible particles whose effects were due to their size and shape. In Germany at about the same time a physician named Becker reported on his numerous observations of chemical reactions and made a distinction between simple and composite materials; unlike Boyle, he did not emphasize weight and other quantitative factors. The name of "affinity" was given to the attractions between the constituents of composite materials.

In the eighteenth century the process of combustion became the crucial problem. For most of the period the predominant explanation was that combustible materials contained an element, named "phlogiston" by the German chemist Stahl, which was released in burning. This theory took account of the visible fact of flame, but "phlogiston" proved impossible to isolate or otherwise prove. The French chemist Lavoisier presented a contrary theory that combustion consisted in the combination with the fuel of an element in air, to which the name "oxygen" was given. Exact measurements, not only of the original fuel and the subsequent ash but also of the air, confirmed the oxidation theory. The way was thus prepared for Dalton, who in the early nineteenth century combined all accumulated chemical data in a systematic theory of distinct elements composed of atoms, which combined according to fixed mathematical ratios to form compounds. This theory became the basis of modern chemistry.

Biology. The study of the structure and functioning of plants and animals made substantial progress. Robert Hooke, by improving the compound microscope, was able to detect the cell structure of plants. Essential processes like plant nutrition from the soil and the role of leaves were glimpsed. The Dutch lens grinder Leeuwenhoek made microscopic studies which included the discovery of sperm cells and of infusoria in water. The doctrine of the circulation of the blood spread and an understanding of the role of the lungs in circulation was seen more clearly.

More difficulty was found with the problem of species, which was connected with the origin of life. John Ray, a brilliant English botanist, in his *Methodus plantarum nova* (*A New Botanical Method*, 1682), classified plants according to their method of generation, using the structure of the embryos and the first leaves of the cotyledons as his key. He also further developed the notion of the species as a group within which reproduction was possible.

Francesco Redi, by a carefully controlled experiment in which maggots did not appear on rotting meat when adult flies were prevented from depositing their eggs thereon, gave strong support to the germ theory of generation, which held that all life arose only from other living things. Even after this demonstration, belief persisted for a long time that life, especially the supposedly simpler forms like insects, arose spontaneously under favorable circumstances.

During the eighteenth century the work of classification begun by Ray was made systematic by the Swedish botanist Linnaeus. His classification helped to show a continuity of species each little different from those adjacent to it; he thereby laid the basis for the notion of an evolution of species. The Frenchman Lamarck explained the origin of species as resulting from the purposeful adaptation and perpetuation of favorable characteristics.

III. Philosophy

The achievements of science, especially the great Newtonian synthesis, accelerated the triumph of rationalism and empiricism: two linked but distinct movements in philosophy.

The Popularization of Philosophy. Philosophy became the activity less of professional metaphysicians in the universities than of gifted "amateurs," i.e. persons of independent means who debated the great questions for their own sake. Immensity of erudition became rarer and skill in persuading the "intelligent layman" more important. Indeed, the test of effective communication became to explain a difficult subject to a lady of intelligence without tiring her interest. The manner was set by Fontenelle, the permanent secretary of the French Academy of Sciences, whose *Entretiens sur la pluralité des mondes* ("Chats about the Multiplicity of Universes," 1686), was a dialogue expounding the Cartesian cosmogony. The Italian Algarotti summed up the trend a half century later in his *Neutonianismo per le dame* (*Newtonism for the Ladies*, 1733).

Certainty and Skepticism. The central purpose of most philosophical inquiry continued to be to discover a firm basis for human knowledge and conduct, or to confirm one which was felt to be already granted to mankind. The large majority of Europeans still believed and practiced Christianity in one of its forms, accepting it as established by divine revelation and providence. Most thinkers, however, although they continued to be Christians in some sense of the word, were seldom satisfied with the traditional arguments in behalf of Christianity and sought some more certain basis for their beliefs. Their purpose was not to bring all things into doubt but to remove doubt wherever possible. They used arguments from reason and experience, thus paralleling the methods of the physical scientists: indeed, many of the scientists, Newton at their head, were deeply concerned with proving the truth of Christianity, though their general emphasis upon rationalizing their faith strained the fabric of traditional theology.

This quest for certainty did not arise out of thin air but came from the endeavor to reply to a persistent skeptical stream of thought. Descartes' *Discourse on Method*, the handbook of the rationalists, had been an effort to turn the skeptics' weapon of doubt against them. Bishop Bossuet had skeptics in mind when he inveighed against an "unfortunate incredulity" which was "an unending error, a risk-all boldness, a deliberate dizziness, in a word, a pride that cannot accept its proper cure, which is legitimate authority." Skepticism nonetheless continued to influence various kinds of thinkers: the brave souls who pushed their arguments to the logical extreme; the facile debaters who used the sharp edge of skepticism against their opponents' argumentation and did not see that the same sword could be used against themselves; and spirits in the tradition of Montaigne, like the exiled French Huguenot Pierre Bayle and after him the Scot David Hume, who opposed all fanaticism, Protestant, Catholic, or rationalist.

The Certitude of Reason. Bossuet's target in his criticism of the skeptics also included the rationalists, one of whom summed up their creed in the sentence, "By obeying reason we depend on no one but ourselves and so, in a sense, we, too, become as gods." * Their trust in reason, and under reason's rule in experience, was virtually absolute. They took confidence in reason and experiment because Newton, to their mind, had proved beyond question the power of these two ways of thought. They believed in the law of nature, in the sense that the universe was a totally ordered system, and in the laws of nature, the specific determinate relationships among particular objects which could be discovered by human minds and stated, for physical objects, in mathematical terms, and for moral and social objects, in terms equally rigorous, universal, and absolute. They therefore rejected Bossuet's "legitimate authority"—the Roman Catholic church—by denying the evidence for its legitimacy; they rejected any transcendant authority beyond and to some extent in conflict with human reason, but did not go all the way with the skeptics who denied the very notion of absolutes.

They called rationalism the only "true and useful philosophy," and rejected all other approaches—authoritarian, mystical, historical, skeptical— either as imposing unproved and unprovable limits upon the power of human beings to know the world and achieve their purposes, or as needlessly cribbing such power. Father Malebranche, a French member of the Catholic order of Oratorians, sought the evidence for his faith in Cartesian rationalism, but his statement of principles held good for rationalism in general: men, he said, "must never assent to any ideas save those so evidently true that they cannot be rejected without inward hurt and secret reproaches of reason." He rejected all authoritarian restriction upon rational analysis: "freedom to philosophize and to reason upon common ideas should not be taken from

* Claude Gilbert, *Histoire de Caléjava* (1700), p. 57, quoted by P. Hazard, *The European Mind, 1680–1715* (London 1953), p. 154.

men," for it was "a right as natural as breathing." Malebranche drew the conclusion that the proof of Christianity lay not in miracles—by definition events contradictory to reason and experience—but in "rational explanation." Similar views were held by the Protestant rationalists and scientists in England of the same period, such as Robert Boyle. The danger to traditional religion in these doctrines lay not merely in a general change of atmosphere, but in such works as the *Histoire critique du vieux testament* (*Critical History of the Old Testament,* 1678), by Richard Simon, a French Catholic scholar; in it the Bible was subjected to the same tests of rational analysis that were used by editors of other ancient manuscripts of less sacrosanct character.

Deists, Atheists, and Materialists. The new science and the new rationalism served to generate a number of distinct, though overlapping, systems of thought which frankly disavowed Christianity.

In philosophy this system took shape as materialism. The materialists took the atomistic philosophy characteristic of the new physics, and the Newtonian refusal to inquire beyond phenomena, and declared that the world of physical objects, the objects experienced through the senses, was and could be the only ultimate reality. Following Descartes, they explained living organisms as machines—*l'homme-machine* ("the man-machine")—in the phrase used by one of the best-known of them, La Mettrie. They considered mind or soul a product of the physical organism, being either a kind of by-product secretion or possessing an active and directive role. Many of the materialists were also atheists who denied the meaning of the concept of God or at least the existence of God.

More widespread and influential by far than the handful of atheists, who had to publish their works anonymously or under false names, were the deists. They affirmed the existence of God and usually shared a number of other conceptions with traditional Christians, particularly divine creation of the world and an after-life beyond death with rewards and punishments for the acts of the present life. They emphasized God as First Cause, the creator and organizer of the universe and of its eternal immutable laws with whose operation he did not interfere. They differed from Christians, however, in rejecting the entire conception of a personal intervention of God in human affairs, most notably the doctrine of His incarnation as Jesus Christ and the establishment of a church through which redemption from sin was offered to men.

The Critics. These various views, though held by a majority of intellectuals, came under criticism not only from the side of the old orthodox religions but also from thinkers who accepted one or more portions of the new thought in order to analyze, judge, and rebut or modify it.

Locke's system of sensationalist psychology, which affirmed that all man's knowledge came through the senses, provided the basis for the criticism of George Berkeley, an Anglican bishop in Ireland. Berkeley drew the conclusion that logically there was no proof at all of the existence of an external world of matter: all objects existed only in thought. He therefore explained the world of experience as existing primarily in the mind of God. Berkeley's critique was troubling to the more sensitive of the thinkers he criticized, but the very absoluteness of his idealist metaphysics made it difficult to accord with the mind-matter dualism of common experience, just as difficult as was rigorous materialism.

A criticism subtler, broader, and in ultimate effect more destructive was made by David Hume. He too took Locke's primacy of sense data as his starting point, but drew the conclusion that both mind and sense data are uncertain organizing principles for knowledge. The notion of natural law and causality rests, according to Hume, on no better proof than the habitual coincidence of events in sequence or simultaneity. Our efforts to prove anything are in the strict sense meaningless, said this supreme skeptic, in a thrust at arrogant reason. He also used skeptical arguments to blow apart the pretensions of the deists' "natural religion," and ended with the paradoxical—and perhaps tongue-in-cheek—conclusion that the old revealed religions were more satisfactory precisely because they trusted faith, not reason. Yet Hume was a skeptic willing to take the world as it seemed to be, neither nihilist nor revolutionary but a mild reformer and conservative.

Hume's critique was taken up in the closing decades of the eighteenth century by an obscure professor of philosophy at Königsberg, in East Prussia. Immanuel Kant shared the general aspirations of the eighteenth-century philosophers in politics and their acceptance of the new science, but at the same time he desired to buttress the religious belief to which they were increasingly hostile. He did so by systematically differentiating the world of appearances ("phenomena"), with which science was alone concerned, from the world of unknowable reality ("noumena," or things-in-themselves), which were the concern of faith.

After Kant, idealist philosophy took complete hold in the German universities, which became during the revolutionary age after 1789 the seat of the most influential formal thinkers. They differed from Berkeley, whose thoroughgoing idealism they shared, in a lack of concern for refuting materialists, and in the self-confident construction of immense systems of analysis.

IV. Political and Social Thought

Two problems—the relationship between freedom and authority, and the nature of the "good society"—dominated political and social thought during the period from the Peace of Westphalia (1648) to the Peace of Vienna (1815).

The School of Authority. After the turbulence of rebellions and civil war in the middle decades of the seventeenth century, the re-established monarchical regimes eagerly sought the buttressing of theories defending their legitimacy. These arguments rested in part upon the claim that government by kings possessed inherent or divine authority, and in part upon the assertion of their social utility.

The argument from utility was best presented by the Englishman Thomas Hobbes, writing during the period of the Commonwealth. Hobbes took as the basis of his analysis the commonplace historical notion, derived from classical and medieval thought, that men had originally lived without a state and had created government by a compact or treaty. He painted this primal society without a political power in the harsh hues of England as he saw it in civil war—a society in which utter selfishness (mitigated only, if at all, by ties of family) was dominant, where men fought each other for property, power, and life, where none was strong enough to be safe, where life was "nasty, brutish, and short." To escape this "war of all against all," men agreed among themselves to give up their individual powers to a single person (or body of persons) to rule over them as sovereign. The interest of the prince in his own preservation compelled him to maintain law, order, and peace in his country and thereby to assure his subjects the tranquillity and safety they needed in order to enjoy their estates. No incidental tyranny of a monarch could outweigh this greatest of boons; the grant of power to the prince was perpetual and irrevocable.

Such an argument, with its stress on gross utility, was repugnant to the traditionalists, for it stripped from monarchy its qualities of magical mystery, its origin in deeds of power, its religious aura; the most dangerous aspect of Hobbes's theory was that in defending monarchy it subjected it to the test of service. Service was, indeed, still the heart of the alternate argument in defense of authority—but stated less baldly, and with emphasis upon service to God as well as the people. But judgment of how well the kings performed their duties lay not with men but with God: monarchy existed by divine right. This doctrine was not at all new, except in the neatness with which its various arguments were harmonized, especially by Bossuet: it rested upon the dictum of St. Paul that "the powers that be are established of God," as it had been modified by the political theorists from the twelfth through the seventeenth centuries. These latter had countered arguments of papal supremacy over princes with the teaching that the secular princes drew their authority *directly* from God, and even possessed rights of supervision over the church. Monarchy was divinely instituted, divinely maintained, divinely safeguarded. Political authority could not be resisted by subjects on any pretext whatever. To be sure, tyranny was reprehensible, but it was seen, in the manner of the Old Testament prophets, as punishment for the misdeeds and impiety of the people; only God could punish a tyrant. Absolute authority did not destroy freedom but rather created it, for "liberty" consisted only in living in a stable orderly society under an undisputed legitimate ruler.

But, as a defense for absolute monarchy, the "divine right" doctrine, like Hobbes's "contractual" theory, had crucial weaknesses. For one thing, it built upon the foundation of religion at a time when belief was shifting character and losing ground; for another, it neglected (as did almost all political theory) the fact that monarchs looked upon their states and their power as birthrights to use as they pleased and often treated the doctrine of the service function of the state as an insult and an offense to their majesty.

The School of Liberty. The basis of the contrary political doctrine was this emphasis upon the human situation of the king, like other men often selfish, wilful, and wayward. Liberty, not authority, was its battle cry. It was a doctrine widely held in various forms in the half-century after the Peace of Westphalia: by the Whigs and their theoretician Locke in England; by the critics of absolute monarchy in France—some Huguenots in exile and others dissatisfied aristocrats; by the republicans in the United Provinces; by defenders of the Estates against the encroachments of the imperial princes in Germany.

John Locke was the most eminent and influential of these theorists, particularly in his *Treatises on Civil Government* of 1690. Like Hobbes he assumed a "state of nature" before the formation of government, when "natural law" held sway. Each man was not then a king unto himself but was under the rule of "right reason," which defined his duties and rights. Such "natural law" was not defined in statute, expounded by courts, and enforced by a higher power, but was "written in the hearts of men," with each man "a judge in his own case," inevitably interpreting the law to suit his own interests and defending his rights by his own means. The result was anarchy, painted by Locke in less somber terms than by Hobbes but nonetheless an unsatisfactory state of existence.

As did Hobbes, Locke saw the remedy as a "social contract" among free men to entrust their rights of judgment and enforcement to a government. Power was delegated to the ruler on condition that he protect the people's interests in their life, liberty, and property; if he became a tyrant and deprived the people of any of these ultimate rights, he violated the primal contract and entered into a state of war with his subjects, who might legitimately overthrow him. But revolution was for Locke the ultimate argument in defense of the rights of the ruled, not the ordinary means of political action. The proper way to defend these rights was to organize government so that the powers of making law and controlling the executive authority always remained in the hands of the people, or more precisely, of their chosen representatives.

With Locke the doctrine of popular sovereignty, which had been used in earlier periods as a kind of logical underlay to the analysis of political authority, was brought to the very forefront of political debate.

The Skeptics and the Wits. Locke furnished the arsenal of fundamental ideas for most of the eminent political thinkers of the eighteen century. They called themselves "philosophers" (*philosophes*, in French); later in the century the German term *Aufklärung* (Enlightenment) was applied to their movement. The *philosophes* (it is customary to call the Enlightenment thinkers by the French word, for the term "philosopher" now implies in English a central concern with formal metaphysics) added little that was basic to Locke's concepts but elaborated them in an efflorescence of theoretical detail and defended them with a verve quite beyond the attainment of the grave Englishman.

The *philosophes* applied with implacable rigor the test of utility to existing political and social institutions. They rejected arguments from history and tradition as invalid unless confirmed by proof that the institutions under debate served the common good. They seldom made their assaults upon the castles of entrenched privilege by open charge, using the weaponry of formal debate, for explicitness might bring censorship or punitive state action into play against them. Instead they dug at the foundations of the existing order, particularly the habit of uncritical obedience and assent to what existed; and they laughed away their foes' defenses, using the literary devices of parody and satire. Though not themselves skeptics, they gladly used the weapon of skeptical doubt and they found a rich store of such arms in the works of Pierre Bayle, particularly the enormous confusion of his *Critical and Historical Dictionary* (first edition, 1695-1697), whose corrosive arguments were concealed in notes and commentaries heaped one upon another in every article. But they wrote with all the purity of the French classical style, with its transparency, its terseness, its easy flow. In their tales they also employed fashionable devices for holding readers' interest: their scenes were laid in strange lands or they brought naive, fresh-eyed strangers to Europe; and they spiced their stories with erotic gallantry. They constantly reassured their reader that he, like the writer, was a "reasonable man," the marksman and not the target. For the standard of judgment of the *philosophes* lay in the opinions of "rational" man, by which they of course meant themselves, not in the description and analysis either of actual conduct or of transcendent eternal values.

The New "Heavenly City." Despite their use of the tool of skepticism, the *philosophes* had as positive a system of beliefs and values as their traditionalist opponents. Theirs was a vision of a "heavenly city" on earth, a better society that could be achieved within reasonable limits of time by the energies and intelligence actually available to men. It derived its ethical elements from Christianity, emphasizing the plain virtues of honesty, decency, mutual love, and trust, but it based these values not on an immediate enactment of God as given in revelation but on man's own reason and character. It rejected outright the orthodox Christian emphasis upon the inherent depravity of fallen man, affirming to the contrary man's innate goodness. But outdated institutions, motivated by selfishness and fostering obscurantism, distorted and thwarted this innate goodness.

The *philosophes* envisioned a world of reasonable people, each with his own modest patrimony and earning his own livelihood; well-educated, especially in useful knowledge but knowing classical antiquity well enough to take to himself the philosophy of the Greeks and the civic virtues of the Romans; informed about the affairs of his own state and participating, to some extent, in the government. It was a society open to talents and virtue, where men would be at the same time citizens of their own land and of the world; war, with its unreasoning barbarism, would be banned from this society of calm "good sense." Over all lay the common objective: happiness on earth rather than hereafter, happiness as its own reward instead of pains and trials in this life for the sake of future happiness. Leibniz had clearly stated the aim of the "heavenly city" early in the eighteenth century: to love God meant to work for the happiness of mankind, to build the kingdom of God upon earth.

Enlightened Despotism. There was more agreement about the general character of this ideal society than about methods of achieving it. Some looked to the absolute monarchs of Europe to be its creators, and urged them to be "enlightened despots"; others made the abolition of absolutism the indispensable prerequisite, for only a free people, by means of free institutions, could remove the injustices by which the monarchs benefited and for which they were responsible. But the two groups were alike in believing implicitly that society was shaped by law, and hence that the lawgiver had in his power the determination of human institutions, customs and attitudes.

Foremost among the adherents of "enlightened despotism" was Voltaire. His admiration for the English system of government was based primarily on its religious tolerance, the freedom of speech and press given to Britons, the reliability and honesty of its fiscal operations, the encouragement given by it to productive enterprise. He did not believe, however, that these boons were necessarily linked to the English system of representative government. He profoundly distrusted the common people, whom he looked upon as a passionate, irrational, violent mob only too ready to follow the worst causes.

It was safer and easier to look to the kings to wield their powers of state on behalf of reform.

His ideal of the "enlightened despot" was a philosopher-king, one such as Plato had depicted in the *Republic,* in the eighteenth century was embodied in Frederick II of Prussia. Voltaire was ready, too, to support the consolidation of the French monarchy at the expense of the privileged orders and institutions, in order that it might be able to undertake the work of reform. But in his own career he experienced the harsh fist beneath the Prussian king's velvet glove and came to the realization that his big hopes were vain, that the most the wise man could hope for was to "tend his own garden"—the sad sagacity with which he ended the gaily told cruelties and crudities of *Candide.*

Enlightened Liberty. Those who placed their confidence in political liberty took England as their model, not only for its results but also for its structure. Locke's treatises on government were their political bible and representative parliaments the essential institutions of state. The most characteristic and influential of these thinkers was Montesquieu. In his *Spirit of the Laws* (1748) he differentiated the proper political systems of countries according to their geographic condition, but held England, with its parliamentary system, its division and balance of powers, to be the ideal general form. Often, however, assemblies of Estates were treated by Montesquieu and most others of his school as exactly equivalent to the British Parliament, despite the disparity of functions and powers which had resulted from their divergent historical development. The term "people" was used in a loose vague way to mean those without legal privilege, in the nomenclature of France the "third estate."

Only with the publication of Rousseau's *Social Contract* in 1762 did the theory of popular sovereignty, in the sense of rule by the whole community, take hold of broad sections of the public. Characteristic of Rousseau's thought was an appearance of rational clarity, and a content of vague though powerful feeling. He made the people the only legitimate sovereign, and made the sovereign so omnipotent that no individual retained rights independent of it; he cast aside Locke's doctrine of an eternal "right reason" which bound all men and all states to a "natural law" independent of their decisions, and instead made public morality simply a matter of the source of decision, not its content. Although he followed Montesquieu in differentiating the proper forms of government according to their geographical extent and character, he took the direct democracy of his native Geneva as the purest form of popular sovereignty.

The New Conservatism. For most of the eighteenth century, the *philosophes* dominated the intellectual scene of Europe. Resistance to their doctrines came mainly from the traditional authorities, whose denunciations consisted usually in the repetition of worn and weary arguments. Even among officials many of the doctrines of the Enlightenment came to be accepted, especially those that emphasized increased efficiency in the central government by reducing or removing traditional privileges.

The onset of the French Revolution reversed the situation. The theories of the *philosophes* became the accepted dogmas of the revolutionary governments, defended by propaganda but no longer analyzed and expounded by their adherents. The opponents of the revolution, however, were jarred by its successes into re-examining their assumptions and their argumentation. The most effective statement of their views was made by Edmund Burke, the English Whig, in his *Reflections on the Revolution in France*, written within a year after the meeting of the Estates General in 1789.

Burke put blame for the revolution squarely on the Enlightenment. Its essential error, in his opinion, was to set abstract theory over living practice, to derive its views of the good society from considerations of the nature of society in general rather than from what each country had evolved in the course of its own history in meeting its particular needs. He took the argument of utility and turned it against the innovators. Their ideas rested upon the too narrow base of their personal thinking, while the historical institutions of a country incorporated the collective wisdom of many generations, beyond the ability of any single critic fully to grasp. Reform was wise and effective only when directed to improving the existing order, not to replacing it outright. To replace a functioning state in the hope of building a totally new society according to theoretical precepts was madness. He attacked egalitarianism as false and harmful: the safety of each man's property, large or little, lay in protecting the right of each to his own.

Burke's ideas were expanded and developed for the next quarter-century with sustained vigor by conservative thinkers. In France, François René de Chateaubriand defended Christianity by a subtle variant of the argument from utility, on the grounds of its beauty rather than its truth. Joseph de Maistre, a Piedmontese, renewing the "divine right" theory which had fallen into disuse, denied that any grounds existed for prying into the mysteries of state; absolute monarchy rested upon the will of God and was linked to the immutable truth of the Roman Catholic Church. German thinkers like Friedrich Gentz emphasized the historical side of Burke's argument.

Thus the age of Enlightenment ended with the reinvigoration of conservative thought. The mind of Europe was split more deeply than at any previous time since the Reformation, and in some respects the cleavage between liberal and conservative was wider than that which had separated Catholic and Protestant.

28

France in Revolution: I

1787 - 1795

In the quarter century from 1787 to 1815, a revolution swept through France, destroying the Old Regime and creating a new order of society. Only from a distance does the revolution seem a single immense event; at closer hand it becomes a series of political, social, economic, and moral revolutions.

I. The Crisis of the Old Regime, 1787-1789

Before the Old Regime was overthrown, it fell, tripped by the tangled knot of institutions which made the smallest measure of reform seem to threaten the whole structure of society.

Fiscal and Economic Crisis. The king's immediate problem in 1787 was to avoid bankruptcy. The year before, the royal treasury had spent about 625,000,000 livres, though income had been no more than 500,000,000. But the deficit could no longer be covered by loans; the credit of the government was shattered. To reduce expenditures seemed impossible. Sixty per cent of revenue went to pay interest on the accumulated debt, and the government could not and would not live within the remaining forty per cent. The royal family would permit no savings at its expense, but the total cost of the court was in any case relatively small. The lower classes, who comprised more than 90 per cent of the population, were already taxed as heavily as ingenuity and inhumanity permitted. The clergy, about 130,000 in number, and the nobility, no more than 400,000 at most, contributed far less to the royal treasury in proportion to their wealth than any other group; they were totally exempt from the most burdensome taxes, notably the taille.

The fiscal problem was made more difficult by the economic crisis which gripped France. A decade-long series of crop failures had cut the cash income of the peasantry and interfered with the collection of taxes, feudal dues, and rents. The urban economy suffered a contraction of its vital rural market; widespread unemployment among artisans and wage workers ensued. The resulting discontent among the urban poor made them readier to riot, just as the peasantry were stirred to restive bitterness by the efforts of their landlords to collect the usual rents to the last penny and to add any forgotten dues which search of the manorial records could prove to have once existed.

The Revolt of the Nobility. The king's need was the aristocracy's opportunity. If Louis XVI would accept the domination of the privileged orders, they would make moderate concessions to him in the matter of taxation. Otherwise, they were ready for resistance.

When the Assembly of Notables convened on February 12, 1787, Calonne, the prime minister, presented a program of reforms which left royal absolutism essentially untouched. The notables, although selected by Calonne, refused to put their privileges upon the sacrificial block; instead they demanded that the king summon the Estates General, which they said alone could adopt new taxes and make fundamental changes. When the assembly deadlocked with the minister, Louis responded by dismissing both.

Loménie de Brienne, archbishop of Toulouse and Calonne's principal antagonist, replaced him but was no more able to solve the crisis. He too ended by making proposals for reform modeled on Turgot's and Necker's; he too was rebuffed by the *parlements*, which refused to register the reform decrees. When he attempted to break the magistrates' resistance by a royal *lit de justice*, they declared such enforced registration null and void; when they were exiled to the provinces and a new high court was set up in their place, they responded by a new "Fronde." The judges, although by office preservers of the king's authority, incited the population in Paris and other cities to street riots and to attacks upon troops attempting to enforce his commands. The soft-souled monarch capitulated. He agreed to convene the Estates General, dismissed Brienne and brought Necker, whose reputation as a miracle-maker was intact, back to office. The first of the revolutions—the aristocratic rebellion—triumphed.

Wrangle over the Estates General. Until this moment the aristocratic opponents of royal despotism had received the enthusiastic and almost unanimous support of the Third Estate. This unity had been maintained even though the bourgeoisie—the untitled townsmen of wealth, or talent, or both— felt strong resentment against the increased arrogance of the nobility. "On every side the roads are closed off," was the way Barnave, who later became a revolutionary leader, described the aristocracy's monopoly in the army, the church, and the state.

The aristocracy now demanded that the Estates General retain the ancient pattern of three distinct orders, each voting separately, the consent of all being necessary to any decision. The commoners quickly saw that voting "by order" meant preservation of the special rights and exemptions of the privileged classes; once again the Third Estate would be called upon to shoulder the whole burden of redeeming the fiscal troubles of the state. They therefore demanded not only that the Third Estate have as many deputies as the two other orders together, but that voting be conducted "by head," that is, in a single assembly. This arrangement would assure the Third Estate a majority as soon as it received the support of even a small number of liberal clergymen and nobles.

The commoners gained enhanced confidence and boldness from a pamphlet published early in 1789 under the title, *Qu'est-ce que le Tiers État? (What Is the Third Estate?)*. Its author, the Abbé Sieyès, was a minor ecclesiastic estranged from his own order. He urged the commoners to be ready to take upon themselves the tasks and the powers of the entire Estates General.

> The assembly of the Third Estate (he wrote) represents twenty-five million men and deliberates upon the interests of the nation. The two other estates, even should they unite, have power only from some 200,000 individuals and think only of their privileges. It will be said that the Third Estate cannot constitute the *Estates General*. All to the good! It will become a *National Assembly*.

Elections and Grievances. Again the government decided to avoid a clear-cut decision. It assented to doubling the representation of the Third Estate but not to the merger of the three orders into a single assembly. At the same time it broke with tradition by granting a vote to all who paid direct taxes, although historically the Third Estate had represented almost exclusively the town patricians and the holders of government office. For the first time the mass of the peasantry were called upon to participate in shaping the policy of the country.

The sense that the king was eager for his people's counsel was strengthened by the instructions to the various electoral assemblies to prepare statements of grievances (*cahiers de doléances*). These *cahiers* brought to the surface the hardships and hopes of a whole nation: all attacked royal despotism and favored some kind of constitutional monarchy, without any tinge of republicanism but with general desire for wide provincial and communal autonomy. In their specific complaints the *cahiers* differed widely. The clergy demanded preservation of Roman Catholicism as the state religion and increased independence of the church in the administration of its affairs. The nobility wanted both "liberty" and the strengthening of their privileges. The bourgeoisie wanted freedom too, especially for business enterprise, but they also stressed equality of all before the law, before the tax collector, and in appointment to government offices. The peasantry requested reduction of their various compulsory obligations and the elimination of the newfangled methods of restricting communal agriculture, notably enclosures. Significantly, however, the delegates of the Third Estate included almost no peasants but a very large majority of lawyers and other professional and business men.

II. Constitutional Monarchy, 1789-1792

The convocation of the Estates General was the prelude not only to political overturn but also to a transformation of French society. This change was achieved within the framework of constitutional monarchy, but this mode of government, on which almost the entire nation was agreed in 1789, disappeared in little more than three years.

The Great Hope. As the deputies to the Estates General assembled in Versailles at the beginning of May, 1789, the nation dreamed and hoped with fervent optimism.

The good life, the good society were at hand. Freedom, justice, and happiness would be achieved, for with the king's consent the nation was confidently taking the conduct of its affairs into its own hands. The teachings of all the great thinkers of the century would guide the legislators in their work of reform and recovery. Reason would inspire them. Since all men's interests were fundamentally the same, dispassionate examination would create unity of decision and efficacy of action.—So felt most politically aware Frenchmen.

Only a handful of doubters remembered the ferocity of the debate over the organization of the Estates General and foresaw not the dawn of a golden age but the renewal of struggle. Queen Marie Antoinette, with her mind fixed on the question of power—the dangerous ultimate question in politics—asked: "Will the Estates General be the masters of the king, or will the king be the master of the nation?" A thoughtful conservative, the writer Rivarol, saw the situation of the king otherwise: "When you wish to prevent a revolution, you have to want one and make it yourself." Whether Louis XVI would "make a revolution himself" or permit his ministers to do so, only the course of the Estates General would show.

THE TENNIS-COURT OATH. Drawing by Jacques-Louis David, 1791. The Louvre, Paris.

The French revolutionaries, still living on the artistic and intellectual heritage of the Renaissance, were in the habit of seeing themselves in the character of Roman republicans, as can be seen in this drawing of the dramatic event of June 20, 1789. The same rhetorical poses and gestures which the artist David gave to his earlier depictions of classical antiquity are here assigned to his contemporary fellow-revolutionaries. (Bettmann Archive)

The National Constituent Assembly. The monarch who came before the Estates General when it began to meet on May 5, and in the subsequent sessions, was no such "revolutionary from above" as Rivarol hoped for. The general representation of the nation was treated as the Assembly of Notables had been, neither commanded nor conciliated. It was soon evident that only funds were really wanted; discussion of constitutional reform was promised after the emergency was met: but then, as many realized, the deputies could be dismissed before they had done anything. "The penury of the treasury is the nation's treasure," was the witty comment of one deputy: the king would knuckle to the people's demands only under the compulsion of his financial necessity.

On the immediately crucial question of voting, the monarch reaffirmed the tradition of voting by order. The Third Estate took up the challenge. It declared itself to be the National Assembly, as Sieyès had urged, asserted that the other estates had lost the right to a separate organization, and demanded that the nobles and the clergy join the single assembly. To reinforce this claim, it declared that all taxes collected without its consent would be illegal and called upon the people to refuse to pay them. From the standpoint of

615

the old monarchical law, this declaration was virtual rebellion, little softened by the proviso that for the time being, so long as the assembly sat, existing taxes might continue to be collected.

On June 20, barred from their meeting place and fearing disbandment, the Third Estate—or National Assembly—met in a nearby tennis court and took an oath "not to separate . . . until the constitution of the kingdom is established and consolidated upon firm foundations." On June 23, Louis XVI attempted a compromise: the Estates General would have the right to consent to all taxation thereafter; the three orders might meet together *if* they all desired; but they would have no right to legislate or to write a constitution. He reminded the deputies that their decisions had no force without his consent, that he, not they, was the true "representative of the nation." He then commanded the three estates to go to their separate meetings. The Third Estate, with a minority of the clergy and nobility, remained in place. "The assembled nation cannot be given orders," declared their presiding officer. The deputies proclaimed their persons to be inviolable and their decisions irrevocable.

As the queen had foreseen, the question of sovereignty was posed. The king, characteristically, sidestepped the issue. A report that Parisians were trooping to Versailles shook his nerve: he really wanted to be left alone to hunt and to enjoy his leisure, not to be harried into hard decisions. On June 27, he instructed the clergy and the nobility to meet with the Third Estate. Emboldened, the National Assembly on July 9 added the formidable word "Constituent" to its title, thereby asserting that its basic task was to draw up a formal written constitution for France. France was far on the way to becoming a constitutional monarchy, another Britain in a continent still largely filled with absolute kingdoms.

The Fall of the Bastille.   Louis XVI was seized with dismay and fright. He capitulated to the counsels of his youngest brother, the count of Artois, who urged that the Third Estate be cowed by a show of force. Regiments of soldiers moved into encampments around Paris and Versailles. On July 11, Necker and three liberal colleagues were dismissed; Necker himself was ordered to leave France within twenty-four hours. The news came to the would-be reformers in the National Assembly as a herald of disaster. They huddled in anticipation of a royal *coup d'état*. The least punishment they could hope for was to be sent home; for many there would be worse. And their brave words were coming to nothing.

Salvation came from Paris. The populace of the great city, distressed by the increasing cost of food and frightened by the threat of military attack, had begun to organize its own defenses. A hunt for weapons began; the Arsenal and the gunshops were stripped bare. On July 14, a crowd went to the great fortress of the Bastille to seek more weapons. Misunderstandings

STORMING OF THE BASTILLE, JULY 14, 1789. Etching by Pierre-Gabriel Berthault after a drawing by Prieur, about 1800.

The elements of the dramatic scene are easily visible in this print: the mob armed with scythes and other improvised weapons, the French Guards with rifles and bayonets and bringing up cannon, the drawbridge across which the attackers are swarming, the penetration of the fortress itself, and the defenders' cannons smoking on the high ramparts. (Achenbach Foundation)

and mutual fear led to shots from the garrison, which killed or wounded some 150 of the crowd. The hatred felt for the Bastille as the symbol of royal despotism broke loose. The fortress was stormed with the aid of mutinous soldiers, several of its garrison were massacred, and the few prisoners in its cells were released.

The fall of the Bastille, in itself a minor incident, almost instantaneously became a great myth of triumphant revolution: the People had stormed the bastion of Tyranny, a new Age of Liberty was beginning. The news swept through France and Europe, arousing great excitement and either joy or wrath, according to the hearer. The fall of the Bastille was more than myth, however. Everywhere in France it was followed by municipal revolutions, as the bourgeoisie seized power from the royal officialdom. Revolution meant not only the transfer of authority, but also its diminution and destruction, as the population began to obey laws and pay taxes only as they pleased. The events of July 14 also demonstrated the effectiveness of insurrection as a means of political action, a lesson already taught by the aristocrat-led insurgency of 1788.

The king, flinching before the popular uprising, ordered the troops away from Paris and Versailles and gave his approval to the National Assembly. Thus he let it be thought that he was at last committed to the transformation of France into a constitutional monarchy. But almost at the same hour he was sending to his cousin, Charles IV of Spain, a formal disclaimer of whatever he might do after July 15, 1789.

The Great Fear. The reorganization of French society was begun not by the legislators but by the common folk in the countryside. All during the month of July the peasantry were gripped by fears of "brigands" reported to be moving across the countryside, ready to despoil and kill; they seized arms and rallied for self-defense. When no brigands appeared, they turned upon the landlords' mansion houses, destroying the manorial records and on occasion massacring landlords and bailiffs. The movement received the name of the "Great Fear."

The government dared not use force to halt the violence of the peasantry, lest it be accused of oppressing the common people. Yet the National Assembly, whatever the antipathy of a majority of its members for the manorial system (included, in contemporary French terminology, within the phrase "feudal regime"), did not relish the lawless destruction of property. On the night of August 4, the National Assembly in a dramatic session acted to calm the peasantry and yet to save the rights of property. Noble and clerical deputies vied with each other to propose the abolition of all the varied rights which made up the manorial and feudal systems. At the end of a week, a summary formula was adopted: "The National Assembly totally abolishes the feudal regime."

There had been sly method, however, in the welter of sacrifices. Once the initial ardor was past and the work of specific legislation began, "total" abolition turned out to be something less. A distinction was drawn between "personal" obligations, such as the labor *corvée*, which were abolished outright without compensation, and "real" obligations, recognizing the "eminent domain" of the manorial lord in the land; the peasant proprietors were authorized to buy out "real" rights at rates favorable to their owners, who were often townsmen or even well-to-do peasants.

The changes in the economic and legal system of French agrarian life were fundamental. The whole complex network of feudal and manorial tenures, with its multitude of dues, rents, and services, was replaced by the system of freehold ownership. The peasantry were thankful to the Revolution for this boon—but their land hunger was by no means appeased and they did not scruple to resist the revolutionary governments which offended other vital interests of theirs. The landless peasantry, about one-quarter of the rural population, found their status little if any better than before; they continued to earn a meager livelihood by working for those with land.

The Declaration of the Rights of Man. The National Assembly then returned to debating a constitution. The victory of the Third Estate assured that the constitution would not be what the aristocrats had wanted, a reaffirmation of the ancient "fundamental laws" of the French monarchy along lines favorable to them, but rather the instrument for creating new institutions based on new principles. Without waiting to complete the formidable task of elaborating a constitution, the Assembly accepted the proposal of the marquis de Lafayette, most famous and honored of the "Americans" (as the aristocrats who had served under General Washington in the cause of American independence were called) to draw up a French equivalent of the Bill of Rights. It would be, he said, "a declaration of the natural rights of man and those of man living in society."

The Declaration of the Rights of Man and the Citizen, enacted on August 26, became the charter of French liberty. It was a distillation of the political thought and experience of more than a century; though abstract in form, it was carefully directed against the specific practices of absolute monarchy which had become hateful. It enunciated a series of general principles, especially in the first three clauses: the freedom and quality of all persons, with "social distinctions" permitted only when resting upon "general utility"; the function of the state as the "preservation of the natural and inalienable rights of man," these being "liberty, property, security, and resistance to oppression"; and the principle of national sovereignty, barring all inherent political authority in any individual or group other than the whole people of France.

Other clauses established equality of the law for all; gave all citizens the right to "concur" in legislation either personally or through representatives; opened public offices to all upon the basis of "virtues and talents"; forbade arbitrary arrest and otherwise made justice more rational and less cruel. Freedom of opinion, religion, speech, and press were established, though subject to limits established by law to protect "public order" and prevent "abuse." Property was declared to be "a sacred and inviolable right"; expropriation was permitted only for public purposes and upon condition of adequate prior compensation.

The New Order of Society. While the slow work of writing a constitution proceeded, the reorganization of French society upon a new basis was not delayed. Before the end of the year 1789, the Assembly passed a series of statutes fundamentally transforming the national institutions and bringing a New Regime into being.

Government in the localities was given to locally elected officials. The provinces, with their variegated origins, privileges, and traditions, and the more recently established "generalities" (the administrative districts of the intendants) were discarded; in their place, 83 (ultimately more than 90) departments were created, lacking historic roots but deftly adapted to the convenience of the population. The system of justice was reorganized; the *parlements*, with their venal judgeships, and the manorial courts, were abolished outright; the new magistrates, elected by the population in their jurisdiction, received their salary from the state and charged no fees to perform their duties. The tax system was basically overhauled—instead of the old taxes, with their irregularities, inequities, and oppressiveness, three new direct taxes were introduced: a uniform land tax, an impost upon industries and another upon merchants. Titles of nobility, the quintessence of the special status of the aristocracy, were abolished.

Only the monarch retained his title, and even that lost its absolutist form. Instead of "Louis, by the grace of God, King of France and Navarre," it became "Louis, by the grace of God and the constitutional law of France, king of the French." A decree adopted on October 1 reaffirmed the sovereignty of the nation but declared France to be a hereditary monarchy; the king was the servant of the people and the law. He received in principle the bulk of the executive power and a suspensive veto for the duration of two legislatures.

A Little Less than King. Louis XVI, with Marie Antoinette ever ready to strengthen his resolve, balked at accepting the role of constitutional monarch thus assigned to him. He continued to believe that the people, in tampering with his ancient powers, were rebels, against whom force was the only real argument. He soon discovered that force was an argument which worked both ways.

Paris had continued to seethe with discontent. Revolutionary turbulence had frightened numerous foreigners and aristocrats into departure and hence had dried up one of the sources of employment for many Parisians. The continuing rise in the price of bread worsened the situation. News that officers of the regiment of Flanders, which was on duty at Versailles, had clamorously demonstrated their readiness to crush the revolution, touched off fears that the shortage of food was due to a royal plot to starve Paris into submission. On October 5, a mob of Parisian women, many of them stallkeepers at the great market of Les Halles, trooped to Versailles to demand bread and to bring the king back with them. They were followed by the National Guard, a body of civilian volunteer soldiers commanded by Lafayette. A clash between the royal guards and the crowd led to bloody fighting, which was terminated only when Lafayette appeared before the rioters with the royal family. The king, queen and dauphin—dubbed "the baker, the baker's wife, and the baker's apprentice" (*le boulanger, la boulangère, et le petit mitron*)—rode to Paris, accompanied by the exultant crowd, the National Guard, and Lafayette riding at the side of the royal carriage.

The king took up residence at the palace of the Tuileries. Two weeks later the National Assembly followed, taking up improvised quarters in a riding-school arena. The shift of the capital to Paris was a fateful event. It placed both the monarch and the Assembly in the midst of a restive population, which was readier than ever to express its fears and seek its aims by brute force. Mob action and insurrection were becoming part of the pattern of revolutionary development.

The Revolution in Imbalance. The National Assembly was appalled at the violence of the "October days." It quickly enacted legislation empowering municipal authorities to order troops to fire upon mutinous crowds after a red flag of warning was displayed. Its readiness to reassert authority did not, however, win it the confidence of the king.

Louis feigned acceptance of his new position, but his purpose was only to buy time; somehow, he hoped, a new situation would come about. He permitted some of the leading constitutional monarchists—notably Mirabeau, who had been a leader of the Third Estate during the struggle for the National Assembly, and Lafayette—to act as guardians of the crown's position, but scorned their proposals in practice.

Meanwhile, France continued to be gripped by political turmoil. Public opinion was no longer the subtle elusive force it had been under the Old Regime; now it was tangible fact. It was the multitude of newspapers, of a variety of political beliefs, reporting events with more passion than truth and arousing their readers' aspirations and passions; the political clubs, where political issues were debated, plans of action were formulated, and leadership was given to the various segments of the nation; the spectators crowding into the galleries of the legislative chamber, following the debate or tumultuously participating by invectives and cheers; the petitioners massed before the bar of the Assembly, presenting demands with imperious insistence. The threat of armed violence lay close to the surface of political controversy. Weapons were in the hands not only of the army and the National Guard but also of ordinary citizens.

Faced with such conditions, the constitutional monarchists of all shades —the "patriots" who emphasized the sovereignty of the nation as well as the "monarchy-men" (*monarchiens*) who favored strengthening the crown— desired to restore calm and order as much as the king. But the "patriots," who dominated the National Assembly, sensed Louis's insincerity even when they could not prove it, and refused to trust him or his ministers. The assembly chipped away at the royal authority but, bound by its monarchism, was unwilling to put any other executive power in its place. The result was to intensify even further the instability of public life, clearing the path for continuation of revolution.

The Civil Constitution of the Clergy. The conflict of the monarch and the National Constituent Assembly was sharpened by the religious policy adopted by the legislature. The Assembly was moved in its religious legislation by the spirit of the Enlightenment, with its emphasis upon tolerance, and by the desire to assume the centuries-old powers exerted by the Most Christian Kings over the Roman Catholic church in France and expressed in the doctrines of Gallicanism.

Freedom of religious opinion was proclaimed by the Declaration of the Rights of Man. A decree adopted on Christmas Eve, 1789, granted complete equality as voters and officeholders to Protestants; similar status was given to Jews in 1790 and 1791. These laws touched the position of the church within the state but not its internal affairs. Measures of intervention began early in 1790 with the abolition of monasticism, a key institution in Roman Catholicism. It was followed by expropriation of the immense wealth of the church, mostly in land; the seizure was prompted by the fiscal emergency, which grew steadily worse after the onset of revolution. The confiscated land was used to provide a backing for the paper currency, called *assignats*, established by the Assembly. The revenues hitherto received by the clergy from their holdings were to be replaced with salaries paid by the state. The capstone of the religious legislation was the Civil Constitution of the Clergy, adopted on July 12, 1790. It provided for reorganization of the bishoprics to coincide with the new departments of civil government and declared that all churchmen were to be elected by the voters of their districts. No powers of nomination, investiture, or discipline were left to the papacy; French bishops might do no more than notify the pope of their election.

Schism in Religion. In adopting the Civil Constitution of the Clergy, the majority in the assembly had no feeling that they were violating the religious principles of Roman Catholics. The protests of numerous bishops sitting in the assembly, particularly against the provision for the election of priests, were brushed aside: churchmen, becoming state officials, ought to come under the same rule of election by those they served that was set down for other public servants. The notion of separating church and state was almost unheard of and received no consideration; it was taken for granted that religion was a necessary cement for society. Being within the state, religion was subject to its decisions.

Surprise and indignation ensued, therefore, when numerous churchmen, not only high prelates but also humble parish priests, refused to swear fidelity and allegiance to the new constitutional legislation, including the Civil Constitution. There was little or no understanding of the grounds of resistance: that the papacy held the "keys of the kingdom" of heaven, that the priesthood was a separate order of men, over and not beneath the laity, that the church was an international organization not subject to political commands in matters of doctrine. The "nonjurors," as the recalcitrants were called, were

The Departments of France
in 1791

confirmed in their resistance by a papal bull issued by Pius VI condemning the Civil Constitution and suspending from office the bishops who had accepted it.

The Assembly reacted in surprise, anger, and fear when the simple folk in many parts of the country clung stubbornly to their nonjuring priests and refused the ministrations of the "constitutional" clergy, as those who accepted the new legislation were called. The attempt of the state to favor the "jurors" was to little avail. The schism between them and the nonjurors proved bitter and implacable. The refractory clergy and their loyal parishioners became a feeding ground for counterrevolution, a source of some of the most difficult resistance that the revolutionaries were to face for a decade.

The Constitution of 1791. The Assembly meanwhile went forward with the writing of a formal fundamental organic law for France. On September 3, 1791, the first written constitution in the history of the country was adopted. It confirmed the new order created by the revolution. France became a constitutional monarchy, with the king holding executive authority. The legislative power was given to a single chamber, the Legislative Assembly. Despite the proclamation of the equality of all Frenchmen in the Declaration of the Rights of Man, a line was drawn between the political rights given to those with and those without property. Only those who paid a direct tax amounting to at least the value of three days' labor became "active citizens" entitled to vote; all others became "passive citizens," protected by the law but with no right to "concur" (in the words of the Declaration of Rights)

623

in its enactment. The active citizens, about four and a quarter million in number (as against the three million passive citizens), did not choose deputies directly but only electors who in turn selected representatives to the Legislative Assembly. These electors were required to have substantially greater wealth than "active" citizens; only about 50,000 in all France were rich enough to become electors.

It was not easy for Louis XVI to give his approval to the constitution, which made permanent the replacement of absolute by constitutional monarchy. But he was driven to acceptance by the virtual certainty that his refusal would result in its being brought into force by the sole authority of the Constituent Assembly, and that he would lose his throne. On September 28, expressing the hope that the revolution was over, he proclaimed the constitution. Three days later the Legislative Assembly, which had already been elected, held its first meeting.

In form, the revolution—the transfer of sovereign power from one group to another—was indeed over. A new legal order came into being. Its principal creators and beneficiaries were the bourgeoisie. Now the time had come for them to enjoy the benefits of the new regime: prosperity, leadership, and power. Instead of these boons, the bourgeoisie and its political representatives found themselves faced by enduring crisis.

The Sans-Culottes. The revolution was the work not only of the bourgeoisie but also of the disparate, inchoate group called "the people"—artisans, wageworkers, small businessmen, adventurers on the make, even some criminals. They differed from their bourgeois "betters" in speech, manners, and dress. Because they wore trousers and not the breeches of the upper classes, the derisive name *sans-culottes* (without breeches) had been given them; but they made it into a term of pride.

The sans-culottes came into increasing conflict with the bourgeoisie, with whom they had been allied against the Old Regime. Their passion for revenge, their readiness to kill, breaking forth into revolutionary massacres, appalled the order-loving bourgeoisie. Even more important was their divergence over the issue of freedom of business enterprise. The bourgeois were mainly pupils of the Physiocrats and favored unrestricted transport of commodities and unhampered play of supply and demand in setting prices; the sans-culottes, on the contrary, demanded that the state assure them their daily bread and their other needs in adequate quantities and at prices they could pay. The National Assembly gladly cast into the discard the guild system, with its restraints upon production, and it also forbade, by the Le Chapelier Law of January 14, 1791, the organization of workingmen into leagues or unions to enforce higher wages, particularly by means of strikes.

The sans-culottes, though they generally gave their support to the radical political clubs, notably the Jacobins, nevertheless constituted a separate political force with its own leaders. Most famous of these was Marat, the fiery editor of the revolutionary journal *L'Ami du Peuple* (*The Friend of the People*). Others were Jacques Roux, a Catholic priest who became a fervid revolutionary, and Hébert, a demagogue seeking his private advantages in public disturbances.

Émigrés and Plotters. At the opposite extreme from the sans-culottes were the *émigrés*, aristocrats who went into self-inflicted exile, and conspirators seeking the overthrow of the revolution.

The movement of nobles out of France had begun in the very first month of the revolution; the most notable was the king's youngest brother, the count of Artois. The *émigrés* had congregated as near to the frontier as possible, wherever the rulers gave them welcome. Turin, the capital of Savoy-Piedmont, and then Coblenz, in the German archbishopric of Trier, became their principal centers. Emperor Leopold II, though the brother of the French queen, gave the aristocratic refugees a courteously cold shoulder: the *émigrés* not only had abandoned the French royal family in its time of need; they bitterly denounced every action of conciliation between king and nation, which Leopold thought wise and necessary.

The *émigrés* lived in rampant luxury as long as their funds, or their creditors' patience, held out; then they importuned their hosts for aid. The purpose of returning home at the head of armies to overthrow the revolution never left their minds; they formed a volunteer corps in the Rhineland and beseeched the European monarchs to wage a crusade to re-establish the Old Regime.

Within France conspiracies were formed among the bolder of the *ci-devants* (the "former" noblemen) who remained in the country. They drew upon a variety of supporters: those embittered by expropriation of their wealth or loss of their status; those set against the revolutionary leaders by personal quarrels; those moved by the wish to defend the nonjuring church; and, not least, those wide circles of the people who did not wish their persons or their wealth to be conscripted in the service of the revolution. The sense of omnipresent plotting increased the disquietude of the revolutionaries.

The King's Flight Foiled. The one great initiative taken by Louis XVI, an attempt to flee France, shattered the unstable equilibrium which had prevailed under the National Assembly. The thought of flight had been in the king's mind at least since the Parisian women had invaded Versailles and dragged the royal family to Paris in September 1789. But he had not squeezed his courage to the point of action. When, in April 1791, a crowd prevented him from leaving the Tuileries to attend Easter services at Saint-Cloud palace, outside the capital, Louis realized that he was a prisoner, despite the provisions in the constitution for his personal inviolability. He decided at last to escape.

Even at such a time the king and queen insisted on a measure of royal grandeur and ease in their flight. They had a heavy coach built for their party, which included not only the royal couple and their son, but ladies-in-waiting and a hairdresser. A day's delay in departure and a leisurely pace en route to the eastern frontier led to disaster. When the royal party halted at Varennes, a postmaster's son identified the ill-disguised monarch, called for help, and brought the escape to a stop. The National Assembly sent an escort of its own, which brought the king, the queen, and their companions back to Paris.

Descent into War. The dilemma of the constitutional monarchists momentarily saved the king from the consequences of his failure. They dared not dethrone him lest they open the way to a republic, with its threat of renewed turmoil; so they pretended that he had been kidnaped and allowed him to reign on. They then focused their fire upon the sans-culottes and the radicals of the Jacobin club, who began to demand the dethroning of the king, the establishment of a republic, and the resumption of a vigorous revolutionary policy. On July 17, 1791, a crowd petitioning the Assembly for a popular referendum on the king's status was fired upon by the National Guard. The breach was complete—between the republican "patriots" and the sans-culottes on the one hand, and the constitutional monarchists on the other. But the monarchists still could not trust their royal prisoner. The worsening of economic conditions and the perennial emptiness of the treasury made the task of government more difficult still.

Their nemesis, however, was the changed attitude of the European monarchies toward France. Until the flight to Varennes, only Gustavus III of Sweden and Catherine II of Russia, at the very ends of Europe, had echoed the *émigrés'* call for a crusade. Pitt in England, the emperor in Austria, and most of the king's ministers in Prussia, all looked upon the debacle of authority in France as their opportunity to press forward to new conquests and acquisitions, uninterrupted by the intervention of what had been once the greatest power in Europe. But the king's attempt to escape France made it impossible to pretend that he had made his peace with the revolution; and reigning monarchs were understandably concerned lest attacks upon kings by subjects became a contagious example. Nonetheless negotiations for military action in favor of Louis XVI faltered upon the unwillingness of Leopold II to use more than words on the French monarch's behalf. Leopold joined with Frederick William II of Prussia in a declaration, issued at Pillnitz on August 21, 1791, warning the French that failure to restore their monarch to liberty would entail action of the European states against them. The threat sounded worse than it was intended, for Leopold had slipped in a clause that such action would occur only "when and in the case that" all the powers concurred, which English unwillingness to join in a crusade would undoubtedly prevent. But the subtlety was lost on the French, who demanded that the emperor retract the declaration of Pillnitz.

War Declared. The threats from abroad, combined with the outbreak of a counterrevolutionary rebellion in the western district of the Vendée, created a crisis in the French government, which passed into the hands of the Legislative Assembly elected under the new constitution. The faction of republicans which dominated the Jacobin club—known as Brissotins, after their leader Brissot, or as Girondins, because the most influential of them came from the department of the Gironde, around Bordeaux—used the opportunity to drive the monarchists out of the government and to established their own ministry.

Then, facing a less conciliatory policy from Austria after the death of Leopold II early in 1792—his successor, Francis II, was no liberal at all—the Girondins enthusiastically declared war, on April 20, 1792, upon "the king of Bohemia and Hungary" (thus avoiding a war upon the Empire, and hence all the German states). The declaration was supported by the king and the monarchists, who hoped that their command of the army would enable them to recapture political control of France; as well as by the stalwart revolutionaries, who hoped war would "unmask the traitors" and thereby drive the revolution on. Only one Jacobin, Robespierre, overcame his first fever for war and warned that it would destroy the revolution, by turning the peoples of other lands against the French and by placing power within the country increasingly in the hands of the generals, who would ultimately establish a military dictatorship.

Overthrow of the Monarchy. War soon proved to be no promenade of triumphant French revolutionaries but a series of defeats at the hands of the imperial forces commanded by the duke of Brunswick, as well as a continuation of the counterrevolutionary rebellion in the Vendée. The French army had been disrupted by years of revolution, the flight of numerous officers, the absence of supplies, and the lack of clear firm leadership. There had been treason, too, for the queen had transmitted the French military plans to the Austrians.

The Legislative Assembly struck at the dangers closest to home. On May 27, May 29, and June 8, it voted three decrees, the first dissolving the king's constitutional guard, which had become a center of counterrevolution; the second ordering the deportation of all nonjuring priests, as inspirers of counterrevolution; and the third establishing a camp of 20,000 National Guardsmen near Paris to protect the capital against military attack, which was feared even more from Lafayette, who commanded an army at the front, than from the Austrians. The king, impatiently awaiting the arrival of Brunswick's troops, refused the proffered aid of Lafayette; instead he began to strike himself at the revolution; he vetoed the decrees deporting the nonjurors and establishing the camp of guardsmen, and dismissed the Girondin ministers. On June 30, he withstood a mass petition to the Tuileries organized by the Girondins in protest against his veto.

His energy came too late. On July 25, the duke of Brunswick published a proclamation drawn up by an *émigré*. It threatened the French with the total destruction of the city of Paris if any harm came to the person of the king. The reply was an insurrection of the Parisian sans-culottes, supported by the Jacobins, on August 10. The king's guards were massacred in the Tuileries; the king himself fled to the Legislative Assembly for safety. The insurrectionists invaded the Assembly hall, demanding the monarch's dethronement. The deputies would go no further than to suspend him, but conceded the summoning of a new assembly, called the Convention, to govern France and draw up a new and more democratic constitution. The vote in the elections for the Convention was given to all citizens. Lafayette, losing all hope of saving the monarchy, fled to the Austrians; they sent him to prison as one of the makers of the revolution. The cause of constitutional monarchy—that system of balance between monarch and nation which had been almost everyone's hope in 1789—was shattered.

III. The Jacobin Republic, 1792-1795

Revolutionary republicanism took over. France fought a coalition of enemy states while civil turmoil raged within the country. The revolution was at its crisis: it could either re-establish authority and thereby save its achievements, or its manifold foes would crush it and undo its work.

The Crisis of the Revolution. When the Convention met for the first time on September 21, 1792, its immediate needs were to take control within the country, and to organize the military defense of the nation.

The sans-culottes of Paris, with the Commune of the capital serving as their organized agency of action and expression, were virtually a second government. They had arrested the king and put him in the prison known as the Temple to await his fate. They established their own committee of watch to imprison those suspected of royalist sympathies; the Extraordinary Tribunal hurriedly created by the Legislative Assembly to take the trial of suspects out of the hands of the Commune aroused the sans-culottes' wrath by adhering to normal standards of judicial procedure, instead of condemning them out of hand. The progress of the invasion and the counterrevolutionary rebellion—Brunswick captured the great frontier fortress of Verdun, while the Vendée was in arms against the revolution—aroused fears that the imprisoned suspects would break out and attack the defenders from behind as soon as Brunswick neared the capital. On September 2, mobs took control of the Paris prisons and during a week of almost incessant bloodshed slew more than a thousand suspects after a pretense of trial by self-constituted "courts."

These "September massacres" confronted the bourgeois revolutionaries who dominated the Convention with one of their fundamental problems: the sans-culottes, by their violent deeds, had repeatedly saved the revolution; how could they be brought under control without striking down one of the essential supports of the revolution? Part of the answer came on September 20, the day before the Convention met, when French forces met and defeated a Prussian force at Valmy. Consolidation of revolution within France depended upon the ending of the military threat from outside.

The Girondins. The Convention opened by proclaiming the abolition of the monarchy and establishing a republic. This was the last action on which there was agreement, for the Convention immediately split into furiously hostile factions, the Girondins, who held the principal ministries of state, and the Mountain, as the radical Jacobins were called because they seated themselves on the highest tiers of benches in the assembly hall.

The Girondins and the "Mountaineers" came from the same general class of the population, but represented different attitudes and feelings. The Girondins, for all their verbal vehemence, were in fact dedicated to ending the revolution as quickly as possible and restoring public order. They were closely linked to business interests, especially in the provinces, and expressed the growing anxiety of the outlying country that Paris, where the sans-culottes were in control, was driving the revolution from its primary purpose, the defense of property, to the very opposite, an attack upon property. The Girondins desired the re-establishment of constitutional rule, with safeguards for individual liberty, as set down in the Declaration of the Rights of Man. They lacked, however, the requirements for leaders in a time of emergency: a single-minded readiness to strike; a certainty in oneself; determination; ruthlessness.

The Jacobins. These were the very qualities of the Jacobins: for the Jacobin club and the Jacobin name became the sole possession of the Mountaineers after the secession of the Girondins. The Jacobins drew their strength from the dream of building, at once, the Heavenly City of the Enlightenment *philosophes:* not for them the Girondin purpose of making the world safe for the man of business and the professions. The Jacobin ideal was a nation of small property owners, engaged in productive enterprise, living modest and virtuous lives. The means to achieve this utopia was the revolution; those who did not share the aim could not be true to the revolution, while those unwilling to use the harsh methods of revolution were untrue to the aim.

The Jacobins acknowledged the sans-culottes as necessary allies in the revolution, because they furnished the insurrectionary violence by which it was defended and driven forward. But they did not share the san-culottes' often almost purposeless violence and cruelty, nor their hatred of all wealth.

The Plain. Neither Girondins nor Jacobins formed the actual majority in the Convention, where delegates from the Parisian sans-culottes were a small minority. Most of the deputies were committed to the revolution as the means of defending the New Regime, that is, the social and economic transformations incorporated in the Declaration of Rights and the Constitution of 1791. Not originally republicans, they were ready to be republicans when the defection of the king made it impossible to remain constitutional monarchists. They lacked the lofty principles of the Girondins or the utopianism of the Jacobins; their interest lay in preserving the concrete gains of the revolution for the bourgeoisie. Like the Girondins and the Mountaineers they were fervent nationalists. Because they sat on the lower seats in the assembly hall, they received the nickname of the Plain. The Mountaineers, contemptuous of their hesitations, called them the Marsh. Plain or Marsh, they had numerical command of the Convention and to win their votes in one or another way became essential for the Girondins, who wished to remain in office, and the Jacobins, who wanted to take their place.

The Struggle for Power. A fierce struggle ensued between the Girondins and the Jacobins. At first the initiative lay with the Girondins, because their essential moderation was closer to the spirit of the Plain. But they fell victim both to the maneuvers of the Jacobins and to their own incapacity.

The fate of the king became a partisan issue. The Jacobins demanded that he be tried for treason. The Girondins decided to save the king, in part to defeat the Jacobin policy and in part to sway towards themselves the large section of the nation which remained royalist in feeling. The Jacobins, led by Robespierre, drove the issue to decision, especially after papers were discovered in a secret chest which proved that Louis XVI had appealed for foreign military aid to crush the revolution. The king was tried and found guilty by a unanimous vote, except for 31 absent and 11 abstaining members. But only 361, exactly a majority, voted for the death penalty. On January 21, 1793, "Louis Capet," once king of France, lost his head under the guillotine.

The Convention followed by a series of measures to defend the revolution: the proclamation of a levy *"en masse,"* a conscription of all men for service, military, or other; the raising of 300,000 additional troops; the formation of a Revolutionary Tribunal and of local revolutionary committees as well as a Committee of Public Safety at the center. The struggle between the Girondins and the Jacobins did not abate. The Jacobins called upon Paris for aid, the Girondins replied with a threat to destroy the city and transfer the capital elsewhere. The sans-culottes rose in revolt, and on June 2 compelled the Convention to place 29 Girondin members under arrest.

A series of executions of Girondin deputies, in violation of their constitutional inviolability, followed. The guillotining of the Girondins was followed by that of dissident Jacobins, notably the would-be conciliator Danton, who had been one of the outstanding organizers of the revolutionary defense. With them to the guillotine went the leaders of the sans-culottes of Paris, including Hébert, who had been implicated in conspiracies or who had disputed the domination of the Jacobins. The Mountain was in sole and total command at last.

The Committee of Public Safety. The victory of the Mountain consolidated the predominating position taken in the government by the Committee of Public Safety. It was only one of the various committees established by the Convention to replace the executive agencies inherited from the constitutional monarchy. The Committee of Public Safety formulated general policy and carried it into action; it became the master of all the branches of government and of the Convention itself.

It was a group of twelve equal members. Though formally without individual assignments, each applied himself to special tasks usually with the full powers of the whole committee. The public spokesman of the committee was Robespierre, the dominant figure in the Jacobin club. His passionate oratory and parliamentary skill helped to make the Convention obey the will of the committee. More than anyone else, he embodied the Jacobin spirit. So wholly given over to the attainment of the ideal society that he was called "the Incorruptible," he saw all who stood in the way as evil. In the service of his aim, he was ready to sacrifice himself and his fellow men. Yet vanity crossed his heroic qualities with petty vengefulness, so that although he could win hosts of devoted disciples he also aroused passionate hatred.

The Committee's accomplishment as the effective government of France depended equally upon the work of its administrator members, of whom Carnot was the most important. A former officer of the royal army, Carnot became the "organizer of victory," directing the rebuilding of the French army, which had been shattered and demoralized by years of revolution and defeat, into a powerful and effective force. He did not share the Jacobin dream; politically he was one of the Plain, and he resisted Robespierre's readiness to hold the sans-culottes in line by egalitarian promises directed against property owners.

The Reign of Terror. The overwhelming fact faced by the Convention and the Committee of Public Safety was that much of the nation was bitterly hostile to the revolution, and most of its friends wished to be saved without undue exertion on their part, with no danger to themselves or their possessions. Yet the disorganization of France was extreme, while its danger was great. The authority of the government was widely flouted. The payment of taxes was partial and sporadic, so that the treasury was emptier than before the revolution; the *assignat* paper currency continued to come off the printing presses, but its value fell constantly. Farmers refused to supply food to the armies and the cities in exchange for *assignats;* the manufacture of other articles of necessity fell off at the same time.

In the face of such immense difficulties, and impelled by an overwhelming desire to punish those responsible, the Committee resorted to terror as a means of government. The guillotine—the new, efficient instrument of execution—became the instrument of a revolutionary "reason of state." The end of revolutionary victory was declared to justify all means, even the introduction of admittedly tyrannical methods of government and justice. Robespierre summed up the attitude in a ringing phrase, "There is no liberty for the assassins of liberty."

A Reign of Terror ensued. In the course of little more than a year, between one hundred thousand and three hundred thousand persons were imprisoned, often on merest suspicion; at least 17,000 died after judicial sentence of death, and perhaps 20,000 or more were slain with less formality. The "Terror," though it touched every part of the country, was fiercest where war and counterrevolution were closest.

The Revolution Completed and Defended. In order to bind the population more tightly to the cause of the revolution, the Convention completed the abolition of the Old Regime. The vestigial recognition of "real" obligations under the old manorial system was discarded; the property rights of the new proprietors in their land became absolute. There were many more such owners, as the expropriated lands of the church and the confiscated lands of the *émigrés*—called "national wealth"—were sold off, with the *assignats* taken in payment at face value. The hoary old system of weights and measures, where each little town or district had its own standards, was replaced by a simple uniform "metric" system based on multiples of ten.

These changes proved enduring. Of briefer existence were other innovations. A revolutionary calendar took the place of the old Roman-Christian calendar; it renamed the months and years, extended the week to ten days, and numbered the years from the beginning of the Republic instead of the birth of Christ. The calendar continued in use for little more than a decade. Attempts to create revolutionary pseudo-religions were even more short-lived. The "de-Christianization" movement of Hébert contributed to his downfall.

A new constitution was drawn up in 1793, which provided for universal manhood suffrage and other principles of the most extensive democracy. But it was not put into operation because of the existing emergency; instead, on October 10, 1793, the government was proclaimed to be "revolutionary until peace," that is, subject to no rules or limits in its work of defense and reorganization. Under the guidance of the Committee of Public Safety, and with the Terror to compel obedience to its decrees, this work was performed

The Conquests of Revolutionary France, 1792-1799

with extraordinary speed and success. The control of central government was absolute, beyond anything achieved even by Louis XIV. War became the business of the nation, not just of the state. The military forces received new recruits under the levy *en masse* and became a people's army, fighting, like Cromwell's "Ironsides" a century and a half earlier, for a cause. The production of weapons and other military supplies was increased with the aid of numerous scientific advisers. Food supplies were brought in from the countryside; military requisitioning parties seized the harvest whenever, as frequently occurred, the peasants would not deliver their produce at the fixed "maximum" price. The commanders of the army were aided, encouraged, and watched by "representatives on mission," who were members of the Convention sent with full powers to act wherever needed, at the front or in the provinces.

By the spring of 1794, the results of this enormous activity began to show in the campaigning. French armies ceased to retreat and began a series of spectacular victories, advancing into territories all along the western and northern frontiers. The energies of France, for centuries the "great nation" in Europe, were no longer bound in by the self-restricting institutions of the Old Regime.

Thermidor: the Fall of Robespierre. As the sense of danger passed, the compelling pressure upon the majority of the Convention to accept the dictatorial domination of the Committee of Public Safety was removed. The result was the downfall of Robespierre, who embodied the rule by terror and revolutionary government above and outside the law. The initiative in turning the Convention against him was taken by Tallien, a member implicated in corruption while a representative on mission. His denunciation of Robespierre as a tyrant on July 27, 1794, broke the spell. Robespierre's proposal to condemn "traitors" within the Assembly without singling them out by name left a wide swath of fright, since none felt safe, and opened the way of acceptance of Tallien's call.

Robespierre was arrested together with his brother and closest associates. Briefly rescued by a force from the Commune of Paris, Robespierre was recaptured by troops sent by the Convention: the sans-culottes failed to rise in insurrection because the execution of Hébert and others of their leaders had broken their confidence in the Jacobins. Robespierre and his friends died under the guillotine the next day.

The government was shifted to the hands of other Jacobins, called Thermidoreans because Robespierre had fallen during the month named Thermidor in the revolutionary calendar. Though Jacobins, they could no longer govern by terror: it had become the abomination not only of the immense majority of the nation but also of the Convention. With terror gone, the mechanism of government slowed. The authority built up in less than two years began to fall apart. Nonetheless the invaders were beaten. Prussia, a principal member of the hostile coalition, accepted peace at Basel in April 1795, followed by the United Provinces in May and by Spain in July. The landing of an army of English and *émigré* troops at Quiberon Bay, in Brittany, in June was a threat from the coast, but a republican force destroyed the invasion on July 21. (See ch. 29, p. 639.) Under the security of this relative calm, the Convention devised a new constitution—the Constitution of Year III, the third of the revolutionary series—designed to consolidate the gains of the revolution, to bring turmoil and disorder to an end, and to assure the unhampered rule of the bourgeoisie of wealth and talents.

29

France in Revolution: II

1795 - 1815

By 1795 THE DESTRUCTION of the Old Regime in France had been completed and the framework of a new society laid down, but the French Revolution was not yet over. The tasks of consolidation and defense remained. During four trouble-scarred years the Directory, a government republican in form and bourgeois in interests, created by the Constitution of the Year III, attempted to re-establish peace and order. When it failed, the fate of the revolution passed into the hands of a military adventurer, Napoleon Bonaparte. His price for preserving the new social order was to make France the instrument of his ambition to be master of France, Europe, perhaps the world. Bloodshed and violence were resumed on an immense scale. Yet, when the Emperor Napoleon fell from power and glory in 1815, the survival of the New Regime was still in question.

I. The Directory

The Directory, which took power late in 1795, embodied the two great hopes of the Thermidoreans. One was to ensure the domination of the new "notables," the bourgeoisie. The other was to terminate revolutionary politics

—the pattern of insurrection and terror, of lawlessness of rulers and ruled alike.

The New Notables. Under the Old Regime the bourgeoisie had been an almost inchoate congeries of distinct, often hostile groups; the Revolution had welded them into a single, relatively coherent class. Wealth became the one universal standard of rank and status; the innumerable special privileges and liberties of the Old Regime no longer set barriers between the segments of the propertied class. Money flowed from one kind of enterprise into others without the legal and social restrictions which had hampered business activity under the monarchy. Bankers and great merchants rose to the top of the social scale.

The satisfaction of the bourgeoisie with the social and economic transformations wrought by the Revolution was shared by the property-owning peasantry. They had achieved total emancipation from the remnants of manorialism and serfdom; they owned their lands outright. By the purchase of "national wealth"—the confiscated lands of church and nobility—they had rounded out their possessions.

Bourgeoisie and peasantry alike were tired of the convulsions and terrors of the preceding half-decade. They wanted calm and peace so that they could safely enjoy the benefits of the new society, but without paying heavy taxes or making other sacrifices. This was the paradox of the Directory: though governing for the bourgeoisie and the peasantry, it could not count upon their unflinching support in time of need. It remained a government *for* the propertied classes, not *by* them.

Government of Checks and Balances. As a system of authority, the Directory was a republic resting on a limited democracy. Like the constitution of 1791, the organic law of 1795 gave the ballot only to those who paid direct taxes, reserving to them the name of "citizens." But even this winnowed-out electorate was not permitted free play in the choice of representatives to the new legislature. Before disbanding, the Convention had decreed that two-thirds of the members of the new assemblies—the Council of the Ancients and the Council of Five Hundreds—must be selected from its own ranks. When a large majority of the voters gave their choice to others who were untainted with participation in the government of the Terror, the handful of re-elected Convention deputies met separately and selected their colleagues in the new legislature. An aura of mistrust between the political nation and the political authorities hung over the new government from its first beginnings.

In structure the Directory was profoundly unlike its revolutionary predecessors. It was artfully designed to prevent the recurrence of the dictatorship of a minority or an individual. The division of the legislature into two chambers doubled the hurdles to be crossed by proposed laws. The legislature chose the executive authority—the Directory in the specific sense—

but lost control over it once the five Directors were named. And since the five were equal in rights, none among them could enforce his will upon the others. The ideal of checks and balances was so perfectly met that only the full-hearted concord of all elements of government, or the extralegal domination of one over the others, could assure the effective conduct of the business of state.

Despite these barriers to purposeful policy, the Directory inaugurated a whole series of measures to consolidate the reforms of the revolution. Jurists were appointed to unify the laws into a single national code. The mechanism of effective taxation—the assessment and the collection of taxes by paid agents of the state—was introduced; the resumption of regular tax payments by the population, which had often ceased after 1789, began to fill the void in the national treasury. The functions, responsibilities, and powers of the separate ministries of state, never wholly clear under the Old Regime and often disregarded by the government of the Committee of Public Safety, were now made specific.

These were accomplishments of lasting importance, but did little or nothing to ease the constant political crisis. The Directory remained as unstable as any of its revolutionary predecessors.

The Revival of Royalism. The revival of royalism was the major peril to the new government within France. The death on June 8, 1795, of the imprisoned "Louis XVII," the son of the late king, gave the royalists another martyr. They proclaimed the count of Provence, eldest brother of Louis XVI, as his successor; he took the title of "Louis XVIII."

Royalism had been hurt and silenced during the Reign of Terror; but it had not been destroyed. The aristocrats, repenting the quarrel with the monarchy which had brought them to disaster along with Louis XVI, were now almost all fervent adherents of the restoration of absolute monarchy; most of the one-time constitutional monarchists who had gone over to the republican cause had been commoners. Royalism continued to hold the affection of many nonnobles as well; for some it was the continuation of long-held principles, for others a catch-all of the antipathies created by a half-decade of revolution. It was, too, the political expression of intransigent Roman Catholicism. As the past receded, the Old Regime took on in the memory of the counterrevolutionaries an appearance of greater stability, order, and happiness than it had in fact possessed.

The royalists, though self-proclaimed advocates of the restoration of order, were as ready as the most vehement Jacobin to use force to achieve their means. On the eve of the establishment of the Directory, they had made two great efforts to overthrow the republic. One was the insurrection of October 5, 1795 (13 Vendémaire Year IV by the revolutionary calendar) in Paris, where a rising of 20,000 royalists was defeated only by the intervention of the military forces, commanded by a young artillery officer, Napoleon Bonaparte. The other was a rebellion of the Chouans (as the Vendée rebels in the West were called) which was aided by the army of English and *émigré* troops landed at Quiberon Bay. It was defeated by another young republican officer, General Lazare Hoche.

Unsuccessful with arms, the royalists turned to the achievement of power within the republican political system. The limitation of the electorate enhanced their chances, since the propertied classes were deeply troubled by the rise of sans-culottist egalitarianism (although royalist commitment to the restoration of the lands of the church and the nobility made those who had acquired "national wealth" fearful of monarchical restoration). Young royalists, dubbed "the gilded youth," made personal attacks upon Jacobins and other republicans in the streets of Paris and other cities. In April 1797 the royalists, open and disguised, succeeded in winning a majority in the legislature. When they elected a director of their own political hue, the remaining directors organized a *coup d'état* on September 4 with the aid of troops. The legislature, under the threat of arms, was compelled to deport 53 deputies and to accept the voiding of elections in 49 departments; in all, 198 royalists lost their seats. Repression, lacking the fierceness of Jacobin terrorism, left the royalists a still threatening danger.

Babeuf: A New Jacobinism. Jacobinism represented a peril to the Directory from the other side. With the fall of Robespierre, it began to change character. Its hold on the propertied classes weakened until only the dreamers and the doctrinaires remained faithful; more and more Jacobinism became the possession of the sans-culottes, who wished to re-establish the dictatorial revolutionary government on a popular base which had existed in 1792-1794.

The increasingly sans-culottist temper of the new Jacobinism was displayed by the "Conspiracy of the Equals," led by the visionary journalist François Émile Babeuf. He put aside the earlier sans-culottist program which favored state intervention to keep prices down, to assure the supply of bread and other foodstuffs, and to provide employment; instead he raised his vision to a total reorganization of the economic structure of society. At first he advocated adoption of the "agrarian law," that is, confiscation and redistribution of landed property upon an equal basis. Later he turned to agrarian communism, that is, common ownership of the land; tillage would remain individual, but consumption would be put on an equal basis, and each would draw upon a general storehouse to which all would contribute their produce.

Though Babeuf's message was concerned with agrarian life, it was heard principally by urban artisans and workmen. Most of them, however, paid little attention to its communal theories: they remained concerned only with the political objective of bringing back the "good old days" when Robespierre governed France. The Directory, soon informed by its police of Babeuf's conspiracy, decreed the death penalty for advocacy of the "agrarian law" or similar communist programs. In May 1796, most of the leading conspirators were arrested. Those who remained free fell into a trap laid for them by the police when Babeuf attempted to organize a rebellion of the troops in a military encampment near Paris in September. Hundreds of Jacobins were arrested; a small number were deported to the French tropical colony of Guiana; Babeuf and one friend were guillotined in May 1797.

The next year Jacobinism took its revenge upon the Directory by winning a majority in the elections for the Ancients and the Five Hundreds. The Jacobin trump was the outbreak of economic crisis. The continuation of war made even worse the inflationary difficulties resulting from abandonment of state controls over the economy, notably the "law of the maximum." The collapse of the assignats and the return to hard currency replaced inflation by severe deflation, with employment falling off dangerously and the market for farm products sharply reduced. Once again the Directors in power resorted to a military coup in order to eject the hostile majority in the legislature.

The Emergence of Bonaparte. Though both royalists and Jacobins were put down, one great problem still remained: how to end the war which France had been waging since 1792. Even battlefield victories did not seem sufficient to achieve this end. Prussia, the United Provinces (Holland), and Spain had withdrawn from the first coalition in 1795; Sardinia (Piedmont) made peace the next year. France was actually able to make an alliance with the Spanish Bourbons in 1796, thanks to their wrath over British incursions into the Spanish colonial empire, but England and Austria remained active enemies.

Military operations took a new turn with the appointment of Bonaparte as commanding general in Italy in 1796. By a series of brilliant campaigns and a measure of luck, he was able to force Austria to make peace at Campoformio the next year; though French armies in Germany contributed greatly to the defeat of Austria, Bonaparte, displaying his extraordinary talent for manipulating public opinion, garnered the laurels of victory for himself. Taking the diplomatic initiative from his annoyed civilian masters in Paris, he laid down the terms of peace, which were built about the construction of Italian republics as satellites of France.

The following year he agreed to lead a French expedition to Egypt, a dependency of the Ottoman empire, in the expectation that French power on the Nile would destroy English naval predominance in the Mediterranean and provide a stepping stone from which to strike at the British colonial empire in India. Bonaparte reached Egypt with his army, escaping the cruising British fleet under Nelson; but the great English admiral surprised and destroyed the French naval forces at the Egyptian port of Abukir on August 1, 1798. Bonaparte's effort to strike up along the Levant coast to Turkey failed at Acre, in Syria; finally, trapped in Egypt with a useless army, he decided to return alone to France, as was permitted by his instructions.

General Bonaparte Takes Over. Bonaparte, once back in France, discovered that he was not a general in disgrace for failure but a hero because he had twice escaped the British navy. He was, furthermore, a hero for whom a group of conspirators within the government had plans. The inability of the Directory to assure itself a majority within the nation and in the legislative assemblies constantly thwarted its endeavors to stabilize conditions and to pursue a steady policy. Sieyès, who had returned to political life and become one of the Directors, after living in safe obscurity during the Reign of Terror, was the leader of the plotters. His basic remedy for the turmoil of French politics was to cut away the dependence of the government upon elections; authority, he now proclaimed, must come from above, and confidence from below. His fertile mind concocted various constitutional arrangements in which the propertied classes would be allowed to vote for deputies, while the legislator's powers would be severely limited.

In order to carry through this final *coup d'état*, which would openly transform the French republic into a self-perpetuating oligarchy, Sieyès needed the support of the military. The generals, however, had become increasingly independent of their nominal superiors in Paris; they drew their supplies and their funds less and less from the ever-inadequate national treasury, and more and more by requisitions and outright seizures from the conquered territories. Bonaparte, a general without an army, appeared the best instrument for Sieyès's purpose. A coup was arranged on November 9, 1799 (18 Brumaire Year VIII); the legislature was brought to heel by military detachments, and consent was given by rump meetings of the assemblies for drafting a new constitution. The proclaimed purpose of the coup was "to organize order throughout the administration, to re-establish domestic tranquility, and to achieve a firm and honorable peace."

II. The Emperor Napoleon

The *coup d'état* of 1799 turned out to be different from all its predecessors. General Bonaparte took power for himself, re-established order and tranquility, but also brought back absolute monarchy in his own person and involved France in immense wars of conquest.

General Bonaparte. Bonaparte, France's new master, was a Frenchman only by accident. He was born in the Mediterranean island of Corsica in

1769, only a year after it was bought by France from its former owner, Genoa. His native language was Italian; to the end of his life he kept slipping into earthy Italian phrases. His family was one of the leading Corsican clans, which took part in the resistance led by Pasquale Paoli against French domination; but after the rebellion failed, the Bonapartes were one of the first families to rally to the French side. They were rewarded by official favors, including the appointment of Napoleon to the French cadet school at Brienne in 1779. In 1784, upon graduation, he received a commission as a sublieutenant of artillery and went on to study for a year at the Champ de Mars military school in Paris, then to serve at various garrisons.

He had already displayed many qualities of his personality. He combined a mind of classical precision with the temperament of a passionate dreamer. He was vain and resentful: he was short of stature, spoke French with an accent among those who took pride in elegance of speech and diction, was poor and of dubious nobility among aristocrats of wealth and standing, and served in a branch of the army which required technical competence of a high order but gave little prestige. His feelings toward France verged on hatred; he spoke of "French tyranny" and remained at heart a Corsican.

His ties with Corsica were broken when he opposed the attempt of Paoli to bring the island over to the English side in 1793. When the Paoli revolt succeeded, he was compelled to flee with his family to France. During the government of the Committee of Public Safety, he was close to the Robespierre group; he admired particularly the forthright energy of Robespierre, although he did not share the sympathy that the "Incorruptible" had for common folk, who were never more than "rabble" in Bonaparte's eyes. Fame touched Bonaparte fleetingly when he directed the reconquest of the port of Toulon from the English in 1793. But the fall of Robespierre resulted in his brief imprisonment.

His fortune changed after his release. He wooed and married the widowed Josephine de Beauharnais, whose husband, a *ci-devant* noble, had been guillotined two years before. She brought Bonaparte the political sponsorship of a leading Thermidorean, Barras, whom he aided in suppressing the royalist rebellion of October 1795. The next year he received the command of the army of Italy, where he showed not only his brilliant abilities as a field commander but also his predilection for personal policy in disregard of the civil government to which he was subordinate.

First Consul Bonaparte. It was this general, readier to command than to obey, whom Sieyès thought to use as his docile instrument in the new government. Sieyès soon learned who was master. When he drew up a draft constitution which divided executive power evenly among three consuls, Bonaparte brushed it aside; he dictated his own charter of government, which gave all essential powers of decision and control to himself as First Consul.

Asked what there was in the new constitution, wags replied, "There is Bonaparte!" Sieyès was helpless, for the army gave its loyalty to Bonaparte, and it was now brute force which determined who would govern.

Yet Bonaparte's political program was in many respects similar to that of the Directory. "We have finished with the romance of the revolution," he announced. The time had come to consolidate what was "substantial and possible" in the changes of the previous decade. He told a delegation of notables that his would be "a government of social defense, the friend of order, respectful of property in all its forms, and peaceful in its foreign policy." He was sensitive to the need to conciliate the nation, or at least the notables. "A first consul is not like those kings by the grace of God who look upon their states as an inheritance," he declared. He therefore continued and strengthened the work of administrative reform which had been begun by the Directory. The great change came in the vigor with which policies were enforced. The sense of authority returned to the state. It was a sign of the times that the payment of taxes became regular and complete.

Enemies Within. The general docility of the population was far from universal. Bonaparte continued to face bitter opposition from several camps.

One was a group who remained faithful to the first ideal of the Directory: to create a regime in which governmental authority was combined with personal freedom. The despotic temper of the First Consul, who became consul for life in 1802, soon persuaded them that liberty for the individual was in some way linked to political freedom. The strength of this group lay largely in the talents of its members, notably the well-known writer Madame de Staël, daughter of the former French royal minister, Necker, and Benjamin Constant, one of her paramours, who combined the gifts of a novelist and a political thinker. Their weakness was their isolation from any political force ready for action even at peril to itself. Bonaparte therefore scorned them as "ideologues," mere talkers; but he watched them closely and did not scruple to punish them for their bolder words.

More dangerous were the Jacobins, as all who remained attached to the ideal of the revolutionary republic were now called. They were not afraid to act: insurrection was one of their principles. But they too had become isolated from the wide public. Only among the soldiers did they retain a following, but it was quite insufficient to turn the army from Bonaparte, particularly as he continued to win victories in the field. The police easily tracked down Jacobin conspirators and arrested them before they could turn words to deeds.

The gravest peril to the Bonapartist government came from the royalists. They felt that he had cheated them of their own opportunity to regain power. They combined readiness to act with new eloquence and intellectual powers: René de Chateaubriand, the most eminent living French man of letters, was their most effective advocate after he broke with Napoleon. They had significant popular support, especially in western France, where the Vendée revolt flared up again.

Royalist conspiracies against the life of the First Consul were rife. An attempt to blow him up in the street on December 24, 1800, left him unscathed but killed and wounded scores of bystanders. In 1803 and 1804 another conspiracy was organized to kidnap Bonaparte in Paris, and to slay him if he resisted. A French royal prince was expected to arrive in France to take over the government in the name of "Louis XVIII." When the duke of Enghien, a member of the Condé branch of the Bourbon dynasty, came to Ettenheim, in Baden, a small German principality on the French border, he was mistaken by the French police for this unnamed prince. On the command of the First Consul, a French cavalry detachment raced into Baden and seized Enghien, who was tried as a traitor and shot. The action shocked the European monarchs, for the kidnaping of Enghien was a flagrant violation of Baden's sovereignty; it showed Bonaparte's disregard of all conventions or principles except that of his self-interest and it reinvigorated hatred for France among the European potentates. Talleyrand, the witty and cynical *ci-devant* noble, bishop, and revolutionary who was now Bonaparte's foreign minister, commented scathingly, "It's worse than a crime; it's a mistake."

"Emperor of the French." Bonaparte's reply to the threats against his life was to make himself a hereditary dynastic monarch. He hoped thereby to discourage assassination attempts, since he would be followed in due course by an heir (in the absence of a son, he named his brothers to succeed him). He was reluctant to face the fact, seen by his more hard-headed officials, that his power, however absolute, was wholly personal in origin and character and would not survive him. But Bonaparte was prodigiously vain and wanted the outward panoply of power. He did not take the title of "king," for he did not want to appear to reverse the revolution; he adopted instead the title "Napoleon I, Emperor of the French." The title "emperor" implied equality with the Holy Roman Emperor and summoned up recollections of Rome and of Charlemagne.

The coronation ceremony at Notre Dame cathedral in Paris on December 2, 1804, was symbolic of the personal and political status of the emperor. He persuaded Pope Pius VII to come to Paris for the consecration ceremony, but at the last moment took the crown from the pontiff's hand and put it on his own head.

Napoleon proceeded to play the part of a monarch in the traditional pattern. He transformed his clan of Bonapartes into a brand-new imperial family. They took to their new ranks if they had been born to the purple; they quarreled over their precedence and their rights, and gave little gratitude to their benefactor, who was in their eyes only the fourth son of the

NAPOLEON THE FIRST, EMPEROR OF THE FRENCH. Engraving by Louis Lacoste, about 1805.

The "lean and hungry look" worn by General Bonaparte has been replaced in this print by the plumpness of Emperor Napoleon. The look of self-satisfaction remains, unmarred as yet by the fierce struggles of the next decade. (Achenbach Foundation)

family. Empress Josephine's family by her first marriage were also incorporated into the imperial family; indeed, her son Eugène de Beauharnais brought more ability to his work than most of the born Bonapartes.

The emperor also organized a court, where members of the old nobility (to whom amnesty had been given) mingled with a new imperial nobility of army officers and government officials. But Talleyrand, who remembered well the old days, disliked the military air in the new court and smiled, like his fellow *ci-devants*, at the clumsiness of the imperial nobles when faced with the requirements of an elaborate court etiquette.

The Ambiguous Settlement. The Napoleonic court, with its mingling of ancient and recent vintages, characterized the entire settlement attempted by Napoleon in France. It was an ambiguous merger of the Old and the New Regimes. Napoleon was the defender of the New Regime insofar as it had transformed the social and especially the economic structure of France; he emphasized the revolutionary principle of a society where "careers were open to talent." But he disdained the political idealism that had marked the first years of the French Revolution, the hope of a world in which men of good will would freely join together for public tasks. He was totally committed to

645

the necessity for an overriding authority to impose a single will upon the people, whom he denied all share in the work of governing. He was no believer in social egalitarianism, but favored the preservation of the division of society into classes. He therefore re-created a noble class, but based it upon wealth and service to the state; it lacked for the moment the castelike exclusiveness of the *ci-devant* aristocracy. He was, in fact, bringing into being a kind of simplified Old Regime, adapted to the legal and economic framework built by the Revolution. He was accomplishing what Louis XVI had neither wished nor been able to do.

His true ideal was that of "enlightened despotism." Like the reforming monarchs of the later eighteenth century, he was a "revolutionary from above," using the power of the state to make the necessary reforms in government, society, and economic life. Like them, too, he could not dissociate the quest for fame from the interests of the nation. He claimed, as they did, to be "the first servant of the state," but essentially looked upon the state as his own possession and instrument. But he was an upstart dynast without historical roots; no centuries-old tradition of dynastic loyalty bound the nation to him, only the prestige of his battlefield victories and his ability to crush all opposition within France. It was this that he recognized when he uttered the paradoxical complaint that he had the misfortune not to be his own grandson. His greatness was of his own making: that was his glory and his weakness.

The Revolution Consolidated. In a sense, the work of consolidating "the substantial and the possible" in the Revolution was not even Napoleon's own achievement. It was a continuation of projects initiated during the Directory, or even earlier, performed largely by those who had been entrusted with these responsibilities before Napoleon took power. Nonetheless it was his authority and his encouragement which enabled them to carry their work to completion. The most important of these projects were the adoption of a Civil Code—also called the Code Napoleon—and the administrative reorganization of the government.

The Civil Code was a systematic restatement of the laws governing private life in France. It laid down clear rules on the organization of the family and the control of its property; Napoleon intervened to strengthen the rights of husbands and fathers and to permit divorce. In general the Civil Code reflected the social principles of the Declaration of the Rights of Man: equality of all citizens before the law, without distinction of order or status (with the exception of the imperial family) ; the sanctity of private property; uniformity of justice in all parts of the land, freedom of conscience. It assured individual rights, but not the rights of the nation. Cambacérès, who was the most influential of the codifiers, summed up its meaning: "Three things are necessary and sufficient to man in society: to be the master of his person; to have property in order to meet his needs; to be able to dispose of both his person and his property to his own greatest benefit." The egalitarian tone of the earlier revolutionary changes was abandoned.

The reorganization of government was based upon the almost total elimination of local initiative and privilege in favor of the power of the central authority. The remnants of federalism inherited from the revolution were abolished; a coherent system of centralized government was introduced, on the pattern of the intendancies of the Old Regime. A prefect, appointed by and responsible to the central government, was placed in charge of each department. The prefects became the key officials of state, between the ministers, who were the direct agents of the imperial will, and the local population.

The Napoleonic regime attempted few economic innovations. The most important was the creation of the Bank of France in 1800; like its namesake in England, it linked private and public credit, and issued paper money. The continental system, though a continuation of the mercantilist policies of the French monarchy of the Old Regime, was primarily a war measure (see below, pp. 654-655).

The Revolution Reversed. Insofar as the relationship between ruler and ruled was concerned, Napoleon totally abandoned the revolutionary ideal of national sovereignty expressed through representative institutions as well as the "enlightened" ideal of personal freedom, safe from the intrusion of persons in political power. He reverted to the practice of monarchy as absolute, personal, and arbitrary as that of Louis XIV, but if anything more efficient and ruthless.

Napoleon profoundly distrusted all independent opinion. He looked upon newspapers as a necessary evil, limited their number to a minimum and placed them under constant censorship. As far as possible, he sought to make them mouthpieces of official attitudes, accepting the news as it was rearranged and often twisted by government departments. The courts were allowed a measure of independence. Judges were appointed for life, but they knew that their hopes of advancement depended upon hewing to the emperor's policies. The Napoleonic government did not confine itself to the normal processes of justice, even those established by itself. The resurgence of brigandage was put down by the institution of provost courts, from which there was no appeal and which were not bound by the usual rules of evidence. Political opposition was silenced by means of arbitrary arrest. The *lettre de cachet*, one of the most abhorred instruments of the police power under the Old Regime, was re-established in practice and used with a frequency that had not been known for almost a century.

The police became the key agency of internal government. Espionage upon citizens of every rank and walk of life was even more widespread than it had ever been under the Old Regime. "Watch everyone except me!" was Napoleon's order. For much of the reign the leader of the police was Joseph Fouché, a born intriguer, quick to adapt himself to changing currents of politics, ruthless and cynical in public life though at home the soul of sobriety. Fouché's spy network reached almost everywhere. Yet Napoleon did not trust Fouché and created several other networks of spies to check not only the population but also each other. Fouché's command of the most effective armed agency within the state, apart from the army, and his readiness to act on his own—for he never learned to kowtow to the emperor—made him a dangerous servant. Napoleon grew more and more to fear him, and finally dismissed him.

The Concordat.   Napoleon's cynical realism became ill-concealed hypocrisy when it came to deciding the place of religion within the state. Himself a deist without interest in philosophic or religious problems as such, having no sense for moral issues (for self-indulgence was his highest principle of conduct), he looked upon the church—which meant in France primarily the Roman Catholic church—only as a public institution. Like Voltaire he emphasized its role in preserving existing society. "I do not see in religion the mystery of the incarnation but the mystery of the social order," he declared. "It ties to Heaven a notion of equality which prevents the poor man from massacring the rich man." He added that "skillful conquerors never become embroiled with the priests." He never forgot that the conflict between the French revolutionaries and the Roman Catholic church had aroused some of the fiercest and most persistent resistance faced by the revolutionaries.

One of Napoleon's first major acts of policy after becoming first consul was to negotiate a religious settlement, or concordat, with the pope, Pius VII. This was concluded on July 16, 1801. It terminated the separation of church and state which had been in effect for six years. Roman Catholicism was recognized as the religion of the majority of Frenchmen; bishops were to be named by the French state and given their spiritual investiture by the pope; the state would provide salaries for the bishops and for one priest in each parish, but the church abandoned its claim for restitution of its confiscated wealth; finally, churchmen were to take an oath of loyalty to the state. Similar organic laws were given to the Protestant and Jewish communities in France.

But Napoleon's hope to win over the clergy was only partly satisfied. They accepted their new privileges but did not cease their efforts to obtain control of education and to expand their influence upon public matters. Tension continued, and became very sharp in the final years of the reign after the emperor confiscated the papal state for his kingdom of Italy and placed the pope under arrest.

The Mind of France.   Napoleon's narrowly political attitude was also displayed toward the intellectual and artistic life of France. He remained out of touch with the newest trends. In his own taste an unrepentant classicist, he abhorred the romanticists, even though their emphasis upon intensity of feeling corresponded to a profoundly important aspect of his own nature. But it was in grandiose action rather than in artistic experience that he found outlet for his passions: "I am not a man but a historical personage!" he boasted.

For him artists, writers, and thinkers were at best useful in strengthening the domination of the state, and no less in exalting the emperor within the state. He continued to support and encourage the painter David, who had been the artistic spokesman for the revolutionary regime. In the verbal arts, he was annoyed and somewhat puzzled that all the superior talents were at best neutral and usually downright hostile to him. "I have the hacks for me and the geniuses against me," he lamented. He gave both trust and support to the scientists, mathematicians, and engineers: their ideas had no obvious political overtones and coincided with the deep rational part of the emperor's nature.

The major educational measure of Napoleon's reign was the creation of a single national system of education in 1806, under the name of the Imperial University. It included not only the established universities, like the Sorbonne in Paris, but also the secondary schools (the *lycées* and *collèges*) which were incorporated into it and became subject to its strict and precise direction of subject matter and methods. This was one of the issues of sharp conflict with the Roman Catholic church, which had begun to re-establish its own system of secondary education. But Napoleon, who looked to the schools to furnish him with army officers and government officials, would not brook ecclesiastical interference in their training.

III. The Empire of Napoleon

However important the domestic policy of Napoleon, it was as a conquering warrior that he won fame and held power.

The Great Captain. Napoleon was the last of the great captains in European history—a general who led his army in person on the battlefield, and gave it victory by the precise aptness of his tactical conceptions, by his resolute, even reckless vigor of execution, and not least by the spur of his presence upon the troops. He was not a creative military mind but a commander marvelously skillful in using the instrumentalities of warfare—human, technical, and intellectual—which were available to him.

Napoleon's instrument of victory was a France again stronger than any other state in Europe, as in the days of Louis XIV, and steeled by an intense nationalism. He was not beset by lack of numbers, the bane of all commanders under the Old Regime: the revolution, by the introduction of conscription, placed at his disposal the manpower of France, and after his conquests he compelled the subject potentates of Europe to furnish him with contingents of troops. He was able to send more than a hundred thousand soldiers into a single battle, and to wage battle after battle; his opponents were forced to match or offset his numbers, or go down to defeat. Yet he applied before they did the tactics created during the revolutionary period for such large combat forces. He made no effort to align his troops in the neat array of an extended battle line, but sent them forward in huge columns behind swarms of skirmishers, with the purpose of smashing through the enemy's line in order to destroy him.

Unlike so many of the eighteenth-century generals, who accepted battle only when maneuver failed, he sought out the clash of arms in order to bring the campaign, and with it the war, to a swift conclusion. He was prompted not only by his impetuosity of character but also by considerations of resources. For he faced financial difficulty in maintaining large-scale warfare over any period of time, and fell far behind his predecessors in preparing for war. He emphasized the importance of supplies in his celebrated dictum that "an army marches on its stomach," but he sent his troops marching to battle ill-clothed, ill-fed, and with the most slender preparations for their subsequent supply. He had to win quickly, lest he lose slowly. He was a great commander but a bad quartermaster.

The Peace of Amiens. When Napoleon took power, his two principal foes were England and Austria. England, which continued its basic strategy of maintaining its command of the sea and building a coalition of continental power to overbalance the strength of France, was the most dangerous barrier to Napoleon's ambitions. But it lay for the moment beyond his reach, across the Channel. However, Austria, a land power, was open to his assault. He organized a double-pronged attack upon the Hapsburg state, from the north by way of southern Germany, and from the south by way of Italy. He took personal command of the Italian campaign, crossed the Alps in mid-May 1800, and fought the battle of Marengo a month later. His hasty temerity brought him to the brink of defeat, but the arrival on the field of fresh forces under Generals Desaix and Kellermann snatched victory from the Austrians. Napoleon unembarrassedly painted the triumph as his own, and his reputation remained intact. The Austrians were not finally driven out of the coalition, however, until Moreau, the commander on the German front, defeated them at Hohenlinden on December 3. It was Moreau's victory which enabled Napoleon to conclude the peace of Lunéville with the Austrians on February 9, 1801. It gave the French the left bank of the Rhine, the "natural frontier" which had become a central aspiration of the revolutionary war program, and extended the territories of the vassal Cisalpine Republic created by Napoleon in Italy.

England meanwhile consolidated its command of the seas. By bombarding Copenhagen without a declaration of war, Nelson drove Denmark out of the league of neutrals which resisted British interference with their trade. The assassination of Tsar Paul in Russia completed the break-up of the league. Nonetheless the rise of economic difficulties in Britain, and a willingness to test if not to trust the peaceful intentions of the First Consul, made it possible for peace to be concluded at Amiens on March 25, 1802. England received Ceylon, taken from the Dutch, and Trinidad, which had been seized from the Spaniards, but agreed to withdraw from other conquests, including the strategic Mediterranean island of Malta, as well as Egypt, which had fallen to English arms the year before. France was committed to remaining within its frontiers. It was fundamentally a peace upon the basis of acceptance of the existing balance of forces, a peace without victory for either side.

National Interest and Personal Ambition. Until and unless mutual confidence developed, the peace of Amiens was no more than a truce. The British were not opposed to the maintenance of peace providing that the European market was reopened to them and they retained their predominance in the overseas empires. The French disturbed their equanimity by failing to make a commercial treaty with them, by reconquering Santo Domingo in the Caribbean from the Negro rebels who held it, and by acquiring Louisiana from Spain. Nonetheless these actions were insufficient to goad the English to renewal of war.

Napoleon himself had spoken words of peace on taking office. The interest of the French nation lay in the utilization of peace to strengthen the revolution-torn and revolution-changed fabric of French society. Napoleon's own program of consolidation required not only his concentrated attention and effort but also the easing of the financial strains upon the nation. But the First Consul held himself ready for war. His excuse was that he needed "brilliant actions, and hence war," in order to hold the respect and fear of those he ruled. The deeper motive to which he responded was that he sought war for itself, as an opportunity of releasing his energies in action and for satisfying his boundless vanities, rather than for the sake of the gains, territorial and political, for which it was nominally waged. He was a dreamer whom the world could never satisfy—but a dreamer who commanded France, the greatest nation in Europe, at a time when its powers had been multiplied by revolutionary change.

The Resumption of War. Napoleon was therefore reluctant to restrain his policy of adventure and expansion. He continued to annex territory in Italy and arranged the political reorganization of Switzerland and Germany.

Britain sent him an ultimatum on April 28, 1803, demanding that he abide by the conditions of peace. Napoleon disdained even to reply, and war came.

At first Napoleon planned to strike at England itself, for the lack of any continental ally for the island kingdom actually deprived the French of a convenient theater of action on land. He strengthened the "Army of England" at Boulogne, on the Channel coast, but found he could not transport it without wresting command of the sea from the British navy. He enticed the British forces from the Channel by sending a French fleet to attack the British Antilles, but when Villeneuve, the French admiral, returned to Cadiz, he was blocked by Nelson, as bold and resourceful a commander at sea as Napoleon was on land. The French fleet, together with the allied Spanish ships, sailed out at Napoleon's explicit command, and was destroyed by Nelson off Cape Trafalgar on October 21, 1805. Not only was the planned invasion of England thwarted, but moreover British maritime superiority became so great that it was not imperilled again during the entire course of the war.

The English victory at Trafalgar was the sign for Russia and Austria to break with France. Tsar Alexander, who had succeeded his father Paul in Russia, took offense at Napoleon's disregard of his interests, especially in Germany. Austria was angered by the proclamation of the Empire in France in 1804 and by Napoleon's proclamation of a kingdom of Italy, with himself as monarch. The Emperor of the French responded with a whirlwind campaign against the Austrians, driving through southern Germany to Vienna and on to Austerlitz in Moravia, where he crushed their last army in the field on December 2, 1805. By the treaty of Bratislava (Pressburg), Austria abandoned all influence in Germany and abandoned Venetia to Napoleon for his Italian kingdom.

In Germany Napoleon used his newly won military dominance to enforce a reorganization of the ancient German state. Emperor Francis II announced the extinction of the Holy Roman Empire. The princes of western Germany entered a Confederation of the Rhine, with Napoleon as protector. Prussia, faced with the loss of her influence in northern Germany and confident in the power of the army created by Frederick II and nurtured in his tradition after his death, responded by war on October 1, 1806. On October 14, Napoleon and his subordinate Davoust shattered the once-great Prussian power in dual battles, at Jena and Auerstedt. Berlin fell on October 27.

Russia continued war alone, but an indecisive battle at Eylau in February, 1807, was followed by a Russian defeat at Friedland on June 13. In July Tsar Alexander met with Napoleon on a raft in the middle of the Niemen river at Tilsit. On July 7 they agreed on terms for peace. Russia became an ally of France against Britain, acknowledged the reduction of Prussian territory, and accepted French military occupation of what had been Prussian

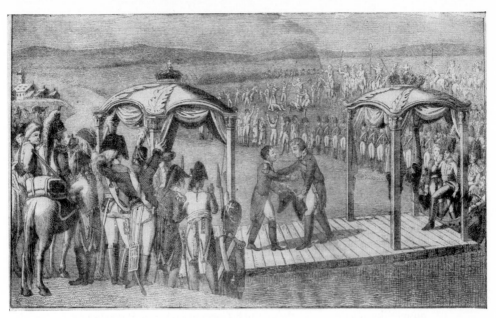

NAPOLEON AND ALEXANDER EMBRACE AT TILSIT.   Etching by an anonymous German artist, about 1807.

This crude contemporary print illustrates the meeting of the emperors of France and Russia on a raft in the Niemen river at Tilsit in 1807. *(Achenbach Foundation)*

Poland, which Napoleon proceeded to transform into the vassal grand duchy of Warsaw. Prussia was forced to make peace on these terms and even to become a French ally too.

The Grand Empire. The peace of Tilsit enabled Napoleon to complete the organization of a Grand Empire. This included an Empire of France which extended from Hamburg on the North Sea to Rome in the South; in it Napoleon ruled directly. Beyond lay a band of vassal states, created by Napoleon and granted by him to his brothers, his sisters, and their husbands —the Napoleonides. The most fantastic kind of dynastic overlordship prevailed. Though nominally sovereign, these various kings, dukes, and princes were established by the decree of the emperor of the French. Yet they were proud of their rank and often sought to implant themselves in the countries over which the caprice of history had placed them. If they dared to place their subjects' interests ahead of the emperor's orders, if they felt, as the emperor's brother-in-law Murat once said, that they were not kings in order to take orders, they quickly discovered that it was Napoleon who held effective power. They could not marry except as the head of the imperial house permitted; Lucien Bonaparte, who defied his imperial brother by choosing his own wife, was left without title or realm.

The emperor kept the kingdom of Italy for himself, though governing through his stepson Eugène. In Naples the throne was taken from the Bour-

653

bons by decree of the French emperor in 1805; his brother Joseph ruled until 1808, when he was shifted to Spain, and Napoleon's brother-in-law, Joachim Murat, became king. In Spain, which had been leagued with France since 1796, Napoleon's scorn for this "wretch of an ally" prompted him to force abdication of Charles IV and his heir and son Ferdinand in 1808; Joseph was then given the throne of Madrid by another imperial decree. The Batavian republic was converted into a kingdom for brother Louis in 1804; but in 1810 when Louis refused to enforce his brother's decrees at the expense of his subjects, he was forced to abandon Holland and the country was incorporated into the French empire. In western Germany a new kingdom was put together out of Hanover and the remnants of Prussian Rhenish territory for brother Jerome, who divorced his American wife and returned from Baltimore to become "king of Westphalia." The grand duchy of Warsaw was the only important territory not ruled by one of the Napoleonides; it was given to the king of Saxony, but he was expected to act with the same puppetlike obedience as they. Such German states as Bavaria and Baden also became appendages of the Grand Empire.

The vast edifice was outwardly impressive, but it rested upon the rifles of Napoleon's soldiers and nothing else. The Napoleonides remained foreigners in the eyes of their subjects and intruders into the ranks of royalty in the eyes of the older dynastic families. But the Grand Empire fed Napoleon's vanity and his sense of clan, and it provided a measure of control in conquered countries without requiring direct administration by French officialdom.

The Continental System. Though Napoleon governed, directly or indirectly, virtually all of western Europe, he could not feel safe in his empire until he had driven England out of the war. As long as it retained the will to fight and the control of the seas, it could tempt European states into attempts to throw off the Napoleonic domination, and its wealth could provide them with the sinews of war. Without a fleet, the emperor could not hope to strike at Britain directly; but he felt confident in a weapon of indirect attack, the measures of economic warfare which received the name of the "continental system."

The weak link of the British economic structure, Napoleon believed, was its dependence on credit. If the faith of the British people in their paper currency and the soundness of the Bank of England could be sapped, a fiscal emergency could be created which would bring down the government, or at least so weaken it that it would accept the emperor's peace terms. By a series of decrees issued at Berlin in 1806 and Fontainebleau and Milan in 1807, Napoleon forbade the import of all goods of English origin, or which had in any way come through British blockade control. These measures were made more effective by the conflict over maritime trade which broke between

Napoleon's Grand Empire, 1812

England and the United States, and resulted in war in 1812. The years 1807 and 1808 were marked by economic difficulties in Britain, and a full-scale economic crisis developed in 1811; the continental system seemed at the point of success. But England made good the loss of the European market by conquering the markets of Latin America and the Levant. It also broke through the continental system with a vast smuggling enterprise in collusion with the European peoples subject to Napoleon's domination. Indeed, the emperor himself legalized the smuggling by granting licenses for the import of English goods after 1809; though he thereby replenished his treasury, he ruined the blockade as a means of economic warfare.

The Revolt of Spain. The year 1807 was the apogee of Napoleon's power. Yet, although he was master of half of Europe and ally of most of the remaining countries, including Russia, his power was not safe or stable. England continued her implacable opposition, and Alexander of Russia was not willing to accept second place in Europe to the upstart emperor of the French. It was in Spain, however, that the Napoleonic empire began to weaken.

In 1807 a combined French-Spanish empire had conquered Portugal, and French forces remained in Spain to protect the lines of communication. Their presence aroused popular resentment, which burst into rebellion in 1808 when Joseph Bonaparte was proclaimed king of Spain in place of Charles IV. Napoleon met his tactical match for the first time in Spain, where guerrilla and regular forces combined to defeat the imperial divisions which had conquered the greatest powers on the European continent. The bulk of the Spanish fighters were *guerrilleros,* members of small bands who slashed at French communication lines and destroyed isolated enemy detachments, but slipped away when attacked by large regular units. The *guerrilleros* alone would not have been able to do more than sap the strength of the French army of occupation; breaking the French was the work of a small force of regular British infantry. The British troops were commanded by Sir Arthur Wellesley, later duke of Wellington, who adapted the long-discarded infantry square (see ch. 1, p. 13) for the use of skilled musketry. Where Napoleon depended upon numbers and his own genius for command, neglecting the training of troops, Wellington was a harsh disciplinarian and pertinacious drillmaster whose soldiers took the mettle of forces considerably outnumbering them.

In 1809 Spain became an open wound in the side of the Grand Empire, steadily draining its strength as it faced tremendous exertions in central and eastern Europe. Austria, encouraged by Napoleon's defeats in Spain, re-entered the war. Once again he drove through Bavaria into the Hapsburg homelands and compelled Francis I (as the former Francis II, now emperor of Austria, entitled himself) to make peace at Schönbrünn (October 14, 1809). France received as the spoils of war a cluster of southern Slavic lands around the northeastern coast of the Adriatic sea; Austria made other cessions of territory to Bavaria, Russia, and the grand duchy of Warsaw. At the suggestion of his chancellor, the devious Metternich, Francis offered to Napoleon the hand of his daughter, Archduchess Marie Louise, in the expectation that Austria would gain time thereby until the fortunes of politics and war changed. Napoleon, anxious for an heir (Josephine was still childless by him) and delighted to contract a marriage alliance with one of the most ancient dynasties of Europe, divorced Josephine and married Marie Louise in 1810.

The Invasion of Russia. The marriage with Marie Louise exacerbated the already embittered relations of Napoleon with Tsar Alexander, who felt that it was the French emperor who had garnered the major advantages in the peace of Tilsit. Alexander was troubled by the French predominance over Germany, where Prussia remained under the guard of occupation troops; the French-controlled grand duchy of Warsaw thwarted his own ambition to rule all Poland; and the continental system, which he had entered at Napoleon's behest, was causing severe hardship to the Russian economy, which depended upon the exchange of its farm and forest products for the manufactured goods of England.

Napoleon decided to act before Alexander took the initiative, and under-took the boldest and most immense of all his campaigns—an invasion of

"ARTHUR, THE CONQUEROR OF NAPOLEON." Engraving by Thomas Burke, after a drawing by Edward Francis Burney of a bust by Peter Turnerelli, published (?) June 18, 1815.

The hero of this print is the Duke of Wellington. Since the date of publication is the day of Wellington's triumph at Waterloo, the publisher, James Daniell, was either extraordinarily lucky in his command of coincidence or did not scruple to predate this work. The Duke's "iron" character may be sensed in this portrait. *(Achenbach Foundation)*

Russia. He drew contingents from every part of the Grand Empire, including 20,000 Prussians and 30,000 Austrians; his total force numbered 700,000, of whom only a third were French. The invasion began on June 22, 1812. Napoleon planned to close with the Russians in battle and destroy them by force of superior numbers and tactics; but the Russian commanders, though ordered to attack and smash the invader, were reluctant to accept the great captain's challenge. The Russian army retreated steadily, managing to survive the two great battles of Smolensk (August 16) and Borodino (September 5-7). Napoleon's strategy of pinning his opponent, which had been created in the narrow confines of northern Italy and applied in the much-compartmented territory of Germany, failed in the vast open spaces of Russia. His lines of communication were constantly imperiled by the assaults of Russian peasant partisans, who fought in the same slash-and-run manner as the Spanish *guerrilleros.*

On September 14, Napoleon reached Moscow, but he had not conquered Russia. Alexander did not sue for peace, as the emperor of the French expected. Napoleon lingered in Moscow until October 19, when the destruction of a large part of the city by fire made him decide to acknowledge his defeat by withdrawing. For two tortured months the Grand Army retreated, fighting its way past Russian harassment and in the final weeks through deep snow and frigid weather. When it crossed over into the grand duchy of Warsaw in December, it was a remnant of 200,000; there remained in Russia 400,000 dead and more than 100,000 prisoners.

The Empire Collapses. The failure of the Russian campaign was the signal for the uprising of subjugated Europe against the French conqueror. The Russians were joined by the Austrians, the Prussians, and the Swedes (who were commanded by their crown prince, the former French Marshal Bernadotte). To resist the allies, rather than accept their terms for peace, consisting in the abandonment of most of the Grand Empire, Napoleon formed a new army. His own victories over the Prussians (at Lützen on May 2) and the Russians (at Bautzen on May 21) were indecisive; but Wellington's triumph at Vittoria in Spain on June 21 caused the total withdrawal of the French from the Iberian peninsula. The huge "battle of the nations" at Leipzig on October 16 was a costly defeat which was followed by the collapse of the Grand Empire.

Once again offered peace upon the basis of France's "natural frontiers," Napoleon accepted too late and had to fight on. In 1814 the war was carried onto French soil, where the allies successfully followed Bernadotte's strategy of defeating Napoleon's lieutenants while avoiding action with the emperor himself. Even in these final months, Napoleon refused to make peace upon the basis of the frontiers of France in 1792, before the revolutionary and imperial conquests. "Leave France smaller than I received it? Never!" he exclaimed. But he was helpless to do otherwise. Paris capitulated to the allies on March 20. On April 6 the emperor abdicated. The allies granted him the small Mediterranean island of Elba in personal sovereignty, together with the title of emperor.

IV. The Tragedy Ends Twice

The grand adventure of Napoleon Bonaparte and the great travail of the French nation were not yet at an end, however. The emperor returned to France, ruled for a hundred days, met final and irrevocable defeat at Waterloo, and sailed away to exile at Saint Helena and to death. The Bourbon king, Louis XVIII, came back to attempt in his own way to reconcile the Old Regime and the New.

Louis XVIII. Uncertainty prevailed over the succession to the departed emperor. There was little wish for the restoration of the Bourbon monarchy among either the people of France or the allies. Nonetheless Louis XVIII came back to France and ascended the throne of his ancestors, thanks to a compromise with the imperial senate, which took authority in the interim. He refused to take the senators' proffer of the throne conditional upon acceptance of a new constitution creating a limited parliamentary monarchy. He proclaimed himself king by the grace of God, but granted as a "concession" a charter of government including a parliament and responsible ministers of state; the electorate was limited, however, only to the wealthiest landowners and businessmen, numbering fewer than 15,000 for the whole of France.

The new king himself was ready to "royalize the Revolution," that is, to rebuild his monarchy upon the basis of retention of the economic and the administrative changes of the previous quarter-century. He took over the system of ministries and prefects as it had been worked out by Napoleon, and acknowledged the irrevocability of the sales of "national" land. The *émigrés* who returned to France in the king's entourage were less conciliatory; it was they, not he, who deserved the bitter charge that the Bourbons had "learned nothing and forgotten nothing." They began to enforce return of their confiscated lands without compensation to the new owners and otherwise to restore the Old Regime wherever possible. After six months the passive acceptance of the restored monarchy had turned to widespread bitterness.

The Hundred Days. News of dissatisfaction in France provided the banished emperor with the opportunity for which he had been waiting. He sailed from Elba on February 25, 1815, landed in France on March 1. A triumphant march followed across the country to Paris. Louis XVIII fled to Ghent. The European monarchs, assembled at Vienna in a peace conference, rejected Napoleon's offer to avert war upon the basis of the status quo, declared him an outlaw, and ordered their armies into action against him.

Napoleon's only hope was to reach and destroy the principal allied force in Belgium before the other armies of the coalition arrived. With 150,000 troops he faced 220,000 Anglo-Hanoverians and Prussians under the supreme command of Wellington. Napoleon launched his attack upon Wellington's principal force at Waterloo, south of Brussels, on June 18; the Anglo-Hanoverians repeatedly withstood the massed charge of the French, until the arrival of Prussian reinforcements resulted in the emperor's total defeat. He fled to Paris, abdicated once more, and sought to take ship at Rochefort for the United States. Refused passage, he sought safety on the British ship *Bellerophon*, which took him to the distant south Atlantic island of Saint Helena. There he remained, a chained eagle, reliving the past and creating a myth of himself as the soldier of the French Revolution, until he died in 1821.

Louis XVIII returned again to Paris. As he entered the gate of Saint Denis, an official welcomed him: "One hundred days have passed since Your

Majesty left his capital amid tears." For France they had been a hundred useless days. The allies had already decided the terms of a general settlement for Europe in the Peace of Vienna (see ch. 30, p. 684), they made France pay the price of the interlude of Napoleon's return by worsening the terms of peace with France. The first treaty of Paris, adopted on May 30, 1814, had left France with its frontiers of 1792 plus some additional lands, including Nice, Savoy, Avignon, and Chambéry. The new treaty of Paris, adopted on November 20, 1815, took from France the strategic Saarland territory and gave it to Prussia; Savoy returned to Sardinia-Piedmont; an allied army of occupation was to remain in the northern fortresses for a period of three to five years; and France agreed to pay a war indemnity of 700,000,000 francs.

France in 1815. The country which returned to the rule of Louis XVIII was one greatly changed from that over which Louis XVI had reigned. The intricacies of social structure characteristic of the Old Regime were replaced by the simplicities of the New Regime. The aristocracy were restored to their titles, and regained much of their wealth, but they were confronted by a bourgeoisie that had tasted power and was confident in its own abilities to play a leading role in society. The common folk, though silent for the time being, remembered that they had thrust their way into public affairs and retained their hope and dream of reshaping the world according to their own desires. The peasantry asked for little but to enjoy the benefits of what they had gained.

Economically France was tired but not exhausted. It had been the leading economic power on the continent for more than a decade. Yet it lagged far behind Britain in industrialization; the revolution had cleared the ground for change, but had not brought about any significant change in the methods of production, either in the countryside or in industrial activity.

The political situation was even more confused. The charter granted by Louis XVIII introduced a parliamentarism more advanced even than that created by the constitution of 1791; but it was given by a monarch who reaffirmed that he held his crown by divine right, not by the gift of the nation. Yet most of the basic provisions of the Declaration of the Rights of Man— equality before the law and individual liberty—remained in force. Fraternity, however, was less present than ever. France remained two nations, one aspiring to the re-creation of the Old Regime, the other to the reinvigoration of the New. France faced her future with a divided soul.

30

Europe in an Age of Revolution

1789-1815

IN THE QUARTER CENTURY from 1789 until 1815, the Old Regime throughout Europe faced the most tremendous challenge it had ever known. Revolutionary France presented to the peoples the ideal of a new society based on freedom, equality, and brotherhood to take the place of the stale and oppressive old order. Imperial France, with its conquering armies, threatened the very existence of the states.

I. Europe on the Eve of Revolution

Unlike France, the other nations of Europe in 1789 were not gripped by revolutionary crisis, unable to live as they had been and desperately seeking a more effective pattern of political and social organization. Yet all was not serene: they too faced problems; for many, more intractable than those of France.

Economy and Society. European economic life retained its characteristic multiplicity within a larger unity. It had resiliency in the rural areas, where agriculture and handicrafts were the basis of nearly complete self-sufficiency, which could be gravely damaged only by the sharpest oppression of tax collector or conqueror, or by the worst of crop failures. It also had perilous fragility owing to the vastly increased size and complexity of its commerce. Industry and a rapidly growing portion of agriculture produced for a market embracing all Europe; if the production or the flow of goods was disrupted at one place, the effects were soon felt elsewhere. The total productivity of the European economy had increased immensely during the eighteenth century; the population had expanded at a similar rate. Prosperity was widespread, although the economic and political crisis in France spread shadows of uncertainty.

The social structure of European life, though in broad outline what it had been for hundreds of years, was significantly changed in detail. The class division of society still set off the major groups of the population according to their economic function, their wealth, their speech and dress, their rank and privileges, their aspirations, purposes, and expectations. But the lines of division were often less clear than they had been; they were easier to cross and hence more bitterly defended.

The peasantry everywhere remained the most numerous class, eager to own the land and resentful of surviving manorial dues and obligations. In western Europe the peasants were usually personally free, but in eastern Europe the grip of serfdom was becoming tighter. The business and professional classes—the "bourgeoisie" as they were coming to be called—were growing in numbers. In many countries, notably England, the Netherlands, and Scandinavia, they were gaining in wealth and prestige, but elsewhere they were frequently still a small, weak, despised minority. The nobility remained the dominant class—politically, socially, and usually economically— yet it often felt hard-pressed by the bourgeoisie, which was demanding equality before the law and in the service of the state. Thus the social tensions of France were largely duplicated beyond its frontiers, but with less sharpness of outline and less virulence.

Politics. As compared to the seventeenth century or even the first half of the eighteenth, there was little struggle or controversy outside of France over the institutions of the state. The sovereign territorial state was triumphant almost everywhere; feudalism in the strict sense had become a mere formality. The European states nonetheless retained the imprint of their past. Politics was the affair of rulers and ruling classes, seldom of the people. The monarchies belonged to dynasties, the republics to cliques of patricians. Where subjects participated in government, they were represented in assemblies of Estates; only in Great Britain had the basic forms of the modern parliamentary system been evolved.

Yet the governments were generally concerned for the welfare of those they ruled, although how this purpose could be reconciled with the self-interest of the rulers and of the noble and patrician classes was a puzzling and potentially explosive question. "Enlightened" doctrines, usually in the moderate form given them by Montesquieu but sometimes even in the bolder version of Rousseau, were the stock in trade of political discussion. Rulers often accepted these principles, especially insofar as they aided them to make the state stronger and more efficient. They thereby facilitated the entry into political debate of doctrines less easily adapted to their purposes: these were the theories of popular sovereignty and utilitarianism. Thus it was that the Old Regime was almost disarmed intellectually when the revolutionary challenge came. This weakness was all the more dangerous because political institutions, which sufficed for normal circumstances, remained often woefully inadequate for the stresses of a revolutionary age.

II. The Challenge of France

No sooner had the revolution broken out in France than the appeal of its ideas and its example began to endanger the Old Regime elsewhere in Europe. This peril was limited, however, so long as the revolutionaries were locked in their own quarrels and had not reconstituted the military might of France. Once the authority of the state was effectively re-established, how-ever, the danger of conquest by the "great nation" was added.

The Threat of Conquest. It was this military challenge from revolution-ary and imperial France which became the crucial immediate problem for the European states. The threat was novel in character: defeat brought the prospect of total destruction of the state and the transformation of society, not merely the loss of a province or the payment of a war indemnity.

There was historic irony in this situation. When revolution had begun in France, the potentates of Europe had gloated over the debacle of French power and had proceeded with their plans of aggrandizement in the com-fortable certitude that France could not interfere. But France rose again to be the "great nation" of Europe. In the two decades between 1793 and 1815 it brought into the field the mightiest armies which had ever been assembled by a European state. France's power was due to the ability of its govern-ments of the revolutionary epoch, after the initial years of flaccid authority, to draw more effectively than any other state—with the sole exception of England—upon the strength of the nation.

A challenge of such dimensions could not be met simply by waging war in the fashion practiced before the revolution. The cautious calculation of means and ends characteristic of the generals and statesmen of the Old Regime was inadequate for holding off, far less for subduing, armies which seemed to be oblivious to problems of reserves and supplies, which fought to destroy a foe and not just to dislodge him, which risked all to gain a single total victory. To win against France it was necessary to match French power.

Sometimes it could be matched through better use of the old means of warfare, by increasing numbers, by improving training, tactics, and strategy: this was the English way, brought by Nelson and Wellington to a level of effectiveness equal to or greater than that of revolutionary and imperial France. But this strategy succeeded because England had the sea and a wall of ships to protect it and because it had continental allies to attract and absorb the main blow of French arms. When continental states retained the old ways of warfare, they succumbed to the French attack. The French empire was pulled down in the end by a combination of revolutionary methods of warfare—popular insurrections and guerrilla operation—and the old techniques of army combat as improved by the lessons of a master teacher, General Bonaparte; and by the formation of an immense coalition of powers, according to the traditional balance-of-power strategy.

The Export of "Jacobinism."   The states had to meet the test of ideas as well as of arms. They had to be able to hold the allegiance of the peoples against the appeal of the new ideas. France, under the Emperor Napoleon no less than under his overtly revolutionary predecessors, was a living proof that a new kind of society, built on the principles of legal equality and national brotherhood, was not only possible but was actually more effective in the hard trial of war. For this efficiency, the armies of the Directory and the Empire—governments dedicated to the extirpation of Robespierrist and sans-culottist Jacobinism within France—nonetheless were accused by their enemies of exporting "Jacobinism." The complaint was not without an ironic truth, if Jacobinism is meant, as to the critics it meant, the creation of a new order of society. The complaint applied much less to "Jacobinism" as the French used the word: the theory and practice of insurrection and terror in order to maintain the dictatorship of a minority on behalf of and in the name of the majority, with the goal a more just reorganization of society.

The collaborators of the French did not even manage to create their own dictatorships. They attained modest power as henchmen of the conquerors, in regimes constructed on the French models of the moment, and serving French interests. Yet these regimes did familiarize the peoples with a system of government and society unlike that which they had known; it was no great leap of imagination for them to conceive the new order serving not France but their own nation. Thus the French soldiers and administrators gave a large part of Europe its first unforgettable experience of the new pattern of society.

The Stiffening of the Old Regime.   The challenge from France did not result everywhere in the introduction of the New Regime, even in fragments; indeed it brought to a quick end the experiment of enlightened despotism in most of the countries where the rulers had dabbled in the transformation of existing institutions according to the precept of efficiency and utility. The Enlightenment lost almost all its royal and aristocratic adherents, for they now attributed the revolution in France to the doctrines of Montesquieu, Voltaire, and Rousseau. The theory that the state rested on a "contract," explicit or implied, binding it to serve those it ruled, was now rejected as subversive and false because it had been used in France to justify the overthrow of monarchy and the destruction of the old society. The rulers were less willing than ever to permit subjects to share in power either by the older method of assemblies of Estates or by the newer technique of parliamentary government.

Yet immobility proved successful only in Russia, farthest of all European countries from France and best protected from French power by the vastness of its territory. Austria adopted the same policy of avoiding change but could not win by its own resources. England actually had advanced a long way toward the New Regime within the framework of the old order; the outbreak of war in 1793 halted but did not reverse the process, and the half-old, half-new institutions of Britain met the needs of the revolutionary era. Prussia's experience was the very opposite: its institutions, so successful for Frederick II, collapsed in 1806 and had to be patched up by partial reforms which enabled the state to use more effectively the energies and the intelligence of its people.

The Emergence of Nationalism. Part of the challenge from France was the strength drawn by its new leaders from a new source—nationalism. This was belief in and practice of two closely associated doctrines, the first that the state belonged to its people and the people to its state, the second that allegiance to one's own state and people was the highest of all loyalties. Nationalism was a force unknown to the old society, or if known usually feared by the rulers. It resulted from the passionate involvement of the people —the burghers and the common folk alike—in the destinies of their country. It was an essential element in the extraordinary vigor of France. There the state ceased to be the affair of a handful of men; it became the possession, actual or yearned for, of every man, who sought from it attainment of his dreams of prosperity, dignity, glory, and vanity. The bounds of Frenchmen's loyalty stretched from the village and town to the outermost confines of the whole nation. Even though this passionate French nationalism was in practice often restrained, diverted, or even reversed by other forces, it brought about an unprecedented devotion of the great mass of the population to the French state.

Nationalism did not remain the possession of France alone. France spurred the creation of nationalism in the other countries of Europe, sometimes by its example, sometimes by its oppressions, sometimes by both at once.

Even to those to whom France brought hope, it also brought one of the cruelest disappointments—brutal and cynical exploitation by "liberators." Wherever France ruled, the governments were compelled to make immense payments of tribute; the burden at once fell upon the people in addition to all those they already bore. The incessant demands of the French emperor for military contingents was an even more bitterly resented "blood tax." In Italy and Spain, the stripping of art treasures from the museums, of books from the libraries, of manuscripts from the archives, in order to swell the holdings of Paris, was a bitter humiliation for the educated classes. These shared resentments heightened the sense of national identity. And from the victories of the soldiers who served as French imperial auxiliaries, though dearly paid for, their countrymen took a new sense of pride in military achievement; this was especially true of the Italians and the Dutch, who had long since lost the tradition of martial duty and valor.

Nationalism also penetrated the countries which the French defeated but did not incorporate into the "Grand Empire." Sometimes, to be sure, it was thrust aside. The Hapsburgs, ruling a multinational empire, refused to risk using it. In Prussia, fear of nationalism contributed to delaying and hampering the Stein reforms, which saved the Hohenzollern state from utter destruction (see below, p. 673). But in Spain and Russia, a crude popular nationalism, with little or no encouragement from the traditional dynasties, rallied the peoples against the invaders and helped to save the old order of society. In Britain, nationalism strengthened the staunchness of Englishmen in their long ordeal of war with France; but it made many Irishmen rebels ready for alliance with France. Nationalism was still no more than a primitive, half-defined force, but it already loomed up as a giant of immense potentialities.

III. The Response of the Nations

The nations faced by the challenge of the revolutionary age responded in ways as many and varied as their particular histories, institutions, and immediate situations.

Great Britain. Britain's position was unique. It was the one land that France could not reach with its armies; indeed, command of the seas enabled England to extend its own colonial empire at the expense of the continental powers. It was the one land that matched France in economic resources though not in population, so that it was able to support its own military efforts as well as those of its allies. Last, it had already largely incorporated the social and economic changes to which we give the name of the "New Regime."

The Great Debate. The initial response of most Englishmen to the revolution in France was favorable, often even enthusiastic: the French were understood to be paying the English the compliment of imitation. The clear political purpose of those who took command in the National Constituent Assembly was to rebuild the French state upon the model of the English constitutional monarchy. The outbreaks of mass violence aroused qualms, but popular rioting was a familiar occurrence in England.

Only Edmund Burke, in his *Reflections on the Revolution in France* (1789), responded to the French events with neither enthusiasm nor mere mild distaste. With the whirling words of a prophet, he denounced the French revolutionaries for their deeds but no less for their purposes: their acts, he warned, were cruel and evil because their goal was to build according to theoretical precepts a totally new society upon the ruins of the old. The English must stand by their own practice—to retain the old ways as embodying the greater wisdom of experience, to change only when necessary and then within the framework of the old. But Burke's warning fell on ears that would not hear, or heard only in order to refute. The Scotsman James Mackintosh replied in 1791 with his *Vindiciae Galliae (A Defense of France)*, which defended the Constituent Assembly as seeking no more than the political liberties which the British already possessed. A more savage rejoinder to Burke came from the pen of the gifted pamphleteer Thomas Paine, who had served the Americans as a propagandist in their war of independence. In his *Rights of Man* (1791), Paine defended the French by attacking the British system of government: it was representative only of oppressive royalty and decadent aristocracy, and was no model for popular rule.

In 1793, the onset of war with France confirmed Burke's tirade against the revolution in the minds of most Englishmen. The English ruling class, and with it a majority of the nation, looked with increasing horror at the Reign of Terror in France. The ensuing life-and-death combat with France compelled Britain to take on the unfamiliar part of the defender of the old order in Europe. In so doing, the very character of British public life, the very constitution that Burke lauded, came into question.

The Parties and the Leaders. The war against France—a struggle of a kind England had not known since the days of the Armada, a fight for national interest combined with ideological combat—transformed the conditions of British public life.

William Pitt, the prime minister since 1784, put aside the program of reforms to become Britain's war leader. He gave his great gifts as a parliamentary leader and an administrator to the task of defending, not improving, the British constitutional monarchy. The Tories, by temperament and doctrines upholders of the old order, regained the initiative in Parliament, especially since Pitt, though in spirit still a political free lance, came more than ever to depend upon their votes. The Whigs, already weakened by their dissensions over the American Revolution, began to break apart as a political force. On the one side were the aristocratic Whigs, as deeply committed to the defense of the existing order of society as any Tory; their strength dwindled in the nation and in Parliament, however, for they no longer had any clear line of separation from the Tories except the allegiances of "connection" and family. On the other side were those who emphasized the Whig principle of national sovereignty and found themselves closer than they liked to the radical democrats, with their fervent admiration for France and their readiness for violence. These Whigs had their spokesman in Pitt's old foe, Charles James Fox. Without giving his unqualified approval to the French revolutionary regimes, Fox continued to minimize the danger which they represented for England and to urge that peace be sought upon the basis of a "hands-off" policy. The upsurge of economic difficulties, especially in 1796, increased support within the nation for this policy of ending the war without victory or defeat; but it never won the votes of a majority in Parliament.

The Constitution in Abeyance. Fox and Pitt clashed, too, over the kind of domestic policy needed by Britain in the age of the revolutionary challenge. The same egalitarianism and independent popular political movements which had emerged in France were already present in Britain and were encouraged by the French example. They found expression through various political clubs —some old Whig societies dating from the time of conflict with the Tories, others new organizations modeled on the "corresponding societies" of the American revolution—which attempted to organize popular resentment over the wartime hardships. The anxiety caused among the ruling classes by the agitation of these "Jacobins," as the popular radicals were called, was heightened by an attack upon the person of the king while he was riding through London to open Parliament in 1795, and by two mutinies of the fleet in 1797.

Despite the protests of Fox that the very liberties which Englishmen were fighting to defend were being thrown away, a series of statutes restricted the Englishman's cherished rights of free speech, free press, and free assembly. A number of the radicals paid for their brave words on the gallows or by transportation to the penal colony of Australia. But the sense remained strong even among the Tories that the withdrawal of these freedoms was a temporary war measure, to cease when the emergency was past.

Ireland: Rebellion and Union. It was not in England that revolutionary France found allies among British subjects resolute and numerous enough to be a real peril to the British state, but in Ireland. There opponents of rule from London included not only the great majority of Catholics, a landless, disfranchised peasantry, but also the landowning Protestants who elected the Irish Parliament sitting in Dublin. The plaint of the Protestants was that the Dublin Parliament was subject to the decisions of the English government, which consistently put English interests, especially in economic matters, before those of Ireland.

An uprising against English rule broke out in 1798, under the leadership of the movement known as "United Irishmen." The rebels counted on military assistance from France to enable them to drive out the English regulars; but the French expedition led by General Hoche met contrary winds, arrived too late and in too small force, and was easily defeated by the English garrison. Though the rebellion was crushed, the resentments which had fed it were still active: another insurrection was likely to come, perhaps in more favorable circumstances.

It was this concern for future security which prompted Pitt to attempt to remove the threat from England's back. He decided that only "emancipation" of the Catholics—giving them the right to vote and to hold office—would make them loyal subjects. Since the Catholics, once enfranchised, would outnumber the Protestants in any strictly Irish Parliament, Pitt advocated the union of Ireland with Great Britain in a single state: there was no danger of the loss of a Protestant majority in a united Parliament. Pitt was able to win enactment of Irish union in 1800 but could not overcome the refusal of George III to consider Catholic emancipation. Rather than resist the monarch, whose sanity was fragile, Pitt resigned his office. Thus the Irish difficulties led indirectly to the downfall of the great English war leader. His successor, Addington, was a politician of small capacities who served on the king's terms. Addington's one achievement was to end the war with France in 1802, by the peace of Amiens.

The War against Bonaparte. The peace of Amiens was only an interlude, for neither in Britain nor in France were the rulers willing to pay the price demanded by the other for lasting peace. Fighting resumed in 1803. Britain fought with even more doggedness against Napoleon than it had against the frankly revolutionary regimes. He was scorned as a usurper to whom the imperial title was refused (the government called him "General Bonaparte" and the people "Bony")—at the same time that he was feared for his successes on the battlefield. Addington soon proved to be incompetent at waging war and was replaced by Pitt and a narrowly Tory ministry. Pitt was ill; his wizardry had vanished. The one achievement of his last cabinet was Nelson's victory over Trafalgar in 1805, but even this was balanced by Napoleon's triumph at Austerlitz.

After Pitt's death early the next year, a "Ministry of All the Talents" took charge. One of its members was Fox, who had no reservations about the necessity to combat the military adventurer who now ruled France. This ministry, despite its proud name, had little success. The next government was formed by the Whig Grenville, but he fell when the king again refused to consider Catholic emancipation. A series of Tory ministries followed, with talents considerably less than Pitt's but sufficient in the end to the task of defeating France.

Britain fought with success a war of unprecedented difficulty on the economic front. Napoleon's "Continental System" cut off Britain from its great European market, but it failed to topple the credit and fiscal system of the island kingdom. The stability of the pound was maintained even though the gold standard was given up; the Treasury and the Bank of England worked in close collaboration to protect the credit mechanism which had become essential in British economic life. The overseas empire of Spain was opened wide to British traders, who also took control of the Dutch imperial possessions; thus the loss of the market on the continent of Europe was made good to a large extent. The London government replied to the "Continental System" with a counterblockade of its own, based on a series of orders in council, which brutally compelled neutrals to serve British war interests or stay off the seas. Indeed, extensive smuggling in collusion with shippers, merchants, and officials of the continental countries enabled the British to ship huge quantities of goods through the French blockade.

Meanwhile the transformation of Britain into an industrial and urban land was proceeding ever faster under the spur of the war; with it the ambiguity of the order of society became greater. Peace therefore meant not the cessation of political controversy but rather its resumption under new conditions.

Holland. Across the North Sea in the Dutch Republic, the French challenge fell upon a nation weakened by political dissensions and lagging in economic development. The victory of the hereditary stadholder, William V, over his "Patriot" foes in 1787 was short-lived, because his rescuers, England and Prussia, were no longer able to hold off French intervention after the outbreak of war in 1793. In 1795 the "Patriot" party took its revenge with the aid of the French revolutionary armies. William fled to England, whence he encouraged the Dutch colonies to accept English occupation. The States General abolished the stadholderate and reorganized the government as the "Batavian Republic," on the French model. Stability did not result, and conditions became worse after Napoleon came to power in France. Economic hardship resulted from the exorbitant demands of the French, the loss of revenues from the colonies, and the inclusion of Holland within the French blockade directed against England.

Dutch disobedience to his commands led Napoleon to bring the country into his vassal empire in 1806. Louis Bonaparte came to rule the "kingdom of Holland." He surprised both his brother and his subjects by taking Dutch interests to heart. His resistance to Napoleon's "Continental System," which was violated in Holland by massive smuggling, led the exasperated emperor to enforce his superior authority in 1810. Louis abdicated and the Dutch provinces were incorporated directly into the French state.

When Napoleon's empire began to break up in 1813, William of Orange was re-established with the title of sovereign-prince; he later became "king of the Netherlands," with a constitution providing for a parliamentary monarchy on the English pattern. His kingdom was extended to include Belgium —the former Austrian Netherlands—at the insistence of the English, who wanted a more effective barrier against France. The division of the Low Countries was ended after two centuries. The question remained whether the Dutch and the Belgians, who had grown so apart in interests and affections, could live together in a single state and become once more a single nation. It was an omen of trouble that William's charter, which was unanimously accepted in Holland, met considerable resistance in Belgium.

Belgium. In the Austrian Netherlands the revolution called forth by the reforms of Joseph II was conducted by people looking both ways, some back to the Old Regime and some forward to the New. They retained power only long enough for their quarrel to emerge, before the country was recaptured in 1790 by the troops of Leopold II. The new emperor returned to a safer, slower policy; he re-established the old forms of government, with the participation of the provincial Estates. In 1792 the Belgian provinces were conquered by the French armies and a year later were incorporated into the French republic. The Old Regime was abolished; the new institutions created by the revolution were introduced without exception. For two decades the southern Netherlands remained a part of France distinguished only by the distrust felt by the rulers in Paris for a population noticeably less enthusiastic and reliable than that of the regions which had been French before the revolution. In 1815 the Belgian provinces were given to the new kingdom of the Netherlands.

Germany. The revolutionary quarter century was for Germany a time first of ignominy and then of regeneration. The Holy Roman Empire ceased to exist, but the two major powers which had already taken shape with it— Austria and Prussia—continued to form the poles of German political life.

The Revolutionary Period. As in England, the first reaction of many in Germany to the revolution in France had been enthusiasm and joy over the dawn of a new epoch. But hostility had been even stronger from the start. For one thing, the tradition of political liberty was weak or nonexistent. For another, numerous princes and lesser nobles with holdings in Alsace were wrathful over the expropriation of their feudal and manorial rights (August 4, 1789) by the French National Assembly. War between the German states and France resulted, however, over the issue of the *émigrés* who had taken refuge in the Rhineland and were preparing a counterrevolutionary crusade. It developed into a struggle between the Old and the New Regimes. The proud self-assurance of the Prussians was first damaged at Valmy in 1793 and was shattered when they made peace with France in 1795. Austria in its turn met defeat and made peace in 1796-1797. The French then pushed their frontier to the Rhine.

There was as yet no sense in Germany of a need to adapt policy to new conditions: the princes and their ministers continued to plan in terms of wars fought by small professional armies in order to acquire additional territory and subjects. Yet the challenge from France was not just another episode in the duel of princes but struck at the very character and existence of the Old Regime. The brief episode of a revolutionary republic formed at Mainz in 1793 was a lesson which the German princes disdained to read: its organizers were native Germans, chiefly intellectuals nourished on the Enlightenment; but, though few in numbers and with little influence on the public, they were able to take power because they were backed by a triumphant French Army. The episode also had a lesson for those who accepted the aid of the "revolution from without": when the French forces were defeated and withdrew from Mainz, the power of the German "Jacobins" disappeared like smoke in the breeze.

Extinction of the Holy Roman Empire. The losses suffered by the Germans until 1800 were painful rather than disastrous, consisting principally in French acquisition of the region on the left (western) bank of the Rhine. Napoleon in Germany was more than a conqueror: he was a destroyer as well. He repeatedly brought Austria and Prussia to their knees and compelled them to look on while he reorganized Germany. He redistributed the territories of western Germany by means of a "recess" adopted at his behest by the imperial diet in 1803. The principal victims were the ecclesiastical princes and the "immediate" knights, who were "mediatised," that is, they ceased to be vassals of the emperor and became subjects of neighboring princes into whose states their tiny territories were incorporated. Napoleon also created two new principalities in the Rhineland, the "grand duchy of Berg" and the "kingdom of Westphalia," for his kinsmen. In 1806 he consolidated his overlordship over the "third Germany"—Germany apart from Austria and Prussia —by establishing a "Confederation of the Rhine"; this was a league of the lesser German princes under his leadership and protection.

Francis II, the ruler of Austria and Holy Roman emperor, recognized the collapse of the old political order in Germany. In order to safeguard his rank, he took the title of hereditary "Emperor of Austria" (as Francis I) in 1804, then, two years later, proclaimed the extinction of the Holy Roman Empire. For the first time in a thousand years Germany ceased to have even the semblance of statehood.

Allies Despite Themselves. After the battles of Jena and Austerlitz, Prussia and Austria fell almost as low as the other German states. Francis I

The enemies of France included those who held to the tradition of Charles III but had not accepted service under Joseph Bonaparte. They favored political, economic and social modernization of Spain without disturbing its character as an exclusively Catholic country. Recruited principally from the ranks of educated officers and government officials, they called themselves "Liberals"—this was the first use of the name "Liberal" to describe adherents of the principles of the Enlightenment and the New Regime. In 1812, while the Liberals were in control of the Cortes convened by the "central junta," they drew up a constitution providing for the establishment of a constitutional monarchy, along the lines of the British parliamentary system but with the king retaining large powers of initiative and control.

In 1813, when Ferdinand VII returned to Spain to reclaim the throne he had abdicated six years before, he struck down the Liberals with ruthless hatred, although they had served long and well in the war of liberation against Napoleon, to whom he had truckled. Many were arrested and some were executed. The constitution was cast aside; the Old Regime was re-established in every possible detail. Unlike Louis XVIII, the Spanish Bourbon king truly deserved the taunt that he had neither learned nor forgotten anything. Whether Spain could remain as immobile as her ruler was a question decisive for her future history.

The Ottoman Empire. The empire of the Ottoman Turks was distant from the center of revolutionary change in France, but it too faced the challenge of the Grand Nation as well as the pressure from Russia closer by. Napoleon's expedition to Egypt showed the weakness of the sultan's control over his outlying dominions, but this danger soon passed. The repeated penetration of Russian armies into the Balkans created a peril not so quickly shaken off. The sultan accepted the alliance of England or France according to the vagaries of European diplomacy—for whoever was Russia's foe was his friend. He was successful in protecting the Turkish heartland in Asia Minor and the vital passageway of the Straits, but could not put down the rebellions of the subject peoples in the Balkans, notably the Serbs, except by granting them autonomy under their own princes.

IV. The Settlement at Vienna

The task of re-establishing stability in Europe after a quarter-century of turmoil and change fell to the leaders of the victorious states, who met at Vienna in 1814 and 1815.

The Congress of Vienna. The Congress of Vienna was the supreme achievement of the diplomacy of the Old Regime. The statesmen of all the powers assembled to negotiate the terms of peace after the greatest war that

Europeans had experienced in a thousand years or more. In addition to the foreign ministers and a horde of lesser officials, spies and adventurers, the rulers of Austria, Russia, and Prussia came in person; only the kings of England and France among the great powers were absent. The pleasantness of life under the Old Regime, at least for the powerful and the wealthy, was visible in the social festivities which went on almost endlessly. "Congress dances," was the brief description of what the world saw, and the phrase summed up one aspect of the conference.

But the "Congress" worked, too, at the humdrum and difficult job of transforming military victory into the terms of peace treaties. There was actually never a congress in the literal sense of a formal organization of all the powers represented; but the statesmen of the great powers—Russia, Austria, Prussia, England, and to some extent France—met as a group, as well as with the spokesmen of the lesser states. The fundamental decisions were made only by the "big five."

The negotiations followed the pattern of the old diplomacy. The principals were dynasts, who held the states by birthright or acquisitions, not the peoples, who were merely subjects and had no voice in affairs (except in parliamentary Britain and now, by a paradox of historical development, in France). Territories were assigned to one or the other state in the first place on the basis of three chief considerations. One was its military performance in the war just concluded, as well as on a calculation of its strength in the new relationship of forces. Another was the principle of compensation, so that if one state acquired territory, other states received equivalent gains, the difference in the numbers, wealth and skills of the population, the resources of the region involved, and not least its military-strategic potentialities, all being taken into account, with the result of maintaining the desired balance of forces among the powers. Last was the principle of "legitimacy," extracted by Talleyrand from the practice and law of the Old Regime. "Legitimacy" meant that rule over given states belonged rightfully to the dynasties which had reigned over them before the revolution. Although this principle was the primary basis for the restoration of the Bourbons in France, it was disregarded without compunction when it came to restoring to their former possessors the confiscated territories of the "immediate" knights, the imperial cities, and the ecclesiastical principalities in Germany. The principle of nationalism, proclaimed by the French revolutionaries even though frequently disregarded by them, received no consideration at all: it was no part of the political conceptions of the Old Regime.

This disregard for the legitimacy of others than themselves was displayed when the great powers wrangled over the future of Poland and Saxony. Russia insisted upon having the major part of Poland as its reward, to the wrath of the Prussian king, who had lost his Polish territories to the "grand

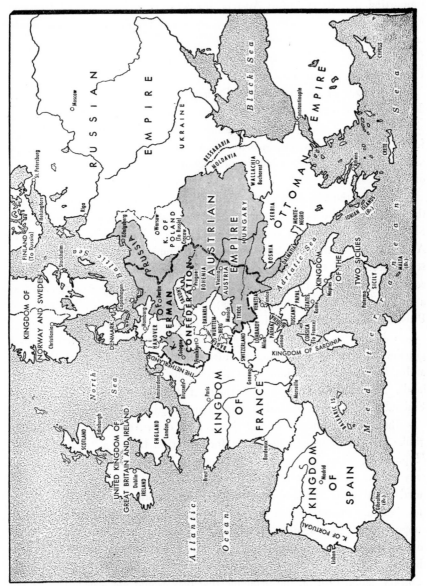

Europe after the Vienna Settlement (1815)

duchy of Warsaw." Frederick William was willing to be recompensed for this loss by receiving the territory of the king of Saxony, who had been so unwise as to accept the title of grand duke of Warsaw from Napoleon. Talleyrand, as the representative of Louis XVIII, made his point for legitimacy by supporting the Saxon cause; Austria, not wishing an extension of Prussian territory to its own frontiers, did likewise. Blustering threats and talk of war ensued, but cooler second thoughts quieted the war fever: a compromise gave Prussia a large swath of Saxon territory as well as the Rhineland between Frankfurt and the Dutch border.

The Peace of Vienna. After the many weary months of dancing and debating, the Congress achieved a settlement, set down in a series of treaties signed on June 9, 1815, and establishing the political organization of Europe for half a century. Though in principle a restoration of the states of Europe as they had been before 1792, in practice it was restoration for the benefit of the victors only.

In Italy, the kingdom of the Two Sicilies and the kingdom of Sardinia, the papal state, the grand duchy of Tuscany, and Lombardy—the old duchy of Milan—were returned to their former rulers; but Venice was given to Austria to form the Hapsburg province of Lombardy-Venetia, while lesser states were given to Marie Louise, Napoleon's estranged wife, and to other scions of the Bourbon and Hapsburg dynasties. Germany was reorganized as a confederation of thirty-eight states; Austria played the leading role and Prussia the secondary part in it, but all members retained their sovereignty, except insofar as the confederation received the right to intervene against popular movements attempting to infringe on the sovereignty of the monarchs. Holland and Belgium were merged into the kingdom of the Netherlands. Sweden withdrew from Germany but gained Norway. Russia held Finland and the re-established but dependent kingdom of Poland.

The Holy Alliance. Among the treaties drawn up at Vienna was one unlike any that Europe had known for centuries. It was a "Holy Alliance" proposed by Tsar Alexander, in the hope of basing the new settlement not only on the shifting interests of the states but also upon the divinely instituted moral order. This treaty proclaimed the brotherhood of spirit among the signatory monarchs and implied that they had the duty and the right to support each other against threats to the existing order of Europe. It remained as innocent of specific obligation as it was lofty in principle, so that the rulers of Austria and Prussia signed with a smile. The English, on the contrary, stood firm on the principle that they would not accede to a treaty which consisted only in a statement of principles and had no practical importance.

The British statesmen foresaw the impact of the Holy Alliance on the mind of the European public more accurately than did the signers. It was soon assumed to have a secret purpose, the destruction of nationalism and liberalism everywhere, and came to be in men's imaginations the very essence of the Vienna settlement.

Europe in 1815. Despite the intentions and the efforts of the statesmen assembled at Vienna, they were not able to put Europe back together in the shape of the Old Regime precisely as it had been in 1789. The old order was shattered as irrevocably as Humpty-Dumpty after his fall. What the peace-makers were able to achieve was a political consolidation of Europe. In it Great Britain, France, the Netherlands, Denmark, Sweden (and, to a limited extent, Russian Poland and Finland) were parliamentary monarchies, while Austria, Prussia, Russia, Spain, and the Two Sicilies remained absolute mon-archies. It was a Europe dominated by the same powers which were pre-eminent in 1789.

Yet conditions had changed profoundly. France, though defeated, had replaced or reformed most of the institutions which had created difficulties under the old monarchy. England had achieved the complete domination of the seas which had been her foremost aspiration for a century and a half. At the same time she continued to play the role of arbiter among the states, with the aim of preventing any one state on the continent from assuming dominance over all the land powers—that "hegemony," in the language of political theoreticians, which Louis XIV had been accused of seeking and which Napoleon had so nearly achieved. Russia, Austria, and Prussia resumed the positions which they had held during the previous centuries—all first-rate powers, economically backward but militarily strong.

The social and economic innovations which had already taken place were not reversed, but the powers hoped to halt all further change. For the moment, this hope seemed possible of attainment. Europeans were bone-weary after the long wars; they wanted peace, order, and stability, so that they could rebuild their lives and fortunes; they were for the most part willing to trust their rulers with power if they used it wisely. This was an oppor-tunity beyond price for the monarchs, who again ruled their lands with strong hands.

Yet they could not neglect without peril to themselves and harm to their countries a fact most of them would not accept. This was that the ideas of the revolution had sunk deep into the minds of men. Europeans were less willing than ever to have their rulers use the states for private advantage. They had been touched by the dream of equality and greater justice and it could not be erased. The nations had risen to political awareness, thereby calling into question the ancient pattern, now re-established and confirmed, of dynastic autocratic monarchy. There was, finally, a memory of vast poten-tialities—the memory of a people's seizing power and ruling in its own name, displacing its king and assuming that great, harsh, and infinitely attractive burden of the State, and with it command over men's lives, fears, and hopes.

This was the deep swell of historic tides that continued to run beneath the placidity of Europe on the morrow of Napoleon's fall. It was a promise of events no less immense in scope, in drama, and in human meaning than those which had filled the last three centuries.

Suggestions for Further Reading

IN HISTORY the richest delights and greatest values come from sampling the whole wide range of historical literature; a book such as this can be no more than an introduction. By further reading, the details of personality, process, institution, and event can be learned—those details which are utterly necessary for painting in one's mind a picture of the past that has color, form, and vitality. By further reading, the meaning of the past can be explored, in a never-ending process of analysis and judgment which lifts history above antiquarian curiosity to become an essential part of man's self-awareness in the dimension of time. In the fields of the arts, literature, and thought, experience of the primary works is irreplaceable: no words can adequately describe or analyze music not heard, painting not seen, or almost equally works or thought not read. "Further reading," therefore, is no mere adjunct of this book: to promote it is its very purpose.

It is impossible, however, to lay down a fixed, uniform pattern of reading for all students to follow—and equally impossible, it may be hoped, to force such a pattern upon their instructors. The resources of libraries vary as widely as do the interests and skills of readers. Students therefore should consider the library catalogue their first resource in the choice of further reading, together with reading lists from their instructors. Beyond these, brief commentaries on the most important books will be found in the forthcoming revision of the *Guide to Historical Literature*, prepared by specialists in the various fields of history under the sponsorship of the American Historical Association. No less valuable and considerably more detailed are the bibliographical essays in the pertinent volumes of the series *The Rise of Modern Europe*, edited by William L. Langer and noted below as "Langer series," and the bibliographies in two French historical series, *Clio* and *Peuples et Civilisations*. The reviews in the *American Historical Review*, the *English Historical Review*, the *Journal of Modern History*, the *Journal of the History of Ideas*, and the *Times Literary Supplement* (London) give criticism of new works as they appear, as well as models for reviewing.

The purpose of the following lists is to suggest, within the immense number of available books, those works in English which are most likely to

687

be useful to a student at the undergraduate level. I have emphasized the more recent books, which are usually more up-to-date in scholarship and interpretation, though not to the exclusion of older books. I have not attempted to include contemporary works and sources, except as represented in several modern anthologies of readings; nor have I attempted to suggest specific works of art and music. Because of the importance of the student's gaining experience in personal judgment in his reading, I have not added evaluative comment to the titles, lest he be unduly guided thereby. The lists follow the division by chapters, except for an introductory section on general histories and historical atlases; but works concerning material in several chapters are given under the first appropriate chapter, with a reference to other chapters in parentheses after the title.

Historical Atlases

Fox, E. W., ed., *Atlas of European History* (1957).

Palmer, R. R., ed., *Atlas of World History* (1957).

Shepherd, W. R., *Historical Atlas* (8th ed., 1956).

General Works

Barker, E., Clark, G. N., and Vaucher, P., eds., *The European Inheritance* (3 vols., 1954).

Beloff, Max, *The Age of Absolutism, 1660-1815* (1954).

Brinton, C., *A Decade of Revolution, 1679-1799* (1934). (Langer series)

Bruun, G., *Europe and the French Imperium, 1799-1814* (1938). (Langer series)

Cambridge Modern History (13 vols., 1902-12).

New Cambridge Modern History (10 vols., 1958—). Only partly supersedes the preceding.

Clark, G. N., *Early Modern Europe from about 1450 to about 1720* (1957).

———, *The Seventeenth Century* (2nd ed., 1947).

Dorn, W. L., *Competition for Empire, 1740-1763* (1940). (Langer series)

Europe: A Visual History (1959).

Eyre, E., ed., *European Civilization, Its Origins and Development* (7 vols., 1934-39).

Friedrich, C. J., *The Age of the Baroque, 1610-1660* (1952). (Langer series)

Gershoy, L., *From Despotism to Revolution, 1763-1789* (1944). (Langer series)

Hayes, C. J. H., *The Historical Evolution of Modern Nationalism* (1931).

Kraus, M., *The Atlantic Civilization: Eighteenth Century Origins* (1949).

Madariaga, S. de, *Portrait of Europe* (1952).

Mosse, G. L., *et al.*, eds., *Europe in Review* (1957). A book of readings.

Mowat, R. B., *A History of European Diplomacy, 1451-1789* (1928).

Nussbaum, F. L., *The Triumph of Science and Reason, 1660-1685* (1953). (Langer series)

Ogg, D., *Europe in the Seventeenth Century* (6th ed., rev., 1954).

Oman, C., *The Sixteenth Century* (1937)

Palmer, R. R., *The Age of the Democratic Revolution: A Political History of Europe and America, 1760-1800* (1959—).

Petrie, C., *Diplomatic History, 1713-1933* (1949).

————, *Earlier Diplomatic History, 1492-1713* (1949).

Roberts, P., *The Quest for Security, 1715-1740* (1947). (Langer series)

Turner, G. B., ed., *A History of Military Affairs in Western Society since the Eighteenth Century* (1953).

Weber, E., *The Western Tradition from the Renaissance to the Atomic Age* (1959). A book of readings.

Wolf, J. B., *The Emergence of the Great Powers, 1685-1715* (1951). (Langer series)

Chapter I. Patterns of People and Power

Brinton, C., *The Anatomy of Revolution* (1938). (Chs. 11, 28)

Buer, M. C., *Health, Wealth and Population in the Early Days of the Industrial Revolution* (1926) (Ch. 26)

Butterfield, H., *The Statecraft of Machiavelli* (1940). (Ch. 7)

Carr-Saunders, A. M., *World Population: Past Growth and Present Trends* (1936).

Clark, G. N., *War and Society in the Seventeenth Century* (1958).

Earle, E. M., *et al.*, eds., *Makers of Modern Strategy: Military Thought from Machiavelli to Hitler* (1943).

East, W. G., *An Historical Geography of Europe* (3rd rev. ed., 1948).

Fuller, J. F. C., *The Decisive Battles of the Western World* (3 vols., 1954-1956).

Goodwin, A., ed., *The European Nobility in the Eighteenth Century* (1953).

Griffith, G. T., *Population Problems of the Age of Malthus* (1926).

Hamilton, F. S., *The Vanished Pomps of Yesterday* (1921). Courts and courtiers.

Liddell Hart, B. J., *The Decisive Wars of History: A Study in Strategy* (1929).

Mahan, A. T., *The Influence of Sea Power upon History, 1660-1783* (1890).

Mattingly, G., *Renaissance Diplomacy* (1955).

Meinecke, F., *Machiavellism* (1957).

Mitchell, J. B., *Historical Geography* (1954).

Nef, J. U., *War and Human Progress: An Essay on the Rise of Industrial Civilization* (1950). (Chs. 2, 26)

Oman, C., *History of the Art of War in the Sixteenth Century* (1937).

Pearl, R., *The Natural History of Population* (1939).

Pounds, N. J. G., *An Historical and Political Geography of Europe* (1947).

Preston, R. A., *et al.*, Men in Arms: *A History of Warfare and Its Interrelationship with Western Society* (1956).

Richmond, H., *The Navy as an Instrument of Policy, 1558-1727* (1953).

Ritter, G., *The Corrupting Influence of Power* (1952).

Stevens, W. O., *A History of Sea Power* (1942).

Vagts, A., *A History of Militarism: Romance and Realities of a Profession* (1937).

Whittlesey, D. S., *The Earth and the State: A Study of Political Geography* (1939).

———, *Environmental Foundations of European History* (1949).

Chapter 2. The Development of Commercial Capitalism, 1500-1650

Clapham, J., *A Concise Economic History of England, from the Earliest Times to 1750* (1949). (Ch. 26)

Clark, G. N., *The Wealth of England from 1496 to 1760* (1947). (Ch. 26)

Clough, S. B., *The Economic Development of Western Civilization* (1959) (Ch. 26)

———, and Cole, C. W., *Economic History of Europe* (3rd ed., 1952). (Ch. 26)

Ehrenberg, R., *Capital and Finance in the Age of the Renaissance* (1928).

Fanfani, A., *Catholicism, Protestantism and Capitalism* (1936). (Ch. 4)

Gras, N. S. B., *History of Agriculture in Europe and America* (1925). (Ch. 26)

Hamilton, E. J., *American Treasure and the Price Revolution in Spain, 1501-1650* (1934). (Ch. 12)

Heaton, H., *Economic History of Europe* (rev. ed., 1948). (Ch. 26)

Hyma, A., *Christianity, Capitalism and Communism* (1937). (Ch. 4)

Lodge, E. C., *Sully, Colbert and Turgot: A Chapter in French Economic History* (1931). (Chs. 8, 17, 18, 26)

Lyashchenko, P. I., *History of the National Economy of Russia to the 1917 Revolution* (1949). (Ch. 26)

Nef, J. U., *Industry and Government in France and England, 1540-1640* (1940).

O'Brien, G. A. T., *An Essay in the Economic Effect of the Reformation* (1944). (Ch. 4)

Packard, L. B., *The Commercial Revolution, 1400-1776: Mercantilism, Colbert, Adam Smith* (1927). (Ch. 26)

Renard, G. F., and Weulersse, G., *Life and Work in Modern Europe, 15th to 18th Centuries* (1926). (Ch. 26)

Robertson, H. M., *Aspects of the Rise of Economic Individualism: A Criticism of Max Weber and His School* (1933). (Ch. 4)

Sée, H., *Modern Capitalism: Its Origin and Evolution* (1928). (Ch. 26)

Singer, C., *et al.*, eds., *A History of Technology*, vol. III, *From the Renaissance to the Industrial Revolution, c. 1500-c. 1750* (1957). (Ch. 26)

Strieder, J., *Jacob Fugger the Rich* (1931).

Tawney, R. H., *The Agrarian Problem in the Sixteenth Century* (1912). (Ch. 10)

———, *Religion and the Rise of Capitalism* (1926). (Chs. 4, 5)

Weber, M., *The Protestant Ethic and the Spirit of Capitalism* (1930). (Chs. 4, 5)

Chapter 3. Letters and Arts in the Age of the Renaissance, 1450-1650

Allen, J. W., *A History of Political Thought in the Sixteenth Century* (1957).

Allen, P. S., *The Age of Erasmus* (1914).

Armitage, A., *The World of Copernicus (Sun, Stand Thou Still)* (1947).

Baumer, F. L., ed., *Main Currents of Western Thought* (1956). A book of readings. (Ch. 27)

Bazin, G., *A Concise History of Art* (1958). (Ch. 27)

Blunt, A., *Art and Architecture of France, 1500 to 1700* (1954).

Bowle, J., *Hobbes and His Critics: A Study in Seventeenth Century Constitutionalism* (1952). (Ch. 11)

———, *Western Political Thought*, vol. I (1947). (Ch. 27)

Brinton, C., *Ideas and Men: The Story of Western Thought* (1950). (Ch. 27)

Bukofzer, M. F., *Music in the Baroque Era* (1947). (Ch. 27)

Burckhardt, J., *The Civilization of the Renaissance in Italy: An Essay* (3rd rev. ed., illustrated, 1950).

Bush, D., *Classical Influences in Renaissance Literature* (1952).

———, *The Renaissance and English Humanism* (2nd ed., 1958).

Butterfield, H., *The Origins of Modern Science, 1300-1800* (1949). (Ch. 27)

Caspari, F., *Humanism and the Social Order in Tudor England* (1954) (Ch. 10)

Cassirer, E., et al., eds., *The Renaissance Philosophy of Man* (1948).

Ferguson, W. K., *The Renaissance* (1940).

Fleming, W., *Arts and Ideas* (1955). (Ch. 27)

Fletcher, J. B., *Literature of the Italian Renaissance* (1934).

Francke, K., *A History of German Literature as Determined by Social Forces* (1913). (Ch. 27)

Gade, J. A., *The Life and Times of Tyco Brahe* (1947).

Gierke, O. von, *Natural Law and the Theory of Society, 1500 to 1800* (1957). (Ch. 27)

Gilbert, A. H., *Machiavelli's Prince and Its Forerunners* (1938).

Gombrich, E. H. J., *The Story of Art* (1958). (Ch. 27)

Hall, A. R., *The Scientific Revolution, 1500-1800: The Formation of the Modern Scientific Attitude* (2nd ed., 1956). (Ch. 27)

Hamilton, G. H., *Art and Architecture of Russia* (1955). (Ch. 27)

Hampshire, S., ed., *The Age of Reason: The Seventeenth Century Philosophers* (1956). (Ch. 27)

Harbison, E. H., *The Christian Scholar in the Age of the Reformation* (1956). (Ch. 4)

Hauser, A., *The Social History of Art* (2 vols., 1951). (Ch. 27)

Hearnshaw, F. J. C., ed., *The Social and Political Ideas of Some Great Thinkers of the Renaissance and the Reformation* (1925). (Chs. 4, 5)

———, ed., *The Social and Political Ideas of Some Great Thinkers of the Sixteenth and Seventeenth Centuries* (1926). (Ch. 27)

Highet, G., *The Classical Tradition: Greek and Roman Influences on Western Literature* (1949). (Ch. 27)

Holt, E. G., ed., *A Documentary History of Art* (2 vols., 1957-59). (Ch. 27)

Huizinga, J., *Erasmus and the Age of the Reformation* (1957). (Ch. 4)

———, *The Waning of the Middle Ages* (1924).

Koyré, A., *From the Closed World to the Infinite Universe* (1957). (Ch. 27)

Kristeller, P. O., *The Classics and Renaissance Thought* (1955).

Kubler, G., and Soria, M. S., *Art and*

Architecture in Spain and Portugal and Their American Dominions, 1500-1800 (1959). (Ch. 27)

Kuhn, T. S., The Copernican Revolution: Planetary Astronomy in the Development of Western Thought (1956).

Láng, P. H., Music in Western Civilization (1941). (Ch. 27)

Leichentritt, H., Music, History and Ideas (1938). (Ch. 27)

Martin, A. von, Sociology of the Renaissance (1945).

Myers, B. S., Art and Civilization (1957). (Ch. 27)

Panofsky, E., Meaning in the Visual Arts (1955). (Ch. 27)

——, Studies in Iconology: Humanistic Themes in the Art of the Renaissance (1939).

Pevsner, N., An Outline of European Architecture (1951).

Philipps, M. M., Erasmus and the Northern Renaissance (1949). (Ch. 4)

Powell, N., From Baroque to Rococo (1959). (Ch. 27)

Randall, J. H., The Making of the Modern Mind (rev. ed., 1940). (Ch. 27)

Reese, G., Music in the Renaissance (1954).

Robb, D. M., and Garrison, J. J., Art in the Western World (3rd ed., 1953)

Russell, B., Wisdom of the West (1959). (Ch. 27)

Sabine, G. H., A History of Political Theory (rev. ed., 1950). (Ch. 27)

Santillana, G. de, ed., The Age of Adventure: The Renaissance Philosophers (1959).

Sarton, G., Six Wings: Men of Science in the Renaissance (1957).

Sellery, C. G., The Renaissance: Its Nature and Origins (1950).

Smith, P., The History of Modern Culture (2 vols., 1930). (Ch. 27)

Sypher, W., Four Stages of Renaissance Style: Transformations in Art and Literature, 1400-1700 (1955). (Ch. 27)

Taylor, H. O., Thought and Expression in the Sixteenth Century (2 vols., 1920).

Tilley, A. A., The Dawn of the French Renaissance (1918).

Timmers, J. J. M., A History of Dutch Life and Art (1959). (Chs. 15, 27)

Toffanin, G., History of Humanism (1954).

Westrup, J. A., An Introduction to Musical History (1955). (Ch. 27)

Whitfield, J. H., Machiavelli (1947). (Ch. 7)

——, Petrarch and the Renascence (1943).

Willey, B., The Seventeenth Century Background (1934). (Ch. 27)

Wittkower, R., Art and Architecture in Italy, 1600-1750 (1958). (Ch. 27)

Wölfflin, H., The Art of the Italian Renaissance (1903).

Chapter 4. Religious Reformation: The Emergence of Protestantism, 1500-1650

Bainton, R. H., Here I Stand: A Life of Martin Luther (1950).

——, Hunted Heretic: The Life and Death of Michael Servetus (1953).

——, The Reformation of the Sixteenth Century (1952).

——, The Travail of Religious Liberty (1958).

Bender, H. S., Conrad Grebel, c. 1498-1562: The Founder of the Swiss Brethren, Sometimes Called Mennonites (1950).

Bergendorff, C. J. I., Olavus Petri and the Ecclesiastical Transformation (1521-1552) in Sweden (1928). (Ch. 16)

Boehmer, H., *The Road to Reformation: Martin Luther to the Year 1521* (1946).

Creighton, M., *A History of the Papacy from the Great Schism to the Sack of Rome* (new ed., 6 vols., 1903-05).

Eels, H., *Martin Bucer* (1931).

Fife, R. H., *The Revolt of Martin Luther* (1957).

Grimm, H. J., *The Reformation Era, 1500-1650* (1954). (Ch. 5)

Harbison, E. H., *The Age of the Reformation* (1955). (Ch. 5)

Holborn, H., *Ulrich von Hutten and the German Reformation* (1937).

Hughes, P., *A Popular History of the Reformation* (1957). (Ch. 5)

MacKinnon, J., *Calvin and the Reformation* (1936).

———, *Luther and the Reformation* (4 vols., 1925-30).

McNeill, J. T., *The History and Character of Calvinism* (1954).

Manschreck, C. L., *Melanchthon: The Quiet Reformer* (1958).

Mosse, G. L., *The Reformation* (1953). (Ch. 5)

Pascal, R., *The Social Basis of the German Reformation: Martin Luther and His Times* (1933).

Pastor, L. von, *History of the Popes* (34 vols., 1906-41). (Ch. 5)

Pauck, W., *The Heritage of the Reformation* (1950).

Schapiro, J. S., *Social Reform and the Reformation* (1909).

Schwiebert, E. G., *Luther and His Times* (1950).

Seebohm, F., *The Oxford Reformers: Colet, Erasmus and More* (1914).

Chapter 5. Religious Reformation: Anglicanism and Catholic Reform, 1517-1660

Brodrick, J., *The Origin and Progress of the Jesuits* (1947).

Brook, V. J. K., *Whitgift and the English Church* (1957).

Campbell, W. E., *Erasmus, Tyndale and More* (1949).

Dudon, P., *St. Ignatius of Loyola* (1933).

Evenett, H. O., *The Cardinal of Lorraine and the Council of Trent* (1930).

Haller, W., *The Rise of Puritanism* (1938). (Ch. 11)

Henderson, G. D., *Religious Life in Seventeenth Century Scotland* (1937). (Ch. 11)

Hughes, P., *Rome and the Counter-Reformation in England* (1942).

———, *The Reformation in England* (3 vols., 1951-54).

Hutchinson, F. E., *Cranmer and the English Reformation* (1951).

Janelle, P., *The Catholic Reformation* (1949).

Jedin, H., *A History of the Council of Trent* (1957—).

Jordan, W. K., *The Development of Religious Toleration in England* (2 vols., 1932-36).

Knappen, M. M., *Tudor Puritanism* (1939).

Parker, T. M., *The English Reformation to 1558* (1950).

Pollen, J. H., *The English Catholics in the Reign of Queen Elizabeth* (1920). (Ch. 10)

Powicke, F. M., *The Reformation in England* (1941).

Read, C., *Social and Political Forces in the English Reformation* (1953).

Schenck, W., *Reginald Pole: Cardinal of England* (1950).

Smith, H. M., *Henry VIII and the Reformation* (1948).

Chapter 6. Europe beyond the Seas, 1492-1650

Arciniegas, G., *Amerigo and the New World: The Life and Times of Amerigo Vespucci* (1955).

Beazley, C. R., *Prince Henry the Navigator* (1895).

———, *The Dawn of Modern Geography*, vol. III (1906).

Benson, E. F., *Ferdinand Magellan* (1930).

Bourne, E. G., *Spain in America* (1904).

Boxer, C. R., *The Christian Century in Japan, 1549-1650* (1951).

Brebner, J. B., *The Explorers of North America, 1492-1806* (1955).

Chapman, C. E., *Colonial Hispanic America* (1933). (Ch. 25)

Crouse, N. M., *French Pioneers in the West Indies, 1624-1664* (1940).

Dulles, F. R., *Eastward Ho! The First English Adventurers to the Orient* (1931).

Gillespie, J. A., *History of Geographical Discovery, 1400-1800* (1933). (Ch. 25)

Hanke, L., *The Spanish Struggle for Justice in the Conquest of America* (1949).

Haring, C. H., *The Spanish Empire in America* (1947). (Ch. 25)

Hart, H. H., *Sea Road to the Indies* (1950). Portuguese pioneers.

Hughes, E. R., *The Invasion of China by the Western World* (1938). (Ch. 25)

Innes, A. D., *The Maritime and Colonial Expansion of England under the Stuarts (1603-1714)* (1932). (Ch. 25)

Jayne, K. G., *Vasco da Gama and His Successors, 1460-1580* (1910).

Klerck, E. S. de, *History of the Netherlands East Indies* (2 vols., 1938). (Ch. 25)

Lanning, J. T., *Academic Culture in the Spanish Colonies* (1940). (Ch. 25)

Madariaga, S. de, *The Rise of the Spanish American Empire* (1947). (Ch. 25)

Means, P. A., *The Spanish Main: Focus of Envy, 1492-1700* (1935). (Ch. 25)

Morison, S. E., *Admiral of the Ocean Sea* (2 vols., 1942). A life of Columbus.

———, *Portuguese Voyages to America in the Fifteenth Century* (1940).

Newton, A. P., *The British Empire to 1783: Its Political, Social and Economic Development* (1935). (Ch. 25)

———, ed., *The Great Age of Discovery* (1932).

Nowell, C. E., *The Great Discoveries and the First Colonial Empires* (1954).

Pannikar, K. M., *Asia and Western Dominance: A Survey of the Vasco da Gama Epoch of Asian History* (1954).

Parry, J. H., *Europe and a Wider World, 1415-1715* (1949). (Ch. 25)

Penrose, B., *Travel and Discovery in the Renaissance, 1420-1620* (1952).

Prestage, E., *The Portuguese Pioneers* (1933).

Quinn, D., *Raleigh and the British Empire* (1942).

Rose, J. H., *et al.*, eds., *The Cambridge History of the British Empire* (1929-59), vols. I, II, IV, VI, VII, VIII. (Ch. 25)

Rowse, A. L., *The Elizabethans and America* (1959).

Sanceau, E., *Henry the Navigator* (1946).

———, *Indies Adventurer: The Amazing Career of Alfonso de Albuquerque, Captain-General and Governor of India (1509-1515)* (1936).

———, *The Land of Prester John, a Chronicle of Portuguese Exploration* (1944).

Willcox, W. B., *Star of Empire: A Study of Britain as a World Power, 1485-1945* (1950). (Ch. 25)

Williamson, J. A., *Europe Overseas* (1939). (Ch. 25)

———, *The Age of Drake* (1938).

———, *Sir Francis Drake* (1951).

———, *Sir John Hawkins* (1950).

Wrong, G. M., *The Rise and Fall of New France* (2 vols., 1928). (Ch. 25)

Wyndham, H., *The Atlantic and Slavery* (1935). (Ch. 25)

Chapter 7. The States of Italy, 1494-1650

Ady, C. M., *Lorenzo dei Medici and Renaissance Italy* (1955).

Ady, J. M., *The Perfect Courtier: Baldassare Castiglione, His Life and Letters, 1478-1529* (1927).

Bellonci, M., *The Life and Times of Lucrezia Borgia* (1939).

Browning, O., *The Age of the Condottieri: A Short History of Medieval Italy from 1409-1530* (1895).

Chabod, F., *Machiavelli and the Renaissance* (1958).

Collison-Morley, L., *Italy after the Renaissance: Decadence and Display in the 17th Century* (1930). (Ch. 24)

Koenigsberger, H., *The Government of Sicily under Philip II of Spain* (1951).

Krey, A. C., *A City that Art Built* (1936). A study of Florence.

Muir, D. E., *Machiavelli and His Times* (1936).

Schevill, F., *The Medici* (1949).

———, *A History of Florence* (1936).

Woodward, W. H., *Cesare Borgia, a Biography* (1913).

Chapter 8. France: The Cruel Century, 1483-1589

Baird, H. M., *The Huguenots and Henry of Navarre* (2 vols., 1903). (Ch. 9)

Battifol, L., *The Century of the Renaissance* (1916).

Bridge, J. S. C., *History of France from the Death of Louis XI* (5 vols., 1921-36). To 1515.

Church, W. F., *Constitutional Thought in Sixteenth Century France* (1941).

Major, J. R., *The Estates General of 1560* (1951).

Neale, J. E., *The Age of Catherine de Medici* (1943).

Palm, F. C., *Calvinism and the Religious Wars* (1932).

Reynolds, B., *Proponents of Limited Monarchy in Sixteenth Century France: Francis Hotman and Jean Bodin* (1931).

Sedgwick, H. D., *Henry of Navarre* (1930). (Ch. 9)

———, *The House of Guise* (1938).

Thompson, J. W., *The Wars of Religion in France, 1559-1576: The Huguenots, Catherine de Medici and Philip II* (1909).

Wiley, W. C., *The Gentleman of Renaissance France* (1954).

Williams, H. N., *Henri II: His Court and Times* (1910).

Chapter 9. France under the Early Bourbons, 1589-1661

Bailly, A., *The Cardinal Dictator: A Portrait of Richelieu* (1936).

Boulenger, J. R., *The Seventeenth Century* (1920). (Ch. 17)

Doolin, P. R., *The Fronde* (1935).

Godley, E. C., *The Great Condé: A Life of Louis II de Bourbon, Prince of Condé* (1915). (Ch. 17)

Guérard, A. L., *The Life and Death of an Ideal: France in the Classical Age* (1928). (Chs. 17, 18)

Hassall, Arthur, *Mazarin* (1903).

Lough, J., *An Introduction to Seventeenth Century France* (1954). (Ch. 17)

Merriman, R. B., *Six Contemporaneous Revolutions* (1938). (Chs. 11, 12, 15, 16)

Richelieu, C. J., *Richelieu: His Rise to Power* (1940).

Simpson, L. B., *The Struggle for Provence, 1593-1596: A Sidelight on the Internal Policy of Henry IV* (1929).

Slocombe, G. E., *The White Plumed Henry, King of France* (1931).

Wedgwood, C. V., *Richelieu and the French Monarchy* (1950).

Chapter 10. Britain: The Tudor Period, 1485-1603

Baumer, F. L., *The Early Tudor Theory of Kingship* (1940).

Bindoff, S. T., *Tudor England* (1950).

Black, J. B., *The Reign of Elizabeth, 1558-1603* (2nd ed., 1959).

Chambers, R. W., *Thomas More* (1949, 1958).

Elton, G. R., *England under the Tudors* (1955).

——, *The Tudor Revolution in Government* (1953).

Falls, C. B., *Elizabeth's Irish Wars* (1950).

Ferguson, C. W., *Naked to Mine Enemies: The Life of Cardinal Wolsey* (1958).

Handover, P. M., *The Second Cecil* (1959).

Harbison, E. H., *Rival Ambassadors at the Court of Queen Mary* (1940).

Harrison, D., *Tudor England* (2 vols., 1953).

Mackie, J. D., *The Early Tudors, 1485-1558* (1952).

Magnus, P., *Sir Walter Raleigh* (1956).

Mattingly, G., *Catherine of Aragon* (1941, 1960).

——, *The Armada* (1959).

Neale, J. E., *Elizabeth I and Her Parliaments* (2 vols., 1953-57).

——, *Queen Elizabeth I* (1934).

——, *The Elizabethan House of Commons* (1949).

Nobbs, D., *England and Scotland, 1560-1797* (1952).

Pollard, A. F., *Henry VIII* (2nd ed., 1951).

Prescott, H. F. M., *Mary Tudor* (rev. ed., 1953).

Read, C., *Mr. Secretary Cecil and Queen Elizabeth* (1955).

——, *Mr. Secretary Walsingham and the Policy of Queen Elizabeth* (3 vols., 1925).

——, *The Tudors: Problems and Personalities in Sixteenth Century England* (1936).

Rowse, A. L., *The England of Elizabeth: The Structure of Society* (1950).

——, *The Expansion of Elizabethan England* (1955).

Smith, L. B., *Tudor Prelates and Politics, 1536-1558* (1953).

Wilding, P., *Thomas Cromwell* (1935).

Williams, C. H., *The Making of the Tudor Despotism* (1935).

Willson, D. H., *King James VI and I* (1956). (Ch. 11)

Wright, L. B., *Middle Class Culture in Elizabethan England* (1935).

Zeeveld, W. G., *Foundations of Tudor Policy* (1948).

Chapter 11. Britain: The Crisis of the British Monarchy, 1603-1660

Allen, J. W., *English Political Thought, 1603-1660* (1 vol. pub., 1938).

Ashley, M., *England in the Seventeenth Century (1603-1714)* (1952). (Ch. 20)

———, *Cromwell's Generals* (1955).

———, *The Greatness of Oliver Cromwell* (1957).

Belloc, H., *Charles the First, King of England* (1933).

Bowen, C. D., *The Lion and the Throne: The Life and Times of Sir Edward Coke (1552-1634)* (1957).

Coonan, T. L., *The Irish Catholic Confederacy and the Puritan Revolution* (1954).

Davies, G., *The Early Stuarts, 1603-1660* (1937).

Davies, J. D. G., *Honest George Monck* (1936). (Ch. 19)

Frank, J., *The Levellers* (1955).

Gibb, M. A., *Buckingham, 1592-1628* (1935).

Gooch, G. P., *Political Thought in England from Bacon to Halifax* (1950). (Ch. 19)

Haller, W., *Liberty and Reformation in the Puritan Revolution* (1955).

Hardacre, P. H., *The Royalists during the Puritan Revolution* (1956).

Hexter, J. H., *The Reign of King Pym* (1941).

Hill, C., *Puritanism and Revolution: Studies in Interpretation of the English Revolution of the Seventeenth Century* (1958).

Kearney, H. F., *Strafford in Ireland, 1633-41* (1959).

Mathew, D., *Scotland under Charles I* (1955).

———, *The Age of Charles I* (1951).

———, *The Jacobean Age* (1938).

Schenck, W., *The Concern for Social Justice in the Puritan Revolution* (1948).

Tanner, J. R., *English Constitutional Conflicts of the Seventeenth Century, 1603-1689* (1928). (Ch. 19)

Trevor-Roper, H. R., *Archbishop Laud, 1573-1645* (1940).

Wedgwood, C. V., *The Great Rebellion* (1955—).

———, *Oliver Cromwell* (1947).

———, *Poetry and Politics under the Stuarts* (1960). (Ch. 19)

———, *Strafford* (1936).

Young, G. M., *Charles I and Cromwell: An Essay* (1935).

Zagorin, P., *A History of Political Thought in the English Revolution* (1954).

Chapter 12. Spain in Greatness and Decline, 1474-1664

Brandi, Karl, *The Emperor Charles V: The Growth and Destiny of a Man and of a World-Empire* (1939). (Chs. 13, 15)

Chudoba, B., *Spain and the Empire, 1519-1643* (1952). (Chs. 13, 14)

Davies, R. T., *The Golden Century of Spain, 1501-1621* (1937).

———, *Spain in Decline, 1621-1700* (1957). (Ch. 24)

Klein, J., *The Mesta: A Study in Spanish Economic History, 1273-1836* (1920). (Ch. 24)

Livermore, H. V., *A History of Portugal* (1947). (Ch. 24)

Maass, E., *The Dream of Philip II* (1944).

Merriman, R. B., *The Rise of the Spanish Empire in the Old World and in the New* (4 vols., 1918-34).

Nowell, C. E., *A History of Portugal* (1952). (Chs. 24, 30)

Salmon, E. D., *Imperial Spain* (1931).

Seavel, H. L., *The Great Revolt in Castile: the Communero Movement of 1520-1521* (1929).

Tyler, R., *The Emperor Charles the Fifth* (1956). (Chs. 13, 15)

Walsh, W. T., *Isabella of Spain* (1931).

———, *Philip II* (1937).

Chapter 13. Germany: The Balancing of Faiths and States, 1483-1555

Andrews, M. (Christopher Hare, pseud.), *Maximilian the Dreamer: Holy Roman Emperor, 1459-1519* (1913).

Carsten, F. L., *Princes and Parliaments in Germany: From the Fifteenth to the Eighteenth Century* (1959). (Chs. 14, 21, 22)

———, *The Origins of Prussia* (1954). (Ch. 14)

Hitchcock, W. R., *The Background of the Knights' Revolt, 1522-1523* (1958).

Holborn, H., *A History of Modern Germany: The Reformation* (1959). (Ch. 14)

Seton-Watson, R. W., *A History of the Czechs and Slovaks* (1943). (Chs. 14, 21, 22).

Thomson, S. H., *Czechoslovakia in European History* (1943).

Valentin, V., *The German People, Their History and Civilization* (1946). (Chs. 14, 21, 22, 30)

Chapter 14. Germany in the Age of the Thirty Years' War, 1555-1648

Beller, E. A., *Propaganda in Germany during the Thirty Years' War* (1940).

Gardiner, S. R., *The Thirty Years' War, 1618-1648* (1897).

Schwarz, H. F., *The Imperial Privy Council in the Seventeenth Century* (1943). (Ch. 21)

Watson, F., *Wallenstein, Soldier under Saturn* (1938).

Wedgwood, C. V., *The Thirty Years' War* (1939).

Chapter 15. The Netherlands United and Divided, 1477-1648

Barbour, V., *Capitalism in Amsterdam during the Seventeenth Century* (1950). (Ch. 24)

Barnouw, A. J., *The Pageant of Netherlands History* (1952). (Chs. 24, 30)

Blok, P. J., *History of the People of the Netherlands* (5 vols., 1898-1912). (Chs. 24, 30)

Cartellieri, O., *The Court of Burgundy* (1929).

Geyl, P., *The Revolt of the Netherlands (1555-1609)* (2nd ed., 1958).

———, *The Netherlands Divided (1609-1648)* (1936).

Griffiths, G., *William of Hornes, Lord of Hèze, and the Revolt of the Netherlands, 1576-1580* (1954).

Iongh, J. de, *Mary of Hungary, Second Regent of the Netherlands* (1958).

Tremayne, E. E., *The First Governor of the Netherlands, Margaret of Austria* (1908).

Wedgwood, C. V., *William the Silent: William of Nassau, Prince of Orange, 1533-1584* (1944).

Chapter 16. North and East Europe, 1483-1650

Andersson, I., *A History of Sweden* (1956). (Chs. 24, 30)

Dastrup, F., *History of Denmark* (1947). (Chs. 24, 30)

Field, C., *The Great Cossack: The Rebellion of Stenka Razin against Alexis Michaelovitch, Tsar of All the Russias* (1947).

Florinsky, M. T., *Russia: A History and an Interpretation* (2 vols., 1953). (Chs. 23, 30)

Graham, S., *Boris Godunof* (1933).

———, *Ivan the Terrible: Life of Ivan IV of Russia, called the Terrible* (1932).

Halecki, O., *Borderlands of Western Civilization, A History of East Central Europe* (1952). (Ch. 24)

———, *A History of Poland* (1943). (Chs. 24, 30)

Hrushevsky [Grushevskii], M. S., *History of Ukraine* (1941). (Chs. 23, 30)

Kerner, R. J., *The Urge to the Sea: The Course of Russian History* (1942).

Kirchner, W., *The Rise of the Baltic Question* (1954). (Ch. 24)

Klyuchevsky [Kluchevsky], V., *A History of Russia* (5 vols., 1911-31). (Ch. 23)

Larsen, K., *A History of Norway* (1948). (Chs. 24, 30)

Lybyer, A. H., *The Government of the Ottoman Empire in the Time of Suleiman the Magnificent* (1913).

MacMunn, G. F., *Gustavus Adolphus, The Lion of the North* (1931).

Merriman, R. B., *Suleiman the Magnificent* (1944).

Miliukov, P., *Outlines of Russian Culture* (3 vols., 1942). (Ch. 23)

Nowak, F., *Medieval Slavdom and the Rise of Russia* (1930).

Reddaway, J. A., *et al.*, eds., *The Cambridge History of Poland* (2 vols., 1941-50). (Chs. 24, 30)

Roberts, M., *Gustavus Adolphus, 1611-1632* (2 vols., 1953-58).

Oechsli, W., *History of Switzerland, 1499-1914* (1922). (Chs. 24, 30)

Stavrianos, L. S., *The Balkans since 1453* (1958). (Ch. 24)

Sumner, B. H., *A Short History of Russia* (1949). (Chs. 24, 30)

Vaughan, D. M., *Europe and the Turk: A Pattern of Alliances, 1350-1700* (1954). (Chs. 24, 30)

Vernadsky, G., *A History of Russia*, vol. IV (1960).

Wittek, P., *The Rise of the Ottoman Empire* (1938).

Chapter 17. France under the Grand Monarch, 1661-1715

Abercrombie, N., *The Origins of Jansenism* (1936).

Ashley, M., *Louis XIV and the Greatness of France* (1953).

Blennherhassett, C. J., *Louis XIV and Madame de Maintenon* (1910).

Cole, C. W., *Colbert and a Century of French Mercantilism* (2 vols., 1939). (Ch. 26)

Grant, A. J., *The Huguenots* (1934).

Halévy, D., *Vauban, Builder of Fortresses* (1925).

King, J. E., *Science and Rationalism in the Government of Louis XIV, 1661-1683* (1949).

Lewis, W. H., *The Splendid Century: Life in the France of Louis XIV* (1954).

Packard, L. B., *The Age of Louis XIV* (1929).

Petrie, C., *Louis XIV* (1940).

Poland, B. C., *French Protestantism and the French Revolution: A Study in Church and State, Thought and Religion, 1685-1815* (1957). (Chs. 18, 28, 29)

Saint-René Taillandier, M., *The Royal Ark: Louis XIV and His Court* (1931).

Sanders, E. K., *Jacques Bénigne Bossuet* (1921).

Tocqueville, A. de, *The Old Regime and the French Revolution* (1955, paperback ed.). (Chs. 18, 28)

Voltaire, *The Age of Louis XIV* (many eds.).

Chapter 18. France: Throes of the Grand Monarchy, 1715-1787

Barber, E., *The Bourgeoisie in Eighteenth Century France* (1955).

Castelot, A., *Queen of France: A Biography of Marie Antoinette* (1957). (Ch. 28)

Cobban, A., *A History of Modern France*, vol. I (1957).

Dakin, D., *Turgot and the Ancien Régime in France* (1939).

Fay, B., *The Revolutionary Spirit in France and America: A Study of the Moral and Intellectual Relations between France and the United States at the End of the Eighteenth Century* (1927).

Ford, F. L., *Robe and Sword: The Regrouping of the French Aristocracy after Louis XIV* (1953).

Gooch, G. P., *Louis XV* (1956).

Gay, P., *Voltaire's Politics: The Poet as Realist* (1959). (Ch. 27)

Lodge, R., *Studies in Eighteenth Century Diplomacy, 1740-1748*. (Chs. 20, 22)

Matthews, G. T., *The Royal General Farms in Eighteenth Century France* (1958).

Meng, J. J., *The Comte de Vergennes: European Phases of His American Diplomacy, 1774-1780* (1932).

Mornet, D., *French Thought in the Eighteenth Century* (1929).

Padover, S. K., *The Life and Death of Louis XVI* (1939). (Ch. 28)

Palmer, R. R., *Catholics and Unbelievers in Eighteenth Century France* (1939).

Sée, H., *Economic and Social Conditions in France during the Eighteenth Century* (1927).

Soltau, R. H., *The Duke de Choiseul* (1909).

Stryienski, C., *The Eighteenth Century* (1916).

Wade, I. O., *The Clandestine Organization and Diffusion of Philosophic Ideas in France from 1700 to 1750* (1938).

Wilson, A. M., *Diderot: The Testing Years, 1713-1759* (1957).

Chapter 19. Britain under the Later Stuarts, 1660-1714

Ashley, M., *Marlborough* (2nd ed., 1956).

Beloff, M., *Public Order and Popular Disturbances, 1660-1714* (1938).

Bryant, A., *King Charles II* (1931).

Churchill, W. S., *Marlborough, His Life and Times* (6 vols., 1933-38).

Clark, G. N., *The Later Stuarts, 1660-1714* (2nd ed., 1955).

Cranston, M., *John Locke: A Biography* (1957). (Ch. 27)

Feiling, K., *British Foreign Policy, 1660-1672* (1930).

———, *History of the Tory Party, 1640-1714* (1924).

Hartmann, C. H., *Charles II and Madame* (1934).

Malcolm-Smith, E., *British Diplomacy in the Eighteenth Century, 1700-1789* (1937). (Ch. 20)

Morley, I., *A Thousand Lives: An Account of the English Revolutionary Movement, 1660-1685* (1954).

Ogg, D., *England in the Reign of Charles II* (2nd ed., 2 vols., 1955).

———, *England in the Reigns of James II and William III* (1955).

———, *William III* (1956).

Renier, G. J., *William of Orange* (1933).

Trevelyan, G. M., *England under Queen Anne* (3 vols., 1930-34).

———, *The English Revolution, 1688-1689* (1938).

Turner, F. C., *James II* (1948).

Chapter 20. Britain: Consolidation and Change, 1714-1789

Briggs, A., *The Age of Improvement, 1760-1820* (1959). (Ch. 30)

Butterfield, H., *George III and the Historians* (rev. ed., 1959).

———, *George III, Lord North, and the People, 1779-1780* (1949).

Eyck, E., *Pitt versus Fox: Father and Son, 1735-1806* (1950). (Ch. 30)

George, M. D., *England in Transition: Life and Work in the Eighteenth Century* (1953). (Ch. 26)

Jones, G. H., *The Main Stream of Jacobitism* (1954).

Maccoby, S., *English Radicalism, 1762-1785: The Origins* (1955).

Marshall, D., *English People in the Eighteenth Century* (1956).

Michael, W., *England under George I: The Beginnings of the Hanoverian Dynasty* (1936).

———, *England under George I: The Quadruple Alliance* (1939).

Namier, L. B., *England in the Age of the American Revolution* (1930).

———, *The Structure of English Politics at the Accession of George III* (2 vols., 1929).

Pares, R., *King George III and the Politicians* (1953).

Petrie, C., *The Jacobite Movement* (2 vols., 1948-50).

Piette, C. J. *John Wesley in the Evolution of Protestantism* (1937).

Plumb, J. H., *Chatham* (1953).

———, *England in the Eighteenth Century (1714-1815)* (1950). (Ch. 30)

———, *The First Four Georges* (1956). (Ch. 30)

Robertson, C. G., *Chatham and the British Empire* (1946). (Ch. 25)

Robbins, C., *The Eighteenth Century Commonwealthman* (1959)

Rose, J. H., *William Pitt and the National Revival* (1911). (Ch. 30)

Sherrard, O. A., *Lord Chatham: Pitt and the Seven Years War* (1955).

Stephen, L., *History of English Thought in the Eighteenth Century* (3rd ed., 2 vols., 1949). (Ch. 27)

Sykes, N., *Church and State in Eighteenth Century England* (1934).

Taylor, G. N. S., *Robert Walpole and His Age* (1931).

Walcott, R., *English Politics in the Early Eighteenth Century* (1956).

Watson, J. S., *The Reign of George III, 1760-1815* (1959). (Ch. 30)

Williams, B., *Stanhope: A Study in Eighteenth Century War and Diplomacy* (1932).

———, *The Whig Supremacy, 1714-1760* (1939).

Chapter 21. Germany: The Rise of Prussia and Austria, 1648-1740

Atkinson, C. T., *A History of Germany, 1715-1815* (1908). (Chs. 22, 30)

Bruford, W. H., *Germany in the Eighteenth Century: The Social Background of the Literary Revival* (1935). (Ch. 22).

Craig, G. A., *The Politics of the Prussian Army, 1640-1945* (1955). (Chs. 22, 30)

Dorwart, R. A., *The Administrative Reforms of Frederick William I of Prussia* (1953).

Ergang, R. R., *The Potsdam Führer: Frederick William I, Father of Prussian Militarism* (1941).

Fauchier-Magnan, A., *The Small German Courts of the Eighteenth Century* (1958). (Ch. 22)

Fay, S. B., *The Rise of Brandenburg-Prussia to 1786* (1937). (Ch. 22)

Frischauer, P., *Prince Eugene, 1663-1736: A Man and a Hundred Years of History* (1934).

Marriott, J. A. R., and Robertson, C. G., *The Evolution of Prussia: The Making of an Empire* (1937). (Chs. 22, 30)

Rosenberg, H., *Bureaucracy, Aristocracy, and Autocracy: The Prussian Experience, 1660-1815* (1958). (Ch. 22)

Schevill, F., *The Great Elector* (1947).

Chapter 22. Germany: The Rivalry of Prussia and Austria, 1740-1790

Gaxotte, P., *Frederick the Great* (1941).

Gooch, G. P., *Frederick the Great: The Ruler, the Writer, the Man* (1947).

——, *Maria Theresa and Other Studies* (1951).

Goodwin, M. C., *The Papal Conflict with Josephinism* (1938).

Henderson, W. O., *The State and the Industrial Revolution in Prussia, 1740-1870* (1959). (Ch. 26)

Kerner, R. J., *Bohemia in the Eighteenth Century* (1932).

Krieger, L., *The German Idea of Freedom* (1957). (Ch. 30)

Link, E., *The Emancipation of the Austrian Peasant, 1740-1792* (1949).

Moffat, M. M., *Maria Theresa* (1911).

Morris, C. L., *Maria Theresa: The Last Conservative* (1937).

Padover, S. K., *The Revolutionary Emperor, Joseph the Second, 1741-1790* (1934).

Reddaway, W. F., *Frederick the Great and the Rise of Prussia* (1904).

Shanahan, W. O., *Prussian Military Reforms, 1786-1813* (1945). (Ch. 30)

Stanhope, G., *A Mystic on the Prussian Throne: Frederick William II* (1912). (Ch. 30)

Chapter 23. Russia as a Great Power, 1676-1796

Gooch, G. P., *Catherine the Great and Other Studies* (1954).

Grunwald, C. de, *Peter the Great* (1956).

Kaus, G., *Catherine the Great* (1935).

Klyuchevsky, V., *Peter the Great* (1959).

Lobanov-Rostovsky, A., *Russia and Europe, 1789-1825* (1947). (Ch. 30)

Menshutkin, B. N., *Russia's Lomonosov: Chemist, Courtier, Physicist, Poet* (1952).

O'Brien, C. B., *Russia under Two Tsars,* *1682-1689: The Regency of Sophia Alekseevna* (1952).

Putnam, P., ed., *Seven Britons in Imperial Russia (1698-1812)* (1952). (Ch. 30)

Robinson, G. T., *Rural Russia under the Old Régime* (1949).

Soloveytchik, G., *Potemkin* (1947).

Sumner, B. H., *Peter the Great and the Emergence of Russia* (1950).

——, *Peter the Great and the Ottoman Empire* (1949).

Chapter 24. The Lesser States in Decline, 1650-1789

Blok, P. J., *The Life of Admiral de Ruyter* (1933).

Godley, E. C., *Charles XII of Sweden: A Study in Kingship* (1928).

Harcourt-Smith, S., *Cardinal of Spain: The Life and Strange Career of Alberoni* (1944).

Herr, R., *The Eighteenth Century Revolution in Spain* (1958).

Hovde, B. J., *The Scandinavian Countries, 1720-1865: The Rise of the Middle Classes* (2 vols., 1943).

Laskowski, O., *Jan III Sobieski, King of Poland, 1629-1696* (1941).

Lefèvre-Pontalis, G. A., *John de Witt, Grand Pensionary of Holland* (2 vols., 1885).

Lord, R., *The Second Partition of Poland* (1915).

Noether, E. P., *Seeds of Italian Nationalism, 1700-1815* (1951). (Ch. 30)

Peers, E. A., *The Church in Spain, 1737-1937* (1938). (Ch. 30)

Shay, M. L., *The Ottoman Empire from 1720 to 1734 as Revealed in Dispatches of the Venetian Baili* (1944).

Chapter 25. Europe beyond the Seas, 1650-1815

Coupland, R., *The American Revolution and the British Empire* (1930).

Crouse, N. M., *The French Struggle for the West Indies, 1665-1713* (1944).

Furber, H., *John Company at Work: A Study of English Expansion in India in the Late Eighteenth Century* (1948).

Harper, L. A., *The English Navigation Acts: A Seventeenth Century Experiment in Social Engineering* (1939). (Ch. 26)

Karraker, C. H., *Piracy Was a Business* (1953).

Kaufmann, W. W., *British Policy and the Independence of Latin America, 1804-1828* (1951).

MacLachlan, J. O., *Trade and Peace with Old Spain, 1667-1750* (1940).

Moon, P., *Warren Hastings and British India* (1947).

Pares, R., *War and Trade in the West Indies, 1739-1760* (1936).

Parkinson, C. N., *War in the Eastern Seas, 1793-1815* (1954).

Priestley, H. I., *France Overseas through the Old Regime* (1939).

Reichwein, A., *China and Europe: Intellectual and Artistic Contacts in the Eighteenth Century* (1925).

Rowbotham, A. H., *Missionary and Mandarin: The Jesuits in the Court of China* (1942).

Schuyler, R. L., *The Fall of the Old Colonial System: A Study in British Free Trade, 1770-1870* (1945).

Williamson, J. A., *Cook and the Opening of the Pacific* (1946).

Chapter 26. The Emergence of Industrialism and Capitalism, 1650-1815

Ashton, T. S., *An Economic History of England: The Eighteenth Century* (1955).

———, *The Industrial Revolution, 1760-1830* (1948).

Beer, M., *An Inquiry into Physiocracy* (1939).

Buck, P. W., *The Politics of Mercantilism* (1942).

Clark, G. N., *The Idea of the Industrial Revolution* (1953).

Corti, E. C., *The Rise of the House of Rothschild* (1928).

Hamilton, E. J., *War and Prices in Spain, 1651-1800* (1947).

Hammond, J. L., and Hammond, B., *The Skilled Labourer, 1760-1832* (2nd ed., 1920).

Henderson, W. O., *Britain and Industrial Europe, 1750-1870: Studies in British Influence on the Industrial Revolution in Western Europe* (1954).

Mantoux, P., *The Industrial Revolution in the Eighteenth Century* (rev. ed., 1928).

Nef, J. U., *Cultural Foundations of Industrial Civilization* (1958).

———, *War and Human Progress: An Essay on the Rise of Industrial Civilization* (1950).

Singer, C., *et al.*, eds., *A History of Technology*, vol. IV, *The Industrial Revolution, c. 1750-c. 1850* (1958).

Small, A., *The Cameralists: The Pioneers of German Social Policy* (1909).

Chapter 27. Arts, Thought, and Science in an Age of Reason, 1650-1815

Becker, C., *The Heavenly City of the Eighteenth Century Philosophers* (1932).

Berlin, I., ed., *The Age of Enlightenment: The Eighteenth Century Philosophers* (1955).

Bishop, M., *Pascal: The Life of Genius* (1936).

Boas, M., *Robert Boyle and Seventeenth Century Chemistry* (1958).

Bruun, G., *The Enlightened Despots* (1929).

Cassirer, E., *The Question of Jean-Jacques Rousseau* (1954).

———, *The Philosophy of the Enlightenment* (1951).

Cobban, A., *Edmund Burke and the Revolt against the Eighteenth Century: A Study of the Political and Social Thinking of Burke, Wordsworth, Coleridge and Southey* (1929). (Ch. 30)

———, *Rousseau and the Modern State* (1934).

Figgis, J. N., *The Divine Right of Kings* (1896).

Frankel, C. W., *The Faith of Reason: The Idea of Progress in the French Enlightenment* (1948).

Gough, J. W., *John Locke's Political Philosophy* (1950).

———, *The Social Contract: A Critical Study of Its Development* (1936).

Green, F. C., *Jean-Jacques Rousseau: A Critical Study of His Life and Writings* (1955).

Halévy, E., *The Growth of Philosophic Radicalism* (1955).

Havens, G. R., *The Age of Ideas: From Reaction to Revolution in Eighteenth Century France* (1955).

Hazard, P., *The European Mind, 1680-1715* (1953).

———, *European Thought in the Eighteenth Century* (1954).

Hearnshaw, F. J. C., ed., *The Social and Political Ideas of Some English Thinkers of the Augustan Age, A.D. 1650-1750* (1928).

———, *The Social and Political Ideas of Some Great French Thinkers of the Age of Reason* (1930).

Kohn, H., *The Idea of Nationalism* (1944). (Ch. 30)

Manuel, F. E., *The Eighteenth Century Confronts the Gods* (1959).

Martin, K., *French Liberal Thought in the Eighteenth Century: A Study of Political Ideas from Bayle to Condorcet* (2nd ed., 1954).

Robinson, H., *Bayle, the Skeptic* (1931).

Sullivan, J. W. N., *Isaac Newton, 1642-1727* (1938).

Torrey, N. L., *The Spirit of Voltaire* (1938).

Chapter 28. France in Revolution: I, 1787-1795

Acton, John E. E. D., Lord, *Lectures on the French Revolution* (1910).

Aulard, F. V. A., *The French Revolution: A Political History, 1789-1804* (4 vols., 1910). (Ch. 29)

Bowers, C. G., *Pierre Vergniaud: Voice of the French Revolution* (1950).

Brinton, C., *The Jacobins: An Essay in the New History* (1930).

Bruun, G., *Saint-Just, Apostle of the Terror* (1932).

Dupre, H., *Lazare Carnot, Republican Patriot* (1940).

Eagan, J. M., *Maximilien Robespierre: Nationalist Dictator* (1938).

Elliott, J., *The Way of the Tumbrils* (1958).

Garrett, M. B., *The Estates General of 1789* (1935).

Gershoy, L., *The French Revolution and Napoleon* (1933). (Ch. 29)

Goodwin, A., The French Revolution (1953). (Ch. 29)

Gottschalk, L. R., *Jean-Paul Marat: A Study in Radicalism* (1927).

———, *The Era of the French Revolution (1715-1815)*. (Ch. 29)

Greer, D., *The Incidence of the Emigration during the French Revolution* (1951).

———, *The Incidence of the Terror during the French Revolution* (1935).

Harris, S., *The Assignats* (1930). (Ch. 29)

Hearnshaw, F. J. C., ed., *The Social and Political Ideas of Some Representative Thinkers of the Revolutionary Era* (1931).

Lefebvre, G., *The Coming of the French Revolution, 1789* (1947).

Madelin, L., *Danton* (1921).

Mahan, A. T., *The Influence of Sea Power upon the French Revolution and Empire, 1793-1812* (2 vols., 1892). (Ch. 29)

Mathiez, A., *After Robespierre: The Thermidorean Reaction* (1931). (Ch. 29)

———, *The Fall of Robespierre, and Other Essays* (1927).

———, *The French Revolution* (1929).

Mayer, J. P., *Political Thought in France from the Revolution to the Fourth Republic* (1949). (Ch. 29)

Palmer, R. R., *Twelve Who Ruled: The Year of Terror in the French Revolution* (2nd ed., 1959).

Rudé, G. F. E., *The Crowd in the French Revolution* (1959).

Salvemini, G., *The French Revolution* (1954). (Ch. 29)

Stewart, J. H., ed., *A Documentary Survey of the French Revolution* (1951).

Thompson, J. M., *Leaders of the French Revolution* (1929).

———, *The French Revolution* (5th ed., 1955). (Ch. 29)

———, *Robespierre* (2 vols., 1935).

———, *Robespierre and the French Revolution* (1953).

Woodward, E. L., *French Revolutions* (1934).

Chapter 29. France in Revolution, II: 1795-1815

Bainville, J., *Napoleon* (1932).

Brinton, C., *The Lives of Talleyrand* (1936).

Butterfield, H., *Napoleon* (1956).

———, *The Peace Tactics of Napoleon, 1806-1808* (1929).

Cachard, H., *The French Civil Code* (1930).

Deutsch, H. C., *The Genesis of Napoleonic Imperialism* (1938).

Geyl, P., *Napoleon, For and Against* (1949).

Guérard, A. L., *Napoleon I, a Great Life in Brief* (1956).

Heckscher, E., *The Continental System: An Economic Interpretation* (1922).

Holtman, R. B., *Napoleonic Propaganda* (1950).

Kircheisen, F. M., *Napoleon* (1932).

Mackesey, P., *The War in the Mediterranean, 1803-1810* (1957).

Madelin, L., *The Consulate and the Empire* (2 vols., 1934-36).

Markham, F. M. H., *Napoleon and the Awakening of Europe* (1954). (Ch. 30)

Mowat, R. B., *The Diplomacy of Napoleon* (1924).

Oman, C., *Studies in the Napoleonic Wars* (1929).

Puryear, V. J., *Napoleon and the Dardanelles* (1951).

Thompson, J. M., *Napoleon Bonaparte: His Rise and Fall* (1952).

Thomson, D., *The Babeuf Plot: The Making of a Republican Legend* (1947).

Walsh, H. H., *The Concordat of 1801: A Study of the Problem of Nationalism in the Relations of Church and State* (1933).

Zweig, S., *Joseph Fouché, The Portrait of a Politician* (1930).

Chapter 30. Europe in an Age of Revolution, 1789-1815

Aldington, R., *Wellington* (1943).

Anderson, E. N., *Nationalism and the Cultural Crisis in Prussia, 1806-1815* (1939).

Aris, R., *A History of Political Thought in Germany from 1789 to 1815* (1936).

Bryant, A., *The Age of Elegance, 1812-1922* (1950). Britain.

———, *The Years of Endurance, 1793-1802* (1942). Britain.

———, *Years of Victory, 1802-12* (1944). Britain.

Buckland, C. S. B., *Metternich and the British Government from 1809 to 1813* (1932).

Cecil, A., *Metternich, 1773-1859: A Study of His Period and Personality* (3rd ed., 1947).

Cobban, A., ed., *The Debate on the French Revolution, 1789-1800* (1950). Britain.

Gooch, G. P., *Germany and the French Revolution* (1920).

Grenfell, R., *Nelson the Sailor* (1949).

Grunwald, C. de, *Napoleon's Nemesis: The Life of Baron Stein* (1936).

Gulick, E. V., *Europe's Classical Balance of Power: A Case History of the Theory and Practice of One of the Great Concepts of European Statecraft* (1955).

Hayes, R., *Ireland and Irishmen in the French Revolution* (1932).

Heriot, A., *The French in Italy, 1796-1799* (1957).

Kukiel, M., *Czartoryski and European Unity, 1770-1861* (1955).

Langsam, W. C., *The Napoleonic Wars and German Nationalism in Austria* (1930).

Marriott, J. A. R., *Castlereagh: The Political Life of Robert, Second Marquess of Londonderry* (1936).

Nicolson, H. G., *The Congress of Vienna: A Study in Allied Unity, 1812-1822* (1946).

Raeff, M., *Michael Speransky, Statesman of Imperial Russia* (1957).

Reiss, H. S., ed., *The Political Thought of the German Romantics, 1793-1815* (1955).

Rose, J. H., *William Pitt and the Great War* (1914).

Scott, F. D., *Bernadotte and the Fall of Napoleon* (1935).

Simon, W. M., *The Failure of the Prussian Reform Movement, 1807-1819* (1955).

Strakhovsky, L. I., *Alexander I of Russia: The Man Who Defeated Napoleon* (1947).

Sweet, P. R., *Friedrich von Gentz, Defender of the Old Order* (1941).

Tarlé, E. V., *Napoleon's Invasion of Russia, 1812* (1942).

Van Loon, H. W., *The Fall of the Dutch Republic* (1913).

——, *The Rise of the Dutch Kingdom, 1795-1813* (1915).

Wangermann, E., *From Joseph II to the Jacobin Trials* (1959).

Webster, C. K., *The Foreign Policy of Castlereagh, 1812-1815: Britain and the Reconstruction of Europe* (1931).

Index